JACK CHAMBERS

Milestones :
The Music
and Times
of Miles Davis

Quill
William Morrow
New York

TO SUSAN
for all the good reasons
and then some

The author is grateful to Jack Maher and Deborah Kelly of
Down Beat and to Frank Driggs for their help with the
photographs in *Milestones 1*, and to Louise and Dale
Dickson for their hospitality in Chicago. Every effort has
been made to identify and acknowledge the photographers
whose work is presented here.

Copyright © 1983, 1985 by Jack Chambers

Originally published separately as *Milestones 1: The Music and
Times of Miles Davis to 1960* and *Milestones 2: The Music and
Times of Miles Davis since 1960*

Library of Congress Cataloging-in-Publication Data

Chambers, Jack.
    Milestones: the music and times of Miles Davis/Jack Chambers.
        p.   cm.
    Reprint. Originally published: New York: Beech Tree Books,
c1983–c1985.
    Includes bibliographical references.
    ISBN 0-688-09602-6
    1. Davis, Miles. 2. Jazz musicians—United States—Biography.
I. Title.
ML419.D39C5   1989
788.9'2165'092—dc20
[B]   89-10819
                                                                    CIP

Printed in the United States of America

First Quill Edition

1   2   3   4   5   6   7   8   9   10

Milestones 1:
The Music
and Times
of Miles Davis
to 1960

Contents

Miles Davis at the Newport Jazz Festival, 1955; from left, Percy Heath, Thelonious Monk, Zoot Sims, Davis, Gerry Mulligan, and Connie Kay (Robert Parent, courtesy of *Down Beat*)

Preface

You can't judge Miles on *Relaxin'* and *Cookin'* only and not on *Miles Smiles* and not on *Bitches Brew* or just on *On the Corner*. You look at the man's work and you see *Sketches of Spain*, a string orchestra, the quintet, a rock date. That to me is what an artist does, he gets interested in many areas over his life, which is all related by a single thread, which is his sound.   Dave Liebman

For the final chapter of her book *Jazz People*, the English photographer and journalist Valerie Wilmer chronicled her meeting with Miles Davis. The entire interview consists of the following three lines of dialogue:

Later!
But Mr Davis ...
Look, baby, when I said 'later' I meant LATER!

A reader approaching Wilmer's interview with no preconceptions about Miles Davis – that is, a reader who happens to be the highest lama of Tibet or the lowest mutant of the Ozarks – might simply wonder what his hurry is all about. But most people have preconceptions about Miles Davis and will find the interview revealing, because it shows him to be what they already believe him to be – prickly, private, angry, rude, arrogant, and caustic. It is surprising that so many people in the world should 'know' all this about a man who has revealed so very little of himself, at least offstage. On stage, of course, Davis has given us one of the best-defined and most personal images in the history of jazz. For the first twenty-five years of a career that began in earnest in 1945, and perhaps also in the still poorly understood years preceding and following his retirement from 1975 to 1981, in both his spontaneous improvisations based on standard themes and his own composed themes, Davis has consistently shown himself to be wary, brooding, introverted, wry, gentle, and sensitive.

The discrepancy between the character revealed on stage and offstage has not, of course, escaped attention. The novelist James Baldwin calls him "a miraculously tough and tender man" and claims that "Miles's disguise would certainly never fool anybody with sense, but it keeps a lot of people away, and that's the point." But if he has succeeded in keeping people away from him in his private life, he has never even attempted to keep them away from his music. He has persistently worked his way into the forefront of modern jazz movements, never shying away from the leader's role and never hesitating to dictate the course of the music. His career swings through the entire post-war history of jazz, crystallizing its main currents all the way from bebop to jazz-rock.

In Nat Hentoff's definition, "Jazz is a continual autobiography, or rather a continuum of intersecting autobiographies." The autobiographies are told in music, and the music – as Davis has reminded us several times – speaks for itself. But the "autobiography" of Davis – his music – is already so rich and varied that even his most diligent listeners are in danger of losing their way. There is a need for a guide to the music as it has unfolded, and also, I trust, for a biography of the "miraculously tough and tender man" who has provided the music. In the end, the man and his music are one and the same. In spite of Davis's recalcitrance with would-be chroniclers, he has left enough clues along with his music, albeit sprinkled far and wide, for the story to come clear. It has its contradictions, and it is vague at some points, but no more so than many biographies of much more willing subjects. In fact, it is so complete that it might surprise Davis himself, who takes some pride in the fact that he does not "give stories."

"It's nothing personal," Davis once told Joe Goldberg, "but I don't give stories. If Jesus Christ himself came down from the cross and asked for a story, I'd say, 'I'm sorry, I don't have the time.' You have to write it, that's your business, so just write about the music, about whether you like it or not. Write what you know, or what you don't know, like everybody else." As a statement of policy, Davis's words are clear and unequivocal. There is little doubt that he means them, and he has been more or less consistent about holding to them throughout his career. Valerie Wilmer was neither the first nor the last prospective interviewer whom Davis rebuffed.

However, he has not been absolutely rigid. As might be expected of a man who has been one of the most prominent musicians in the world for over thirty-five years, he has often been asked for interviews, and he has occasionally consented – or perhaps relented. There are at least fifteen interviews in existence, all of them longer than the one with Valerie Wilmer and some of them quite extensive, including even a "self-portrait" (1957) – a press release from Columbia Records in Davis's own words, which were culled from a taped interview with George Avakian. There are also, of course, many smaller items, such as Leonard Feather's "blindfold tests" with Davis for *Down Beat* magazine and reminiscences by Michael Zwerin, Max Gordon, and others.

The quality of these sources, naturally, varies enormously. In some of the interviews, Davis's distaste for the whole affair is almost palpable, and the information he surrenders is largely opaque: for instance, when Harriet Choice of the *Chicago Tribune* asks him how he knows which musicians are right for his bands, he answers, "The same way I know what girl I want to screw." Even some of the long interviews have their problems. The best known is the 1962 *Playboy* interview, because it inaugurated the highly touted series of interviews in that magazine, and perhaps also because the interviewer, Alex Hailey, later became a celebrity with the publication and television adaptation of his book *Roots*. But that interview is not all it is cracked up to be. In at least a couple of instances, there is a curious similarity between what Hailey puts into the mouth of Miles Davis and what Marc Crawford elicited from Davis's father for *Ebony* magazine the year before. One point of similarity is shown in this parallel text:

CRAWFORD	HAILEY
Davis's father: When he was in high school he played trumpet. In school competitions he was always the best, but the blue-eyed boys always won first and second prizes ... The officials, Miles and everybody else knew he should have had first prize.	*Davis:* In high school, I was the best in the music class on the trumpet. I knew it and all the rest knew it – but all the contest first prizes went to the boys with blue eyes.

There can be little doubt that Hailey ransacked Crawford's article in order to find some of the words that Davis speaks in the *Playboy* interview, rather than vice versa, not only because Crawford's article ante-dates Hailey's, but also because of textual evidence. In at least one instance Hailey has taken Crawford's quotation from Davis's father and put it in the mouth of Davis himself, where it comes out as gibberish:

CRAWFORD	HAILEY
Davis's father: Historically, way back into slavery days, the Davises have been musicians and performed classic works in the homes of the plantation owners. My father, Miles the first, was born six	*Davis:* The slave Davises played classical string music on the plantation. My father, Miles the first, was born six years after the Emancipation. He wanted to play music, but my grandfather

years after the Emancipation and forbade me to play music because the only place a Negro could play then was in barrel houses.

wanted him to be more than an entertainer for white folks.

Any assertion by Miles Davis that *his* father was Miles Davis the first and that he was born six years after the Emancipation is utter nonsense, and Miles Davis would know that better than anyone, except perhaps his own father, whose father in turn these facts concern.

The *Playboy* interview is neither the most revealing nor the most interesting interview with Davis, despite the publicity it received. Several of the others contend for that honor: Nat Hentoff's may reveal more about Davis's music of the time (1958) than any other, and Sy Johnson's may reveal more about his character at the time (1976) than any other, but my personal favorite is probably the interview with Julie Coryell, in her book *Jazz-Rock Fusion* (1978), which is long and chatty and full of fresh topics.

In any event, there exists a fair amount of first-person information on Davis – almost enough to make an autobiography, by assembling Davis's own words from the various sources – almost, but not quite. I have done that wherever possible, letting Davis speak for himself.

Along with the various interviews, the most useful source has been Jorgen Grunnet Jepsen's *A Discography of Miles Davis* (1969), which provides a listing of the studio recordings and recorded performances of Davis up to May 1968, as far as they were known at the time. Like all of Jepsen's discographies, this one provided a wonderful foundation for the rest of us to work from. My copy now contains hundreds of corrections, most of them on miniscule details, as well as the dozens of additions to the known works prior to May 1968 that have become known more recently, and also, of course, the dozens of additions since 1968. Michel Ruppli's discography finally provided a successor to Jepsen's when it appeared in *Jazz Hot* in 1979. Brian Priestley's discography, appended to Ian Carr's *Miles Davis: A Biography*, updates the entries to 1981 and also clears up some old mysteries. My own discography below updates and corrects some of the main entries but omits the discographical freight of master numbers and complete issues, readily available for those who want them in Jepsen's and Ruppli's listings. I am grateful to Jan Lohmann for letting me hear some of the more important private recordings in his collection and for helping me with information about the discographically difficult period 1970–5.

There are four earlier book-length studies of Davis. *Miles Davis*, by the English reviewer Michael James, was published in 1961 and reviews all of Davis's recorded works that James had access to. Although the list of works has more than quintupled since then, James's little book remains a very useful guide to the music that it covered. *Miles Davis: A Musical Biography*, by Bill Cole, was roundly condemned by its reviewers when it appeared in 1974, mainly because it contains errors galore, beginning with the incorrect birthdate. (Most authors err by one day, copying the mistake from Leonard Feather's *Encyclopedia of Jazz*; Cole errs by three weeks.) Cole's book cannot really be counted among the sources. Ian Carr's *Miles Davis: A Critical Biography* appeared in England early in 1982 and in the United States several months later (with its subtitle inexplicably shortened to *A Biography*). Carr, a British jazz trumpeter, highlights his narrative of the main events of Davis's life with his sensitivity to jazz style and trumpet technique, especially when dealing with Davis's fusion music of the late 1960s, the main influence on Carr's own music. *'Round about Midnight: A Portrait of Miles Davis*, by Eric Nisenson, also appeared in 1982. A paperback categorized by its publisher as a celebrity biography, it is less concerned with Davis's music than with his style and less concerned with his life than with his image, and Nisenson portrays both the style and the image succinctly.

My book is organized in two volumes, which subdivide Davis's long and extraordinarily productive career into its main phases. *Milestones I* traces the emergence of the teenaged Davis from East St. Louis, Illinois, into post-war New York City, where he joined the ranks of the bebop revolutionaries, worked out his individual style, and took his place in the forefront of jazz music by late 1959. Davis's activities during this period are covered in two main movements: the first, under the heading "Boplicity," details his apprenticeship, first in his hometown and later under the aegis of Charlie Parker and Dizzy Gillespie, culminating in his first masterwork with the short-lived experimental nonet of 1948; the second, titled "Miles Ahead," concerns his creative recess during his years of heroin addiction and his dramatic return to form in the 1950s, culminating in the years of the first great quintet and the sextet. *Milestones II* takes up his music and his times from 1960, also in two main movements: it begins, in "Prince of Darkness," with his formal reorganization of bebop in the second great quintet and continues in "Pangaea" with his restless search for further formal expansions, leading to fusions with free form, rock, and other music.

The book thus presents Davis to the reader in the variety of personae – bebop prodigy, hipster, fashion plate, autocrat, activist, rock star – he has offered for public consumption and his music in the shifting guises he has chosen as his medium. Through all the personae and the guises, all these surfaces, shines the single, expansive, encompassing spirit that is Miles Davis. The business of a biographer is to present the surfaces as faithfully and as comprehensively as he can and hope that the spirit is ultimately recoverable by his readers from them. That has seemed a tall order, when the subject is Miles Davis and the surfaces comprise so many lifestyles, itineraries, associations, bands, recordings, and all the rest. Yet those of us who have lived through a fair amount of the history that this book documents have managed to see through all the diversity with which Davis's career has presented us to the spirit pervading it, and so I can hold out some hope that my readers will be able to do the same when it is compressed into print.

I am beholden to Colette Copeland, Dale Dickson, Bernard Lecerf, Jan Lohmann, Dan Morgenstern, and Chuck Netley, for sundry favors which made this book better than it would otherwise have been. No financial assistance was sought or received for the research and writing of *Milestones* I and II.

ABBREVIATIONS

The following standard abbreviations have been used in the discographical entries:

arr	arranger	gtr	guitar
as	alto saxophone	perc	percussion
b	bass	pno	piano
bs	baritone saxophone	ss	soprano saxophone
clnt	clarinet	tba	tuba
comp	composer	tbn	trombone
cond	conductor	tpt	trumpet
dms	drums	ts	tenor saxophone
flt	flute	vcl	vocal
frh	french horn	vib	vibraphone

PART ONE
BOPLICITY

The history of both jazz and jazzmen is that of creative purity gradually corrupted by success. In his youth, the great jazz musician has to struggle to impose his art; if he succeeds in doing so, he must struggle daily *against* his own success. How many men have won *this* struggle? Charlie Parker undoubtedly did, because he never reached the peak of success and because he died at the age of thirty-five. [Thelonious] Monk and Miles Davis may win it, either because of their tough, incorruptible characters, or because they took Pascal's advice and fled success rather than try to stand up to it.   André Hodeir (1962)

The Charlie Parker Quintet at the Three Deuces, 1948; from left, Tommy Potter, Parker, Max Roach (behind Parker), Miles Davis, and Duke Jordan (William Gottlieb, courtesy of *Down Beat*)

1

Tune-up
1926–44

Music is the song I love,
And nothing comes between.
Melodies are à la carte,
But they reach my selfish heart.
  Miles Davis (February 1976), quoted by Julie Coryell (1978)

"Childhood? Who wants to remember that?" asked Miles Davis in 1981. And he added, "I was born like this."

At the time he had just turned 55, and he was sitting uneasily for an interview with George Goodman, Jr, of the *New York Times*, part of the promotional hullabaloo surrounding his imminent return to the concert stage after more than five years of retirement. He was garbed in a white cap, a red jump suit, and cowboy boots, the kind of ultramodish attire that he had been affecting for more than a decade, ever since the average age of his audience was halved by his appearances at rock emporiums. Even so, his appearance seemed thoroughly unfamiliar because he wore a moustache for the first time in almost thirty years and a goatee for the first time ever. It was, to that extent, a new face that Davis had prepared for the public after so many years out of sight, and for the part of his public with any memories at all it would be one more rebirth to reckon with. His altered appearance as well as his disdain for discussing his childhood – or, for that matter, anything else that had happened to him more than a few months ago – was part and parcel of the same Davis creed: the refusal to look back, to pay any homage at all to the past or even to waste much time deploring it, and the utter absence of nostalgia. It is a creed that Davis professes consistently, so that from a distance his career and his life seem suffused by a Heraclitan obsession with change and flux. In truth, Davis's creed has less to do with Heraclitus than with Charlie Parker, and it is less a philosophical stance than a gut reaction to growing up black in mid-century America. It is middle-aged hipsterism, more articulate and reasoned than in the hip youth of the bebop revolutionaries, when it meant merely mumbling and turning away, but its highest values remain much the same – a cool, detached, unfeeling, impersonal response to the vagaries of life, whether good or bad. Expressions of sentiment are considered signs of weakness. Talking openly about the past invites the flow of feeling, and so Davis has avoided talking about it as far as he can. But just as in his art Davis has never been successful in submerging his feelings, no matter how cool and detached the surface of the music, so in his life he has not been able to avoid talking about the past entirely. Over the years he has offered details that, together with the recollections of other, less reluctant witnesses, can be pieced together to make a surprisingly coherent and far from unrevealing collage of his middle-class upbringing in the American Midwest. If he has stopped well short of giving us what Holden Caulfield called "all that David Copperfield kind of crap," he has revealed more of his childhood and adolescence than he ever imagined that he would, and certainly more than anyone had any right to expect.

Miles Dewey Davis III was born in Alton, Illinois, on 26 May 1926. His father, a dentist with ambitions that went well beyond even the comfortable limits enjoyed by most men of his profession, came to realize, at the very moment that his first son came into the world, that his ambitions required an urban arena, and he moved his family 25 miles south to East St. Louis when young Miles was only one. In East St. Louis he divided his energies between his dental practice in the city and a two-hundred-acre farm in the countryside near Milstead, Illinois. Miles Davis's mother, Cleota Henry Davis, was a taciturn woman, whose social ambitions almost matched her husband's business ambitions. Besides Miles, the Davises had a daughter, Dorothy, two years older, and in 1929, after they had been settled in East St. Louis for two years, their third child, Vernon, was born.

According to Miles's father, who was known locally as Doc Davis, his oldest son's musical ability and his leadership were inherited directly from the Davis side of the family. "By genetics and breeding Miles is always going to be ahead of his time," he told Marc Crawford in 1961. "Historically way back into slavery days, the Davises have been musicians and performed classic works in the homes of the plantation owners. My father, Miles I, was born six years after Emancipation and forbade me to play music because the only place a Negro could play then was in barrel houses. My father was the most efficient double entry bookkeeper in Arkansas before the coming of the adding machine and white men came to his home under cover of night for him to fix their books. He was later driven from his extensive holdings." "My grandfather made a hundred dollars a day during the Depression," Miles Davis told Julie Coryell. "When his kids got old, he gave them land." Those land holdings no doubt provided the collateral for the comfortable conditions in which Doc Davis's family was raised.

There was nevertheless a price to be exacted from a black man who was too successful in Arkansas at the turn of the century. So Davis's grandfather was removed from his land, probably because his holdings outstripped too conspicuously those of his white neighbors or perhaps because his bookkeeping jobs made him too knowledgeable about the business dealings of the whites. For whatever reason, Miles Davis's grandfather lived much of his adult life under the threat of violence from white men. One of his sons, Frank, who inherited less business acumen from his father than did Doc Davis, served as his father's bodyguard. The experience of white antagonism thus became part of the patriarch's legacy no less important than his worldly ambition, and it was passed down to his sons, and to his grandsons, just as forcibly.

Besides Frank, Doc Davis also had a second brother, Ferdinand, who is warmly remembered by his nephew. Unlike Frank, the bodyguard, and even more than Doc Davis himself, Ferdinand was a man of culture and a citizen of the world. "My uncle went to Harvard and studied in Berlin," Davis told Julie Coryell. "He was the editor of *Color* magazine. He used to tell me everything ... He talked to me about Caesar and Hannibal ... He was a brilliant guy. He made me feel dumb." Ferdinand seems to have been more than willing to fill in the gaps in his nephew's education, but there were some gaps that Miles Davis's mother felt were better left unfilled. His association with his uncle Ferdinand became a minor source of conflict between Miles and his mother. Davis recalls, "My mother said, 'Oh God, Ferd and you together!' (He had a suite downtown.) I said, 'We're the only ones in the family with any brains' – Ferd, me, and my father."

If Doc Davis could hardly compete with his brother's flair in the eyes of his son, he still had credentials of his own that were impossible for his son to undervalue. He graduated from Arkansas Baptist College, Lincoln University in Pennsylvania, and Northwestern College of Dentistry, making up at least in quantity what he may have lost in his son's eyes by not going to Harvard. "Three degrees," his son points out, "and he finished when he was twenty-four." Besides that, he alone inherited the bent for business, his father's business sense sitting less easily on his brothers. "My father told them to always count their money," Davis says. Counting his own money became increasingly difficult for Doc Davis during young Miles's youth and adolescence. In East St. Louis he began to specialize in dental surgery in the city and in special breeds of pork on the farm, with great success in both. "My father is worth more than I am," Davis claimed in 1962, when he himself was earning a six-figure salary. "He's a high-priced dental surgeon with more practice than he can handle – because he's good at his business – and he raises hogs with pedigrees. It's a special breed of hogs with some funny name I would tell you, but I never can remember it."

Of his mother, Davis has had much less to say, and not much that is positive. Mother and son seem to have had a fairly stormy relationship, and they certainly did not share any confidences. He had been away from home living in New York for about ten years before he discovered that she knew any music at all. "I didn't know until after I'd gone back there for a visit a few years ago that my mother even knew one note of music," he told Nat Hentoff. "But she sat down one day and played some funky blues. Turned out my grandmother used to teach organ. I was surprised my mother could play because she always looked as if she'd hit me everytime I played my horn." He has occasionally conceded, as he did to Cheryl McCall, that "she was a very beautiful woman," but he qualifies even that praise: "My mother was pretty and very blank-faced ... *no expression*. She looked at me when I played the trumpet. She'd say *When are you gonna play something that I can understand?*" Mrs Davis was only participating in a form of hypocrisy that was widespread among bourgeois blacks all over America for most of the century following Emancipation. Its source was a deep-seated dread among black parents that their own children would be sucked back into the social vortex of barge-toting and bale-lifting from which they had worked against great odds to free themselves. Rightly or wrongly, they believed that the surest way for their offspring to slip backward was by playing any of the forms of black music – ragtime, marches, dance tunes – the parents had left behind in their scramble up the social ladder. Thousands of middle-class black youngsters felt the parental pressure. Doc Davis received it as an edict from his own father in Arkansas around the turn of the century, and in succeeding decades the same pressure was exerted – unsuccessfully, thank God – on Duke Ellington in Washington, Earl Hines in Pittsburgh, Fats Waller in New York, Hampton Hawes in Los Angeles, and countless other sons and daughters on whose shoulders lay the burden of upward social mobility.

It must nevertheless have been clear to Davis that his mother was not dead set against *all* music. His sister and his brother also studied music as children, and his sister did so with their mother's blessing. "My sister Dorothy studied music for ten years – she says her mother wanted to keep her off the streets," he told Julie Coryell. "My brother Vernon went to the Roosevelt Conservatory in Chicago for three years. He went to Howard University too. He played trumpet and piano." Davis claims that he taught his brother to play the trumpet so he could join him in the high school marching band. For Vernon, as for their sister Dorothy, music became an avocation, not a profession.

The city where the Davis children were raised, East St. Louis, sits on the east bank of the Mississippi River, as does the town of Alton, where Miles Davis and his sister were born. The river at this point coincides with the state line, separating Illinois on its east bank from Missouri on its west. The river also forms a natural city limit for East St. Louis, but the urban landscape does not simply end there. Indeed, it seems to erupt across the river, the site of St. Louis, Missouri, the biggest city to be found within hundreds of miles in the Midwest. In spite of the physical barrier of the river and political barrier of the state lines, East St. Louis is really just an appendage of metropolitan St. Louis, as its name implies. The urban sprawl of St. Louis takes on the appearance of an urban oasis amid a vast expanse of corn and cattle country. Kansas City, the nearest urban center of comparable size, is 246 miles away to the west; Chicago is a little further, 278 miles due north; New York is 930 miles to the east, and Los Angeles is twice as far away, to the southwest.

Apart from the fact that it is the place where Miles Davis was raised, for jazz buffs the main distinction of East St. Louis comes from the title of the Bubber Miley-Duke Ellington composition *East St. Louis Toodle-oo*, the theme song of the Ellington orchestra in the late 1920s and a staple in its repertoire for many years. The composition has nothing to do with East St. Louis. Ellington told Stanley Dance that the tune was born when the band traveled to New England and saw a sign advertising Lewando Cleaners. Someone in the bus sang out *"Oh, Lee – wan – do!"* and every time the bus passed the sign after that the musicians set up a chorus. The chorus grew into the arrangement that eventually became known as *East St. Louis Toodle-oo*. At the time of its first recording by the Ellington band in 1927 it featured a solo by the St. Louis trumpeter Louis Metcalf. Metcalf's prominence probably accounts for the title. Years later Ellington mused, "It would have been better if we had called it *Lewando* and got some advertising money from it."

"East St. Louis was so bad," Davis told Leonard Feather, "that it just made you get out and do something." That impression was no doubt formed after the Davis family moved into a white neighborhood, when Miles was in elementary school. "About the first thing I can remember as a little boy," he said later, in a story repeated endlessly by jazz journalists, "was a white man running me down the street hollering, 'Nigger! Nigger!' My father went hunting him with a shotgun." Doc Davis has told the same story, adding, "I got my shotgun, but I could never find him." And he concluded, sadly, "I don't think Miles, a sensitive boy, ever forgot it, or our troubles." The incident was a malevolent ripple on what would have been, for a white child, a smooth surface. "You're going to run into that Jim Crow thing regardless of how wealthy you are," Davis has said. "I can't buy no freedom. Having money has helped me once in a while, but I'm not looking for help ... There's no excuse for being poor anyway. You see, you're not supposed to wait on anybody to give you nothing. My father taught me that."

Davis learned the lessons of his father very well, from the beginning: "I have never been what you would call poor. I grew up with an allowance, and I had a big newspaper route. I saved most of what I had except for buying records." The newspaper route is obviously a source of pride to him, because he has mentioned it to interviewers several times. He was ten years old when he started working on it, and soon "it got bigger than I could handle because my customers liked me so much. I just delivered papers the best I could and minded my business, the same way I play my horn now." He was beginning to discover other strengths in his personality, especially at the farm. "He liked long walks in the country," his father remembers, "and hunting and fishing. He was an excellent horseman and if he was ever thrown he'd remount immediately and master his mount." That steel resolve would show up even more forcefully in a few years, when he began playing trumpet on 52nd Street beside such technical wizards as Charlie Parker and Dizzy Gillespie.

There was increasing friction between his mother and father, and very often it seems to have centered around young Miles. "When I was eleven, my mother said, 'Spank Miles.' And my father would say, 'For what?' She'd say, 'He's crazy.' He'd say, 'Remember that.'" The friction, which would eventually lead to a legal separation, was aggravated by Cleota Henry's inclination to pit her own wishes against those of her eldest son and then to call in her husband to arbitrate. She seemed doomed to lose, for Clark Terry, who knew the Davis family before he left St. Louis, has said, "Doc Davis was the type of guy who believed his son could do no wrong."

For Miles's thirteenth birthday, his mother talked about getting him a violin, but his father decided that he should have a trumpet instead. According to Davis, "Once my father was fixing a music instructor's teeth, who said, 'Send Miles around. I go to the grade school every Wednesday. Buy him a trumpet.'" That conversation was apparently enough to convince Doc Davis, and his son went along with him. "My mother said, 'Why don't you play the violin!' I said, 'If I take a violin out on the streets, I'll have more knockouts than I have now.'" Looking back on the incident, Davis sees it as a kind of power struggle between his parents: "My mother wanted to give me a violin for my birthday, but my father gave me a trumpet – because he loved my mother so much!" That same year saw a deeper disruption of his relations with his mother: "Me and my mother fell out when I was thirteen. We were close at one time; we could talk to each other, but you know, I wasn't going to take none of that shit from her just because she was my mother ... It was a matter of either talk straight to me or not at all. When she did, we became real tight ... [My father] just told my mother to leave me alone." From that time he seems to have reacted against her every wish, but that did not deter her from expressing her views.

The one positive recollection Davis has of his mother stems from her bringing jazz into the house. "My mother bought two records – Duke Ellington and Art Tatum," he says. "She hit on the right thing, didn't she?" Her choices seem altogether out of character from everything else we know of her.

Young Miles seems to have taken immediately to the trumpet he received for his birthday, although the lessons given by the itinerant school teacher were far from inspiring. "Once a week we would hold notes," Davis recalls. "Wednesdays at 2:30. Everybody would fight to play best." Learning to play the trumpet soon came to occupy more of his time than the school schedule allotted to it: "I used to spit rice to school every day and back, or spit half a pea – it makes you used to playing the trumpet." For Davis, the monotony of the school lessons was soon relieved, again through the intercession of his father. "Lucky for me, I learned to play the chromatic scale right away," Davis says. "A friend of my father's brought me a book one night and showed me how to do it so I wouldn't have to sit there and hold that note all the time."

Soon after, he began to take private lessons. Again, the choice of teacher was dictated by the fact that Doc Davis was doing some dental work for a trumpet teacher, but the choice was excellent. Elwood Buchanan had recently returned from a stint in the trumpet section of some touring dance bands, including Andy Kirk's orchestra. He steered Davis toward jazz music: "He used to tell us all about jam sessions on the showboats." St. Louis was visited regularly by showboats traveling the Mississippi, bringing musicians from New Orleans and other ports. When he got a little older, Davis spent some time on the showboats, sometimes joining in the jam sessions and always learning directly from the old pros, but Buchanan gave him the taste for jazz on the showboats from the beginning.

Buchanan also directed Davis's attention toward certain players whose styles were to have an abiding influence on his own mature style – Bobby Hackett and Harold Baker. Hackett, a white cornetist from New England, was only eleven years older than Davis, but he had been playing professionally around New England and New York since 1929, when he was fourteen. Indentified as a disciple of Bix Beiderbecke, Hackett played with a spare, singing tone that swung gently but insistently. In 1939–41, when Buchanan was telling Davis about him, Hackett's reputation was still largely a local one on the eastern seaboard, but because of Buchanan's exposure to Hackett's work when he was on the road, he became a formative influence for Davis. Almost a decade later, when Davis was firmly entrenched as a member of the bebop revolution and Hackett was entrenched in the opposing swing establishment, Hackett surprised some of his cohorts by remarking, "The other night I started to think I was sounding like Miles Davis, and I liked it." Tit for tat.

Harold Baker, a St. Louis native, known throughout his career as Shorty, was a member of some of the best bands in the land during the 1930s, including those of Don Redman, Teddy Wilson, and Andy Kirk. Although Baker had played in the Duke Ellington orchestra for part of 1938, his long tenure with Ellington (1943–51, 1957–9) was still to come when Buchanan was telling the young Miles Davis about him. Once described by Ben Webster, Baker's colleague in the Ellington band, as "the greatest unrecognized trumpet player in the world," Baker had a masterly technique that gave him complete control of the horn at all tempos but was most effective when he played ballads, later the forte of Davis as well. Although he was never the featured soloist in Ellington's trumpet section, over the years he produced a significant body of recorded solos that consistently shine in their lyrical embellishments of the melody. His tone is bolder than Hackett's, but still sharp and clear. It survives in the work of Miles Davis. "I recall how often, when Miles first came on the New York scene," says songwriter Mort Goode, "the men in Duke's band, Johnny Hodges and countless others, pointed up the similarities and the warmth." Mary Lou Williams, the pianist and arranger who was married to Baker, says, "Harold Baker was terrific when he played a slow tune and Miles always said, I heard him say: 'Oh, if I could only play as sweet as Harold Baker.'"

Buchanan's choice of models for his student went against the grain at the time, when the most influential trumpet styles derived from Louis Armstrong's hot, ebullient playing. Armstrong's lessons had been carried into the swing bands in several highly personal versions, by the likes of Charlie Shavers, Buck Clayton, Rex Stewart, and Roy Eldridge. These men and almost all the other top trumpeters of the day shared Armstrong's energy and verve, and sought his great range and bold tone. For most young trumpeters, those elements were essential, and by the time Miles Davis arrived in New York those essentials would be transliterated very successfully into the bop idiom by Dizzy Gillespie.

Partly because of Buchanan's influence, the hot trumpet tradition would be much less important for Davis. Buchanan was directing his attention toward an alternative tradition, much less fashionable, featuring a lighter tone, a narrower range, and a more lyrical bias. The patriarch of this tradition is Leon (Bix) Beiderbecke, a Midwesterner from Davenport, Iowa, who died in 1931 when he was only twenty-eight, leaving behind just a few recordings that show his style to any advantage and several others that, however prized by his admirers, mainly reveal his propensity for recording with mediocre bands. Compared to the incomparably corporeal Armstrong at the head of the other tradition, Beiderbecke seems a mere wraith. In the years of Miles Davis's early adolescence, Beiderbecke's memory survived best in a few mythic anecdotes on the theme of alcoholic self-destruction. The few trumpeters who claimed to be following him included only a couple of Chicagoans whose technical competence was openly doubted and the up-and-coming Hackett.

Harold Baker's style obviously shared the main features of Beiderbecke's, but it probably never occurred to him that he might be considered Beiderbecke's descendant, however indirect. Instead, Baker was an exponent of the distinctive style of trumpet-playing that had been heard in St. Louis for years. A curious *Kulturbund* makes St. Louis a wonderful, and inexplicable, breeding ground for lyrical jazz trumpeters. The list of St. Louis trumpeters is long, and everyone on it shares (to a greater or lesser extent) the essential features that are so handsomely realized in Baker's style, even when the men belong to different generations. Clark Terry, six years older than Davis, is another St. Louis trumpeter and, except for Davis, probably the best known. Terry admits the influence of the older players in his hometown, listing among them some who are virtually unknown beyond the city limits. He offered the following list in an interview with Stanley Dance: "Levi Madison, who I think played one of the prettiest trumpets I ever heard. He was older than Shorty Baker, but he had a very similar tone. Then there were Dewey Jackson, George Hudson, Crack Stanley, Mouse Randolph, Bobby Merrill, Sleepy Tomlin, who was with Jimmy Lunceford at one period, and Joe Thomas, who lives in New York now." The list can be extended by adding the names of Louis Metcalf, Charlie Creath, Ed Allen, and, of course, Elwood Buchanan. All of them were the precursors of Clark Terry and Miles Davis, but the list does not end with Terry and Davis. The most prominent St. Louis trumpeter since Davis is Lester Bowie of the Art Ensemble of Chicago. As a player of free form music, Bowie is seldom heard in a context where one can make comparisons with his St. Louis forebears, but the sound is clearly there. In a telling instance, the drummer Lenny White listened to an unidentified record as part of a blindfold test in *Down Beat*, and while he failed to identify either the Art Ensemble or Bowie, he commented, "The trumpet player's been listening to Miles Davis." He heard the sound of St. Louis in Bowie's playing.

For Miles Davis, the sound of St. Louis and the sound of the Beiderbecke tradition came together in Buchanan's taste, and they were crystallized in his teaching: "'Play without any vibrato,' he used to tell us. 'You're gonna get old anyway and start shaking,' he used to say. 'No vibrato!' That's how I tried to play," Davis recalls. "Fast and light – and no vibrato."

Buchanan encouraged Davis even when he seems to have been incapable of putting together a lesson. "I used to make a lot of noise, but my instructor liked me 'cause he liked the way I played," Davis told Julie Coryell. "He used to say, 'Little Davis, come here.' I'd say, 'What do you want?' He'd say, 'Do nothing 'til you hear from me; pay no attention to what's said –' Every time he'd get drunk, that's what he'd sing – that song." The song, *Do Nothing 'til You Hear from Me*, was a popular hit for Duke Ellington and lyricist Bob Russell in 1943; its melody was Ellington's *Concerto for Cootie*, written as a solo showcase for trumpeter Cootie Williams three years earlier.

Around 1943, Davis was clearly outstripping the teachings of Buchanan and was set to move on. However, he never found a better teacher, apart from the musicians he hung out with when he first arrived in New York, and he never forgot the lessons he learned from him, including even his attitude toward the instrument. "The approach to the trumpet by my instructor in St. Louis, Elwood Buchanan, is so slick," he told Don DeMicheal years later. "You can't help but play fast if you approach the trumpet like he does. He approached the trumpet like he was really going to play it – and he did."

Davis had made excellent progress under Buchanan's tutelage. Only the recognition was sometimes missing. "In high school I was the best in the music class on the trumpet," Davis says. "I knew it and all the rest knew it – but all the contest first prizes went to the boys with blue eyes." Doc Davis recalls the same situations: "Miles always had to settle for third prize. The officials, Miles and everybody else knew he should have had first prize. You can't treat a kid like that and tell him to come out and say the water isn't dirty." Young Miles saw the dirt all right and resolved to avenge himself by working twice as hard. "It made me so mad," he says, "I made up my mind to outdo anybody white on my horn. If I hadn't met that prejudice, I probably wouldn't have had as much drive in my work. I have thought about that a lot. I have thought that prejudice and curiosity have been responsible for what I have done in music ... I mean I always had a curiosity about trying new things in music – a new sound, another way to do something, things like that."

He was also finding musicians closer to his own age who shared his curiosity. "My best friend was a man named Duke Brooks," he says. "We used to have great days. He was a real genius. He played piano like Bud Powell although he never saw or heard him." Another friend, identified by Davis simply as Bruz, seems to have done his share in imparting the values of St. Louis trumpet-playing to him. "I'd say, 'Man, you really sound bad,' and Bruz would laugh. He was one of the baddest of the bad. He would play very few notes – a man of few, but choice, statements – musically, I mean. I learned a lot of shit from him." Bruz was probably Irving Wood, a trumpeter a few years older than Davis whose nickname is elsewhere recorded as Broz.

Davis's second teacher, Gustav, the first trumpet with the St. Louis Symphony Orchestra who is identified by Davis as Gustat and by Clark Terry as Gustaph, emphasized technique and probably complemented Buchanan's emphasis on style as a result. "Gustat could run chromatic scales in two octaves," Davis says, "seventeen times in one breath." Their first meeting was not very promising. "I went to Gustat and played one note. He said I was the worst trumpet player he ever heard in his life. I said, 'That's why I'm here – I'm the pupil, you're the teacher.'" In spite of his prickly manner, the new teacher obviously had a heart. Clark Terry remembers, "I could never afford the famous St. Louis teacher, Gustaph, but I would go and ask him questions and he would never turn me down.

He knew who I was, a kid from a poor neighborhood, and he helped me with my problems." Another of Gustav's students was Levi Madison. Davis echoes Terry's praise for Madison, calling him "one of Gustat's best students": "He'd play all those pretty notes. Boy, we used to have fun. God damn! maybe 'cause we were at home." Unfortunately, Madison chose to stay at home, and as a result his playing went unrecorded.

Like Elwood Buchanan, Gustav also made a lasting impression on Miles Davis, although in a much less personal sense. He has remained a reference point to whom Davis could turn after he moved away from St. Louis. He has also directed other trumpeters to him, including Dizzy Gillespie. "When Dizzy got fucked up in the mouth, I told him to go to Gustat," Davis recalls. "He sent him to a doctor who gave him a shot inside of his mouth." Gustav also gave Davis the mouthpiece that he has used since he was a teenager. "Someone told me to have it copied," he said recently, and he was lucky in taking the advice. "As soon as I did, Jim Rose, my road manager, lost it [the original one]."

Around 1941, Davis met Clark Terry for the first time. It was not an auspicious meeting, but the irony of the situation clearly delights Terry, and he has told the story many times. "I was with a band led by a one-legged piano player named Benny Reed," Terry says. "We were playing at a Carbondale, Illinois, night club known as the Spinning Wheel. One afternoon we were engaged to play at a picnic grounds where there was an athletic competition between various southern Illinois high schools. There were several school bands in attendance with their teams. One of the bandleaders, who had the East St. Louis outfit, was an old friend of mine." In other accounts, Terry has identified the East St. Louis band-leader as "an old drinking buddy." He continues, "He wanted me to meet a little trumpet player he admired very much and eventually brought the kid over to introduce us. The kid started right in asking questions – how did I do this, or that?" Terry remembers that the young Davis was simply eager, but not at all pushy or aggressive in his queries. "He came up to me very meekly," Terry says, "and said, 'Pardon me, Mr. Terry, but would you tell me something about the horn? I'd like to know how you do certain things.'" "We talked," Terry says, "but my mind was really on some girls dancing around a Maypole." "And I was so preoccupied with all the beautiful schoolgirls around that I said, 'Why don't you get lost – stop bugging me,' which is something I never normally do." "I kind of fluffed the kid off," Terry adds. If the incident had happened a few years later, Terry might well have earned an enemy for life, but as it happened, Davis was young and apparently willing to accept being "fluffed off" in order to learn. His own account of his meeting with Terry shows no hard feelings – far from it. "Around that time I met Clark Terry," he says. "He was playing like Buck Clayton in those days, only faster. I started to play like him. I idolized him."

Soon after that meeting, when Davis was only sixteen, he began playing professionally around St. Louis. His precocious career was helped, no doubt, by the fact that many of the older, more experienced musicians were leaving town with the armed services, as the United States geared up for and then joined the Second World War. Davis's first regular job as a trumpet player was exactly the one that he most desired at the time, and he landed it through a combination of audacity and sheer luck. In a bull session with some of his friends he had been denigrating some of the local St. Louis bands and lauding Eddie Randle's Blue Devils, calling them "the only band in town," when some of his friends decided to call his bluff and dared him to ask Randle for a job. "You know how I take dares," he told Julie Coryell. "I called him and he said, 'Come on over.'" Davis was hired, and he worked with the band for three years.

Very little is known about the band because it stayed so close to home, which was one of the reasons that it could be the working band for a high school sophomore. Its members definitely included some musicians who deserved to be heard further afield, according to Davis. He has said that the band's saxophonist, Clyde Higgins, "played like Bird and could read anything, but Jimmy Lunceford wouldn't hire him 'cause he was too black. They only wanted to hire handsome cats." The band's book seems to have been made up mainly of what would later be known as rhythm and blues. In 1969, Davis told an interviewer, "You don't have to be a special kind of player to play rock. That's what we were playing when I first started playing with Eddie Randle's Blue Devils in St. Louis – played the blues, *all* the time."

Playing regularly in the band accelerated his development. Clyde Higgins's wife, Mabel, who played piano with the Blue Devils, helped him, and he became more and more preoccupied with what he could learn from instructional books. "I used to buy a lot of books on theory," he says. "Also, people would show me different things – like Mabel Higgins, who showed me some things on piano – a great woman; she was fat but great. I spent a lot of time learning this shit – reading a lot of books, canceling on a lot of people I thought I liked." And, of course, he was playing in public regularly and learning in a practical way, for which there has never been a substitute in the education of a jazzman.

In a very short time, he came a very long way. Clark Terry again supplies the telling details: "I was used to going up to the Elks Club in St. Louis to jam," he says. "One night, as I was climbing the long flight of stairs, I heard a trumpet player flying about on his horn in a way I couldn't recognize. Eddie Randle had the band, and I knew everyone in it but this little trumpet player. After I got over by the stand it dawned on me I'd seen the fellow before. As I said, 'Aren't you –?', he broke in with, 'Yeah, I'm the kid you fluffed off in Carbondale.'" The incident took place within a year of their first encounter in Carbondale.

Terry befriended him, and for the year remaining before Terry was drafted into the navy and stationed in Chicago, he opened up the doors of the St. Louis jazz scene for him. Davis recalls: "He'd come over to my house and ask my father if I could go with him, you know, and he'd take me to a session. Man, we'd play from six o'clock to six the next morning." In no time at all their sessions together at a club called the Moonlight Inn were important local events. "When Clark Terry and I were friends, in order to get inspiration, he would play with me. He could play real fast. People would hear that we were playing and the place would be full. I wasn't drinking or anything then ... Clark used to play so fast 'cause he played out of a clarinet book, and I used to play out of a piano book and a French book on clarinet. I'd play a whole page in one breath. He'd play everything down the scale. Sometimes, just to tease him, I'd play what he'd play. We had a ball."

Terry joined the navy in 1942 and stayed until 1945, serving most of that time as a member of the navy band in Chicago, where he could make it back to St. Louis on leave if he wanted to. After the war, he returned to St. Louis and played locally for a while, but by then Davis had left for New York. "I tried to get him to come to New York," Davis says, "but I couldn't. He came three years later." By the time Terry arrived in New York, Davis was already recognized as one of the young stars.

Terry has defended the character of his young friend against his later critics. "He was a nice, quiet little kid then, and I think the changes in him are a cover-up. Deep down, basically, he's a beautiful cat ... If he seems to go to great lengths to conceal it, he's probably been given a hard time by people who've mistreated him and he feels he doesn't have to accept these things any more."

The jam sessions that Terry introduced him to were often on the showboats, the ones that Davis had heard about from Elwood Buchanan. "The boat would stop in St. Louis and Clark would call me up and say, 'Let's go to the session.' I had to get the okay from my father. So we'd go to a session; we'd jam all night. Guys would drink whiskey, change drums. Drummers would do all kinds of tricks with their sticks; trumpet players doing different shit – playing high notes, changing keys. They didn't care what you wanted to play – 'Let's play!'" Some of the men who impressed him are now dim legends in the early annals of the music. "Fats Pichon was a fat cat who played piano; Stanley Williams was just a little lighter than me, with straight black hair. They could swing like a mother-fucker – those funky meters, the way they play today. I said, 'Oh, shit, that's how bad I want to be.'"

Not all the players Davis met were from New Orleans; some were from Kansas City, which had replaced New Orleans as the incubator of jazz style in the previous decade, and some were from Oklahoma. Davis remembers two trumpeters particularly: "Alonzo Pettiford was one of the best trumpet players I've ever heard; he could play real fast. But my main man used to play sax and trumpet. His name was Charlie Young. All those guys who came from Kansas City and Oklahoma, they were playing eastern music," meaning the music of New York City. It was probably the other way around; the musicians in New York were absorbing the lessons of the Midwesterners, who were gravitating there all the time. Alonzo Pettiford's brother, Oscar, a superb bassist and also one of the few men capable of playing jazz on a cello, had left for New York before Miles Davis made it to the showboats.

The greatest player to come out of Kansas City before Charlie Parker, tenor saxophonist Lester Young, nicknamed "the President" by Billie Holiday and known as Prez to the other musicians, was also based in New York by this time. Several commentators have noted the stylistic similarities between Lester Young and Miles Davis, even though none of them was aware of the close encounters the two had in St. Louis. Sadik Hakim, Young's pianist, who was known at the time by his Christian name, Argonne Thornton, recalls: "One of the things I guess people don't realize is that Lester contributed much to the way Miles plays. When I first went with Lester Young, we used to go to St. Louis quite a bit when we traveled; it was one of the cities we stopped in and played in frequently. I remember Miles used to come and listen to Shorty McConnell [the band's trumpeter], and he used to come and bring his horn and play. He was very young, of course. But he'd sit in and he really dug Prez at the time and I think much of his style, if you listen to him closely, was from Prez. He took many of the things Prez did and transferred them to his style, which we know as the cool style, which Miles is famous for."

Another musician who provided a valuable lesson for Davis was Fats Navarro, then an almost unknown young trumpeter. Davis's recollection links Navarro with the music of New Orleans, but Navarro was not from the center of creole culture at all but from Florida. "Fats Navarro was in a band with Andy Kirk and Howard McGhee that played in town," Davis remembers. "He started that whole style from New Orleans. Fats is a creole; nobody ever mentions him. He's one of the greatest trumpet players I ever heard. He could also play saxophone like Coltrane. He didn't imitate anybody – he had his own style, he created it." For Davis, Navarro's example reinforced the importance of developing an individual style.

His early exposure to good musicians, established ones as well as unknowns, leads Davis to disparage the usual view that bebop started in New York in the early 1940s. "Nobody started a style," he said, "it just happened. It happened when I was thirteen. Everyone who came from Oklahoma, Kansas City, New Orleans, and St. Louis played like that." Undeniably, however, New York became the focal point for the experiments with aggressive rhythms and innovative harmonies known as bebop, and the style spread outward from there.

Inevitably, Davis's precocious contact with touring musicians contributed to more than his musical education. "Music was easy," he has said, and it could not occupy all of his time. "I was fascinated by the musicians, particularly guys who used to come up from New Orleans and jam all night. I'd sit there and look at them, watch the way they walked and talked, how they fixed their hair, how they'd drink, and of course how they played." He quickly came to realize that a man's style was not confined to his music. More than that, in music he found that he could support the lifestyle to which he was attracted. Because the other members of Eddie Randle's band held day jobs in the steel mill and elsewhere, Davis became the band's "musical director," charged with setting up and rehearsing the music for the acts they accompanied. The responsibilities brought him a pay raise. "When I was about sixteen, I was making $85 a week with Eddie Randle's band," he recalled, although on other occasions he has raised the remembered salary to $100 and $125, and lowered the remembered age to fifteen. "I was driving my father's car and I had ten suits. I got them from the pawnshop. I'd get them down to $20 a suit – Brooks Brothers and so on." At the age of sixteen he was already on his way to the lifestyle that would someday encompass Ferraris and the best-dressed list of *Gentleman's Quarterly*.

By contrast, Clark Terry at about this same age, a few years before Davis, had found himself in totally different circumstances. "I worked myself up on a paper route, and another for hauling ashes and tin cans, even going out of my neighborhood, maybe a mile away," Terry recalled. "I worked in a bowling alley setting pins. Every night and weekends I'd be working. Eventually, out of my savings, I bought a $15 bike – $10 down and a dollar a month." It seems a far cry from wearing Brooks Brothers suits and driving your father's car, but the contrast does not end there. The hard-earned bicycle turned out to be, as Terry said, "my undoing. We were supposed to hand over the money we earned and when my father found out about it he was furious. 'Whoever sees him first,' he told the others, 'tell him now he's got a bike to keep riding on it!' He meant it, definitely, and it seems I've been riding on it ever since, because I never went home from that point on." Part of the difference between Terry and Davis, but only part, was a matter of timing; Terry's adolescence was spent in the Great Depression but Davis was just young enough that he could spend most of his in the years of full employment brought on by the war.

As Davis's sense of style in other matters blossomed, so did his sense of style in music. He started to get noticed by visiting musicians by the time he was sixteen. Incredible though it seems, Kinney Dorham, another aspiring young trumpeter living in Austin, Texas, heard about Davis while they were both high school students, through a neighbor who spent some summers in St. Louis. Sonny Stitt, only two years older than Davis, arrived in St. Louis touring with Tiny Bradshaw's band. In between sets at the club where he was playing, he dropped into the Rhumboogie nightclub where Randle's Blue Devils were accompanying the floor shows and his attention became fixed on Miles Davis. Davis says that Stitt approached him at intermission and said, "You look like a man named Charlie Parker and you play like him too. Come on with us." Stitt then went back to his boss and coaxed him to make Davis an offer. "The fellows in the band had their hair slicked down, they wore tuxedos, and they offered me $60 a week to play with them," Davis says. "I went home and asked my mother if I could go, but she said no, I had to finish high school. I didn't talk to her for two weeks." Later on, in 1943 and 1944, Davis had similar offers from Illinois Jacquet, whose band toured out of Houston, and from A.J. Sulliman, whose band, McKinney's Cotton Pickers, was a final attempt at reviving one of the most popular recording bands of a decade before. All of them were told that they would have to wait until he graduated from high school.

That day was not far off. Davis maintains that his work at Lincoln High School was not a particular problem for him because he possesses a photographic memory: "See, if I had a book, I could look at it and remember the whole page. It came to me like that. I can remember anything – telephone numbers, addresses. Even today I can just glance at them and remember. That's the reason I used to take care of band payrolls; I could remember all the tabs and shit." The school regimen, as he remembers it, was easy, even though he was out playing music most of the night. "I was awake until five in the morning, then in class at nine, talking about Shakespeare. Miss Johnson, my teacher, was too hip – she saw me with a girl and said, 'That bitch ain't nothing.' I didn't fuck until I was eighteen. I made all As, and I got out of school and said, 'Fuck it!' I didn't make my own graduation. My father didn't care. He just said, 'Anything you're going to do, do it well.'"

His parents were now separated, and Davis's growing independence was matched by a growing sense of responsibility, especially for his sister, Dorothy. He claims that he taught her mathematics even though she was two years ahead of him in school. He also claims to have paid for part of her education at Fisk University, in Nashville, Tennessee, starting when he was sixteen. Around the time that Davis moved to New York to start his own further education, Dorothy graduated from Fisk as a qualified teacher.

As might be expected of a young dude in a Brooks Brothers suit, Davis was soon attracting attention for reasons other than his music. His account of Miss Johnson's advice to him in high school, although it is couched very much in the idiom of Davis himself, no doubt has its basis in fact. He has described another early encounter as well: "Ann Young, Billie Holiday's niece, said, 'Let me take you to New York and buy you a new horn.' But I was making $125 a week and buying slick suits in pawnshops, and I had just bought a horn, and I wasn't fucking." These references to the age at which he "started fucking" are curious. They crop up, apparently unsolicited, in several interviews he gave in the 1970s, and usually, though not exclusively, when his interviewer is female. That might suggest that he is tossing them into the conversation for their shock value – especially when, as in the interview with Harriet Choice for the *Chicago Tribune*, he makes an outlandish remark and then asks, "You gonna print that?" Moreover, his claims seem to have no basis in truth. His claim that "I didn't fuck until I was eighteen" is pure fiction, because almost two years before that, in 1943, he was already an expectant father. He was probably married that year, at the age of sixteen (although the *New York Times* primly referred to the arrangement as a "relationship" in contrast to his later marriages). His young wife, Irene, gave birth to a daughter, Cheryl, in 1944, and to his two sons, Gregory in 1946 and Miles IV in 1950. Davis became a grandfather in 1968, at the age of forty-two.

In June 1944, when he was graduating *in absentia* from high school, Davis left St. Louis for the first time with a band, Adam Lambert's Six Brown Cats. Lambert's band, an obscure New Orleans group playing a modern swing style, had finished a long engagement at the Club Silhouette in St. Louis, where Joe Williams, who much later became the featured vocalist with Count Basie's orchestra, was their singer. As they were about to leave for a two-week engagement at the Club Belvedere in Springfield, Illinois, their trumpet player, Tom Jefferson, grew homesick and decided to return to New Orleans. Davis was recommended to replace him. He recalls, "There was a school teacher in St. Louis who was a hell of a trumpet player. They needed someone in Springfield, Illinois, who could read and he told them about me. That's where I made my first hundred dollars. Sometimes we'd play for strippers, then a guy would come in and tell jokes." After the two weeks in Springfield, Lambert's Brown Cats moved on to Chicago but Davis returned home.

His return to St. Louis put Davis in the right place for what would be the best musical experience of his St. Louis years. The Billy Eckstine orchestra was scheduled to play for two weeks at the Riviera in St. Louis that July. Although the public would not know it for another year or so, most musicians in the United States already knew that the Eckstine band was a collection of the finest young jazz talent in the country. The band provided the steady jobs for many of the insurgents who were leading the bebop revolution in New York. In the summer of 1944, the band had just been formed, and the two weeks at the Riviera proved to be crucial for its development. Art Blakey joined the band there as its drummer, filling a chair that had been suspect before he arrived. In New York most of the musicians were preoccupied with playing after-hours and with other diversions, and the engagement in St. Louis allowed the band to work together with some concentration of effort. Eckstine says, "That is where we really whipped the band together – in St. Louis. We used to rehearse all day, every day, then work at night."

According to Dizzy Gillespie, the band's musical director and lead trumpet player, they were originally scheduled to play at the Plantation Club instead of the Riviera. Gillespie recalls the strange set of circumstances leading to the change of venue: "The Plantation Club in St. Louis was a white club," he points out. "They fired Billy Eckstine's band because we came in through the front door. We just walked right in with our horns, in front. And the gangsters – St. Louis was a stronghold of gangsterism – said, 'Them guys got to go.' So we changed jobs with George Hudson. He came over and played for them. Clark Terry was with that band. We went over to work at another place." If Gillespie's memory is correct, the band seem to have made a good deal for themselves out of the situation, for the Riviera, where the Eckstine band played in July 1944, is described by Clark Terry as "a big, plush sort of place where Ellington swears he originally wrote *Sophisticated Lady*."

Miles Davis, who had turned eighteen that spring, ended up playing with the Eckstine band during their stay. He recalls the events leading up to his temporary engagement this way: "A friend and I went to see them. I had my horn with me; we'd just left rehearsal. As soon as I walked in, this guy runs up to me and says, 'Do you have a union card?' It was Dizzy. I didn't even know him. I said, 'Yeah, I have a union card.' 'We need a trumpet player. Come on.' I wanted to hear him. I could always read, so I got on the bandstand and started playing. I couldn't even read the music at first from listening to Dizzy and Bird. The third trumpet man was sick; I knew the book because I loved the music so much, so I played with the Eckstine band around St. Louis for about three weeks. After that, I knew I had to go to New York." These events were reconstructed a little differently by Eckstine. "Miles used to follow us around in St. Louis," he says. "He used to ask to sit in with the band. I'd let him so as not to hurt his feelings, because, then, Miles was awful. He sounded terrible, he couldn't play at all." Later he added, "You couldn't hear him past the reed section."

The two accounts are irreconcilable, but there are probably elements of truth in both. The teenaged Davis was no doubt a less accomplished musician than the New York pros with whom Eckstine was used to working, but if Davis were as utterly incompetent as Eckstine suggests, he would certainly not have been received so enthusiastically by Gillespie and Parker when he turned up in New York a few months later. Eckstine's version may have been revamped in the telling, perhaps to add a touch of irony to his early encounter with the trumpeter

Eddy Randle's Blue Devils at the Rhumboogie Club, St. Louis, 1943; Miles Davis, age 17, in the far right of the back row (courtesy Frank Driggs collection)

Billy Eckstine and Charlie Parker at the opening of Birdland, August 1949 (courtesy of *Down Beat*)

who would soon be heralded as a rising star. In any event, Davis was recruited by Gillespie to replace an ailing regular. Buddy Anderson, the third trumpeter in the section, discovered that he had tuberculosis soon after the band arrived in St. Louis. He returned home to Oklahoma City and retired from music altogether. Davis filled his chair while the band was in St. Louis, and when it moved on to its next engagement at the Regal Theater in Chicago, Gillespie recruited Marion Hazel to replace Davis.

Davis's brief stint with the Eckstine band was his first brush with the leaders of the jazz vanguard of the day. It sharpened his urge to leave East St. Louis for New York, a move that had been a matter of considerable controversy within his family ever since his graduation from high school. His mother wanted him to join his sister at Fisk. "You know how women are," Davis shrugs. "She said they had a good music department and the Fisk Jubilee Singers." Davis responded by taking home the latest edition of the *Esquire Jazz Book* and brandishing it at her. "I looked in the book, and I asked my mother, 'Where's all this?'" "That's where I wanted to go," he says. Finally, to settle the dispute, "I got hold of my father, and got permission to go to New York, where I enrolled at Juilliard." His intention to attend the Juilliard School of Music should have assuaged his mother, but there is no indication that it did.

When Miles Davis left East St. Louis in 1945, the war was still raging in the Pacific, although there was a growing hope that its end was finally in sight. In the next decade, Davis would visit his family fairly frequently, and after that, his returns to the area would be surrounded by the aura of triumph, with a hail of advance publicity for his club dates and concerts, and line-ups around the block for reserved seats. His father would grow in stature in the post-war boom, running for state representative but losing, and increasing his wealth until his son, when he was perhaps the best-paid jazz musician in the history of the music, could point to him with filial pride and say, "He's worth more than me." Of his mother, Davis has had little more to say than this of her remaining days: "When my mother was sick I went to see her in the hospital. I knew she was dying of cancer. But when she died I didn't go to the funeral." Miles Davis sums up his roots in East St. Louis by declaring, "I don't believe in families. Like, if I die, my money ain't going to go to people just because they're close relatives. The people that are closest to me are the ones that helped me to do what I do, not just because somebody's my brother. If I had a lot of money, I wouldn't leave everything to my brother or sister just because they're related to me." Looked at dispassionately, that view of the family is perhaps very rational, and one might even imagine the pragmatic Doc Davis beaming at his first-born son for expounding it. Miles Davis put East St. Louis behind him irrevocably when he boarded the train for New York. He would return fairly frequently, but always as a visitor.

Davis's move to New York, like so many of his moves, was perfectly timed, thus making it much easier for him to cut off his ties with the place where he had spent a secure and relatively comfortable youth. The new sound of bebop was just moving out of the Harlem night spots where it took shape and was settling into the downtown jazz clubs on 52nd Street – *The* Street, it was called. Within a few years it would be everywhere, even on Broadway, where it would have its own clubs. Bebop gradually displaced both the swing bands and the traditional Dixielanders, who fought a tough rearguard action to keep it out. In the bebop explosion, many young unknowns would rise to prominence in jazz. Miles Davis would eventually be the foremost among them, and he had been well prepared for his rise to the top by what he had learned in St. Louis. He recognized that himself. "When I got to New York, I thought everybody knew as much as I did," he said, "and I was surprised. Wasn't nobody playing but Dizzy and Roy [Eldridge]. The guys who *were* playing, you didn't even know or hear of. Same way in my hometown. I was fifteen and guys would come to hear me play because they heard about me." Now, three years later, at eighteen, he was on his way to New York, where almost no one had heard about him. Three years after *that*, when he turned twenty-one, everyone in the world who knew anything about the music at all would have heard about him.

2

52nd Street Theme
1945–6

I used to make the rounds and play many places – Victoria at 141st and Seventh, the Harlem Club on 116th between Lenox and Seventh, places on Eighth Avenue. There were about fifteen places where we'd go ... It was a wonderful time. But 52nd Street was better. Uptown we were just experimenting. By the time we came down our ideas were beginning to be accepted. Oh, it took some time, but 52nd Street gave us the rooms to play and the audiences ... 52nd Street was a mother. I say mother – and I don't mean motherfucker, though it was that, too.   John Birks 'Dizzy' Gillespie

Miles Davis traveled to New York City with another aspiring young trumpeter from St. Louis, a young man remembered only by his first name, Henry. He too was planning to enrol at the Juilliard School of Music, but he apparently did not share Davis's ulterior motive of making his way into the thriving jazz scene that was then in full bloom in Harlem – which even to Davis must have seemed a faint hope. The first hurdle was to pass the audition at Juilliard so that they could be admitted into the summer semester. "There was an entrance exam," Davis recalled for Julie Coryell. "I played a song called *Youth Dauntless* – I don't know what that means, but it was very fast. My best friend Henry was taking the exam too. He said, 'If I don't get in, my mother will kill me!' I said, 'What are you gonna play?' He said, 'Clyde McCoy's *Sugar Blues*.' We both got in but he just couldn't play – he turned out to be a good writer. He was pretty cool, but he just looked wrong playing the trumpet."

As soon as the entrance exam was passed, Davis started searching for Charlie Parker, the alto saxophonist whom he had listened to in awe when he was sitting in with Billy Eckstine's orchestra the summer before. Parker was known to his friends as Bird, an abbreviation of Yardbird, the nickname he sported from his hometown days in Kansas City because of his prodigious appetite for fried chicken. He already carried an underground reputation as the best young jazz player alive, but that reputation would not begin to surface for a few more months, when his recordings of *Groovin' High* and *Shaw Nuff* with Dizzy Gillespie for Savoy Records (made in February 1945) became available. For the time being, his reputation was confined mainly to the Harlem habitués of Clark Monroe's Uptown House, Minton's Playhouse, and the other night spots that featured jam sessions with the young upstarts, and to the handful of young blacks who had been aware enough to seek out the Billy Eckstine orchestra, as Miles Davis had, when it made its inaugural tour.

In 1945, Parker was still close enough to anonymity to be hard to find. "I spent my first week in New York and my first month's allowance looking for Charlie Parker," Davis recalls. He finally caught up with him at a jam session at a place called the Heatwave in Harlem. If the search seemed difficult, its result must have made Davis feel that it was all worthwhile. Parker not only recognized Davis, but he greeted him expansively and hung out with him for the rest of the night. When he finished playing for the night, Parker packed up his horn and went with Davis back to his rooming house, where they talked some more and finally caught some sleep. The next day, when Davis returned from his classes, Parker was still there, and they decided to share the apartment on a regular basis. Charlie Parker had moved in.

The immediate attraction of the guru of the jazz vanguard for the untried Juilliard student begs for an explanation, but it will probably remain a mystery. Apart from the music they played, the two men had almost nothing in common. Parker was twenty-four and Davis was eighteen. Parker had been educated on the streets of Kansas City and had been enmeshed in night life since the age of fifteen, when he moved out on his widowed mother; she had doted on his every whim and supported his every indulgence from the day he was born, even though it meant abject poverty for her. Davis had been exposed to the rawest elements of the night but had to return home to a family that took some pains to impress upon him that he was expected to bear its high standards. Parker had gluttonous appetites for food and drink and sex, and the appetites were usually visible – the dregs of his indulgences accumulated on his clothes until the suit finally wore out and he could beg or borrow a replacement. Davis, already a father, drank a little but was not very interested in it, and he was proud of the small closetful of suits he owned. Parker began using heroin when he was little more than a boy and was addicted to it by the time he was fifteen; Davis knew some heroin addicts in the St. Louis nightclubs but was not interested in it himself – not yet. Apart from their music, the two had little in common.

An uncynical view of Parker's attraction to Davis and the attention he gave him would simply claim that Parker saw in Davis the promise of remarkable musicianship, which of course he later realized. Probably no one has ever taken that view seriously, because too much is known about the character of Parker. In the personality of an abysmally spoiled youngster growing into an insatiable adolescent junkie, regardless of his musical genius, there is hardly room for sponsoring a young disciple. Parker was notoriously selfish in almost every close relationship throughout his entire life, whether with musicians who idolized him, fans who worshipped him, or women who adored him. Parker's story includes countless tales of his borrowing another musician's saxophone when his was pawned, playing a job with it, and then pawning the borrowed one; or of women nursing him back to health from a narcotic or alcoholic stupor and then waking to find him gone, sometimes with their silverware, fur coats, and money. As the poet Ted Joans puts it, "He took from those he loved as well as from those he had only just met." The wonder is that Parker never ran out of dupes, and many people allowed him to work his con on them more than once. But then, he was not just a psychopath, but also a genius. He stands as one of the greatest improvisers in the history of jazz. He possessed a gift so enormous that it prevailed through most of the health and personality problems that wracked him. Because of Parker's genius, almost no one has ever thought to ask why the young Miles Davis should have admitted a character like Parker so easily into his private life – the question has always been about Parker allowing Davis into *his* life. Davis arrived in New York with rooms for Parker to live in and an allowance of $40 a week for Parker to spend. Although Parker, throughout his adult life, was notorious for singling out his young idolators and treating them with cruel condescension – making them carry his saxophone case, hold doors for him, run trifling errands, and otherwise demean themselves – nothing we know about Davis suggests that he would play that role. The point that Parker saw in Davis someone who was relatively well fixed has more credibility, and Parker did take some of his money and pawn some of his belongings. Davis was willing enough to share his allowance with Parker and his other new friends. "I blew it takin' care of Bird ... and all them guys," he told Cheryl McCall. "They didn't have any money, *I* had the money. Got so bad I used to tell them, just keep some of it, 'cause those guys asked me for money."

For Parker, rooming with Davis may or may not have meant that he had ready access to the money he needed to support his appetites, but it certainly also meant the companionship of a young musician who respected his abilities and gave him some cause for self-respect. For Davis, the arrangement meant ready access to the vital music scene in which Parker was already a leader, and a conspicuous entry into it.

Just a few months earlier, the burgeoning new style of the young blacks in Harlem had moved downtown, to fabled 52nd Street, where its thunderstruck white audience would christen it bebop or rebop, eventually shortened to just bop.

The surfacing of the new music would soon send up a clamor that would some-times end in fist fights over the relative merits of bop versus the traditional two-beat music that originated in New Orleans. The Street had itself been the nightclub center for more traditional jazz styles, especially swing, during the pre-ceding decade. But the wartime clientele of servicemen from all over the country were moved less by swing music than were the more genteel downtowners they were crowding out of the clubs; several of the managers on 52nd Street had switched to striptease and pop vocalists to keep the audiences coming in. The switch away from jazz did not, however, sit well with some of the managers, probably because the girlie shows brought in crowds that were tougher to handle but also, according to Arnold Shaw in *The Street That Never Slept*, because some of the managers were genuine music fans. The Onyx, at 57 52nd Street, tried bringing in a bop band as an alternative to striptease. The first bop band on The Street was a quintet led jointly by Dizzy Gillespie and bassist Oscar Pettiford, with Don Byas on tenor saxophone, George Wallington on piano, and Max Roach on drums. To the managers, the business proved good enough to warrant a second look. After that, bop groups began working at the Three Deuces and the Spotlite, across the street from the Onyx, as well.

The real birth of bop as a 52nd Street fixture happened in the winter of 1944–5 when Parker and Gillespie led a quintet, with Al Haig on piano, Curly Russell on bass, and Stan Levey on drums, at the Three Deuces. The audacious melodies and breakneck rhythms had the jazz fans agog. For the next three years, until the jazz clubs moved a few blocks away to Broadway, there was always at least one bop band playing somewhere on The Street as long as the clubs were not darkened by the periodic clean-ups of the vice squad. When Parker was not working in the band, he was usually there sitting in with them. Starting in the spring of 1945, Miles Davis was often at his side. "I used to follow him around, down to 52nd Street, where he used to play," Davis says. "Then he used to get me to play. 'Don't be afraid,' he used to tell me. 'Go ahead and play.'" Sometimes Davis could over-come his nerves and get up on the bandstand, but even then his efforts were wary. "I used to play under him all the time," he says. "When Bird would play a mel-ody, I'd play just under him and let him lead the note, swing the note. The only thing that I'd add would be a larger sound. I used to quit every night when I was playing with that guy. I'd say, 'What do you need me for?' That man could swing a whole band. One of the record companies should have recorded him with a good big band. Then you would have heard something!"

Parker's insistence that Davis get up and play is one piece of evidence that his interest in the young trumpeter was not entirely self-serving. He had himself been through a period when his talent was less than fully formed and the older musicians had given a rough ride. He had refused to give in. Now, he was refusing to allow Davis to give in. Budd Johnson, the tenor saxophonist whom Parker had succeeded in the Earl Hines band and was with him now in Eckstine's band, saw the parallel: "Well, when Charlie started to play the saxophone in Kansas City, when the cats would see him come around, they'd say, 'Oh no, not this cat again, man! I mean, look –' And they did the same thing with Miles Davis on 52nd Street. 'If this cat's gonna get on the stand, I'm not gonna play, man.' That's how bad he sounded." Johnson's comment is one of the few direct statements that corroborates Eckstine's criticism of Davis in St. Louis. Far from quitting now, Davis was putting himself through the paces that would bring him up to The Street's standards before much longer. And he was doing a lot more than just forcing himself to get up on the bandstand. "Every night I'd write down chords I heard on matchbook covers," he says. "Everybody helped me. Next day I'd play those chords all day in the practice room at Juilliard, instead of going to classes."

Then suddenly, and certainly prematurely, Davis found himself in a recording studio with a band led by a reedman named Herbie Fields. Under other circumstances, it might have proven to be a break for the young trumpeter, a chance to be heard by a wider public before his career had properly started. However, he played almost as if he were trying to be inaudible. It was, to put it mildly, a forgettable recording debut. The recordings were made by Savoy, an aggressive independent label, and the details are as follows:

Herbie Fields' Band with Rubberlegs Williams
Miles Davis, tpt; Herbie Fields, as, ts; unknown rhythm section; Rubberlegs Williams, vcl. New York, 24 April 1945
That's the Stuff You Gotta Watch (Savoy 564); *Pointless Mama Blues* (Savoy 564); *Deep Sea Blues* (Savoy 5516); *Bring It on Home* (Savoy 5516)
Jepsen and Ruppli both list John Mehegan, pno; Al Casey, gtr; Slam Stewart, b; and Lionel Hampton, dms; Priestley lists Teddy Brannon, pno; Leonard Gaskin, b; and Eddie Nicholson, dms.

Davis's recording debut, a month before his nineteenth birthday, catches him in the uncertain mood that he described when he played beside Parker on 52nd Street. (These sides have never been reissued, and the originals are very hard to find, and so I have heard only *That's the Stuff You Gotta Watch* and *Pointless Mama Blues*; even if there is a marked improvement in his playing on the other pieces, it will still probably raise the level only to the pedestrian.) On both of the first tunes, Davis uses a mute except for the opening ensemble of *Pointless Mama Blues*, and he sounds as if he is facing away from the microphone. By contrast, the vocalist, Rubberlegs Williams, is a bawler, and Herbie Fields, playing tenor saxophone on both pieces, displays a raucous, rough tone, very much in the rhythm-

and-blues idiom. Davis can barely be detected playing wispy obbligatos on the vocal choruses, and he lays out entirely when Fields solos. The earliest discographies listed Snooky Young as the trumpeter on these sessions, but since then Davis has admitted that he was the trumpeter. He confessed, "I was too nervous to play, and I only performed in the ensembles, no solos." Still, if one concentrates on the trumpet line, it is possible to pick out typical little figures played by Davis occasionally, especially at the close of the vocal choruses on *Pointless Mama Blues*.

Rubberlegs Williams is credited in some accounts as a blues shouter, but that calling seems much too generous on the evidence of these recordings. He comes off instead as a comedy singer, making weird vocal noises and slyly underlining the mild innuendos of his jive lyrics. The records were clearly an attempt by the small Savoy label to get a hit with a novelty song, a genre the public had recently shown they would buy when other labels put out such cornball items as *Open the Door Richard* and *Cement Mixer (Putt-ee Putt-ee)*. Williams, a show-business veteran who performed low comedy in minstrel costume and dresses, had been approached earlier by the producers of Continental records for a similar project. The song for Continental, recorded in January, was called *I Want Every Bit of It*, and it seems to have met with the same lack of success that these Savoy sides were to have. On *I Want Every Bit of It*, Williams's accompanists included Dizzy Gillespie and Charlie Parker as well as several other top musicians. Probably Gillespie was invited to play on the Savoy date and declined, suggesting Davis as his substitute.

The leader of the recording session, Herbie Fields, remains a shadowy figure. Considered at the time to be a rising star on 52nd Street, he was, as it turned out, very close to the peak of his career instead. He had returned to New York in 1943 from the army, where he was a bandleader, and at the time of these recordings was featured with Lionel Hampton's band. Fields's return to civilian life was followed almost immediately by one of the few triumphs of his career, as he was awarded the *Esquire* New Star for alto saxophone in 1945. One of the few recollections of Fields from these times comes from Jimmy Heath, the tenor saxophone player, who complained that "the cool school was an effeminate kind of playing; they were the ones who didn't try to swing hard," and then added, as if by way of explanation, "Herbie Fields used to put pancake make-up on his face to travel with Lionel Hampton." As a white man in a black band, Fields used to darken his complexion artificially, but there was certainly no hint of effeminacy in Fields's playing, and no coolness either. In any event, after his promising start in the mid-1940s, Fields soon disappeared from jazz altogether. He committed suicide in 1958.

Not surprisingly, Davis's studies at Juilliard were not going very well. Diverted by making his recording debut and concerned with surviving on 52nd Street, he paid little attention to the Juilliard program, which increasingly seemed simply irrelevant to him. "I didn't believe it," he told Julie Coryell. "They showed me some things I already knew when I was fourteen about theory and all that shit." When he did leave the practice room to work on the program, he found it less than challenging: "I did Juilliard summer school in one night – Mozart's *Requiem in E-flat*; I took it apart musically, with Hindemith's *Kleine Kammermusik* for an introduction." Inevitably, he soon concluded, "All that shit they were teaching wasn't doing me a damn bit of good." He persisted, however, for about a semester and a half, probably out of deference to his father, who had gone out on a limb to send him there.

It is often assumed that Charlie Parker was mainly responsible for the music that Davis was learning, probably because of their shared accommodation in the first year and Davis's stint in the Parker quintet later on, in 1947–8. Ross Russell, who recorded Davis with Parker in four sessions during 1946–7, says, "Parker's music was the alpha and omega of Miles Davis's trumpet style and musical system." But Russell's statement could apply equally well to dozens of musicians Davis's age, on whom Parker's influence was undeniably great. That influence touched Davis no less than it touched virtually all of his contemporaries, and also no more. Parker was a teacher solely by his example. "He never did talk about music," Davis has said. More important to his development were the musicians who did talk about music with him during these crucial years, and the first – and perhaps the most important – was Dizzy Gillespie.

No less than Parker, John Birks Gillespie seems to have been interested in Davis's development from the moment he arrived in New York. Gillespie, who was saddled with the nickname Dizzy because of his crazy antics whenever he was onstage, has always been a comparatively stable and reliable individual among jazzmen, despite the nickname. If Parker was the spirit of the bop movement, Gillespie was its head and its hands. He looked out for the interests of the younger players who were yearning to join in, and he seems never to have given a thought to the fact that he and Davis, who was nine years younger, might someday be seen as contenders or rivals by a fickle jazz audience. Gillespie's long and distinguished career has been sullied somewhat by his neglect in the superficial popularity polls conducted annually by such magazines as *Down Beat*, *Esquire*, and, later on, *Playboy*, in which top awards went to Davis rather than Gillespie year after year; it was not until 1956 that Gillespie was voted top trumpeter in the *Down Beat* readers' poll, and the only other years he was so voted came in 1977 and 1979, when Davis was in temporary retirement. Fortunately, the musicians are more likely to assign such contests their true value, which is nothing at all. If, in the view of a segment of their listeners, Gillespie has spent much of his career in Davis's shadow, that is a strange irony, for no one spent as many hours discussing music and working out technicalities with Davis in these formative years. It is only since 1979, with the publication of Gillespie's memoirs (with Al Fraser), *To Be or Not to Bop*, that the early involvement of the two trumpeters became widely known.

While Davis was sharing his apartment with Parker, Gillespie's house was the daytime gathering place of the boppers. "My house was full all the time," Gillespie says. "Miles used to stay there. He didn't have a bed there because there was no room to have a bed for him. But as soon as he'd get up – boom, he was over there. Kinney Dorham, Max [Roach], everybody. Any one of the guys of that era – Monk, all of them – came by my place, which was a clearinghouse for our music." It was Gillespie who urged Davis to learn to play the piano. "Miles ... used to ask me, 'Man, where do you get them notes?' 'Off the piano,' I'd say. 'That's your ass if you don't play the piano, you can't find them. You might luck up on them sometimes, but if you play the piano, you'll know where they are all the time. You might get lucky and find one every now and then just from playing your own instrument, but if you know the piano you'll know where they are all the time. You can see them.'"

Davis learned Gillespie's lessons quickly, and their relationship soon became useful to both. In Gillespie's memoirs, the two men remembered Davis coming upon an Egyptian minor scale in a theory book and going immediately to Gillespie's house to show it to him. "Egyptian minor scale, that's right," Gillespie recalled. "He was going to Juilliard then. You see, music is so vast, like rhythms and harmonics in our music. Imagine, if you just study that, and study what it has done. And it's infinite." The lesson that Gillespie appears to be proudest of was the playing of minor harmonics in a chord, the so-called flatted fifth, taken to be one of the hallmarks of bebop. Gillespie points out, "It wasn't considered a 'flatted fifth' then, it was considered a half step ... That's what Rudy [Powell] taught me [in 1938], and that has governed my playing ever since. And that's one of the distinctive things about Miles Davis, that he learned from me, I'm sure. Because I showed him on the piano the pretty notes in our music." He adds, "There are some nice notes in a chord, man, so now Miles knows how to hold one note for hours. That's how Miles got all those pretty things he plays. It resolves all the time, that one note. To find out where the notes resolve, you don't have to play every chord. You can hold one note and it'll take care of three chords, because it's in all of them. And pretty notes, too." Gillespie is generally credited with introducing the flatted fifth into bebop as a major stylistic device, and it became a feature of every bopper's style, not just Davis's. But Davis learned it directly while most other musicians were forced to pick it up from Gillespie's records and performances. "We used to hang out together, man, every night," Davis says, "so the shit, you know, rubbed off."

Naturally, much of the discussion between the two centered on their individual styles. In one well-known exchange, they reveal their essential differences. "I asked Dizzy, 'Why can't I play high like you?' 'Because you don't hear up there,' he said, 'you hear in the middle register.' And that's true. There are times when I can't even tell what chords Dizzy is working on when he's up high, and yet he'll tell me what he's playing is just an octave above what I do." Dave Burns, a trumpeter in Gillespie's big band later in the 1940s, sums up the relationship by saying, "If there wasn't a Dizzy Gillespie, there wouldn't have been a Miles Davis. He wouldn't have played that way because he wouldn't have heard Dizzy." Even though their mature styles are poles apart, Burns is probably right. Davis's mature style is not in any meaningful sense derived from Gillespie's, and their technical abilities differ markedly, with Gillespie one of the most gifted pyrotechnicians on his instrument in the history of jazz (or any other genre), but the harmonic basis of their music and their use of rhythm mark their school tie. The influence was by no means one-sided. "I used to tell Dizzy, 'Play in the low register 'cause your low register is out of tune,'" Davis recalls. "See, he and I could talk. Nobody else could tell him. Dizzy's like a relative."

Gillespie was not alone in working with Davis. The musical world Davis entered when he sought out Charlie Parker was a free school. "Monk would write out chords for me, Tadd Dameron, and Dizzy, who advised me to study piano, which I started to. I had some background in understanding progressions from a book I'd bought in St. Louis, *Georgia Gibbs Chord Analysis*." The book, written by a pop singer and picked off the rack of a St. Louis music shop, seems to have been more useful than the training he was supposed to be getting at Juilliard.

As the summer session came to a close and the fall semester got under way, Davis found that he was being accepted more readily by the older musicians on The Street, and as a result he became more involved than ever in the clubs. He had developed his own nightly routine, and he usually showed up without Parker at his side. Coleman Hawkins was playing an extended run at the Downbeat Club, at 66 52nd Street, and his trumpeter, Joe Guy, frequently failed to show up. Davis became a regular substitute, although he still worked free. Around this time, Davis recently told George Goodman, Jr, Hawkins hired him as a kind of non-playing musical director for one of his recording sessions. Davis's job was to spot mistakes Hawkins's sidemen made when they played his arrangements in the studio. Generally, Hawkins seems to have filled the role of patron for Davis. "He would buy a coat for $300 and sell it to me for $15," Davis says.

A few doors away from the Downbeat Club, another tenor saxophonist, Eddie Davis, known as Lockjaw, led a group at the Spotlite that included Rudy Williams on alto, and if Joe Guy was on the stand with Hawkins that night, Davis knew he was welcome to sit in at the Spotlite. According to one report, he accepted a job with Eddie Davis at the Spotlite around this time and played regularly for a month. If so, it was his first paid job in New York.

As often as not, when Davis showed up on The Street he was with Freddie Webster, a trumpeter with the Benny Carter and Jimmy Lunceford bands, among others. Already twenty-eight, Webster was still waiting for the break that would help to publicize his talent, by recording a featured solo or leading a group on 52nd Street. It was a break that never came. In the meantime, he was not bothered much by personal ambition, satisfied to know that other trumpeters recognized his talent for what it was. Even Dizzy Gillespie said that "Freddie Webster probably had the best sound on a trumpet since the trumpet was invented – just alive and full of life." And everyone on The Street knew, as Sadik Hakim put it, that "Miles Davis definitely thought a lot of Freddie Webster and wanted his tone and was influenced by his style." Unfortunately that tone and that style were never documented satisfactorily before Webster died, suddenly and mysteriously, in Chicago in 1947, when he was only thirty. According to George Hoefer, when Webster was a fixture on the New York scene in 1945 he "frequently played at Minton's. Webster had a singing tone with a beauty that especially appealed to Davis. Musicians still talk about the shows at the Apollo when Webster was playing with the Jimmy Lunceford band. When the band played *Stardust*, Webster would be featured in a solo played from the balcony." Davis was not the only trumpeter affected by Webster's sound. Years later, in a blindfold test for *Down Beat* magazine, Thelonious Monk identified a record by Gillespie as characterizing the Webster sound. "That was the Freddie Webster sound, you know, that sound of Dizzy's," he told Leonard Feather, later adding: "Well, if that's not Diz, it's someone who plays just like [Webster]. Miles did at one time too ... Yes, that's the Freddie Webster sound." Webster's influence on Gillespie has seldom been mentioned, but his influence on Davis often is, although it can never be fully appreciated because of the sparsity of recorded evidence from Webster. If we take Davis literally, probably the best recorded instance of Webster's tone and style is heard in Davis's solo in *Billie's Bounce*, recorded in November 1945, a solo that Davis says he likes just because he sounds like Webster.

The little that is known about Webster suggests that he was a complex character. Born in Cleveland, Ohio, in 1917, he grew up with the composer-pianist Tadd Dameron, who was born there in the same year. He worked in Chicago and elsewhere in the Midwest before joining up with the touring bands that would eventually take him to both coasts. Art Pepper, the Los Angeles alto saxophonist, toured with him in Benny Carter's band in 1942. "Freddie Webster was a nice looking, kind of strange looking, little cat," Pepper says. "I had a strong affection for him. He was a little man who could back up the little man complex. His playing was incredibly beautiful. And he always carried an automatic pistol. He felt that because he was black and because of his size, somebody was going to push him into a corner and he'd need an equalizer." Davis may have responded to

Webster's style in more ways than one. Pepper's suggestion of Webster's abrasive personality no less than his beautiful trumpet-playing might well have described the Miles Davis of a few years later.

For Davis, another great virtue of Webster's playing was its economy. "Freddie didn't play a lot of notes," Davis told Nat Hentoff. "He didn't waste any. I used to try to get his sound. He had a great big tone, like Billy Butterfield, but without a vibrato. Freddie was my best friend. I wanted to play like him. I used to teach him chords, everything I learned at Juilliard. He didn't have the money to go. And in return, I'd try to get his tone." Davis's admiration for Webster's self-editing in his playing, a trait that even Gillespie lacked, harks back to his training from Elwood Buchanan and comes up time and again throughout his career. The musicians who earn Davis's highest praise are always those who articulate melodies by a few carefully placed notes rather than by virtuoso runs at great speed. That sensitivity to economy that he heard in Webster signals the beginning of a break from his first 52nd Street models, although it would take a few years to integrate the economy he admired into his own style.

While Webster took over as Davis's main colleague and collaborator in the intensive learning program he was going through, for both of them Gillespie stood out as the master. "Freddie Webster and I used to go down every night to hear Diz," Davis recalls. "If we missed a night, we missed something. Stand up at the bar, throw a quarter, and name the note that it came down on. That shit be going down so fast, and we'd be testing ourselves." Later on he recalled: "We really studied. If a door squeaked, we would call out the exact pitch. And every time I heard the chord of G, for instance, my fingers automatically took the position for C sharp on the horn – the flatted fifth – whether I was playing or not." The tests at Juilliard seemed more and more superfluous.

About Juilliard, Davis says, "Originally I went there to see what was happening but ... I found out nothing was happening." He earned a chair in the student orchestra, but even that proved tedious. "Up at Juilliard I played in the symphony, two notes, 'bop bop,' every ninety bars, so I said let me out of here and then I left." Any conflict he had felt back in East St. Louis about where his musical future lay had been resolved by the head-to-head confrontation of the jazz clubs and academe. "I realized I wasn't going to get in any symphony orchestra," he says. "And I had to go down on The Street at night to play with Bird or Coleman Hawkins, so I decided to go that way – all the way." There remained, of course, the awkward job of telling Doc Davis about his decision. Even with a father who had been so supportive in every decision he had taken so far, this one had an ominous feel to it. It was certainly not the kind of discussion that could be carried out on the telephone, and Davis did not even let his father know that he was on his way home. He just appeared.

In a conversation with Dizzy Gillespie and Al Fraser some thirty-four years later, Davis remembered the confrontation. "My father looked up one day and I was back in St. Louis. 'What the fuck're you doing here?' he said. I said, 'I'll explain. A guy named Dizzy Gillespie and Charlie Parker, Yardbird –' 'Yardbird Parker and Dizzy Gillespie?' he said. 'What're they doing?' 'Well, they're playing a new kind of music, and I can't get that – I can't learn that at Juilliard.' Because everything at Juilliard, I knew."

His father's response, he has reported elsewhere, was gratifying. "Okay – just do it good," he said. "If you need a friend, call me." Davis quit Juilliard as soon as he returned to New York, probably in October 1945.

If it seems obvious to us that Davis's disaffection for Juilliard was basically because they were training musicians for a kind of music that he did not want to play, that realization seems never to have entered his mind. "I was allowed to quit Juilliard," he has said, "because they stretch everything out there, and I did improvisation, and I had imagination." In his view, the trumpeters who stayed behind and eventually graduated "haven't got tones good for anything – they have a legit sound, and it's a white sound." He has even, on one occasion, proposed his own alternative education system for training musicians, and, not surprisingly, individuality gets top priority. As an educator, he told Don DeMicheal, "I'd have different guys for different things. Get Dizzy for the freedom in music, and a white guy who's stricter on tradition and form, and learn both of them. Then you go your own way ... Let it come out the way it comes out, not the way you [the educator] want it to be." Although Davis would almost certainly deny it, his own musical education in 1945 very nearly measured up to the system he propounded as an ideal to DeMicheal. He had Gillespie, of course, and also Parker, Hawkins, Webster, and all the others, helping him to discover the "freedom" in music, and he had his instructors at Juilliard, "stricter on tradition and form," as well.

Once he had cut himself loose from Juilliard, Davis worked in various groups all over the city. Since he was well connected on The Street, there was probably even a choice, perhaps slim, of jobs for which he could try. Away from The Street, his friend Freddie Webster was playing with John Kirby's band at the Café Society Downtown, giving him a link there, and of course there were always the clubs in Harlem. The prospects looked good, but because of some very lucky timing his prospects turned out to be better than ever. As it happened, Charlie Parker found himself in need of a trumpet player at almost the very moment Davis found himself in need of a job.

The move downtown for the new music was already a year old, and the exposure had done wonders. While the jazz periodicals were laced with hate mail and caustic critical comment, a few younger writers, among them Barry Ulanov and Leonard Feather, the co-editors of *Metronome*, were coming forward with spirited defenses. Neither the amount of publicity, even if it was mainly bad, nor the distaste of the older fans – the reactionaries, who would soon be branded 'moldy figs' – had done the club owners any harm. Young people, many of them just back from the armed services, were flocking to the clubs, anxious to be part of the new movement. White musicians such as the clarinetist Tony Scott, pianist George Wallington, and drummer Shelly Manne were beginning to catch on, too, and swelling the ranks of the initiates. The 52nd Street clubs even had the luxury of line-ups when Charlie Parker and Dizzy Gillespie were fronting a quintet. Parker was becoming an idol. Everywhere he played, he was followed around by a coterie of fans, some of them lugging Wollensak wire recorders, the predecessors of tape recorders, to catch what they could of his playing on those cumbersome outfits. There were also the women of the street willing to meet him in the musicians' room in the twenty minutes between sets, the errand boys of the dope peddlers, and sometimes even the big-time peddlers themselves, pushing samples on him, and of course there were the musicians, addicts, pimps, salesmen, students – they all turned up. Their adulation came as no surprise to Parker, and their gifts aroused no particular gratitude. He accepted both with cool detachment, as if he had been a seigneur all his life. But all the attention was not doing his health much good, or his reliability. Often he did not show up to play at all, and sometimes when he did he was in terrible condition. Gillespie sat him down every chance he got and tried to get him to sort out his priorities, and when Parker was in his more coherent moods he readily agreed to a basic arrangement that involved his showing up, playing every set, and staying sane until the night's work ended. And then he would miss the next set or fail to show up the next night. As the co-leader of their quintet, Gillespie had to face the crowds that had been promised both Gillespie *and* Parker, to scuffle to find a pick-up player to fill in for him, and to negotiate with the irate club owners about the docked payrolls and the broken contracts. Eventually Gillespie had had enough. He knew that he could sustain the jobs with his own name. He and Parker agreed that they would carry on making records together when the chance came, but they would split up the quintet as a working unit and go their separate ways in the clubs.

The word about Gillespie and Parker's split-up spread among the club managers, and when Parker went looking for work he took Davis with him. "He used to talk to people about work and they'd say, 'You don't have a trumpet player,'" Davis recalls. "And he'd say, 'Here's my trumpet player right here.'" As a result, Parker moved into the Three Deuces for a short engagement in October 1945, leading a quintet with Davis, Al Haig, Curly Russell, and Stan Levey. The rhythm section was the same one that the Parker-Gillespie quintet had used in the same club earlier. Later that month, Parker moved over to the Spotlite, keeping Davis and Levey with him but picking up Sir Charles Thompson on piano and

Leonard Gaskin on bass. That engagement might have settled into a long run if the police had not closed down the Spotlite along with some of the other clubs on The Street in early November.

At first, the musicians and everyone else assumed that the closing was temporary, just one of the police department's periodic clean-ups of the area. This time, however, The Street remained closed for several weeks, and the pressure from the police when it did reopen kept it from ever fully recovering its status. It was the beginning of the end for the jazz clubs on 52nd Street, although no one could know that at the time.

Almost as soon as the Spotlite closed, Parker simply moved his quintet uptown, to Minton's in Harlem, and they kept right on playing. Davis gained confidence every night. The crowds were usually noisily partisan to Parker, but every night Davis noticed more of the listeners obviously attentive to his solos as well, and some of them looked for him between sets, wanting to talk about the music and, especially, wanting to hear him talk about *his* music. He was still struggling with some of the trumpet parts – especially on the tough lines of such tunes as *Cherokee* and Gillespie's *Night in Tunisia*, which Gillespie maneuvered through with such élan – but only a handful of listeners, including Freddie Webster and Gillespie when they were there, knew that he was faking them.

It was probably between sets at Minton's that Teddy Reig, the producer for Savoy, approached Parker about a recording session. They agreed to record some of Parker's tunes and set the date for 26 November, a Monday, which was a day off from Minton's. The pay was set at union scale, which was more than Savoy usually paid, but the union stewards were watching the little label closely, suspecting that they were taking too many liberties in some of their sessions.

The circumstances surrounding the recording session were straight out of a Sennett comedy, even if the stewards were watching. Fortunately, external circumstances never seemed to bother Parker, and the session resulted in some superb bebop. For Davis, now nineteen, the recordings gave his career the kind of fillip that would make him one of the best known of the young boppers. Ross Russell, who would later record some of Parker's best work for his own independent label, Dial, calls this Savoy date "the definitive session toward which bop had been striving." The details are as follows:

Charlie Parker's Reboppers
Miles Davis, tpt; Charlie Parker, as; Dizzy Gillespie, pno (on *Billie's Bounce* and *Now's the Time*); Sadik Hakim, pno (on *Thriving on a Riff*); Curly Russell, b; Max Roach, dms. New York, 26 November 1945
Billie's Bounce (five takes); *Now's the Time* (four takes); *Thriving on a Riff* (three takes) (all on Savoy SSJ 5500; master takes only on Savoy 2201; alternate takes on Savoy 1107)

Thriving on a Riff has sometimes been issued as *Thriving from a Riff*; the former title was on the original release on 78 rpm. The other titles recorded at this session, with Gillespie instead of Davis on trumpet and Hakim on piano, are *Warmin' up a Riff*, *Ko Ko* (two takes), and *Meanderin'*; all are issued as above.

The first problem arose over finding a piano player. It was long believed that the piano player was supposed to be Thelonious Monk, who could not be found. However, Teddy Reig recalls that Bud Powell was supposed to play and that Parker knew in advance that Powell would not be able to make it; according to Sadik Hakim, Powell had gone home to Philadelphia. Reig says, "See, in those days you didn't just tell a guy, 'Like, we're gonna have a date at four o'clock,' and he'd show up. You had to go round him up, from about one o'clock on. When I finally got to where Bird was, around Dewey Square and Seventh Avenue, he had Dizzy with him. I say, 'What the hell is he doing? Where's he going? You coming down with us, John?' And he said something about he was gonna play piano, seeing that Bud couldn't make it." The problem of the missing piano player, then, seemed to be solved, until they picked up Davis. They started to talk about what they would record, and Parker named *Ko Ko*, a melody based on the chord changes of *Cherokee*. Davis balked, saying he did not play it well enough to record it, but Parker insisted on keeping it in, probably because he had already accepted Reig's $300 advance to provide four original compositions for this session. When Parker remained adamant, Davis told him that Gillespie would have to play the trumpet part, which meant that they would still need another piano player for *Ko Ko*. Someone finally found Sadik Hakim at a place called Hector's Cafeteria. (It is largely because of Hakim's presence that the complicated personnel shifts finally got sorted out; fifteen years later, when students of jazz were locked in debate about who played what, Hakim came along to settle the debates, saying, "All anybody had to do to find this out was ask me." He was hardly an obvious candidate to ask, however, because his name did not appear on the studio sheets; neither he nor Parker was a member of the New York local at the time, and union rules stipulated a non-union quota of one for recording sessions. Hakim was listed as Hen Gates on the original labels.)

Even if Gillespie and Hakim had not been conscripted, they would probably have found their way to the studio. Word of the session, which was Parker's first as a leader, had spread outward from Minton's, and the recording studio bulged with Parker's regular complement of hangers-on. All kinds of characters were circulating through the studio, and Parker would occasionally dispatch one or more of them on some errand, sending them out for hamburgers and whiskey. The session, as might be expected, lasted much longer than the three-hour union limit.

The first take of the opener, *Billie's Bounce*, a medium blues named for Billie Miller, the personal secretary of Parker's manager, Billy Shaw, showed the promise that the session would finally fulfil, even though Davis faltered on the lead behind Parker near the end of the theme statement and Parker was bothered by a squeaky reed on his solo. Following Parker's solo, Davis enters with a strong broad tone, surprising to hear after his tentative playing on the opening, and Max Roach, the drummer, raises his level behind him, providing a little lift for the soloist. It is a masterful piece of drumming, probably Roach's best showing until the two takes of *Ko Ko* at the end of the day, and it shows off Davis neatly. The second take ends abruptly because of reed problems during Parker's solo, but the third take is complete, and it features a very bold solo by Davis, his best on the open horn all day. As luck would have it, Parker stumbles opening his own solo by being too adventuresome and then suffers through more squeaks, with the result that this take, showing off Davis so well, was not released at the time. Parker also aborted the fourth take during his solo, but the fifth one was completed and became the master take, featuring a very blue solo by Parker but also catching Davis fluff a note in the ensemble and build his solo, which is adequate, on some distinctly Gillespie-like phrases. Davis later said that he counted his solo on *Billie's Bounce* among his favorites "because the trumpet sounded like Freddie Webster"; he was probably referring to his superior solo on the first take, which was released as the alternate. The resemblance to Webster may reside in more than just the open tone. Benny Bailey, a trumpeter who knew Davis well soon after this in California, says: "I happen to know for instance that on the recording of *Billie's Bounce* which Miles made with Charlie Parker in Los Angeles [*sic*], his solo was exactly the one Freddie played for this particular blues. Evidently Miles said he was nervous on the date and couldn't think of anything to play so he did Freddie's solo note for note." If Davis was following Webster's model, that might explain why his solo on takes 1 and 3 are played with so much confidence.

Now's the Time, another blues, has been discussed reverentially in recent years because its militant title came to be seen as an intimation of the black nationalism behind the bop movement, which had to be covert then. The first take ends almost as soon as it begins because Davis enters late in the theme statement, and the second take struggles through an inept statement of the theme by both horns before stopping, probably on a signal from Reig in the control booth. The third and fourth takes are both complete. The third, issued as the alternate, is weak for all soloists: Parker plays a series of blues clichés, Davis toils over long, awkward lines and seems to slow down the tempo, and Curly Russell, the bassist, thumps out a wooden chorus. It is thus remarkable – and one of the real joys of listening to these takes in succession – to hear how all the looseness falls away on the very next take, which became the master. Davis's solo again features a broad tone, but Parker's solo preceding him is so dazzling, with its flashing runs, that it seems to echo well after it has ended anyway. Still, Davis's solo on the master turned out to be his best effort on *Now's the Time*, and it did his reputation no harm when it was released soon afterward.

Billie's Bounce and *Now's the Time* are so firmly entrenched among the classic recordings of jazz that it is difficult to imagine the impact they had when they were made available to the largely unsuspecting jazz public outside New York. Every jazz buff who heard them reacted strongly – whether positively or negatively – to their unsettling harmonies and tough rhythms. Frank Sanderford, a Chicago journalist who later became a close friend of Parker, describes his own reaction this way: "My jazz tastes then were rather old – Lester Young was the last innovation. I had listened for a few times to a couple of Bird records. The first time I heard *Now's the Time* I wondered if the musicians were 'birding' me, if they were having a private little joke of their own. Of course, I later found out that that was an important part of the whole thing. But aside from any wry humor and sardonic wit, there emerged a beautiful sadness, tinged with anger at times, all clothed in an exactness of craftsmanship that had never before been expressed in jazz." Not all the fans with "old" tastes were so open-minded. The reviewer of *Billie's Bounce* and *Now's the Time* for *Down Beat* (22 April 1946) was scathing: "These two sides are excellent examples of the other side of the Gillespie craze – the bad taste and ill-advised fanaticism of Dizzy's uninhibited style ... The trumpet man, whoever the misled kid is, plays Gillespie in the same manner as a majority of the kids who copy their idol – with most of the faults, lack of order and meaning, the complete adherence to technical acrobatics ... Good, bad or indifferent, the mass of Gillespie followers will love these sides, for even bad music is great if it's Diz. This is the sort of stuff that has thrown innumerable impressionable young musicians out of stride, that has harmed many of them irreparably. This can be as harmful to jazz as Sammy Kaye." Clearly, the battle lines were drawn. To follow Gillespie, according to the moldy figs, was to court disaster.

With the advantage of hindsight and the perspective afforded by having the alternate takes as well as the masters available, it is possible to detect the germ of Miles Davis's individualism in these recordings. Even so, it is little more than a hint, and the dominant impression of Davis on these records derives a bit uncomfortably from Gillespie. Even as good a listener as Whitney Balliett could only hear Gillespie's influence in what the nineteen-year-old Davis played on this day; Balliett wrote in *The New Yorker* in 1958, "Davis's debut, some twelve years ago, with such musicians as Charlie Parker and Max Roach, was wobbly. His approach consisted largely of an awkward blotting up of the work of Dizzy Gillespie. He had a shrill, mousy tone, he bungled more notes than not, and he always sounded as if he were playing in a monotone." But there is something in the style that is distinct from Gillespie. It may or may not be "an awkward blotting up" of Freddie Webster, but it certainly does nothing to devalue Parker's recording debut as a leader.

The third number on which Davis plays, *Thriving on a Riff*, is built on the changes of *I Got Rhythm* and was better known at live performances later on as *Anthropology*. Davis is muted on all three takes and seems to have no problems steering through the peppy theme. Only the first take has both an opening and closing ensemble by the horns. The second and third takes open instead with a solo by Davis, and the second ends soon after it begins. The order of the parts on the first take is the same as for *Billie's Bounce* and *Now's the Time*, with an ensemble, a long solo by Parker, a shorter one by Davis, and the ensemble again. Parker plays well, but Davis gets involved in a long line during his solo and breaks it off abruptly when he runs out of breath. On the other complete take, the third, issued as the master, the arrangement has been altered to allow Hakim to solo: it begins directly with Davis's solo, moves to Parker's, and then to Hakim's before the closing ensemble. In order to stay within the three-minute limit of 78 rpm recordings, something had to be sacrificed to allow Hakim his solo space, and the opening ensemble went. It might have been more merciful to sacrifice Davis's solo instead, because he was clearly rattled by opening directly with his solo, and he struggles near the beginning at the point where he had stopped completely on the previous take. The solo is otherwise quite attractive, but the opening mistake is completely exposed. It is a little hard to believe – again, with the advantage of hindsight – that there could have been serious debate for so many years about whether the trumpeter on *Thriving on a Riff* was Gillespie or Davis. The aural evidence is clear, and most listeners guessed correctly that it was Davis. A British discographer advanced the following argument: "The trumpet, in addition to being a little off-mike (intentionally?), appears to be either unfamiliar with, or unable to play the theme, and misses a good many notes ... Dizzy is unlikely to have been fazed by the relative simplicity of *Anthropology*, of which he is credited as co-composer. In short, while the *Thriving* solos don't sound at all like Gillespie, they clearly *could* be by Miles."

This first Savoy session with Parker was hardly an unalloyed triumph for Davis, and it was not even as successful as it might have been if things had gone just a little differently – if take 3 or even take 1 of *Billie's Bounce* had been released before take 5, if the original arrangement of *Thriving* had been pursued instead of the one that forced him into an opening solo, and so on. And there was still the matter of Davis having to surrender his trumpet to Gillespie on *Ko Ko*, in full view of the assembled fans. By the time that happened, however, most of the fans, and most of the musicians too, were oblivious to the change. Between *Thriv-*

ing and *Ko Ko* there was a long delay while someone went eight blocks away searching for Parker's Rico #5 reeds, to eliminate the squeak once and for all. During the delay, the party in the studio continued, and by the time the recording resumed, Davis was asleep on the floor, completely unaware of Gillespie's facile manipulation of the trumpet part that had stumped him. Almost thirty-five years later, Davis just shook his head at the recollection of that introduction that he could not master. "That's the damnedest introduction I ever heard in my life," he told Gillespie and Al Fraser. For Gillespie it was no problem at all. He sailed through it in the recording studio.

The police shutdown of 52nd Street continued after Parker's engagement at Minton's ended. The piano player in Parker's group at Minton's, Sir Charles Thompson, was hired to stay on with a trio afterward, and he hired Davis. The third member was drummer Connie Kay. The odd instrumentation – trumpet, piano, and drums – did not bother Thompson, who seemed to live with contradictions most of the time. Originally from the Midwest like so many of the other 52nd Street veterans, Thompson had conferred his knighthood on himself, probably to give jazz another rank to go along with its dukes, counts, and kings. He spent most of his career in the company of swing players such as Buck Clayton, Illinois Jacquet, and Roy Eldridge, who valued his Basie-style piano, but that piano style also included echoes of Bud Powell, and Thompson kept busy by working with the boppers as well. He knew very well that at Minton's he did not have to worry about showing up on the bandstand with unusual or awkward instrumentation, because the working members of the band were never alone on the bandstand for very long. Connie Kay remembers the parade of players very well: "We'd play one set and generally that was it. The rest of the evening it would be people sitting in – Charlie Parker and Dizzy Gillespie, Milt Jackson, Georgie Auld, Red Rodney. I remember when Ray Brown first came there. Freddie Webster came in all the time and showed Miles how to get those big oooh sounds, those big tones Miles uses now."

When Thompson's gig ended, Coleman Hawkins took over the bandstand at Minton's, and he also hired Davis. Probably Sir Charles Thompson stayed on with Hawkins as well, and perhaps Tommy Potter was the bassist. Davis was teamed for the second time with Hawkins, the first master of the tenor saxophone, this time for pay. Hawkins, from St. Joseph, Missouri, near Kansas City, was only forty-one in the late fall of 1945, but he was revered as the first man to prove that the tenor could be used as a solo horn in jazz. Until he made his first records with the Fletcher Henderson orchestra in the early 1920s, the tenor was seldom used as anything but an ensemble instrument; once Hawkins showed the way, tenor soloists popped up all over the place, and the tenor soon became the most common wind instrument in jazz. The style that Hawkins pioneered featured a broad, breathy tone, carried over from the days when the instrument's function was to give depth to the ensemble, but his brilliance came from his ability to modulate the barrel-house tone with great delicacy. He was a great interpreter of ballads, and his recording of *Body and Soul* remains one of the most celebrated ballad performances ever. It is no coincidence that Davis had a close connection with Hawkins during this first, formative year in New York. "I learned to play ballads from Coleman Hawkins," he has said. "He plays all the chords and you can still hear the ballad." For Davis, Hawkins was one more of the great teachers that The Street provided.

Around the time that Davis was playing with Hawkins in Harlem, his living arrangement with Parker ended. Parker had met a waitress named Doris Sydnor, a young woman with an apparently fathomless maternal feeling toward him, and he moved into her apartment at 411 Manhattan Avenue, where Sadik Hakim was also boarding. Davis was thoroughly fed up with Parker's problems off the bandstand. "I used to put him to bed sometimes with the needle still in his arm and him bleeding all over the place," Davis says. There were other problems too. "Bird was really selfish," Davis said later. "If you had some dope, he'd want all of it. If you had some food, he'd want all of *that*." Parker was treating Davis the way he treated most of his friends and acquaintances, but as long as they were sharing living space Davis was especially vulnerable. "He used to pawn my suitcase and take all my money," Davis says. "He was a dirty motherfucker, man. I loved to listen to him, but he was so fucking greedy. Just greedy – you know how greedy people are. But he had a hell of a mind." In spite of Parker's behavior and Davis's blunt reactions to it, the two men somehow remained full of respect for one another and their professional association continued unchanged.

As soon as Parker moved out, Freddie Webster moved in with Davis, and their informal seminars on the music of The Street carried on night and day. Davis tried to supplement his education on the The Street with more formal training. He sought out William Vachiano, a respected teacher of advanced students in New York, but the experience only soured him further on formal instruction. "Vachiano, my teacher in New York, would always say, 'Play *Tea for Two*.' The motherfucker wouldn't teach me," Davis complained to Julie Coryell. "I'd say, 'Man, I'm paying you – teach me something!'" Davis's battles with the celebrated Vachiano later grew into a minor legend among New York musicians. Marc Levin, a multi-instrumentalist who plays jazz-based experimental music, studied with Vachiano in 1958 and heard the rumors then. "Everybody studied with William Vachiano," Levin says. "Miles Davis studied with Vachiano, but I heard at the time that Vachiano had a lot of trouble with Miles Davis." And vice versa, apparently.

It was not only in the more formal educational context that Davis balked at what he was hearing. Mary Lou Williams, then a fixture in the Café Society Downtown, recalls, "I knew a guy who taught me all the sounds of [John] Coltrane in the 40s. His name was Milton Orent and he knew so much that he couldn't play. He was going to learn jazz and then I learned from him, writing and sounds and things. When Sarah Vaughan and people would come up, Milton would sit at the piano and play some way-out changes. Miles used to come up too and he .didn't like it. Milton played way-out sounds like Coltrane and that was when I was in the Café Society." In the late 1950s, Davis would foster Coltrane's development in much the same way as his own was fostered by Parker, but this contact with the unknown piano player whom Mary Lou Williams insists on comparing to Coltrane left him cold – perhaps because he "knew so much that he couldn't play." For all his efforts, Davis's schooling was always more successful when it was in the hands of practicing musicians.

Davis was also forming alliances with musicians closer to his own age, and they would soon direct bebop toward the next stage of its development. One of his closest friends was Max Roach, the Brooklyn-born drummer, who was just over a year older than Davis. Roach was already being touted as Kenny Clarke's successor as the top bop percussionist. Together, Davis and Roach were fast becoming a clique within the clique surrounding Parker, and Parker knew it. Tony Scott remembers an incident that must have happened at the Three Deuces or the Spotlite that fall, although it is not certain when Roach was in these bands, the drummer of record being Stan Levey. As Scott recalls it, "One night he was playing The Street with Miles and Max, and I took out my clarinet and started to assemble it, when Miles turned to me and said, 'Bird don't like no one to play with him.' 'Okay,' I said, and sat down. After a set, Bird spotted me and said, 'Tony, what's the matter with you? Do I have to give you an engraved invitation every time? Come and play a few with us.' I told him what Miles had said. He said, 'Miles and Max have been bugging me lately. I'm gonna fire those guys.' And he did. But such a magnificent combination could not be separated for long. They went to California," Scott says, soon after that, but not together.

The Street remained closed throughout November, and there was no indication that it might reopen in December or for a long time after that. Unlike the sporadic clean-ups in the past, this one was instigated not only by the vice squad but also by the military authorities, who were annoyed by continual reports about servicemen who were rolled, beaten, or conned there on overnight leave. The musicians soon began to feel the pinch. It was all very well for them to sit in at Minton's and the other Harlem clubs for a few nights, but none of them could survive for long without pay. Whenever they got together now, there was talk about leaving New York for a while to find some work, and California came up often in the conversation. Finally, Gillespie took the idea of a California tour to his agent, Billy Shaw, who liked it and got on the phone to an acquaintance in Los Angeles, a nightclub-owner named Billy Berg. Shaw convinced him that the new music would be a sensation in his club and promised to send him the all-star band with Parker and Gillespie that had packed the Three Deuces off and on since late 1944. Berg agreed, offering the band eight weeks at his club starting the second week of December. When Shaw passed the news along to Gillespie, however, he found him less than pleased about having to put up with Parker on the bandstand again, but neither Shaw nor Berg would consider leaving Parker out. Gillespie had to settle for a compromise, keeping Parker in the band but adding Milt Jackson, the vibraphonist from Detroit, to give the band an extra solo voice on nights when Parker failed to show up. The deal was confirmed, and the sextet, with Al Haig, Ray Brown, and Stan Levey as the rhythm section, left for California by train the first week of December.

Davis headed home to East St. Louis soon after that, arriving in time to spend Christmas with his family. He was still there in January when Benny Carter brought his big band into the Riviera in St. Louis, and Davis joined the band's trumpet section. Carter's band were a rarity, along with Stan Kenton's, because they used Los Angeles as their home base rather than New York. When Davis joined, the band were scheduled to work their way back to the west coast by late February or early March. As soon as he found that he would be traveling to Los Angeles, Davis phoned Parker there to tell him the news. Parker, who was lining up a recording date with Ross Russell of Dial Records, began promising him that he would be able to include the young trumpeter in his band as soon as he arrived.

The Carter band returned to Los Angeles to play an engagement at the Orpheum Theatre, and after that they broke up temporarily. Carter took a smaller group from the band to play local engagements during the lay-off, and he included Davis, along with trombonist Al Grey and tenor saxophonist Bumps Meyers. This small band played on a radio broadcast from Los Angeles on Sunday 31 March, and a tape that exists in some private collections catches them running through the standards *Just You Just Me*, *Don't Blame Me*, and *Sweet Georgia Brown*.

By the time of the broadcast, Davis had already made contact with Parker and begun playing with him at an after-hours spot called the Finale Club, where Parker had been hired as the contractor for the house band. Parker had landed at the Finale Club when Gillespie and the other members of his New York band returned home after the engagement at Billy Berg's, in the first week of February. Gillespie had doled out airline tickets to each of the men but Parker failed to show up at the airport. A venerable legend says that Parker cashed in his ticket almost as soon as Gillespie was out of sight in order to buy narcotics, but Ross Russell points out that during his last weeks at Berg's Parker had been toying with the idea of settling in California and may not have intended to catch that flight. He had persuaded Foster Johnson, the retired vaudevillian who managed the Finale Club, to put him in charge of hiring the club's musicians. The venture was so short-lived that it would probably have been completely forgotten if Parker had not been associated with it and if Russell, a documentor of early bop in general and of Parker in particular, had not been among its clientele. It was at 115 South San Pedro Street, in the section of the city then known as Little Tokyo but already being annexed to the nearby black neighborhood. Its low ceiling was a reminder that it had formerly housed a Japanese club, but under Johnson's management it had been turned into a bottle club that was supposed to be used only by members, who could bring in their own liquor and buy ice and mix from the club. The private memberships cost $2 at the door and were in effect for one night only. The club lasted no more than three months. Russell says, "It was closed by the vice squad of the Los Angeles Police Department just as it had established itself as *the* after hours rendezvous for resident and visiting jazz musicians."

Davis was fined by the local musicians' union soon after he arrived in Los Angeles for doubling at the Orpheum with Benny Carter and the Finale Club with Charlie Parker. Forced to make a choice between the two groups, he chose to resign from Carter's band and stay with Parker.

One musician who sometimes visited the Finale Club after his own job was over, trumpeter Art Farmer, remembers the band that Parker assembled and also recalled their uneasy reception by the local press: "Bird had a group consisting of Miles Davis on trumpet; my brother Addison [Farmer] on bass; Joe Albany, piano; and Chuck Thompson, drums ... Some chick who was writing for a Negro newspaper came down one night to review the group. She was escorted by Dootsie Williams, a trumpet player who acted as some sort of musical consultant. It was their considered opinion that Bird was saying nothing. What's more, his manner was arrogant and he was not too approachable. He had with him, she wrote, a little black, wispy trumpet player who had better technique than Bird. The bass player, she graciously said, had an indefatigable arm. But Bird just played flurries of notes without any content." Farmer continues, "I showed the paper to Bird not knowing what to expect, perhaps great indignation. He just gave a bitter little grin and said, 'She's probably all right, but the wrong people got to her first.'"

The Finale Club band made a radio broadcast, probably in early March, with the personnel that Farmer remembers there. The performance was preserved on acetate lacquer discs, a direct-to-disc process used before magnetic tape became widely available. Although the lacquers inevitably suffered over the years, they were cleaned up as far as possible and transferred to vinyl almost thirty years later, by Tony Williams of Spotlite Records. The details are as follows:

Charlie Parker Quintet
Miles Davis, tpt; Charlie Parker, as; Joe Albany, pno; Addison Farmer, b; Chuck Thompson, dms. The Finale Club, Los Angeles, probably March 1946
Anthropology [*Thriving on a Riff*]; *Billie's Bounce*; *Blue 'n' Boogie*; *All the Things You Are*; *Ornithology*
(all on Spotlite SPJ123 [side 2])

The first two compositions are carried over from the repertoire that Parker and Davis played at Minton's and recorded for Savoy in the fall. Beneath the surfaces of the lacquers, it is easy to pick out a much more relaxed Davis, relieved of the pressures of a recording studio and a restless audience of New York musicians. Surprisingly, at the Finale Club he plays everything with a muted horn – even *Billie's Bounce*, which he originally recorded with a broad, open sound. The other three tunes, recorded by Davis here for the first time but not the last, are all framed in arrangements a little more interesting than the conventional first two, which simply state a theme, line up solos by Parker, Davis, and Albany in turn, and close out with the theme again. On *Blue 'n' Boogie*, a Gillespie composition, Albany solos first, presumably to get him out of the way before the horns take up the riff-style arrangement. At the start of Parker's solo and at the end of his first chorus, the trumpet and alto punctuate the break with a four-bar unison passage, and after Davis's first and second choruses they do the same, using a completely different riff. After a short bass solo by Farmer, the two horns play an extended duet passage, leading into the out chorus. The relative complexity of this arrangement and its flawless execution suggest that it had been a staple for the two hornmen for some time, probably back in New York. *All the Things You Are* is also carefully arranged, with the alto saxophone stating a three-note motif before and during the trumpet statement of the melody; at the bridge, the alto takes over the melody line, picking up its motif again at the end of the bridge. It is different from a later treatment, featuring Davis when he was with the Tadd Dameron band and recorded in May 1949, which is based on John Lewis's arrangement for Dizzy Gillespie's big band; but the prominence of Davis here in the theme statement and the basic device of framing the melody with a motif both suggest that the 1946 arrangement might well be Davis's own. The remaining tune is *Ornithology*, which would be recorded again for Dial later in the month.

The Finale Club sessions featured a variety of players, many of them musicians who had moved to Los Angeles from the Midwest a few years earlier, such as

Howard McGhee from Detroit, the Farmer brothers from Iowa, and Sonny Criss from Memphis, as well as the cream of the local talent, including bassist Red Callender and Callender's protégé, Charles Mingus. Mingus was smitten by the genius of Parker and only slightly less impressed by Davis. In his autobiography, *Beneath the Underdog*, Mingus recalls a session that took place apparently soon after Davis arrived in Los Angeles. Like the rest of Mingus's autobiography, the scene mixes fantasy and fiction with fact, but it does provide a novel impression of the young trumpeter. The session included Parker, Davis, tenor saxophonist Lucky Thompson, reedman and flutist Buddy Colette, pianist Dodo Marmarosa, Mingus, and drummer Stan Levey. It opens with an announcer welcoming Davis: "And will all you people give Miles Davis a hand – Miles is just in from New York. Come on now, everybody – Miles Davis! Give him a good California welcome!" As the band proceeds to play *Billie's Bounce*, Parker calls out the names of the soloists in their turn: "Blow, Miles." After his chorus, Davis says, "I done blew, motherfucker. Now you got it, cocksucker. Blow, Lucky." A little later, he turns to the other horn players and says, "When are you motherfuckers going to stop talking and start playing, instead of just Dodo and Stan over there jacking off?" To which Mingus replies, "Miles, you're so vulgar," and Davis says, "I want to hear Bird blow, not all this dumb-ass conversation." A little later, he directs his ire at the audience which is also talking instead of listening: "Ladies and gentlemen, will you all shut up and just listen to the motherfucker blowing!" Mingus chides him: "Careful, man, you can't say that." "Schitt [*sic*], man," Davis replies, "I put my hand over the mike on 'motherfucker.'" Whatever its truth, Mingus's portrait shows Davis confidently aggressive among his peers even at this time.

Soon after Davis got settled in, Parker set the date for his recording session with Dial. Ross Russell had contacted Parker and the other members of the New York sextet when they first started at Billy Berg's, hoping to get them to record for Dial. The musicians were willing, and Parker made it to the chaotic rehearsal session but failed to show up at the recording session the next night. A few days later, he went to Russell at his office in the Tempo Music Shop on Hollywood Boulevard and suggested they try again, this time with Davis. Parker and Russell signed an informal agreement, dated 26 February, binding Parker to Dial Records for a year. The first recording session was set for 1 p.m. on 28 March. Parker's hand-picked septet were supposed to rehearse the night before at the Finale Club, but they ended up arguing bitterly and nothing much was accomplished. At the studio the next day, the men drifted in nursing grudges as well as hangovers. They took more than an hour setting up their instruments and getting in place, but the session produced the first of a series of recordings for Dial that are generally conceded to contain the very best of Parker's recorded work. The details are as follows:

Charlie Parker Septet
Miles Davis, tpt; Charlie Parker, as; Lucky Thompson, ts; Dodo Marmarosa, pno; Arv Garrison, gtr; Victor McMillan, b; Roy Porter, dms. Los Angeles, 28 March 1946
Moose the Mooche (takes 1, 2, 3); *Yardbird Suite* (takes 1, 4); *Ornithology* (takes 1, 3, 4); *A Night in Tunisia* (takes 1, 4, 5)
(all on Spotlite 101, except take 3 of *Moose the Mooche*, on Spotlite 105; master takes on Archives of Jazz 503)
Other takes from this session are lost. Take 3 of *Ornithology* was originally issued as *Bird Lore*; take 1 of *A Night in Tunisia* was originally issued, and is still commonly referred to, as *Famous Alto Break*.

The recording session went on until 9 p.m., despite the union limit of three hours. Russell remembers "Miles Davis, wooden and deadpanned, not playing much on his solos but warming the ensemble parts with his broad tone." He says also that the numerous flawed takes "were in all cases the fault of the sidemen, especially Miles Davis, who was slow to learn new material." Russell's recollections may be slightly jaded – he and Davis were never very friendly. Nothing in the surviving recorded evidence supports his claim that most of the ruined takes were Davis's fault or that he did not play well on his solos. It was largely because of what he played on the master takes that he won *Down Beat*'s New Star award for trumpet in 1946 and Thompson and Marmarosa won the same citations for their instruments.

  Moose the Mooche is an uptempo romp named by Parker for his Los Angeles connection, a character identified by Russell in *Bird Lives!* as Emry Byrd, to whom Parker signed over half of his composer's royalties from the corporation that Dial was setting up on his behalf. That deal turned out to be a windfall for the connection, especially because *Yardbird Suite*, a graceful, hip melody, became something of an anthem for boppers. Davis, muted as he is on all these sides, plays a stunning solo on the master take (the fourth), helped more than a little by the fact that the arranger, presumably Parker, has him play sixteen bars, lay out while Lucky Thompson plays eight, and return for eight more before giving way to Thompson again. The contrast between Davis's muted sound and Thompson's robust, breathy tenor saxophone works superbly, bringing to mind the contrast that Davis would later exploit when he played alongside the saxophonists John Coltrane and Julian Adderley in his peak years, 1955–9. *Ornithology* succeeds almost as well as *Yardbird Suite*, although the composition lacks the polish. On *A Night in Tunisia*, Dizzy Gillespie's best-known composition, the three horns make an orchestral setting, with Davis flawlessly negotiating the melody in the opening and closing ensembles. Compared to his work on the Savoy session only four months earlier, Davis seems to have made a quantum advance, but then, even the playing of Parker is much more polished and sure here, suggesting that the conditions of the production more than the individual development deserve the credit. Indeed, Parker's playing shines so consistently on these sides that it fairly blinds one to the achievements of his sidemen, as excellent as their playing often is. The first release from this session, a 78 rpm pairing of *Ornithology* and *A Night in Tunisia*, was rushed through production and released within a month. Almost everyone who heard it recognized it as a significant event in the development of jazz.

In California, Davis soon found that he was being sought out by the younger musicians, the men his own age or just slightly older. Having put in a year on The Street absorbing the lessons that are only available from more experienced jazz-men, Davis owned knowledge that the California musicians had not come across before, and he shared it with them as freely as the men on The Street had shared it with him. "Miles was giving me quite a bit of help musically," Benny Bailey recalls. "The first time I heard them playing was on *Lady Be Good*, just an old standard, but what they did with the chords I thought was amazing, and very confusing to me. They were adding chords and, you know how bebop was going then with the minor sevenths and flatted fifths, well I didn't understand that and Miles was really the first guy to pull my coat to what to do, how to get the most out of a tune by changing the chords." A few years later, Bailey joined the trumpet section of Dizzy Gillespie's superb big band.

In April, Davis appeared with Parker in a concert at the Carver Club, on the campus of the University of California at Los Angeles. The other players included Britt Woodman on trombone, as well as Lucky Thompson and Arv Garrison, both holdovers from the Dial session. The fact that Woodman was in the band suggests that the bassist was probably Charles Mingus, his best friend.

In spite of the Dial recordings and the steady work at the Finale Club and other places, by the spring the jazz scene in California was definitely clouding over. Parker was very heavily in debt to his connection, who obviously had not been moved to kindness by the dedication of *Moose the Mooche*. Parker was also getting burned on some of the dope he was injecting. He was incapacitated quite often, and he was ballooning in size. The storm clouds settled in when the musicians showed up for work one night and found the Finale Club padlocked. Foster Johnson claimed he had been shaken down by the police once too often and he simply closed up the place. Parker disappeared immediately and was located only after a long search by Howard McGhee, who found him living in a garage in the heart of the ghetto and subsisting on local port wine, which he drank from gallon jugs. Eventually, McGhee and his wife persuaded Johnson to let them reopen the Finale Club, and for a few days Parker was back at work there, in a quintet with McGhee, Marmarosa, Red Callender, and Roy Porter. Then Parker's connection was arrested and jailed. In an effort to clean himself up, Parker gave up heroin, but he also began to drink awesome quantities, first gallons of cheap port and later whiskey by the quart. Some kind of disaster seemed inevitable when he appeared for his second Dial recording session on Monday 29 July with a band organized by McGhee. Parker could hardly play, and his tortured attempt at playing *Lover Man* was later described by Russell as "the raw notes of a nightmare." Later that night he set fire to the bed in his hotel room and was arrested wandering around naked; he was eventually confined to Camarillo State Hospital in a rehabilitation program. He would stay there for seven months.

Through all of these goings-on, Davis's position as Parker's trumpeter had been taken over by Howard McGhee. By the summer, Davis was working in bands that usually included Charles Mingus. In August, he was featured in a band fronted by Lucky Thompson at the Elk's Ballroom on Central Avenue, the main thoroughfare of the Watts district in Los Angeles. Thompson leased the Ballroom three nights a week, running advertisements that announced "the brilliant young trumpet player, Miles Davis, last heard here with Benny Carter." Mingus was the bassist. The engagement lasted only a few weeks, however, and then Thompson left the city with Boyd Raeburn's band.

Probably during the Elk's Ballroom engagement, Davis and Thompson took part in a recording venture led by Mingus under the sobriquet Baron Mingus. The details, as far as they are known, are as follows:

Baron Mingus and His Symphonic Airs
Probably Miles Davis, Vern Carlson, tpt; Henry Coker, tbn; Boots Mussulli, as; Lucky Thompson, ts; Buddy Colette, ts, flt; Herb Carroll, bs; Buzz Wheeler, pno; Charles Mingus, b; Warren Thompson, dms; Herb Gayle, vcl (on *He's Gone*). Los Angeles, probably August 1946
He's Gone (Fentone 2002); *The Story of Love* (Fentone 2002, Rex-Hollywood 28002); *Portrait* (unissued)

The release details are taken from Jepsen's 1969 listing, but some sources claim that none of these titles was ever issued. They would be among the very rarest jazz records if they ever were available. The spectacle of the large, gifted Mingus passing himself off as the baron of jazz, thus hauling himself into the ersatz but celebrated royal family of jazz, seems ludicrous but is not at all out of character. Davis recalls the Mingus panache with undisguised admiration. "Mingus is a *man*," he says. "He don't do nothin' half way. If he's gonna make a fool of himself, he makes sure he makes a damn fool of himself." In the summer of 1946, when Davis was just becoming known and Mingus was still entirely unknown outside his home area, the two men gravitated toward one another. "Mingus and I were really *close,*" Davis says. "We used to rehearse all the time in California." No jazzman can survive on rehearsals alone, of course, even if he is working out the skills and the style that will eventually carry him to the forefront of his art, but Davis's days of rehearsing with Mingus and scuffling for jobs in Los Angeles helped him to pass the time until he could earn his ticket back to The Street.

For Davis, it was another instance of being in the right place. Billy Eckstine's band arrived in Los Angeles in the fall, probably September, to play some local engagements. As luck would have it, Eckstine needed a trumpeter to fill his solo chair in California, and Davis was already there, ready and waiting. The vacancy came about because Fats Navarro, who had taken over Dizzy Gillespie's chair in the band when Gillespie left New York for California, wanted to complete his tenure in the New York local of the musicians' union and was unable to leave the city. Eckstine says, "When we went out as far as California, he decided he wanted to stay in New York and work his card out. So I got in touch with Miles Davis; he was out there working in a group with Bird, who also had left me by then." Even though Eckstine had lost several of his leading players from the original band, his touch for finding excellent young musicians had not left him. The 1946 orchestra that Davis joined included saxophonists Sonny Stitt, Gene Ammons, and Cecil Payne, and it was still buoyed by the rhythm section of Linton Garner, Errol's brother, on piano, Tommy Potter on bass, and drummer Art Blakey. As far as Eckstine was concerned, this band just carried on the strong individual talents he had assembled in the spring of 1944 and had kept together despite the considerable economic odds against it. After two and a half years, he realized that this western tour would determine once and for all whether he was going to continue his quest for success as a bandleader as well as a vocalist. By now, there was no doubt at all about his ability to succeed as a vocalist. He was already very close to the top of that field, a star whose record sales and popularity put him in the league with Bing Crosby, Frank Sinatra, Dick Haymes, Jo Stafford, and Dinah Shore. They owed their start to the big bands just as he did, for the bands put them before the public in the first place. Only Eckstine, however, still clung to his roots as a band singer, all the others having put the big bands behind them as soon as they could make it on their own. Eckstine loved leading a band, considered himself a musician rather than a star, and felt comfortable in the company of jazz players, but he must have realized that his vocalizing subsidized his bandleading, and that choosing to go with the former alone made good sense financially for him. He may have seen the Hollywood sojourn as the final effort to vindicate his career as a bandleader.

Besides playing in ballrooms and supper clubs, the orchestra with Davis also recorded some of Eckstine's hit songs in Hollywood. The details are as follows:

Billy Eckstine and His Orchestra
Miles Davis, Hobart Dotson, Leonard Hawkins, King Kolax, tpt; Walter Knox, Chippy Outcalt, Gerry Valentine, sometimes Eckstine, tbn; Sonny Stitt, John Cobbs, as; Gene Ammons, Arthur Samson, ts; Cecil Payne, bs; Linton Garner, pno; Connie Wainwright, gtr; Tommy Potter, b; Art Blakey, dms; Billy Eckstine, vcl. Los Angeles, 5 October 1946
Oo Bop Sh'Bam (two takes) (both on Savoy SJL 2214 [1976]); *I Love the Loveliness* (Savoy SJL 1127 [1979]); *In the Still of the Night* and *Jelly Jelly* (Savoy SJL 2214)

Similar personnel, perhaps including Ray Linn, tpt, plus strings. Los Angeles, 6 October 1946
My Silent Love; Time on My Hands; All the Things You Are; In a Sentimental Mood (all on Savoy SJL 2214)

All these titles were originally released as 78 rpm pairings on the long-forgotten National label, Eckstine's recording company from the beginning of the days with his own band in 1944. The recording session of 5 October includes some of the best big-band playing ever documented in a studio by a band of Eckstine's. Eckstine's marketability had nothing to do with his band's swinging, a fact that becomes painfully obvious to any jazz listener after the most cursory review of his National recordings. Still, on *Oo Bop Sh'Bam*, a bebop riff with a line of nonsense syllables for a vocal refrain, written by Dizzy Gillespie and Gil Fuller when they were with Eckstine in the Earl Hines orchestra, the band cut loose and Gene Ammons takes an effective solo. *Jelly Jelly*, a blues written by Eckstine and Hines that was Eckstine's very first vocal hit (in the Hines orchestra's recording), also works well for Ammons and allows the sections to swing. The remaining tracks offer little of jazz interest. Occasionally, as on *My Silent Love*, one can pick out a few bars of a trumpet lead that are possibly Davis's work, but ironically the only extended trumpet solo, lasting eight bars in the middle of *Time on My Hands*, features an orthodox player sticking close to the melody. Three decades after the recording, Eckstine identified the trumpeter as Ray Linn, a veteran of the touring bands who had settled into the Hollywood studios by this time.

Eckstine's band must have been allowed more playing room at personal appearances or his lineup of top-flight jazz players would surely have drifted away. The gap between the band's jazz potential and their invariably staid recordings is enormous. Art Blakey, in an interview with Arthur Taylor years later, bemoaned what the record company missed in studio sessions with the orchestra. "Nobody got to hear it," he said. "They didn't get recorded, and the records they did make were sadder than McKinley's funeral. Even the horses cried. Because it wasn't recorded right; they recorded a big band on two mikes, which was very unfair. They weren't interested in the band. They were interested in Billy Eckstine.

Later on they wished they had recorded the band right, because the biggest stars in jazz were playing in it." A persistent rumor maintains that Eckstine holds a collection of taped performances by his band; every jazz fan hopes that they will show the band's mettle when they are finally made public. Presumably the experience of those live performances kept Davis interested, along with the discipline of playing in a well-drilled big band. His assumption of the solo chair formerly held by Gillespie and Navarro stands as a symbolic coming of age for the young trumpeter. His success must have been all the more satisfying because Eckstine had been sharply critical of his ability two years earlier. Now Eckstine had to change his opinion. "By the time we got to California," he said, "he had blossomed out. He'd been going to Juilliard, and playing with Bird, so he came in and took over the same book, the solo book which was originally Dizzy's. Miles stayed with me until I broke up, which was in 1947."

Also in October an all-star sextet from the band recorded four titles with two vocalists who worked the Central Avenue bars. The music has never been issued on record, but the sextet included Davis and Ammons, the band's best soloists, along with their rhythm section, and they played three takes of each of the four unidentified songs, two of which were sung by Earl Coleman and two by Ann Hathaway. Hathaway remains unknown, but something is known of Coleman from two songs he recorded with Charlie Parker a few months later, soon after Parker was released from Camarillo. Ross Russell had lined up a large band of local musicians for Parker to record with on a Dial session marking his return to active playing, but Parker showed up with Coleman at his side and insisted that the singer should be allowed to record two of his songs, *This Is Always* and *Dark Shadows*. Russell finally had to give in, and then he sat back helplessly as the singer, an Eckstine sound-alike, fumbled take after take, finally getting satisfactory versions of the songs after two hours and twenty minutes. Unlike the recordings with Davis and the other members of Eckstine's band, Coleman's recordings with Parker were issued (all five complete takes of the two songs are on Spotlite 102). They reveal a hefty baritone voice and an extravagant phrasing that seem to parody Eckstine's style. Coleman's vibrato often quavers right into the next bar, and his songs with Parker come out as paeans from a trembling lover. There is little hope that his songs with the band that included Davis will be any more interesting, if they are ever uncarthed.

The Billy Eckstine orchestra, including Davis, made their way back toward New York late in 1946. Chicago, naturally, was one of the stops along the way, and it was probably the last stop before the band broke up temporarily for Christmas. Davis stayed in Chicago for a while, playing an engagement at the Jumptown Club with his bandmates Gene Ammons and Sonny Stitt. For Davis, this Chicago stopover at Christmas was the first in what would become a career-long pattern. Except for a few years when his health or personal problems made the Chicago trip impossible, he has arranged his schedule so that he plays in a club or a concert there around Christmas every year. Davis's sister Dorothy lives there, teaching in a Chicago public school and, since her marriage to Vincent Wilburn, raising her family. Ever since his first Christmas away from East St. Louis, Davis has made sure that he would be in the vicinity during the holiday season.

The Eckstine orchestra reassembled in New York in the new year to finish off their commitments for January and February. After that, Eckstine disbanded permanently and struck out on his own as a featured vocalist. The disbanding put an end to Eckstine's aspirations as a bandleader and also cut off the relatively secure jobs that the band had provided for so many of the rising stars of the bebop revolution. Unencumbered by his band, Eckstine headed back to California in April, where he made his final recordings for the National label with a studio orchestra, including the hit records *Blues for Sale* and *Solitude*. (Jepsen's discography and other sources list this session as taking place in New York before disbanding and include Davis in the orchestra, but Eckstine corrected the listing when the sides were reissued in 1976 on Savoy SJL 2214.) After that, he signed with MGM Records, turning out a string of commercially successful records over the next five years, when the appeal of his highly mannered singing began to wane.

Thanks to Eckstine, Miles Davis was back in New York, and back on 52nd Street, where the music was again being played. The Street had remained shut down for several weeks in 1946, and then it had begun to show signs of life again, as first one club and then another was allowed to reopen. Now, almost a year later, there was a fair amount of night activity although it was still not bustling as it had before the shutdown. Some of the clubs remained dark, and in the ones that had reopened the managers were keeping closer tabs on their trade, as the police department also was. Hopes were high that The Street would eventually recover its old panache, but the new strictures were never to be fully relaxed, and the anarchy of the night life it had supported for so long was gone for good.

Much of the excitement among the musicians on The Street still centered around Dizzy Gillespie, who was experimenting with bebop in a big-band format. His experiment was lauded as the next logical step in the progress of bop, and he showed uncanny sense in enlisting Walter Gil Fuller, a writer for the Eckstine band, as his musical director right from the beginning. As straw boss and composer-arranger, Fuller took the responsibility for hiring musicians and compiling a book as seriously as Gillespie did, and the band generated excitement among musicians and jazz listeners almost immediately. Part of the musical activity on The Street consisted of watching for developments coming out of the Gillespie band and participating in working them out further. One of Davis's first jobs after the Eckstine band folded came from an attempt by Illinois Jacquet and Leonard Feather to produce some big-band bebop. The details are as follows:

Illinois Jacquet and His Orchestra
Miles Davis, Joe Newman or Russell Jacquet, Marion Hazel, Fats Navarro, tpt; Gus Chappel, Fred Robinson, Ted Kelly, Dicky Wells, tbn; Ray Perry, Jimmy Powell, as; George Nicholas, Illinois Jacquet, ts; Bill Doggett or Leonard Feather, pno; Al Lucas, b; Shadow Wilson, dms. New York, March 1947
For Europeans Only; Big Dog; You Left Me Alone; Jivin' with Jack the Bellboy
(All originally Aladdin [78 rpm]; reissued on Imperial LP 9184)

The recording session brings together Davis and Navarro, whom Davis had replaced in Eckstine's orchestra. As habitués of 52nd Street, their paths had crossed many times and would again on several occasions before Navarro's death three years later. Ted Kelly, George Nicholas, and probably some of the others in the band were members of Gillespie's band at the time and had returned not long before this from that band's inaugural tour, a whirlwind trip through the southern states during which they played sixty one-night stands.

In the south, the Gillespie band had been received with a lot of befuddlement and some outright hostility, but now that they were back in the city, things were looking up. Billy Shaw, the manager, arranged a week's booking at the McKinley Theater in the Bronx for early April. Gillespie and Fuller saw the engagement as their best chance to make a breakthrough with the band and win over an audience that would be large enough and enthusiastic enough to keep the band together full-time. They were taking no chances with the players, hiring the best men around, bar none. Max Roach, the band's drummer on the southern tour as well as at the McKinley Theater, shakes his head in disbelief when he recalls Gillespie's original New York band: "When Dizzy had his first big band, here's the kind of brass section we had. He had Freddie Webster, Kinney Dorham, Miles Davis, Fats Navarro. That's the trumpet section." With Gillespie added, that section must rank among the most powerful of all time. Just as the rehearsals were getting under way, the band seemed to get an unexpected boost by the reappearance of Charlie Parker. He had been released from Camarillo in February, and after hanging around on Central Avenue and recording two separate sessions for Dial in Los Angeles, he made his way back to the east coast by train, stopping over in Chicago and playing with some local bands along the way. Fuller hired Parker as soon as he arrived. After all, Parker's sound was part of the fabric of the band itself. "We wanted it to sound like what Dizzy and Bird were doing,"

Fuller explains, "but the sound had to be translated into a big band sound." With Parker in the band, joining the best boppers on The Street, Fuller and everyone else expected to hear a glorious realization of that goal.

Parker lasted only one night. Although he had only been out of Camarillo for about six weeks, he was involved with narcotics as heavily as ever by the time he got to New York. Gillespie, feeling the pressure to make his big band succeed, was in no mood to tolerate the same old nonsense he had to put up with from Parker in the past. Fuller remembers the band's opening night at the McKinley: "Charlie Parker came in the place and had this shit in him and sat up there through the whole thing till his solo comes, and when his solo comes, Bird puts his horn in his mouth and [plays] 'doodle-loo-deloodle-loo,'" Fuller says. "And Dizzy, on stage with people in the audience, said, 'Get that mothafucka off my stage!' Because he didn't want the whole band tagged as a bunch of junkies, you know. He wouldn't let me put him in there anymore; he just wasn't gonna have that. Because Bird would always get high, man, and start nodding right on the bandstand. And you're playing the whole thing with no first saxophone player."

Gillespie remained adamant about keeping the band clean, or at least making it appear to be clean, and to him that meant keeping Parker out of it. Fuller went to him to plead Parker's case, no doubt passing along all kinds of promises that Parker had made, but Gillespie had heard it all before and would not give in. "That was a helluva band," Fuller says, "but again, we wanted Charlie Parker for writing the tunes. And I told Dizzy, 'Shit, man, it'd be worthwhile just to give him a hundred dollars a week and let him write tunes for us than be worried with him.' But we didn't have the money at that time. There was nobody putting the money up." They would just have to get along without Parker, and they could, as Gillespie knew very well.

No matter how savagely Parker abused himself, he seemed to come back full of strength. This time, though he could not have predicted it, he did not even have to reach down very deeply to tap those mysterious resources, because the conditions were all in his favor. While he was relaxing at Camarillo, out of circulation, he was not forgotten. His Dial recordings, especially *Yardbird Suite* and *Ornithology*, were the sensations of 1946. The new audience for bop, once a coterie but now growing by leaps and bounds, could not hear them often enough. Parker's seven months of inactivity added an aura of mystery that did nothing to diminish his audience. And now The Street was open again, and the managers were looking for small bands that might be able to bring the crowds back. To some club owners, Parker looked like the man to do that.

And so, in April 1947, Charlie Parker assembled a small band. He hired Tommy Potter from the defunct Eckstine band to play bass and Duke Jordan to play piano. As soon as the Gillespie orchestra finished its engagement at the

McKinley Theater, Parker enlisted Max Roach as his drummer and Miles Davis as his trumpeter. Together, they comprised the Charlie Parker Quintet, Parker's first working unit and the only one that would ever have any semblance of permanence. The quintet immediately became the most influential small band of the day.

3

Ornithology
1947–8

Once upon a time, my time, a few years ago now ...
There was a young cafe-au-lait colored bird, who blew
sax, and his earth name was Charles Parker
   Ted Joans

The first and the best of the Charlie Parker quintets was formed in April 1947, soon after Parker returned to New York from California. Their first engagement was at the Three Deuces, the setting for many of Parker's past successes and a fitting site for his triumphal return. They were originally booked to play opposite the Lennie Tristano Trio for two weeks, but their engagement was extended beyond that, and then beyond that again, until their billing read that they were there "indefinitely." The Three Deuces thus became home base for the group for the rest of the year, with occasional tours outside New York to Philadelphia, Washington, Baltimore, Boston, Detroit, Chicago, Milwaukee, and St. Louis. When they finally left the Three Deuces and moved over to a new jazz club called the Royal Roost, it was not so much a shifting of allegiance from one club to the other as it was shifting away from 52nd Street to the new home for New York's jazz clubs, Broadway.

As jazz bands large and small go, the first Charlie Parker Quintet had a fairly stable and settled personnel for the next twenty months. The piano chair seemed to be a problem at first. Everyone in the group wanted Bud Powell as the pianist, and their first recordings, less than a month after getting together, included Powell, but everyone knew that he could not keep up the nightly pace that was required because of chronic mental problems, which were categorized in the jargon of the time as "nervous breakdowns." Powell's history of unreliability made even Parker's record look good. Later, the group used John Lewis, Gillespie's piano player in the big band, on a recording session, and Tadd Dameron and Al Haig, who played some club dates with them. One reason for the vacillation over the piano player was that Miles Davis did not think highly of the playing of the man whom Parker chose for the job, Duke Jordan. Jordan, whose given names were Irving Sydney but who was known only as Duke to musicians and fans alike, came from Brooklyn, like Max Roach, and had been around Monroe's Uptown House at the time of the first significant bop experiments and later worked on The Street in several bands. Davis may have played beside him earlier in one of Coleman Hawkins's groups, since Jordan sometimes found work with Hawkins. Jordan's own recollection is that he was recruited by Parker for the quintet in "late 1946," which cannot be right because Parker was still in Camarillo; even though he did not record with the quintet until October 1947, he was probably its original working pianist, beginning in April. Despite playing around New York for several years before this, Jordan had never met Parker until the night he was hired by him, when he was playing at the Three Deuces in a trio led by guitarist Teddy Walters. He remembers it happening like this: "I was working down at the Three Deuces with a guitarist. Charlie Parker came in one night and he said, 'Wow, listen to that guy playing,' and when the set was over he asked me would I like to play with his band. He was forming a new band and as I had heard of Charlie Parker I naturally said yes, and it turned out that it was the band with Tommy Potter, Max Roach, Miles Davis and myself."

The bassist, Tommy Potter, had been with the Billy Eckstine orchestra in California, along with Davis. Like Jordan, he too was replaced during the working life of the first quintet, when Curly Russell took over as bassist in the fall of 1948, but Potter returned soon after and eventually stayed with Parker into 1949, after the first quintet had broken up.

The working life of the first quintet is measured by the time that the other two members, Miles Davis and Max Roach, stayed with it. Both joined at the beginning and both left together as well, in December 1948. With Parker, they formed the nucleus of the quintet which is respected as one of the great small bands in the history of the music. Their importance in the band is reflected in the pay scale, although not very decisively: at the Three Deuces, Parker received $280 a week, Davis and Roach $135 a week each, and Jordan and Potter $125 a week.

Parker's hiring of Davis to fill the second horn chair has sometimes elicited some mild criticisms, usually from Parker fans who consider that the pyrotechnics of someone such as Gillespie might have complemented Parker's style better than the more subdued and cerebral style that Davis was rapidly developing. The criticisms often mention that Fats Navarro was also available at the time, on the assumption that Navarro's style was closer to Gillespie's, which may be true, and that he was technically more accomplished than Davis, which is probably false, although he was better technically than Davis showed at the time of his 1945 recordings with Parker on Savoy. What is always missing from such criticisms is any justification for the premise that Parker might have been heard advantageously beside someone who reflected Gillespie's style more closely. Parker recorded most of his finest work beside Davis, not beside Gillespie, and that was probably not accidental. The stylistic similarity of Parker and Gillespie had to be artistically stifling with any concentrated contact. "They played the same chords, they played the same chords," Davis emphasized later. "Dizzy and Bird played the same thing. They used to play lines together just like each other. You couldn't tell the difference." Parker and Davis provided a play of contrasts, with Parker making bold variations and Davis making understatements, Parker playing triplets and Davis leaving spaces, Parker gushing and Davis tentative. They were complementary rather than competitive. One of the first critics to point out the crucial importance of Davis to Parker's music was André Hodeir, who noted: "Miles Davis is the only trumpeter who could have given his music the intimate character that is one of its essential charms." Parker must have been aware of that, if only intuitively, because Ross Russell recalls that Davis was "Charlie's first and only choice on trumpet."

It is probably worth wondering why Davis and Roach and the others so willingly joined up with Parker. By the time he reached New York on Easter Monday, 7 April, he was saddled with a heroin habit again. His attempt at playing with the Gillespie band that first week gave no hope whatever for his settling into even a minimally stable lifestyle. Perhaps the members of the quintet expected no more than two weeks employment, the term of the original deal Parker made at the Three Deuces. And perhaps they had very few options in the shrinking market for jazz musicians. But both Davis and Roach could have found places in the Gillespie band, which was playing an exciting book and gaining support rapidly. Neither man seems to have entertained thoughts of joining Gillespie or anyone else once Parker made his offer, and the reason was almost certainly that Parker was the greatest musician of the day. The music they produced with him would more than make up for the mundane problems of working for him. Barry Harris, the pianist from Detroit who sat in with Parker's band during this period, sums up the feeling: "It wasn't frightening at all to play with him – just the opposite – he was the one to make you feel relaxed. That's why you take all the musicians who played with Charlie Parker, who played their best with Charlie Parker. They haven't played better since. Most of them. Miles and all of them. Because he was the leader. And he had that quality, that charisma they call it nowadays. It was a life force thing." Harris undeniably overstates the case: Davis and Roach went on to make individual marks that would eventually overshadow their playing with Parker, although Jordan, Potter, and members of later quintets such as Kinney Dorham, Red Rodney, and Walter Bishop probably never played better than they did with him. For Davis and Roach no less than the others, however, their playing was elevated by the standards of his performance; if they had not gone on to other achievements their work beside Parker would have guaranteed their mark in the history of the music. They might not have gone beyond that level if they had not had his extraordinary talent so constantly in view throughout these years.

Within a month after forming the quintet, Parker was in the recording studios making four sides for Savoy. He was still under contract to Dial, and Russell was trying to work out the details for fulfilling his contract by long distance, but contractual obligations never impressed Parker. On 8 May, a Thursday, Parker assembled his All Stars, with Bud Powell on piano, for the session:

Charlie Parker All Stars
Miles Davis, tpt; Charlie Parker, as; Bud Powell, pno; Tommy Potter, b; Max Roach, dms. New York, 8 May 1947
Donna Lee (five takes); *Chasin' the Bird* (four takes); *Cheryl* (two takes); *Buzzy* (five takes) (all on Savoy S5J 5500 and on BYG 529 130 and BYG 529 131; master takes on Savoy 2201; alternate takes on Savoy 1107)

For the first time, Davis contributed a composition. All these titles were credited to Parker on the original 78 rpm issues, and the mistake was perpetuated on numerous reissues, but *Donna Lee* is the work of Davis (although even its most recent issue, on Savoy 2201, lists Parker as its composer on the label, even while correcting the mistake in the album notes). *Donna Lee* provides the first hint of Davis's growing interest in composition. The information that he, not Parker, is the composer came not from either of them but from Gil Evans, who approached Parker and was directed to Davis when he wanted to pick up the lead sheet for *Donna Lee* in order to write an arrangement of it for Claude Thornhill's orchestra. The suspicion that Davis wrote this piece was felt even before Evans volunteered the information. Med Flory, the alto saxophonist who wrote arrangements based on many of Parker's most famous solos for the saxophone section known as Supersax in the 1970s, heard *Donna Lee* as part of a blindfold test in *Down Beat* and remarked, "It doesn't sound like a Parker chart. It sounds like Miles wrote it." The confusion over authorship has not been helped by the fact that *Donna Lee* is named for bassist Curly Russell's daughter whereas *Cheryl*, written by Parker, is named for Davis's daughter, but these titles were assigned, apparently quite arbitrarily, by producer Teddy Reig. *Donna Lee* features very long unison lines by the two horns, based on the chord changes of *Indiana*. Neither Parker nor Davis preserves the structure of the opening melody in his solo, and Parker's solos on all takes consist of several short phrases strung together, a distinct contrast to the unbroken phrases of the written ensemble.

A more distinctive composition from this session is *Chasin' the Bird*, based on *I Got Rhythm*, in which Parker and Davis play the melody as a canon, Davis introducing his statement one bar after Parker has begun. The effect is very distinctive, and possibly unique in the jazz of the day. The structure of the round – the "chase" of the title – is repeated for two choruses and then broken by an improvised chorus and repeated again. Parker plays the improvised break in the introduction, but in the out-chorus it is taken, with some difficulty, by Powell on the first two takes; on the successful third take, Davis rather than Powell comes in to improvise the break on the out-chorus.

The other two tunes, *Cheryl* and *Buzzy*, are relatively straightforward blues variations. The first take of *Cheryl* is a false start, and after that the band needed only one complete take to be satisfied, a notably unusual occurrence in a Parker recording session. The other blues, *Buzzy*, went to the opposite extreme and required five takes. Coming at the end of the session, the number of takes seems to have taken a toll on the players. On the fifth take, released as the master, Parker's and Davis's lack of interest is quite audible, although Powell's chorus and Potter's walking bass line are very attractive. Davis's solos especially are much better on the early takes than on the fifth.

The recording session, which gave Davis better exposure than anything he had recorded in the previous ten months with Billy Eckstine and others, supplies further proof that his distinctive style was rapidly developing. The fiery phrases of Gillespie and the liquid tone of Freddie Webster, which both seemed to be calques on his style, are largely eliminated, even though he plays an open horn through-out. Barbara Gardner comments: "By 1947 Davis had filtered from his heretofore Gillespieish playing all that was not natural to himself." In some ways, the distinctiveness of his sound put him at a slight disadvantage with the fans of the day who had grown to accept the Gillespie style as the standard for trumpeters. Med Flory says, "Like a lot of guys, I didn't dig Miles at the beginning when he replaced Diz. It didn't sound like Miles had any chops ... At the time, I thought Miles ruined a lot of trumpet players who tried to imitate him instead of Diz, but I realize now that those guys were never gonna play like Diz anyway, so at least Miles gave them a shot at something to hang on to. Miles is a totally musical guy, which I didn't appreciate at the time." Indeed, the other trumpet players and then the listeners began to alter their appreciation of how a jazz trumpet should sound during Davis's tenure with the Parker quintet, to the extent that Whitney Balliett could claim, a few years later, that "nine out of ten modern trumpeters are true copies of Dizzy Gillespie or Miles Davis."

In all his recording sessions with Parker, including this one, Davis was unlucky because his own solos never determined which take of a composition would be released as the master. Very often, his best solo occurs on the earlier takes, a fact that was generally recognized only years later, with the release of collations of all the existing takes. The reviewer Ronald Atkins notes that Davis often "could not retain his form over several takes, although he often managed a confident, organically developed solo at his first or second try, for instance on *Cheryl*. On later versions his tone lost some of its resonance, and, being unable or unwilling either to play around with the same phrases or to invent new structural relationships, his solos became disjointed. One can follow this process on *Donna Lee*, *Barbados* and *Perhaps*. Because so few of his best solos were issued at the time, Davis's reputation suffered. The good ones that were put out – *Blue Bird*, *Cheryl*, *Another Hair-Do* – were all early takes." In the 1950s, when he was approaching his peak both as a soloist and as a leader, Davis began recording everything in a single take, a practice that seemed to everyone around him to be reckless; looking back at his superiority on the early takes with Parker, one sees his later method as a custom-made accommodation of his own limitations.

At the Three Deuces, the audience always included a number of musicians, and part of the attraction for them was the chance that they might be invited to get up on the stand and play with Parker on some of the later sets. Parker remained receptive to the practice of sitting in, a practice he had grown up with in Kansas City and kept up in Harlem, but Davis and Roach and perhaps some of the others were less than happy with it. Dave Lambert, the bop singer, remembers going to hear Parker and being uncertain about who his regular band members were. Lambert says, "Sometimes when I went to hear Bird, he'd be on the stand with a group of about four men, and there'd be another four or five waiting to sit in and jam. Bird was never discourteous to a musician. He never told them verbally to get off the stand; instead he would call a number – *All the Things You Are*, in the key of E – and start off *pow* in a ridiculous tempo and in a tough key, and the guys would just walk off the stand ... The musicians just petered off, and the men were separated from the boys." The practice of excluding amateurs by playing difficult pieces probably increased as Davis and Roach made their objections clearer to Parker.

A glimpse of the clique that was developing in Parker's band comes by way of Jimmy Heath, the tenor saxophonist and composer, who in his early days also played alto and other saxophones and was tagged with the nickname Little Bird. In 1947–8, Heath played with Howard McGhee in a quintet that modeled its style on Parker's quintet. They were often booked into the Three Deuces when Parker was on tour, and Heath has frequently recalled an occasion when Parker's quintet were scheduled to take over from McGhee's at the Deuces. "Milt Shaw of the Shaw agency called me and said, 'Charlie Parker's not going to make the gig tonight, and you're Little Bird, so can't you come in and play for Bird?' Now, Miles and Max were in this band. I went through the floor, because in those days it wasn't like today when young musicians don't have that much respect for the older cats – they just come right up and try to blow you out. But in those days there was some respect happening, so I just told the guy, 'Look, I can't be playing in Charlie Parker's band, in his place.' And I didn't go." Heath refers to Davis and Roach as "older cats" but they were only a few months older than he was. Such was the rank, perhaps, conferred on them by their positions in the quintet.

For Davis, another advantage of his high profile in Parker's band was the chance to lead his own recording session for Savoy, which happened during the summer. "Miles was ready," Teddy Reig says. "Give Miles credit, he had to put up with a lot working with Bird and really, like, we owed him this date because of all the shit he took." Reig also saw the date as an opportunity to display Parker's talent on the tenor saxophone, which he had played in Earl Hines's band in 1943. But the session was by no means just a Parker date under the nominal leadership of Davis. Davis took the leader's role seriously, and as a result the recording became a milestone in his personal development. He wrote and arranged four compositions for it and called two rehearsals at Nola Studios on Broadway prior to entering the recording studio. For the first rehearsal, Parker nonchalantly stopped off at a bar where musicians hung out and borrowed a tenor saxophone from a man named Warren Luckey. "I had to watch out for that tenor to make sure Bird didn't hock it," Reig recalls. Parker also borrowed an instrument on short notice for the other rehearsal and for the recording session. Apart from the two rehearsals, he did not work on his tenor technique at all. Not surprisingly, at the recording session he starts out very tentatively; on *Milestones*, the first composition recorded that afternoon, he plays very little. More surprisingly, by the end of the session he plays the bigger horn like one of its masters; he seems to gain confidence with each take played, until he finally seems to be completely in control. Parker's metamorphosis into a tenor master comes as a surprise to fans who associate him only with the alto, but it was obviously expected by Davis, who selected him for the band and made no special concessions for his unfamiliarity with the new instrument in writing the arrangements. All the members of the band Davis assembled for his debut as a leader have his personal stamp of approval: the two favored members of the quintet, Parker and Roach; John Lewis, a university-trained pianist and composer whose extended work, *Toccata for Trumpet and Orchestra*, would be played by the Gillespie band in concert later in the year; and bassist Nelson Boyd, only nineteen years old, from the Tadd Dameron band. The details are as follows:

Miles Davis All Stars
Miles Davis, tpt; Charlie Parker, ts; John Lewis, pno; Nelson Boyd, b; Max Roach, dms.
New York, 14 August 1947

Milestones (three takes); *Little Willie Leaps* (three takes); *Half Nelson* (two takes); *Sippin' at Bell's* (four takes)
(all on Savoy s5J 5500 and on BYG 529 131; master takes on Savoy 2201; alternate takes on Savoy 1107)
There is a fourth take of *Little Willie Leaps*, apparently released under the title *Wailing Willie*, but it is not available.

There has been confusion about the composer credits on this session, especially for *Milestones*, for which Parker has often been credited (as he is on the BYG release listed above, though not on Savoy, beginning with the releases listed above), but Davis is its composer. The character of the music differs strikingly from the sessions under Parker's leadership. Generally, Davis places more emphasis upon the arranged sections, in spite of the three-minute time limit for 78 rpm issues. The tempos, too, are more restricted, staying within the bounds of medium tempo.

Milestones is a mellow original, unrelated to Davis's better-known composition with the same title recorded in 1958. It is ironic that this tune should have been incorrectly attributed to Parker for several years, because none of the compositions is more unlike his style, or, perhaps better, none is more like the style that Davis would bring to the fore a year and a half later, the 'cool' reaction to bebop. Its arrangement also breaks up the solo pattern typical of the recordings under Parker's leadership, by having Parker play after Davis (and also after Lewis) instead of at the beginning.

The careful preparation and rehearsal prior to the recording session show especially in the few takes that were required: each composition gets only two complete takes, the extra one on *Little Willie Leaps* being a false start, and the extra one on *Sippin' at Bell's* aborting during the opening solo by Parker. *Little Willie Leaps*, built on the changes of *All God's Children Got Rhythm*, receives two very different treatments in its two takes. The first is played at a slower tempo and features a relaxed solo on the open horn by Davis. The second is faster, perhaps because the first was considered long at just over three minutes, but probably because the producer wanted more variety of tempo for purposes of coupling up the tunes in the 78 rpm release. Although the faster second take was released as the master, all the players sound a bit uncomfortable on it compared to the first.

Half Nelson is similar to Tadd Dameron's better known *Lady Bird*, which was still unrecorded when Davis's session took place; its title suggests that Nelson Boyd, who was Dameron's regular bassist, had a hand in working out the composition, but Davis alone is credited as the composer. Parker constructs excellent solos on both takes, showing technical facility on the tenor saxophone that almost rivals his wizardry on the alto. Sonny Rollins acknowledged the influence of

Parker's tenor-playing on his own style, and it must surely be his work on *Half Nelson* that impressed Rollins. *Sippin' at Bell's*, a blues that pays homage in its title to a Harlem bar, is a faster-paced tune notable for the controlled, understated solos by both Davis and Lewis. Their similarity in approaching their solos on this tune shows clearly why Davis advocated Lewis's piano style during this period.

The critical reactions to this debut for Davis as a leader have, with the advantage of hindsight, given them a central place in charting his development. As usual, critic Martin Williams's account is very incisive and well worth quoting at length. "The atmosphere of these performances is more relaxed, the themes are more fluent and more legato, and, although Davis had clearly learned from Parker and Dizzy Gillespie, he seemed to be reaching back to the easy, introverted phrasing of Lester Young," Williams wrote. "Davis's themes ... have a built-in harmonic complexity. *Sippin' at Bell's*, for example, is a twelve-bar blues, but it is so written that the soloist has to find his way through an obstacle course of some eighteen assigned chord changes in a single chorus. And the shifting structure of *Little Willie Leaps* ... almost throws so able a man as John Lewis. There is an effective tension on these recordings between the surface lyricism of Miles Davis's solo melodic lines and the complexity of their underlying harmonic outline. The wonder of it is that a man who plays with such apparent simplicity as Miles Davis would have wanted such technical challenges. But he did, and he learned a great deal from the experience. And once he had learned it, he showed an artist's wisdom in forgetting, but still knowing, what he had learned." This recording session marks the first time that Davis was not dwarfed by the mastery of Parker beside him: "In these fresh surroundings, at medium tempos over complex and fast-changing chords, Davis' melodic gift bloomed," J.R. Taylor noted. "For once, he matched Parker's work instead of complementing it."

When the recordings were released, the critical perception of Davis's work by both reviewers and fans was still somewhat jaded by the fact that Davis's style was different from the faster, tougher style of Gillespie and of his disciples Navarro and Dorham. However, the tide was changing, especially as Davis gained control of the elements of his style, which removed it even further from Gillespie's. He was finding adherents among other trumpet players and fans wherever he was heard and, in the Parker quintet, he was heard widely. The attraction toward Davis's style was first felt only by insiders but it soon became public knowledge. The first significant notice of it was given by Ross Russell in an article for the *Record Changer* the following year, 1948. Russell's comments seem a remarkable prognostication. "There is a mounting body of evidence," he wrote, "that Davis is leading the way or even founding the next school of trumpet playing. Nothing could be further from the Eldridge-Gillespie school than the Miles Davis trumpet. He plays a 'soft' horn. He has consistently been overlooked by critics because he lacks the virtuosity of his contemporaries. Davis seldom uses the upper register, preferring to play almost wholly 'within the staff.' His tone is broad and warm. Davis's sound, and his sense of chord changes and rhythm suspensions, are very close to the Charlie Parker alto style – he has played much with Parker in the past three years. As an idea man and influence, Miles Davis has just come into his full powers. If his grasp of the instrument still leaves something to be desired, he has shown considerable improvement ... since his first record (*Billie's Bounce*), and is certainly the trumpet to watch."

Apart from the music they played, Charlie Parker and the members of his first quintet also developed a particular approach to the presentation of their music. Unlike Gillespie, who sometimes wore funny hats and danced on the bandstand while keeping up a constant patter with his audience, the Parker quintet had no interest whatever in the compromises of show business. Their presentations revolved around inside jokes and private gestures – what Frank Sanderford called 'birding' the outsiders. Parker led the assault on conventional stage manners, and from him it soon spread outward until it became one of the hallmarks of the bebop revolution. "It was the bebop tradition to freeze out strangers," Coleridge Goode recalls. "It was *their* tradition. I think it stemmed from hearing that Parker would turn his back [on the audience]. So it was wear shades and turn your back and shut yourself off from the people. And just play." Parker's stage manner became a set routine, and it has been described countless times, with approbation or resentment, depending upon the disposition of the describer. But the routine was the same. Ross Russell says, "Charlie worked from a set of stock remarks considered hilarious by the cognoscenti, but less well understood by the public and sometimes resented by them, not to mention night club owners. These were delivered in a George Arliss voice and couched in stilted, stiff-collar phrases. As the set opened, the crowd would be told: 'Ladies and gentlement, the management of —— Club has gone to *enormous* expense to bring you the Charlie Parker Quintet.' The weighting of the word made the management sound like pikers ... When enthusiastic applause followed a good performance he would tell the audience, 'Thank you, ladies and gentlemen, ordinary applause will suffice.' The groundwork for later patronization of the public, to be made a fine art by Miles Davis, was being laid." Parker was, in spite of his stage manner, an extrovert; Davis, an introvert, would eventually cut off all communication with the audience beyond the playing of his music and in doing so would arouse such controversy that it sometimes threatened to distract all attention from what he was playing.

Early in the life of the quintet, August Blume, an avid fan, witnessed a unique entrance staged by Parker. "I was struck by the presentation at the Apollo Theater in 1947. There was a big banner proclaiming Buddy Johnson and his

Band, and, in little letters, Charlie Parker's Quintet. The Apollo Theater in Harlem really gave you your money's worth. I saw two African movies, with people running around in headdresses, and then came the live show. On a rolling stage, the resplendent Buddy Johnson Band emerged. When they finished, the curtain came down, and you could hear the clatter and noise of backstage changing. I was eagerly awaiting Bird and his group. The curtain rose, but the stage was bare. Then the guys came out pushing their instruments before them like prop men. Duke Jordan rolling out the piano, Max Roach with his drums on a little platform on wheels, Tommy Potter dragging his bass, Miles Davis shuffling out, and then Bird with his horn. Yard simply walked over to the microphone, announced the number, tapped his foot three times, and detonated a musical powder keg." The grand entrance of the Buddy Johnson Band, needless to say, was erased from memory by the time the quintet played their first notes.

If the members of the quintet were self-contained in their stage manner, they were equally wrapped up in the music they made. The legend persists that they once played on while a fire smoldered in the club where they were working. "The customers stumbled out through the smoke-filled vestibule as firemen lugged their hoses in through the doorways," Alun Morgan claims. "Apparently unaware of the mass exodus Parker, Davis, Jordan, Tommy Potter and Max Roach continued their way through a number which had started before the fire warning."

While 52nd Street and Harlem were the main venues for presenting the music, Brooklyn became a new scene for hanging out. Max Roach and Duke Jordan had been raised there, and several younger musicians were emerging from there and would soon be heard outside their borough. One of these was Randy Weston, who was only a few months younger than Davis but took a few years to decide that he wanted to play piano professionally. In the meantime, he manned a luncheonette called Frank's, one of four owned by his father in Brooklyn, and he specialized in catering to the boppers after hours. "We had the hippest juke box anywhere in New York," he says. "Cats would finish a gig in Manhattan and take the subway down for a cup of coffee and a hamburger. We had Stravinsky and Bird on that juke box, man, and the conversation was heavy every night." Among the regulars that Weston recalls were Davis and Roach, Dizzy Gillespie, Leo Parker, and Bud Powell.

In 1947, Davis finally recorded with his old mentor, Coleman Hawkins. The result, for listeners interested in the development of Davis, was disappointing, because he and the other young musicians in Hawkins's pick-up band are relegated to the background, playing chords behind Hawkins's rich tenor in much the same way as they might have for a featured vocalist. The music has none of the easy egalitarianism that Davis enjoyed playing beside Parker, who might have taken a star turn just as Hawkins does here, but never did. The details are as follows:

Coleman Hawkins All Stars
Miles Davis, tpt; Kai Winding, tbn; probably Howard Johnson, as; Coleman Hawkins, ts;
Hank Jones, pno; probably Tommy Potter or Curly Russell, b; probably Max Roach,
dms. New York, June–November 1947
Bean-A-Re-Bop; Phantomesque; The Way You Look Tonight; Isn't It Romantic
(all on Queen-disc Q-038)
The recording company was a small independent label, Aladdin.

All the titles are carefully arranged. *Phantomesque*, an original ballad by Hawkins, features Ellingtonian voicings behind Hawkins's lead, and the other two ballads, *The Way You Look Tonight* and *Isn't It Romantic*, have simpler and more subdued contributions from the band. On *Bean-A-Re-Bop*, a jump tune credited to Hawkins and his piano player Hank Jones, Hawkins joins the ensemble after a fashion but his huge sound dominates it almost as if he were playing the lead. Only on this title do Davis and Winding get heard, splitting a chorus between them after Hawkins's solo chorus. Perhaps the lack of solo space was a blessing, since Winding comes off laborious and struggling in his sixteen bars, and Davis is hardly any better in his. The session was thus completely dominated by its leader, as were so many others in his long and prolific career.

By the fall of 1947, Ross Russell had worked out the details for getting Parker to fulfill his contract with Dial. Russell moved to New York and carefully laid out the scheme for recording sessions that would be the apex of Parker's career. All the sessions were held at the WOR Studios, with the technical details in the hands of Doug Hawkins. "The working conditions over there were always very good," Russell says. "Hawkins sometimes seemed as important as another musician because he was so fine technically. He was a Juilliard graduate, and he also had a great deal of patience and understanding of what jazz musicians are trying to do." Instead of bringing in outsiders for the recording sessions, such as Bud Powell on the earlier Savoy session and John Lewis and Nelson Boyd on Davis's Savoy session, Russell insisted on recording the regular quintet, which made an important difference. "The most important thing about the records we made in New York, I think, is that they were made by a working band, Bird's own band, men that he had selected by choice, and a rhythm section that would be hard to surpass even today," Russell says. "There was almost complete one-mindedness among the musicians, so that everything they played had a lot of cohesion and was very subtle."

Russell organized three sessions, all to take place within the relatively short span of about eight weeks. The first, on a Tuesday evening in October, began ominously. Parker showed up early, appearing nervous and irritable, and demanded $50 from Russell. As soon as Russell gave it to him, he turned it over to a man who had been watching in the background and went into the washroom to prepare the heroin he had bought. But by the time the rest of the quintet arrived he was settled and ready to get started. The session turned out to be a model of efficiency, requiring only fifteen takes over a four-hour span to complete six titles (instead of the usual four) – four originals by Parker and two ballads:

Charlie Parker Quintet
Miles Davis, tpt; Charlie Parker, as; Duke Jordan, pno; Tommy Potter, b; Max Roach, dms. New York, 28 October 1947
Dexterity (two takes); *Bongo Bop* (two takes); *Dewey Square* (three takes); *The Hymn* (two takes); *Bird of Paradise* (three takes); *Embraceable You* (two takes)
(all on Spotlite 104)
A third take of *Dexterity* was recorded at this ession, but has since been lost. In numerous issues and reissues, these sides have had various titles: take 1 of *Bongo Bop*: *Charlie's Blues*; take 1 of *Dewey Square*: both *Prezology* and *Air Conditioning*; both takes of *The Hymn* have appeared as *Superman*, and take 1 of *Bird of Paradise* as *All the Things You Are*.

Among the originals, *The Hymn* ranks as one of the finest examples of Davis's playing as well as being a superlative example of Parker's genius. Parker assigns himself the unenviable task of opening the tune directly with his solo, at a fast tempo, before he and Davis state the theme at half-tempo. In the ensemble passages and during most of Davis's solo, the piano lays out, a device that lightened the group sound and that Davis frequently employed with his own bands during the next two decades. *Bird of Paradise* is played first as a straightforward version of *All the Things You Are*, in the arrangement recorded at the Finale Club in Los Angeles. On the second and third takes, it is transformed into an original melody based on the chord changes of *All the Things You Are*, with only oblique hints of the original melody. Because of the transformation, of course, Parker could take composer credit, and royalties, for *Bird of Paradise*. One might wonder, however, why the same process did not happen on *Embraceable You*. This slow ballad, one of Parker's finest improvisations on a ballad, is played with such invention that the original melody is heard only in fragments, apart from the eight bars played as a coda by Davis and Parker.

The title *Dexterity* refers to Dexter Gordon, the Los Angeles tenor saxophonist whom Parker and Davis had got to know during their stint in California the year before. He had arrived in New York earlier in 1947 and was active in the clubs of 52nd Street. During a period of inactivity for the Parker quintet, both Parker and Davis worked as sidemen with Gordon. "I worked with Bird at a place called the Spotlite with my sextet, with Miles and Bird, Stan Levey, Bud Powell, Curly Russell and Baby Laurence," Gordon recalls. "Laurence was the show but he was really part of the band ... He danced bebop. The way those cats danced, man, was just like a drummer. He was doing everything that the other cats were doing and maybe more. Blowing eights, fours and trading off. He just answered to the music. There were several cats at that level but he was the boss. Baby Laurence. Fantastic." Parker probably based the melody of *Dexterity* on a theme played by Gordon at that time.

The title *Dewey Square* refers to the area on 117th Street where Parker lived in a hotel after returning from California. He lived there for about a year, with Doris Sydnor, who devoted herself to nursing him and generally trying to coax him into better health. She seems to have received little reward for her efforts. Budd Johnson recalls a visit to Parker's apartment: "One day Bud [Powell] and Miles ran into me and told me that Bird was laying up at the Dewey Square hotel with pneumonia. We all went up to visit him, the boys first bringing the patient a fifth of Seagrams. When we got there, he was lying with water running off his face like a faucet. He had just polished off a bottle of wine with some person, and his wife Doris was frantic with worry. Our visit produced a burst of energy in him, and he arose and embraced us including the bottle. When his wife told him to get into bed, he put her out of the room."

The second New York recording session for Dial, just one week after the first, on Tuesday 4 November, again produced excellent results. Parker was late, but efficient when he arrived. He again recorded six compositions and took only a little more than three hours. Three of the tunes were standard ballads, requiring no elaborate ensembles or difficult tempos. The details are as follows:

Charlie Parker Quintet
Miles Davis, tpt; Charlie Parker, as; Duke Jordan, pno; Tommy Potter, b; Max Roach, dms. New York, 4 November 1947
Bird Feathers (one take); *Klakt-oveeseds-tene* (two takes); *Scrapple from the Apple* (two takes); *My Old Flame* (one take); *Out of Nowhere* (three takes); *Don't Blame Me* (one take)
(all on Spotlite 105; master takes of the last four titles are on Archives of Jazz AJ 503)
Thirteen takes were recorded; missing are the first two of *Bird Feathers* and the first of *Scrapple from the Apple*. *Bird Feathers* has also been released under the title *Scnourphology*, and the first take of *Out of Nowhere* as *Nowhere*.

The title *Klakt-oveeseds-tene* (given here in Parker's spelling, as it is listed on the Spotlite release) is a set of nonsense syllables, written out for Russell without comment when he requested a title. The composition is an ingenious march cadence on which Davis, muted, plays a line over Parker's low harmony. The ensemble resembles Dexter Gordon's *The Chase*, a well known tenor saxophone duel between Gordon and Wardell Gray recorded earlier by Dial in Los Angeles. The fact that no one is certain whether Parker or Gordon and perhaps Gray originated the line shows the scant attention that composition was given during this period; the tenormen know that they started playing *The Chase* while Parker was hanging around Central Avenue the year before, and all three of them may have had a hand in developing the theme that eventually became well known by two different titles.

The three ballads are structured the same way. Parker opens, playing the melody with embellishments and then improvising two choruses before Davis is heard at all; Davis then plays a chorus and restates the melody, with Parker in the background, to end it. *My Old Flame* and *Don't Blame Me* were completed in one take each, and *Out of Nowhere* would have been too, except that Jordan was alloted a chorus between Parker and Davis on the first take and the playing time ran to almost four minutes. The second take eliminated Jordan's chorus altogether but somehow managed to cut only eleven seconds off the recording time, and it was necessary to play it again with a shorter allotment of space for Davis. Parker plays superbly on all three takes, and astonishingly distinctively, but for all the other players, the overlong first take is probably the best.

By the second half of 1947, the success of the Gillespie orchestra and the Parker quintet was being widely felt and was spilling over onto musicians who had been obscure figures in the original movement and to younger players coming up. One result of the success was an increase in opportunities to play, especially in one-night, all-star settings. Jackie McLean, fifteen years old and a mere beginner on the alto saxophone that would soon put him on the bandstand, remembers one all-star concert at Lincoln Square, a large ballroom that occupied the site where New York's Lincoln Center sits now. McLean had raised the $1.50 admission fee but was denied entry because he was under age and had to persuade Dexter Gordon to take him in through the stage door. "I'll tell you who was on the bill that day," McLean says. "Art Blakey, Kenny Clarke, Max Roach, Ben Webster, Dexter Gordon, Sonny Stitt, Red Rodney, Charlie Parker and Miles Davis. But Miles didn't even play with Bird on that set. Bird was playing with Ben Webster and Dexter Gordon and Freddie Webster on trumpet. Fats Navarro was playing with Sonny Stitt. Miles was playing with Bud. All this on one day." It was up to the audience to convert the dance hall into a concert hall, McLean recalls. "You could bring up folding chairs – they had rows of folding chairs close to the bandstand and near the back, away in the back, there was an open area to pass around in. People could dance if they wanted to, but most people used to take their folding chairs and move them up near the front to be near the music. That's what they were there for, not dancing." The presence of Freddie Webster at this concert must mark one of his final appearances in New York. He died in Chicago before the year ended.

Soon after the November recording session, the Charlie Parker Quintet traveled to Detroit for an engagement at a club called El Sino. The engagement, which resulted in a cancellation, illustrates the kinds of situations that seemed to be part of the lives of Parker and his men and also, incidentally, explains why Parker would show up for the next Dial recording session, in December, with a new and superior saxophone to play. As often happened when Parker had to move away from his New York contacts, he had some problems in Detroit in making the connections for his heroin supply. He showed up at the club one night hardly able to play and after a noisy argument with the management stomped out of the club. Back in his hotel room, in a fit of rage, he threw his saxophone onto the street below, smashing it. When these incidents were reported to Billy Shaw, he threatened to abandon Parker for good but, as he had done before and would do again, he eventually gave in to Parker's pleading and gave him one more chance, buying him a new Selmer saxophone into the bargain.

Back in New York, the final Dial session took place in the same studio, WOR, with Doug Hawkins again at the controls. On the evening of Wednesday 17 December, when the recording was scheduled, Ross Russell was suffering from influenza. However, he had attended the rehearsals leading up to the recordings, which were necessitated by the addition of trombonist J.J. Johnson to the regular quintet. Including Johnson had been Russell's idea: "I was always interested in the trombone, and I thought that J.J. Johnson was just the end. I liked the idea of getting him into a date, and Bird thought it was a pretty good idea." This time Parker set up a real challenge for the band, calling for five originals and only one ballad, but the band responded by completing the session under the union limit of three hours:

Charlie Parker Sextet
Miles Davis, tpt; J.J. Johnson, tbn; Charlie Parker, as; Duke Jordan, pno; Tommy Potter, b; Max Roach, dms. New York, 17 December 1947
Drifting on a Reed (three takes); *Quasimado* (two takes); *Charlie's Wig* (three takes); *Bongo Beep* (two takes); *Crazeology* (three takes); *How Deep Is the Ocean* (two takes) (all on Spotlite 106)
Several takes, probably amounting to little more than false starts, have been lost, including the first and third takes of *Drifting on a Reed* and *Charlie's Wig* and the first take of *Bongo Beep*. Alternative titles abound: *Drifting on a Reed* was introduced by Parker in his club dates as *Big Foot* and is probably at least as well known by that title; its first take was released as *Giant Swing*, and the second take as *Air Conditioning*; the second take

of *Quasimado* (of which all takes have sometimes been referred to as *Quasimodo*) was released as *Trade Winds*; and *Bongo Beep* has had a rough history, being mistakenly issued as *Bird Feathers* and as *Dexterity* on different occasions.

For some reason, the music recorded at this session is not quite up to the consummate standards of the two previous Dial sessions. Although the addition of the trombone gives the ensemble passages of *Quasimado* a little extra awkwardness, this minor ballad, based on *Embraceable You*, would not have been significantly more attractive played by the quintet alone. Elsewhere, it is impossible to find fault with J.J. Johnson, who fits in well and executes his difficult parts on such fast numbers as *Charlie's Wig* and *Bongo Beep* with characteristic ease. Davis's playing on the earliest available take of *Drifting on a Reed* seems nervous, as he plays many more notes than is usual for him and threatens to slip into the style of Gillespie again, which he otherwise seems to have put behind him. More than anything specific, the whole session is marked by a lack of spirit. Only *Crazeology*, which is a tune usually known as *Little Benny* after its composer, Benny Harris, features risk-taking in the solos, but solo space is alloted to all six players and no one gets much room to move.

Only a week before Christmas, the quintet left New York again for Detroit, to fulfill the broken contract at El Sino. This time Parker made it through the engagement without incident. Among the musicians who sat in with the quintet in Detroit was Betty Carter, the bop singer who left Detroit soon after this with Lionel Hampton's orchestra. Carter, in what is definitely a minority opinion from this time, remembers Davis still struggling with his technique. "I sat in with him in Detroit before he had even learned to play the trumpet," she says, "when his notes were really tit for tat. I had to have the experience of sitting in with Charlie Parker and those guys. When they came to town, I'd be the first one there standing in line – a real fan, but a musician too. Because music was growing on me – it was magnetizing me." She was not the only one in Detroit, which was then showing the first signs of becoming a flourishing jazz community. Aspiring young musicians always turned out there for performances by the Parker quintet, making a good audience and a convivial atmosphere.

While in Detroit, Parker was approached quietly by Teddy Reig to make another recording for Savoy. Parker had been told in no uncertain terms by Billy Shaw that once his obligation to Dial was complete he was to leave the independent labels in favor of a contract with one of the giants of the recording industry. However, Parker and everyone else knew by now that the American Federation of Musicians, in a show of strength under the tough leadership of James D. Petrillo, was calling for a recording ban starting on the last day of 1947, just a little more than a week away. For Parker and the others, the opportunity for quick cash from recording dates looked unlikely in the months to come, and they readily agreed to Reig's offer. The Savoy session, with the regular quintet, took place on the Sunday before Christmas:

Charlie Parker Quintet
Miles Davis, tpt; Charlie Parker, as; Duke Jordan, pno; Tommy Potter, b; Max Roach, dms. Detroit, 21 December 1947
Another Hair-Do (four takes); *Blue Bird* (three takes); *Klaunstance* (one take); *Bird Gets the Worm* (three takes)
(all on Savoy S5J 5500; master takes on Savoy 2201; alternate takes of *Blue Bird* and *Bird Gets the Worm* on Savoy 1107)

The session has all the marks of a quickie production. The arranged material is at an absolute minimum: *Another Hair-Do* opens and closes with a simple riff; *Blue Bird* has twelve bars of a standard blues played by Davis at the opening; and both *Klaunstance* and *Bird Gets the Worm* open with very fast improvisations by Parker and have no themes at all. The whole affair is just a blowing session and probably took no more than two hours to complete. Duke Jordan is saddled with a piano badly in need of tuning. Yet in spite of all the adversities, the music recorded is always interesting. A good example is provided by Duke Jordan's solo on the final take of *Bird Gets the Worm*, in which he avoids exposing the untuned piano any more than is necessary by halving the time of this recklessly fast piece, thus playing relatively few notes but still making a solid contribution that is one of the highlights of the day's work. The whole session consists of solos loosely strung together, but they are generally excellent.

When the engagement at El Sino ended, Parker left for California, where he joined Norman Granz's Jazz at the Philharmonic (JATP) for a concert tour of the southwest. The other members of the quintet went their separate ways for the Christmas break, with Davis probably heading to Chicago. They reassembled in New York early in the new year to resume their booking at the Three Deuces.

Charlie Parker returned from his JATP tour full of the confidence that came with star billing in such an assemblage of jazz players. On tour he had even slipped off to Mexico and married Doris Sydnor, missing a concert unannounced to do so and arousing the ire of Norman Granz as a result. The January issue of *Metronome* magazine named him the best alto saxophonist of the year, his first win ever in the periodicals. Both his JATP billing and his *Metronome* award drew more attention to the quintet, by now already well established as a working unit and as a drawing card in the clubs. But in spite of all these favorable portents, a cloud seemed to hang over Parker, and it had nothing whatever to do with the recording ban, which would last eleven months. Instead of reaching out to grasp the success that was now so close at hand, Parker seemed compelled to avoid it altogether, or, perhaps more accurately, he seemed predisposed to sit back and wait for success to envelop him rather than to make any effort at grasping it. The more adulation he felt, the more disdain he showed. The more attention he drew, the more private he became. To some extent, his unorthodox response worked wonders for him, building his legend among the hipsters who worshipped him from the front-row seats, but it took its toll among those who were closer to him, his sidemen and managers, who had to contend with a lot more than his music if they hoped to stay in contact with him.

For one thing, the exposure to narcotics was constant. Duke Jordan says, "Wherever we would be, the pushers were with us. The grapevine, as far as drugs is concerned, is very quick, very swift, and as soon as Bird hit town, someone would contact him. 'I know where something really good is,' they would say, sometimes calling the hotel at five or six in the morning, and Bird would go with them." When he returned, sometimes as much as twelve hours later, he was often incapable of playing.

During an engagement at the Argyle Show Bar in Chicago, the problems seemed to be endless. Sadik Hakim, scheduled to play with Lester Young in Chicago the next week, traveled there early "to hear Bird and Miles." One evening he accompanied Parker to the club and watched as he received an ominous reminder that he had an overdue debt to his heroin connection. "Bird came in, early for once – no one else in his band was there," Hakim recalls. "He had left his horn at the club. Now Bird had very good connections in Chicago, but this time he apparently forgot to pay them. He opened his horn case to find all the keys torn off or broken."

Frank Sanderford heard Parker in person for the first time during this engagement at the Argyle, an expensive club, and remembers it vividly. His recollection provides an insight into the closed circle that the quintet maintained. "The place was packed but somehow I managed to get a seat at the bar, directly facing the band," Sanderford recalls. "Bird was tired, only occasionally playing a short solo. A few times it seemed to me he might fall over backwards. The fellows with him would shoot side glances his way, look quickly at one another with guilt not quite being covered by hastily formed masks of derision. It was difficult to tell if they were concerned or fearful and, if so, for themselves or their leader." Somehow, Parker caught Sanderford's eye and signaled to him to make his way to the musicians' room at the end of the set. Sanderford continues, "I managed to squeeze through the crowd to a small, dark room where the musicians lounged. As I came in, they looked surlily at me. It was hot, the musicians whispered among themselves, I heard snickers." What Parker wanted him for, it turned out, was to run out and pick up a hamburger for him. Parker's request was condescending and brought sneers from the others, but Sanderford ran the errand. When he returned with the hamburger, the musicians had hardly changed their expressions. The scene was finally disrupted by the management. "Suddenly, the manager appeared and demanded in querulous tones for their return to the stand," Sanderford says. "Slowly, resentfully, they went out."

But being "tired" and unsteady on his feet was only part of Parker's Argyle adventure. Duke Jordan picks up the story: "Bird came in one night, late and drunk. He couldn't play. He was too juiced. So the quartet, me, Max, Miles and Tommy finished out the evening. The club owner figured that he could get away without paying the band. Bird went up to the union to see if he could get money for the sidemen at least. He was in the office of the colored president of the local. A deal must have been cooked up between the club owner and this official, because the man suddenly whipped out a gun and said to Bird, 'Get the hell out of here or I'll shoot you up your ass.' Charlie left, saying, 'I'll be back.' He was about to make good his promise when I stopped him downstairs from the guy's office and told him not to be foolish, that the man would not hesitate to use his gun. He took my advice. We didn't get any money, but our leader was alive." Eventually Parker got his revenge, after a fashion. In an incident that Ross Russell calls "the jazz scandal of 1948," one night at the Argyle Parker set down his saxophone and strode off the bandstand, with all eyes in the lounge on him, and into the lobby, where he entered a telephone booth and proceeded to urinate at great volume and length – "as from a stallion," in Russell's phrase. The pool of urine flowed out of the booth and onto the carpet, and then Parker emerged, smiling broadly as he buttoned up. It is interesting to think that "the jazz scandal of 1948" should not be the withholding of wages from Parker's sidemen by the manager of the Argyle, and not the collusion and armed threat of a union official, but a sophomore prank by Parker that failed to touch the core of any issue – even if it did afford some comic relief.

As winter turned to spring, jazz musicians were bothered increasingly by two problems. One was, of course, the recording ban, which continued with no sign of a let-up. For jazz, a performer's medium rather than a composer's, the recording ban had especially damaging implications. The other problem was the general decline of 52nd Street as a venue for jazz. The Street had never recovered from the shutdown of November 1946. The real offences that brought it about – the murphy men, the prostitution, the mugging of drunks, the narcotics peddling – continued, and the police were applying pressure on the managers for both real and imagined infractions, adding to the managers' woes and probably to their under-the-counter payments as well. It was a bleak time, and virtually all the jazz that was played at the time evaporated as it bounced off the smoke-stained walls of a few clubs. The Charlie Parker Quintet fared a little better than most other bands. In New York it played regularly in the few clubs that still booked jazz, especially the Onyx and, of course, the Three Deuces. Moreover, some home-made tapes of the quintet's performances at both clubs survived the buffeting of the years – although just barely – and provide a glimpse of what it was playing in live performances:

Charlie Parker Quintet
Miles Davis, tpt; Charlie Parker, as; Duke Jordan, pno; Tommy Potter, b; Max Roach, dms. Probably the Onyx Club, New York, ca spring 1948
Theme [52nd Street Theme]; *Shaw Nuff*; *Out of Nowhere*; *Hot House*; *This Time the Dream's On Me*; *A Night in Tunisia*; *My Old Flame*; *52nd Street Theme*; *The Way You Look Tonight*; *Out of Nowhere*; *Chasin' the Bird*; *This Time the Dream's On Me*; *Dizzy Atmosphere*; *How High the Moon*; *Theme* [52nd Street Theme]
(all on Prestige PR 24009)

Same personnel, plus Kenny Hagood, vcl (on *All the Things You Are*). Three Deuces, New York, ca March 1948
52nd Street Theme; *Dizzy Atmosphere*; *My Old Flame*; *All the Things You Are*; *Half Nelson*; *52nd Street Theme*; *52nd Street Theme*; *Big Foot* [Drifting on a Reed]
(all on Spotlite SPJ 141 [1979])

These recordings are not from complete sets or probably even from the same evenings, but are a conglomeration of pieces played by the quintet at various times. They were made from radio broadcasts using a hand-held microphone with a wire recorder, and the sound is barely listenable. The men who made the tapes, Bob Guy and Jimmy Knepper (who later played trombone with Charles Mingus's band and others), were Parker fanatics who edited the transcriptions by shutting off the machine during the performances whenever Parker was not playing. No title is a complete performance. But in spite of the heavy editing and the terrible sound reproduction, the tapes fill a gap in the material from 1948.

Judging from the titles recorded, the nightly repertoire of the quintet includes surprisingly few of the compositions recorded for Dial and Savoy the previous year. Only *Chasin' the Bird*, *Drifting on a Reed*, Davis's *Half Nelson*, and the ballads *Out of Nowhere* and *My Old Flame* show up. Where, one wonders, are *The Hymn*, *Donna Lee*, *Milestones*, *Bongo Bop*, *Scrapple from the Apple*, and all the others? Instead of playing the original works of the working quintet, Parker tends to call for the best works of a short-lived earlier quintet, the one that he and Dizzy Gillespie had fronted on 52nd Street in 1945: *Shaw Nuff*, *Dizzy Atmosphere*, and *A Night in Tunisia*, all by Gillespie, *Hot House* by Tadd Dameron, and the bop chestnut *How High the Moon*. Davis is heard best on *The Way You*

Look Tonight, *Dizzy Atmosphere*, and *How High the Moon*, because he states the theme and trades fours with Parker and sometimes Roach, contributions that the men running the recording machine could not eradicate. On all the tunes, the editors cut him off abruptly less than a bar into his solo.

How recordings such as these came to exist belongs to ornithology. The butchery of the tapes resulted from devotion so ardent that it blinded Guy and Knepper to the talents of all other musicians. In 1981, Knepper just shook his head at the recollection: "When Bird came along, the musicians in my circle were enchanted by him. The effect was that we couldn't listen to anybody else. People that played with Bird – even Diz – sounded silly. They sounded like they were children, playing the game that he was master of. Whoever was on those early records with him would sound childish. That kind of stunted my diversification, my catholic tastes. It was only years later that I could appreciate what Diz and others did."

Knepper and Guy were only two of several amateur recordists of Parker's music. Unfortunately, most of the others lost themselves and their caches of wire recordings in the next decade. These were the hipsters who worshipped Parker. Many of them were, like him, heroin addicts, and most of them gloried in his antics – the George Arliss announcements, the nodding onstage, the Argyle Club urination – almost as much as they admired his genius. Chief among the ornithologists was Dean Benedetti, who aspired to be a jazz alto saxophonist until the first time he heard Parker play; according to legend, he immediately discarded his own saxophone and thereafter followed Parker wherever he went or preceded him wherever he was going and set up his wire recorder on the spot. He recorded Parker from the washroom at Billy Berg's, the basement at the Onyx, and anywhere else he could find an electrical outlet where Parker was playing. Like Guy and Knepper, who probably learned from him, he is said to have recorded only Parker, not his sidemen. He died, again according to the legend, in mysterious circumstances in Sicily in the late 1950s. Intensive searches for his trunkful of Parker solos have always come up empty.

The phenomenon of the Parker fanatic has no precursor or successor in the history of jazz, and it becomes more difficult to grasp as it recedes in time. Bob Dorough was a music student in New York when it was happening, and, happily, is an articulate lyricist as well as a singer and piano player. He captures something of the spirit of the time in his notes for the album reissuing his vocal version of *Yardbird Suite* (Bethlehem BCP-6023). "Oh, it was *crazy* how we dug Bird," he says. "We'd give up pork chops for beans to have cab fare and admission to Birdland (cheep). We'd follow him whenever we could, session-gig-or-concert. And you'd give up a night's work when word came 'round that Bird was playing at the William Henry – a jam session with the cats, all the Bird-lovin', ordinary, jazz-blowin' cats. I mean, even tho' we thought of Bird as a sort of god, it seems he was occasionally induced to visit and blow with lesser mortals ... We'd all crowd into this basement pad at 136th and Broadway, bringing provisions and contributions, wine, pot, snacks, just to hear and be there – and, sometimes, *you'd get to play two or three tunes with Bird!* Wow! DONNA LEE! CONFIRMATION! HALF-NELSON! And it was *taped*. Even if you weren't there that night you could listen over and over again. Not content to buy his every recorded solo we collected tapes and exchanged them – and *listened* to them. We loved every note he played. We loved the squeaks of his reed. We loved other people too, especially the giants and the survivors, Diz, Miles, Thelonious – but we really dug Bird – it was like idolatry – it was crazy. I tried to keep *my* head up; make my 8:00 o'clocks, do my homework, make a little money, experience some of the vast musical scene (non-jazz) going on in New York City, etc. But my cold-water flat family gang was eggin' me on and we were Bird-happy, Bird-struck, and Bird-bent – and mostly tryin' to learn to blow a little. Small wonder that, sitting in a musicology class one day at Columbia University, I suddenly realized that the musicologists were out *there*, man, following Bird around with the Wollensack, recording every note he played – *that* was musicology-in-the-field; collecting the work of a genius who would soon sing his last song. A few days later I quit school." Dorough went on to work as a singer-pianist in Europe and then back home, setting the kind of low-key personal standards that would lead Miles Davis, improbable though it may sound, to commission a song from him in 1962. He is one of the survivors himself, like Jimmy Knepper but unlike most of their "Bird-happy, Bird-struck and Bird-bent" cohorts and, of course, unlike Bird himself.

At the same time that Parker's coterie was gathering, an epidemic of narcotics addiction began to spread among the jazz musicians. Narcotics have long been part of the night-life subculture, endemic to pimps and prostitutes, petty and grand thieves, and the fringe of outsiders who make up the night people. Jazz musicians have been members of that subculture ever since their music was installed as a diversion in the bordellos of New Orleans, and they were charter members by the time jazz spread to the American heartland as an entertainment in Prohibition speakeasies. Most jazz musicians were exposed to drugs, many of them experimented with them, and some became hard users as far back as the 1930s, including Charlie Parker. Now, in the late 1940s, as bebop was elevating jazz to the status of concert music instead of pop entertainment or dance music, addiction became more widespread. Paradoxically, one cause of the spread was the new status of jazz, which gave the musicians rank as artists instead of mere entertainers in the eyes of their peers. Parker was certainly influential, being lauded as a genius and emulated as an addict. Howard McGhee, the trumpeter who was close to Parker in California, describes the new exposure of musicians such as himself in this way: "The era that we came up in, with Dizzy and Miles and all those cats, everybody was trying to be tight with us because they liked us and dug what we were doing. They said, like, 'McGhee's my friend,' but the cat might not even realize that he was more of an enemy by turning me on. Nowadays I know, because I'm a little different than I was then, but the average cat figures that he's doing you a favor by making stuff available. Every day he's there and you just get deeper and deeper until pretty soon he's gone and *you*'re asking where *he*'s at. They leave you out there on a limb."

The Street played a role in the narcotics trade as well. Tony Scott, who had gone there to sit in as a serviceman throughout the war, was back there as a working musician after his discharge, and he watched the decline. "The Street started to slow down after the war ended, after V-J Day," he says. "But while everybody was coming back, for another year anyway, things were pretty flush. There was always a bad element, but it got worse and worse after the war and into the late forties. It was a hotbed, for example, for narcotics. Marijuana was the main thing then. The bad element used to take especial advantage of out-of-towners and soldiers and sailors. The police started to make some arrests, and warnings were given, and things were made harder and harder on the club owners, and every once in a while something bad would happen. There began a move away from The Street." Scott feels that the problem was not only with the habitués of the clubs themselves, but also in the attitudes of the owners. "It seemed like the feeling just went out of the smaller clubs on 52nd Street," he says. "The war had ended and it was more profitable for the club owners to switch to all-girlie shows. And so The Street gradually became a place for strip joints. I remember Bud [Powell] had left The Street to take a group into the Roost on Broadway with Miles Davis, who had come onto the scene. The last jazz club folded by about 1948. And The Street was no more."

"I got off The Street about that time," Monte Kay recalls. Kay, a publisher who was also an avid jazz fan, had been running weekly jam sessions at Kelly's and elsewhere on The Street since 1942. He too became disillusioned with the aura surrounding the jazz clubs there. "It had developed a clip-joint attitude that was rough on the kids, including myself," Kay says. "If you stayed for more than fifteen minutes, they hustled you for another drink. But I was convinced there was an audience for bop." Kay started the move away from 52nd Street to Broadway, just around the corner, where jazz had never before been featured prominently. He remembers the circumstances that opened up Broadway to bop: "One night – it was a Saturday – I went into the Royal Roost, a chicken joint on Broadway and 47th Street owned by Ralph Watkins. Jimmy Lunceford was playing. Though he had an outstanding band, the place was practically empty. Watkins was skeptical about the modern stuff. But I managed to talk him into letting me and Symphony Sid produce a concert on an off night. He picked Tuesday, and we did a concert with Bird, Tadd Dameron, Miles Davis, Fats Navarro and Dexter Gordon." Kay also started the policy of admitting minors and others into a non-drinking section of the club, where for 90¢ they could sit and listen without being harassed or jostled by waiters; the idea of the non-drinking section, called the bleachers, was later adopted by another Broadway club, Birdland, which became even better known than the Royal Roost and survived much longer. After the success of Kay's Tuesday-night bop concerts, the Roost began billing bop bands regularly and Tadd Dameron, who was managed by Kay, was hired to front the Roost house band. For 52nd Street, the shift of jazz to Broadway was another serious blow in its protracted decline.

While the music played by Parker's quintet revealed new strengths the longer it worked as a unit, personal differences among its members surfaced more forcefully as it entered its second year of existence. Part of the problem came from Parker's remoteness; he was never available to take the initiative when a decision had to be made or to smooth out differences when they came up. "We all know what Bird's habits were because he'd had them since he was fourteen years old," Ray Brown says. "That preoccupied a lot of his time off the bandstand; it took up most of his social life; it dictated the type of friends that he was to have. Unfortunately, he was relegated to just dealing and running in certain areas to get what he wanted to get, to keep up with his needs." The leader's role was assumed more and more by Davis, not always with the full approval of the others. Davis saw it simply as a necessity, because of Parker's absence.

"He never did talk about music," Davis complained. "I always even had to show Duke Jordan, the pianist in the band, the chords." Davis was never satisfied with Jordan's playing and agitated to have him replaced by someone with a stronger theoretical background. Jordan, with typical gentleness, remembers the awkward situation he found himself in: "The group got on very harmoniously except for slight altercations with Miles. He and Max formed sort of a little clique. They were both getting $135 a week, ten more than me and Tommy. Miles was making it at Juilliard, and he was tight with John Lewis, and he wanted Bird to substitute John for me in the group. But Bird silenced him by quietly and firmly saying that he chose the guys and Miles could form his own outfit if anything displeased him. That was all that was heard from Miles." Jordan's recollection that Davis was "making it at Juilliard" reflects on what Jordan considers to be at the root of Davis's disaffection for his playing, since Juilliard was well in the past by now. John Lewis, who had been Davis's choice on his own Savoy date a year earlier, had a more successful university career, having graduated from the University of New Mexico in 1942. Lewis was in the eye of a similar storm over the replacement of a piano player in 1946, when Dizzy Gillespie chose Lewis to replace Thelonious Monk in his orchestra over the objections of Gil Fuller. The two situations, so similar in their essentials, underline the changing perception of their music by certain jazz musicians, who were beginning to realize that the new complexity of the music demanded some training beyond merely surviving in jam sessions.

As the tensions within the quintet grew, they were exacerbated by Parker's erratic behavior, which caused all the members grief. Even when the quintet were booked for a long engagement, the sidemen had to worry about getting paid. "At some clubs Bird was actually paid by the set, it was that risky a thing that he would show," says guitarist Jimmy Raney. "His horns presented a problem – they were in hock so often. At the Three Deuces, the porter had a job assigned to him, to go to the pawnshop every day and get Bird's horn for the job, and then return it to the shop after the job."

In spite of the unpredictability of the leader and the hard feelings between Davis and Jordan, the personnel had remained the same for sixteen months. By the late summer of 1948 that stability grew too precarious to last much longer. Someone, presumably Parker, had to make a decision: either Davis and Roach had to go, or Jordan and Potter had to go. In spite of Jordan's recollection of Parker's support for him against Davis, it was he and Potter who left. Davis and Roach were emerging as important musicians in their own right, and they drew an audience wherever they played; this latter consideration must have weighed heavily with Billy Shaw, if Parker consulted him. If the arrangement was intended to restore personal cohesion among the members of the quintet, it failed. Davis and Roach were fed up with Parker's vagaries and, armed with the confidence that they could move out on their own and be successful, were less tolerant when Parker's behavior robbed them of their pay and made havoc of their music. They remained with Parker somewhat uneasily.

Jordan was replaced by John Lewis for the one recording session of the year, in September, clearly a nod in Davis's direction, and by Tadd Dameron, another close associate of Davis's, for a Royal Roost date in September, when Dameron filled in temporarily while doubling as the piano player in his house band. Jordan's permanent replacement was Al Haig, who joined Parker in December and stayed until mid-1950. Haig was almost certainly Parker's choice rather than Davis's. He had been with Parker in the first bop quintet on 52nd Street and in the sextet that traveled to Los Angeles. He was also, like Jordan, a piano player schooled in the clubs, with very little academic training. Potter's replacement was Curly Russell, but in December, just before Davis and Roach left the quintet for good, Potter was rehired. The timing of Potter's return and of the departures of Davis and Roach is probably not accidental.

While Haig and Russell were in the group, the quintet played at the Three Deuces again – probably for the last time. Parker seemed quite unmoved by the occasion. Guitarist Tal Farlow, who played opposite the quintet in a band led by vibraphonist Margie Hyams, recalls Parker at the Three Deuces with a sense of awe because of his playing and with a sense of disbelief because of his antics. One night, Farlow remembers, "Bird came storming into the club after a lengthy absence. The management tried to get him up on the stand immediately. He wouldn't be rushed. We were standing in the rear of the place. Margie, Miles Davis, Al Haig, Curly Russell and I watched the comedy unfold. Bird had some sardines and crackers, and was eating them with a sense of relish, while the management pleaded with him to come to the stand. They got to the point where they were cajoling and begging him. He kept offering them sardines and crackers. We laughed 'til our sides hurt. Finally he came out and played."

Starting in September, the quintet usually played on Broadway. One of the advantages of playing at the Royal Roost was a weekly radio broadcast. Remote broadcasts similar to the one from the Roost had been an integral part of the swing era in the 1930s, popularizing the big dance bands, especially Benny Goodman's, and creating an audience for them far from the big urban centers where the broadcasts originated. They had also been important for the small swing bands during the heyday of 52nd Street, and they were expected to work as well for the bop bands at the Roost. The Roost remotes were instigated by Symphony Sid Torin, Monte Kay's co-promoter, who hosted a popular rhythm-and-blues program on station WHOM in the early 1940s and was the first broadcaster to promote bebop on the air when he played, and touted, the first records by Gillespie and Parker in 1945. During the recording ban of 1948, the Roost remotes were doubly significant, providing listeners with one of the few sources of current music outside the clubs themselves. Whenever a transcription of one of the remotes has been preserved, by wire recorder or disc recording or, increasingly, the new-fashioned tape recorders, its value in filling in the development of the music during the ban is inestimable. Many of the remotes were traded back and forth among fans over the years; some of them have been transferred onto records more recently, sometimes licensed by the producers for limited issues and sometimes marketed as unauthorized or bootleg albums.

From September until December, when he left the quintet for good, Davis appears on several broadcasts from the Royal Roost, sometimes with Parker and sometimes with a band of his own. Only those broadcasts with Parker are discussed in this chapter, and those without Parker will find their place in the next chapter. The Roost broadcasts by Davis with his own band belong to a different phase from the one chronicled in this chapter. The two phases are clearly separable. Davis was, in these final months with Parker, moving in two different musical directions – introducing an influential reaction to bebop and wrapping up his own involvement beside Parker in the main current of bebop.

Davis's first broadcast from the Roost with the quintet took place on a Saturday in September. Parker's quintet, as has been indicated above, takes on an unfamiliar look for the occasion, with Tadd Dameron and Curly Russell in place of Jordan and Potter:

Charlie Parker All Stars
Miles Davis, tpt; Charlie Parker, as; Tadd Dameron, pno; Curly Russell, b; Max Roach, dms. Royal Roost, New York, 11 September 1948
52nd Street Theme; Ko Ko
(*Ko Ko* issued on Le Jazz Cool JC 101)
Jepsen (1969) lists the date of this broadcast as 4 September, but several Parker discographies correct it as shown.

Le Jazz Cool issued three albums based on Parker's broadcasts from the Royal Roost and elsewhere, some of them with Davis and some without, several years ago. They are now unavailable.

Just a week after this, while Davis was engaged at the Royal Roost with his own band, a nonet, which would make its broadcasting debut that same night, Davis spent the afternoon in a recording studio with the Parker quintet, for the first time in almost nine months. The recording ban was still in force, and the recording had to be done clandestinely. Herman Lubinsky of Savoy had contacted Parker and set the recording dates with him. Why he chose to violate the ban is not clear. Possibly he knew that Davis and Roach were set to leave Parker's band and he wanted to record the quintet before it broke up. Or perhaps he was simply fed up with waiting for the end of the strike which by now looked interminable. He and Parker agreed to record eight titles, all of them originals by Parker, in two sessions, the first on Saturday 18 September, and the second the following Friday:

Charlie Parker All Stars
Miles Davis, tpt; Charlie Parker, as; John Lewis, pno; Curly Russell, b; Max Roach, dms. New York, 18 September 1948
Barbados (four takes); *Ah-Leu-Cha* (two takes); *Constellation* (five takes)
(all on Savoy S5J 5500; master takes on Savoy 2201; alternate takes on Savoy 1107)
Davis does not play on the fourth title recorded at this session, *Parker's Mood* (five takes).

Same personnel and place, 24 September 1948
Perhaps (seven takes); *Marmaduke* (eight takes); *Steeplechase* (two takes); *Merry-Go-Round* (two takes)
(all on Savoy S5J 5500; master takes on Savoy 2201; alternate takes on Savoy 1107)
For several years the dates of these two sessions were listed incorrectly as 29 August and

August-September, respectively, but the Savoy company ledgers have now confirmed the dates listed above.

These recordings, the last ones made for Savoy by either Parker or Davis, rank among the best the two men made together. It is worth comparing them with the first recordings they made together, also for Savoy, in November 1945. There, the fumbling young Davis had to give way to Dizzy Gillespie because he could not master the introduction to *Ko Ko;* here, he dispatches the intricate heads of *Barbados* and *Marmaduke* with apparent ease, and he solos confidently at all tempos. On listening to the fast *Constellation* from this session, Med Flory noted: "This was 1948, and by this time, Miles was playing very well, way up high, very fast, as together as anybody can get." For most listeners, *Parker's Mood,* a soulful blues played by Parker backed only by the rhythm trio, is the highlight of these final Savoy sessions, and it is hard to argue with that opinion when Parker, one of the greatest blues players, is so near the top of his form. Of the other sides, all by the quintet, *Ah-Leu-Cha* remains a striking performance of an interesting composition. Structurally, it is identical to *Chasin' the Bird,* recorded for Savoy in May 1947, with the two horns playing simultaneous counter-melodies for sixteen bars and then Parker playing the release alone for eight bars before the two horns restate the counter-melodies for the final eight. If one listens to *Chasin' the Bird* right after *Ah-Leu-Cha,* the maturity attained by the first Charlie Parker Quintet becomes obvious: *Chasin' the Bird* is, by comparison, a ragged ensemble, with the two horns seeming to miss the timing of the counter-melodies perceptibly, if only by a millisecond. On *Ah-Leu-Cha,* the horns are in phase, and the melody sounds rich and full. *Ah-Leu-Cha* has been relatively neglected among the compositions Parker recorded with the first quintet, but unjustly so. One of the few recordings of it since the original one is by Davis and his first quintet with John Coltrane, made several years after this one, in October 1955, a few months after Parker died. It is the only Parker composition to be recorded by Davis after leaving Parker's quintet.

Soon after the clandestine Savoy sessions, Parker left New York again to tour as a featured soloist with Norman Granz's Jazz at the Philharmonic. By the time he returned to fill an engagement with the quintet at the Royal Roost, the recording ban had finally ended. The settlement between the American Federation of Musicians and the recording companies came in November, and the companies began tooling up for the new season. Billy Shaw got Parker to sign an exclusive contract with Mercury Records, where Norman Granz was the jazz producer, but there was no immediate move by the company to record the quintet.

The documentation for the final weeks of the quintet's existence comes instead from the surviving Roost broadcasts, with their home-made sound and radio production. Davis made three broadcasts with Parker in December, two of them on Saturdays – 11 and 18 December – and the other on a Sunday – 12 December:

Charlie Parker All Stars
Miles Davis, tpt; Charlie Parker, as; Al Haig, pno; Tommy Potter, b; Max Roach, dms.
Royal Roost, New York, 11 December 1948
Groovin' High; Big Foot [Drifting on a Reed]; Ornithology; Slow Boat to China
(all on ESP-Bird-1; *Groovin' High* and *Ornithology* on Le Jazz Cool JC 101; *Big Foot* on Le Jazz Cool JC 102)

Same personnel and place, 12 December 1948
Hot House; Salt Peanuts; Half Nelson; White Christmas; Little Willie Leaps
(*Hot House* on Le Jazz Cool JC 103; other titles unissued)
The unavailable titles from this broadcast should not be confused with the broadcast of 25 December, when the same titles were played. The later broadcast had Kinney Dorham on trumpet replacing Davis.

Same personnel and place, 18 December 1948
Chasin' the Bird; Out of Nowhere; How High the Moon
(all on MEEXA 1776; *Chasin' the Bird* and *Out of Nowhere* on Le Jazz Cool JC 102)

The broadcast versions of the various compositions have a refreshingly spontaneous quality, as might be expected. Some of them are given perfunctory performances, as *Groovin' High* is here, with Parker idly attempting to leap an octave instead of sticking to the harmony on the out-chorus. Others are surprising because of the transformations they have undergone since their earlier recorded performances; here, *How High the Moon* is played over a latin beat, and *Out of Nowhere* is played at a fast tempo. Davis and Roach set up a pattern on several of these tunes (*Big Foot, Ornithology,* and *Chasin' the Bird*) in which Davis plays four-bar phrases in a descending scale and Roach thumps the bass drum at the conclusion of each phrase; the effect is bumptious, even if it was obviously enjoyed by the two players. The repertoire is expanded by comparison with the Onyx recordings earlier in the year. The most satisfying performances are versions of Parker originals recorded the previous year, *Big Foot, Ornithology,* and *Chasin' the Bird*. The quintet's repertoire also included at least two of Davis's originals from the previous year, *Half Nelson* and *Little Willie Leaps*.

Five days after the last of these broadcasts, on 23 December, Davis quit the band for good. "Miles and Bird were hardly speaking," says Ross Russell. "Christmas week the internal tensions within the group came to the surface. Complaining to me that 'Bird makes you feel one foot high,' Miles Davis stalked off the stand, not in an ordinary huff, but never to return. Max Roach quit the same night." But Roach was persuaded to stay on for at least two more nights, until his replacement, Joe Harris, who had recently left the Gillespie orchestra, could take over. Roach appears on the broadcast from the Roost the next Saturday, Christmas day, but the trumpeter in the band is Kinney Dorham (whose given name, McKinley, is sometimes rendered as Kenny). As soon as Davis quit, Parker dispatched a handsome young singer who was appearing with his band at the Roost, an unknown named Harry Belafonte, to Dorham's apartment on Sugar Hill with the message that the job in Parker's band was available. Dorham, a Texan, had played in several modern bands, including Russell Jacquet's, Billy Eckstine's, and Dizzy Gillespie's, but his main ambition was to join Parker's group. He was proud to state: "I took Miles Davis's place. He recommended me for the spot."

Russell claims that "events had proved that the presence of Miles in the same band with Charlie presented insoluble personality conflicts." Maybe so, but it is easy to overemphasize the differences between the two men. Certainly they remained in fairly close contact with one another after the split, occasionally playing together and even recording together again in both 1951 and 1953 (and also twice in 1949, when both were members of large bands assembled for recordings). There is certainly no evidence of animosity in Davis's recommending Dorham as his replacement, and even less in Parker's accepting the recommendation.

Parker's continuing regard for Davis's trumpet style and the contribution it made to the group sound is not shown so clearly in his selection of Dorham, whose style is closer to Gillespie's, but it is reaffirmed in his selection of Red Rodney as Dorham's replacement in 1950. Rodney seemed a surprising choice to many commentators, but the choice is surely explained by Rodney's appreciation of the style of Miles Davis. "I loved Miles Davis, I thought he was most beautiful," Rodney says. "I thought he changed the sound of the trumpet. He made it much more lyrical. He was a great creative jazz artist." After Davis, Rodney was perhaps the most satisfactory trumpeter to work regularly beside Parker, because he came the closest to giving Parker what Davis had given him – warmth of tone and a cool contrast to Parker's fire.

In the weeks immediately following Davis's resignation, Davis and Parker remained at close quarters. Parker stayed at the Royal Roost with his quintet until the middle of March; for two weeks in February and one more in March, the group appearing opposite Parker's was Tadd Dameron's Big Ten, featuring Miles Davis. Later in March, Parker's quintet and the Miles Davis–Tadd Dameron Quintet traveled together to France, where they took their turns on the stage of the Paris Jazz Festival. If Parker and Davis were no longer partners in the music they made, their circle nevertheless remained unbroken.

The early association of Miles Davis and Charlie Parker is unique in jazz annals. In an art form that does not have its own academic tradition, it is not at all uncommon for one great player to learn at the elbow of another great player. One thinks of the boyish Louis Armstrong rising out of the band of King Oliver, his patriarch on the cornet, and of John Coltrane searching doggedly for the harmonies he could hear but not yet play in the bands of Miles Davis in the 1950s. These examples, along with the example of Parker and Davis, are only the best known in an art form that, of necessity, has had to improvise its own apprentice system. But Oliver sent for Armstrong to join him in Chicago because he had already heard the genius in his playing, as anyone could hear it, almost from the first note. And Davis kept rehiring Coltrane, against his better judgment and common sense, as we shall see, because he knew, as some others also knew, that Coltrane would eventually break through that harmonic barrier. What did Parker see in the young Davis that assured him of his talent? What could he possibly see in a young man afraid to join in the jam sessions, hanging back in the shadows? Whatever it was, Parker's instinct was unerring. Davis's climb into the front rank of jazz musicians took about three years – only slightly longer than it took Armstrong, and much quicker than Coltrane's sluggish rise would be. By the time Davis walked off the bandstand and left the Charlie Parker Quintet in December 1948, he had already laid the foundation that would make him Parker's peer in the development of jazz. It had happened at the Royal Roost, with an experimental nine-piece orchestra that played together in public for only two weeks. To piece together that part of Davis's story, we must go back again to the summer of 1948.

4

Move
1948–50

Jazz sort of needs movements. They always remind some people of some things they haven't been paying any attention to, or bring about something new that is real crazy.
  Thelonious Monk

Jazz music was not the only art form in ferment in the New York of the 1940s. The city had borne the brunt of the Great Depression in the previous decade, and then the war, believed almost unanimously to be a war worth shedding blood in, a "just" war, came along and dispelled the Depression like a foul odor. In the United States the war was viewed not as a concerted effort by the Allied Forces against the malevolent Axis so much as an exercise of American courage and ingenuity to head off powers opposed to freedom and democracy. During the Depression, President Roosevelt had proclaimed that his fellow citizens had "nothing to fear but fear itself," and now, less than a decade later, many of them journeyed to the Old World to defend their inalienable rights against the forces of evil. In preventing the fascists from conquering the world, the Americans believed – as their movies, their newspapers, and their politicians gave them every reason to – that they were inadvertently conquering the world themselves, if not exactly by and for democracy, then by Coca Cola and Chiclets and know-how. The mood, despite the blood being shed, was euphoric, and the arts, finding themselves surrounded by euphoria for the first time in ages, were thriving. Jackson Pollock painted canvases with tubes instead of brushes, and for the first time there was an internationally known entity called American art, with a host of rising stars such as Willem de Kooning, Clyfford Still, Franz Kline, Robert Motherwell, and Grace Hartigan. In American theater, Eugene O'Neill had loomed as a solitary giant before the war, but during and after it he was not merely joined but supplanted by such new playwrights as William Saroyan, Tennessee Williams, Arthur Miller, and William Inge. Fiction flourished, with

Hemingway reborn, it seemed, by the war, and a host of tough new writers: Ralph Ellison, James Jones, and Norman Mailer. And the brilliance of all of them was matched, in their different ways, by the leaders of the bebop revolution with their American – *distinctively* American – music. Out of Lester Young and Charlie Christian a brand-new sound had emerged, the work of many minds: Kenny Clarke, Thelonious Monk, Bud Powell, Oscar Pettiford, and, especially, Dizzy Gillespie and Charlie Parker.

But the war ended – not suddenly, on a given day when some politicians signed some treaty or other, but imperceptibly, the way really important things happen. The men returned from overseas, not all at once but one by one, and the women threw out their coveralls and their Red Cross uniforms, not all on the same day but sooner or later. Instead of lining up to punch in at the munitions factory or to pick up the weekly ration of bacon, people started lining up instead to put their names on the waiting list for Hoovers and Chevrolets and suburban bungalows. The boom was every bit as high as the bust of the 1930s had been low. By 1948, some people could put their feet up and say, hey, look at us, first a depression and then a world war – what next?

Some of them were artists. Andrew Wyeth looked out his window and saw not only his own reflection but also trees and fields *and* his own reflection, all at once. Carson McCullers and J.D. Salinger and Truman Capote discovered that they were not so tough, maybe, as Hemingway's batmen, and they worried about that for a while, and then they stopped worrying. In the theater, whose headquarters, Broadway, would soon be shared with improvising musicians, the change was not so much in what was being written as in how it was being declaimed: the young actors studied by day at Lee Strasberg's Actors Studio, where they learned that the business of acting lay not so much in delivering the sense of the play, as the Lunts and the Barrymores had done so nobly for so long, as it did in delivering the sensibility of its action. There would be an entity, undreamed of until now, called American acting, as soon as the actors could find the parts. And they would find the parts.

The young actors studied and worked on Broadway, when they could afford the lessons and find the work. The rest of the time, which was most of the time in the beginning, some of them hung out at the apartment of the actress Maureen Stapleton, in a crumbling brownstone on fading 52nd Street, beside Leon and Eddie's, the old show-biz hangout that had lost the celebrities and was surviving, barely, on strippers. On a hot summer night, the actors could sometimes hear the overtones from Oscar Pettiford's group across the street or the applause for Charlie Parker's quintet down the street. But they had to be listening for it, and most of the time when they were at Stapleton's place they were not listening; they were talking about how it *should* be in the theater or how it *would* be some day, and they were most of all acting, trying out gestures and postures and deliveries on one another. The young actors who drifted in and out of there, as unemployment permitted, included, among many others now forgotten, David Wayne, Tom Ewell, Julie Harris, Jerome Robbins, Kevin McCarthy, Kim Stanley, Montgomery Clift, and Marlon Brando. At Maureen Stapleton's place, they and their friends constituted what would have been called, in eighteenth-century Europe, a *salon*. Eventually they changed the art of acting in the United States, and soon after that they changed it throughout the world.

At the same time there was a jazz salon – too precious a word for it, and one that none of its members would use, but the only word the language has for what it was. It was three blocks north, on 55th Street, where the rents were lower, and it belonged, in the sense that he held the lease for it, to Gil Evans, an arranger for Claude Thornhill's dance band. The one-room basement apartment belonged to Evans in almost no other sense. "I just left the door open," Evans says, "and people came in and out all the time for the next couple of years." Dave Lambert, the jazz lyricist and singer, says, "It was shared by around nine people. There was Gil, myself, my wife and daughter, Specs Goldberg the drummer, and Gerry Mulligan." And they were only the regulars. Irregularly, there were many more. "Being right near 52nd Street which was swinging at the time," Lambert explains, "Max, Miles and Bird would fall by, and, as soon as someone would get up from a bed, another person would jump on it. The people would lie crosswise so they could fit more bodies. It was a struggle, but fun." It was a struggle, apparently, just to get to the place. Lambert says, "You had to go down a short flight of stairs, pass a Chinese laundry, through a boiler room, and there it was – home."

"I don't know how Gil ever got anything done, because there were people there twenty-four hours a day," says Blossom Dearie, who rehearsed and sang with Lambert at the time. "Charlie Parker lived there for a while, and you'd generally find Dizzy Gillespie and Miles Davis and Gerry Mulligan and John Lewis. Or George Handy would be there, or George Russell or Barry Galbraith or Lee Konitz." George Russell remembers the place as a haven and a direct reflection of Gil Evans's personality. "A very big bed took up a lot of the place; there was one big lamp, and a cat named Becky. The linoleum was battered, and there was a little court outside. Inside, it was always very dark. The feeling of the room was timelessness. Whenever you went there, you wouldn't care about conditions outside. You couldn't tell if it was day or night, summer or winter, and it didn't matter. At all hours, the place was loaded with people who came in and out. Mulligan, though, he was there all the time. He was very clever, witty and saucy, the way he is now." Mulligan's wit often depended upon sarcasm, and Russell recognizes that there were tensions not far from the surface in him and in all of them, except Evans. "Gerry had a chip on his shoulder," he says. "He had more or less the same difficulties that made all of us bitter and hostile. He was immensely talented, and he didn't have enough of an opportunity to exercise his talent. Gil's influence had a softening effect on him and on all of us. Gil, who loved musical companionship, was the mother hen – the haven in the storm. He was gentle, wise, profound, and extremely perceptive, and he always seemed to have a comforting answer for any kind of problem. He appeared to have no bitterness."

Gerry Mulligan, the arranger and baritone saxophonist, was a year younger than Miles Davis. He had arrived in New York as a member of the Gene Krupa orchestra in 1946, while Davis was in California. His major accomplishments consisted of two arrangements recorded by the Krupa orchestra, *How High the Moon* in May 1946 and *Disc Jockey Jump* in January 1947. The frustrations that Russell mentions seemed to dog the young Mulligan especially, and even though he found a few opportunities to display his precocious talent in notable settings, he had to wait four more years, until 1952, before he gained public and critical recognition. That recognition, when it came, was enthusiastic and persevering, but by the time it arrived, Mulligan might justifiably have given up on it. He had already had, besides the arrangements for Krupa, two very attractive arrangements recorded by the Elliot Lawrence band, *Between the Devil and the Deep Blue Sea* and *Elevation*, in 1949 (reissued, with the Krupa sides, on Columbia PC 34803). Between these, he wrote arrangements for Miles Davis's nine-piece band that grew out of the Evans salon, and with that band he also displayed a highly personal and swinging sound on the baritone saxophone. For some reason, all his talents went unnoticed by most listeners until he moved to California and broke through, and in 1948, when he was living in Evans's apartment, he was struggling. Dave Lambert remembers him leading open-air rehearsals at the time. "Mulligan was rehearsing a band in Central Park," Lambert says, "because he had no money to rent a rehearsal studio. They would play in the grass till the cops came and chased them." Acclaimed now as one of the crucial arrangers and composers of postwar jazz, his formative experience was in the salon. "We all gravitated around Evans," he says. Mulligan calls Gil Evans Svengali, an anagram of his name.

The man who hosted the salon was, on the surface, an unlikely Svengali. George Russell's metaphor, "haven in the storm," fits better, and if the salon bustled like a cyclone, Gil Evans was its eye, its calm and unruffled center. Born Ian Ernest Gilmore Green in Toronto on 13 May 1912, of Australian parents, he soon moved to the Pacific coast, where he spent his youth in British Columbia, Washington, and California. His surname, Evans, was conferred on him by his stepfather. He led his first band in Stockton, California, in 1933, and a few years later, in 1936–7, his band became the house band at the Rendezvous Ballroom in Balboa Beach. Evans has always been a reluctant leader, unwilling and perhaps temperamentally unable to put up with the extramusical grief of dealing with booking agents and club managers. His first band was taken over in 1937 by the band's singer, Skinnay Ennis, and Evans remained with it as its arranger and director, a role that suited him better even if, in the pop music scheme of things, it reduced to anonymity his crucial creative contribution to the sound and the style of the band. As the band became more successful under Ennis, playing regular radio spots with Bob Hope as well as the Rendezvous dances, Evans was joined by a second arranger, Claude Thornhill, who stayed until 1939 and then left to form his own band in New York. In 1941, Thornhill sent for Evans to write arrangements for his new band. They were just becoming established when Thornhill enlisted in the army, where he stayed from 1942 until 1945; Evans enlisted soon after and stayed from 1943 until 1946, rejoining Thornhill when he was discharged.

In the new band, they experimented with combinations of instruments, adding french horns and a tuba to the stock sections of dance bands, and filled its ranks with several jazz soloists, including alto saxophonist Lee Konitz, clarinetist Danny Polo, guitarist Barry Galbraith, and trumpeter Red Rodney. Besides the obligatory dance band fare, Evans prepared meticulous arrangements of some of the current compositions being played on 52nd Street, including Sir Charles Thompson and Illinois Jacquet's *Robbin's Nest*, Gillespie and Parker's *Anthropology*, Parker's *Yardbird Suite*, and Davis's *Donna Lee*. Although the band's style did little to win over the jitterbuggers, relying instead on subtlety and understatement to a degree unheard of in the field, musicians and other discerning listeners soon realized what was happening. "Thornhill had the greatest band, the one with Lee Konitz, during these modern times," Miles Davis said in 1950, adding, "The one exception was the Billy Eckstine band with Bird." Evans was credited by the insiders for the band's essential musicality. He was earning the private praise of musicians eight or ten or – in Davis's case – fourteen years younger than himself. Reedy and pale and pensive, Evans thus discovered his musical fraternity not only among such arrangers as Mulligan, Johnny Carisi, and George Russell, but also among the volatile young blacks of the bebop revolution.

The respect that he earned was stranger still because, unlike most of the other great arrangers of jazz, Evans was not an instrumentalist. Although he played piano with bands he sporadically led during the 1960s and 1970s, he had almost never played publicly before that. He showed no interest in working to attain performing skills on the piano until around 1952, when he was already forty, and even then he hardly attacked the task; fifteen years later he told Leonard Feather, "Miles has asked me to play at different times, but I never had the nerve to do it." His arranging skills are, incredibly, self-taught, and so is his piano technique. "I never played scales and exercises, never in my life," he says. "I can sit down at the piano and just look at it for hours, maybe hit a note here and there. I can't just sit down and play." His lack of formal training may be a key to his originality, for he can arrange harmonies that no one else has ever arranged and cluster instrumental groups that no one has ever sectioned before. "He knows what can be done, what the possibilities are," Davis says. An orthodox academic background might only have limited those possibilities for him. Indeed, with an academic background, Evans would almost certainly never have hosted the 55th Street group at all, for the salon was partly his own graduate school. "I was always interested in other musicians," Evans told Nat Hentoff. "I was hungry for musical companionship, because I hadn't had much of it before. Like bull sessions in musical theory. Since I hadn't gone to school, I hadn't had that before."

If Evans is a reluctant leader and player, he is no less reluctant as a composer. It is all part of the essential anarchism of his character. He has never regimented himself to compose or arrange on any schedule, and he is not disturbed by writer's block any more than he is by writer's cramp. He simply does not conceive of himself as a producer of any kind. "If I feel the need for some emotional development, well, I think about music and play and even write," he says. "But as far as the product is concerned, there is no product." As for meeting deadlines, he says, "If it's the right time to do it, it works out fine." The wonder is that Evans, with his approach, should have produced any lasting work at all.

Evans's recorded materials are remarkably sparse and tend to cluster around certain productive moments of his career – 1957–9, 1963–4, and perhaps a couple of others – but some of the little work he has produced ranks with the very finest orchestrations in jazz, perhaps even placing him alongside Duke Ellington among the great arrangers. But any mention of Ellington in the same breath simply underscores again the anomaly of Evans's position. Not only was Ellington enormously prolific as an arranger, but he was an arranger only because he was first a composer; he was an arranger of his own compositions. Evans, in a professional career which – incredibly – spans as many years as Ellington's did, has managed only a handful of original compositions, and his greatest achievement is in arranging other people's. In this respect, he differs not only from Ellington but from almost every other major composer-arranger in jazz as well. Leonard Feather says, "He is perhaps the only great writer in jazz history who has always tended to work as an arranger of the works of others and rarely as a composer of his own material."

The list of Evans's original compositions can easily be listed (with the dates when they were recorded): *Blues for Pablo* and *Jambangle* (1957); *Gone* (1958); *La Nevada, Sunken Treasure, The Pan Piper, Saeta, Solea,* and *Song of Our Country* (1960); *The Flute Song* and *El Toreador* (1963); *Barracuda* and *Isabel* (1963 or 1964); *Las Vegas Tango* (1964); *Spaced, Proclamation* and *Variation on* the Misery (1969); Zee Zee (1973); and perhaps a few others in less accessible places. If the list is supplemented by the compositions written by Evans in collaboration with Miles Davis, his only collaborator and probably the only person capable of motivating Evans to compose at all, it is increased by these: Boplicity (1949); Miles Ahead (1957), an arrangement of Davis's 1953 composition; Song #1 and Song #2 (1962); Hotel Me (1964); Petits Machins (1968) or Eleven (1973) – two titles for the same composition; General Assembly (1969); and perhaps a few others. Nevertheless, what the list lacks in quantity it partly compensates for in quality, because many of these works are sumptuous and memorable compositions. One thinks of Boplicity, Miles Ahead, Blues for Pablo, Gone, La Nevada, Saeta, and Barracuda among the finest moments of recorded jazz.

Evans's originality does not require original compositions for its demonstration. His arrangements of other people's compositions simply sparkle with his individualism; they overflow with invention. Even such old chestnuts as St. Louis Blues and It Ain't Necessarily So, so well known that they might seem to have lost all charm, and such jewels of the jazz literature as Lester Leaps In and Manteca, so familiar in their original, classic arrangements, have been resuscitated by Evans so that listeners might think they had never heard them before. Among the composers Evans has arranged, he has certain favorites. Most surprising, and an indication of Evans's catholic taste, is Kurt Weill, from whom Evans has made brilliant use of the melodies of My Ship (1957), Bilbao Song (1960), and a weirdly funereal The Barbara Song (1964). In the late 1970s and after, Evans has shown a predilection for arranging the rock themes of guitarist Jimi Hendrix, and he has liberally selected works by composers between the two distant poles represented by Weill and Hendrix. He has often chosen to arrange works by the men who made up the salon on 55th Street in 1948, to their considerable advantage: Miles Davis, of course, most of all, but also Johnny Carisi (Springsville), J.J. Johnson (Lament), John Lewis (Concorde and Django), and George Russell (Blues in Orbit and Stratusphunk). Beyond these rather scattered relations, one searches in vain for any telling thread that determines Evans's selection of material. He has obviously ranged throughout the world of music with something close to absolute freedom, from the most tawdry pop tunes (Under the Willow Tree for Thornhill and I Don't Wanna Be Kissed for Davis) to themes from minor classics (Moussorgsky's Pictures at an Exhibition as The Troubador for Thornhill, and the second movement of Rodrigo's Concierto de Aranjuez for Davis). His tastes have been unencumbered by convention or bias, and his career has been almost untouched by self-promotion or self-aggrandizement. And he has managed, on his own terms and at his own pace, to produce a body of work that holds its own proud place in jazz.

That accomplishment might have been out of the question if he had never met Miles Davis. Just as Davis could stir up Evans's will to compose, so he has also been able to stir him to produce most of the arrangements on which his reputation stands. No one else has been capable of doing it, at least not consistently. A lucrative contract from Verve Records in the 1960s calling for four albums of music from Evans terminated after one album and a few out-takes; by way of contrast, Evans has collaborated with Davis on five albums and several additional tracks of released material, and on at least that quantity of unreleased material.

Davis met Evans in 1947, sometime after Davis's *Donna Lee*, recorded in May of that year, was released by Savoy. Evans approached Davis to ask him for the lead sheet of *Donna Lee*, so that he could make an arrangement of it for the Thornhill band. Davis agreed, on condition that Evans get him a copy of his arrangement of *Robbin's Nest*, recorded by Thornhill on 17 October, so that he could study it. The two men thus discovered the basis of their mutual respect. As Davis puts it, simply, "He liked the way I played and I liked the way he wrote." Evans agrees, although he puts it less simply. "We had this thing – this sound – in common," he told Zan Stewart. "We heard the same sound in music. Not necessarily the details; the first thing you hear when somebody plays or writes things or even talks is the sound, the wave form, and having that in common made it possible for us to be good collaborators."

Still, it is hard to guess how Davis reacted to Evans's arrangement of *Donna Lee*, which was recorded by Thornhill on 6 November as a piano solo by Thornhill accompanied by the band's rhythm section – Barry Galbraith on guitar, Joe Shulman on bass, and Billy Exner on drums. In contrast to the pert rendition by the Parker quintet, Thornhill plays it at a very slow, dreamy tempo. Davis's melody is transformed almost beyond recognition. Thornhill's version is not entirely surprising: he cultivated the dreamy quality in the band's book. "At first, the sound of the band was almost a reduction to inactivity of music, to a stillness," Evans notes. "Everything – melody, harmony, and rhythm – was moving at a minimum speed. The melody was very slow, static; the rhythm was nothing much faster than quarter-notes and a minimum of syncopation. The sound hung like a cloud." As the style grew more mannered Evans became bored by it, and it is ironic that his arrangement of Davis's melody should come to stand as a prime example of Thornhill's mannerisms. Finally, as the cloudy style dominated the band's sound more and more, Evans decided to leave Thornhill. "The sound had become a little too sombre for my taste, generally speaking, a little too bleak in character," he said. "It began to have a hypnotic effect at times. The band could put you to sleep." He resigned in the summer of 1948. Although Evans says that his leaving was friendly, Thornhill immediately reorganized the band and gradually eradicated Evans's contribution to its book. By 1953, bassist Bill Crow told Ian Crosbie, "Some of the Evans charts were used only as punishment, when the band was getting sloppy or drunk." That same year, 1953, Thornhill, troubled by depression and alcoholism, disbanded for the last time.

Looking back on the Thornhill band, Bill Borden, another of its arrangers, remarked, "Gil Evans changed the face of the band but, I think, undermined Claude's confidence in himself." The attention that Evans was getting from the young musicians on 52nd Street and Broadway might have encouraged Thornhill to find an alternative direction for the band that would again stamp it as his own creation rather than Evans's. By the late summer of 1948, Evans was seeking a band to write for that would allow him to express himself more fully. At the same time, Miles Davis, increasingly disturbed by the tensions in the Parker quintet, was also looking for a band that would allow him to exploit his own strengths as a soloist. The discussions in the salon about experimenting with new voicings and discovering some new dynamics for improvised music suddenly took a more practical turn.

Evans originally hoped that Charlie Parker, who spent as much time at Evans's place as he did anywhere else and thus qualified as a resident, might be the one to lead the salon's theoreticians in their assault on the world outside, but he soon abandoned that hope. "Months after we had become friends and roommates, he had never heard my music, and it was a long time before he did," Evans told Nat Hentoff. "When Bird did hear my music he liked it very much. Unfortunately, by the time he was ready to use me, I wasn't ready to write for him. I was going through another period of learning by then. As it turned out, Miles, who was playing with Bird then, was attracted to me and my music. He did what Charlie might have done if at that time Charlie had been ready to use himself as a voice, as part of an overall picture, instead of a straight soloist." Davis, of course, was ready.

The members of the salon all agreed that the perfect band for what they wanted to accomplish would need to have nine players, with the standard bop quintet of trumpet, saxophone, and rhythm supplemented by a second reed instrument and three more brass. The added instruments were all to be in the lower ranges – trombone, french horn, tuba, and baritone saxophone – which pretty well dictated that the other reed instrument would have to be an alto saxophone, which has a lighter sound and a higher register than the tenor. That choice of instruments was determined before Davis entered the discussions. "Gil Evans and I spent the better part of one winter hashing out the instrumentation for that nine-piece band," Gerry Mulligan says, adding, "but Miles dominated the band completely; the whole nature of the interpretation was his." It was a subset of the instrumentation of the Thornhill orchestra, which normally had eighteen or more pieces in it. Davis considered Thornhill's full band to be merely cumbersome rather than functional, especially because Evans was capable of grouping the voicings to get as much sound from fewer instruments. "Gil can use four instruments where other arrangers need eight," he says, and that was the proportion – half the instruments that Thornhill used – that was decided on. The only hope that the band had of playing in public lay in limiting the number of players as far as possible. Even nine men would seem extravagant to club owners used to paying trios, quartets, and quintets. However, "this was the smallest number of instruments that could get the sound and still express all the harmonies the Thornhill band used," Evans says. "Miles wanted to play his idiom with that kind of sound."

Without Davis, all the talk about the band would almost certainly have remained just that. He brought a new element into the salon, an ambition to translate the discussions into practice. "He took the initiative and put the theories to work," Mulligan says. "He called the rehearsals, hired the halls, called the players, and generally cracked the whip." Because he was better known among the managers of jazz clubs after working beside Charlie Parker for so long, he eventually got the band some public exposure beyond the rehearsal studio.

Gil Evans calls him "the complete leader" of the band, because "he organized the band, sold it for a record contract, and for the Royal Roost where we played." The record contract was with Capitol, one of the handful of large companies that dominated the record industry at the time, along with Columbia, Decca, Victor, and Mercury. As soon as the recording ban ended, Davis signed a contract to record twelve compositions for Capitol with the nonet. By the time the recording sessions started, the nonet had long since disbanded, having played their two weeks at the Royal Roost in September and finding no more opportunities for club dates. Fulfilling the contract proved to be a problem, as it became impossible to reassemble the original members for the three sessions required, and both the new members and the original members required rehearsals prior to each session because learning the complex charts amounted to much more than just reviving faded memories.

The first session did not take place until 21 January 1949, four months after disbanding, and the others were on 22 April 1949 and 9 March 1950. As a result, the impact of the nonet on critics and other musicians was dissipated. Only the few hundred who saw them live at the Royal Roost were fully aware of what they were attempting, and even for them their style was so innovative that their real accomplishment could hardly be appreciated. For most of the jazz world – musicians, critics, and listeners alike – their influence was not an impact at all but an insinuation; the recordings appeared at wide intervals and were not put together in a collection until May 1954, when Capitol released a ten-inch album

containing eight of the compositions. The band were ahead of their time when
they were first assembled, but by the time the recordings had eased their style
into the jazz consciousness, their time was ripe.

Miles Davis forged ahead on the nonet project in the summer and fall of 1948,
fighting the practical and commercial outlook of the day, urging Evans and the
other arrangers to prepare their charts, and becoming the organizer and task-
master for eight other musicians who were mostly, like him, employed in other
bands. He was fully aware that he had discovered his own métier. In Gil Evans
and the other members of the salon, he found the individuals gifted in theory and
harmony who could continue his own education beyond what he had learned
from Gillespie, Monk, Webster, and the others, including, of course, Juilliard and
William Vachiano. He also discovered a musical setting that suited him better
than the hard-core bebop he played nightly with the Parker quintet. Bob Weinstock, who started Prestige Records soon after this time, says, "Gil Evans had a
tremendous influence on Miles' musical thinking. Miles always spoke of Gil
Evans, and he kept telling me, 'Get Gil Evans, get him to do an album. He's
beautiful.' I think that Miles found his true element there, at *that* time. Here was
a chance for all his sensitivity, compared to Bird's savageness and deep fire and
emotion, which was overpowering Miles every time they played on the same
stand; here was an outlet for Miles Davis to let out the sensitivity that he had as a
musician."

The nonet also provided a chance for him to discover his abilities as a composer. "I didn't start writing until I met Gil Evans," he says, apparently overlooking *Donna Lee*, which provided the occasion for their first meeting. "He told me
to write something and send it to him," Davis recalls. "I did. It was what I played
on the piano. Later I found out I could do better without the piano. I took some
piano lessons at Juilliard, but not enough. If you don't play it good enough, you'll
be there for hours and hours." The first effects of Evans's interest in Davis's
composing can be heard, at least faintly, in the four original compositions Davis
recorded in August 1947 – *Milestones*, *Little Willie Leaps*, *Half Nelson*, and
Sippin' at Bells – which are arranged for the instrumentation of a bop quintet but
show hints of the salon style in their moods and tempos. Over the years, Davis has
proven to be an important and interesting composer, with several jazz standards to
his credit. He has nevertheless made his priorities clear. "There's a certain feeling
you can get from playing that you can't get from composing," he says. "And when
you play, it's like composition anyway. You make the outline." In the nonet, the
control and clarity of his improvising often match the careful arrangements.

Some of the thornier problems in recruiting musicians for the nonet were
solved simply by recruiting players from the Thornhill band. Bill Barber, a graduate of Juilliard and the Manhattan School of Music, had been playing the tuba in

Thornhill's band for more than a year by the late summer of 1948, and he came highly recommended by Evans and the others who knew him. Mulligan says, "He used to transcribe Lester Young tenor choruses and play them on tuba." Sandy Siegelstein, one of Thornhill's french hornists, played at the first rehearsals with the band at Nola Studios, although he was not with the band when it played at the Royal Roost. By then he had been replaced by Junior Collins, about whom the only ready information comes from Mulligan's assertion that he "could play some good blues."

The members of the salon naturally became players in the nonet. John Lewis, one of the arrangers, was the piano player, and Gerry Mulligan, another of the arrangers, played baritone saxophone, as he occasionally had in the Gene Krupa orchestra and other big bands. In the smaller band, Mulligan had a chance to expose for the first time his ability as a soloist, revealing the personal sound and light touch that would mark him as one of the most interesting soloists ever to play that cumbersome horn.

Membership in the salon was not enough in itself to guarantee membership, any more than was membership in Thornhill's band. Lee Konitz, an alto saxophonist with an almost fragile sound compared to the bold sound of Parker and his followers, was one of Thornhill's best soloists, especially on Evans's arrangements of *Anthropology* and *Yardbird Suite*, and he was also entrenched in the jazz avant-garde of the day, not only participating in the discussions of the salon but also working and studying with pianist Lennie Tristano. Still, Davis's first choice for the alto saxophonist in the nonet was not Konitz but Sonny Stitt, whose style was very much in the mold of Parker. Stitt, had he been included, might have made an enormous difference to the band's sound, not only because of his individual contribution but also because his presence alongside Davis, Lewis, bassist Al McKibbon, and drummer Max Roach, all of whom were involved nightly in playing bebop, might well have tipped the balance and made their sound much more bop-oriented and bop-derived than it ended up being. Fortunately, Davis listened to Mulligan's advice and ended up asking Konitz instead of Stitt. "Gerry said to get Lee Konitz on alto because he had that light sound too," Davis says. Davis's hiring of Konitz meant that he had to absorb some criticism when he was away from the salon. "When I hired Lee Konitz, some colored cats bitched a lot about me hiring an ofay in my band when Negroes didn't have work," he says. "I said if a cat could play like Lee, I would hire him, I didn't give a damn if he was green and had red breath." Davis's attitude about following a color line in hiring players for his bands has consistently been the one he expresses here: the first consideration is talent, not color. Even during the 1960s and 1970s, when his public pronouncements on racial matters were zealous, his musical priorities often led him to hire white players.

Al McKibbon, the bassist, had replaced Ray Brown in the Gillespie orchestra in 1947, where he formed close ties with John Lewis, his partner in the band's rhythm section. Max Roach not only was a member of the Parker quintet with Davis but also shared his enthusiasm for what the salon was working toward. He was part of that circle, and his interest in composing probably dates from this period, although he did not record any original works until a few years after he had played with the group. Kenny (Pancho) Hagood was the tenth man in the nine-piece band; he was Gillespie's band singer, and he was added for some vocal choruses.

The remaining instrumental chair was the trombonist's, and filling it proved, surprisingly, to be a problem. J.J. Johnson, a member of the salon, would seem to have been an obvious choice, and later on he recorded with the nonet in their two later sessions. In the summer and fall of 1948, however, he was a member of the Illinois Jacquet band, and he was apparently either traveling with it or playing full-time at a New York club when the nonet were rehearsing. For a couple of decades the trombonist who worked with the nonet at the Royal Roost was incorrectly listed as Ted Kelly, a member of Gillespie's orchestra. Kelly may have been Davis's choice for a while, but he did not play with the band and seems not to have made any of the rehearsals with them either, at least none of those directly connected to the two-week engagement at the Royal Roost. Improbably, the trombonist in the working nonet was an eighteen-year-old college freshman who was home on vacation in the summer of 1948 when he was recruited by Davis. His name was Michael Zwerin, and he later wrote some interesting jazz journalism, including this account of his own recruitment into the celebrated nonet: "I was sitting in at Minton's Playhouse one night when I saw Miles standing, listening, in the back. When I was packing up my trombone, he asked me if I could make a rehearsal the next day at Nola's Studios." As simply and unexpectedly as that, Zwerin found himself in the nonet. (Later, Davis made similar unexpected approaches to several other musicians, some of whom went on to become key members of his bands.) The hiring of such an unknown and untried trombonist as Zwerin probably resulted from the unexpectedness of the public debut of the band.

"That whole thing started out just as an experiment," Davis recalls. "Then Monte Kay booked us into the Royal Roost on Broadway for two weeks." The band assembled for the first time at Nola Studios above Lindy's restaurant on Broadway, where some of the Savoy recordings were made, including the clandestine ones with Parker the next month, September, during the recording ban. Zwerin remembers that "Miles was pleasant and relaxed but seemed unsure how to be a boss. It was his first time as a leader. He relied quite a bit on Evans to give musical instructions to the players." Zwerin's impression of Davis's uncertainty may indicate only that at the time Zwerin did not realize the extent to which the whole project was a collaboration between Davis and the arrangers rather than simply Davis's project. Zwerin adds, "Miles must have picked up his famous salty act sometime after that, because I don't remember his being excessively sarcastic that summer."

By the time the band opened at the Roost, Zwerin and everyone else should have been fully aware of their collaborative nature, if only because of the billing they were given on the sidewalk sign outside the club. "There was a sign outside – 'Arrangements by Gerry Mulligan, Gil Evans, and John Lewis,'" Evans recalls. "Miles had it put in front; no one before had ever done that, given credit that way to arrangers."

The sign on the sidewalk was a concession that Davis got from Monte Kay and the Roost's owner, Ralph Watkins, from whom he could hardly expect many more favors. Booking the nonet had been a kind of concession, not only because of the size of the band, which increased its payroll, but also because the managers had no reason to expect any commercial payback from its engagement. "At the time the Royal Roost was probably the only nightclub in the country that would have taken a chance with this new and forbidding type of jazz," Nat Hentoff points out. That Kay and Watkins took the chance is a credit to their commitment to the music and also probably a sign of the goodwill Davis had earned while working there as a member of the Parker quintet, which played there in alternate weeks with the nonet and was scheduled to return there in December. The nonet took second billing to the Count Basie orchestra and probably helped initially to draw some of the bop fans who might otherwise have avoided showing up to hear Basie's Kansas City swing style. Whether the nonet could keep those fans coming after they had a taste of their subtle style is another matter.

The dates of the Royal Roost engagement were discontinuous. The radio broadcasts, now issued on record, are dated 4 September and 18 September, both Saturdays, with an intervening Saturday, the 11th, taken up by the Charlie Parker quintet with Tadd Dameron on piano. (A third broadcast, made on Saturday the 25th, also features Davis but with neither Parker nor the nonet; he is heard with Lee Konitz and a rhythm section, suggesting that a sub-group of the nonet were rehired for the following week. Some commentators, including Hentoff, have claimed that the nonet played at the Royal Roost for three weeks, against all the assertions of the men who were in the band, probably on the assumption that the last aircheck was also a nonet date.) If the dating of the broadcasts is correct, then the nonet played the first of their two weeks from 30 August until 4 September, and the second 13–18 September, with the Parker quintet filling the hiatus, 6–11 September; otherwise, the dates of the broadcasts may need correcting, with 11 September being the right date for one of them. Apart from this uncertainty, the details are as follows:

Miles Davis Nonet
Miles Davis, tpt; Michael Zwerin, tbn; Junior Collins, frh; Bill Barber, tba; Lee Konitz, as; Gerry Mulligan, bs; John Lewis, pno; Al McKibbon, b; Max Roach, dms; Kenny Hagood, vcl (on *Why Do I Love You?* and *Darn That Dream*). Royal Roost, New York, 4 September 1948
Why Do I Love You?; *Godchild*; *S'il vous plait*; *Moon Dreams*; *Hallucinations* [Budo] (incomplete)
(all on Ozone 2 and on Durium-Cicala BLJ 8003)

Same personnel and place, 18 September 1948
Darn That Dream; *Move*; *Moon Dreams*; *Hallucinations* [Budo]
(all on Alto AL-701 and on Durium-Cicala BLJ 8003)
Hallucinations is Bud Powell's original title for this theme, and it is apparently identified by that title in the announcements from the Royal Roost (not included on these recordings); when it was recorded by the nonet for Capitol on 21 January 1949, it was titled *Budo*, and Miles Davis was credited as its co-composer along with Powell.

All but two of the arrangements played on the broadcasts from the Royal Roost were later among the twelve sides recorded for Capitol Records. The exceptions are *Why Do I Love You?* and *S'il vous plait*. This additional material on the radio broadcasts, which only became generally available in the 1970s, thus provides the first clue about the band's repertoire beyond the material on the Capitol recordings. *Why Do I Love You?*, with a vocal chorus by Kenny Hagood, contains a highly forgettable lyric, but Gil Evans's arrangement does a good job of de-emphasizing it. The opening chorus, strictly instrumental, features harmonic layers by the horns under Davis's lead, which gives way to a trombone lead for a few bars at the bridge (the only bars in which the trombone is featured in any composition). Evans's touch is obvious in the shifting textures behind the trumpet lead and also, after Davis's solo and Hagood's vocal chorus, in an elaborately arranged ending using stop-time. (The audience begins to applaud after the vocal chorus, where vocal arrangements normally end, but stops short when the band keeps playing.) For better or worse, Evans seems to have drawn the arranging chores for only the slow dance tempos; while neither Mulligan nor Lewis could have handled them as well, it might have been interesting to hear Evans's work at faster tempos too. The only other vocal arrangement for the nonet that has survived, *Darn That Dream* (on both the broadcasts and the recording) is by Mulligan; it is a more straightforward arrangement for a vocalist, subjugating the band to Hagood's lead, and is much less interesting instrumentally than *Why Do I Love You?*

The other arrangement that never made it into the recording studio, *S'il vous plait*, is a fine example of the nonet's style. An uptempo instrumental, it sections the horns into the brass and the reeds, and the melody is stated in counterpoint by the brass playing a motif in half-time while the reeds weave a lively second motif around it. (Jepsen's discography identifies this as *Chasin' the Bird*, Parker's composition using counterpoint, but there is no melodic similarity.) The arranger has been identified as Miles Davis (by Chris Sheridan, in *Jazz Journal*) but on the basis of aural evidence alone, one might guess that it is Mulligan, since he used counterpoint extensively, almost as a trademark. Whether the arranger is Davis or Mulligan, the arrangement makes an excellent frame for solos by Konitz, Davis, and Mulligan, the latter two playing over an arranged background of riffs. The reason for its not making the transition to studio recording might be its length, since the version played at the Roost lasts well over four minutes, but other compositions last almost as long in the broadcast version and were successfully pared down for the recorded versions. One is grateful, naturally, to have it preserved in any version at all, but it is hard not to mourn its omission from the Capitol sessions. Luckily, the home-made tapes of the Royal Roost broadcasts are nowhere near the worst examples of their genre and are quite listenable. On the 4 September broadcast, the piano is drastically underrecorded, and the tuba and the bass go almost unnoticed on both broadcasts. However, the broadcasts have a kind of spontaneity altogether missing from the recordings, which are polished to a point just short of distracting, and, of course, the broadcast versions feature longer and more varied improvisations.

Formally, the music played by the nonet departs sharply from the conventions for bebop performances of the day, and the difference was fully intended. After several years, the bebop format had become static, revolving primarily around twelve- or thirty-two-bar theme statements followed by a round of solos by all hands. The tempos were limited more and more to medium and uptempos, and the solos at any tempos included phrases of eighth- and sixteenth-note runs, very often recognizable in the work of lesser players as originating in the recorded solos of Gillespie and Parker. In every respect, Davis's nonet proclaimed a revaluation of bebop standards. Tempos ranged from fast on *Budo* and *Move*, both arranged by Lewis, to very slow – unusually slow for the jazz of the day – on *Moon Dreams*, arranged by Evans. The theme statements often took up several choruses, thus drawing attention to the arranged material rather than hurrying past it, and many of the solos were wholly or partly contextualized by arranged material in the background. And in Davis and Konitz, and only slightly less noticeably in Lewis and Mulligan, the band featured soloists who played quarter-notes most of the time and frequently incorporated rests as stylistic devices. "The group's musical approach has been subject to repeated analysis because it represented the first viable alternative to bop," says Max Harrison. "Several of the pieces – *Move*, *Budo*, *Venus de Milo* – were mainly vehicles for improvisation, yet it was more significant that the sounds of all instruments were fused in a texture whose parts moved with a supple fluidity that contrasted with the hard, bright, darting lines of bop."

Curiosity was piqued by the unorthodox band, and Barry Ulanov of *Metronome* magazine, who was more receptive to the newer music of the day than most other writers in the periodicals, asked Lee Konitz for an explanation of the nonet's style. Konitz's answer seems much more abstruse than does the music it was intended to explain: "Let's say we change the punctuation of a 32 bar structure, like carrying the second eight bars over into the bridge, making our breaks somewhere within the second eight and in the middle of the bridge instead of at the conventional points. Or better, since we have already altered the construction of the line, we re-paragraph a paraphrase. And that leads to the next logical point, to continuity and development. Because you've got to think in terms of both, so that everything holds together, so that you get not four choruses, but a four chorus statement." Is that clear? Not really.

Much clearer is the reaction of Count Basie, who listened to the nonet night after night for two weeks as he waited to take the stand with his orchestra after it finished. "Those slow things sounded strange and good," Basie remembers. "I didn't always know what they were doing, but I listened, and I liked it." So did several others in the audience during those two weeks, especially other musicians.

Probably the most important listener was Pete Rugolo of Capitol Records, whose company was then anticipating the end of the recording ban. Capitol, with the other large firms, had ignored bebop so far, while such small labels as Dial and Savoy, directed by men who were music fans as well as businessmen, took the initiative and recorded it. For the corporations, that situation was tolerable as long as the music had only a cult following, but since bop recordings had taken a commercial upturn the corporations had to begin competing. Rugolo spoke to Davis at the Royal Roost and, as soon as the ban ended, signed him to the contract for twelve sides. Although completing the contract took almost a year and a half, without it the influence of the nonet would have been peripheral and indirect; instead, their influence was central and direct, even though it was slow in making itself felt.

In the meantime, Davis carried on with other projects. He had recorded with the Charlie Parker Quintet for Savoy on 18 and 24 September, the first of those dates being the last Saturday of his nonet's engagement at the Roost. He was also leading a band at the Roost when the second Savoy session with Parker took place, and he is heard again on the remote broadcast from there for Saturday 25 September, with an all-star quintet drawn from the ranks of the nonet. The details are as follows:

Miles Davis All Star Quintet
Miles Davis, tpt; Lee Konitz as; John Lewis, pno; Al McKibbon, b; Max Roach dms;
Kenny Hagood, vcl (on *You Go to My Head*). Royal Roost, New York, 25 September 1948
Broadway Theme [52nd Street Theme]; *Half Nelson*; *You Go to My Head*; *Chasin' the
Bird*
(all on Session 101)
The broadcast opened and closed with incomplete versions of *Jumpin' with Symphony Sid*,
played as the theme, which are not included on the recording.

This aircheck is exceptionally well recorded, and the music is outstanding. The
piano and the bass are, for once, clearly audible throughout. Lewis plays a very
boppish accompaniment on *Broadway Theme*, which is the tune usually entitled
52nd Street Theme and credited to Thelonious Monk, although it was used by
dozens of bands as a closer when they played in clubs on 52nd Street and later on
Broadway (where it apparently underwent a change of title to accommodate the
change of venue). It was treated very much as communal property by the bop
musicians, useful especially at jam sessions because everybody knew it and could
play its conventional harmonies before launching into the string of solos. Davis's
bands used its familiar strains as a set closer until 1964. It is used here as an
opener, suggesting that this band was a pick-up group, relying on the communal
repertoire of bop rather than their own book.

The rest of the material is the familiar fare of the Parker quintet. On *Chasin'
the Bird*, Lewis displays a deft touch, leaving lots of space but toying ingeniously
with the melody. Konitz plays his contrapuntal line tentatively, as he does the
arpeggios around Kenny Hagood's vocal on *You Go to My Head*. Hagood's swag-
gering baritone, in the manner of Eckstine but without Eckstine's mannerisms, is
recorded so well that his lisp is noticeable. By contrast with the nonet broadcasts
of the preceding Saturdays, all the material except the ballad is uptempo, and the
arranged sections are minimal. The emphasis is on the solos, with Max Roach
taking a solo turn on all three bop standards, trading four bars or eight with Davis
and Konitz in turn. If there was any remorse about disbanding the nonet a week
before, it certainly does not show up in the playing of this band, which is ebullient
and inventive.

In December, Davis was back at the Royal Roost with the Parker quintet.
Parker's engagement there was long, lasting well into 1949, but Davis, as we have
seen, cut it short for himself by walking off the stand on 23 December, leaving
the quintet, with which he had played for twenty months, for good.

Davis immediately went back to the Three Deuces, where he joined Oscar
Pettiford's band, which also included trombonist Kai Winding, with whom he

would play several recording dates during the next year. He then moved with Pettiford's band to Broadway, where they opened a new jazz club called the Clique. It was owned by the owners of the Three Deuces, Sammy Kay and Irving Alexander, who were hoping to make the transition from 52nd Street to Broadway. Pettiford's band for the occasion were exceptional, including Davis, Fats Navarro, Dexter Gordon, Lucky Thompson, and Bud Powell, but the musicians made discordant music together, according to the historian Marshall Stearns; he remembers this engagement as a display of the worst excesses of the bop movement. The forty-five-minute sets were taken up mainly by one or two interminable solos while the other horn players disappeared from the stand. "Everybody was carving everybody and taking thirty minute solos to prove it," Lucky Thompson told Stearns, and Oscar Pettiford just said, "Nobody bothered about the audience." The owners were apparently as unlucky with their other featured bands as well, because they were forced to shut down the Clique after six months, in July 1949. Certainly it was not the Clique's location that caused its failure, because it was taken over by new management that summer and reopened as Birdland, perhaps the best-known jazz club of all time.

Less than two weeks after leaving Parker's group at the Royal Roost, Davis was back in the recording studio with Parker, but under unusual circumstances. The editors of *Metronome* assembled an all-star band almost as soon as the recording ban ended, on Monday 3 January, the first working day of the new year. The selection of players was remarkable, bringing together several men who, although they were not yet widely known, would exert a tremendous influence in jazz throughout the next decade. Davis was one of these, of course, and with him were J.J. Johnson and Kai Winding, the trombonists, and the drummer Shelly Manne. Winding and Manne and the bassist for the date, Eddie Safranski, had been featured with the Stan Kenton orchestra, which had made a popular impression with a voluble, brass-dominated style. Pete Rugolo, Kenton's chief arranger before he joined Capitol as producer, was appointed as the arranger and leader of the Metronome All Stars. Other players included the leaders of the current music – Parker, Gillespie, and the leader of his own highly individualistic branch of jazz, Lennie Tristano:

Metronome All Stars
Miles Davis, Dizzy Gillespie, Fats Navarro, tpt; J.J. Johnson, Kai Winding, tbn; Buddy DeFranco, clnt; Charlie Parker, as; Ernie Caceres, bs; Lennie Tristano, pno; Billy Bauer, gtr; Eddie Safranski, b; Shelly Manne, dms; Pete Rugolo, cond. New York, 3 January 1949
Overtime (two takes); *Victory Ball* (three takes)

(The first takes were both released on RCA Victor 20-3361, the alternate takes on RCA Victor LPT 3046.)
Davis, Navarro, Johnson and Caceres do not play on the first two takes of *Victory Ball*.
Rugolo arranged *Overtime*, and Tristano arranged *Victory Ball*.

With so many soloists working within the confines of the three-minute limit of these 78 rpm recordings, the musical interest of this session is predictably limited. Probably in an attempt to solve this problem, the first two takes of *Victory Ball* were made without Davis, Navarro, Johnson, and Caceres, which may also give a rough indication of the pecking order of the horn players. *Overtime* is reputedly so named because Parker pretended that he was unable to master the arrangement, causing numerous false starts that eventually put the session two and a half hours over the three-hour time limit imposed by the union and dramatically increasing the musicians' cheques by the new pay scale won by the recording ban of the American Federation of Musicians. Unfortunately, the complete session, if it was preserved, has never been collated. Perhaps the main interest of this music comes from the trumpet section, which brings together all three leaders of the younger generation of trumpet players for the only time. In their consecutive choruses on *Overtime*, Gillespie, Navarro, and Davis all play similar passages on open horns, so that it is not easy to tell where one of them ends and the other begins. This point was not lost on Gillespie, who cites this recording as evidence that the styles of Davis and Navarro derive from his own. "I know that each of them sounded like me because we played on a record together, the three of us, and I didn't know which one was playing when I listened – the Metronome All Stars date," Gillespie said. "I didn't know which of us played what solo because the three of us sounded so much alike." Davis, who later played with Navarro at Birdland, also noted that he and Navarro tended to alter their styles in each other's company. "He and I used to play together and we'd sound alike," Davis says, "but when we played separately, we didn't sound alike." The similarity among musicians with such highly personal approaches to their instruments in other contexts probably attests to the strength of their musical roots on 52nd Street, and the Metronome All Star session provides, if nothing else, a permanent record of it.

Later in January, Davis was back in the recording studio for the first of his sessions with the nonet for Capitol. Four months had elapsed since the nonet had disbanded, and assembling the players was a problem. Kai Winding replaced young Michael Zwerin, who had gone back to college, and Parker's piano player, Al Haig, and the bassist Joe Shulman from the Thornhill band came in as replacements for John Lewis and Al McKibbon, who were touring with the Gillespie orchestra. The recording session was called for a Friday afternoon:

Miles Davis Nonet
Miles Davis, tpt; Kai Winding, tbn; Junior Collins, frh; Bill Barber, tba; Lee Konitz, as;
Gerry Mulligan, bs; Al Haig, pno; Joe Shulman, b; Max Roach, dms. New York, 21
January 1949
Jeru; Move; Godchild; Budo
(all on Capitol M-11026)

It seems unusual, to say the least, that no arrangements by Gil Evans were
recorded at this first session, considering his importance in the development of
this music. *Jeru* and *Godchild* are Mulligan's arrangements (the former titled by
Davis, who called Mulligan "Jeru"), and *Move* and *Budo* are Lewis's. Perhaps the
decision about what to record was made by the producer, Pete Rugolo. Certainly
the medium tempos (both of Mulligan's) and the faster tempos (Lewis's) stood a
better chance of commercial success than Evans's slower arrangements.

No matter who made the decision, it cannot be faulted by its results. All four
compositions are perfectly played – and impeccably recorded, as they had to be if
all the nuances were to be preserved. The arranged sections are typically lengthy,
both in the introductions and conclusions and also as frames for the solos. While
the arrangements dominate, the solos are equally flawless, and they are so beautifully integrated into the arrangements that they have often been overlooked by
commentators, or at least undervalued. There is no lack of what is sometimes
called jazz feeling, and the band, especially its soloists – Davis on all four compositions, Mulligan on all but *Move*, Konitz and Roach on *Move* and *Budo*,
Winding on *Godchild* and *Budo* – are not unduly restrained, although they are
certainly disciplined. Perhaps the most striking example is Max Roach on *Move*,
who plays with enormous drive throughout but also manages a paradoxical delicacy. In that, he epitomizes the achievement of the nonet, and he is only one of
nine players who accomplish it on these recordings. The arrangements should
probably be credited with setting the tone, because they oblige the players to work
within a well-defined context, but no one had any reason to expect that the
players would meet the challenge so forcefully. Gil Evans has said, "These
records by Miles indicate what voicing can do, how it can give intensity and
relaxation." With the problems of shifting personnel and a drawn-out schedule,
Davis required consistency and concentration from all his sidemen, and they
responded. Mulligan said, much later, "I count myself fortunate to be there and
I thank whatever lucky stars were responsible for placing me there. There's a
kind of perfection about those recordings." Apparently Rugolo and the Capitol
executives recognized it as well, because they rushed them into print. *Move* and
Budo, John Lewis's uptempo arrangements, were released within a month (as

Capitol 78 rpm 15404); *Jeru* and *Godchild* came out in April (as Capitol 60005). Those buyers who listened carefully heard a new spirit in American improvised music.

In February, Davis was back at the Royal Roost, playing opposite the Parker quintet as a member of Tadd Dameron's Big Ten. Dameron was a gifted arranger and composer, among the best that bop had, and playing in his band allowed Davis to function in a musical context that was similar to the nonet in its attention to arranged materials as well as in its size. The circumstances surrounding Davis's joining Dameron's house band, a plum job because it was steady and at the heart of the musical activity, were not so happy. Dameron's regular trumpeter was Fats Navarro, but Navarro was heavily addicted to heroin and often suffered from assorted other ailments as well, especially heavy colds, which left him weakened. Navarro, born in Florida in 1923, had spent his youth there playing in regional bands and soon earned a reputation as a facile soloist among visiting musicians. He arrived in New York with Andy Kirk's orchestra in 1943. In 1945, he was chosen by Billy Eckstine as Gillespie's replacement in his big band, at Gillespie's urging, and the ease with which he stepped into that key role was the talk of all the musicians in the band.

His addiction soon made reliability a problem and also kept him chained to the New York area, where he could find his supplies. As a result, Davis replaced him in the Eckstine orchestra for their California tour. Now he was replacing him again, although Navarro still played for Dameron whenever he could. Davis stood in for him in Dameron's band for most of the winter of 1949 and is heard on two Saturday broadcasts from the Royal Roost in February and one in early March, as well as on an April recording session. Much of Dameron's writing for the Roost band revolved around Navarro's trumpet lead and his soloing strength, making Davis's task as his replacement far from easy; but Davis's playing on the broadcasts is confident and competent:

Tadd Dameron Big Ten
Miles Davis, tpt; Kai Winding, tbn; Sahib Shihab (Ed Gregory), as; Benjamin Lundy, ts; Cecil Payne, bs; Tadd Dameron, pno; John Collins, gtr; Curly Russell, b; Kenny Clarke, dms; Carlos Vidal, bongo. Royal Roost, New York, 19 February 1949
Focus; April in Paris; Good Bait; Sid's Delight [*Webb's Delight*]
(all on Beppo BEP 503)

Same personnel and place, 26 February 1949
Miles; Casbah
(both on Beppo BEP 503)

Probably the same personnel, same place, 5 March 1949
Good Bait; The Squirrel
(both unissued)

The broadcast repertoire consists of Dameron originals recorded for Capitol around this time. Dameron had recorded *Sid's Delight*, announced here as *Webb's Delight*, and *Casbah* in January with Navarro in the band, just three days before Davis's nonet session. The recordings with Navarro and the aircheck with Davis, although the arrangements are the same, have a very different sound, as Navarro dominates the ensembles in a way that Davis never does. Although the versions with Davis feature a better blend in the ensembles, they also fail to subdue the vibrato of altoist Sahib Shihab as thoroughly as the versions with Navarro did, and the band sounds, for brief moments, as if a refugee from a sweet band, perhaps Carmen Lombardo himself, had sneaked into it. Davis solos on all the numbers except *April in Paris*, a feature for guitarist John Collins, and he is showcased by Dameron's arrangements of the infectious *Good Bait*, which became a standard bop tune, and the ballad called *Miles*.

Davis was still playing in place of Navarro when Dameron's band was called for its second Capitol recording session, in April. The band is the one that played at the Roost except that J.J. Johnson, back in New York after touring with Illinois Jacquet, replaces Winding, and a vocalist, Kay Penton, is added for two titles, no doubt as part of Capitol's scheme to commercialize bebop:

Tadd Dameron and His Orchestra
Miles Davis, tpt; J.J. Johnson, tbn; Sahib Shihab, as; Benjamin Lundy, ts; Cecil Payne, bs; Tadd Dameron, pno; John Collins, gtr; Curly Russell, b; Kenny Clarke, dms; Kay Penton, vcl (on *What's New* and *Heaven's Doors Are Open Wide*). New York, 21 April 1949
John's Delight; What's New; Heaven's Doors Are Open Wide; Focus
(all on Capitol CAP M-11059)

Kay Penton was a clear-voiced but undistinguished band singer, with no affinity for bebop. Dameron's arrangement of *What's New*, with its attractive pop lyric, is mundane, and so is his arrangement of *Heaven's Doors Are Open Wide*, for which he wrote both the words and music. Dameron's Tin Pan Alley clichés in his lyric for *Heaven's Door Are Open Wide* thinly disguise some vaginal imagery:

Heaven's doors are open wide ...
There's love inside;

... You know I'm here
So wake up, dear,
Make my dream come true,
Heaven's doors are open wide, to you.

Surprisingly, Davis does not solo on any of the titles. *John's Delight* showcases John Collins, and *Focus*, an intriguing thirty-eight-bar melody that resolves into standard thirty-two-bar solos in 4/4 time, also has Collins soloing where Davis soloed on the Royal Roost version. The only indication of Davis's presence comes from the ensembles, especially in the trumpet lead on the out-chorus of *John's Delight* (where Davis is heard hitting a clinker once) and throughout *Heaven's Doors*. Otherwise, he is silent.

The next day, Davis returned to the Capitol studio with his nonet. J.J. Johnson returned with him, replacing Winding who had originally replaced Zwerin. Sandy Siegelstein from Thornhill's band replaced Junior Collins on french horn. The Gillespie band were back in New York, so John Lewis could take his place at the piano, but Al McKibbon had been replaced in Gillespie's band by Nelson Boyd, who now replaced him in the nonet as well. Kenny Clarke also returned to the Capitol studio for the second straight day, replacing Max Roach, who had returned to the Parker quintet in late January. Of all the changes, the loss of Roach might appear to be the most crucial, though no more so than the loss of John Lewis on the first date, and on that occasion the music did not suffer noticeably. Clarke is as adept as Roach technically, and more experienced, and the two men shared many stylistic traits as a result of Clarke being Roach's tutor in the beginning:

Miles Davis Nonet
Miles Davis, tpt; J.J. Johnson, tbn; Sandy Siegelstein, frh; Bill Barber, tba; Lee Konitz, as; Gerry Mulligan, bs; John Lewis, pno; Nelson Boyd, b; Kenny Clarke, dms. New York, 22 April 1949
Venus de Milo; Rouge; Boplicity; Israel
(all on Capitol M-11026)

Four different arrangers are featured on this date; *Venus de Milo* is Mulligan's, *Rouge* Lewis's, *Boplicity* Evans's, and *Israel* Johnny Carisi's. *Venus de Milo* is a relatively straightforward showcase for Davis's trumpet, as the title punningly suggests. The memorable little melody is stated by a trumpet lead, followed by Davis's solo, and then Mulligan spells him for a couple of choruses before he leads the ensemble out. Davis's tone is full and bold, recalling the early takes of *Billie's Bounce*, which he said sounded like Freddie Webster.

Rouge was never released on 78 rpm by Capitol, waiting around in their vaults until the first microgroove release in 1954. Certainly it would have done the nonet no harm had it appeared immediately. The arrangement is tight and apparently difficult, and there is a suggestion of tentativeness in the concluding section, especially by Clarke and perhaps also by Mulligan, who suddenly seems to break ranks for one bar in the ensemble before being absorbed into it again. But there is some fine playing. Its strengths are in Lewis's use of a peculiar little fanfare that opens the recording decorously and then recurs at unexpected moments throughout it, and in the solos by Lewis, Konitz, and Davis, which are polished variations on the theme.

Boplicity was written by Davis and Evans, but on its original release was attributed to Cleo Henry, Davis's mother. It moves along through numerous shifts of texture as the various horns are rearranged into new alliances, in what can only be described as a *tour de force* by Evans. Asked in 1950 to name his favorite example of his own work, Davis answered, without hesitating, *"Boplicity*, because of Gil's arrangement." André Hodeir says, *"Boplicity* alone is enough to make Gil Evans qualify as one of jazz's greatest arranger-composers."

For all its brilliance, *Boplicity* was overshadowed by *Israel* at the time of their release in October, and not altogether unjustly. Carisi's composition sounds impossibly complex, with the melodic line played first by a section made up of Davis, Konitz, Johnson, and Siegelstein, and then repeated while a second section led by Mulligan and an amazingly supple Barber introduces a counter-melody. Eventually, several melodies weave into one another. Davis's solo ranks as one of his very best on record to this time. Martin Williams has singled it out along with his solo on *Move* from the first date for special praise: "If [these recordings] proved nothing else, they would prove that Miles Davis, already an interesting and personal soloist, could produce two great improvisations, each one great in a different way. His blues solo on *Israel* is a beautiful example of classic simplicity of melody and a personal reassessment of the mood of the blues. His chorus on *Move* is a striking episode of meaningful asymmetry, and it has some phrasing that is so original that one can only say that, rhythmically, it seems to turn back on itself while moving steadily forward."

The pairing of *Israel* and *Boplicity* in an October release by Capitol seems almost an embarrassment of riches for jazz fans. The other pieces recorded with them, however, were not released at the time; *Rouge*, as already mentioned, was withheld for five years, and *Venus de Milo* was put out only a year and a half later, weakly backed by Kenny Hagood's vocal on *Darn That Dream*.

Tadd Dameron, an outstanding composer-arranger in his own right, was moved by what he heard from the nonet. "Davis is the farthest advanced musician of his day, and *Boplicity* is one of the best small group sounds I've heard," he said. As the two men continued to work together, Dameron's regard for Davis's contribution to his band led him to share the leader's duties, and eventually the joint leadership was acknowledged in the name of their band. It was called the Miles Davis–Tadd Dameron Quintet, and it was organized for a festival in Europe. Charles Delaunay, the principal organizer of Le Festival de Jazz 1949, to take place in Paris in the week of 8–15 May, had arranged for the Charlie Parker Quintet to headline the festival along with Sidney Bechet's band. Tadd Dameron and Miles Davis were invited to share the billing, and they put together a quintet that was a cross between a pick-up group and a set band. Davis and Dameron chose Kenny Clarke from Dameron's Big Ten, giving the group a core of players whose names were known to European jazz buffs. They added James Moody, the tenor saxophonist formerly with the Gillespie band who was then living in Europe, and a bassist selected by Delaunay. The bassist's name was Barney Spieler, an American expatriate studying at the Conservatoire national de musique de Paris but also an experienced player with visiting American jazz groups, including Benny Goodman's. With the Charlie Parker Quintet, which now included Kinney Dorham, Al Haig, Tommy Potter, and Max Roach, and the Miles Davis–Tadd Dameron Quintet, the festival already had some of the very best modern players, and to them were added Don Byas, who had stayed behind in Europe after touring there with Don Redman's band in 1946, and the best European piano player, Bernard Peiffer. Bechet's band included trombonist Russell (Big Chief) Moore, and the traditional styles were also represented by the boogie-woogie piano player Pete Johnson and cornetist Jimmy McPartland. Swing was represented by Oran (Hot Lips) Page, trumpeter-singer, supplemented by European swing musicians such as England's Carlo Krahmer and Belgium's Toots Thielemans. It promised to be a gala occasion.

The American contingent arrived by air only the day before the opening. The Davis-Dameron quintet played in the opening concert on Sunday, 8 May and again the next night, the 9th, taking two days off and returning for matinée and evening performances on Thursday, 12 May; after another day off, they returned Saturday evening, the 14th, and again played both a matinée and evening performance on the final day of the festival, Sunday 15 May. In what has become a venerable tradition at European jazz concerts, most if not all the performances were recorded privately. Some twenty-eight years later, the best of the private recordings of the quintet were selected and issued by Columbia Records:

Miles Davis–Tadd Dameron Quintet
Miles Davis, tpt; James Moody, ts; Tadd Dameron, pno; Barney Spieler, b; Kenny Clarke, dms. Salle Pleyel, Paris, 8 May 1949
Rifftide; Good Bait; Don't Blame Me (omit Moody); *Lady Bird*
(all on Columbia 34804)

Same personnel and place, 9, 12, 14, or 15 May 1949
Wah Hoo; Allen's Alley; Embraceable You (Moody on coda only); *Ornithology; All the Things You Are*
(all on Columbia 34804)
Performances of *The Squirrel, Crazy Rhythm*, and *Perdido* (probably *Wah Hoo*, which is based on *Perdido*'s changes) and a second version of *All the Things You Are* have not yet been issued.

Davis and Moody's problem of playing ensembles together with virtually no rehearsal was solved mainly by avoiding it altogether. On *Good Bait*, Moody plays the melody alone and Davis plays the bridge alone; on the ballads, *Don't Blame Me* and *Embraceable You*, Moody sits out altogether. When they do play together, it is on bop standards such as *Rifftide, Wah Hoo*, and *Allen's Alley*, but even that precaution does not help on *Lady Bird*, which features a ragged ensemble. The French critic Henri Renaud says, "James [Moody] was an unassuming, even shy man and the prospect of playing with such a figure as Miles nearly scared him to death." Moody is definitely subdued, and his only striking turn is on *All the Things You Are*, recorded late in the festival; the quintet uses an arrangement based on John Lewis's arrangement for Gillespie's band, where Moody must have played it several times.

Dameron is equally subdued on these recordings, and Davis dominates the band in every sense, even to the extent of his announcing the titles for the audience, a practice he gave up completely after he developed what Zwerin calls "his famous salty dog act." He plays an aggressive bebop style, not at all characteristic of his work in New York with the nonet and Dameron's Big Ten; his solos are marked by eighth- and sixteenth-note runs into the upper register, almost as if he set out to prove something to someone – perhaps to Parker. The striking difference in his approach became the main topic of reviewer's comments when these performances were issued years later. "Playing with a fiery attack that is closer to Fats Navarro than anyone else, his solos represent probably the best bebop he ever played," Michael Shera wrote in *Jazz Journal*. Scott Yanow, writing in *Record Review*, said, "His multi-note runs on uptempo numbers resemble the style of Gillespie ... It is on the ballads that Davis sounds most individualistic, coming close to the style he would perfect in the Fifties." The same reviewer calls the Paris Jazz Festival recording "the best pre-1954 Miles Davis album." That judgment seems remarkably short-sighted, considering the recorded work with Parker and especially with the nonet, but it does point out the excellence of his playing here, which should finally lay to rest the claim that he developed the warm, controlled style of his mature playing because he could not cope with the pyrotechnical Gillespie style. Here he not only copes with it, but he shows considerable mastery of it. Like all great artists, he knew exactly what he was doing when he set aside the stylistic elements in vogue in his formative years.

Apart from these tracks with the Miles Davis–Tadd Dameron Quintet, Davis also participated in the jam session that brought the festival to a close. It is as much a traffic jam as a music jam and does not reveal anything of his playing (or much of anyone else's):

Festival Jam Session
Aime Barelli, Bill Coleman, Miles Davis, probably Kinney Dorham, Oran (Hot Lips) Page, tpt; Russell (Big Chief) Moore, tbn; Hubert Rostaing, clnt; Sidney Bechet, Pierre Braslavsky, ss; Charlie Parker, as; Don Byas, James Moody, ts; Al Haig, pno; Hazy Osterwald, vib; Jean (Toots) Thielemans, gtr; Tommy Potter, b; Max Roach, dms. Salle Pleyel, Paris, 15 May 1949
untitled blues
(on Durium-Cicala BLJ 8024 and on Spotlite 118)

Le Festival de Jazz 1949 certainly succeeded in disseminating the newer currents of American music to Europe, along with some traditional elements, which were already well entrenched there. Parker and Davis became European celebrities and were received with considerable pomp in Europe ever after. They might well have been received that way anyway, because of their status in the development of jazz music. A few of the other musicians, including Kinney Dorham and Al Haig, hardly went on to achieve what Parker and Davis did but they too remained favorites in Europe, and Haig owed his second career in jazz, beginning in 1973, after more than fifteen years of obscurity, to the enthusiasm of European fans, who sought him out and encouraged him to play bebop professionally again. Tadd Dameron went from the Paris festival to London, where he spent some weeks working with the Ted Heath orchestra, writing some charts for them and improving the charts they were already using. The festival also instigated a number of more or less permanent exchanges. Toots Thielemans emigrated to the United States in 1951, and Bernard Peiffer in 1954. Sidney Bechet settled in Paris in 1951. Kenny Clarke, who had lived in Paris for several months in 1946, staying behind when his colleagues in the Gillespie band returned after their tour, settled there permanently in 1956, joining Bechet and Don Byas, among others, and eventually becoming an elder statesman in the growing community of jazz expatriates.

When the festival ended, Davis returned to New York with Kenny Clarke, Charlie Parker, and the rest of the American contingent. The time away and the easy camaraderie with musicians as diverse as Bechet and Hot Lips Page must have made it doubly difficult for them to settle back in at home, where there was a growing hysteria about the direction that jazz was taking.

Reviewers and fans were split decisively into two camps. One camp advocated traditional jazz as the only "real" jazz music, and the other acclaimed bebop as the culmination of decades of "progress" in American music. Almost everyone who had more than a casual interest was aligned on one side or the other, usually vociferously so. Most of the journalists who covered jazz in America, or in Europe, were traditionalists, except for the few who had formed their tastes during the era of the big dance bands, and thus stood a bit apart from the warring camps, as did many of the musicians who had emerged from the big bands – the so-called swing, or mainstream musicians. Band leaders such as Earl Hines, Cootie Williams, and Jay McShann employed boppers in the beginning and sometimes played arrangements of bop compositions, and men such as Coleman Hawkins, Roy Eldridge, and Ben Webster played alongside the younger musicians without qualms.

The mainstream players suffered most from the controversy. As the public and the press became polarized, the very malleability of the mainstream players left them without an audience that could identify with them. The traditionalists, known as moldy figs among the modernists, discovered the trumpeter Bunk Johnson and later the clarinetist George Lewis on the backstreets of New Orleans and lauded their technically limited playing as evidence of the authentic roots of jazz. Their advocacy of two-beat music over all other jazz created in turn an audience for the Chicagoans whose style was based on traditional New Orleans playing – men who gathered around Eddie Condon – and also for younger men who embraced the New Orleans players as their direct influence, among them Turk Murphy, Wally Rose, and Bob Wilber. The modernists looked, of course, to Charlie Parker and Dizzy Gillespie as the fount of jazz music, conveniently ignoring Parker's occasional nod toward Lester Young and Gillespie's frequent praise for Roy Eldridge. As the bickering heated up, it became more and more difficult to convince anyone that there were virtues on both sides, much less that both were authentic jazz.

In this irrational climate, the recordings of the Miles Davis nonet eventually exerted a steadying influence, winning over even some critics who had previously been opposed to the new music, such as John S. Wilson of the *New York Times*, as well as hundreds of fans who were similarly, although more quietly, opposed. Davis was himself a surprisingly open commentator on the controversy, considering the depth of his involvement in the bop movement. "I don't like to hear someone put down Dixieland," he told Wilson. "Those people who say there's no music but bop are just stupid. It just shows how much they don't know. I never played Dixieland myself. When I was growing up I played like Roy Eldridge, Harry James, Freddie Webster and anyone else I admired. You've got to start way back before you can play bop. You've got to have a foundation."

Davis found himself in a privileged position among some of the anti-boppers, who began to cite him as an exception to all the things they found wrong on the other side. John Hammond, the discoverer of Count Basie and Billie Holiday in the 1930s and many other great jazz players, got caught up in the debate and threw his not inconsiderable weight onto the side of the traditionalists. Looking back on it about three decades later, in his memoirs entitled *On Record*, he offered this reason for his stance: "Bop lacked the swing I believe essential to great jazz playing, lacked the humor, and the free-flowing invention of the best jazz creators. In their place it offered a new self-consciousness, an excessive emphasis on harmonic and rhythmic revolt, a concentration on technique at the expense of musical emotion. Instead of expanding the form, they contracted it, made it their private language. I extend this judgement even to such giants as Bird Parker, Monk, and Coltrane." And then Hammond added, "The superlative Miles Davis is exempted."

In the midst of all the hullabaloo, Davis unfortunately did not immediately resume the recording project with the nonet. Although he returned from Europe to find that club engagements were hard to come by, he devoted his time instead to getting together a large band, co-led by Dameron, and organizing their book and personnel. Little is known about the band because they never got past the rehearsal phase, but there were reportedly eighteen pieces. The personnel included trumpeters Red Rodney and Bernie Glow; trombonists Matthew Gee, Kai Winding, and Johnny Mandel; reedmen Allen Eager, Charlie Kennedy, Zoot Sims, and Cecil Payne; and a rhythm section with John Collins, Nelson Boyd, and Rossiere (Shadow) Wilson. With Tadd Dameron's ability as a composer and arranger and Miles Davis's strength as a leader as well as a soloist added to that list of players, the band looked very promising. The fact that they disappeared without a trace, never getting a booking or being recorded even on home equipment, is cause for regret. Perhaps they would have charted new directions for jazz as had the nonet, which also came perilously close to existing only as a rehearsal band.

Certainly the project was badly timed. All around there were signs that the age of big bands was ending. Concert dates for larger groups were scarce, and payrolls were becoming impossible to meet. Within a year, Count Basie would be forced to disband his orchestra, which he had led continuously since 1935, and reduce his working unit to a septet. The most modern of all the bands, Dizzy Gillespie's, would also disband, thus robbing Gillespie of the musical context that best suited his playing. "Everybody was sorry about that, man; cats were crying, not making any money. So was I," Gillespie says; and then he shrugs, "The fad was finished." For the Davis-Dameron big band, the fad never even began.

The winds of change were moving too strongly in the other direction and were being felt from other experimental quarters besides Davis's nonet. Lennie Tristano, a Chicago-born pianist, settled in New York after the war and began playing in the clubs on 52nd Street and elsewhere. Because he was blind, white, academically trained, and a natural teacher, he could hardly escape the notice of young and curious musicians, and before long he had his own coterie of pupils and disciples, including Lee Konitz, tenor saxophonist Warne Marsh, guitarist Billy Bauer, and drummer Denzil Best, the composer of the nonet's *Move*. Like Davis and Dameron and several others, Tristano was signed by Capitol Records when the recording ban ended. On 16 May, at Tristano's third recording session of the spring, his sextet, including all the musicians named above and bassist Arnold Fishkin, recorded two free-form tracks called *Intuition* and *Digression*. They had neither a set of chord changes nor a fixed tempo, but the sextet had been working for some time at discovering form and developing coherence extemporaneously, and Tristano reckoned that they were now ready to record their experiments. The producers at Capitol apparently thought otherwise upon hearing the result, which they felt had no commerical possibilities, and they refused to pay Tristano's men for the recordings or to release them. The recordings then became something of a cause when Symphony Sid Torin got hold of the masters and began to play them on his radio show. Finally Capitol was forced to make them available (and, of course, to pay Tristano for them). When they were reissued on microgroove in the early 1970s (on Capitol M-11060), Tristano commented: "These two sides were completely spontaneously improvised. A lot of people who heard them thought they were compositions. To my knowledge Miles Davis is the only noted musician who acknowledged in print the real nature of the music on these sides." Davis's response is an early indication of his awareness throughout his career of new directions in the music.

Though jobs were scarce throughout the rest of 1949, Davis worked, with or without Dameron, in several limited engagements in clubs. One of these is probably the source of an unidentified recording featuring Davis playing *Embraceable You*, which he had also used as a ballad showcase in Paris. The few available details are these:

Miles Davis Band
Miles Davis, tpt; unidentified trombone, tenor saxophone, piano, bass, drums. Unknown place and date
Embraceable You (Session LP 101)

The recording was made in a very noisy setting. Before the ballad begins, a tenor saxophone is heard noodling idly, and then the piano introduction begins and the saxophone player stops. Someone, apparently Davis, calls an instruction to the pianist – "Break it up, break it up" – who then introduces block chords. The track is an extended trumpet solo; only in the final statement of the melody are the tenor and (probably) trombone heard, playing harmony.

On Christmas night, Davis played in a concert at Carnegie Hall called the Stars of Modern Jazz Concert, promoted by Leonard Feather – his third Christmas jazz concert at Carnegie Hall, and the last. The main attractions were Sarah Vaughan and the Charlie Parker Quintet, with some new faces: Red Rodney for Dorham, and Roy Haynes for Roach; Roach played instead with one of the pick-up bands assembled for the concert. Lennie Tristano and his coterie were also there, including Konitz, Marsh, and Bauer, with Joe Shulman on bass and Jeff Morton on drums. One makeshift group put tenor saxophonist Stan Getz and trombonist Kai Winding in front of Parker's rhythm section, and the other one, with Miles Davis, was a septet:

Stars of Modern Jazz Jam Session
Miles Davis, tpt; Benny Green, tbn; Sonny Stitt, as; Serge Chaloff, bs; Bud Powell, pno; Curly Russell, b; Max Roach, dms. Carnegie Hall, New York, 25 December 1949
Move; Hot House; Ornithology (incomplete)
(all on IAJRC 20)

The concert was taped by Voice of America, the United States radio network in Europe, and parts of it were broadcast the next year. The recording of the concert issued by IAJRC in 1976 was reconstructed from the files of Voice of America and assorted home-made tapes from European collectors. The band with Davis plays at the beginning and the end of the concert, with the rhythm section alone starting off (with *All God's Children Got Rhythm*) and then being joined by the horns for *Move*, the uptempo number from the nonet's repertoire that became Davis's most recorded tune for the next few years. At the end of the proceedings, the seven pick-up players return to play two bop standards, *Hot House* and *Ornithology*, but the recording of the latter ends during the third solo, when the Voice of America tape ran out. The music by the group that includes Davis is standard fare, with perfunctory recitations of the melody by apparently unrehearsed ensembles and then the queue for solo turns. Jam sessions like this one became a fixture at concerts because they were part of the successful formula used by Granz's Jazz at the Philharmonic; fortunately the Stars of Modern Jazz Concert did not go so far as to emulate the JATP's excesses by bringing in honkers and gut-bucket specialists to excite the crowd, a function then being filled for JATP by Illinois Jacquet and Tommy Turk.

Leonard Feather, the English jazz writer who emigrated to New York in 1939, now marvels at his youthful nerve in promoting the concert. "Now that I look back on it, I wonder why I had the courage to do it, because it was a risky thing to do at the time," he says. "And I put my own money into it. I don't know what it came to, maybe a couple thousand dollars, which at that time was a lot to put into a concert." He adds, "But I had some other people involved, Monte Kay and Symphony Sid; we became involved together in putting these concerts on." The fact that the third Christmas concert was the last further underlines the state of recession into which jazz was slipping. However, all three concerts turned profits. "They did very well, surprisingly well, surprising in view of the fact that there was so much active, really nasty opposition to the music, particularly in the media," Feather says. "The daily press was just death on it; they didn't even acknowledge its existence." Indeed, the concert was mentioned neither in New York's major daily newspapers nor in the jazz magazines. Feather adds, "With the exception of *Metronome* and an occasional write-up in *Down Beat*, most of the musical press were violently opposed to it. Some very small magazines which wielded some power in jazz circles used to run whole articles attacking me and attacking bebop in general and attacking anything which was not New Orleans – Bunk Johnson and them. That's what was called the 'War of the Moldy Figs.'"

By early 1950, Miles Davis began mixing with the up-and-coming young players in jazz. He had almost always played with men older than he, apart from isolated exceptions such as bassist Nelson Boyd, who was even more precocious. Now, increasingly, there were younger men around the clubs, men such as Sonny Rollins, a tenor saxophonist from Harlem who was three years younger than he. Rollins had made his recording debut early in 1949 as part of the bebop round-up conducted by Capitol Records. He turned up, unheralded, in the band of bop singer Babs Gonzales on 20 January, along with J.J. Johnson and Benny Green, and burned a chorus on both of the tunes Gonzales's band recorded that day, *Capitolizing* and *Professor Bop*. Rollins's choruses are easily the most interesting music on either piece, but he moved to Chicago soon after and stayed there for the rest of the year, returning to New York early in 1950, where he played in the house band at a Harlem club. It was there that Davis first met him. "Miles already had a considerable reputation by that time," Rollins says. "He'd heard a few of my records and of course I'd heard him, so you could really say that we already knew each other." Davis was very impressed and invited Rollins to join his band for an engagement at the Audubon Ballroom later in the month. That band also featured Art Blakey, who had just left the Lucky Millinder band and was back in town.

Davis's interest started Rollins on the course that would soon lead to wider recognition, even rivaling Davis's stature for a short period late in the decade, but it was probably not difficult for Davis to pick him out as a musician of great potential. As a high school student in the Sugar Hill district of Harlem, Rollins already exuded the charisma that marked his personal and musical style as a professional. Tall and imposing, his presence seems automatically to attract attention both on the bandstand and off it, although Rollins has never learned to feel comfortable with the attention. For all the admiration given him, he suffers bouts of self-doubt, but his admirers see only the power and the presence. Jackie McLean, who was a high school freshman when Rollins was a senior, says, "He influenced everybody uptown, playing every instrument."

Sugar Hill, when Rollins and McLean were growing up, was just beginning to fade as Harlem's hub of affluence and culture. Coleman Hawkins lived there, and so did Bud Powell, Teddy Wilson, and a covey of Ellingtonians including Duke and his sister Ruth, Billy Strayhorn, and Mercer Ellington. Their neighbors included the two finest poets of the Harlem Renaissance, Langston Hughes and Countee Cullen, the novelist Ralph Ellison, and Roy Wilkins and Walter White, executives of the National Association for the Advancement of Colored People. In his program notes for the 'Sugar Hill Penthouse' movement of the suite *Black, Brown and Beige*, Duke Ellington crowed, "If you ever sat on a beautiful magenta cloud overlooking New York City, you were on Sugar Hill." Bounded by 145th and 155th streets, with the Polo Grounds, home of the New York Giants baseball team, on its periphery, Sugar Hill became populated by black families only in the 1920s, years after the rest of Harlem was solidly black. It flourished in the 1930s, but by the end of the 1940s many middle-class blacks were no longer settling in Sugar Hill or any other part of Harlem, choosing instead the borough of Queens and the further suburbs. The last significant group of artists nurtured in Sugar Hill were the young jazz musicians who emerged in the wake of the bebop revolution, and among them Sonny Rollins was the lodestar.

Jackie McLean remembers, "There were a lot of musicians in our neighborhood like [drummer] Arthur Taylor, [pianist] Kenny Drew, Connie Henry, who played bass for a while, Arthur Phipps, who also played bass, and [alto saxophonist] Ernie Henry, and there were guys who used to come from out of the neighborhood to see what was happening, like Walter Bishop [later Parker's pianist]. Sonny was the leader of all of them." They were all close to Miles Davis in age, if not in experience, and soon after he met Rollins, Davis began spending his spare hours with them. "When Miles came to town," McLean says, "he began to hang out up there on the Hill with us." Most of the young musicians Davis befriended there, including Rollins and McLean, used heroin and other narcotics, which became readily available on the Harlem streets after the war.

Another relative newcomer whom Davis met at this time was John Coltrane, a Philadelphian who joined the Dizzy Gillespie orchestra in its final year as an alto saxophonist, even though his preference was clearly for the tenor saxophone. Coltrane and Rollins, destined to be touted as rivals by the jazz press because they were both gifted players on the same instrument, first played together with Miles

Davis, probably at the Audubon Ballroom early in 1950, with Art Blakey on drums. Rollins says, "Coltrane and I first met in 1950 in New York, where we worked together for a few memorable gigs with Miles Davis. I really had to listen carefully to him. I often wondered what he was doing, where he was going." Coltrane was already engaged in the painstaking search for musical form that would eventually elevate him to the ranks of the greatest improvisers jazz has had. As for the rivalry with Rollins, it seems always to have been trumped up for press copy, as might be expected from the personalities of the two men. Rollins says, "Later we became good friends. Good enough friends for me to borrow money from him, and Coltrane and Monk were the only two people I would ever ask for a loan." For more than a decade, Rollins and Coltrane were Davis's top choices to join him as the leading horns in his small bands, whenever he was in control of the hiring for the engagements he played.

Although many of the clubs that had recently supported jazz were shifting their entertainment policies, making the short-term prospects for jazz musicians bleak, the news was not all bad. In particular, Broadway continued to open up as the central location for jazz activity in New York, following the success, commercial as well as musical, of the Royal Roost. One new club, Bop City, opened at Broadway and 49th Street, billing itself in neon lights as "the jazz center of the world," and Birdland, in the same block, opened as almost a carbon copy of the Royal Roost, featuring a bullpen for listeners who did not want to drink and a weekly remote broadcast of live music. Birdland, named of course for Charlie Parker, would prove to be a force in jazz presentation, surviving until 1965, an amazing length of time as jazz clubs go; by the time it finally closed, both the Royal Roost and Bop City would be distant memories.

Davis played at Birdland in February, in an all-star band whose nominal leader was Stan Getz, a tenor saxophonist with a casual, lyrical style derived from Lester Young. Getz had become well known in Woody Herman's orchestra, especially for his playing on *Early Autumn*, a hit in 1948. Around this time, Getz recalls, "J.J. Johnson and I had a cooperative band together with Miles Davis, Bud Powell, Max Roach and Curly Russell." The band that broadcast from Birdland on Saturday 10 February substitutes Tadd Dameron for Powell and Gene Ramey for Russell. The details are as follows:

Stan Getz-Miles Davis Sextet
Miles Davis, tpt; J.J. Johnson, tbn; Stan Getz, ts; Tadd Dameron, pno; Gene Ramey, b; Max Roach, dms. Birdland, New York, 10 February 1950
Conception; Ray's Idea; Max Is Making Wax; Woody'n You
(all on Ozone 1)
On the remaining title from this date, *That Old Black Magic*, Getz is featured with the rhythm section; Davis and Johnson are not heard.

The aural evidence proves that this band was not simply a pick-up group. On all the pieces except Getz's ballad showcase, *That Old Black Magic*, where he is the only horn, the sextet execute relatively long and detailed arranged sections, including background riffs behind the soloists in several places. The spirit of Davis's nonet is evident in the band's musical priorities. The compositions played mark the first appearance in Davis's repertoire of three compositions destined to show up in later recordings as well. None is an original by Davis, but all come with pedigrees. Two belong to the Gillespie big band book, *Woody'n You* and *Ray's Idea*, and *Conception* is George Shearing's, recorded by him in July 1949. *Woody'n You* was actually somewhat older than is suggested by its fairly recent prominence in Gillespie's repertoire (recorded by his orchestra in December 1947), having been written and arranged by Gillespie for the Woody Herman orchestra – as its title rather awkwardly indicates – a few years earlier. *Ray's Idea* is a collaboration by bassist Ray Brown and Gil Fuller. Of all the compositions played here by the sextet, Shearing's *Conception* receives the most interesting arrangement, involving shifting leads between the trumpet and saxophone and sequences of altered time. The arrangement freely borrows Gil Evans's devices and is entirely worthy of Evans himself, but the credit for the arrangement belongs to Davis, a fact that emerged three weeks later, when this arrangement was recorded by the nonet on the final Capitol session. Directly or indirectly, Evans's craftsmanship reverberates throughout Davis's arrangement.

This Birdland aircheck represents the only surviving document of the collaboration between Getz and Davis, although the collaboration apparently lasted several weeks. Regrettably, it does not include a recorded instance of their playing a ballad together. Both men are recognized as masters at interpreting ballads, although the recognition of Davis was less secure than it would later become. Getz was already acclaimed for his ballad playing, and for that reason he took the leader's privileges by playing the ballad alone. Giving Getz those privileges might seem to be an unusually generous gesture, especially in a cooperative group that accords both Davis and Getz a single vote in such matters. The prospect of Davis and Getz working cooperatively in a band might fire the imagination of any jazz historian, because both men are notoriously prickly personalities, accepting no nonsense, real or imagined, from any quarter. That alone would seem to guarantee a difficult relationship, but they seem always to have held one another in the highest regard, perhaps because they share a melodic gift that leaves them with very few rivals. Davis says, "I like Stan because he has so much patience, the way he plays those melodies – other people can't get nothing out of a song, but he can. It takes a lot of imagination, that he has, that so many other people don't have." Their mutual respect comes through clearly in the few recorded minutes that have survived from the hours they spent working together in 1950.

Finally, on 9 March, a Thursday, a version of the Davis nonet convened in the Capitol recording studios to fulfill the third and final session that had been contracted almost sixteen months earlier. Surprisingly, the changes in personnel were not even as extensive as they had been for the second date. The only entirely new face was Gunther Schuller, the french hornist, who replaced Sandy Siegelstein (who had originally replaced Junior Collins). Schuller, less than a year older than Davis, had had a strict conservatory background and was a member of the orchestra at the Metropolitan Opera when he recorded with the nonet. He was nevertheless deeply interested in jazz and he went on to make several ambitious attempts at fusing jazz and symphonic music. He eventually became, along with John Lewis, one of the key figures in third stream music, an interesting hybrid that attracted less interest than it deserved from both jazz and symphonic music fans. In 1950, Schuller was just preparing to earn the credential that would give him some credibility among jazz listeners when he surfaced with his proposals for fusion, by playing with the nonet.

Apart from Schuller, the only changes were to bring back the two rhythm players who had worked with the nonet at the Royal Roost, Max Roach and Al McKibbon, and to add Kenny Hagood for a vocal arrangement:

Miles Davis Nonet
Miles Davis, tpt; J.J. Johnson, tbn; Gunther Schuller, frh; Bill Barber, tba; Lee Konitz, as; Gerry Mulligan, bs; John Lewis, pno; Al McKibbon, b; Max Roach, dms; Kenny Hagood, vcl (on *Darn That Dream*). New York, 9 March 1950
Deception; *Rocker*; *Moon Dreams*; *Darn That Dream*
(all on Capitol M-11026)

The four compositions were, not surprisingly after so long a hiatus, less interesting than the preceding ones. Some of the edge had undeniably been lost since the original Royal Roost engagement. At the previous recording sessions, it must have seemed a possibility that success in the recording studios could lead to the reactivation of the nonet on a permanent basis. Some records had been released, eliciting great interest in some circles and producing a modest commercial success, but too much had happened in the meantime to hold out any hope for the nonet, which by now would require revival, not merely survival.

Yet the recordings were as impeccably rehearsed and as carefully arranged. One might question Davis's choice of *Darn That Dream*, with Hagood's vocal and an arrangement by Gerry Mulligan, instead of *Why Do I Love You?*, if a vocal track had to be recorded. The version of *Why Do I Love You?* that survives from the Royal Roost broadcast has a more intricate, almost arabesque, arrangement by Gil Evans, which makes it more interesting musically, but perhaps its intricacy was the very reason that it was overlooked in favor of the straightforward *Darn That Dream*. At least Capitol seemed pleased with *Darn That Dream*; it was released in November, coupled with *Venus de Milo* from the April recording session. A reviewer in *Down Beat* considered Kenny Hagood to be "too tense" but lauded the arranger, whom he took to be Gil Evans: "Here is an arranger who has learned the individual instruments and their sound possibilities." Well and good, but the nonet's book also included *S'il vous plait* and perhaps other compositions that might have represented so much better what the nonet had accomplished.

Deception was arranged by Davis and credited to him as composer, although, as its title obliquely confesses, it is really George Shearing's *Conception*; *Rocker* is Gerry Mulligan's, and *Moon Dreams*, also played on both of the Roost remotes, is Gil Evans's. The recording of *Deception/Conception* points up the fact that the intervening months had somewhat altered the intentions of these recording sessions. Instead of providing a permanent document of the music of the nonet, *Deception* introduces brand-new material, since it could not have been part of the original repertoire, having been recorded by Shearing some nine months after the nonet's public appearances. In its style, the arrangement is worthy of the nonet, showing how thoroughly ingrained in Davis's music that brief phase of his career had become. The emphasis is upon the arranged sections to an unusual degree, with the band playing the arranged introduction twice in its entirety, leaving room only for Davis and a very cautious J.J. Johnson to solo.

Mulligan's *Rocker* became a post-bop favorite, showing up later in the year in an arrangement for Charlie Parker with strings – Norman Granz's latest attempt to enshrine Parker – and in various arrangements by Mulligan for his own groups, as well as in the repertoires of many house bands. Its bouncy, good-natured swing typifies Mulligan's best music, and in the next decade or so he would provide an abundance of that.

Moon Dreams, Gil Evans's retooling of a schmaltzy ballad by Chummy Mac-Gregor, the pianist for Glen Miller and other sweet bands, sounds like an academic exercise in writing for the instruments of the nonet. Its thick, deliberate blend of the six horns inches along romantically. Occasionally one of the horns moves out of the blend to establish a lead for four bars or eight bars and then recedes back into it again – first Davis, and then Konitz, and then Mulligan – but there are no solos. It is a *tour de force* for the arranger, a brilliant display of inimitable talents. *Moon Dreams*, a kind of musical still life, is easy to admire but impossible to love.

The legacy of the Davis nonet was now, finally, complete. On the surface, the nonet had accomplished very little: a two-week engagement at the Royal Roost, and twelve recorded titles lasting about three minutes each. To accomplish even that, a total of no fewer than twenty musicians, counting Hagood, had played in the band, and two more, Johnny Carisi and of course Gil Evans, had also contributed to the writing. In the two weeks at the Roost, probably fewer than a thousand heard the group in person, and perhaps a few thousand more heard the remote broadcasts. Many of them must have just scratched their heads on hearing the nonet's sounds, and perhaps some others, mostly musicians, nodded theirs.

As the 78 rpm records came out, one by one, spread over a year and a half until there were finally eight sides available – four releases – a few fans probably watched eagerly for the next one, but with so few releases most people just heard the latest one somewhere and picked it up or simply missed it altogether. The nonet certainly did not blitz their audience. And yet, in the unaccountable way that quality sometimes perseveres, the nonet changed the face of jazz, and not especially slowly. Of course it was not *only* the nonet that forged the change, by any means. At the Stars of Modern Jazz Concert on Christmas day, while Davis was putting in the night with a pick-up group playing bebop, both the Lennie Tristano Quintet with Lee Konitz and the Stan Getz–Kai Winding Quintet were displaying a brand of careful, thoughtful chamber jazz that would very soon be known far and wide as cool jazz, which the nonet had pioneered. Their influence was felt directly by members of both those groups, since Winding and Konitz had both played in the nonet, but the style of music they played was partly their own creation too. And by the time Gerry Mulligan moved to California in 1952, he found dozens of musicians playing that same cool style, and most of them knew all about his role in that nonet and could hum every bar of *Israel* and *Boplicity* and *Venus de Milo*. Jimmy Giuffre and Sonny Criss and lots of other musicians on the west coast felt that the nonet had helped them to see more clearly the direction they had been moving in, without actually showing them that direction. The style of the nonet trickled into the jazz mainstream from so many sources that it soon formed one of its currents. By the time eight of the Capitol recordings were collected for release on a ten-inch LP in May 1954, under the title *Birth of the Cool*, they were already justly celebrated.

The rumor nevertheless persists that the nonet went unheralded and unheard, which is not true even of the live performances by the group and is much less true of the recordings. Thus Max Harrison has written: "Even if the music's commercial failure was unavoidable ... it still might have been expected, in view of the wealth of new resources, to affect other jazzmen. This it scarcely did at all ... The jazz community, in fact, turned aside, as so often, from an area of potentially major growth, and the error was confirmed by the jazz press of that time, which disliked the Capitol titles because of their refusal to sink into some convenient pigeonhole. Altogether, people began to forget about Gil Evans: his brilliance had been made obvious, but several years passed before anyone was reminded of that fact." Contrary to all of Harrison's claims, the recordings sold well enough to merit their quick release and continual reissue, their influence on other musicians was subtle, largely because of the distended recording schedule, but very significant, and the jazz press, not especially receptive to newer styles, gave more space to the nonet than might have been expected. *Down Beat*, for instance, published analyses of Davis's solos on *Godchild*, *Israel*, and *Move* and of Lee Konitz's solo on *Move*, by Bill Russo and Lloyd Lifton in four columns of its series "Jazz on Record." It also printed a letter from the pianist Herbie Nichols that said, "Miles proves melody and harmony in sufficient amounts will win out in the end."

A more accurate appraisal of the influence of the nonet comes from another English reviewer, Mike Butcher, who said in 1957: "Without exaggeration, it can be said that ninety per cent of the world's small, avant garde jazz groups – and many of the big bands, too – have been influenced by the Davis combo scores ever since, right up to this day." Nat Hentoff says, "These records were comparable in their impact on a new generation of jazz musicians to the Louis Armstrong Hot Five and Hot Seven records of the 1920s, some of the Duke Ellington and Basie records of the Thirties, and the records made by Parker and his associates in the early and middle Forties."

That impact, it must be admitted, was not entirely positive. The nonet's style also had a negative effect, and bebop, at least in the short term, suffered for it. André Hodeir, probably the first critic to assess the historical significance of the nonet's recordings, explained some of the positive effects and implied the major negative effect on bebop: "Quite apart from their value as pure jazz, sides like *Boplicity* and *Godchild* direct jazz toward a language that seems to hold great potential riches; *Israel* shows a fertile determination to investigate polyphonic writings; *Jeru* boldly calls for a re-examination of form, construction, and meter ... There may well result from all this, sooner or later, a completely renewed jazz that, without renouncing its tradition, would find its justification in a new classicism, which bop seems no longer capable of bringing about." For the time being, bop suffered by comparison to the cool chamber jazz of the nonet, and bop already had more enemies than it needed. The bop players, as musical revolutionaries affirming values such as intensity and virtuosity, had let the antipathy toward their music fall where it may among the established jazz clientele of the day. The latter were made up of a majority raised on the offerings of the big dance bands, a jazz style often on the fringes of vaudeville and pop music and sometimes wholly engulfed by them. Bebop came along and made its brash assertions in a tone and temper alien to that style – brazen, energetic, unsolicitous, unyielding, unbowing. It was a musical world as alien to most dance band fans as were the backstreets of Harlem where it had been nurtured.

Now, the nonet found a ready audience not only among the musicians, who appreciated their musical values, but also among the old fans, who found them comparatively accessible, orderly, and melodic. Nat Hentoff said: "The counter-revolutionary aspect of the Davis discs was that they again put the stress on ensemble playing. The soloist was still permitted to improvise, but he did so within a cohesive framework of relatively complex, freshly written ensemble material. The rhythmic and harmonic innovations of Parker, Gillespie and the rest were retained by the new men, but they aimed for a lighter and more flowing rhythmic pulse than had emerged from the guerrilla warfare that had sometimes existed in the early modern-jazz rhythm sections, and a considerably more sensitive and varied dynamic range. Some of the leaping cry and slashing spontaneity of the beginnings of modern jazz were lost, but the records established a standard for coping once again with the problem – solved by the early New Orleans bands for the first time, and by Ellington and Basie for theirs – of maintaining each player's individuality and at the same time emphasizing the organized expression of the group. The Davis records were an arranger's triumph." This interpretation puts the most optimistic face forward in assessing the achievement of the nonet.

But there is another side. Many of the bop values that were being supplanted by the cool music seem quite undeniably to be values that belong to the essence of jazz. One is improvisation, which is essential in the root sense of the term – a defining property of jazz – and while improvisation is retained, of course, in the cool paradigm, its role is greatly diminished, perhaps to the point that in the hands of some musicians it is no longer as highly valued as arranged music. Another is rhythm, which has undergone many changes in the history of jazz and has been the harbinger of further change on several occasions, but in cool music there is the beginning, at least, of a tendency to smooth out the rhythm and flatten its accents.

Neither rhythm nor improvisation is devalued to the extent that it flaws the work of the nonet, unless it is in *Moon Dreams*, which has no improvisation and virtually no pulse, but the tendency was there, and subsequently, in the hands of less gifted players and especially less talented arrangers, both elements would be disastrously devalued. The two sides of the cool movement were perceived by Hodeir, when he not only saw the possibility of "a completely renewed jazz" in the nonet's experiments but saw that "it is also possible to believe that music so essentially intimate and excessively polished may lose some of jazz's essential characteristics and cease to be anything but a devitalized successor. Only time will tell which of these two hypotheses corresponds to what the future actually holds."

Exactly the same peril lurks in the shift in emphasis on individual styles that the members of the nonet brought to the fore. The pyrotechnical displays of the boppers were supplanted by the highly personal musings of the cool musicians, a decidedly positive effect when undertaken by musicians of the caliber of Davis and Konitz. The danger arises when it is undertaken by lesser musicians. As Mike Butcher puts it, "The copyists who had emulated Diz and Bird now, in many cases, began to idolize Miles and Lee." Among lesser musicians, that idolatry sometimes led to something akin to a rejection of technique, and some musicians playing cool jazz felt no need to strive technically or emotionally for improvisational effects.

All the deleterious effects lay in the future. The nonet recordings embody the essential values of jazz music and give them a remarkably full and creative expression. There is about them, as Gerry Mulligan said, "a kind of perfection," comparable, as perhaps a dozen critics and historians have pointed out, even to Armstrong's Hot Fives and Hot Sevens. They are, of course, in no way blameworthy for the weaker elements of the tradition that they fostered. Remarkably – almost incredibly – when those weaker elements threatened to predominate, some four years later, it would be Davis who would, once again, supply the antidote.

For Davis, the nonet recordings stand as the first of his consummate achievements in a career that includes several. It was 1950, and he was only twenty-four years old. Accolades were already commonplace. In California, an entire school of musicians looked to him as the source of their music. Shelly Manne, who was prominent among them, recalls that time. "I think the main influence on West Coast Jazz, if one record could be an influence, was the album Miles Davis made called *Birth of the Cool*," Manne says. "That *kind* of writing and playing was closer to what we were trying to do, closer to the way a lot of us felt, out on the west coast. What we wanted to do was represented by that album. It had a lot to do not only with just improvisation and swing. It was the main character of the music we liked – the chance for the composer to be challenged too. To write some new kind of material for jazz musicians where the solos and the improvisation became part of the whole and you couldn't tell where the writing ended and the improvisation began. The spaces were right, it was lighter, maybe a little more 'laid back' kind of music. Maybe a little cooler, but still swinging. I felt that it was a good period, a creative period at that time."

Davis was suddenly being compared to Dizzy Gillespie, so recently his mentor, to Gillespie's disadvantage. "Years ago speed was everything," says Barret Deems, the traditional drummer. "The faster you were, the better you were. Not much else counted as far as the public was concerned. Technique was very important in the Thirties. Everybody tried to be a virtuoso. The drummer who played the fastest, the trumpeter who blew the highest – they were the best. Now it's the ideas that are important. It's what you do with the technique you have that counts. That's why Miles could be as big an influence as Diz, even though Diz has ten times the chops. It was the ideas, the stories they were telling." For Deems the difference was in ideas, but for Gil Fuller it was the tone. "As a musician, Dizzy didn't have the tone that everybody else had," he says. "He concentrated more on technique than he concentrated on tone and the kind of sound he had. His sound and tone wasn't as big as, say, Freddie Webster's. Or you could say that his tone wasn't like Miles's, because Miles tried to sound like Freddie Webster when he started out. And Miles had a softer tone. When you look at Miles as a whole, Miles didn't have the technical facility for getting over the horn like Dizzy had. So, I mean, like you develop in one area and you don't develop in the other. It's like specializing in something. Dizzy specialized in technique. Other fellas specialized in tones." For James Lincoln Collier, the difference is in Davis's use of rests as a stylistic device. "Where Gillespie, and the beboppers in general, exposed long, rolling lines sometimes lasting ten or eleven bars, Davis played in fragments, dropping short phrases in here and there over the ground beat, sketching rather than making complete pictures." And he adds, perhaps too grandly, "The development of this spare style was Davis's major contribution to jazz." Whatever the objective value of such comparisons, at least they show the shift in taste triggered by the style of the nonet. Davis emerged as the leading trumpeter in jazz, and one of its major figures.

Davis's rise to prominence would affect more than his music. As a young man, introverted and shy, Davis found himself respected by musicians both older and younger than he and courted by fans and the jazz press. Several people who knew him at the time say that cataclysmic personality changes resulted. Ross Russell's critical appraisal of Davis's music in 1948, when Davis was appearing as a sideman with Parker on Russell's Dial issues, had been both generous and clairvoyant. Russell, who was not much liked by Davis and thus hardly a sympathetic observer, offers this portrait of the new leader in *Bird Lives!*: "The one-time 'junior' of the first Charlie Parker Quintet and the leader's unwilling errand boy, Miles was now artfully turned out in tailored British tweeds. Miles made *Playboy*'s list of best-dressed men, and drove an imported sports car. As a member of the Parker Quintet, he had found ample opportunity to study the art of the put-on from one of its masters. Miles now reshaped this experience to create the new image of the combo leader, aloof and *disengagé*. Miles did nothing so crude as to mistake a telephone booth for a men's room. He simply turned his back on the audience at the finish of his solos and walked off the bandstand to sit alone at a back table, indolently smoking a cigarette and staring with stony contempt at the customers. Outwardly, he seemed unemotional, unconcerned, and indifferent. Inside, he seethed with hostility. He worked out with boxers so that he could take care of himself in a brawl, forgetting, until an agent put him wise, that one good belt in the mouth could end his career ... One of his favorite ploys was to shake hands with an old colleague, apply an excruciating jiujitsu grip, and, as the other writhed in his grasp, hiss, 'I never liked *you*.' Or comment, in his snaky voice,

'Man, you're getting old.' The new Mr. Cool was small, tweeded, and nasty, the new culture hero, driving a sports car with a trunkful of custom-fitted golf sticks." Russell's description telescopes the trappings of Davis's private life so that they seem to have arrived at once, along with success. The best-dressed award, the sports car, the boxing workouts, even the "snaky voice" are all in the future and in themselves quite innocuous. What is missing entirely from Russell's account is any indication of or appreciation for the talent that supported such a lifestyle – Davis's music. For that, one might turn to André Hodeir again, in a remark that presages the brilliant continuation of Davis's career. "In the intelligent and allusive style of many of his solos, the young trumpeter shows a concern for alternation and contrast that augurs well for what he may create in the future," Hodeir says, referring specifically to his solos with the nonet. "Davis's phrasing has a variety that must be called rare."

That rare talent had barely begun to reveal itself in the nonet recordings. It would reveal itself, in a seemingly unending flow of creativity and explorations, for more than two decades. Such a long period of creative growth is unusual in any art form, but perhaps more unusual in jazz than in most others, where the conditions of employment take an excruciating toll on the artist's energy and resources. Jazz is a young person's art, by and large. If Davis had retired or simply coasted throughout the remainder of his career, his place in its history would have been secure. As the trumpeter beside Charlie Parker at the very height of Parker's enormous powers, and as the leader and featured soloist of his own nonet, Davis had already made an indelible mark.

For a while, it appeared that those achievements would stand as the apex of his achievement. Soon after the final recording session by the nonet, Davis's behavior became noticeably erratic, he frequently showed up unprepared and fumbling at engagements, including recording sessions, he disappeared and could not be found for weeks at a time, and he soon found himself struggling for any employment at all. Like Sonny Rollins, Jackie McLean, Gerry Mulligan, Stan Getz, and dozens of other jazz musicians, Davis was hooked on heroin. The story of how he fought off his addiction and eventually returned to his music not only recovered but reborn, to achieve new heights, is the subject of the next part.

PART TWO
MILES AHEAD

The music
From the trumpet at his lips
Is honey
Mixed with liquid fire.
   Langston Hughes

Miles Davis with Charles Mingus's Jazz Workshop; from left, Mingus, Ernie Henry, Teo Macero, and Davis (Robert Parent, courtesy of *Down Beat*)

5

Down
1950–4

The only jazz has come out of oppression and drug addiction and so on, although there have been individuals who weren't particularly poor: Ellington and Miles Davis, for example. When Miles was impoverished it was rather by choice than necessity, but in spite of his troubles he has consistently made excellent music throughout the years. So I don't feel that the lilies necessarily have to grow in a stinking swamp.   Archie Shepp

"I got hooked after I came back from the Paris Jazz Festival in 1949," Davis says. "I got bored and was around cats that were hung. So I wound up with a habit that took me over four years to break."

He makes becoming addicted to heroin sound easy, and it certainly was. Almost everyone associated with the bebop revolution used narcotics, so that needle tracks along one's arm became a member's insignia. One of the few who kept clean was Dizzy Gillespie, who thus became a spectator to the self-destruction around him. "Dope, heroin abuse, really got to be a major problem during the bebop era, especially in the late forties, and a lotta guys died from it," he says, and then he remembers the black humor that made the scene a little more bearable: "Cats were always getting busted with drugs by the police, and they had a saying, 'To get the best band, go to Kentucky.' That meant that the 'best band' was in Lexington, Kentucky, at the federal narcotics hospital." Another trumpeter, Benny Bailey, says, "Getting high, and so on, that was always the danger. A lot of cats were trying to be like Charlie Parker, including myself, to see how high they could get. That was a pretty dangerous period."

Looking back, the wonder is not that Davis became addicted to heroin but that he did not become addicted until the late spring of 1949, soon after his twenty-third birthday. He had been closely allied with Charlie Parker as a nineteen-year-old, and Parker was, by all accounts, the leader of the drug cult, by example if not by design. He had been using heroin and other narcotics since he was fifteen, before he left Kansas City, and by the time Davis met him, he was using enormous quantities. Even so, Parker was by no means an isolated figure among the musicians, even at the beginning. Gene Ramey, the bassist who played with Parker in Kansas City and left there for New York with him in Jay McShann's band, believes that Parker kept a degree of control over his habit until he made contact with the New York musicians. "In the McShann years, Bird was generally in control of his habit," Ramey recalls. "He wasn't scratching his face, which was always an obvious sign. It was very rarely you would see him nodding and that sort of thing, but you could tell. The other guys who were trying to be like him by using it were the ones who showed it worse ... But when Bird got to New York and was hanging out with Tadd Dameron, they were experimenting with everything. He was even soaking the reed in his mouthpiece in Benzedrine water. That was a waker-upper. The drug was a go-to-sleeper." Parker's partner in drug experiment, by Ramey's recollection, Tadd Dameron, was of course Davis's closest musical associate immediately after he left Parker's quintet.

It was apparently not the direct influence of either Dameron or Parker that led to Davis's addiction. Somehow he resisted that. Instead, it was the younger musicians he worked with after returning from Paris. They included Sonny Rollins and the circle of his Harlem friends; Max Roach and another pace-setting drummer, Art Blakey; Stan Getz, who would be arrested attempting to rob a drugstore in 1954; Gerry Mulligan, who was arrested for possession in Los Angeles in 1952 – to name a few who survived and are consequently remembered. Davis's partner when he started using heroin, he told Cheryl McCall in 1981, was Gene Ammons, the Chicago-born tenor saxophonist who was the star soloist in Billy Eckstine's band when Davis was in it. "Gene Ammons and I done that, we just started doin' it," Davis said. "First we started snorting it, then we started shooting it, and I didn't even know what was happening." Ammons was only a year older than Davis but he had made a brilliant start with Eckstine. Because of his addiction, he spent most of his career close to home in Chicago. In 1962 he was arrested on a narcotics charge and sentenced to fifteen years in prison. He served seven of those years before he was released, but he had less than five years left after that to resume his career before he died of cancer in 1974.

For Davis, the addiction seems bitterly ironic. Ever since he arrived in New York he seemed to be destined to be a leader, not a follower. But now, after sharing the front line with the likes of Parker and Dameron on the bandstand, he appeared ready to trade his hard-earned equality by joining Parker's sycophants in the search for a chemical high. Heroin was, of course, readily available among the night people who inhabit jazz clubs, and had been for years, and some jazz musicians would inevitably have been among its users under any circumstances. But in the late 1940s in New York and Los Angeles, far more modern jazz musicians

Sonny Rollins (courtesy of *Down Beat*)

Sonny Rollins and Thelonious Monk at the Five Spot (Marvin Oppenberg, courtesy of *Down Beat*)

Gene Ammons (Don Schlitten, courtesy of *Down Beat*)

used it than did not. Beyond any reasonable doubt, one of the reasons for the drastic increase in heroin use and addiction was the idolatry of Charlie Parker.

The effect that Parker had on his young admirers was something that he almost certainly could not comprehend in the beginning, and something that he seems to have sincerely regretted later on. Hampton Hawes, the Los Angeles pianist who spent several years in prison on narcotics convictions before he died at the age of forty-eight in 1977, was an aspiring young musician of seventeen when he was first allowed into his hero's inner sanctum. During Parker's first, ill-fated sojourn in Los Angeles, the young Hawes used to drive Parker to the club where he was playing. "When I came early one night he motioned me to follow him up to his room," Hawes recalled in his autobiography, *Raise Up Off Me*. "I waded through piles of sandwich wrappers, beer cans and liquor bottles. Watched him line up and take down eleven shots of whiskey, pop a handful of bennies, then tie up, smoking a joint at the same time. He sweated like a horse for five minutes, got up, put on his suit and a half hour later was on the stand playing strong and beautiful." The lesson, to the awestruck young piano player, was clear: "Those of us who were affected the strongest felt we'd be willing to do anything to warm ourselves by that fire, get some of that grease pumping through our veins. He fucked up all our minds. It was where the ultimate truth was." He was not the only one to draw that conclusion. Hawes recalls that the addicts on the West Coast had a secret code that they used to identify one another: they whistled the opening three notes of *Parker's Mood*.

The effect was the same in New York. Sonny Rollins, a year younger than Hawes, recalls: "I had gotten into hard drugs at the time, just like everyone else did in the community after the war. Heroin just flooded the community. We all knew Bird used drugs, and it made me feel that it can't be that bad if Bird is doing it. I wanted to be like Bird in every way I could. Later, after I'd been into it a while and I was going through a lot of hassles, I realized that Bird didn't really want people to get involved in that kind of life. By certain looks he would give me, I knew he didn't dig what I was doing. I realized he didn't think it was the hippest thing to do, be a little junkie following him around trying to be like him. He treated me like his son in a way, and I could see that he felt bad about what I was doing." Jackie McLean, the youngest of Rollins's high school friends, got the same message from Parker: "He said that using narcotics would be the one thing that could ruin us, the new group of guys coming up. One night, he even asked me to kick him in front of a club in the Village – he bent over and said, 'Come on, kick me in the ass! All these young guys are messed up 'cause of me, go on, kick me.' It was very embarrassing to me." It also proved to be ineffective as a lesson; McLean was imprisoned on narcotics charges while he was in his twenties.

Heroin abuse became a symbol, one of the trappings affected by the boppers just as dark glasses and pegged cuffs were, except that the heroin was potentially lethal. Probably the only musician ever to deny that it was part of the lifestyle is Miles Davis, an individualist if ever there was one. "You do drugs 'cause you like to," he told Julie Coryell in 1978, "not 'cause it's a lifestyle." However, many other statements indicate that he, no less than every other addict, had to keep on using heroin long after any pleasures it may have held for him were lost. One's choice of intoxicants became a symbol of where one stood in the jazz strata. Many of the swing musicians, the men whose styles were challenged and subverted by the boppers, were heavy users of alcohol, and many of the best of them, including Ben Webster, Lester (Prez) Young, and Coleman Hawkins, suffered bouts of alcoholism.

In the musical fervor of the day, alcohol and drug abuse developed into aspects of the contending ideologies. "The guys who drank whiskey were condemned by the guys on the other side of the street who used dope," Gene Ramey says. "They'd see Ben or Prez or Hawk half-way drunk and say, 'Man, you a drag. You a damned drunkard.' You couldn't turn around and tell a guy who was high and bent all out that he was a dope addict, because that would be squealing! Drinkers like Ben and Roy used to talk about this. 'Man, this guy's hitting me,' they'd say, 'and I can't fight back.'" Heroin became part of the bop style, and even Ramey seems to confuse the music and the drug. "With heroin came the idea that guys had to play with a straight sound, a symphonic sound," he says. "They put everybody down who was playing the other way."

For Davis, heroin addiction happened in the wake of his first creative peak, when his achievements in Parker's greatest quintet and his own nonet were still fresh. Buoyed by that peak, he managed to sustain a high level of creativity for a time, but perceptibly over the next three years he went through a descent that left him technically impoverished. By the time he cured himself, his talent had been dismissed by all but a handful of musicians and fans, and even those who remembered his potential of a few years earlier had long since given up hoping for the return of his powers.

A grim premonition of the course that Davis had started on was ominously close at hand in May 1950, when he led an all-star group at Birdland. Most of the players were drawn from his close associates of the time: J.J. Johnson, Tadd Dameron, Curly Russell, and Art Blakey. The tenor saxophonist was Milton (Brew) Moore, a native of Mississippi with a style derived from Lester Young, who had been on the fringe of The Street scene for several years. And there was also, unexpectedly, a second trumpeter, Fats Navarro.

Theodore Navarro was only twenty-six at the time of Davis's Birdland engagement, but he was making one of his last appearances on that stage or any other.

Seven weeks later he would die, the official cause of death listed as tuberculosis. Throughout the previous year, he had made only sporadic appearances in the jazz clubs, but he apparently felt well enough to play in public for at least part of this week in May, and he certainly needed whatever pay it would bring. Probably Davis took the suggestion to include him to the Birdland managers, who worked out an arrangement for expanding the group to a septet. Such an accommodation was not all that unusual when Navarro was the musician in question, because he seems to have been universally liked, even loved. "He was very sweet," Dizzy Gillespie remembers. "He was like a little baby."

Navarro was also, until a year or so before his death, a very creative trumpeter. Until he lost control of his heroin addiction, Navarro played the trumpet with great strength, detailing facile solos in a clear, full tone. He was expected, along with Davis, to take his place in the line of succession of great trumpeters. Under the circumstances, it might have been natural for Navarro and Davis to have emerged as competitors. Both were highly regarded on The Street a few years earlier, and listeners inevitably debated their relative merits; both were young, Navarro being only two and a half years older than Davis, and both started out as disciples of Gillespie. But Navarro seems to have had no competitive instinct, even before his addiction drained away all his worldly ambition, and his benign personality seems to have defused any competitive instinct in those around him. He and Davis learned from one another directly as well as indirectly. "He's one of the greatest players I ever heard," Davis told Julie Coryell. "I used to show him some things. He couldn't play a ballad. He would always play the same things, so I loosened him up. I told him what it was he was trying to play and couldn't. I showed him: I said, 'It's this chord right up here. You don't have to play the same thing every time you play this part; play something different right here – invert the chord.' That's the way I used to talk to him. He used to call me 'Millie'; he'd say, 'Millie, why can't I play something different on *I Can't Get Started*?' I said, 'Because you don't know what you're doing. You know in the end of the part that turns around – the first eight bars – you have to go back.' He didn't know how to do that, so I showed him what it was. 'All you have to do is run these two chords differently and you can go back.' He said, 'Oh.' Then he said, 'Thanks.' Fats and I would jam all night. It's nice to do something you like."

To all appearances, the two men were opposites. In spite of the similarity of their styles when they recorded together for the Metronome All Stars in January 1949, which caused Dizzy Gillespie to remark that he could not tell his own solo from either of theirs, their mature playing developed quickly, and they soon came to sound unlike Gillespie and one another. Davis's introspective, spare lines contrast with Navarro's powerful, long statements, at least when he was relatively healthy. The ebullience of Navarro's style suited his personality perfectly. "He was a fat, lovable character, playing the most beautiful horn," singer Carmen McRae remembers. "He was jovial and always laughing; he was typical of his size. He was really big before he got on the stuff. You should have seem him. They called him 'Fat Girl' because he was sort of a cherub, big fat jaws and a fat stomach." By the time he appeared alongside Davis at Birdland, any resemblance to the cherub of a few months earlier was gone. He weighed about 100 pounds, where formerly he had carried 175 pounds on his short frame, and his hacking cough seemed to rattle his bones. The fact that he could summon the energy to play at all surprised most of his friends, but the fact that he could occasionally still rip off some passable solos, with at least some of the old spirit, amazed them.

What remains of Fats Navarro's performance at Birdland has to be reconstructed in part from the incomplete transcripts made on Wednesday 17 May. The details are as follows:

Birdland All Stars
Miles Davis, Fats Navarro, tpt; J.J. Johnson, tbn; Brew Moore, ts; Tadd Dameron, pno; Curly Russell, b; Art Blakey, dms. Birdland, New York, 17 May 1950
Wee [*Rambunctious Rambling*] and *Deception* [*Poohbah*] (Alto 701); *Hot House* [*Miles' Midnight Breakaway*] (Session 101); *Eronel* [*Overturia*] and *Slow Broadway Theme* (Session 102)
The titles in brackets identify the titles on the Alto and Session releases, which came out in 1974; soon after, all or most of these tracks were also released together as one side of an album on the Beppo label. On *Deception*, Johnson and Moore do not solo, but the saxophone can be heard in the background on the out-chorus.

The transcripts of these performances are particularly disjointed, and many of the details have been subject to debate. *Hot House* is missing the opening theme; it begins with Davis's solo. *Slow Broadway Theme* is tagged onto the end of *Eronel*, probably signaling the end of the broadcast, but it is cut off abruptly. The original tapes presumably include an announcer's remarks at the beginning and the end of the broadcast, the former superimposed on *Hot House* and the latter on *Slow Broadway Theme*. The identification of these transcriptions as a single broadcast and the date of the broadcast itself are not completely certain. One of the mysteries of these transcripts arises on *Deception*, where only the trumpets and the piano solo; Davis leads off, followed immediately by a second trumpeter, apparently Navarro, but he in turn is followed by what sounds like a third trumpeter, whose presence has so far been unacknowledged. If *Deception* includes one trumpeter too many, *Hot House* closes with one too few. It features good bop solos by both Davis and Navarro separated by solos from Moore and Johnson, but on the closing choruses only Johnson, Moore, and Davis return to trade bars with Art Blakey; Navarro has vanished.

These discographical puzzles should not, however, overshadow the fact that beneath the din of the home-made recording some spirited bebop reverberated through Birdland that night. Especially on *Eronel*, an extended version of a theme composed by Sadik Hakim but invariably credited to Thelonious Monk, the players show their form in leisurely solos. Navarro sounds out of breath when his turn begins but he gathers strength as he goes along and in the end he manages to capture some of the boyish exuberance that marked his best playing. The solo was probably the last one that he ever recorded.

If the date of Davis's Birdland engagement with Navarro is correct, then it coincides with his first work ever in the recording studios of Columbia Records, the corporate giant with which he would be associated for all his later career. The occasion was a series of ballad recordings by Sarah Vaughan, and the results indicate that Columbia's producers recognized the commercial potential in Vaughan's flashy vocal style. Vaughan's accompanist, Jimmy Jones, assembled a good band to play his arrangements on these recordings but kept the band in tight check behind her. The recordings make a superb showcase for Vaughan:

Sarah Vaughan with Jimmy Jones's Band
Miles Davis, tpt; Benny Green, tbn; Tony Scott, clnt; Budd Johnson, ts; Jimmy Jones, pno; Freddie Green, gtr; Billy Taylor, b; J.C. Heard, dms. New York, 18 May 1950
Ain't Misbehavin'; *Goodnight My Love*; *It Might As Well Be Spring*
(all on Columbia CL 745)

Same personnel, except Mundell Lowe, gtr, replaces Green. 19 May 1950
Mean to Me; *Come Rain Or Come Shine*; *Nice Work If You Can Get It*
(all issued as above)

Sarah Vaughan and Jimmy Jones had been featured in the Stars of Modern Jazz concert at Carnegie Hall on Christmas day, 1949, where Davis and Benny Green were also on the bill, and Jones probably invited them then to rehearse for these recording sessions. The band were used very cleverly to Vaughan's advantage, making these ballads among her finest recordings. For the musicians, the hours in the Columbia studios no doubt helped to keep the pot boiling, but gave them little opportunity to show off *their* talents for the larger audiences. All four horns take eight-bar solos between the vocal choruses on *Ain't Misbehavin'*, which is the closest that any of the recordings comes to using the jazz format. Davis is heard most prominently on *It Might As Well Be Spring*, where he plays an effective obbligato behind the first twenty-four bars of Vaughan's vocal, and on *Nice Work If You Can Get It*, where he plays the solo interlude between the vocal choruses in a nicely controlled, full tone. These tracks offer proof, if further proof is needed, of his growing mastery of the ballad form, and especially his ability to project a sensitive and thoughtful interpretation in only a few notes.

For the country at large, 1950 was a kind of turning point. The exhilaration of the post-war years was abating. Economically, supply was finally catching up to demand, and there were automobiles, refrigerators, washing machines, and bungalows in the suburbs for everyone who wanted them, and that meant practically everyone. Where Manhattan had been invaded nightly by servicemen in uniforms just a few years before, it was now occupied daily by men in grey flannel suits, many of them ex-servicemen, who commuted to Long Island or Connecticut or New Jersey as soon as the office closed. The nightclub audience dwindled, and the audience for live jazz dwindled even further. The Street was already a fading memory, something that the younger musicians only heard about; its clubs changed owners and changed names frequently, but their bill of fare remained essentially the same – comedy and striptease.

Sometime in 1950, Davis led the last bop band on 52nd Street. The finality of the occasion made it almost a symbolic act, what Ira Gitler called "a last gasp for the modern" on The Street. The host club was the old Onyx, now known as the Orchid or Black Orchid. For the valedictorians, Davis chose another habitué of The Street, Bud Powell, and a couple of relative newcomers, Wardell Gray on tenor saxophone and Sonny Stitt on alto and tenor saxophones. When they finished their last set on whatever Saturday night in 1950, The Street's long association with jazz closed with them. Beginning soon after that, the brownstones that had housed the basement jazz clubs since 1934 were torn down, to be replaced by lofty office buildings providing daytime spaces for even more commuters.

The big bands also continued to fail. Count Basie was forced to disband in 1950, reducing his working unit to a septet with some bop-oriented players including Clark Terry and Wardell Gray. One of the casualties was guitarist Freddie Green, the rhythmic soul of the Basie bands from the beginning; he would be invited to rejoin Basie in 1951, when Basie expanded to an octet, but for the time being, he scuffled for work like so many others of the swing generation, playing occasional recording dates (as he did for Sarah Vaughan's Columbia session with Davis) whenever he could get them.

Dizzy Gillespie's orchestra also disbanded in early 1950. The orchestra had made some memorable music, some of it on records but much of it unfortunately recorded only in the memories of the musicians who played it and the listeners who happened to be there at the time. One performance involving Davis as a guest soloist is recalled by Cecil Payne, the baritone saxophonist with the orchestra since 1948. "The reason why I remember the concert with Dizzy and Miles," Payne says, "was because when Miles came up to the bandstand, we were playing a number that Miles didn't actually know. And when Miles started taking the solo, Dizzy was calling the chords off in his ear. And when he called the chords off, Miles was playing them and running them all through the thing. They really knew what they were playing," he says, adding, "Yeah, it was remarkable."

In an attempt to fill the void after Gillespie's band were finished for good, the managers of Birdland tried out an all-star big band for one week, probably in the spring or early summer of 1950. Billy Taylor, the pianist in the band, remembers: "Everyone was in it – the personnel consisted almost entirely of sidemen who wanted to be leaders, or had been leaders from time to time. I think the trumpet section consisted of Dizzy Gillespie, Miles Davis, Fats Navarro, Kenny Dorham and Red Rodney; the trombones were J.J. Johnson, Kai Winding and Benny Green, and the saxes included Gerry Mulligan and Lee Konitz; the rhythm section was Art Blakey and Al McKibbon and myself." This personnel overlaps at many points with Davis's recorded groups in the spring of 1950, including five members of the nonet that recorded for Capital on 9 March (Johnson, Mulligan, Konitz, McKibbon, and Davis) and four members of the Birdland septet in May (Navarro, Johnson, and Blakey, as well as Davis).

Birdland's managers undeniably gathered an aggregation deserving of the epithet all-star but, collectively, as Taylor also remembers, the music they made was a mixed blessing. "They were all marvelous musicians and the solos were the greatest," Taylor says. "The only trouble was that when they tried to play the arrangements (using Dizzy's big band book) they sounded awful." They sounded so awful that no one wanted to be named as the leader, leading to a chain of buck-passing that made the story worthy of a place in Leonard Feather and Jack Tracy's *Laughter from the Hip*. "Birdland wanted to bill it as 'Dizzy Gillespie's Dream Band,'" Taylor continues, "but Dizzy said, 'No, that's not my band, don't put it under my name.' So they decided to use the name of Symphony Sid, who ran the radio show out of Birdland, and call it Symphony Sid's Dream Band. And Sid said, 'No, don't put my name on it – I'm not responsible.' I guess none of the other musicians wanted their name on it either, so they just couldn't name a leader. They wound up calling it just 'The Birdland Dream Band.' That sure was a strange dream – I guess everybody was relieved when they woke up the following week." So far, perhaps mercifully, no transcriptions of the band have been issued, although some must certainly have been made.

While the opportunities for jazz musicians to make a living were drying up in New York, Davis's addiction to heroin was increasing. In the early fall, he left the city to tour with Billy Eckstine, whose stylized vocals were in vogue on the supper club circuit. The tour came to a disastrous climax for Davis when he and Art Blakey, the drummer in the band, were arrested in Los Angeles in September for possession of heroin. The jazz press had so far turned a blind eye to the growing problem of narcotics addiction in the ranks of the musicians, even though the reporters and columnists closest to the scene were well aware of it. Now the mood of the press was changing. The problem had grown alarmingly, with the pathetic wasting away of Navarro, who had died in July, and the conspicuous diminution of people such as Billie Holiday and Charlie Parker, among the greatest musicians jazz had known. The press could hardly ignore the problem any longer and remain responsible. *Down Beat*, then the most influential journal covering jazz, chose to break the silence with an editorial in its issue of 17 November. It began: "*Down Beat* has usually not given prominent display to news stories about musicians who run afoul of the law because of their habit. We did not wish to be accused of sensationalism. We knew, of course, that Miles Davis, the trumpet star, and drummer Art Blakey were picked up recently in Los Angeles on a heroin charge. We did not print it." The editorial then continued with a general indication of the rise in heroin abuse among musicians and an exhortation to musicians and club owners to bring the problem under control.

Necessary though the editorializing undoubtedly was, *Down Beat*'s phrasing was certainly unfair to Davis and Blakey, singling them out, and, by doing so, seeming to lay the problem squarely on them, even though they had only been arrested, not convicted. Many club owners, possibly in response to the editorial as well as to the increased vigilance by the police in their clubs, assumed a tougher stance by refusing to hire known or suspected addicts. Because of the editorial, Davis and Blakey were suddenly among the most widely "known" users in the business. Neither man could command his fair share of the available jobs any longer. For Davis, the consequences were disastrous. According to Leonard Feather, "It is doubtful whether he worked more than six or seven weeks in 1951." His documented performances include five recording sessions and only a few more nightclub engagements, including two at Birdland for which broadcast transcriptions have survived. Even if this documentation is incomplete (as it almost certainly is), it still points to a year – and more – of relative inactivity, which in turn probably exacerbated the drug problems. Professionally and personally, Davis's fortunes took an abrupt turn downward.

During the Christmas holidays in 1950 and the first week of January 1951, Davis played at the Hi-Note in Chicago at Clark and Illinois streets, leading the band that accompanied Billie Holiday. Holiday arrived in Chicago from California, where she had probably hired Davis at the end of his Eckstine tour. By this stage of her career, Holiday was notoriously erratic, often failing to show up at all or, sometimes, showing up incapacitated by drugs and alcohol. It is hardly surprising that Davis could find employment at the Hi-Note so soon after the *Down Beat* editorial, since any manager willing to take a chance on Holiday would hardly need to screw up his courage to hire Davis. The engagement was a complete success, and Holiday and Davis played to capacity audiences for every set. The manager of the Hi-Note, Mart Denenburg, praised Holiday warmly. "She's a wonderful person, very easy to get along with, goes on stand on time," he said, refuting all the rumors of the day. "I couldn't ask for more."

For Davis, the stint not only afforded him some weeks of work but also placed him in Chicago for Christmas again. The booking was available only because Anita O'Day, a Chicagoan who was regularly featured as the singer at the Hi-Note, had accepted a booking in Milwaukee for the holidays. She was still in Chicago when Holiday and Davis opened at her home club, and she recalled Davis's visit there in her memoirs, *High Times Hard Times*. As she remembers it, she was sitting at the bar waiting for the musicians to arrive and idly scatting a tune she calls *Cent and a Half*: "After a bit, this good-looking black man got off one of the stools and came over to ask, 'Where'd you get that tune?' 'Oh, I don't know,' I said. 'It's in the air. Kind of a favorite of mine.' 'I wrote it,' he said, matter-of-factly." The man was Davis, although the tune he laid claim to is not one that is identified with him, at least not by that title. In the week before she left for Milwaukee, O'Day says, "we formed a mutual admiration society." O'Day was not so lucky in her relationship with Holiday. Although she idolized Holiday and acknowledged her debt to her as a jazz singer, Holiday seems always to have derided O'Day, treating her as just another second-rate white imitator who would cut her out of the bookings she deserved. O'Day does not mention Holiday's presence during Davis's stay at the Hi-Note.

Davis's professional association with Holiday seems to have begun and ended with the job at the Hi-Note, but he retained an indelible impression of her as a victim who was preyed on by unnamed exploiters. "She was the nicest woman in the world, you know," he said more than a quarter of a century after their booking in Chicago. "All she wanted to do was sing. They picked on her and picked on her to get money out of her." A few years later, when Davis had regained his health and Holiday's was declining rapidly, Davis used to visit her at her home on Long Island. "She was in love with one of my kids and his curly hair – he used to ride my bicycle and watch the horses at Aqueduct." In the years immediately before her death in 1959, Holiday was drinking gin by the quart and taking whatever narcotics she had access to. By all reports, she was not very good company, but for Davis, visiting her with his son in tow, the image that persists is different. "Her mouth was so sensuous," he recalls, "she was pretty and she would say certain words and her mouth would quiver, and she always had this white gardenia and long gloves." He was describing her as she must have appeared in the Hi-Note shows.

Soon after the Hi-Note engagement ended on 7 January Davis was acquitted on the heroin charge in Los Angeles. It was welcome news, of course, but did little to undo the publicity that had followed the charge.

Later that month, on 17 January, Davis put in a marathon session in the studios, recording four titles with Charlie Parker for Verve records, four more with his own pick-up sextet for Prestige, and a single title – as a pianist – in a quartet led by Sonny Rollins, also for Prestige. The frenzy of the day-long recording sessions makes an ironic contrast to the weeks of inactivity that lay ahead.

The reunion with Parker came a little more than a year after Davis had quit his quintet. Parker was now recording exclusively for Norman Granz's Clef and Verve labels, and this reunion session was produced by Granz for Verve. Under his new contract, Parker always recorded with various combinations rather than a set band. The familiar presence of Davis, as well as Max Roach, must have been a blessed relief after more than a year of coping with less familiar musicians in more elaborate productions. Six takes from their recording session, presumably all the complete takes, survive:

Charlie Parker and His Orchestra
Miles Davis, tpt; Charlie Parker, as; Walter Bishop, pno; Teddy Kotick, b; Max Roach, dms. New York, 17 January 1951
Au Privave (two takes); *She Rote* (two takes); *K.C. Blues*; *Star Eyes*
(all on Metro 2356 087)
The surviving takes are the second and third for *Au Privave*, the third and fifth for *She Rote*, the first for *K.C. Blues*, and the second for *Star Eyes*. All others are unissued.

These performance are typical of the Parker quintet's work in the studios for Dial and Savoy in years past. The first two titles are Parker originals that required some rehearsal, though apparently less than most listeners would expect. *Au Privave* opens and closes with unison passages at a medium tempo, executed flawlessly by Parker and Davis on the two surviving takes. The second available take has Davis playing a chorus in an uncharacteristic staccato, laying out a succession of careful notes directly on the beat. As usual, he plays much more interestingly on the early take. *She Rote* opens and closes with a perfunctory ensemble passage over stop time, little more than the minimum felt necessary for introducing the cycle of solos. The last two titles are fillers, invented on the spot, and are in many ways the most interesting. *K.C. Blues* is an improvisation on blues changes and a magnificent performance by Parker, who displays great feeling and intonation on some conventional figures learned undoubtedly in his Kansas City youth. His opening and closing solos are so powerful that the statements by Davis, muted, and Bishop that fill the interval pass by almost unnoticed. Parker's blues style on this track seems obviously to be the direct source for the style of Julian Adderley, who would emerge four and a half years later as one of Parker's most worthy successors on the alto saxophone. The ballad, *Star Eyes*, features an equally brilliant rendition by Parker of the attractive melody, cleverly framed by an introduction and coda played by muted trumpet over latin rhythms.

The pianist, Walter Bishop, remembers this recording date mainly because of the facile manner in which Parker put it all together. "With Bird," he says, "if you didn't know a tune, he would take the time to acquaint you with it. Sometimes we got to a record session without any rehearsal. Bird would have some little bits of marks on scraps of paper. 'Here, Miles, this is how it goes.' We did a number, *Star Eyes*. I didn't know how the tune went, but Bird knew I had big ears. He just ran it down once or twice and I got it." This casual approach is hardly evident in the music. Mark Gardner, the English specialist in Parker's music, was amazed by Bishop's revelation about the casual preparation leading to the recording of *Star Eyes*. "It sounds meticulously rehearsed – Miles's muted trumpet intro riding over Bishop's firm chords and then Bird's soaring melody statement," he says. "*Star Eyes* here becomes a miniature masterpiece."

For Davis, the day's work had barely begun by the time *Star Eyes* was in the can. On this cold and slushy Wednesday, he still had his own recording session for Prestige to look after. It was no ordinary session either, because it marked his first recording under the terms of an exclusive one-year recording contract he had signed with Prestige soon after returning to New York from Chicago. That contract, though it must have seemed like a windfall to Davis, had not been sought by him. Instead, he was pursued by Bob Weinstock of Prestige, who recalls: "Miles sort of disappeared from the scene, and I was on a business trip out to St. Louis, and I knew Miles lived around there. I made some calls, there were a few Davises in the phone book, and I reached his home. They told me he was in Chicago. I said, 'Please, if you should hear from Miles, ask him to call me in New York. I want to record him.' Finally he got in touch with me, and he came back east."

The recording personnel for the first of the three sessions he signed for was settled to Davis's satisfaction, although Weinstock had some reservations about his choice of saxophonist. "He liked Sonny Rollins, as crude as Sonny was at that time," says Weinstock, "and also John Lewis. On his first date, you can hear a very different Miles Davis than on the Capitols." True enough, although the extent of the difference may be greater than any of the musicians really intended, because Davis's best playing of the day was already behind him when he left the Verve studios. The Prestige recordings, although they have strengths of their own, show signs of fatigue, and worse, in his playing:

Miles Davis and His Band
Miles Davis, tpt; Benny Green, tbn; Sonny Rollins, ts; John Lewis, pno; Percy Heath, b; Roy Haynes, dms. New York, 17 January 1951

Morpheus; Down; Blue Room (two takes); *Whispering*
(all on Prestige 7674)
Green does not play on either take of *Blue Room*, and Rollins does not play on the second take. The first take is a composite of two takes spliced together; the masters are now lost, and the reissue of the first take is mastered from a well-used copy of the original release.

Davis's debut for Prestige began moderately well and deteriorated steadily as the evening wore on. *Morpheus*, a John Lewis original, attempts to recapture the nonet style. It features complex ensemble passages broken up only briefly by solo choruses for Davis, Rollins, and Lewis. The contrapuntal theme statement, based on drum figures at the opening and on shifting trumpet-trombone leads in the extended closing, sounds enormously complex and probably is, although the evidence of technical failures and carelessness later in this recording session suggests strongly that this band might have found *any* arrangement too complex on this day. Davis's original twenty-four-bar blues, *Down*, the first of several memorable original compositions he would record during this period, retains some interest mainly because Sonny Rollins strides through his solo turn in a manner that should have served notice that a major talent was emerging, but Davis's tone falters at least twice during his solo and he misses a couple of notes in the closing ensemble. On *Whispering*, a limp, romantic ballad notwithstanding its contribution of the chord sequences for Gillespie's *Groovin' High*, Davis states the melody alone and seems unsure of it throughout.

But the takes of *Blue Room* were technical disasters. Both takes are built around simple restatements of the doleful melody over the spare, tasteful accompaniment of John Lewis. Lewis plays beautifully on both takes. Davis, however, misses notes and fades away into uncomfortable silence; on the second take, he seems to lose his way several times until Lewis rights him by striking assertive chords. The occasional but persistent critical claims that Davis is a technically deficient trumpet player, which are amply refuted by dozens of hours of recorded evidence, may very well rest on these few minutes in the recording studio.

For all the problems, the session has received some generous notices. Barry McRae, reviewing the reissue of these sides in 1975, says, "It hardly seems to matter that Davis was well below form, Rollins was still immature, or that on tracks like *Down* Haynes plods dreadfully." The saving grace, if there is one, is expressed in Michael James's assessment: "Despite obvious technical shortcomings on Davis's part, there is no mistaking the very personal air of sour nostalgia that pervades this performance." Certainly *Blue Room* (take 2), Davis's worst performance technically, is suffused by the anguish of an artist losing control. A few years after this session, in late 1956, the critic Alun Morgan met Davis in

Paris and asked him what had happened on the recording of *Blue Room*. "Hell, man, I was playing badly on that date," Davis replied. "I was – you know."

The remaining record date of the day was a continuation of the one before, with a nominal change in leaders from Davis to Rollins, and a change of piano players. Davis insisted that Weinstock give Rollins a chance to make a recording as leader, and he remained undeterred even when his own recording session ran late and John Lewis had to leave. He simply took over the keyboard himself:

Sonny Rollins Quartet
Sonny Rollins, ts; Miles Davis, pno; Percy Heath, b; Roy Haynes, dms. New York, 17 January 1951
I Know (Prestige 7856)

The single track, lasting about two and a half minutes, is essentially Parker's tune *Confirmation* (as Davis's title *I Know* slyly suggests) without the melody, here credited to Davis as composer. Davis is not at all tentative in the role of piano accompanist, and Rollins bristles through his extended solo, making a good start, however briefly, in his debut as a leader.

Davis's own debut for Prestige did not show nearly as much promise, and no one would have blamed the Prestige company if they had questioned their commitment to record Davis twice more in 1951. Under the peculiar circumstances of the jazz recording industry then, they probably did not entertain such doubts even for a moment. On the contrary, they entered the agreement knowing very well that they would have to put up with certain vagaries in Davis's behavior and inconsistencies in his playing. They knew when they signed him that he was a heroin addict. The apparent paradox of Davis being actively pursued by Prestige and offered a contract for three recording sessions at the very moment when his personal problems were growing and his self-control was diminishing is not a paradox at all. Several recording producers knew that the surest way to turn a profit on jazz recordings, with their limited short-term sales prospects, was to record musicians who would accept a ridiculously small fee as an advance against royalties. If the cash on the line was paltry enough, the companies faced almost no financial risk in producing the records because almost any release by a relatively well-known jazzman would recoup their small investment. Needless to say, musicians suffering from drug addiction were exactly the ones most likely to enter into this kind of one-sided agreement, if their need for cash was great enough, as it usually was. The companies were dealing with artists who, in effect, had no bargaining power at all.

Just six days later, Davis was back in the recording studio, this time for Capitol, with the 1951 edition of the Metronome All Stars. The format was much the same as it was on Davis's first outing with the All Stars two years earlier, with too many good players wedged into too few minutes of playing time. The two tracks that resulted are interesting mainly as an index of the shifting tastes in jazz. Where the 1949 All Stars had played big band bop, the 1951 All Stars pick their way through two carefully arranged pieces:

Metronome All Stars
Miles Davis, tpt; Kai Winding, tbn; John LaPorta, clnt; Lee Konitz, as; Stan Getz, ts; Serge Chaloff, bs; Terry Gibbs, vib; George Shearing, pno; Billy Bauer, gtr; Eddie Safranski, b; Max Roach, dms. New York, 23 January 1951
Early Spring (comp, arr Ralph Burns); *Local 802 Blues* (comp, arr George Shearing) (both on Capitol M-11031)

Early Spring, composed and arranged by Ralph Burns, who had scored a jazz hit with *Early Autumn* for the Woody Herman orchestra and made Stan Getz, its soloist, an 'all star,' is patently modeled on the style of the Davis nonet, featuring ensemble passages with subtly shifting leads and short solos (of eight, twelve, or sixteen bars). *Local 802 Blues* exploits the other main commercial thrust of the previous year, the sound of the George Shearing Quintet; the ensemble is played by the piano and the vibes in unison, the same pretty voicing that the blind English pianist would exploit for the next twenty-five years. The most effective solos are simultaneous improvisations by two of the players, matching Konitz and Davis, and Winding and Roach, among others. The experimental atmosphere in the use of simultaneous improvisation reflects the mood of Lennie Tristano as well, and some of the players – Konitz, LaPorta, and Bauer – were from Tristano's coterie. Considering that both the tracks by the Metronome All Stars add up to only a few seconds more than five minutes of music, the All Stars session makes a surprisingly comprehensive statement about the shift of emphasis in jazz, giving them a historical status that overshadows any intrinsic interest in the music itself.

The next month, Davis led a band at Birdland stocked by his friends from Sugar Hill, including Sonny Rollins and Kenny Drew. They broadcast on Saturday 17 February, but the recordings remain unissued, and further details are unknown. This is probably the Birdland engagement at which Davis introduced the young alto saxophonist Jackie McLean to downtown jazz audiences. In any event, sometime before McLean's twentieth birthday in May, Davis included him in a band he led at Birdland. McLean had made impressive progress on his horn but the prospect of playing at the most famous jazz club of the day definitely unnerved him. On the first night of the engagement, with Dexter Gordon and other jazzmen sitting in the audience, he bolted from the bandstand toward the washroom but was sick to his stomach halfway there. But his playing made an impression on the audiences, and he was soon being hailed as a rising young talent. His rapid development over the next year was a direct result of Davis's exposing him to audiences, and at least indirectly to the lessons he learned playing beside him. "Miles influenced me with his choice of notes and the way he played, even though I couldn't copy anything directly from his concept," McLean says.

In March, Davis recorded for Prestige again, but as a sideman. It is a surprising session because of his thorough relegation to a supporting role behind the leader, Lee Konitz. In a sense, the real leader for the first half of the session is George Russell, the composer and arranger of the first two titles, who was making a return to music after suffering a relapse of the tuberculosis that had dogged his health since he was a teenager. For the Konitz session, Russell prepared two charts of considerable complexity, and Konitz assembled a sextet made up of four Tristano students, counting Konitz himself, plus Davis and Max Roach, thus providing Russell with players literate enough to negotiate his charts:

Lee Konitz Sextet
Miles Davis, tpt; Lee Konitz, as; Sal Mosca, pno; Billy Bauer, gtr; Arnold Fishkin, b;
Max Roach, dms; George Russell, comp, arr (on *Odjenar* and *Ezz-thetic*). New York,
8 March 1951
Odjenar; Ezz-thetic; Hi Beck, Yesterdays (omit Roach)
(all on Prestige 7827)

Odjenar, named for Russell's wife, the painter Juanita Odjenar, features weaving counter-melodies by saxophone, trumpet, and guitar, with no fixed time, creating a solemn mood; Konitz steps out from the interplay to solo over a slow 4/4 rhythm. *Ezz-thetic*, a title alluding to the heavyweight boxing champion of the day, Ezzard Charles, is appropriately tougher, and a *tour de force* for both Russell and Konitz. The composition and the solos are superimposed on rapid, solid brushwork by Max Roach; over it, Davis plays two slim melodic figures repeatedly while Konitz plays what might be called an obbligato except that it is in the foreground. The set piece gives way to a burning Konitz solo for several choruses, surely one of the most impressive turns he has ever recorded, while Davis reappears at intervals playing the melodic figures behind him and then has sixteen bars to himself before the close. These pieces are miniature masterpieces in the corpus of George Russell, whose presence as an active contributor in jazz has been much too infrequent.

The remaining two titles are much less ambitious, and less interesting. *Hi Beck*, credited to Konitz, is really an improvisation on *Pennies from Heaven*; Davis is allowed a full chorus following Konitz, his longest solo during this session. On *Yesterdays*, Davis plays the introduction before Konitz comes in to state the attractive melody and play variations on it; Davis returns only to play four bars leading up to the closing chord.

While the music is undeniably interesting, its strengths are very closely circumscribed. For Russell, it is a show of strength after a period of inactivity, and a new revelation of arranging skills to rival those of Gil Evans, without calling forth in any way the elements of Evans's style. For Konitz, it is an incisive display not only of skill but also of feeling, from an improviser whose inclination throughout a long and well-documented career has been to favor skill. For the others, it seems to have been an exercise in self-effacement. They function adequately in the background of the two Russell compositions, although Bauer plays his countermelody on *Odjenar* stiffly and Davis fluffs some notes playing behind Konitz's solo on *Ezz-thetic*. Otherwise, they do not get heard much and for Davis, if not for the others, that is uncommon. Under the circumstances, however, it was probably not unwelcome.

Davis's recording session with Konitz was a relief from the periods of inactivity that were beginning to crop up more frequently and to last longer. Birdland also provided him with a few more weeks of work in 1951, in early June and again in late September. For the first engagement, he surrounded himself with some familiar faces. Some of the music they made has been preserved, albeit in low fidelity, from the regular Saturday radio broadcast:

Miles Davis All Stars
Miles Davis, tpt; J.J. Johnson, tbn; Sonny Rollins, ts; Kenny Drew, pno; Tommy Potter, b; Art Blakey, dms. Birdland, New York, 2 June 1951
Move [Moo]; *Half Nelson* [Two]; *Down* [*The Blues, Mick's Blues*]
(all on Session 102, Ozone 7, and Beppo 501)
The titles in brackets identify these tracks on some of the microgroove issues. On the Session 102 issue, but not on Ozone 7, a few bars of the closing theme are heard after *Down*.

The sound on all issues is flat and indistinct, with obtrusive drums throughout (surely only partly the fault of the unbalanced taping). The most notable feature is the strained attempt at providing arranged sections as an adjunct to the usual sequence of solos. The repertoire is otherwise very familiar, with *Half Nelson* brought forward from 1947 and *Move* from 1948 as well as Davis's good blues, *Down*, recorded five months earlier. All the players handle the familiar fare readily enough except for the new ensemble sections, probably introduced to give a semblance of the nonet's music. On *Move*, the horns play a ragged riff between drum breaks toward the end, and the ensemble eventually breaks down completely when Davis enters ahead of the others; he saves face by persisting with a statement of the melody, calling the others in to close the tune. On *Half Nelson*, the short ensemble following Kenny Drew's recitation of some patented Bud Powell phrases features Davis squeaking some attempts at high notes. On *Down*, the horn soloists double the tempo after an initial chorus, but only Rollins succeeds in sustaining the increased tempo on his last chorus, in spite of Blakey's insistent cues. The performances are not just unpolished; they are barely controlled.

For the September engagement at Birdland, after a lapse of almost four months, Davis must have had much less say in the conditions. While Blakey was also hired and the bassist was Charles Mingus, recently arrived from California, probably both Davis's choices, the rest of the band appear to be somebody else's choice. Possibly Davis was not the leader but just a featured performer in the band assembled by the Birdland management, although he assumes the leader's privileges by taking the first solos on the transcriptions preserved from the Saturday broadcast and he clearly had a say in the choice of repertoire:

Miles Davis and Eddie 'Lockjaw' Davis All Stars
Miles Davis, tpt; Eddie (Lockjaw) Davis, ts; George (Big Nick) Nicholas, ts; Billy Taylor, pno; Charles Mingus, b; Art Blakey, dms. Birdland, New York, 29 September 1951
Move [Mod]; *The Squirrel*; *Lady Bird*
(all on Ozone 7 and on Beppo 501)

This band seem strange company for Davis, and yet the music they made is far more rewarding than that of the more compatible band he had taken into Birdland a few months before.

Billy Taylor, a literate player just gaining stature then as an accompanist, had established himself as the regular pianist in Birdland house bands; he strengthens the ensembles by embellishing the melodies with neat phrases and abets the soloists with tasteful chords, but his own solos, for which he has seldom been praised, are equally interesting here, featuring long bop statements with the right hand and a severely economical left hand, which chips in with a chord or two occasionally, sometimes letting a whole chorus pass between chords. Taylor's frugal use of the bass clef anticipates the style that Horace Silver and others would bring to the fore a few years later.

Davis's co-leader, Eddie Davis, had been a regular sideman and frequent leader for a decade in Harlem clubs, including Monroe's Uptown House and Minton's when they were the cradles of bebop, but it would take a stint in Count Basie's reconstituted big band, starting in 1952, to bring him international recognition. His brawling tone on the tenor saxophone, featuring the unashamed use of vibrato, could hardly be more different from the approach of Davis, but the two make an amicable enough pairing. Best of all, Eddie Davis's gusto seems to rub off on all the others, including the trumpeter, inspiring him even to make a challenge out of *Move*, by now a tired old commonplace. On *Move* and Tadd Dameron's *Lady Bird*, Eddie Davis plays extended chase sequences, alternating four-bar phrases with the other saxophonist, Big Nick Nicholas; the chase device, a kind of mock cutting session for the saxophonists, pits the two players against one another directly, and most listeners will probably be surprised to hear Davis pressed hard by Nicholas, a player who never made his mark with a sizeable audience. Among the New York musicians, however, Nicholas was as well respected as any member of the band, having played in several big bands, including Gillespie's band of 1948, and having led the house band in a Harlem club called The Paradise, where he was in a position to hire musicians such as Parker and Monk and to be heard playing beside them.

Easily the most obscure musician was Charles Mingus, who first played beside Miles Davis in Los Angeles five years earlier. Mingus left California in 1950 as the bassist with the Red Norvo Trio, a successful group completed by Tal Farlow on guitar. He quit the trio in New York, partly because of the indignity of being unbilled when the group was advertised as "The Red Norvo Trio featuring Tal Farlow," and he was struggling to find work in New York. It was Davis who arranged the first breaks for Mingus, getting him into the band at Birdland and later making room for him in a recording studio, but apparently Davis was helpful without being particularly friendly. Mingus, in *Beneath the Underdog*, reconstructs a conversation he had with Fats Navarro just before Navarro's death, soon after Mingus arrived in New York. The dialogue at one point turns on Davis's penchant for keeping his feelings to himself. Navarro, in the course of introducing himself to Mingus, says: "You play with Diz and Bird when they was in California? See, I knowed of you before you knowed of me ... You ain't so undiscovered. Miles played once with you. He used to tell about the band you guys had." At this piece of information, Mingus, incredulous, exclaims, "He did? He hardly said a word except with his horn. How cool can you get when you don't even say hello."

Davis's second recording date for Prestige as a leader, in October, became the occasion for Jackie McLean's recording debut. It was also one of the first recording sessions that set out to exploit the possibilities of the new microgroove technology, which finally freed the musicians of the strictures imposed by the three-minute limit of 78 rpm records. Microgroove technology had been available for more than a year, but studio sessions had never altered their time-honored format to accommodate it and the new 33⅓ rpm recordings, pressed onto ten-inch vinyl discs, the same diameter as the 78s, had been used almost exclusively for pressings of live performances. Now producer Ira Gitler brought Davis and his band into the studio to record compositions at whatever length the musicians chose, and the result was enough music to fill two ten-inch long play (LP) records.

In his liner note for the first release from this session (Prestige LP 124), Gitler extols the technological advance for his customers, saying: "This album gives Miles more freedom than he has ever had on records for time limits were not strictly enforced. There is an opportunity to build ideas into a definite cumulative effect."

Gitler's comments apparently attempt to break down whatever consumer resistance might be lurking, a vague fear shared by the rest of the recording industry, which sat back waiting for someone to try the new wares. But the resistance did not materialize, notwithstanding the increase in prices – ten-inch LPs cost about three times the price of ten-inch 78s – and even the most hidebound record buyers needed no persuading. The record-buying public was so receptive that ten-inch LPs gave way almost immediately to twelve-inch LPs, which not only increased the price to almost four times the cost of 78s but also altered the very dimensions that records had typically had since Edison's old cylinders became relics.

Microgroove technology established itself so rapidly that its revolutionary effect on musical forms has gone unnoticed. In jazz, its obvious impact was in destroying once and for all the artifical distinctions between recorded performances and live performances, by permitting, even encouraging, expanded formal frameworks and fully developed improvisations on record. The superficial similarity between jazz and American popular song had been promoted inadvertently by the limits of 78 rpm recording technology from the beginning. Popular song forms fit very comfortably into those limits, probably too comfortably for the fit to be purely accidental, since the song forms themselves became fixed at the same time as sound recording was developing. The succinct form of American song was established by Jerome Kern, Irving Berlin, and other songwriters in the early decades of this century. The lyric was set in only thirty-two bars segmented into four equal movements, probably as much because of the strictures of the early recording technology as because of any intrinsic, structural considerations. Popular song forms that developed *prior* to the recording industry tend to be structurally more complex; operatic and operettic arias, *Lieder*, and narrative folk songs always fit uneasily onto 78 rpm pressings. So, really, did jazz, in the forms it usually took at performances.

For decades, jazz musicians adjusted to the recording strictures by adopting American popular songs as their vehicles for improvisation, and by composing originals with the same structure. Throughout the 1930s and 1940s, when sound recording became a big business, nearly all recorded jazz took that form, so much so that musicians schooled in those years assumed that the thirty-two-bar format belonged to jazz no less than to popular song. Probably because of the musicians' predilection, it continued to dominate in jazz compositions throughout the 1950s, but its grip loosened in the 1960s, and in the 1970s the younger jazz musicians, to whom 78 rpm records were just museum pieces or old junk, seldom used the form at all. (Over the same period, American popular songs also began to depart from the conventional thirty-two-bar form, and any list of the best songs of the 1960s and 1970s will inevitably include several – Don McLean's *American Pie*, Joni Mitchell's *The Circle Game*, Paul Simon's *Dangling Conversation*, Lennon and McCartney's *Eleanor Rigby* – with unconventional forms; the only realm where the thirty-two-bar form retains its currency is in theater music, presumably because Kern, Berlin, and their successors such as Gershwin, Rodgers, and Porter used the form too impeccably for their precedent to be ignored.)

In jazz history, Davis's microgroove recording for Prestige in October 1951 stands as a milestone in introducing the new technology both to musicians and to fans. The session retains a reasonable share of intrinsic interest as well:

Miles Davis All Stars
Miles Davis, tpt; Jackie McLean, as; Sonny Rollins, ts; Walter Bishop, pno; Tommy Potter, b; Art Blakey, dms. New York, 5 October 1951
Conception; Out of the Blue; Denial; Bluing; Dig; My Old Flame; It's Only a Paper Moon
(all on Prestige 7744)
Jackie McLean does not play on *Conception*, *My Old Flame*, and *Paper Moon*. The first ten-inch LP issued from this session (Prestige LP 124) included *Conception*, *Dig*, *My Old Flame*, and *Paper Moon*; the other compositions were issued later on a second ten-inch LP (Prestige LP 140).

This session turned up an ambiguous result, with some excellent work on some titles and some very ragged performances on others. *Dig* made considerable impact upon its release, providing Rollins with an opportunity to record a powerful solo, his best to that date by far; giving McLean a chance to display his distinctive solo style, which juxtaposes short bop phrases in a choppy but coherent sequence; and exposing Davis's best bop style not once but twice, because the new LP format allows him to play at length both before and after McLean. This track again, incidentally, shows how unconcerned the jazz musicians of the day were about composer credits: *Dig*, credited here to Davis, was recorded seven months later as *Donna* and credited to McLean; by either title and author, it is a bebop line superimposed on the chord sequence of *Sweet Georgia Brown*. *Conception*, George Shearing's fine tune already better known as *Deception* from the nonet version of March 1950, where it was credited to Davis, restores not only Shearing's title but also Shearing's name to the piece, although it is played here in the nonet's arrangement. *Denial* is an improvisation on Parker's *Confirmation*, exactly the same gambit used earlier by Davis and Rollins for Rollins's debut as leader, when it was entitled *I Know*.

The recording session began with the well-rehearsed version of *Conception* and then descended perceptibly through various degrees of poorer preparation on the other titles, ending with the standard ballads *My Old Flame* and *It's Only a Paper Moon*. On *Bluing*, a blues improvisation that stretches out to almost ten minutes, Blakey apparently became distracted from his time-keeping chores; he keeps on drumming after everyone else has stopped playing, prompting Davis to turn to him and bark, "Play the endin', man. You know the arrangement." Rollins, on *Bluing* and elsewhere, was bothered by a squeaky reed. Fortunately he continues playing in spite of it on most tracks, including *Dig*, but on *Denial* he drops out after one wooden chorus. According to Ira Gitler, he had at this point given up on his own horn and was trying out J.R. Montrose's, who happened to be in the studio watching. Montrose was not the only spectator; Jackie McLean recalls that "Mingus had come to the studio with Miles that day, carrying his bass on his back, and stood at the piano, running over the tunes." There is no indication that Mingus got to use his bass during the session, but the bassist figures prominently in the background of *Conception*, playing a stop-time figure at the bridge of each chorus behind all the soloists, and it would not be at all surprising to discover that it was Mingus rather than Tommy Potter playing it.

Davis's best work came quite late in the day, long after the rest of the players had given their own best efforts. On *Paper Moon*, the closer, he fails to reach some high notes during his solo, but on *My Old Flame*, the sentimental old ballad that Parker had featured when Davis was a member of his quintet, he is less ambitious technically and more successful melodically. His performance is not up to the standards he set a few years later, or even a few years earlier, but it is good enough compared to his playing elsewhere in this period to be noteworthy, especially coming so near the end of a long recording session that had a party atmosphere from the beginning, and at a time in his life when his self-discipline had deserted him almost completely.

By the fall of 1951 Davis's addiction to heroin dominated his life. It was not only sapping his strength but also costing a great deal of money, much more money than he could hope to make playing music sporadically in clubs and studios. Twenty-three years later he told Gregg Hall, "When I was using dope it was costing me a couple of grand a day and I used to take bitches' money." Max Roach remembered those days too. "Miles was a heroin addict with a stable," he said, and then went on to explain: "I don't know the details, but I know he used drugs and he had to do everything he could to take care of his habit because you couldn't support it by just playing music." "I was a pimp, I had a lot of girls, I was doin' this, doin' that," Davis told Cheryl McCall. "I had more money then than I

have now." His stable included about seven prostitutes, but his business arrangement with them, as he described it for McCall, fell far short of the malevolence
described by crime novelists and moviemakers. "They didn't give all their money
to me," he said; "they just said, 'Miles, take me out. I don't like people I don't like,
I like you, take me out.' That's like a family they like to be in." In turning to
pimping, Davis is not alone among jazzmen. Numerous others also found pimping
one of the more profitable sidelines of the subculture in which they lived and
worked. Jelly Roll Morton and Charles Mingus both talked openly about their
adventures in the skin trade half a century apart, and the number of others who
did not talk about their adventures cannot even be guessed. Certainly the opportunity was always there for the right man. When trumpeter Freddie Hubbard
arrived in New York in 1959 from Indianapolis – "a real country boy," by his own
admission – he was amazed, and more than a bit flattered, by the attention he
received from the prostitutes in the nightclubs where he found work. "I could
have become a successful pimp," he told Leonard Feather; "prostitutes just used
to beg me." It was an opportunity that many jazzmen who needed cash to support
their habits could not pass up.

Even pimping could not always sustain Davis, and he found himself bereft on
several occasions. Clark Terry tried to help on one occasion but found it a doubly
thankless task. "I remember one day on Broadway I found him sitting in front of
one of those ham-and-egg places," Terry told Leonard Feather. "He was wasted,
actually sitting in the gutter. I asked him what was wrong and he said, 'I don't
feel well.' After buying him some ham and eggs I took him around to my hotel,
the America on West 47th Street. I was getting ready to leave on the bus with
Basie's band, and I told him, 'You just stay here, get some rest, and when you
leave, just close the door.' The bus waited longer than I'd expected, so I went back
to the room. Miles had disappeared, the door was open, and all my things were
missing." Terry had been duped in a way that was known and expected by people
who knew junkies, but coming from Davis he was not willing to sit back and
accept it. "I called home, St. Louis, and told my wife to call Doc Davis to see if he
could get Miles, because he was obviously in bad shape and had become the
victim of those cats who were twisting him the wrong way. And you know what?
Doc Davis was very indignant. He told her, 'The only thing that's wrong with
Miles now is because of those damn musicians like your husband that he's hanging around with.' He was the type of guy who believed his son could do no wrong.
So he didn't come to get him."

Although Doc Davis could rise to his son's defense, he was by no means
untouched by his plight. Davis's sister Dorothy says that his addiction sent shock
waves through the family. "Up to this very day," she told George Goodman in
1981, "none of us discuss it publicly."

For the next two and a half years, Davis's movements became far-flung and sudden. Sometimes he left New York to front a local band for a week or so in another city, but more often he just disappeared from the city for parts unknown. Bob Weinstock, whose job at Prestige involved trying to get a quorum of addicts into the recording studios at the right time, says, "In those days a lot of guys used to disappear from the scene for months at a time." The musicians' disappearances were sometimes forced by pressure from narcotics investigators and sometimes by the need to find a new source of narcotics when a man had used up all his credit with the local suppliers or to avoid violence from the people he had duped. For Davis, there was also another, more positive motive, at least later on, for he has said that when he hit bottom he began searching for a place where he could straighten himself out. Eventually he succeeded, but for the time being his ramblings merely added more uncertainty to what was already a chaotic existence. By 1952, Davis's movements had become so unpredictable that apparently even Weinstock could not keep track of him, and his recording contract with Prestige was not renewed.

In the spring, he surfaced in his hometown, where he was taped playing as a guest soloist with a local group:

Miles Davis with Jimmy Forrest
Miles Davis, tpt; Jimmy Forrest, ts, vcl (on *Ow!*); Charles Fox, pno; John Hixon, b;
Oscar Oldham, dms; unidentified bongo player (on *Our Delight* and *Lady Bird*). Barrel-house Club, St. Louis, spring of 1952
All the Things You Are; Wahoo; Our Delight; Ow!; Lady Bird
(all on Jazz Showcase 5004)

This home-made taping, an unexpected document, is more interesting as an example of the company he kept on his catch-as-catch-can tours than for the playing itself, which is a standard rundown of some bop themes. Inevitably it is poor technically, with saxophonist Forrest more favorably picked up on the tape than any of the others and the bass player hardly noticeable at all. The beginning of *Ow!*, including Davis's solo (if there was one), is cut off entirely, leaving Forrest's scat vocal with its commercial references ("Super suds, super suds ...," he sings at the beginning) the center of attention.

Jimmy Forrest, though he was based in his hometown, was by no means unknown beyond its borders. Born in St. Louis in 1920, six years before Davis, he had worked all over the United States during the 1940s as a sideman in the bands of Jay McShann, Andy Kirk, and Duke Ellington before returning to his birthplace. Soon after returning, he recorded a rhythm-and-blues instrumental called *Night Train*, based on Ellington's *Happy-Go-Lucky Local*, which became a popular hit and then went on to occupy a prominent place in the repertoire of bands accompanying striptease acts. Soon after, he settled in Los Angeles and, much later, beginning in 1973, he joined Count Basie as the featured tenor soloist, bringing him a measure of international acclaim before his death in 1980. In many ways, Forrest gets the best of his stint with Davis in St. Louis, and it is not solely because he is better recorded. His solos, in a big bluesy tone but without the bawling mannerisms of rhythm-and-blues players, are bright and witty, full of oblique references to dozens of obscure songs, just as his brief vocal, which he apologetically prefaces by announcing that it is "for kicks only," interlards the nonsense syllables with jingles and blues references. The audience clearly belongs to him, even with one of the best musicians ever to come out of the St. Louis area sharing the stage with him.

The other musicians in the group, when they get a hearing, which is seldom, do not rate at all. They were probably strictly local musicians (although a pianist named Charles Fox had recorded with Dexter Gordon on Dial in 1947) and seemed destined to remain just that. The unidentified bongo player on *Our Delight* and *Lady Bird* may have been an old acquaintance of Davis's who was enjoined to sit in. Drummer Oldham unlooses some hefty bass drum accents on *Ow!*, making his most conspicuous move of the evening a display of a drum style that the New York bop drummers had abandoned years before. Pianist Fox, who gets a solo turn on every track, sticks close to the melody and often uses a stride left hand. For all that, the music is spirited, especially when Davis and Forrest trade four-bar phrases on Benny Harris's *Wahoo* and Tadd Dameron's *Our Delight*. In finding a musician of Jimmy Forrest's caliber in the Barrelhouse Club band, Davis was probably much luckier than he usually was when he played in clubs outside New York.

Sometime in early 1952 Davis toured with a concert package known as Jazz Inc, put together by Symphony Sid Torin. The itinerary is now forgotten, but also on the tour were Milt Jackson, Zoot Sims, and, later, replacing Sims, Jimmy Heath.

Davis's closest associate in New York remained Jackie McLean. The two shared an apartment on 21st Street between 6th and 7th Avenue, and Davis spent some of his time tutoring McLean and promoting his career in his curiously nonverbal manner. Both of them were heroin addicts, but the stronger bond between them was the music they played. When Davis was scheduled to open at Birdland just two days after he returned to New York, probably from the Jazz Inc tour, he gave McLean the responsibility of putting together a band for him. McLean called up two of his Sugar Hill neighbors, pianist Gil Coggins and bassist Connie Henry, to form the rhythm section along with drummer Connie Kay. Alongside Davis and himself in the front line, McLean added Don Elliott, a multi-instrumentalist with a Juilliard background whose main experience was in lounge bands. The group were heard on broadcasts from Birdland on both the Friday and Saturday nights of their engagement, and the transcription was released on record several years later:

Miles Davis All Stars
Miles Davis, tpt; Don Elliott, mellophone (on *Confirmation* and *Weedot*), vib (except on *Confirmation*); Jackie McLean, as (except on *It Could Happen to You*); Gil Coggins, pno; Connie Henry, b; Connie Kay, dms. Birdland, New York, 2 May 1952
Conception [*Evans*]; *Confirmation*
(both on Ozone 8)

Same personnel and place, 3 May 1952
Weedot; *The Chase*; *It Could Happen to You*; *Conception* [*Opmet*]
(all on Ozone 8)
The tracks identified as *Evans* and *Opmet* ('tempo' spelled backwards) are based loosely on George Shearing's *Conception*, yet another *Conception* deception.

Surprisingly, there is no attempt at ensemble playing, even on *Confirmation* and *Conception*, regularly featured in standard arrangements. Instead, Davis states the melody accompanied only by the rhythm section, usually including Elliott's vibraphone. The group approach is thus about as rudimentary as it can be in jazz music, with Davis playing a loose variation of the melody and then striking out in the first of the sequence of improvisations; the other soloists always follow in the same sequence, with McLean after Davis, then Elliott on one or the other of his instruments, and back to Davis again, who either trades four-bar phrases with Connie Kay (on *Confirmation* and *Weedot*) or returns directly to the closing statement of the melody. The absence of ensemble playing and the strict sequence of solos indicate the lack of rehearsal time, and the music is interesting mainly because it documents the growing confidence of Jackie McLean.

For McLean, this Birdland engagement brought recognition that the twenty-year-old alto saxophonist could hardly even imagine just six months earlier. "In 1952 I had a gig with Miles at Birdland, and Bird came on the stand," McLean remembers. "It was the first time I played with him. He was always kind and appreciative of my musical efforts. One evening he kept applauding my solos loudly. I know, because there wasn't much other applause. When I was through with the set, he rushed over and gave me a kiss on the neck." Miles Davis, needless to say, was not so effusive. His relationship with McLean, as close as it was, never really became a friendship in the sense of a meeting of equals. "I looked up to Miles, and he helped me in a lot of ways," McLean says "He was the same way he is now. People say that Miles has gotten arrogant since he became successful, but Miles was arrogant when his heels didn't point in the same direction. I learned a lot from him, both on and off the bandstand. You might say that I was in the University of Miles Davis. I remember once when he got after me about a tune that I didn't know; the tune was *Yesterdays*, and I passed it off by saying that I was young, like, I'll learn it before I die. Miles cursed me out so bad, and he could really curse, that I never used that excuse again." In the years that followed, numerous musicians passed through the University of Miles Davis, and very few of them seem to have gotten any closer to the dean than McLean was able to. For the others, as for McLean, the tuition was too valuable and the lessons were too important to bother much about the distance that he always seemed to put between himself and the people he worked with most closely.

Davis's fury at McLean over *Yesterdays* took place at a recording session in the Blue Note studios less than a week after the Birdland engagement ended. Gil Coggins as well as McLean was retained from the Birdland band for what would prove to be Davis's only studio date of the year:

Miles Davis All Stars
Miles Davis, tpt; J.J. Johnson, tbn; Jackie McLean, as; Gil Coggins, pno; Oscar Pettiford, b; Kenny Clarke, dms. New York, 9 May 1952
Dear Old Stockholm; Chance It [Max Is Making Wax]; Donna [Dig] (two takes); Woody'n You (two takes); Yesterdays; How Deep Is the Ocean
(all on United Artists UAS 9952 [in North America], Blue Note BST 81501/2 [in Europe])
Johnson and McLean do not play on *Yesterdays* and *How Deep Is the Ocean*.

The music recorded on this day, a Monday, is interesting, as is shown by the somewhat surprised tones of its reviewers when it was reissued twenty years later, in 1972. Mark Gardner, reviewing it for *Jazz Journal*, says, "This is durable music which has survived the passing of two decades and the introduction of many subsequent styles without losing any of its brightness and impact"; and then he adds, with the ominous tone of the bebop fan who by 1972 knew he had been deserted by Davis, "I wonder if we will be able to say the same of Miles Davis's current output in 1992." The reviewer for *Down Beat* said: "By 1952, [Davis] could encompass the warmth of *Dear Old Stockholm*, the dancing mood of *Donna*, and the bitter lyricism of *Yesterdays*. The last is a statement which ranks only a little behind Billie Holiday's interpretation of this challenging Kern song, and which has all the tonal (and emotional) edginess that would characterize his ballad playing, masterful, good, and just routine, over the next decade."

As good as the music is, it suffers by comparisons with both earlier and later work by Davis. *Donna* is a peculiarly methodical reading of the bouncy tune recorded under the title *Dig* for Prestige just seven months earlier, and the same deliberate, cautious ensemble playing mars this version of *Woody'n You*, Dizzy Gillespie's swinging composition. The two ballads, tacked on at the end of the recording session in the by-now familiar routine, have a faint pulse, and the emotionalism seems more than a little labored. They nevertheless provide very impressive displays for Gil Coggins as an accompanist, as he improvises harmonies and picks up short phrases from Davis's line for fills. A.B. Spellman called Coggins "one of the greatest piano accompanists of the era," but Coggins left music two years later to sell real estate and returned only sporadically, probably leaving behind too little evidence to justify such an accolade.

The high point of the session is *Dear Old Stockholm*, a beautiful ballad recorded by Stan Getz in Sweden the year before. Davis's arrangement sets off the delicate melody on the trumpet by superimposing it on dramatic ensemble passages. So effective is the arrangement that Davis would resuscitate it four years later in his first recording session for Columbia Records, when his trumpet-playing had the gentle assertiveness that would turn the whole performance into a brilliant recording.

But something was missing. Whatever the physical toll his addiction was taking, its psychological toll was much more obvious. Although he had so recently been acclaimed the top man on his instrument, his ability to retain that stature deserted him, and if jazz listeners in Madison and Montreal and Manchester were unaware of his failing powers, happily misled by the inevitable lag between recording sessions and record releases, there was still no hiding the fact of his failing powers from himself or from the musicians and managers and other insiders. Bad news travels fast, and by the middle of 1952 there were people watching Davis with furrowed brows wherever he played. He soon began to doubt himself.

To make things worse, the rumor mills were working as always in the jazz business, and people were returning to New York full of news about young trumpeters coming along for whom Davis, they implied, was no match. One name beginning to be heard was Chet Baker's. Charlie Parker had hired him for a quintet he formed in Los Angeles between tours with Jazz at the Philharmonic, and they had played together at Billy Berg's in Los Angeles and in some concerts in Vancouver. Baker says, "When Bird went east he told Dizzy and Miles, 'You better look out, there's a little white cat out on the West Coast who's gonna eat you up.'" As soon as Parker returned to the east coast, Baker joined the newly formed Gerry Mulligan Quartet and began playing ingenious counterpoint alongside Mulligan's baritone saxophone and spinning fragile, memorable melodies that made the quartet, and Baker, enormously popular in California. Within a year, the Mulligan quartet's records brought them much the same success in New

York and everywhere else. Although Baker's approach to the trumpet derived directly from Davis's work in the nonet and proved to be strictly limited to that delicate style, his reputation grew formidably, and he soon enjoyed most of the acclaim that had so recently been reserved for Davis.

Another young trumpeter with a growing reputation among musicians was Clifford Brown, then playing in bar bands around Philadelphia. Brown had been encouraged by Fats Navarro when he was a high school novice on his instrument in 1948, and by the time he had completed his apprenticeship playing rhythm and blues he seemed to have no technical limitations at all. He could play the fastest tempos in all registers with little loss of tone, and he could also play attractive ballads – and he was still learning. To further his learning, he intended to move to New York in 1953.

Another highly touted trumpeter was Joe Gordon. Musicians returning to New York from Boston, Gordon's hometown, brought back story after story of Gordon's prowess, especially of his aggressive playing in jam sessions. Gordon arrived in New York in 1952, and one of his first moves, long anticipated by musicians, was to sit in with Davis one evening at Birdland. The result, as told several years later by Cecil Taylor – a fellow Bostonian who admired Gordon and has no love at all for Davis, later a caustic critic of Taylor's avant-garde piano style – may be somewhat embroidered, but it indicates as well as any instance preserved from this period the debilitation of Davis. "Miles heard Joe play," Taylor says, "and then walked off the stand. And Bird ran up to Miles and grabbed him by the arms and said, 'Man, you're Miles Davis.' And Miles sort of came back and stood around shuffling his feet." The incident is all the more revealing with the advantage of hindsight, for Gordon, a trumpeter who made a few good recordings, notably one with Thelonious Monk (Riverside RLP 12-323), before his death in a fire in 1963, was never a serious rival for Davis in either ability or style. He only appeared that way to Davis from his distorted perspective in 1952.

Superficially, 1953 opened with much better prospects. Davis had a new recording deal with Prestige, and that would at least guarantee him some exposure and a little income. He wasted almost no time in starting to fulfill his commitment. Near the end of January he took an all-star band into the Prestige studios for his first session, which was marked by good intentions that, perhaps predictably, got buried in the execution. The sextet assembled by Davis included two tenor saxophonists, one of whom was Sonny Rollins. The other one was identified as Charlie Chan when these sides were finally released almost four years later, but the notes accompanying them made it clear to anyone who could not guess that the man behind the pseudonym was Charlie Parker. Parker was under some pressure, not only because he had an exclusive contract with Mercury, but also because the trumpeter in his regular band, Red Rodney, had been arrested and committed to the federal prison in Lexington. Parker believed that he was being watched by narcotics agents, according to Ross Russell, and he had given up narcotics for the time being and was consuming large quantities of alcohol instead. During the rehearsal period, when he was supposed to be getting used to the new King tenor saxophone that he brought with him to the studio, he drank a quart of vodka. As the confusion in the studio increased throughout the afternoon, the engineer became fed up and announced that he was leaving at 5:30. He told the musicians that the studio would close at 6:00 and that his assistant would look after any recording that might get done in the last half-hour. The musicians had managed to play only two titles, with a grand total of only three complete takes. In the remaining half-hour, they tried Monk's *Well You Needn't* a few times but could not get through it, and finally, with fifteen minutes to go and no chance for straightening out the problems on *Well You Needn't*, managed to make a complete take of another Monk composition, *Round about Midnight*:

Miles Davis All Stars
Miles Davis, tpt; Charlie Parker, Sonny Rollins, ts; Walter Bishop, pno; Percy Heath, b; Philly Joe Jones, dms. New York, 30 January 1953
Compulsion; *The Serpent's Tooth* (two takes); *Well You Needn't* (unissued); *Round about Midnight*
(all but *Well You Needn't* on Prestige LP 7044; reissued on Prestige 7822)
According to Ira Gitler's notes on the original release, Rollins does not play on *Round about Midnight*; however, on aural evidence, the tenor saxophone chorus following Davis's solo is probably Rollins rather than Parker, who solos before Davis; a second saxophone can also be heard playing a few notes in the background on the out-chorus.

The confusion in the recording studio is reflected in the music, although, as always when Parker was a participant, the irregularities had a less disastrous effect on the music than one might expect. In opening the recording session with his original composition *Compulsion*, Davis almost seems to be laying bare the potential problems on the date. Parker is expected to wrestle with his unfamiliar instrument on the fastest tempo that Davis will call all day, and he is also asked to solo immediately ahead of Rollins. Rollins turns out to be enormously more fluent than Parker on this title. On the two takes of *The Serpent's Tooth*, another Davis original, Parker improves noticeably and seems more in control even on the brighter tempo of the second take than on the medium tempo of the first. By the time the band gets around to playing *Round about Midnight*, Parker is capable of treating the tune as a feature, playing the first solo with obvious feeling and a measure of grace that bely his technical limitations on the unfamiliar horn.

Indeed, on *Round about Midnight* the technical limitations belong much more prominently to Davis, who hits half a dozen sour notes playing the melody at the beginning and end.

This chaotic session marked the first appearance of Davis's new favorite among drummers, Philly Joe Jones. Three years older than Davis, Jones attached the name of his hometown to his own given name in hopes of avoiding confusion between himself and Jo Jones, Basie's longtime drummer – though Philly Joe was almost completely unknown. Although he seemed rather old to have made no mark among jazz drummers, he was far from untalented. The best indications of his strengths at his debut session with Davis come on the first take of *The Serpent's Tooth*, where the bop melody played over a medium tempo offers lots of opportunity for assertive drumming. Jones punctuates the phrases of the melody and of the solos with resounding accents and yet somehow manages to remain integral and unobtrusive as well. He shows a rare combination of aggression and sensitivity, a preview of the gifts that he developed magnificently during the next five years behind the leadership of Davis. In 1953, he was as involved in other aspects of night life as in music, and many musicians knew him better as a streetwise hipster than as a drummer.

Three weeks later, Davis was back again in the Prestige studios with an entirely different band. After the fiasco with 'Charlie Chan' and the others, Weinstock took no chances and chose Davis's sidemen himself. The band are an interesting mix of some solid musicians. Only John Lewis and Kenny Clarke had been associated with Davis before this. The two tenor saxophonists, Al Cohn and John (Zoot) Sims, had been together in Woody Herman's Second Herd in 1948–9 as members of the famous Four Brothers saxophone section and both approached their horns in a style derived from Lester Young, as did almost all white tenor players of the day. Cohn was a literate soloist and a fine arranger, and Sims an ebullient, inventive swinger, one of the most consistently pleasing soloists on the instrument all through his long, uninterrupted career. So well did their talents mesh that they were often matched in later recording sessions and led a quintet of their own in the late 1950s. Putting them together for the Prestige session pretty well ensured a listenable result, no matter how uneasy their presence made the leader:

Miles Davis with Al Cohn and Zoot Sims
Miles Davis, tpt; Sonny Truitt, tbn (on *Floppy*); Al Cohn, Zoot Sims, ts; John Lewis, pno; Leonard Gaskin, b; Kenny Clarke, dms. New York, 19 February 1953
Tasty Pudding; Willie the Wailer; Floppy; For Adults Only
(all on Prestige 7674; originally on Prestige LP 154)

All the music is composed and arranged by Al Cohn, and it is unabashedly bright, friendly, and extroverted – a bit of an oddity for Davis. It is also meticulously arranged, requiring some concentration by the players. *Willie the Wailer* is over-arranged, resulting in a cluttered ensemble with the horns crowding the drum breaks. The rest of the music is intricate but not precious. *Tasty Pudding* features Davis, in the only solo apart from a short turn by John Lewis, and it rides over a cushion of harmony provided by the saxophones. It is the one sure sign that Davis is the leader of this session, because elsewhere he shares the solos equally with Sims and Cohn, even alloting them the first solos on *For Adults Only*, where he follows their neo-swing styles with a strangely cautious solo in which he seems to place each note deliberately before going on to the next. On *Floppy*, an uptempo number where the melody is little more than an excuse to get into the round of solos, Cohn and Sims follow their individual turns by alternating part-choruses, a version of the tenor chase used in jam sessions. Though Davis played better than he had for more than a year, the exuberance of Sims and Cohn on that chase sequence consummates the session.

Davis's flurry of recording activity for Prestige preceded another session for Blue Note, in what appears to be a companion session to the one he recorded for that label almost a year earlier. J.J. Johnson returned as trombonist and Gil Coggins returned as pianist, but Jimmy Heath is the reed player in place of Jackie McLean, with Jimmy's brother Percy, who had played with Davis on the Charlie Chan date, and Art Blakey filling out the sextet:

Miles Davis All Stars
Miles Davis, tpt; J.J. Johnson, tbn (except *I Waited for You*); Jimmy Heath, ts (except *I Waited for You*); Gil Coggins, pno; Percy Heath, b; Art Blakey, dms. New York 20 April 1953
Tempus fugit (two takes); *Enigma; Ray's Idea* (two takes); *I Waited for You; Kelo; C.T.A.* (two takes)
(all on United Artists UAS 9952)

These recordings took Davis back into the familiar confines of bebop, featuring reckless tempos on the three titles that required second takes: Bud Powell's *Tempus fugit*, *Ray's Idea* by Ray Brown and Walter Gil Fuller, and Jimmy Heath's *C.T.A.* J.J. Johnson contributed a couple of medium-tempo tunes, *Kelo* and *Enigma*, the latter built on the chord changes of *Conception/Deception*. The only ballad, Fuller's *I Waited for You*, played by Davis and the rhythm trio, was borrowed from the old Gillespie band book. (With *Woody'n You* recorded by Davis for Blue Note in May 1952 and the two Fuller tunes at this session, Davis shows an unexplained predilection for Fuller's music in these Blue Note recordings.) The session was not especially distinguished except for the quantity of music recorded – nine complete takes of six different titles, more than thirty minutes of music. But a listener can hardly fail to pick out the frailty of Gil Coggins's solos on both takes of *Ray's Idea*, the only tracks where he is given solo space, and, more positively, Davis's flowing bebop solo on the alternate take of *Ray's Idea* and Blakey's thunderous drumming on the master take of *Tempus fugit*, a bright spot more easily appreciated by contrast to his relative restraint on the alternate take. Yet a malaise hangs over the session, suggesting that it meant little more to the players than a few hours of work.

So far, 1953 had found Davis amid some very unlikely company, beginning with the tenor-toting Charlie Chan and continuing with the Al Cohn–Zoot Sims pairing. He next turned up at Birdland in a band accompanying a hip vaudevillian, Joe (Bebop) Carroll, a comedy singer garbed in loud-checked suits, a beret, and dark glasses. Carroll had been a member of Dizzy Gillespie's big band in their final years, 1949–51, an adjunct blatantly designed to increase the size of the audience. Most jazz fans tolerated Carroll's presence in the Gillespie band as a necessary evil for keeping the band together in the economic climate of the day. But Gillespie thrived on Carroll's nonsense onstage, willingly playing second banana. After the big band folded, he hired Carroll for his small bands, which hardly needed a burlesque component, and kept right on playing the fool alongside him.

Years after Carroll's role was forgotten, Gillespie kept the jive monologues and the nonsense vocals in his 'act,' often diluting his wizardry as a trumpeter in a way that caused the purists and sometimes the not-so-purists in his audience to shake their heads. In the beginning, the jargon and the costumes caricatured the bebop revolution, taking the trappings of that movement to such extremes that it became laughable. Although the joke did not remain truly funny for more than a fraction of the time that Gillespie has kept on telling it, it is so much a part of Gillespie's *schtick* that his performances are unimaginable without it. If pressed, Gillespie would almost certainly try to vindicate his use of low comedy by saying that jazzmen of his generation were expected to be entertainers, as Louis Armstrong was before them.

The idea of a jazzman surviving by music alone came later, and one of the people responsible for the change was Miles Davis. "He was the first one," according to Gillespie, "that came along in our business and figured he didn't have to smile at everyone, didn't have to tell no jokes or make no announcements, didn't have to say thank you or even bow. He figured he could just let the music speak for him, and for itself." No stage manners could be more diametrically opposed than Davis's and Gillespie's, since Gillespie has spent decades projecting an

Joe (Bebop) Carroll and Dizzy Gillespie (Arthur Zinn, courtesy of *Down Beat*)

Ahmad Jamal (courtesy of *Down Beat*)

onstage character that seems to be a composite of a musician and a clown. The clownish part of that character originated in Joe Carroll. Davis's shared billing with Carroll at Birdland could hardly have been more out of character, but it was arranged by Gillespie and no doubt agreed to by Davis because of his financial needs.

For reasons now forgotten, Gillespie found himself unable to front his band for part of its engagement at Birdland in May, and Davis stood in for him. On the broadcast of Saturday 16 May, Davis is the only trumpeter; on a later broadcast, probably the following Saturday, Gillespie rejoins the band and Davis appears as a guest along with Charlie Parker. So far only one title from these two broadcasts (*I Got Rhythm*, from the first broadcast) is available on record. The details are as follows:

Miles Davis with Dizzy Gillespie's Band
Miles Davis, tpt; Sahib Shihab, bs; Wade Legge, pno; Lou Hackney, b; Al Jones, dms; Candido, conga; Joe Carroll, vcl (on *I Got Rhythm*). Birdland, New York, 16 May 1953
I Got Rhythm; Move; Tenderly; Night in Tunisia; Dig; Lullaby of Birdland (theme)
(*I Got Rhythm* on Chakra CH 100; all other titles unissued)

Miles Davis, Dizzy Gillespie, tpt; Charlie Parker, as; Sahib Shihab, bs; Wade Legge, pno; Lou Hackney, b; Al Jones, dms; Joe Carroll, vcl. Birdland, New York, possibly 23 May 1953
The Bluest Blues; On the Sunny Side of the Street
(both unissued)

On *I Got Rhythm*, Carroll sings a tangential version of the Gershwin tune and then launches into a chorus that includes scat syllables and pop allusions, including the line "How much is that doggie in the window?" from the tawdry novelty song that was earning a fortune for Patti Page on the pop charts. Davis's solo, which follows, repeats single notes and short phrases, along the way tossing in a reference to the theme from *Dragnet*, a radio detective series then popular. Only on his last chorus does Davis sound at all like himself.

Between the two Birdland broadcasts, Davis was making more significant music with a quartet in his third recording session of the year for Prestige:

Miles Davis Quartet
Miles Davis, tpt; John Lewis, pno (except *Smooch*); Charles Mingus, pno (on *Smooch*); Percy Heath, b; Max Roach, dms. New York, 19 May 1953
When Lights Are Low; Tune Up; Miles Ahead; Smooch
(all on Prestige LP 7054; reissued on Prestige 7822)

This session offers little that is novel in Davis's work. He plays lyrically throughout, in good command technically, and he is well supported by the rhythm players; John Lewis and Percy Heath were now regular partners in the newly formed Modern Jazz Quartet, a cooperative unit that originated the year before (as the Milt Jackson Quartet) and would continue under the new cooperative arrangement for more than two decades.

In the perspective of Davis's career, the session takes on more interest. More than any other individual session of the period, it shows him building up the resources he would refine throughout the later part of the decade. Two of the compositions Davis recorded here for the first time, Benny Carter's *When Lights Are Low* and the original *Tune up*, credited to Davis, would remain in his repertoire for several years; he recorded them again in definitive performances for Prestige in October 1956. Davis's other original, *Miles Ahead*, did not remain in his active repertoire, although it deserved a place. It reveals a great deal of Davis's musical development during his first twelve years in New York, because it reinvents his composition *Milestones*, recorded for Savoy in August 1947. As *Miles Ahead*, the original melody has been pared down and clarified (although Davis meanders and misses some notes in the final chorus, apparently searching for the melody he opened with). It will be reinvented yet again by Davis and Gil Evans in 1957, in a big band showcase. *Smooch* is a nonce effort credited to Davis and Charles Mingus, who takes over from Lewis as the piano player. It is a moody, pulseless piece with Davis as the only soloist.

Following this brief flurry of activity in New York early in 1953, Davis again left the city, for an even longer time than usual. His next documented appearance there was not for some ten months, when he would record again for Blue Note. In the interim he seems to have spent some time at home in East St. Louis, and he probably played in clubs in the Midwest as a guest soloist with local rhythm sections, as he had during his previous travels during this period. He spent a large part of the fall and winter in and around Los Angeles. The arrangements for his California sojourn were probably made during his May recordings for Prestige, because two of his sidemen then, Max Roach and Charles Mingus, were already planning moves to California. Mingus still considered Los Angeles home, although he had been away for a couple of years. Roach, who was as dissatisfied with the jazzman's lifestyle in New York as Davis was, decided to make a break by accepting a steady job in the house band at a club called The Lighthouse in Hermosa Beach, California.

Modern jazz in the Los Angeles area was suddenly attracting a large following after years of languishing in the shadow of more traditional styles. Popular magazines such as *Life* and *Newsweek* ran features on its popularity, branding it West

Coast jazz and extolling its virtues as clean-cut, tightly organized, lightly swinging music. It had become the musical counterpart of the Ivy League fashions then sweeping into vogue, featuring narrow lapels, thin ties, and close-cropped hairdos; like the Ivy League accoutrements, the jazz coming from the opposite coast presented the appearance of immaculate neatness. West Coast jazz had given rise to a whole roster of musicians whose names were becoming internationally known. Along with Gerry Mulligan and Chet Baker, whose pianoless quartet had broken up because of Mulligan's imprisonment on a narcotics charge before its records caught on beyond California, the leaders of the style, at least in the beginning, were men who had left the bands of Woody Herman and Stan Kenton to settle in the Los Angeles area. The leading exponents, trumpeter-arranger Shorty Rogers and drummer Shelly Manne, arrived in California by this route and supplemented their jazz jobs with lucrative day jobs in the Hollywood studios. So did many of the others who came out of the big road bands – trumpeters Pete and Conte Candoli, trombonist Milt Bernhart, and saxophonists Jimmy Giuffre, Bob Cooper, Bill Holman, and Bud Shank.

Mixed in with them were a number of musicians raised in the area, especially pianists, including Hampton Hawes, Russ Freeman, and Claude Williamson, whose debts to a younger, healthier Bud Powell were evident in everything they played, and the jarring individualist Dave Brubeck. Art Pepper, the alto saxophonist, was raised in Los Angeles and was also a veteran of the Kenton band; Paul Desmond, a San Franciscan, starred as the altoist in Brubeck's quartet; and multi-reed player Buddy Colette was a childhood friend of Mingus's who stayed at home and for a short time met with better success than the big bassist. Besides Manne, the drummer most closely associated with the style was Chico Hamilton, first noticed in the Mulligan-Baker quartet and then as the leader of his own quintet with Colette. As the cult of West Coast jazz gained breadth and popularity, so did the list of its proponents, until it included classicists such as pianist André Previn and guitarist Laurindo Almeida, who joined the ranks as soon as they could master the rudiments of swing. Along with the pool of capable musicians, West Coast jazz quickly developed its own record producers, among which the most abiding were the labels Pacific Jazz, Fantasy, and Contemporary Records.

Jazz clubs sprang up, many of them short-lived, such as the Haig, where Mulligan's quartet got its start. The longest-lived and probably the most important club was The Lighthouse. Its jazz policy was overseen by Howard Rumsey, a former bassist with Kenton, and he installed Shorty Rogers and Shelly Manne in the house band. Rumsey also inaugurated a record label called Lighthouse when he saw the commercial potential of his house band, pressing an all-star session onto discs of red transparent vinyl to sell to the aficionados who turned up for "our most popular feature of the week – a continuous concert from 2 p.m. to 2 a.m. every Sunday throughout the year." By the middle of 1953, everyone knew that California was a great place to play jazz, and Max Roach, one of the leading lights of the bebop revolution a few years earlier, was joining The Lighthouse band, replacing Shelly Manne.

Roach did not travel west alone. Howard Rumsey told Leonard Feather: "When Max Roach came in from New York to take over Shelly Manne's chair, he drove up with Charles Mingus and Miles Davis in the car with him. Miles was just starting to play again after a long sabbatical back home in St. Louis. He hung around for a while, stayed at my home for a week, and did a couple of guest shots at the club. One of them was recorded, but the stuff was never released; I just heard Contemporary is finally going to put it out." The session with Davis remains unreleased in spite of frequent rumors, dating back to 1953, that it will finally see the light of day. Eventually it will be issued, and only then will another rumor, one of the most persistent in jazz, finally be squelched. For The Lighthouse recording has been eagerly anticipated not only because it contains material from one of Davis's silent periods but also because Davis is believed to share the leadership on the recording with Chet Baker, whose star seemed to be ascending just as Davis's seemed to be flickering. The rumors of a recorded meeting of Davis and Baker, fueled most recently by the listing in a 1980 discography (included in Baker's *Once Upon a Summertime* LP, Artists House 9411) of unissued material from September 1953 by Baker, Davis, and The Lighthouse All Stars, are, sadly, untrue. The two did not meet for another year, when Baker arrived in New York for the first time and looked up Davis, and then the meeting was brief and unmusical. Davis's recording at The Lighthouse probably includes Max Roach and some prominent West Coast players, but Baker is not among them.

Davis did not find many other opportunities to work in California but he stayed, living with Max Roach and hanging around The Lighthouse bar. After a few weeks he had certainly worn out his welcome at The Lighthouse and probably at Roach's apartment as well. The tensions came to a head on Roach's birthday, when Davis staged an impromptu celebration at the bar for which he could not pay. Davis told the story to Julie Coryell: "The cat at the bar says, 'Max says you have to pay the bill.' I said, 'Shit, Max, it's your birthday, you pay the bill.' The bartender said, 'I'm gonna kick your ass 'cause you're a black motherfucker.' It's a funny thing, 'cause I had a knife on me, in my pocket; I had just taken it away from Max, who I was living with. So Max says, 'I'll leave this [situation] with you,' and goes on the bandstand. The bartender says, 'When I get off, I'm gonna kick your ass.' So I said, 'If you're gonna kick my ass, you don't have to wait until you get off – you might as well get off right now!'" The end of the story remains untold.

Some changes seemed inevitable. Davis's decline – his long absences from playing, his technical failings when he did find an opportunity to play, and his preoccupation with extra-musical problems – had been going on unabated for some four years. By now the decline had become obvious even to listeners far removed from Davis's live performances. André Hodeir detected Davis's lack of control from recordings released in France, even though the recorded evidence was sporadic and selective. "The extreme unevenness of Miles Davis's recordings, which seem to give a faithful picture of the great trumpeter's current work, makes it impossible to consider him any longer as a leader," Hodeir wrote. "It is hard to define the reasons for this decline beyond pointing out that they are instrumental in nature, but in any case, far from being affected by it, his historical position is stronger than ever. Trumpeters as different from each other as Chet Baker and Clifford Brown have in common a certain way of proceeding, a certain idea of sonority, that is in a sense their share of the heritage left by Davis's discoveries."

Davis was only twenty-seven, and already his career was being assessed by one of his most astute critics in terms of its historical contribution. Hodeir's assumption that Davis's best work was behind him was shared by many others, and if most listeners could not have reached Hodeir's conclusion with the same clarity, any study of the works of these years, especially compared to the works immediately preceding, could only lead to the same conclusion. Thus Martin Williams, looking back, says: "By the early fifties, it may have seemed that the productive career of trumpeter and flugelhornist Miles Davis was just about over. Between 1950 and 1954 his work had become uneven. Obvious aspects of his style had already been siphoned off and popularized by several trumpeters, particularly on the West Coast." Davis's decline seemed to fit the well-known pattern for a jazz career; jazz artists who do not die young are likely to relax into complacency. He seemed to be a prime prospect for one or the other of those fates.

The listening public was nearly ready to write him off: in the *Down Beat* reader's poll for 1954, Davis barely made the list of top trumpeters, showing up ninth. It was no disgrace to find himself behind such perennial stars as Dizzy Gillespie (second), Roy Eldridge (fourth), and Louis Armstrong (sixth), or even the swing trumpeter Harry James (third), but the other front-runners were about the same age as Davis and had been learning their scales or sitting anonymously in band sections when he was already making innovations. All of them were associated with the West Coast. Maynard Ferguson (seventh) was featured prominently as Stan Kenton's high-note man, and the others, Conte Candoli (eighth), Shorty Rogers (fifth), and the surprising first-place choice, Chet Baker, displayed in their different ways the West Coast sound that was derived from Davis's innovations. Following Davis were Bobby Hackett and Clifford Brown; Brown also won the New Star award among trumpeters.

Whatever anyone else may have thought about Chet Baker taking first place, Baker did not think much of it. "I played some nice things on the first Gerry Mulligan album," Baker concedes. "It was a different style – soft, melodic. I think people were wanting and needing something like that and it just happened that at the time I came along with it and it caught on. But I don't think I was half the trumpeter that Dizzy was, or Kenny Dorham. Clifford was around then, Jesus Christ! So it just didn't make sense to me that I should have won the poll. It was a kind of a temporary fad kind of thing that was bound to work itself out." For Davis, Baker's ascendancy and his own loss of stature were further blows to what was left of his pride. They might have sounded his death knell, and no one would have been very surprised; but they seemed instead to reactivate that slumbering pride. Davis may have been down but he suddenly knew that he could stay down no longer. He was determined to put his heroin addiction behind him once and for all. And in the end it was not a rival trumpeter with a good press agent or a record producer with a handful of nickels and dimes or even a ham-fisted thug with his I.O.U. in his pocket who made him keep his promise to himself when he had failed to keep it so many times before. Instead, it was an athlete with a winning smile and a winning right hook.

Like every boxing fan of the day, Davis particularly admired Sugar Ray Robinson, the longtime welterweight champion who was called the best boxer, pound for pound, of all time. Sugar Ray was a celebrity, a strikingly handsome champion known as a ladies' man. Between fights, he appeared in New York society, photographed by the *Herald Tribune* or the *Times* stepping out of a limousine in a velvet cape and wide-brimmed hat. But when he went to Madison Square Garden to defend his title, any resemblance to that smiling socialite disappeared. He appeared instead as a trim, grim athlete, superbly conditioned and prepared. In the two sides of Robinson, Davis saw everything admirable, and somehow he projected his own dilemma onto the situation that Robinson mastered so gracefully. The main difference, in Davis's mind, was that he had become incapable of defending himself. That much he would learn from the boxer. "Sugar Ray Robinson inspired me and made me kick a habit," Davis said twenty years later. "I said, 'If that mother can win all those fights, I can sure break this motherfuckin' habit.' I went home, man, and sat up for two weeks and I sweated it out." Of Robinson's example he says, "Man, he didn't know it [that he inspired the cure, but] when he started training, he wouldn't make it with chicks. He disciplined himself and all that." He was exactly the model that Davis needed.

If it took Robinson's example to show him the self-discipline he needed, it was Max Roach who goaded him into using it. In the aftermath of his argument with the bartender at The Lighthouse, Davis berated Roach bitterly, and Roach, who had already put up with him at close quarters for a long time, tried his best to placate him. "Max Roach gave me $200 and put it in my pocket, say I looked good," Davis told Cheryl McCall. The money and flattery did not placate him at all; they just made him angrier. "I said that motherfucker gave me $200, told me I looked good, and I'm fucked up and he knows it. And he's my best friend, right? It just *embarrassed* me to death. I looked in the mirror and I said, Goddam it, Miles, come on." Davis left California immediately and headed for his father's farm near East St. Louis. Doc Davis was waiting for him when he arrived. "We walked out in the pasture," Davis recalls, "and he said, 'If you were with a woman and the woman left you, I would know what to tell you; you could get another woman. But this you have to do by yourself, you know that, 'cause you have been around drugs all your life. You know what you have to do.'"

Davis knew very well. He cured himself with the most primitive, and most successful, therapy of all, by locking himself in his bedroom at the farmhouse and suffering while the demons of his addiction contended inside him. For almost two weeks he lay in the darkened room. Once in a while the maid would ask him if he wanted some food sent in and he would shout back, "*Get* outta here," but the rest of the time he lay there in silence, because, he told McCall, "my father was next door and I was sure not gonna let him hear me holler and scream." He described the cure for Marc Crawford in *Ebony*: "I made up my mind I was getting off dope. I was sick and tired of it. You know you can get tired of anything. You can even get tired of being scared. I laid down and stared at the ceiling for twelve days and cursed everybody I didn't like. I was kicking it the hard way. It was like a bad case of flu, only worse. I lay in a cold sweat. My nose and eyes ran. I threw up everything I tried to eat. My pores opened up and I smelled like chicken soup. Then it was over."

He needed a period of recuperation after that, a time for working at his music and staying away from his old connections. New York was no good, and Los Angeles was no better. He liked Chicago, of course, and Sonny Rollins had already disappeared into the bowels of America's second city more than once in his attempts to rehabilitate himself, but the temptations in Chicago rivaled those in New York and Los Angeles. Davis chose Detroit, a city with a huge working-class population serving the automobile industry and, not incidentally, with a vital local jazz scene still largely undiscovered beyond the city limits. In the next few years it would not escape discovery, as it turned out such progeny as pianists Hank Jones, Tommy Flanagan, and Barry Harris, brass players Thad Jones, Donald Byrd, and Curtis Fuller, saxophonists Billy Mitchell and Yusef Lateef, bassist Paul Chambers, drummers Oliver Jackson and Elvin Jones, singer Betty Carter, and many others. The local musicians were good, but they were better than they knew. Detroit still had no reputation as a center for jazz, and Davis's residency impressed the locals. He moved into the Bluebird Inn as the guest artist with Billy Mitchell's house band, which also included Tommy Flanagan and Elvin Jones. Guest soloists normally played at the Bluebird for a month at a time, but Davis stayed for several months. Lonnie Hillyer, the trumpeter, was only fourteen, a student of Barry Harris's, as were many of the Detroit musicians, when he first caught sight of Davis in his hometown. "It was an experience for me – impact," Hillyer recalls. "He lived there for a while in Detroit. I was impressed with all the things kids are usually impressed with – personality as well as the playing, the whole thing, you know, the manner, know what I mean? Appearances – all the glamorous things. Jazz people are the smartest people in the community. They always seem to be a little ahead of everybody else. You have to be *equipped*." Whether or not Davis was equipped when he arrived in Detroit, he certainly was after a few months there. His playing became confident again, he worked out several new compositions, and he lost the desire for drugs as well as the dependence on them. As soon as spring arrived, he felt the need to move back to New York where he could renew the career he had walked out on.

For Davis the years of heroin addiction were over, and only the scars remained. The needle tracks on his arm faded soon enough, but perhaps there were deeper scars, left over from wounds that were never so visible. To someone such as Babs Gonzales, who has watched the healing process more times than he can count, those scars seem obvious. "Miles came from a prosperous upper middle-class home and was even spoiled a little as a boy," Gonzales reasons. "Therefore there doesn't seem to be any reason for the suspicion he has toward people, right? But he knew some grim times before all this success. For one thing, when he was strung out on heroin – and he's one of the very few who broke the habit all by himself, completely without treatment – Miles was desperate enough to fall in with some pitiless people. Some of them exploited him musically, made him play for very little bread, but he badly needed that little bread. Also, the hoods who ran the jazz clubs in New York used to beat up on Miles and Bud Powell and other musicians who were strung out and in hock to them. Miles has always been a proud man, and while they didn't break him, they hurt him for a long time. Ever since then he's been leery about everybody. With exceptions – and they never know who they'll be."

But if Davis's suspicious, sometimes erratic behavior dates from his addiction, to him it must seem a small price to pay. "I ought to be dead from just what I went through when I was on dope," he says. Before, during, and after his days as an addict, he has often found himself surrounded by musicians who are killing themselves by degrees with narcotics. Only a few of them have been more than nodding acquaintances of his once they leave the bandstand for the evening.

With narcotics no longer occupying most of his waking hours or sapping his strength, Davis found himself on a creative peak that he would sustain unbroken for six years. Jazz, or any other art form, has seldom known anything comparable to such sustained invention over such a long period, but Davis himself sees it as nothing more than substituting a real narcotic for a more ephemeral one. "Music," he said, years later, "is an addiction."

6

Walkin'
1954–5

Miles Davis has reached back two generations and brought a seminal style up to date. More than any other player, Miles Davis echoes Louis Armstrong; one can hear it, I think, in his reading of almost any standard theme. And behind his jaded stance, beneath the complaints, and beneath the sometimes blasé sophistication, Miles Davis's horn also echoes something of Armstrong's exuberantly humorous, forcefully committed, and self-determined joy.   Martin Williams

It was a strangely formless musical scene that Miles Davis moved back into in New York in the spring of 1954. It had been a few years, of course, since he had participated fully in that scene, and in those few years several tendencies had taken a decisive turn. The longtime leaders were no longer leading. Charlie Parker was suffering musically as well as physically; his erratic behavior caused him to miss almost as many engagements as he showed up for and often to play terribly when he did show up. The managers of Birdland, the club that had been named for him, would finally ban him after an onstage shouting match with the ailing Bud Powell, and many of his most fervent followers of a few years before had begun drifting away. Dizzy Gillespie, although as healthy and technically proficient as ever, was playing many of the same tunes in the same arrangements he had played ten years earlier, and while no one else played them as well, listeners were looking elsewhere. The West Coast school, with its roots in the Davis nonet and the post-swing bands, attracted the jazz as well as the popular press, and its proponents moved in to take more than an even share of the jobs from the old pros in New York. The same currents that fostered the West Coast school's popularity were also at work in the rest of the country. In New York, people were beginning to notice the band that billed itself as the Modern Jazz Quartet, a cooperative unit made up of John Lewis, Milt Jackson, Percy Heath, and Kenny

Clarke (who would be replaced the next year by Connie Kay). Under Lewis's direction, the MJQ played fastidiously arranged chamber jazz. Their glossy facade allowed the admirers of West Coast jazz to identify with them, but behind the facade, and almost unnoticed in the first waves of enthusiasm they felt, lurked more substantial roots in the blues that made their music more durable than most. The academic strain of Lennie Tristano and his student-followers continued to draw attention, as did the George Shearing Quintet, which spawned more than a few combos riding the crest of popularity on pretty, quasi-jazz ensemble sounds, including such groups as the Australian Jazz Quartet, the Calvin Jackson Quartet, and many others now forgotten.

While no one would deny that some good musicians were involved in the new developments, many musicians complained that the music had become *too* cool – too effete and emotionless. "Musically speaking, the cool period always reminded me of white people's music," Dizzy Gillespie said, decades later. "There was no guts in that music, not much rhythm either. They never sweated on the stand, Lee Konitz, Lennie Tristano, and those guys. This music, jazz, is guts. You're supposed to sweat in your balls in this music. I guess the idea was not to get 'savage' with it, biting, like we were. But that's jazz to me. Jazz to me is dynamic, a blockbuster. They sorta softened it up a bit, but the depth of the music didn't change. Because we had the depth already. You couldn't get too much deeper than Charlie Parker." As for Davis's role as the patriarch of cool music, Gillespie recognized that Davis was no longer truly represented by the music that went by that name. "Miles wasn't cool like that, anyway," he said. "Miles is from that part of St. Louis where the blues come from. Just part of his music is played like that, cool. They copped that part – the cool – but let the rest, the blues, go, or they missed it."

No one knew that better, of course, than Davis himself. Returning to New York full of creative energy, having been humbled in so many ways by club owners and audiences and reader's polls in the past few years, he was ready to declare emphatically that the bebop revolution was not finished, that emotion or guts or whatever one cared to call it belonged in the music no matter how literate its players might have become, and that the music of the present needed to draw on, not turn away from, the great music of the recent past. As usual, he was not inclined to discuss such matters, but his music of the period leaves no doubt about his convictions. Whether or not he believed he would find an audience is impossible to guess. After being practically written off for the previous few years, he must have known that he would have to struggle to regain his audience. He was certainly prepared. With his confidence intact, he played with a new intensity and produced a string of recordings in 1954–5 with moments of great brilliance.

They were only the buildup for what he would accomplish in the second half of the decade, but they crystallized his own mature style and convincingly subverted the more effete aspects of the cool style.

His first recordings back in New York were for Blue Note, early in March. Davis approached Alfred Lion, Blue Note's owner, soon after he resettled and made arrangements for a recording date with a rhythm trio. The details are as follows:

Miles Davis Quartet
Miles Davis, tpt; Horace Silver, pno; Percy Heath, b; Art Blakey, dms. New York, 6 March 1954
Well You Needn't; Lazy Susan; Weirdo [Sid's Ahead]; The Leap; Take off; It Never Entered My Mind
(all on United Artists UAS 9952)

In Percy Heath and Art Blakey, Davis chose rhythm players with whom he had often been associated before, but in Horace Silver he found an important new piano stylist. Silver, who was twenty-three, had been around New York for almost four years, playing in bands lead by Stan Getz and Lester Young, among others, but he remained virtually unknown because he had not found enough opportunities to record. He and Blakey knew one another well, and their musical partnership remained close for a few more years after these recordings, notably in the first edition of Blakey's successful band called the Jazz Messengers, formed about a year later with Silver as the piano player. Silver's presence on Davis's Blue Note date and also on his next three recording sessions during this prolific spring gave him exactly the kind of exposure he needed. His immediate blossoming as a major young talent further enhanced Davis's reputation as a jazz mentor, although more than a little luck was involved in bringing the two men together.

When Davis moved back to New York he lived at first in a hotel on 25th Street, and Silver happened to be living in the same hotel. They got to know one another because Silver had a piano and Davis needed to use it. "I had a little upright piano in my room and Miles used to come in all the time and play it," Silver remembers. It was inevitable that they would talk about music and natural that Silver would become Davis's student. "I learned a lot of things from him about music," Silver says. "He's a hell of a teacher." Silver was obviously an able student, because he became Davis's regular piano player for the time being. By the end of the year, partly as a result of Silver's playing on these recordings, he would be named the New Star on piano in Down Beat's international poll of critics.

On the Blue Note session, Silver is clearly under the influence of Davis, especially when he submerges his already considerable individuality to play in Thelonious Monk's style on *Well You Needn't* and to play conventional ballad accompaniment on *It Never Entered My Mind*. (Conventional though it was, the latter ballad was effectively incorporated into Ralph Burns's soundtrack for the 1974 movie *Lennie*, starring Dustin Hoffman, a melodrama about the ill-starred monologist Lennie Bruce; Burns also used *Well You Needn't* from this session and *Tempus fugit*, the 1953 recording by Miles Davis for Blue Note, in his soundtrack.) Silver's style shows up better on the other four tracks, as he strings together blues-tinged phrases with a facile right hand while the left hand ventures neat, occasional chords almost imperceptibly. The essentials of that style would soon be adopted by dozens of other piano players.

Davis's selection of *Well You Needn't*, one of a dozen or more Monk themes that are among the treasures of post-war jazz, seems almost calculated to redress some of the problems that Davis had so recently put behind him, for this was the tune that Davis and the tenor duo of Sonny Rollins and Charlie (Chan) Parker had failed to make into a presentable version for Prestige a little more than a year earlier. This time, it is more than simply presentable, as a restrained romp sustained by Silver's oblique, splayed imitation of Monk's pianistics. *Lazy Susan*, *The Leap*, and *Take off*, all written by Davis, have their moments too, notably Heath's and Silver's repeated figure in stop time on *Take off* and Davis's decidedly un-cool staccato bursts on *The Leap*. But it is the other Davis composition, *Weirdo*, that stands out. Recorded again in 1958 by his sextet under the title *Sid's Ahead*, *Weirdo* consists of a single declamatory phrase with harmonic variants. As a compositional technique, the phrase and variants soon become characteristic of Davis's best work, showing up time and again in his original compositions. Simple though it is, it provides a versatile framework for what is essentially an improvised art form, the declamatory statement functioning as a kind of proclamation that opens and closes the improvised core and at the same time establishes the mood or context of the improvisations. *Weirdo/Sid's Ahead* is also interesting as a compositional sketch based on the more elaborate *Walkin'*, a composition originally credited to Davis but later correctly credited to Richard Carpenter, which would be given its first and definitive recorded statement by Davis just a few weeks later. The comparative simplicity of *Weirdo* may have been dictated by the limits of the quartet format, but it is nonetheless a virtuous simplicity, as Martin Williams has observed: "In this piece, Davis has abstracted his theme of *Walkin'* and reduced it to an essence of three notes, and he has done it so brilliantly as to make the delightfully original *Walkin'* seem overdecorative." The virtue of musical simplicity has been one of Davis's main themes, both in theory and practice, throughout his career.

Just four days after the Blue Note recordings, Davis returned to the studios, this time for Prestige, with exactly the same rhythm trio, to record two more original compositions and a ballad. This session was his first installment on a new three-year recording contract he had signed with Prestige, a long-term commitment he would come to regret, and the previous Blue Note session had been hastily arranged in order to squeeze in an extra payday before the new contract took effect. Although the sponsoring labels are different, this session is a continuation of the one before it. The details are as follows:

Miles Davis Quartet
Miles Davis, tpt; Horace Silver, pno; Percy Heath, b; Art Blakey, dms. New York, 10 March 1954
Four; That Old Devil Moon; Blue Haze
(all on Prestige LP 7054; reissued on Prestige 7822)

Davis's only concession to his new employers was in saving *Four* for them instead of recording it for Blue Note. A jazz classic, *Four* remained in Davis's repertoire for twelve years and received several other renditions from his own later quintets (*Four* played by five, as it were) as well as by other musicians, including one notable version by Sonny Rollins backed only by bass and drums (*Four* by three, reissued on Quintessence QJ-25241). One of the compositions most closely associated with Davis's name, *Four* has recently been claimed by Eddie (Cleanhead) Vinson, who says that he gave Davis permission to record both it and another of his themes, *Tune up* (first recorded by Davis in May 1953), and then stood silently for more than two decades as both tunes appeared and reappeared in new versions and reissues crediting Davis as the composer. Vinson, now known as a good blues saxophone player, was then more highly regarded as a blues singer and could not use *Four* and *Tune up* in his own recording sessions. Davis remains their credited composer, and both bear his imprint, fairly or not, in the jazz canon. On the original recording, the tune is taken at a slightly slower tempo than it was usually given later, and it has a mellow feel.

Little else of real consequence came out of the Prestige session, probably because Davis had used up so many of his resources so recently for Blue Note. His arrangement of *That Old Devil Moon* tinkers with its song form, imposing stop time on its three A sections and breaking into 4/4 swing only for the B section. The device encodes the melody attractively enough, but it is also sustained throughout the improvisations as well, and the playing seems to get bogged down in the artifice of the form. *Blue Haze* is a standard blues, introduced by Percy Heath's walking bass line for two choruses. Its title comes from the fact that it was recorded with the studio lights turned off as the players improvised in the reflected light from the control booth.

Only a little more than three weeks later, Davis was back again recording for Prestige, this time with Kenny Clarke replacing Blakey, and with an alto saxophonist named Dave Schildkraut added to make the group a quintet:

Miles Davis All Stars
Miles Davis, tpt; Dave Schildkraut, as (except on *You Don't Know What Love Is*);
Horace Silver, pno; Percy Heath, b; Kenny Clarke, dms. New York, 3 April 1954
Solar; You Don't Know What Love Is; Love Me Or Leave Me; I'll Remember April
(first three titles on Prestige 7608; the fourth on Prestige 7054)

The aural evidence suggests that Schildkraut's presence was not particularly welcomed by Davis or the others. He is treated as an appendage to the proceedings, given little contact with the rest of the ensemble on any of the three titles on which he plays. His role in the arranged parts is restricted to playing a simple riff on *Love Me Or Leave Me* and *I'll Remember April*, and even that he plays very tentatively. As a veteran of several big bands including those of Buddy Rich, Stan Kenton, and Pete Rugolo, Schildkraut was certainly a more proficient player than he appears to be on this session, which might otherwise have given his career a boost. He was known at the time only as an imitator of Charlie Parker; in the original notes accompanying these records, Ira Gitler refers to him as "an ornithologist." The music shows that Schildkraut's rote recitation of set phrases, even if the phrases did originate with Parker, cannot add up to an effective solo. Dick Katz, the pianist and critic whose commentary on Davis's work of this period for the *Jazz Review* remains among the most perceptive critiques on any jazzman, notes that Schildkraut, whom he calls "a very gifted but erratic player," "sounds ill at ease, and there is a lack of rapport between the two horns." As a result, Katz concludes, "The session is notable mainly as a superb example of Kenny Clarke's brushwork." It is certainly that, but it is also a superb example of Davis's use of the muted trumpet. Curiously, Clarke stays with brushes and Davis with the mute throughout the entire session, even on the uptempo pieces, *Love Me Or Leave Me* and *I'll Remember April*. Neither of them suffers noticeably for the self-imposed restriction, although it must have made the tunes harder to manage for both of them. Even more striking than anything in the musicians' performances at this session, the most positive result was the exposition of the moody *Solar*, yet another stunning original composition by Davis, with a beautiful melody based on the chord structure of *How High the Moon*. Although Davis seems to have neglected *Solar* as soon as it was satisfactorily recorded, other musicians have rediscovered it over the years and given it the airing it deserves.

All of Davis's hours of recording activity in the spring of 1954 seem like little more than a warm-up for the session he produced in the Prestige studios later in April. He returned this time with a sextet, including the same rhythm team of Silver, Heath, and Clarke, by now a cohesive unit accustomed to the way Davis worked in the studio. To them he added his occasional front-line partner for many years, J.J. Johnson, and the tenor saxophonist Lucky Thompson, with whom he had recorded on Charlie Parker's first Dial session, in California in 1946. The ideas for this remarkable session were worked out in advance on Silver's upright piano in the hotel. (Silver adds that Davis did not own a trumpet and had to borrow one for the recording date; the borrowed trumpet belonged to Jules Colomby, and it leaked, but it certainly did not hinder him at all.) In some intangible way, the mix of musicians and music for this session worked perfectly, and the result, amounting to twenty-one and a half minutes on two titles, is a classic jazz performance. Dick Katz called it "artistic and of lasting value," and Whitney Balliett, reviewing the first appearance of this music on a twelve-inch disc in 1957, noted that it includes "some of the best jazz improvisations set down in the past decade."

There is, however, even more to this music than just the sum of its excellent solos, as numerous critics have pointed out. Martin Williams remarked that "in these excellent performances, so immediately effective even at a casual listening, there is going on a reassessment of the materials, the devices, and the aims of jazz." Ralph J. Gleason agreed, and added that the reassessment was overdue: "As part of the reaction in the years following World War II, jazz seemed lost in the ethereal clouds of intellectualism, its roots no longer in the blues, shaped instead by the specter of European orthodoxy. With one record, *Walkin'*, Miles Davis changed all that and brought back lyricism and melody (and the blues) to jazz. In the same motion he reaffirmed that one could play pretty and still play jazz. It seems unlikely that jazz will ever forget the lessons it has learned from Miles Davis." Frank Kofsky hears *Walkin'* as "the clarion call of the hard bop movement," referring to the revitalization and broadening of the style inaugurated by Parker, Gillespie, Powell, and the other leaders of the bebop revolution that came in the wake of these recordings. "As cool grew increasingly inbred and passionless, its inability to fashion a music of any emotional substance emerged with greater and greater clarity, especially when juxtaposed against the infinitely more demonstrative and muscular hard bop styles," Kofsky wrote. "The massive shift in taste that was heralded by Miles Davis's *Walkin'* in 1954 soon made it clear that all but a few cool stylists had fallen permanently from public favor." Kofsky probably overstates the destructive effect of the revaluation on cool jazz, but not the positive effect of this session on jazz in general. It had, as James Lincoln Collier put it, "a measurable effect on both musicians and the jazz public." The details are as follows:

Miles Davis All Star Sextet
Miles Davis, tpt; J.J. Johnson, tbn; Lucky Thompson, ts; Horace Silver, pno; Percy Heath, b; Kenny Clarke, dms. New York, 29 April 1954
Blue 'n' Boogie; Walkin'
(both on Prestige 7608)

Davis's revival of *Blue 'n' Boogie*, a piece written by Dizzy Gillespie in 1945 and perhaps not played by Davis since he worked with Charlie Parker in Los Angeles in 1946, suggests that his reappraisal of the recent past in these recordings was entirely deliberate, because the theme is itself a bebopper's abstraction of an old barroom swing style. To listeners aware of the recent history of jazz, Davis's new version reverberates with multiple reflections, his 1954 sextet adapting Gillespie's 1945 adaptation of, say, a 1936 Kansas City blowing session. Davis quite literally filters the blues through bebop into a new style, to be called hard bop or neo-bop in the years to come. Dick Katz described the session as a seminar: "*Walkin'* and its companion *Blue 'n' Boogie* are acknowledged to be classics. To me they represent a sort of summing up of much of what happened musically to the players involved during the preceding ten years (1944–54). It's as if all agreed to get together and discuss on their instruments what they had learned and unlearned, what elements of bop they had retained or discarded. An amazing seminar took place."

The use of Lucky Thompson also underlines Davis's purpose, because Thompson, although only two years older than Davis, had modeled his tone and his approach on pre-bop saxophonists. His opening chorus on *Walkin'* reminds the listener, probably deliberately, of Ben Webster, even to the breathy vibrato. Yet Thompson is completely comfortable playing bebop, and he spent most of his career doing just that. His presence here is another multiple reflection.

The reflections do not end there. Katz discerns another ghostly undertone in Davis's voice on *Blue 'n' Boogie*. "Miles's spelling out of triads and general diatonic approach is reminiscent of early and middle Armstrong," he says. "Further, his precise, split-second sense of timing and swing are not unlike those of the early master. Each is a master of economy – few, if any, of their notes are superfluous. Of course, there the comparison stops. The feelings and conception each projects couldn't be more different – for obvious reasons – age being one and Miles's much larger musical vocabulary being another."

Comments such as these risk emphasizing the historical significance and neglecting the music itself, but no commentator is likely to ignore it for long. Especially in *Walkin'*, it is memorable, swinging, free; it is, as Martin Williams says, "immediately effective even at a casual listening," and its effect does not depend on knowledge about the state of the art in jazz on the day it was recorded. Amid a wealth of superior performances, Davis's blues on *Walkin'* is singled out for special plaudits. "Davis's solo work exhibits all the earmarks of his style: it is hesitant, tentative, spare," James Lincoln Collier says; "Davis's style was now mature, the influences melded into a single, unified and unique conception. Both musicians and audiences responded to it immediately." Katz says: "Miles's solo is as good as any he has recorded, before or since. His sound ideas and execution, and the feelings he projects are prime examples of his art. Every idea that Miles states here is clearly formed and will stay with the listener afterwards." For Davis, *Walkin'* and *Blue 'n' Boogie* proclaimed emphatically that he had returned to the forefront of jazz.

In May, still months before *Walkin'* would be heard by the public, Davis's status received another boost with the release of the first significant collection of the nonet sides. Capitol finally put eight of the twelve recordings on a single ten-inch LP called *Birth of the Cool* (Capitol 459), a title that has been attached to all later releases and that immediately became the jazz fans' catchword for all the nonet's studio recordings. *Jeru*, *Godchild*, *Israel*, and *Venus de Milo*, until then available only as 78 rpm records, were included in the collection, along with *Rouge*, *Moon Dreams*, *Rocker*, and *Deception*, released for the first time. Three of the uncollected titles, *Budo*, *Move*, and *Boplicity*, had been released in separate anthologies by Capitol in 1952 and 1953 and were left out because they were still available. Their omission was unfortunate, since they are, with *Israel*, the very best of the nonet's recordings. They were not collected alongside the other eight titles for three more years, when *Birth of the Cool* (Capitol 762) was issued as a twelve-inch LP. The complete set of twelve titles, including Kenny Hagood's vocal on Gil Evans's arrangement of *Darn That Dream*, was collected on a single LP only in 1971, by Capitol's Dutch subsidiary (*The Complete Birth of the Cool*, Capitol M-11026). This piecemeal and disorganized release schedule was caused partly by the low artistic esteem in which jazz has generally been held, which makes the notion of an artist's oeuvre almost laughable to many American recording executives, and partly by the peripheral involvement of Capitol Records in jazz, which has meant that its managers, even more ignorant about jazz than most, did not understand the value of what they were burying in their vaults. But it was also caused partly by the confusing and rapid technological advances in the recording industry at the very moment when the nonet recordings were mastered. In little more than a decade, beginning in the late 1940s, the recording industry moved from wax masters of three-minute performances to acetate (tape) masters of longer performances pressed on microgroove vinyl, and from single (monaural) microphone placement to mike separation (high fidelity) and finally to multi-tracking (stereophonic). The variety of forms that the various titles of the nonet's recordings went through reflects some of the confusion in the industry, and especially at Capitol, during that decade. Still, the collection of eight titles in May 1954, even without the strengths of *Boplicity*, *Move*, and *Budo*, made available the evidence of Davis's considerable accomplishment in the recent past. *Birth of the Cool* helped to fix the attention of jazz listeners on him at a time when he was poised to reveal a great deal more to them.

Davis had put together the rhythm section that he felt could carry his revitalized music to new heights. Horace Silver and Percy Heath had been his constant accompanists since he returned to New York, and, after he tried Art Blakey on a couple of sessions, Kenny Clarke was established as his drummer. They comprised an excellent unit, and even though good bookings were still hard to come by for Davis, he began thinking about putting together his own band. Just as he had no doubt about whom he wanted in his rhythm section, so he knew whom he wanted to share the front line with him. Sonny Rollins, whose commanding stature was matched by a commanding tone, the perfect foil for Davis's delicate sound, had been his first choice for years and would continue so long after it became clear that he would never accept a permanent commitment to Davis's band. In mid-1954, Davis still hoped that Rollins would join his band, when he was in a position to put a band together. A preview of what that band might accomplish came when Davis led this quintet into the recording studio two months after the *Walkin'* session. The results were excellent:

Miles Davis Quintet
Miles Davis, tpt; Sonny Rollins, ts; Horace Silver, pno; Percy Heath, b; Kenny Clarke, dms. New York, 29 June 1954
Airegin; Oleo; But Not for Me (two takes); *Doxy*
(all on Prestige LP 7109; reissued [1970] on Prestige 7847)

This time, none of the compositions was Davis's own. The three originals, *Airegin* (Nigeria spelled backwards), *Oleo*, and *Doxy*, are all by Sonny Rollins. *Airegin*'s infectious bop melody is introduced by Rollins playing a vamp, reminiscent of some of Dizzy Gillespie's pieces. *Oleo*, also bop-oriented, is based on the chord changes of *I Got Rhythm*. (Its title comes from the name of the butter substitute, oleo margarine, which was then being marketed in the United States for the first time.) The arrangement modifies the piano's role by having Silver play only on the bridge all through the piece; in the statement of the melody, the unison line, played by muted trumpet and tenor saxophone, stops while Silver enters to play eight bars with the rhythm; throughout the piece Silver returns to accompany Davis and Rollins only during the bridge of their solos. In constraining the piano player in this way, Davis gives an early example of a device he would later use occasionally with Red Garland and Herbie Hancock. One advantage of having the piano player lay out on *Oleo* is that Percy Heath takes the responsibility for comping (that is, playing accompaniment) throughout, thus making a brilliant exposition of his abilities even on a session where he does not solo at all. The general advantage of having the piano player lay out is that the pianoless accompaniment loosens the ensembles and permits the soloist a broader range of choices than he has when the pianist feeds him harmonies.

Doxy is a sixteen-bar melody with a basic blues feeling, the kind of uncomplicated jazz melody then beginning to be described as funky. The term seemed especially apt for the style of Horace Silver, and Silver's playing on *Doxy* and similar pieces soon made him a favorite among both musicians and fans.

George Gershwin's *But Not for Me* – at first glance just a good pop song chosen to fill out the session – attracted Davis's attention because it was featured in the repertoire of a pianist named Ahmad Jamal, whose trio was beginning to be heard in supper clubs in Chicago and New York. While Jamal never seemed to win the approval of jazz reviewers, his particular genius was soon recognized by many musicians, and by none more forcibly than Davis. In short order, Jamal would become Davis's final formative influence in the line from Elwood Buchanan through Freddie Webster and Dizzy Gillespie to Gil Evans and the other members of his 55th Street salon. In 1954, Jamal's influence on Davis was still nascent, but Davis's selection of his signature ballad is meaningful. The first take, at a sprightly tempo close to the one at which Jamal plays it, seems somehow rushed when played by Davis's quintet, and the second take, at a slower tempo, succeeds much better, in spite of Rollins's squeaking reed. The issue of both takes led Dick Katz to comment, "I don't see the point in releasing both takes of *But Not For Me*. For celebrated performances the documentary value of such releases is real, but in this case, neither take is up to the standard of the rest of the date." Nevertheless, the two takes are different and add to the scant documentation on what might have been intended as Davis's first working quintet.

If Davis did hope to make a permanent band of these men, he was destined to be disappointed. Heath and Clarke were committed to the Modern Jazz Quartet. When Clarke gave up his commitment to the MJQ, it was because he was disillusioned with the situation of the jazz musician in America, and in 1956, a year after leaving the MJQ, he departed for France, where he has lived and worked ever since. Heath never left the MJQ, staying with it until it disbanded in 1974. Silver, the youngest man in the rhythm section, joined Art Blakey's new band, the Jazz Messengers, when it was formed in 1955; his growing reputation, based partly on his work with Davis in 1954, later made it possible for him to lead his own band.

The quintet that Davis led into the Prestige studios in June could have been a scintillating jazz band if they had become a working unit. Judging by their one recording session, they might eventually have become as good as the quintet that Davis finally formed as his working group a year later, in 1955.

Davis was still in no position to support a working band. Notwithstanding his recovery of technique after the years of faltering and the superb taste with which he was now playing, he still had some dues to pay for the neglect of his art. He was temperamentally incapable of helping his cause either by promoting his music in any conventional way or by making a public display of his renewed dedication to it. Long gone were the days when he would introduce titles or sidemen on stage as he had, for instance, at the Paris Jazz Festival in 1949, before his addiction. To some members of the audiences who turned out to hear him as he traveled around playing guest spots, he appeared hostile. To club owners and managers, he appeared disdainful.

Even when his musical reputation was fully restored, his aloofness and his candor brought sharp criticism, although by then it was inevitably mixed with grudging respect. In the mid-1950s, when he needed and deserved a few breaks, the criticism was not tempered with respect. Around this time, a booking agent told Nat Hentoff: "He's basically not a nice guy. His conversation, when he bothers to talk to you at all, is made up mainly of insults. That sonofabitch is bad for jazz. He doesn't give a damn for audiences, and he lets them know it by paying no attention to them. I mean you don't have to wave a handkerchief or show your teeth like Louis Armstrong to let the audience feel you care what they think about your music. But not him." In refusing to make any concessions, he was serving notice that his success would be on his own terms. The front that he showed to audiences and managers was often belied by the music he made for them, with its growing sensitivity and undeniable grace. The critic Dan Morgenstern has said: "Those who know him at all well have found him a generous, kind man whose true self is not revealed by his flamboyant, provocative behavior, but rather by the introspective, complex, often shifting style of his music." But very few people were allowed to see the man behind the music. Davis has been, as Babs Gonzales said, "leery about everybody. With exceptions – and they never know who they'll be."

Even Thelonious Monk proved to be no exception. During a remarkable recording session led by Davis late in the year the two men clashed with such bitterness that the session has become almost as famous as the brilliant music that it produced. The occasion was Christmas eve, and the place was, as usual, Rudy Van Gelder's recording studio in Hackensack, New Jersey. Davis had lined up an all-star band that was billed in all the releases as the Modern Jazz Giants. Percy Heath and Kenny Clarke were among them, along with a third member of the

MJQ, Milt Jackson, and Monk. The session started between 2 and 3 p.m., but by the time Ira Gitler, Prestige's consultant for the session, left for dinner, "not much had been accomplished." Gitler had persuaded the producer, Bob Weinstock, to allow Davis to include Monk's composition *Bemsha Swing* in the day's repertoire. Davis wanted to include it to placate Monk, who was disgruntled because Davis was insisting that Monk should not play behind Davis's solos on the other titles.

Monk brooded throughout the afternoon, which was spent on rehearsals, and when the recording began he became more uncooperative. He found the idea of laying out during Davis's solos humiliating, and as he grew more disruptive he prompted some unfriendly exchanges with the others, especially Davis. At the beginning of the first take of *The Man I Love*, during Milt Jackson's introductory bars, Monk suddenly interjects, "When'm I supposed to come in, man?" The music stops abruptly and the others groan ("Ohhh!"; "Oh no!" and other assorted noises are heard), and one of them says, "Man, the cat's cutting hisself." Monk, in a kind of a whine, says, "I don't know when to come in, man. Can't I start too? Everybody else – ." But Davis cuts him off and calls to Van Gelder in the control booth, "Hey, Rudy, put this on the record – *all* of it." It is on the record, and so is a brief, indecipherable exchange of unpleasantries between Monk and Davis during Monk's solo on the second take of *The Man I Love*. It was rumored that Davis ended up punching Monk, but he did not. When Gitler asked Monk about it later, Monk said, "Miles'd got killed if he hit me." In spite of the discord, or perhaps because of it, some magnificent music was made, by Monk no less than by the others.

The musicians knew that their work that day was superior and that the tension contributed to the result. When Gitler met Kenny Clarke at Minton's later that evening and asked how the session had gone after he left, Clarke said, simply, "Miles sure is a beautiful cat." The British critic Raymond Horricks, writing in the late 1950s, calls these "four of the most inspired jazz performances of the decade." The passage of time has hardly dulled them, especially *Bags' Groove* and *The Man I Love*, both of which survive in two complete takes and both of which remain outstanding examples of the improvisers' art.

That such results could be attained by five musicians who did not come out of a stable, working band seems paradoxical, but these circumstances were so regularly part of the professional jazzman's life that the musicians had to devise ways of coping with it. One way is what André Hodeir calls a "prepared jam session": "One can imagine a good many intermediate stages between the small improvising group whose members are closely united by long experience playing together, and the true jam session in which the participants hardly know one another. There is, for example, the 'prepared jam session,' so called because the musicians involved form a well-defined group and because the music displays structural qualities usually lacking in a true jam session. Here the musicians use introductions and codas that have become traditional with them. Most of the so-called blowing sessions ('just come and blow') recorded during the past few years belong to this category, which has produced some of the greatest masterpieces of jazz, like Miles Davis's famous *Bags' Groove*, with Thelonious Monk, Milt Jackson, Percy Heath and Kenny Clarke." The details of this famous session are as follows:

Miles Davis and the Modern Jazz Giants
Miles Davis, tpt; Milt Jackson, vib; Thelonious Monk, pno; Percy Heath, b; Kenny Clarke, dms. New York, 24 December 1954
Bags' Groove (two takes); *Bemsha Swing; Swing Spring; The Man I Love* (two takes)
(*Bags' Groove* [both takes] on Prestige 7109; all others on Prestige 7150; the complete session available on Prestige PR 7650 [1969])

Bags' Groove, Milt Jackson's celebratory blues (Jackson's nickname is Bags), went through two complete takes, with the first one usually considered slightly superior. Of Davis's solo on the first take, Dick Katz wrote: "Miles's solo is near perfect – a beautiful, unfolding set of memorable ideas, each a springboard for the next. His sound or tone has a real vocal-like quality of expression. His interpretation of the blues here is deeply convincing, and it is without exaggerated 'funk'. He establishes a mood and sustains it." Whitney Balliett notes that it is on medium-tempo blues such as *Bags' Groove* that "Davis is capable of creating a pushing, middle-of-the-road lyricism that is a remarkable distillation, rather than a one-two-three outlining of the melodic possibilities; indeed, what comes out of his horn miraculously seems the result of the instantaneous editing of a far more diffuse melodic line being carried on in his head." As for Davis's making Monk sit silently throughout his solo, Katz says, "His purported rejection of Monk's services as an accompanist is irrelevant. The end result is superb. And when Jackson enters with Monk behind him, the contrast is strikingly effective." Whatever feelings Monk may have been harboring certainly did not affect his own solo adversely. "Monk's solo is one of his best on record," Katz maintains. "By an ingenious use of space and rhythm, and by carefully controlling a single melodic idea, he builds a tension that is not released until the end of his solo." Balliett agrees that "Monk is superb. In the first version his solo is broken by such long pauses that it appears he has left the studio; then he suddenly resumes, with clumps of clattering, off-beat dissonances. In the second version, his pressure up, he engages in a dizzy series of jagged runs." Of the second take, Katz says, "Davis's solo contains several 'pops' which sound like saliva in the horn, which mar an otherwise fine solo. Also, this version is not as concentrated as take 1, but Jackson's solo maintains the high level of the first – take your pick. Monk surprises with a completely different solo – different in approach and feeling. Here he is more concerned with playing the *piano*, less with developing a motif, and is much more extravagant with his ideas. A fine solo, but take 1 was exceptional." Most listeners would be hard pressed to choose between the two takes, and fortunately there is no need to choose, because Prestige has always included both in all releases. "In both versions, Davis's solos, which are played on open horn, have an oblique relentlessness and are full of neat, perfectly executed variations," Balliett says, adding, "This is an indispensable record."

On *Bemsha Swing*, the only title on which Monk was permitted to accompany Davis, a stunning exchange takes place at the transition from Davis's solo to Monk's. Davis closes his solo with some patently Monkesque phrases, which are then picked up by Monk and incorporated into his solo. The exchange is open to a number of interpretations, and the reviewers have offered a couple of possibilities. Dick Katz sees it this way: "Miles seems quite distracted by Monk, and it breaks the continuity of his solo. His discomfort is finally expressed by his quoting a couple of well-known Monk phrases. Monk in turn acknowledges Miles's sarcasm (or compliment?) and lo and behold, they end up playing a duet." Stanley Crouch hears it quite differently; according to him, "In order to tell Monk that he loved him even though he wouldn't allow him to play while he was soloing, Davis quotes some Monk licks in the trumpet section that precedes the piano solo. The rankled giant responds by taking the lick and building an incredible solo of virtuosic colors, turns, harmonies and rhythms that seem to say, 'Excuse me, young man, but if you intend to piddle around with my shit, see if you can ever get to *this*!' By no means was Monk to be undone or outdone. He was ready and had been ready for a long, long time." Whether the exchange signaled détente or war, Monk takes a glorious turn. Few of his many excellent recorded solos match this one in its eccentricity. Whitney Balliett, in an entirely unrelated context, remarked that Monk "approaches a keyboard as if it had teeth and he were a dentist." On *Bemsha Swing*, he makes the keyboard sparkle.

Swing Spring, a stately melody by Davis, was prepared for this session and then promptly forgotten by him, if not by his listeners. Four years later, Nat Hentoff played Davis a version of *Swing Spring* recorded in France by Kenny Clarke and a French band with an arrangement by André Hodeir, and Davis felt the shock of recognition. "That's my tune, isn't it?" he exclaimed. "I forgot all about that tune. God damn! Damn! You know, I forgot I wrote that." After hearing the French version, Davis added, "I think I'll make another record of this tune. It was meant to be just like an exercise almost." He then went to the piano and picked out a scale for Hentoff, explaining, "It was based on that scale there and when you blow, you play in that scale and you get an altogether different sound. I got that from Bud Powell; he used to play it all the time." Davis's description reveals

Swing Spring as one of his earliest compositions based on a scale – that is, a modal composition of the type that George Russell had been investigating – rather than on chord changes. The innovation toward modal organization, allowing more freedom of choice for the improvisers than a progression of chord changes, was an inevitable development in jazz history, because the best players had always strained against the strictures of the chordal form. "Virtually all the superior players are never *chained* by the chordal structure of their material," Dick Katz explains. "The chords are merely signposts. The sophistication in Monk, Rollins and Davis lies in the fact that after years of 'making the changes' they now often only imply them, leaving them free to concentrate on other aspects of improvisation, such as expression, rhythm, etc."

From a system where the chords are only implied, it is a short leap to a system where they are ignored altogether, although it took jazz several decades to make that short leap. The leadership in restructuring the formal basis of jazz naturally fell to performing musicians who had gained the sophistication in running changes of which Katz speaks. While George Russell explored the idea of modal composition in jazz academically, it would be Davis who eventually brought it forcefully into the studios and onto the stages. His most influential modal works were still a few years away when *Swing Spring* was recorded, but when Hentoff played Kenny Clarke's version of it for him in 1958, he was already busy writing and recording the modal works that would influence the next generations of jazz musicians. *Swing Spring* played no part in that movement; Davis seems to have forgotten it again soon after Hentoff's reminder, and he never did re-record it.

On *The Man I Love*, a beautiful Gershwin melody, the first take serves as a kind of model for what the second take is expected to be but is not. The first take opens with a ringing introduction by Jackson which provides an entrance for Davis to state the melody; Jackson then doubles the tempo for his own flowing solo, and Monk follows at the same tempo with a staccato solo, based on the stunning device of spreading the melody over twice the number of bars; Davis re-enters and after a chorus halves the tempo again and plays a haunting variation of the melody. By any standard, take 1 is a marvelous ballad performance, mixing moods and atmospheres and individuals but making a single, consistent entity. It seems nearly perfect, but it has been completely overshadowed – in everyone's account – by the second take, in which things go wrong. (I find myself struggling against great odds to maintain a semblance of objectivity about the second take, because it was the first music by Davis that I ever heard. The record belonged to a high school friend, and when we got it home from the record store and put it on the turntable, we were – I can think of no other word that is nearly adequate – transfixed. For weeks afterward we could hardly wait for the final bell at school – there were days when we didn't bother waiting for it – so we could get back to his place and listen to it half a dozen more times before supper. By now I know very well that is not Davis's 'best' record, much less his most significant, most interesting, or most revealing, but to me it remains, after literally hundreds of listenings, every bit as powerful as the first time I heard it.) The basic elements of the second take are the same as those of the first take, but the nuances of their execution add a powerful new element. Dick Katz describes the development: "After a lovely Jackson introduction, Miles unfolds an exceedingly lyrical introduction of the melody. His use of rhythm and his completely original manner of phrasing here should continue to enrich a listener for years. Jackson doubles the tempo with a four-bar break and takes a fine solo which does not quite sustain interest all the way, probably because of its length. Monk follows with the *pièce de résistance* by getting carried away with his own self-made obstacle course. He tries to rearrange the melody rhythmically by extending the sequence over a number of bars. However, he gets lost (or so it seems to me), and comes to an abrupt halt about the 28th bar or so (long meter). What follows is a model duet between Clarke and Heath which could serve as a lesson in graceful walking for anyone. Along about the 14th bar of the bridge, Miles leads Monk back on the track, and he comes roaring in in his best 1947 style. Miles comes in on his heels with a delightful bit and then surprises by quickly jamming a mute into his horn and continuing – an electrifying effect. A return to the original tempo at the bridge halts the discussion between Monk and Miles and the piece ends on a note of agreement."

What happens at the point where Monk suddenly stops playing is not clear. Katz assumes that he "gets lost," and Alun Morgan concurs: "The pianist tried a bold experiment which, seemingly, was doomed to failure. He attempted to spread the original melody over twice the number of bars, and actually succeeds in doing so until he reaches the middle eight ... In the process of collecting his thoughts, Monk allows two or three bars to slip by and Davis, doubtless under the impression that the pianist's departure from convention has caused him to lose his place in the chorus, enters abruptly with an angry-sounding paraphrase of the melody." But both Katz's and Morgan's accounts overlook the fact that Monk had successfully brought off exactly the same rhythmic device just minutes earlier, on the first take. Monk's losing his way on the second take after finding it on the first seems unlikely, and it seems much more probable that he was willing to stop his solo there out of sheer bloody-mindedness. Raymond Horricks apparently hears it that way too. In his description, "Monk unaccountably ended his solo after only half a chorus, leaving Percy Heath to take up the tune in his stead. Miles didn't feel it that way, and at the far end of the studio picked up his horn and blew it irritably for the pianist to come in again. Monk answered the call and the music righted itself." Whatever the cause, the interlude between Monk and Davis sublimates the tension between the two men into musical terms that cannot fail to be felt by any listener.

On Christmas eve in the Van Gelder studios, Miles Davis and the Modern Jazz Giants created music of unusual power, which was partly a sublimation of the tensions among the musicians, especially between Monk and Davis. "Aware that they were on trial before each other musically, both men approached their solos with anxious intent," Horricks says, "and, in effect, unconsciously, they encouraged each other towards greatness as they played. Miles himself blew with the soul, the sensitivity and something of the lyric vision of a poet." Dick Katz puts it much more simply. "This performance would be absolutely impossible to repeat," he says. "God bless Thomas Edison."

A few years after the clash, Nat Hentoff asked Davis about his feelings toward Monk. "Monk has really helped me," Davis said. "When I came to New York, he taught me chords and his tunes. A main influence he has been through the years has to do with giving musicians more freedom. They feel that if Monk can do what he does, they can. Monk has been using space for a long time." About his decision to make Monk lay out when he was soloing, Davis remained unrepentant. "I love the way Monk plays and writes, but I can't stand him behind me. He doesn't give you any support," Davis claims, adding, "Monk writes such pretty melodies and then screws them up." At the time of that interview, in 1958, Davis was at the peak of the line of development that began in the period covered here, and Monk was at the peak of his own commercial success, finally receiving the critical and popular acclaim that he had long deserved, and appearing regularly in New York at the Five Spot. "You have to go down to hear him to really appreciate what he's doing," said Davis, who was a frequent member of the audience at the Five Spot. Davis's great sextet also regularly featured Monk's compositions *Round about Midnight* and *Straight No Chaser*, and Davis told Hentoff that he was interested in adding more Monk compositions to his repertoire. "I'd like to make an album of his tunes if I can ever get him up here," he said. But the two men, the most formidable jazz artists of the 1950s, never recorded together again after the second take of *The Man I Love*.

As the decade reached its mid-point, jazz activity remained diffuse. There was a potential audience for jazz that was growing by leaps and bounds, made up of young, middle-class whites all over North America and Europe. They had been attracted to jazz initially by the West Coast movement, which was nothing if not accessible music. They had sought it out in the first place as an alternative to pop music, which was dominated by talentless chattels like Tommy Sands and Fabian singing three-chord banalities over a chorus of doo-wahs. At the same time, West Coast jazz was wearing a little thin, apart from Dave Brubeck's Quartet with Paul Desmond and Gerry Mulligan's Quartet with valve trombonist Bobby Brookmeyer, neither of which had ever been part of the core of Hollywood studio musicians who played jazz on weekends.

The spirit of the bebop revolution, which had carried along most of the rising young musicians for more than a decade, was finally spent. Its symbol was Charlie Parker, and his capacity for intoxicants and other forms of self-abuse seemed at last to be reached. No longer the messiah capable of preaching his creative message while nodding out, he often appeared as a stumblebum, hardly capable of forming a sentence. Frank Sanderford, Parker's frequent companion for years whenever he played in Chicago, witnessed the decline. "The last time I saw him was at the Beehive in Chicago," Sanderford remembers. "The owner had asked me to get Charlie to go on. He was in a little room where they stored beer. I went back there; Charlie met me at the door and threw his arms around me as if I were the only person in the world. He couldn't go on the stand, he said; he was in no condition. He looked bad. The house was jammed. I asked him to take a look and see how many people had come just to hear him play, and I opened the door a little. He glared out. 'They just want to see the world's most famous junkie,' he growled. I will always be guilty, because I did get him to go on the stand. He made a few, awful bleating sounds. He couldn't play. He was disgusted, afraid, and frustrated somehow. He was a beaten man." .

Charlie Parker died in New York on 12 March 1955, at the age of thirty-five. His death was not wholly unexpected, but it was sudden. He was supposed to be on his way to Boston for a weekend date as a guest soloist but he stopped off instead at the Manhattan apartment of the Baroness Pannonica de Koenigswarter, the jazz patroness, complaining of stomach pains. The baroness summoned her doctor, and when they could not persuade Parker to enter a hospital, they ministered to him in her living room. The news of his death three days later sent shock waves throughout the jazz world, and beyond it. In New York, Babs Gonzales and four of his friends took the subway lines in different directions and left a trail of graffiti proclaiming "Bird lives!" In Paris, David Amram, the composer, conductor, and musicologist who was then best known as a jazz french hornist, was playing a concert with Raymond Fol, Bobby Jaspar, Lars Gullin, and other European jazzmen when he heard the news. "I went backstage," Amram recalls, "and as the other band was finishing their number, someone came running up and said to Raymond, 'Man, did you hear the news?' 'What's that?' Raymond said. 'Charlie Parker is dead.' We all suddenly seemed to shrink. Everyone backstage quieted down. All the heroin and other drugs were quietly put away. People just stood there in silence while the band onstage, oblivious of this terrible news, kept on wailing." When a reporter got in touch with Miles Davis, all he could think to say was, "New York will never be the same without Charlie Parker."

Inexplicably, many people thought about Davis after they had absorbed the news of Parker's death. Perhaps the reason for it was simply that they were dusting off their old Parker records and inevitably replaying the old Dials and Savoys with Davis on them and remembering the excellence of that band. Parker had done the same just before his death, according to Robert Reisner: "Not long before his death, he was standing on a corner, reminiscing and optimistically planning, 'I'll get my old group together, Max and Miles, Duke and Tommy.' And then he, who created so much of the music, said with a laugh, 'If I don't know the tunes, I can learn them.'" It seemed somehow like a natural progression for the leadership to pass from Charlie Parker to Miles Davis.

"I'm sure that Miles considered himself a leader in the new movement, within our movement, because he wasn't that far away from us to be considered 'away,'" Dizzy Gillespie says. "There was a change in the administration of the music, I guess you would call it, a change in the phrasing. The phrasing went a little differently. Phrasing changes every so often, and you can tell what age the music comes from by the way it's played. But Miles only knew what to play from what had gone on before, then he began to find his own identity." It was not only that he knew what went on immediately before. Approaching the full development of his powers, Davis was making a highly personal amalgam of jazz styles both before and after behop. Whitney Balliett says, "His playing sounds predominantly sweet and restrained, yet it conceals, much of the time, the basic hotness of men like Louis Armstrong and Roy Eldridge."

The essential jazz 'feel' of his predecessors, which Davis retained, was the very element that seemed to be threatened in the cool popularizations going on around him, but there was also something entirely new in his playing, and much harder to define. Gil Evans put it this way: "Miles changed the tone of the trumpet for the first time after Louis – the basic tone. Everybody up to him had come through Louis Armstrong, though they might not have sounded exactly like him, as with Roy Eldridge. But then all of a sudden Miles created his own wave form. It became another sound. Miles didn't even realize this, he just knew he had to have a certain sound. I mean you can describe it any way you like, but it's a different sound and the whole world took it over." Listeners who were willing to pay attention could hear the sound in Davis's music for a year before Parker's death; after his death, many more listeners seemed willing to pay attention. The first palpable result was that Davis tied Gillespie in Down Beat's international jazz critics poll as top trumpeter for 1955; an editorial comment maintained that Davis had surfaced in the poll "practically ... from out of nowhere."

In June, Davis again recorded for Prestige, his first recordings since Christmas eve. This time he fronted a quartet, and some significant new faces replaced the rhythm team he had used throughout 1954. Equally significant, though invisible, was the presence in spirit of Ahmad Jamal. The details are as follows:

Miles Davis Quartet
Miles Davis, tpt; Red Garland, pno; Oscar Pettiford, b; Philly Joe Jones, dms. New York, 7 June 1955
I Didn't; Will You Still Be Mine; Green Haze; I See Your Face before Me; A Night in Tunisia; A Gal in Calico
(all on Prestige LP 7007; reissued on Prestige 7221)

A Night in Tunisia might have been intended as homage to the memory of Parker, with whom Davis had recorded this Gillespie composition in 1946, but, if so, it is certainly an oblique gesture, because Davis plays the bop anthem as a wry abstraction, almost a parody of bebop. Another oblique reference occurs on *I Didn't*, a Davis original based on Thelonious Monk's *Well You Needn't*, to which its title forms a reply.

Green Haze contains a reminder in its title of *Blue Haze*, which Davis recorded with another quartet a year earlier, and like it, *Green Haze* is an extended, extemporaneous blues. Whereas the earlier *Haze* with Horace Silver and company was a basic, funky blues, simple and countrified, the new one is sophisticated and urbane. The essential difference seems to emanate from the presence on this one of William (Red) Garland, on piano. Garland, a Texan, had been around New York and Philadelphia for a few years working as a piano player in pick-up bands, often with Philly Joe Jones. He has a light keyboard touch that does not lend itself to percussive playing, even at quick tempos, which led Whitney Balliett to label him "a bright, dandyish pianist," and it was no doubt that touch that first attracted Davis's attention. The two men met through Philly Joe Jones, who recorded with Davis on the unhappy 1953 session that included Charlie Parker as a tenor player. Garland may also have impressed Davis for entirely extramusical reasons, because he once, according to a rumor that has since grown into a legend, made his living as a boxer. Davis discovered also that Garland was not only a very capable piano player but that he was malleable, in contrast to Horace Silver and Monk. Davis now had a very specific notion of how his piano player should sound – like Ahmad Jamal. "Red Garland knew I liked Ahmad and at times I used to ask him to play like that," Davis has said. "Red was at his best when he did."

Jamal's enormous influence on Davis gets its first significant airing at this session, and it will persist until it becomes an inseparable element of Davis's style. Here, it is most obvious in the choice of tunes. Both *A Gal in Calico* and *Will You Still Be Mine* were part of Jamal's repertoire, and the bright, almost bouncy tempo at which Davis plays them is borrowed directly from Jamal's treatment of them. He had included *But Not for Me* in a recording session a year earlier, and this Gershwin melody would become known as Jamal's song with the commercial success of his 1958 recording of it. Soon to come were several other Davis recordings of titles borrowed from Jamal's repertoire, including *Surrey with a Fringe on Top*, *Just Squeeze Me*, *My Funny Valentine*, *I Don't Wanna Be Kissed*, *Billy Boy*, and the Jamal originals *Ahmad's Blues* and *New Rhumba*. No other individual had exercised so decisive an effect on what Davis played since his early explorations of the Gillespie-Parker bebop repertoire.

Jamal's influence went much deeper than just the selection of titles. Melodic understatement, harmonic inventiveness, and rhythmic lightness were part and parcel of Jamal's style and became central to Davis's style and the style of his finest bands. Davis's debt to Jamal can never be calculated precisely, of course, because Davis possessed all of these traits to some degree long before he heard of Jamal's trio. In Jamal, he recognized a kindred spirit, and he freely used whatever he could from him. Most of the borrowings, apart from the repertoire and large swatches of Red Garland's phraseology, are quite subtle. Martin Williams associates the Davis bands' playing "in two," that is, "accenting the second and fourth beats, once the weak beats, in a kind of upside-down Dixieland," with Jamal's influence, although it is usually credited to Philly Joe Jones, who would be Davis's drummer more often than not for the next three years.

Jamal's impact on Davis's musical thinking was pervasive, and Davis made no effort to conceal his debt. "Ahmad is one of my favorites," Davis said; "I live until he makes another record. I gave Gil Evans a couple of his albums, and he didn't give them back." To Nat Hentoff, who had the temerity to tell Davis that he considered Jamal "mainly a cocktail pianist," Davis simply said, "That's the way to play the piano." He then began playing Jamal's records for Hentoff and pointing out Jamal's strengths: "Listen to how he slips into the other key. You can hardly tell it's happening. He doesn't throw his technique around like Oscar Peterson. Things flow into and out of each other." Julian Adderley later became an advocate of Jamal under Davis's influence and he made the same point: "He has a potful of technique, but he has learned restraint." Davis says, "Listen to the way Jamal uses space. He lets it go so that you can feel the rhythm section and the rhythm section can feel you. It's not crowded." For Davis, Jamal's appeal was unqualified. "All my inspiration today," he said in the late 1950s, "comes from the Chicago pianist Ahmad Jamal."

Jamal was born and raised not in Chicago but in Pittsburgh, in 1930. He began playing the piano at the age of three, and he studied classical piano soon after that and through his teenage years. It was not until he was a student at Westinghouse High School that he decided to concentrate on becoming a jazz player, but by the age of fourteen he was already a member of the musicians' union and a featured local player. While still in his early teens, he is said to have been heard by Art Tatum, who called him a "coming great." His first successes came in Chicago. After touring the Midwest as a member of George Hudson's big band and as the accompanist for a song-and-dance act called the Caldwells, he formed his own trio in 1951 and began working in Chicago nightclubs. Around the same time he converted to Islam and assumed his new name, dropping his christened name, Fritz Jones.

Jamal's trio, comprised of piano, guitar, and bass for the first four years, drew favorable notices playing at a club called the Blue Note and moved into the Lounge of the Pershing Hotel in 1952, where Jamal played regularly for years, with occasional engagements at the Embers in New York and other piano bars and supper clubs throughout the country. The trio also made their first recordings in 1952 (later collected on Epic LN 3631, but now long out of print); among the first titles Jamal recorded were *A Gal in Calico* and *Will You Still Be Mine*. Many of Jamal's musical hallmarks can be picked out on these first recordings, but any listener familiar with his recordings from a few years later will certainly miss the cohesion of the later Jamal Trio, which became an almost uncanny meeting of minds when Jamal altered the instrumentation and began working with Israel Crosby on bass and Vernell Fournier on drums. John Hammond, who touted Jamal's work from the beginning, said, "Ahmad's trio is not just Ahmad, not all piano like Errol Garner. It's a *trio*."

The trio were never better than in 1956–9, the years with Crosby and Fournier. Israel Crosby started with Jamal in his original trio in 1951 but left in 1953 to tour with Benny Goodman and then returned to the trio in 1956. A native Chicagoan, he had a rich history as a jazz bassist before Jamal came along, beginning with the boogie-woogie piano player Albert Ammons in 1935 when Crosby was only sixteen and recording what might be the first jazz showcase ever for the string bass, a composition called *Blues For Israel*, with Gene Krupa's Chicagoans that same year. Vernell Fournier, originally from New Orleans, gained a local reputation in Chicago as the drummer in the house band at the Beehive, where he worked for almost three years before joining Jamal's trio. Despite his exposure in the trio, Fournier never received full credit and remains relatively unknown, but he is a percussionist of extraordinary delicacy. Jack DeJohnette, a much younger Chicago drummer, says, "One day I heard Ahmad Jamal at the Pershing, and I heard Vernell Fournier on drums. His brush work was so incredible – I mean just impeccable."

DeJohnette adds, "Ahmad's always been his own man – way ahead of his time in terms of using space and chord voicings, which is one of the reasons Miles liked him so much. Ahmad knew how to get the most out of his instrument, so that a piano trio sounded like a symphony orchestra. He's a great organizer, and his concept is so sophisticated and intelligent, yet so loose and funky." Jamal's best qualities were all caught in a live recording his trio made at the Pershing Lounge on 16 January 1958, which became one of the best-selling jazz LPs of all time (Argo LP 628; reissued as part of Chess 2ACMJ-407). *Ahmad Jamal at the Pershing* remained on the national top ten list of best-selling albums for 108 weeks.

The popularity of Jamal's record did nothing to mollify his critics, who maintain that he is not a jazz player at all, but it has obviously delighted thousands of listeners, and it certainly had some influence at the height of its popularity. Anthony Braxton, a Chicago teenager at the time, says, "I was into rock and roll – the Flamingos, Frankie Lyman and the Teenagers, that record still arouses memories – that was the music happening in the '50s, and I was a real rock and roll fan. And later I heard an Ahmad Jamal record, *At the Pershing*, and it kind of changed my whole scene." One wonders how many thousands of other listeners first came around to jazz through Jamal.

Notwithstanding the accolades Jamal has received from musicians and fans, most jazz critics have been less than kind to him. Martin Williams led off his review of *Ahmad Jamal at the Pershing* in *Down Beat* by saying, "Apparently this is being marketed as a jazz record"; he concluded that it was not jazz at all but "innocuous ... cocktail piano." Several critics compared Jamal unfavorably to Errol Garner, Jamal's older contemporary from Pittsburgh who also attended Westinghouse High School. Dom Cerulli, also writing in *Down Beat*, said, "Jamal is working an area which Errol Garner works, but without Garner's wit and drive," and Ralph J. Gleason called him "a sort of refined, effete Errol Garner." To his persistent critics, Jamal replies, "Sometimes people don't identify with purity – that's what my music was then and that's what it is now. I've endured some of the harsh statements, but for every harsh statement there have been 99 complimentary ones. What I've done and am still doing is a product of years of blood, sweat and tears, and as long as I am completely secure in the knowledge that what I am doing is valid, then eventually even the most stupid critic has to acknowledge the validity of my work."

Part of the problem critics have with his music, according to Jamal, is that it is understated. "Anybody can play loudly," he says. "It is more difficult to play softly while swinging at that same level of intensity you can get playing fortissimo. To swing hard while playing quietly is one of the signs of the true artist." Almost completely overlooked by the most negative critics is Jamal's flawless technique. It is a virtue that other musicians, especially piano players, talk about with reverence. Cedar Walton says, "I never heard Ahmad even come close to playing anything without a great deal of technique, taste and timing. When he goes across the piano, he just doesn't ever miss a note – there's never any question. For me, that's still a great thrill, just to hear somebody do that."

One of the most bewildering facts of all for Jamal's critics is his influence on Davis. "Miles Davis was clearly influenced by the trio of pianist Ahmad Jamal," Martin Williams concedes. "One can readily understand why, since Jamal is a sophisticated harmonicist and, like Davis, uses space and openness in his music. Despite the impeccable swing of Jamal's group, however, his music seems chic and shallow – all of which is another way of saying that good art, and particularly good popular art, can be strongly influenced by bad." On another occasion, Williams contrasted Davis's musical integrity with what he saw as Jamal's show-biz pyrotechnics. The result is one of the most caustic condemnations that Jamal ever received. "Jamal has the same interest in openness of melody, space and fleeting silence that Davis does," Williams began. "But for the trumpeter these qualities can be aspects of haunting lyric economy. For Jamal they seem a kind of crowd-titillating stunt-work ... Jamal's real instrument is not the piano at all, but his audience. On some numbers, he will sit things out for a chorus, with only some carefully worked out rhapsodic harmonies by his left hand or coy tinklings by his right. After that, a few bombastic block chords by both hands, delivered *forte*, will absolutely lay them in the aisles. And unless you have heard Ahmad Jamal blatantly telegraph the climax of a piece, or beg applause en route with an obvious arpeggio run which he drops insinuatingly on the crowd after he has been coasting along on the graceful momentum of Crosby and Fournier, then you have missed a nearly definitive musical bombast." Faced with this kind of critical reception, Jamal maintained the outward calm of an ascetic, and his music remained as unruffled and good-natured as ever. His consolation came unfailingly from the audiences during his peak years. If that were not enough, he might have recalled Davis's greatest wish: "I'd love to have a little boy someday," he told Nat Hentoff, "with red hair, green eyes and a black face – who plays piano like Ahmad Jamal."

Whatever the critical consensus on Jamal's music, his influence is undeniable. For Miles Davis, who had learned his art at the side of the demonic genius who did more than anyone else to forge the bebop revolution's charter, Charlie Parker, the influence of Jamal expanded that art in an unexpectedly civil direction. Where popular songs had formerly existed in Davis's lexicon primarily for their chord sequences, they now began to function as winsome melodies to be given depth and meaning by an improviser's variations. Where tempos had once raced along recklessly as if to discourage outsiders and second-raters, they now began to be manipulated and disassembled, even admitting sprightly, finger-popping figures that had to be incorporated into the fabric of the new melodies. This direction posed considerable risks, for it gave the music a facile veneer and seemed to invite the improviser to embellish the veneer rather than to probe it. If Jamal sometimes did just that, as so many of his critics claimed, Davis never did. He had learned far too much from Parker and Freddie Webster and Gillespie and Monk in the decade since he arrived in New York to settle now for superficiality. Those early lessons could never be unlearned. Instead, they were integrated into a new conception, and by 1955 Davis's music was as unlike Jamal's as it was unlike Parker's, but it included elements of both. And for the time being, it was largely undiscovered.

The public image of Miles Davis was refracted, like an object catching the sun in a clouded pool. He was regarded as inconsistent and undependable, but the addiction that had made him that way was now cured. His records showed him struggling technically and playing indifferently, but he had recently recorded music that was both technically proficient and passionately stated. He was considered by even the well-informed fans as a figure from jazz's recent past, but he was actively working at a new aesthetic and surrounding himself with important new sidemen. The gap between the public image and the reality narrowed almost overnight.

The setting, improbable though it must have seemed, was Newport, Rhode Island, a small New England city that John Hammond, himself a Vanderbilt, calls "one of the snob communities of this fair land." The occasion was the first annual Newport Jazz Festival, which was inaugurated there in the first week of July 1955. (There had been a two-day trial run the previous summer that never gets counted in the official history of the event.) The impetus for bringing jazz musicians to fashionable Newport for a week-long series of matinée and evening concerts came from Elaine and Louis Lorillard, patrons of the arts who had been involved for years with a summer program of concerts by the New York Philharmonic in Newport. They were interested in extending the community's involvement by adding a series of jazz concerts. As their producer for the jazz festival they chose George Wein, a piano player from Boston who showed unmistakeable entrepreneurial instincts in mounting concerts in Boston, managing and eventually buying jazz clubs there, and producing records for his own small label, called Storyville, which was also the name of his best-known club. Wein organized the Newport Jazz Festival in the first years simply by presenting the best known big and small jazz bands as headliners and filling in the gaps with either lesser-known bands or with all-star groups playing jam sessions.

In 1955, the headliners included the big bands of Count Basie and Woody Herman and the small bands of Dave Brubeck and Louis Armstrong. The all-star group lined up to play at the closing concert, between Basie and Brubeck, were made up of Zoot Sims, Gerry Mulligan, Thelonious Monk, Percy Heath, and Connie Kay. Shortly before the festival began, too late to list him in the program for the closing concert, Miles Davis was added. Perhaps someone noticed that the group for that evening lacked a brass instrument; perhaps Davis, who needed both the work and the exposure, appealed to Wein or one of his acquaintances on the festival board to include him; or perhaps someone who knew about the clash between Monk and Davis the previous Christmas eve thought that their presence together might create a newsworthy situation. Davis arrived to take his turn with the all stars and when he was finished he was suddenly one of the most talked-about and sought-out jazz musicians in the country.

The protocol for the jam session that evening followed the familiar format. The rhythm section started off, and then the horns were added to the rhythm players one by one, until all of them were on the stage. Monk opened with Heath and Kay supporting him on *Hackensack*, and then Mulligan joined them, and then Sims, and finally Davis. "Within the ranks of the professional critics, there was not too much notice taken when he joined the group on stage," Bill Coss, the editor of *Metronome* magazine, remembers. "Professional listeners are blasé, especially when an artist is as unpredictable as Miles; unpredictable, that is, in terms of the relationship between what he can do and what he will do." The group continued with *Now's the Time*, dedicated to Parker's memory, but it was Davis's muted solo on *Round about Midnight* that brought the audience to its feet. "On this night at Newport," Coss continues, "Miles was superb, brilliantly absorbing, as if he were both the moth and the probing, savage light on which an immolation was to take place. Perhaps that's making it too dramatic, but it's my purely subjective *feeling* about the few minutes during which he played. And over-dramatic or not, whatever Miles did was provoking enough to send one major record label executive scurrying about in search of him after the performance was over. And dramatic enough to include Miles in all the columns written about the Festival, as one of the few soloists who lived up to critical expectations." Those expectations had been deflated by the discrepancy between his recent work and the level at which he was working when the critics last took notice. As André Hodeir put it: "Miles Davis's 'comeback' at the 1955 Newport Jazz Festival was hailed as a major event precisely because the halo of glory attached to his name a few years earlier had managed to survive a period of temporary neglect." Davis felt the same about it, but he put it more succinctly. "What's all the fuss?" he asked. "I always play that way."

Davis's career began to blossom again after Newport. Not all of his sudden activity resulted from his Newport coup. He was already scheduled to record with Charles Mingus soon after Newport. He was also busy organizing his own quintet for a debut engagement at the Café Bohemia in Greenwich Village; the Bohemia date was being treated as a trial run, and if the audiences turned out in large enough numbers Davis was ready to book the quintet into jazz clubs in other cities in the fall. All the Newport publicity did was sharpen the public's respect for Davis's current music, practically guaranteeing the turnout of press and fans for at least his opening night at the Bohemia. After that, it would be up to him to keep them coming back.

But there was more, and it came as a direct result of the Newport appearance. George Avakian, the jazz producer at Columbia Records, was the executive whom Bill Coss and the others had seen scurrying around as soon as Davis left the stage at Newport. He contacted Davis and began talking to him about signing an exclusive contract with Columbia. At the moment, Columbia's jazz department was a bit thin: Davis had recorded for the label a few years earlier in the backing band for Sarah Vaughan, but Vaughan had moved on; Duke Ellington had recently left Columbia for Bethlehem Records, a jazz specialty label, but he seemed to be struggling anyway, as did their other stalwart in the jazz department, Louis Armstrong, especially when compared to younger men such as Dave Brubeck, whom they had recently signed. Columbia was definitely interested in updating its jazz representation. In the next few months, Ellington would return, and Art Blakey's Jazz Messengers and Errol Garner would be added to its list. Columbia offered a good opportunity for a jazz musician, because it had lots of working capital brought in by strong popular and classical divisions, and a broad and growing international distribution. Avakian wanted Davis, and Davis let him know that he wanted to join Columbia. Only later did Avakian discover that Davis was still carrying a long-term contractual obligation to Prestige, but by then Avakian had convinced himself that he needed Davis at Columbia and, instead of being deterred, he set out to negotiate a settlement with Prestige for the rest of the contract. Bob Weinstock at Prestige knew as much about Davis's potential as Avakian did, and he made it clear that any settlement would have to be attractive. The negotiations began, but they were not likely to be settled very quickly.

Davis was scheduled to record within a week of his Newport appearance, but he was recording neither for Columbia nor for Prestige. Instead, he was going into the studios for Debut Records, a label owned by Charles Mingus. Mingus had started up Debut in 1952, partly as an outlet for his own music, which was considered too adventuresome to attract an established company. But there was more to Debut than that. Mingus always aspired to manage his own affairs, and he was never reluctant to manage other people's affairs either, given half a chance. His willingness to manage either himself or others, however, was never matched by a commensurate capability for it. The manager's role sat uneasily on Mingus's broad shoulders, which surprised no one who was familiar with his emotional, not to say brawling, response to the world around him. Nevertheless, he had produced his first records as a young man in Los Angeles, including the long-lost sides with Davis in 1946 in the band he called Baron Mingus and His Symphonic Airs, and he would keep on trying right into the 1960s with a label called Charles Mingus Records.

Debut was in many ways the most successful of all of Mingus's record ventures, its status firmly established with the release of a classic recording made at Toronto's Massey Hall in 1953, when Dizzy Gillespie, Charlie Parker, Bud Powell, and Max Roach were reunited for one night only and played magnificently. Mingus was their bassist that night only because Oscar Pettiford, who had played the bass with them on 52nd Street and was originally lined up to play in the reunion band by the Toronto promoters, broke his arm and had to drop out. Mingus planted a tape recorder on the stage and thus preserved an irreplaceable moment in jazz history. It proved to be his greatest accomplishment as a record producer, and it also illustrates his managerial shortcomings as well, for Mingus, who was willing and able to lecture the world endlessly on its abuse of artists such as him, never got around to paying royalties or any fee at all to the other men on the record. It is hard to believe that his failure to pay them was motivated by anything more malicious than sheer mismanagement. Nevertheless, he never really gave up on his managerial ambitions, no matter how successful he became as a performing jazzman, and in that role he was soon to realize many of his ambitions.

By the mid-1950s Mingus was acclaimed as one of the finest bass players around, and by the late 1950s he was equally acclaimed as a significant composer and a superb bandleader. Not that success made life much easier for him; with Mingus, nothing seemed easy. As both musician and manager, his successes no less than his failures proceeded from a personal intensity so fierce that it sometimes erupted into mania. Nat Hentoff described Mingus hovering over his sidemen on the bandstand "like a brooding Zeus making up the scorecard for eternity." Among the more notorious incidents in a career filled with them were Mingus's knife fight with trombonist Juan Tizol while they were playing in Duke Ellington's orchestra, and a few years later, in his own band, Mingus's clobbering Jimmy Knepper onstage because he purportedly misplayed his part.

Charles McPherson, the alto saxophonist who played in Mingus's bands off and on for twelve years beginning in 1960, described what it was like. "Working for Mingus was a challenging situation because he was a very complex personality type – one way one day, another way another day, very intense, very honest – painfully honest," McPherson said. "Sometimes it was frightening: my first night on the gig, because he didn't get all his money from the club owner, he proceeded to take apart a Steinway grand piano with his hands – the insides, the guts, he commenced to plucking steel strings out." For Mingus, it was a recurring pattern. Sensitivity vented itself in brutality, and it was all, to Mingus's mind, in defense of his rights. "Sometimes I think if all black people were like me there wouldn't have been any slaves," he said in his autobiography; "they'd of had to kill us all!"

Few jazzmen have been as willing to take on all comers over such a profusion of principles. One other who has, of course, is Miles Davis. They very idea of Mingus trying to produce a record by Davis summons up a situation for jazz historians to conjure with. In the end, however, Mingus and Davis ignored one another almost completely during the recording session, and the session, like the recording it gave birth to, was about as uneventful as it could possibly be.

Bill Coss, who attended the recording session in order to gather material for the album's liner notes, met Davis at his hotel that Saturday morning at the appointed hour when they were supposed to be picked up by a taxi and taken to the studio. Davis "waited one hour in front of his hotel, leaning detachedly against a fire plug, apparently never doubting that he would be driven to the recording studio, which was only two blocks away, as he had been promised," Coss remembers. Finally the taxi arrived, and Davis settled back for the five-minute ride through traffic. "Then, on the way to the studio, his one major comment: 'I hope I don't have to hit Mingus in the mouth.'" Coss adds: "This, of course, despite the fact that Mingus could carry two of Miles around the block in a half-gallop." When they arrived at the studio they found vibist Teddy Charles still working on the arrangements they were going to record. "Miles moved into a corner and waited," Coss says, while Mingus, who had been haranguing drummer Elvin Jones when they arrived, "alternately fussed and fumed like a great rooster in attendance to a hatching." Somehow, Mingus and Davis kept out of one another's way until the arrangements were finally ready and the recording could begin. The details are as follows:

Miles Davis All Stars with Charles Mingus
Miles Davis, tpt; Britt Woodman, tbn; Teddy Charles, vib; Charles Mingus, b; Elvin Jones, dms. New York, 9 July 1955
Nature Boy; Alone Together; There's No You; Easy Living
(all on Debut DEB 120; reissued [1972] in Europe on America 30 AM 6051, in the United States on Fantasy M6001)
Alone Together is arranged by Charles Mingus; the other three titles, by Teddy Charles.

If most listeners had not been keeping track of the recent developments in Davis's style, Mingus was one who obviously had. The session was clearly calculated to exploit Davis's wistful, romantic ballad playing – too calculated. The tempos are uniformly ponderous, and only *There's No You*, which is a little more spirited than the others, sustains any rhythmic interest at all. To make up for the lack of pace, the rhythm is carried along most of the time by arranged ostinato figures played by Mingus on bass and Britt Woodman on trombone. Elvin Jones, who would soon be earning plaudits for his aggressive polyrhythmic drumming, goes almost unnoticed throughout.

The arrangements seem cluttered and often stilted. In Teddy Charles, Mingus had lined up an arranger with an academic background whose wont was to interpolate European musical devices in jazz contexts, exactly the thrust that Mingus himself, who was always involved in some form or other of musical experiment, favored at the time. Mingus's arrangement of *Alone Together* is hardly less formalistic than any of Charles's. Mingus was starting to counter his infatuation with European forms with devices from American music, especially from Ellington and gospel music, but had not yet discovered how to incorporate them into his arranging, although they were always abundantly evident in his playing. Over these contrived backgrounds, Davis picks his way cautiously, sticking close to the melody most of the time in an aloof, emotionless manner.

When this recording was reissued in Europe in 1972, reviewer Ron Brown called it "an unbelievably lacklustre session." The noncommital attitude of Davis is summed up in an occurrence that Coss noted at the time: "On one take Miles wandered so far afield that he was completely lost. But he made no mention of it, not even a request for another take, although, fortunately, another was made, almost as if he didn't really care, was above caring, whether anyone had discovered the error." (The first take was apparently destroyed, since it has never been released; the entire session produced only twenty-seven minutes of music, barely enough to fill an LP.) Davis, however, is by no means the least satisfactory player on the date. Brown comments also that "Britt Woodman and Teddy Charles play their front-line roles on these slow ballads as if exhausted." "Although Mingus is on form," Brown says, "he's actually responsible for a degree of imbalance, for his forceful soloing exposes his soporific colleagues even more than if the bass player was asleep too."

The recording, though, is not uninteresting. Mingus managed to orchestrate – both literally and figuratively – a context that would expose one aspect of Davis's playing, that of the self-indulgent, bemused lyricist; the tougher, blues-oriented bopper is completely eradicated. The record thus became a kind of starting-point for a peculiar breed of Davis fans, who read into his detached musings not a lack of feeling but some higher order of feeling, perhaps the apotheosis of feeling. They came to share Bill Coss's opinion of this record, that "through it all, none of the musicians show Miles' finality of mood, but they do perfectly match him as if they shared the same secret." (My own copy of the original release, scarred and worn from the countless listenings of a high school clan hoping to tap that elusive secret, has seldom commanded playing time since those days.) The music itself, stacked up against its promise, simply seems anticlimactic.

If Davis seemed uninvolved, he probably had good reason. He was preoccupied with assembling a new band of his own for the engagement at the Café Bohemia, and for the first time since he assembled the short-lived nonet in 1948 he had some realistic hopes of keeping this band together as a working unit. Of course he knew exactly who he wanted for most of the positions, and the main problem was making sure that they were available for the date. Sonny Rollins, naturally, was his choice to share the front line with him, and Red Garland and Philly Joe Jones would form two-thirds of the rhythm section. On the quartet recordings in June, he used Oscar Pettiford on bass with Garland and Jones, and he had used Percy Heath regularly before that, but there was no hope of getting a bassist of that stature. Jackie McLean, however, raved about a young bassist from Detroit with whom he had been working in the George Wallington Quintet. The bassist, whose name was Paul Chambers, had arrived in New York only a few months earlier and had already been seen working with the promising new quintet of J.J. Johnson and Kai Winding before he landed with Wallington. Davis decided to give him a try.

After a couple of informal rehearsals, the new Miles Davis Quintet moved into the Bohemia. Two of the titles they played on the Wednesday of what was probably their first week there have been preserved:

Miles Davis Quintet
Miles Davis, tpt; Sonny Rollins, ts; Red Garland, pno; Paul Chambers, b; Philly Joe Jones, dms. Café Bohemia, New York, 13 July 1955
Bye Bye Blackbird; Walkin' [Rollin' and Blowin']
(both on Chakra CH 100)

Bye Bye Blackbird, which became a perennial favorite in the book for Davis's bands for several years, gets a spare, Jamalesque statement from Davis on the muted horn, his solo dotted with quotations from Leonard Bernstein's ballad *Maria* from *West Side Story*, then the hit of Broadway. Rollins's two choruses are more expansive, even including some sixteenth-note runs. The lack of playing experience for this band as a unit shows up especially in *Walkin'*, another perennial in Davis's book, where the theme is stated only once at the beginning before giving way to the round of solos, which includes not only Davis, Rollins, and Garland, but also a bowed chorus by bassist Chambers, whose contribution throughout is simply outstanding.

Davis must have known from the beginning that he had put together a rhythm team of great potential. Chambers fitted in immediately with Garland and Jones, who were already comfortable with one another, and Chambers and Jones seem to rally in support of Garland's solos, which are usually attractive and always competent but almost never adventuresome, the bass and drums thus adding color and pace to them and saving them from becoming a letdown in the proceedings. Even in these relatively unpolished performances, Davis could hear all the essential elements he wanted in his band. He seems never to have doubted that Rollins's burly tone made the perfect complement for his own playing; and in the rhythm team he heard the kind of unabashed spirit that would set them both off.

It was already a good band at the Bohemia, and beyond any doubt it could become a great one. Best of all, the crowds were there to hear them, attracted at first perhaps by the good notices from Newport but hanging on throughout the entire engagement, even though it was July, the toughest month to draw an audience into a jazz club in any city. Davis went ahead and booked a tour of jazz clubs outside New York for the fall.

Apart from Davis's triumphal entrance at Newport, the jazz event that drew the most notice in the summer of 1955 was the first appearance in New York of a rotund saxophonist named Julian Adderley, better known as Cannonball, with the Oscar Pettiford Quartet at the Café Bohemia in the weeks immediately following Davis's engagement there. Adderley spun out paragraphs of blues-based improvisations on the alto, which looked like a toy up against his bulk, and he did it with such facility that his audiences at the Bohemia, including the reviewers, could hardly resist comparing him to Charlie Parker. Adderley, who was almost twenty-seven, was a high school music teacher in Fort Lauderdale, Florida, and the New York audiences, including most of the musicians in town, could hardly believe that such a talented player could exist outside the hub.

One musician who spent several hours at the Café Bohemia that summer was Davis, and he was impressed enough by what he heard that he took Adderley aside and offered him some advice. "Miles helped me when I first came to New York," Adderley says. "He told me whom to avoid among the record companies, but unfortunately I didn't take his advice." Adderley ended up signing a contract with Mercury-EmArcy that summer, and for the duration of the contract he was told by the label's producers what to record, who would arrange it, and who would publish it. Davis, under contract to Prestige and being courted by Columbia, recommended neither of them. "Al Lion of Blue Note was one man he recommended," Adderley recalls, "and Miles also told me about John Levy," the man who became Adderley's manager. Davis also tried to talk to him about his playing, but without much success. "Miles began telling me something musically about chords, but I sort of ignored him," says Adderley, remembering the glow of his summer as the toast of the New York jazz world. "I was a little arrogant in those days. Then, about three months later, I saw an interview in which Miles said I could swing but I didn't know much about chords. But by that time I'd begun to listen to Sonny Rollins and others, and I realized I knew very little about chords. You can play all the right changes and still not necessarily say anything. Finally, I learned how to use substitute chords and get the sound I wanted."

The attention that Davis paid to Adderley that summer was probably not gratuitous. Sonny Rollins was again grumbling about life in general and threatening to get out of music and out of New York for good. Even though Davis did not believe he would follow through, he was keeping an eye out for a possible replacement just in case, and Adderley must have looked like a good prospect. If so, Davis had a surprise coming, for Adderley was not available, at least not in the immediate future. He was obliged to return in September to his high school job in Fort Lauderdale. By the time he returned to New York to work as a professional musician the following spring, Davis already had a saxophonist and Adderley formed a quintet of his own with his brother Nat, a cornetist. He eventually joined Davis's band, but not until two years after his auspicious summer debut.

Davis's efforts at putting together a permanent band were interrupted one more time that summer by his obligations to Prestige, for which he was set to record another all-star date. Some of the players in the band were longtime studio associates, including Milt Jackson, who was listed as co-leader on the first release of this session, and Percy Heath. Jackie McLean was also along for two of the four tracks, which he composed, and he brought along the drummer from the George Wallington Quintet, Arthur Taylor, yet another of McLean's neighbors from Harlem. The piano player was Ray Bryant, who had played occasionally with Davis in Philadelphia at the Blue Note, where he had been the house pianist for several years before his recent move to New York. The details are as follows:

Miles Davis and Milt Jackson All Stars
Miles Davis, tpt; Jackie McLean, as (on *Dr. Jackle* and *Minor March*); Milt Jackson, vib; Ray Bryant, pno; Percy Heath, b; Arthur Taylor, dms. New York, 5 August 1955
Dr. Jackle; *Bitty Ditty*; *Minor March*; *Changes*
(all on Prestige LP 7034; reissued [1967] on Prestige 7540)

McLean's *Dr. Jackle* is a theme that Davis obviously relished, judging from his long skittish solo here, and he kept it in his repertoire for a few years. The other piece by McLean, *Minor March*, is basic bebop, all the more readily identifiable because of McLean's quotation of some Parker phrases in his solo. The session amounted to one more LP of competent post-bop playing. The most noticeable difference between this session and Davis's other recent recordings comes from the presence of pianist Ray Bryant, who works much more actively in the bass clef than most of the other young piano players of the time. His solo on his own *Changes*, a blues chord sequence with no set melody, is a carefully made, two-handed recital, which previews the best of his later work as a featured pianist.

The record date with a pick-up band again seems to have been little more than a distraction for Davis. His main interest was in lining up his own quintet for the round of club dates starting in September, but he was not making much headway. Sonny Rollins disappeared, as he had threatened to do, and when Davis tracked him down he told him that he was giving up music and moving to Chicago. He would not be dissuaded. Davis began searching for another tenor saxophonist for the quintet. First he tried a young Chicagoan named John Gilmore, a man who had listened carefully to Rollins and learned some of his style from him, although Gilmore was an adventurous player who would not confine himself to styles that were already worked out. He had grown up amid the first winds of an avant-garde movement in Chicago, had played there with a singular organization called the Arkestra led by a mysterious figure who called himself Sun Ra, and had made his first recordings with the Arkestra for Sun Ra's Saturn label earlier in the year. Davis tried Gilmore in a few rehearsals and then tried another tenor player, John Coltrane, on the recommendation of Philly Joe Jones, who had often played with Coltrane in Philadelphia.

Davis knew Coltrane slightly. He had been around New York a few years earlier, playing alto saxophone in Dizzy Gillespie's orchestra and tenor saxophone at some club dates, and their paths had crossed then and later, when Coltrane usually stayed close to home in Philadelphia. Coltrane proved to be a competent player and a very willing sideman, practicing almost constantly between rehearsals, but much of the time he was simply mystified by Davis. "After I joined Miles in 1955, I found that he didn't talk much and will rarely discuss his music," Coltrane said later. "He's completely unpredictable ... If I asked him something about his music, I never knew how he was going to take it." For Coltrane, a serious, almost solemn man, asking questions about the music they were rehearsing seemed as natural as breathing. For Davis, who expected his sidemen to answer their own questions in their own terms as they grew independently within the musical context he determined for them, Coltrane's quizzical attitude went against the grain. The personality differences between them did not make any long-term association look very promising. When Coltrane had to return to Philadelphia to fulfill a playing commitment after rehearsing with Davis for a few weeks, he was probably not surprised to read a newspaper item quoting Davis as saying that he expected Sonny Rollins, who was rumored to have started playing again in Chicago, to join his quintet in time for the fall tour.

Rollins did not return. In his place, Davis reinstated Coltrane at the last minute. Davis probably had little choice in the matter; apart from Rollins, no one but Coltrane knew the band's book. How much longer it took the taciturn Davis to discover that in Coltrane he had discovered an exquisite element for his music no one will ever know for certain. It would take a little while before he could bring himself to laud Coltrane's playing, but he must have known his value much sooner, probably within a few weeks, when the members of the quintet had begun to work as a unit. It did not take much longer than that for Davis's listeners to recognize the superb balance of the new Miles Davis Quintet, and many of them could discern Coltrane's crucial counterweight in that balance. They discovered that the little-known saxophonist had, in Whitney Balliett's phrase, "a dry, unplaned tone that sets Davis off, like a rough mounting for a fine stone."

7

Cookin'
1955–7

With the single exception of Louis Armstrong and the classic discs he made with his Hot Five and Hot Seven, there has been no series of recordings in jazz history that has had the impact of the Miles Davis Quintet and Sextet records, nor the later albums with Gil Evans and the large band ... Seen against the backdrop of all jazz, it is a great achievement; seen against the backdrop of contemporary music as a whole, it is even greater; and against the backdrop of all contemporary art, it is perhaps more significant than we yet realize.   Ralph J. Gleason

Jazz buffs learned that the new Miles Davis Quintet, with John Coltrane, Red Garland, Paul Chambers, and Philly Joe Jones, had something special for them to hear long before all but a handful of them actually heard it. The network that links the cognoscenti had begun its rumblings about Davis's intentions of forming a new 'boss' group soon after he had walked off the stage at Freebody Park in Newport in July. The rumble amplified when the quintet played their first notes in public, which happened shortly after 9 a.m. at a small club called Anchors Inn in Baltimore on Monday 28 September 1955. The quintet's first recordings were made for Columbia one month later, exactly the interval that Davis wanted in order to let the individuals in the band resolve into a working unit, but even these performances the public did not get to hear for a long time because of the contract dispute between Columbia and Prestige. The general public's first taste of the quintet's music came with the release in April 1956 of a November 1955 recording session for Prestige.

By that time, the quintet had played before only a few thousand listeners in several cities in the United States, and the men in the quintet already knew, as almost none of their listeners did, that no matter how successful they became – and they must have realized that they would become, in jazz terms, phenomenally successful – life as a member of the Miles Davis Quintet would never be easy. The tensions within the group, which surely worked to fuel its creative fires, were scarcely evident to outsiders, whether they were following the quintet's itinerary in the pages of *Down Beat* hoping they would come within range of their cities and towns, or riffling through the accumulation of LPs from these years. Davis's artistic course in the last half of the 1950s has the appearance of a steady upward spiral at the head of the cohesive quintet, spelled occasionally by special projects with Gil Evans, and onward into an expansion of the quintet into a sextet that was perhaps the greatest small band in jazz history. (The sextet years are the subject of the next chapter.) Looked at more closely, the progress is not nearly so smooth. In the twenty-seven months from its debut in Baltimore until it became a sextet, the great quintet was disbanded no less than four times when one or more of the sidemen, usually John Coltrane or Philly Joe Jones and sometimes both, fell out of grace with the leader. Davis would then re-form it eventually, sometimes after a period of months. The quintet was a working entity only a little more than half of the time that it held sway over the jazz world.

The quintet remained Davis's reference point through all this period and never failed to satisfy him musically no matter how disgruntled he might become with the members either personally or professionally. In spite of his various attempts to dismantle the quintet once and for all, he relented whenever he had an important performance to make and called the members back to the fold. And, of course, the men never failed to return to him, no matter what curse they had left under. What matters is what remains of the quintet – their music – and the vagaries of their daily existence only help to elucidate the circumstances in which some great music came into being. "This Quintet represented a high-water mark in post-war jazz," says Alun Morgan, an opinion that is virtually unanimous. These years in jazz belonged to the Miles Davis Quintet, even during the weeks when their leader thought that he had banished them from the scene.

After Newport it became a possibility that Davis would be in a position to establish his own band, and he turned immediately to the Shaw Artists Corporation, run by Milt and Billy Shaw, the veteran bookers and managers from the days of 52nd Street. All the jazz veterans knew the Shaws, and the Shaws knew the jazzmen. On the one hand, they knew that Davis had a lot of potential, and on the other hand they knew that he was not a particularly manageable man. In jazz, the managers were accustomed to exercising considerable control over their clients. Of course, the days were past – but just barely – when a successful jazz musician required a street-smart white manager to get any work at all, but the spectre of Irving Mills dictating to Duke Ellington and Joe Glaser piloting Louis Armstrong, which seem now to be chapters more appropriate in the annals of the American Civil War than of the Roaring Twenties, remained vivid in 1955. Davis allowed the Shaw Agency no illusions about the relationship he expected when he took on a manager. "It's all right to be in business with a white man," he said, "but for him to own everything and dictate to you is outdated, and it was outdated when I was born." The Shaws assigned Davis to the dossier of one of their junior partners, a man named Jack Whittemore, and the two struck up an enduring, if sometimes uneasy, partnership. "Jack and I are good friends," Davis says. "Jack asked me, 'Miles, what do you want me to do, which percentage do you want me to take – five, ten, or what?' If I don't feel like paying him shit, I ain't gonna say nothing, but I wouldn't take advantage of him, because of my attitude. And I don't want him to take advantage of me."

Whittemore set up the first itinerary for the new Miles Davis Quintet, putting them in Baltimore from 28 September to 3 October, in Detroit for 5–10 October, into Chicago's Sutherland Lounge starting 12 October, and into Peacock Alley in St. Louis after that. From St. Louis, they would return to New York, presumably having worked out most of their musical kinks. They were booked into the Café Bohemia, the jazz club on Barrow Street in Greenwich Village where Davis had tested the climate for his music in the summer with Sonny Rollins in the band. Davis hoped that they could make their first records during the Bohemia engagement.

The fuss over his tenor saxophonist when the tour was about to begin ruffled Davis a bit, at least momentarily. By the time Sonny Rollins finally begged off, John Coltrane was back in Philadelphia playing a club date with the organist Jimmy Smith. Things were looking up for Coltrane because Smith had asked him to join his band permanently. He was pondering the offer and talking it over with Naima Grubbs, the woman he lived with in Philadelphia, when Philly Joe Jones telephoned from New York to tell him that the tenor chair in Davis's band might still be available. Naima and he decided that, if the offer came, he would go with Davis rather than Smith, because it would give him a better chance to play his music than he was likely to get playing in the shadow of Smith's domineering organ. Philly Joe Jones finally called him again on 27 September and told Coltrane to join the band in Baltimore the next day. Coltrane hastily arranged for Odean Pope, a good local saxophonist, to fill in for him in the week remaining with Jimmy Smith. He left for Baltimore and joined the others in time for a late afternoon rehearsal before starting their first set. For all the haste, the first set went off smoothly enough, and so did the rest of the engagement. "It was just a natural thing," Red Garland said later.

The members of the quintet hit it off when they were not performing. At the end of their week in Baltimore, on 3 October, Naima arrived and she and Coltrane were married, with the others in attendance. As the tour moved into the Midwest they grew closer together. The week in Detroit was important to Davis, who still had close contacts among the local musicians, and it was equally important to Paul Chambers, who was returning home. "We'd hang out together during the day – the whole band," Garland says. "We'd go eat, stop off at a bar, walk around the streets and just have fun. We liked each other. Local musicians would organize a jam session and we'd go to those during the day." Chambers was no stranger to Chicago either, and when the band moved there, he shared an apartment in the Sutherland Hotel with Doris Sydnor, Charlie Parker's widow.

Musically, Coltrane still seemed to have some uneasy moments on the stand, probably because he had joined the group relatively cold. During the Sutherland engagement, a Selmer salesman came in to show Davis his line of trumpets and when he stayed over to hear the quintet he thought he detected that Coltrane was having some problems with his instrument. He arranged to take Coltrane the next day to the Selmer plant in Elkhart, Indiana. This incident was repeated almost ritually by Coltrane every time he visited Chicago thereafter, and then was carried out in almost every city in the world where saxophone manufacturers could be found, in what amounted to an obsessive search by Coltrane for the perfect instrument, the perfect mouthpiece, and the perfect reed. He had been working intensely on his music for years now, and the intensity would continue until the day he died.

That intensity was felt by some members of his audience even in his performances on this first tour, when Coltrane was almost completely unknown. "I saw Trane when everybody was expecting Sonny Rollins in St. Louis, Missouri," Leon Thomas, the improvising vocalist, told Arthur Taylor, recalling the quintet's last stop on their inaugural tour. "East St. Louis had turned out for Miles's gig at the Peacock Alley. Paul Chambers, Philly Joe, Red Garland, Miles and Trane showed up. The people were drug because they didn't know who Trane was. They had never heard of him, and he was a last-minute substitute for Sonny. They knew they wouldn't dig the way he was playing. I was sitting up front, and he just blew me out of the place. Wasn't nobody else after that, nobody!' But Thomas's reaction was not always shared by other members of the audience as their first impression of Coltrane.

For all his work so far, Coltrane still had made scant progress. Andrew White, the tenor saxophonist and 'Coltranologist,' points out that "he was pretty much playing in standard bebop style until he joined Miles Davis in 1955." The union with Davis, which came so close to not materializing, was crucial. "The time spent with Miles, who many musicians accurately called the 'star-maker,' was the starting-point of the Coltrane legacy," White says. "Miles had a way of putting bands together with musicians who were as diverse in their playing as they were in their personal lifestyles. But some sixth sense seemed to give him the ability to bring out the best of everybody ... Many years later, Coltrane recalled that he was pretty much content to sound like anybody else until he joined the Davis band, that Miles had the ability to relax you while keeping you professional at the same time." It was not necessarily Davis's presence that was the catalyst for Coltrane's development. White adds: "He could also have pointed out that when Miles left the bandstand Trane *had* to play – he was the only horn left." Whether or not Davis's absence would have worked so effectively for other players seems doubtful, but for Coltrane it worked perfectly. "It was the constant professional pressure to produce that sparked the level of ingenuity in Coltrane's playing that would soon set him apart from the rest of the tenor players and mark him as the foremost player of the Sixties, a crystallizer of the bebop era, and the so-called 'father of the avant garde,'" White says.

Coltrane's progress as a member of the quintet was by no means unique, although it was undoubtedly the most dramatic – possibly the most dramatic individual development in jazz history, since he was already twenty-nine, his birthday coming the week before he joined the quintet, well past the age when jazz musicians generally attain their mature styles. He was just four months younger than Davis, and Davis had established the main elements of *his* style more than five years earlier. If the other members of the quintet did not progress as dramatically as Coltrane, they nonetheless went through some considerable changes.

Red Garland, whose seemingly modest gifts were prodded purposefully by Davis as he encouraged him to incorporate the beauties he heard in Ahmad Jamal's playing, quickly emerged as one of the most influential piano players of the day. Garland's stature did not come solely from what he took from Jamal, as the French pianist and critic Henri Renaud points out. "Garland is a marvelous pianist in his own right," Renaud says, "an original artist with a very personal and creative approach to melody, rhythm, beat and sound. Yet there can be no denying that about 1955, when he made his first recorded appearance with Miles Davis, he was instrumental in most younger pianists the whole world over going in for both Ahmad Jamal's rhythmic conceptions (the 'Charleston' syncopation) and Errol Garner's harmonic ones ... The Garnerian influence is obviously at work in Garland's system of chord inversions: Garner never strikes the tonic with the left hand's little finger. Here indeed lies the essential differences between the pianistic sound that was prevalent during the Parker era and the one that was to supersede it in Coltrane's time."

Partitioning the joint influences of Garner and Jamal on Garland is not as straightforward as Renaud makes it sound. The harmonic innovation that he traces from Garner was also an important element in the fabric of Jamal's style, and Jamal may well have learned it from Garner, his older colleague from Pittsburgh. But it was Garland, more than either Garner or Jamal, who transmitted the innovation to the younger jazz players, because he had the best forum as a member of the Miles Davis Quintet. Garland "brought a new approach to keyboard voicing," according to Jerry Coker, the saxophonist and educator, who explains it this way: "He omitted the root from the bottom, if not altogether, placing instead a seventh or third (usually) on the bottom, and played the voicings more in the middle and upper rather than the lower portions of the keyboard. Within a very short time, virtually all jazz pianists made a similar change, sometimes modifying Garland's exact voicings. It was plain to see that we were not going to be hearing many root-oriented voicings again, except perhaps in ballads or at important cadence points in faster selections." Clearly, Garner, Jamal, and Garland and their immediate successors such as Bill Evans shared a light touch on the keyboard as compared to such contemporaries as Oscar Peterson, Ray Bryant, and Dave Brubeck. The impression of that light touch probably derives partly from eliminating the root of chords, though that was also part of the stock-in-trade of some older pianists too, especially Billy Taylor and John Lewis, long among Davis's favorite players. With Ahmad Jamal and Red Garland, the technique was used more frequently and became a predominant aspect of their styles.

Paul Chambers was only twenty when he joined the Miles Davis Quintet, but he made his mark within the first few months. In the ensembles, his presence is felt rather than heard, as a sturdy walking bass line that pins down the chordal foundation and frees the piano player's left hand. But it was as a soloist that Chambers drew most attention. "Paul Chambers concentrated all his career on solo work," says Percy Heath, one of the many older bassists who began listening carefully to what Chambers was doing. "I've always liked his solos better than his choice of notes as an accompanist. I have the feeling that his notes are more like tenor saxophone notes." From the start, Chambers took occasional solo turns arco rather than pizzicato, a technique that was rarely used by jazz bassists except for Slam Stewart, who for years had been bowing his solos and humming along in unison, giving him one of the most unique sounds, though hardly the most pleasant, in all of jazz. With Stewart, the use of the bow was considered to be a novelty (he was once part of a jazz vaudeville act – Slim and Slam – on 52nd Street with guitarist Slim Gaillard), but with Chambers it was considered a feat, and those bassists who had had any training in the use of the bow quickly set about sharpening their skills. Chambers was voted the new star on his instrument in *Down Beat's* International Critics Poll for 1956.

Philly Joe Jones was already thirty-two when the quintet was formed, the same age as Red Garland and three years older than Davis, and he had been around the jazz scene on the east coast for several years without making any appreciable impression. Amazingly, his time with Davis would elevate him right to the top rank of modern jazz drummers, where Kenny Clarke, Max Roach, and Art Blakey had been unchallenged for years. A whole generation of rising drummers would emerge imprinted with Jones's style, among them Jack DeJohnette, who would become Davis's drummer in 1968. "I really got into Miles' music,"

DeJohnette remembers, "and Philly Joe was making it happen. Philly Joe was like the acrobatic dancer of the rudiments. He took rudiments and made them swing." The transformation of Jones's drumming came directly from Davis's conception, both for the band and for himself, which suited Jones's bright, pulsating ingenuity perfectly. Jones explains it this way: "Most bandleaders and drummers, they have a marriage. We feel each other and know each other. I know everything he's going to do – almost. After a few weeks it comes that he can't make a move without I know he's going to make it – and I anticipate it. A lot of times Miles would say, 'Don't do it *with* me, do it *after* me.'" The impact on jazz drumming was almost immediate. "During the time Philly was with Miles he started playing that rim shot on four," Horacee Arnold, another drummer, recalls. "You'd get a gig with somebody and they'd say, 'Play the Philly lick' ... You'd go to a record date and they wanted everybody to play what Philly did." Although Jones's technical gifts were considerable, his elevation depended upon their exposure in Davis's deliberately uncluttered ensemble, which left lots of spaces for the drummer to fill. After Jones, Davis would employ other drummers who would also rise from obscurity to the forefront for the same reason, most notably Tony Williams in the 1960s. But Williams, like every other drummer of *his* day, would arrive in the band with the technical arsenal derived directly or indirectly from Jones.

It was not only the drummer, of course, whose role was enhanced by Davis's conception of how a small band should sound. All the sidemen were assigned a function that both challenged the player and drew attention to his work. It has become a cliché to say that for a bandleader such as Duke Ellington the band is his instrument. The cliché works almost as well for Davis, although the dominance of a leader of a small band can be nowhere near as specific as it is for the leader of a large band, where sections must be coordinated internally as well as structurally in the band as a whole. By and large, Davis's success as a leader has the same source as Ellington's and consists essentially in discovering and exploiting the individual strengths of his sidemen. In this, Davis has become a model for a small band leader, a point that is emphasized by Herbie Hancock, who became a successful leader after spending four years with Davis's band in the 1960s. Hancock explains the key to leadership, which he calls "Miles' philosophy," this way: "A lot of bands go through musicians like drinking water, but what I try to do, rather than, for instance, always looking for another drummer to play a specific thing, is try to see what my drummer has to offer already, and function from that." As a basis for building a band, the strategy of exploiting individual talents is, of course, no more than sound common sense. It is not, for all that, easy, judging from the relative lack of brilliant, as opposed to merely adequate, leaders in jazz history. The mystery is how a leader implements the strategy. Davis seems to lead by indirection rather than by direction, seldom or never talking to his sidemen about his music. Even the musicians who have been through his bands have no clear idea about how he pulled the band together. When asked directly about it, Davis himself simply says, "I just bring out in people what's in them."

By the time the quintet returned to New York for their engagement at the Café Bohemia in late October, the five men already had a sense of their collective strength. One frequent visitor at the Bohemia was George Avakian, who was still intent on signing Davis to a Columbia contract. His most vivid memory of that Bohemia engagement was of John Coltrane, whom he had not heard in person before. Coltrane impressed him greatly, and Avakian later described him as a man who "seemed to grow taller in height and larger in size with each note that he played, each chord he seemed to be pushing to its outer limits." Avakian's strong impression of Coltrane was shared by a small but growing minority of listeners wherever the quintet played.

Avakian's negotiations on Davis's recording contract were running into some snags. In his view, Davis was too demanding and Prestige was uncooperative. His reaction was predictable, because Columbia was in a vulnerable position. Finally, he made a little headway by getting Davis to come to terms. Davis's agreement did not come cheaply: he received a $4,000 advance to join Columbia, then a sizeable fee for any recording artist and an unheard-of fee for a jazzman. (In 1981, the *New York Times* stated that the terms of Davis's original contract with Columbia also called for "a reported annual fee of $300,000," a large stipend for a jazz artist in 1980, let alone 1955; so far, the figure has not been corroborated.) Prestige proved to be more difficult. It had Davis under contract for another year, with four LPs stipulated as the year's production, and it would not consider releasing him outright, notwithstanding Davis's expressed wish that he be released. Terms of Davis's contract with Prestige were eventually fulfilled to the letter. During the next twelve months, Davis recorded music for Prestige that was eventually released on five and a half LPs with one title left over. Of these, five LPs and the extra title were by the regular quintet, and the other half-LP was by an all-star quintet. The half-LP was a leftover obligation from 1953, when the recording session with Charlie Parker on tenor had dissolved, leaving less music than was required. The extra title completed Davis's obligations to the company for 1954, when the total studio output had ended up a few minutes short of four full LPs. The first of the quintet sessions amounted to one LP, which completed his obligations for 1955, since two LPs had already been recorded. And the other four LPs, which would be recorded in two marathon sessions in 1956 (along with the extra title), then completed the final year of his contract. The oft-repeated, conventional account of these negotiations in the jazz literature (always unattributed) gives Prestige credit for some generosity, claiming that while it required its four LPs, it waived the year-long term of the contract and released Davis from it as soon as he recorded the required amount of music. It did no such thing. Davis's final recording date for the company, 26 October 1956, was exactly one year after the Café Bohemia engagement when the negotiations took place.

Nevertheless, Avakian won a small concession from Prestige. He was allowed, for inducements unknown, to begin recording Davis at Columbia in six months instead of waiting for the full year to expire. That agreement meant that Davis could start working in the Columbia studios around the end of May 1956; neither Davis nor Columbia, for whom he would record for decades, wasted any time in activating the contract, and he made his first official recordings for the company on 5 June.

These arrangements look fairly straightforward: essentially, Prestige would receive everything it had coming to it, and Columbia won the right to a con-current agreement for part of the remaining contract year, at Davis's request. However, in the recording industry nothing is likely to be as it appears, and the agreement had been violated before the ink was dry on the contract. Davis and his quintet made their first recordings for Columbia on 27 October, while they were still playing at the Café Bohemia. The session was probably arranged by Avakian and Davis as soon as Davis settled his own negotiation with them, pre-sumably on the assumption that Prestige would either negotiate a release with Columbia or give Davis his outright release. When Prestige refused to release him at all, the Columbia session had already taken place.

Columbia was then stuck with an LP's worth of the first recordings of the new Miles Davis Quintet to which it apparently had no legal rights. This suspicion is reinforced by Columbia's circuitous course in issuing the results of the session. The music consists of four bebop compositions played reasonably well, certainly well enough to merit its release in the usual manner under ordinary circum-stances. However, the four titles have never been released together or even listed together. Instead, they have come out at odd intervals between 1956 and 1979. *Ah-Leu-Cha* was issued a little more than a year after it was made, along with titles from Davis's first official Columbia session, and with no indication that it did not date from the same session as the others. *Budo* first appeared in 1957 on an anthology that also included tracks by Louis Armstrong, Dave Brubeck, Eddie Condon, Duke Ellington, Errol Garner, Gigi Gryce and Donald Byrd, J.J. Johnson, Art Blakey's Jazz Messengers, and Turk Murphy – the palpable results of Ava-kian's recruiting program for Columbia's jazz department. *Budo* reappeared on a French CBS recording in the late 1960s. On an American release in 1973, it appeared along with *Little Melonae*, a previously unknown title from the same session (but incorrectly dated as 1958, although *Budo* was correctly dated); the two showed up together again (both correctly dated) in a 1977 release. *Two Bass Hit* remained unreleased – and unlisted – until 1979. It seems reasonable to guess that this schedule was determined by contractual problems at the time the music was recorded.

The Miles Davis Quintet made their recording debut, for Columbia, a few days less than a month after they had made their performing debut in the Baltimore nightclub:

Miles Davis Quintet
Miles Davis, tpt; John Coltrane, ts; Red Garland, pno; Paul Chambers, b; Philly Joe Jones, dms. New York, 27 October 1955
Ah-Leu-Cha (Columbia CL 949); *Two Bass Hit* (Columbia 36278 [1979]); *Little Melonae* (Columbia C32025 [1973]; JP 13811 [1977]); *Budo* (CBS [French] BPG 62637; also available on the issues listed for *Little Melonae*)

The repertoire is uncharacteristic of subsequent recording dates by the quintet and of Davis's recording dates for Prestige in the previous year, which usually mixed ballads and jazz compositions with an imbalance in favor of the ballads. Here, Davis calls three bebop classics and a new bebop title.

Ah-Leu-Cha is Parker's tune, recorded by Davis and Parker in the last days of the original Parker quintet, in 1948; it had hardly been played at all since then by anyone, and Davis seems to have removed it from his quintet's repertoire after the first few months. It deserved a better fate, probably, because it is an affecting uptempo melody based on a counterpoint chase by the two horns. On this version, Philly Joe Jones plays the melody at the bridge, and Davis solos coolly while the rhythm blasts around him.

Two Bass Hit, by John Lewis and Dizzy Gillespie, was recorded by Gillespie's orchestra in 1947, and the quintet pay homage to Lewis's original arrangement by preserving some of his arranged figures in their version. Here and for the rest of the decade, *Two Bass Hit* functions as Coltrane's showcase in the quintet; he is the only soloist apart from a drum break by Jones, and he charges through nine choruses, accompanied by Davis's obbligatos for the last one. Until this recording came to light in 1979, it was still possible for listeners to assume that Davis remained lukewarm about Coltrane's playing for the first months of the quintet's existence, but the fact that he gave Coltrane a showcase from the very beginning and also recorded it at the first opportunity disproves that assumption. In 1975, Davis told Jimmy Saunders, "When I first went into the studio with Coltrane, they asked me, 'What are you doing with a sad-ass saxophone player like him?' So I said, 'Just shut up and get behind the controls – before we leave.'" Davis's confidence in Coltrane is more than vindicated by his long solo on *Two Bass Hit*, which opens with a patented Coltrane charge that seems to carry him all the way through it.

Little Melonae, the only new title, was contributed by Jackie McLean, and it might have helped McLean gain some recognition as a composer if it had been released at the time, especially in conjunction with McLean's other contributions to Davis's repertoire, including *Dr. Jackle*, *Minor March*, and *Dig*. *Little Melonae* features long improvisations by Davis, Coltrane, and Garland (who plays an odd, exotic solo in the lower half of the keyboard) and gives Chambers a chance to be heard in the break at the bridge.

Budo, of course, is yet another version of Bud Powell's *Hallucinations*, as originally revamped for the nonet in 1949. It features Davis on muted trumpet, and an aggressive ride cymbal by Jones, which is either over-recorded or imbalanced in the mix. Although the selection of compositions is far from typical, it was apparently made to give reasonable exposure to each member of the quintet, and it should have assured Columbia that it had made the right move in pursuing Davis.

Davis's apparent haste in moving over to Columbia even before settling with Prestige might seem to be harsh treatment for the small, independent company that had employed him almost continually since 1951, giving him recording exposure when many other companies would not and providing him with some income when he had almost no other. For the time being, of course, he remained in their employ. Three weeks after recording for Columbia, he took the quintet into the Prestige studios to record the remaining LP of his commitment for the calendar year. The details are as follows:

Miles Davis Quintet
Miles Davis, tpt; John Coltrane, ts (except *There Is No Greater Love*); Red Garland, pno; Paul Chambers, b; Philly Joe Jones, dms. New York, 16 November 1955
Stablemates; *How Am I to Know*; *Just Squeeze Me*; *There Is No Greater Love*; *The Theme*; *S'posin'*
(all on Prestige LP 7014; reissued [1963] on Prestige 7254)

Ironically, the 1963 reissue of this recording session came out under the title *The Original Quintet (First Recordings)*; the original issue had been called simply *Miles*.

Most of the session is made up of standards that the quintet seem to have gone in and just played, without many preliminaries, so that in its design this session is a scale model for the remaining quintet recordings for Prestige that would take place the following year. There are no ensembles except on *Stablemates* and *The Theme*. On all the other titles, Garland plays a few bars by way of introduction, Davis enters to play the melody and variations of it, and then Coltrane steps in cold to play his solo. As perfunctory as that scheme seems, the result is more than just desultory. The quintet are already good enough, collectively and individually, that their playing consistently swings and their solos consistently work.

While their best work for both Prestige and Columbia was still to come, their efforts this day were in many ways more satisfying than what they had recorded for Columbia a few weeks earlier. The contrast between these two early sessions would recur throughout the months of concurrent obligations to the two companies: the Columbia recordings were made from staples of the active repertoire and the Prestige recordings more often from standards swotted up for the day; the former balanced improvisation and ensemble skills while the latter used head arrangements to get into the round of solos. Given these differences, Columbia's files of the quintet's recordings should have a clear advantage over Prestige's files from the same period, but jazz listeners would face a difficult task if they had to choose between them.

The quintet's first work for Prestige is best remembered for *Stablemates*, an attractive composition written as a song form by a twenty-six-year-old tenor saxophonist from Philadelphia named Benny Golson, a close friend of Coltrane. Golson was eking out a living playing his saxophone locally, but his main interest was in composing, and Coltrane asked Davis to include *Stablemates* in order to give his friend a boost. It opens and closes with a simple ensemble statement, suggesting at least some minimal rehearsal time on it, but it was apparently not added to Davis's active repertoire. Nevertheless, it gave the attractive melody enough exposure that it was picked up by other bands and recorded several times. The other title that includes an ensemble statement is *The Theme*, the old 52nd Street draft horse with which Davis's bands had long been ending every set. Instead of playing the Monk-like theme once and leaving the stand, they dust it off for an extended blowing session. Between theme statements, Chambers, Davis, and Coltrane each play two choruses, and Jones plays a chorus of his own before the end. Less satisfying are the two standards played as moderate uptempo swingers, *How Am I to Know* and *S'posin'*. Coltrane seems unfamiliar with the former and feels his way through his solo, but Davis, muted for both, and Garland run through the changes on both unreflectingly. *No Greater Love*, which leaves Coltrane out altogether, is played as a pulseless threnody by Davis, a good example of his lyric tone but little else. This song is lifted from Ahmad Jamal's book but Davis's arrangement does not resemble Jamal's, where it comes off as a slow but lilting *tour de force* for bassist Israel Crosby. Jamal's influence is much more clearly felt on *Just Squeeze Me*, Duke Ellington's novelty song from 1946, which is played puckishly by Davis on muted trumpet over Jones's dancing brushwork. Although Coltrane still sounds more than a little self-conscious in this light-hearted context, the song is as good as anything the quintet played at this session, and it points ahead to the good ballad performances with which the quintet would soon enrich Prestige so abundantly.

The recording that resulted from the afternoon's work was released the following April and became the harbinger of the quintet for those fans who were beyond its physical reach. Nat Hentoff reviewed the record in the pages of *Down Beat* (16 May 1956) and gave accolades to *almost* everyone in the band. Miles Davis is, he said, "in wonderfully cohesive form here, blowing with characteristically personal, eggshell tone, muted on the standards, open on the originals." Garland, he says, "plays some of his best choruses on record here" (which must have been a fairly easy judgment, since there were so few others), Chambers "lays down support that could carry an army band," and Jones is "pulsatingly crisp as usual." However, Hentoff gave the record four stars rather than five, in that strange, criticism-defeating polling system that *Down Beat* maintains to this day, and his reason for holding back the fifth star was Coltrane's playing: "Coltrane, as Ira Gitler notes accurately ... is a mixture of Dexter Gordon, Sonny Rollins and Sonny Stitt. But so far there's very little of Coltrane. His general lack of individuality lowers the rating." Hentoff is justified in assessing the album as less than excellent, and he is right in pointing out Coltrane as the individual who, on the day, had the most conspicuous problems (although one wonders about his lack of individuality being the key to them). For the next few years, Coltrane's playing would continue to pose a stumbling block for some listeners, but for others it would prove to be instantly and unstintingly enticing.

Coltrane was sensitive to the cool reception that sometimes greeted his work, whether it came from musicians or fans or reviewers. His response, so characteristic of the man, was to work harder at his music, to spend even more of his waking hours practicing, and to keep on searching for the perfect mouthpiece. "I began trying to add to what I was playing because of Miles' group," he says. "Being there, I just couldn't be satisfied any longer with what I was doing. The standards were so high, and I felt I wasn't really contributing like I should." Musicians started spreading the word about Coltrane in the form of a one-liner that simultaneously mocked him gently and shone with admiration for him. "If you go by Trane's house at any time of the day or night and you don't hear saxophone playing," the line goes, "then you know that John isn't home." He was constantly developing his technique, or his tone, or his approach, and listeners who were in a position to hear the quintet regularly began to notice the difference between his playing in person and on his most recent records.

Nesuhi Ertegun, the producer at Atlantic Records, first noticed Coltrane's development when he spent hours in the audience at the Café Bohemia during the quintet's engagement in the spring of 1956. "Coltrane was already way ahead of any records he'd previously made," Ertegun says. "His music seemed so different from what the rest of the band was playing. The construction of his solos, his advanced harmonics, the strange way the notes succeeded one another, and the speed with which they were played – I found all these things most intriguing, but not all that comprehensible at one sitting." David Amram had returned from Paris that spring and he too caught the quintet at the Bohemia. "When I first met John Coltrane he was standing in front of the Café Bohemia on Barrow Street," he told J.C. Thomas, one of Coltrane's biographers. "This was in the spring of 1956, when Miles Davis was playing there. I went outside during intermission and there was Coltrane eating a piece of pie. I remember his eyes, huge but not staring, friendly and almost bemused. We looked at each other for the longest time, until I said hello and told him how much I liked his music. I'd played with Charles Mingus, and I mentioned this to Coltrane, who said he was quite an admirer of Mingus' music. He also said that one of the things he was trying to do was to take music beyond the 32-bar song form, to constantly develop and improvise on an idea or a simple line, as Indian musicians do with raga. I think it was the most serious musical discussion during the shortest amount of time I've ever had in my life."

As spring turned to summer, the quintet had chalked up enough successes in their personal appearances and with their one record release that they seemed to be a fixture. The sidemen grew together even more. Coltrane, who had come into the group under the aegis of Jones and Garland, was closest to young Paul Chambers, with whom he usually roomed when they were on the road. Davis seemed pleased with what he had wrought – the group sound, the critical attention directed at all his sidemen, and the way they all reacted to his own playing. He found it even less necessary to say anything in particular to them now that they were working well together – or to anyone else. He subscribed to the essential lesson of the hipster about the world beyond the bandstand, that it is Us against Them. He had never questioned Charlie Parker's perspective on that, and he was unlikely to start now. The band was, in his view, self-contained. Even the noisiest of nightclub audiences could not penetrate the band's concentration. "I figure if they're missing what Philly Joe Jones is doing, it's their tough luck," he said. "I wouldn't like to sit up there and play without anyone liking it, but I just mainly enjoy playing with my own rhythm section and listening to them. The night clubs are all the same to me. All you do is go and play and go home. I never know what people mean when they talk about acoustics. All I try to do is get my sound – full and round. It's a challenge to play in different clubs, to learn how to regulate your blowing to the club." Yet he was not indifferent to the effect of his playing on the audience, and he was adept at bringing it around when he wanted to. "I know what the power of silence is," he told Julie Coryell. "When I used to play in clubs, everybody was loud; there was a lot of noise. So I would take my mute off the microphone and I would play something so soft that you could hardly hear it – and you talk about listening!" Sometimes, but not often, he slips up and shows that he is neither indifferent to nor unaware of the world beyond the bandstand. "You can sell anything," he once said. "If you want to sell a car, paint it red. It can be the raggedest car in the world, but somebody'll buy it."

The audience was turning out to be the least of his problems as leader of the quintet. He knew he could satisfy it. The gut issues, the contentions that really affected the quality of life on the bandstand, came from the club owners and managers. Matters had hardly changed since his days on 52nd Street, and Davis began challenging some of the assumptions that were still taken for granted. "Things were changing during the 1950s but you still had to fight almost every step of the way and teach people," Dizzy Gillespie says. "One good example of that is Miles. He found out that he was powerful enough to demand certain things, and he got them. Miles was the first one to refuse to play 'forty-twenty.' In the old days, you would come into a club and play from twenty minutes after the hour to the end of the hour, and then you would come on twenty minutes later and so on. Miles broke that up. He came to Philadelphia once and told the owner he was going to play three shows. The owner didn't want to go for it, and Miles told him, 'Well then, you ain't got no deal.' Now, musicians play only two shows a night in some places. Miles did a lot for musicians." In most clubs, jazz groups now play three sets a night, with at least an hour in between, certainly an improvement over the old system.

The security of the quintet's success gave Davis the leverage to challenge other antiquated conditions as well. Jack Whittemore, his agent, remembers Davis confronting another situation that he felt needed reforming. Whittemore says: "Back in the days when he was only getting a thousand dollars for a concert, Miles was booked into Town Hall. The tickets were selling very well, so the promoter suggested doing two shows instead of one. As was customary in such cases, Miles was to get half fee, $500, for the second concert, but when I approached him with this, he looked puzzled. 'You mean I go on stage,' he said, 'pick up my horn, play a concert, and get a thousand dollars. Then they empty the hall, fill it again, I pick up my horn, play the same thing and get only five hundred – I don't understand it.' I told him that this was how it was normally done, but he was not satisfied. Finally he turned to me and said he'd do it for $500 if they would rope off half the hall and only sell half the tickets. When the promoters heard this, they decided to give him another thousand for the second concert."

Davis's business prowess is for him a source of not inconsiderable pride. In the early 1970s, he helped the singer Roberta Flack in what he saw as a business coup. "I got Roberta Flack $25,000 instead of $5,000 for Atlanta," he boasted to Gregg Hall. "She called me up and she was so mad because her lawyer put her name down to appear for $5,000 on behalf of the Mayor. So I straightened her out ... I told her that when she refused a date she shouldn't say that she doesn't want to make it but instead make her price so high that they either say yes or they say no. She finally got $25,000 – and the place was sold out." Similar dealings by Davis on his own behalf in the second half of the 1950s quickly made him one of the highest-paid jazz musicians of all time.

His dealings with the business side of the jazz world could not often be carried out at a safe remove, as they were for Roberta Flack. Usually they required confrontation, which has ended up in a collision on more than a few occasions. It is the classic case of two unrelenting forces poised on opposite sides of an issue. On the one hand, the managers, owners, and entrepreneurs, especially in the 1950s, were accustomed to dictating the conditions under which jazzmen would work for them, and if any of those conditions were deemed to be negotiable they would certainly not be negotiated with a trumpet player, much less with a black one. On the other hand, Davis demanded all his rights and a few privileges too, and he considered them his due; he was not interested in bargaining for what was his due or in presenting his case tactfully, which was a waste of breath.

The potential for collision was obvious to Davis, and from the earliest days of the quintet he took a step that guaranteed that he would not be totally unprepared when difficulties occurred. He retained a lawyer named Harold Lovett to oversee his interests. Davis's relationship with Lovett became an alliance that is legendary among jazz musicians of Davis's generation. "It's a matter of business maneuver, so to speak," Duke Jordan says. "From what I understand, when Miles formed his new group, the first thing he did was contact a lawyer, a young lawyer who was interested in handling musicians. This particular guy Miles was up with helped him tremendously, so when Miles came up with an idea of – whatever it might be – he would say to his lawyer: 'Hey, look, man, this guy is giving me a hard time. I'm supposed to be here for four weeks but I'm going to be here for two weeks and then quit because I don't dig what's going on. What kind of trouble can I get into if I do this?' And the lawyer would straighten him out." Davis's association with Lovett went well beyond legal advice. "Lovett is probably Miles' best friend and most constant companion," Joe Goldberg wrote in *Jazz Masters of the Fifties*. "He is one of the few people who stuck by Miles during the bad years ... One person remarked of Lovett, 'he makes Miles look like a choirboy,' and another person says that he has heard Miles talk about Lovett admiringly on several occasions, as though Lovett's 'coolness' were the ultimate in behavior. Asked about this, one club owner said, 'I think Miles is much cooler than Harold. Harold tends to worry about Miles, but Miles never worries about Harold.'"

Lovett's work for Davis often involved a lot more than investments and contracts. At a concert in Chicago, where the quintet were appearing as part of a package tour (probably Jazz for Moderns, a touring concert in the late 1950s), Davis walked in one night after the opening curtain had gone up, which was the promoter's deadline, but well before he and the quintet were scheduled to go onstage. When the promoter, who was not on cordial terms with Davis, charged toward him backstage, announcing loudly that he was going to fine him $100 for being late, Davis flattened him with one punch and then walked to the phone to call Lovett in New York.

In the winter of 1956, Davis canceled a scheduled engagement at a jazz club in Toronto at the last minute. When he was asked why, he said, "Because that motherfucker who owns it told me to fire Philly Joe because he's too *loud*! Nobody can tell me what to do with my music." Naturally, some legal hassles followed. And by the time Davis canceled the engagement, Coltrane and Chambers had already left New York for Toronto, where they found they had no place to play.

Soon after the Toronto fiasco, Davis disbanded the quintet for the first time. The main reason was that he had to lay off for a while in order to undergo surgery that would remove a growth on his larynx. It had been bothering him for almost a year, affecting his speech and causing hoarseness. The quintet were scheduled to make a recording in May, so the disbanding was only temporary.

Davis's throat ailment had caused him to speak in a whisper since the previous summer, a marked change from the voice recorded in the angry exchanges with Monk in 1954. Well before the operation, Bill Coss wrote: "The bother and anxiety about a growth in his throat had made the cat-slight Miles speak and talk in such whispers that his always present, kind of nose-thumbing withdrawal seemed nearly complete." The whispers became Davis's permanent mode of speech because he got caught up in a shouting match too soon after the surgery and permanently damaged the larynx. His adversary was a promoter by one account and a co-owner of a record company by another. "I wasn't supposed to talk for ten days," Davis says. "The second day I was out of the hospital, I ran into him [the businessman] and he tried to convince me to go into a deal I didn't want." To make his point clear, Davis found it necessary to raise his voice, for what turned out to be the last time. Leonard Feather claims that his hoarse whisper is "a source of psychological and physical discomfort, and a subject he prefers to avoid" discussing, but in recent years Davis has pointed with quite undisguised pride to the fact that Cicely Tyson, the actress who became Davis's fourth wife in 1981, imitated his voice when she played the feisty 110-year-old lead character in the television drama *The Autobiography of Miss Jane Pittman*, which won her an Emmy award in 1974. Since the operation, Davis's voice has been as distinctive as his trumpet-playing, and it is very much part of his character. The English reporter Michael Watts describes it this way: "Miles' voice is a phenomenon. It's a hoarse whisper, strained through his larynx like a sieve. He dredges it up slowly through the whole of his body, but it barely leaves his lips. It just hangs, a vague sibilance in the air, like the effort of a dying man. At first, it's both incomprehensible and comic. Instinctively you cock your head to one side to catch what he's saying. But gradually, you adjust to its level, as you would twiddle the dials on a radio to get its tuning." The voice certainly makes people attentive to him when he does choose to speak, not unlike his gambit of opening a set in a noisy club with an off-mike muted ballad.

During his period of recuperation, Davis led a pick-up group into the Prestige studios to dispatch the half-LP he still owed the company from 1953. Only Paul Chambers was brought in from the quintet. Although these recordings were slated to be released along with the material recorded in 1953 by the sextet with Charlie Parker on tenor, only Sonny Rollins was brought back from that band. Rollins had finally regained his confidence during the winter in Chicago and had joined the Max Roach-Clifford Brown Quintet, replacing Harold Land, when they were playing at the Beehive there in late December, almost two months after he had turned down Davis's invitation to join his quintet. The Roach-Brown group were almost continuously travelling from city to city, but they were based in New York and Rollins was living there again. He was rounding into his peak individual form, and the group were formidable, playing brittle, aggressive neo-bop. Their constant traveling kept them from putting in as much time in the recording studios as they might have wished, but they had completed three recording sessions for EmArcy in January and February and had another session scheduled under Rollins's name for Prestige just six days after Rollins played there in Davis's group. Those four sessions would be the only studio recordings ever made by the Roach-Brown-Rollins alliance because Brown was killed in a car crash along with the group's piano player, Richie Powell, and Powell's wife, on 25 June. Brown was only twenty-six.

At the moment of Davis's recording, Sonny Rollins was at a pinnacle and he showed up ready to play. Philly Joe Jones had been the drummer on that abortive 1953 date, but he was not recalled for this complementary session. In his place, Davis called in Arthur Taylor. The piano player on that earlier date had been Walter Bishop, a graduate of Parker's bands, but Davis this time brought in Tommy Flanagan instead. The details are as follows:

Miles Davis All Stars
Miles Davis, tpt; Sonny Rollins, ts; Tommy Flanagan, pno; Paul Chambers, b; Arthur Taylor, dms. New York, 16 March 1956
In Your Own Sweet Way; No Line; Vierd Blues
(all on Prestige LP 7044; reissued [1970] on Prestige 7847)

No Line and *Vierd Blues* just happened in the recording studio, although both are credited as Davis's compositions. *No Line*, as its title indicates, has no beginning or end, just a middle. It opens with what might as easily be the fifth chorus of a cheerful uptempo solo by Davis on muted trumpet, and it peters out with Chambers and Taylor left suddenly on their own, and sounding stranded. In between, Rollins, Flanagan, and (again) Davis take their turns. *Vierd Blues* is a slow blues with a minimal head played by the two horns, and it features a notably calm solo by Rollins, as if he is trying to match Davis's calmness before him. *In Your Own Sweet Way* presents an entirely different feeling. This handsome melody by Dave Brubeck is treated with some reverence. Paul Chambers is at the heart of Davis's arrangement, reflecting the novel use of time that makes this melody work so well and interpolating stop-time intervals between the soloists. Davis's muted playing has some rough edges, and there is no doubt that the performance would have benefited from a second take, as would *No Line*, but there were no second takes at this recording session, which was set up to fulfill an old obligation. At the end of *In Your Own Sweet Way*, almost before the last throbbing note of the bass has been taped, Davis rasps, "Yeah, Rudy," to Rudy Van Gelder in the control booth.

Although this record date hardly seems memorable, Tommy Flanagan recalled it twenty-four years later. "It was my birthday, that's how I remember; my twenty-sixth birthday," he told Michael Ullman. "He had the date and I got the call." Most of all, he remembered the spontaneity of the session being broken by Davis's introducing *In Your Own Sweet Way*. "We just cooked," he says. "All except that one Brubeck tune. That came about strangely. Miles had that tune in his back pocket – a sketch of the chords. I remember him telling me how to voice the intro. He always knows exactly what he wants. It makes him easy to work with. If you don't play what he wants, he tells you like this [whispering hoarsely] – 'Play block chords, but not like Milt Buckner. In the style of Ahmad Jamal.' I didn't really get into it too much, but Red Garland really grasped that. I love Ahmad's playing, but I didn't want to play like him ... I know what Miles likes about it – he plays that way himself. With the spaces – it just gives you a lot of room to play inside of. Like Ahmad can repeat a phrase to death, but with taste. Not the kind of monotony that really wears on your nerves – he gets a lot of good out of it." On this occasion, Tommy Flanagan played his short session with Davis sounding not at all like Jamal and very much like himself.

Within two months, Davis was back in the Prestige studio to begin working off his contract obligations for 1956. This time he surrounded himself with the working quintet, and they completed the first of two incredible sessions that would yield enough music to fill all four LPs called for in his contract, with one track left over. The first session, in May, was the more prolific, producing fourteen complete takes in the space of one Friday afternoon and evening. Nevertheless, the music is varied in tempo and form, careful and sometimes brilliant in execution, and usually ingenious in invention:

Miles Davis Quintet
Miles Davis, tpt; John Coltrane, ts; Red Garland, pno; Paul Chambers, b; Philly Joe Jones, dms. New York, 11 May 1956
In Your Own Sweet Way (Prestige LP 7166); *Diane* (Prestige LP 7200); *Trane's Blues* [*The Theme*] (Prestige LP 7166); *Something I Dreamed Last Night* (Prestige LP 7200); *It Could Happen to You* and *Woody'n You* (Prestige LP 7129); *Ahmad's Blues* (Prestige LP 7166); *Surrey with a Fringe on Top* (Prestige LP 7200); *It Never Entered My Mind* (Prestige LP 7166); *When I Fall in Love* and *Salt Peanuts* (Prestige LP 7200); *Four*, *The Theme I*, and *The Theme II* (Prestige LP 7166)
Coltrane does not play on *Something I Dreamed Last Night*, *It Never Entered My Mind*, and *When I Fall in Love*; neither Davis nor Coltrane plays on *Ahmad's Blues*. *Trane's Blues* is a version of *The Theme*. The Prestige issues listed above refer to the first releases of this material, called *Workin'* (7166), *Steamin'* (7200), and *Relaxin'* (7129); the music has been reissued in North America with new catalog numbers at least twice, but the album titles as well as the selections have remained the same.

To record this material, the quintet assembled at Van Gelder's Hackensack studio and Davis called out the titles one after the other, as if they were playing an extended nightclub set. There were no second takes, and even the second recording of *The Theme* at the tail end of the day is not a second attempt at it but merely a brief coda to the whole set; the version that precedes it is a full-blown swinger. Something of the atmosphere was preserved in the recordings by including some of Davis's directions to the men in the control booth: at the start of the version of *The Theme* that was released as *Trane's Blues* he announces, "The blues"; after *It Could Happen to You*, he calls up to Bob Weinstock, "How was that, Bob?," and on being assured that it was fine, he announces, "OK, we're gonna do *Woody'n You*"; and after *Woody'n You*, he is heard asking "OK?," and when he is apparently told in jest to do it over, he says, plainly irritated, "Why?," but Coltrane, nonplussed, is heard saying, "Could I have the beer opener?"

The shifting instrumentation on several numbers is typical of their club performances at this time, with Coltrane usually sitting out on the slow ballads and the rhythm trio taking a feature on their own. Two of the ballads without Coltrane, *Something I Dreamed Last Night* and *When I Fall in Love*, are the least interesting pieces, although not directly because of his absence. Both are played as pulseless ballads in which Davis places his mute within a centimeter of the microphone, and though his ballads in this style were useful in attracting listeners who had previously listened only to ballad singers such as Frank Sinatra and Jo Stafford, they now seem sentimental and cloying. The other ballad without Coltrane, *It Never Entered My Mind*, is entirely different: an ornate arrangement polished by club performances, it features a repeated Chopinesque countermelody on the piano and a repeated stop-time figure on the bass. Davis fashions the melody on his muted trumpet in the space between the piano and bass, but he does not solo, leaving that to Garland, who plays a delicate, static, semi-classical set piece with all the accoutrements of Ahmad Jamal but none of his swing. The total effect is what one might expect if Jamal were to write an arrangement for the quintet, and the unassimilated, even undigested, foisting of Jamal's mannerisms onto the members of the quintet represents the apogee of Davis's fascination with Jamal. Even *Ahmad's Blues*, the rhythm trio's rendition of a tricky, trilled original recorded by Jamal in 1952, retains the individuality of the players better.

The other ballads show the unmistakeable touch of Jamal too, especially in their jaunty beat and their understated melodies. Brubeck's *In Your Own Sweet Way*, which Davis had introduced to the men in the control booth just a few weeks before, this time gets its due. *Surrey with a Fringe on Top*, a silly Rodgers and Hammerstein song from *Oklahoma!*, the charms of which were unearthed by Jamal, gets a surprisingly gritty ride by the quintet that lasts nine minutes and might be the one title from this session, if you could choose only one, you would most want to take with you to a desert isle. Among its glories is the first recorded instance of the arranged dynamism between Davis and Coltrane, as Davis's lacy, romantic exploration of the melody on muted trumpet gives way to a four-bar break in which Coltrane comes roaring in to take over in no uncertain terms. The device, based on a simple contrast that was always implied in the styles of the two men, is exploited consciously here, as it would be in all their finest work together.

In simply rattling off such a quantity of music, Davis was displaying either unbounded confidence – not to say chutzpah – or fathomless desperation. There can be no doubt that he wanted to rid himself of his Prestige contract, but if in doing so he had left behind a legacy of slipshod performances the damage to his reputation might have been irreparable. More likely, he knew the strengths of the quintet, and every nightclub performance with them was, in a sense, a rehearsal for the Prestige sessions, even if some of the titles were new. He was a veteran of the recording studios in a sense that very few performers of the day were. He had been in them often and long, and his approach to recording was formed to some extent by Charlie Parker, who disdained them thoroughly. He was also a pioneer in the microgroove technology. All these factors allowed Davis to become more and more cavalier about recording sessions after the carefully rehearsed nonet sessions of the early 1950s, to the point where he seldom called for retakes, even when they were needed, as in his recent date with Sonny Rollins and Tommy

Flanagan. From now on, his approach to the recording studio, probably buoyed by the success of the first Prestige marathon, would be quite consciously casual, a point that drew the attention of other musicians. J.J. Johnson says, "I've recorded with Miles and I know how he operates. Most of the time, he goes into the studio and one take is it! Goofs or not, there's no second or third take. That's his philosophy on the recording bit." He said so himself, a few years later, talking to Ralph J. Gleason. "When they make records with all the mistakes in, as well as the rest, then they'll really make jazz records," he said. "If the mistakes aren't there too, it ain't none of you."

As if to balance some psychological ledger, Davis and the quintet were in the recording studio for Columbia early the next month. After the outpouring for Prestige, this Columbia session has a frugal look, producing only three titles:

Miles Davis Quintet
Miles Davis, tpt; John Coltrane, ts; Red Garland, pno; Paul Chambers, b; Philly Joe Jones, dms. New York, 5 June 1956
Dear Old Stockholm; Bye Bye Blackbird; Tadd's Delight [*Sid's Delight*]
(all on Columbia CL 949)

This session contrasts with the previous one not only in quantity but also in attitude. Here the resources of the quintet are under tighter control, with solos framed neatly in arrangements and the exuberance of the group's bulls, Coltrane and Jones, reined in. They do not suffer noticeably for the control: Coltrane is set up for his solos on the two ballads so that he loses the awkwardness that is sometimes felt in the Prestige counterparts of these ginger ballads, and Jones sublimates his more raucous tendencies into nimble, showy drumming that never takes the center of the stage but is never far from it. The resuscitation of *Tadd's Delight* – Dameron's bebop theme broadcast as *Webb's Delight* by Dameron and Davis in 1949 and recorded for Capitol as *Sid's Delight* (on M-11059) by Dameron and Fats Navarro that same year – adds to the stockpile of bop tunes by the quintet at Columbia. It suggests again that Columbia was still looking to the Davis quintet as potential leaders in the hard bop movement, then enjoying considerable success in record releases by the Max Roach-Clifford Brown group and Art Blakey's Jazz Messengers. Columbia was about to discover, however, that Davis's real strength lay elsewhere and that its commercial success would dwarf that of the hard boppers. Davis probably knew already what was happening, judging from his treatment of *Tadd's Delight*, which was brief, straight, and only moderately upbeat, a far cry from what the Jazz Messengers might have done with it.

The ballads were a different matter. *Dear Old Stockholm*, played only slightly slower than *Tadd's Delight*, opens with a motif played by Garland and Coltrane and sustained by Garland throughout. Over it, Davis plays the haunting Swedish folk melody discovered by Stan Getz, and Paul Chambers takes the first solo; when Coltrane enters, the rhythm toughens perfectly, but it softens again when Davis returns for his muted solo. All the elements of Davis's beautiful arrangement of this song were already in place when he recorded it for Blue Note in 1952 – Getz's original version (long out of print, but last on Roost SLP 2249) had none of these elements – but by comparison there is a definite coarseness to the motif in Davis's earlier version, when it was played by J.J. Johnson and Jackie McLean, and to Davis's lead work too, played open rather than muted and sounding a little flat. Comparing the two versions, four years apart, shows clearly that Davis's progress lay not in his musical conception but in the refinement and discipline he could now exercise over it. The other ballad, *Bye Bye Blackbird*, an old song that a couple of generations of Americans grew up knowing although it was never a popular hit, is suffused by a blues feeling that popular songwriters often tried for but seldom found, except in the best work of Harold Arlen and perhaps some of Gershwin and Hoagy Carmichael. It also carries vague sociological implications: in the 1930s the few blacks who participated in white activities, such as the semi-professional National Football League, were serenaded with the song by the all-white spectators. Davis's tightly muted rendition seems to be a distillation of everything he ever learned from Billie Holiday: it is sorrowing, and it is pained, but it is not self-pitying. More than that, compared to the two pulseless ballads he had played for Prestige, this one swings.

This Columbia session continued, in effect, about three months later, producing even more magnificent music. This date also served the first public notice – though few people knew about it at the time or for several years after – of Davis's musical reunion with Gil Evans. To all appearances, the date was just another brilliantly successful day in the recording studios for the quintet, which was now beginning to get used to such days. The details are as follows:

Miles Davis Quintet
Miles Davis, tpt; John Coltrane, ts; Red Garland, pno; Paul Chambers, b; Philly Joe Jones, dms. New York, 10 September 1956
All of You (Columbia CL949); *Sweet Sue* (originally on Columbia CL919; reissued on CBS [Fr] 62 637 [1968], Columbia C 32025 [1973], and JP 13811 [1977]); *Round Midnight* [*Round about Midnight*] (Columbia CL949)
Sweet Sue is arranged by Teo Macero; *Round Midnight* is arranged by Gil Evans. The original issue of *Sweet Sue* includes a narration by Leonard Bernstein.

This recording session is partitioned into two parts, with the recording of *All of You* and *Round Midnight* standing in many ways as consummations of Davis's work with the quintet, and the recording of *Sweet Sue* a minor curiosity.

Sweet Sue came about because of Leonard Bernstein, then conductor of the New York Philharmonic and composer of an enormous range of music from the symphony *Jeremiah* to the music for *West Side Story* and the scores for the film *On the Waterfront*. Bernstein also acted during the 1950s as writer, narrator, and performer on the television program *Omnibus*, a Sunday afternoon lecture-entertainment on music which, ironically, was probably more responsible for his nationwide celebrity than his prodigious musical talent. Along with expositions of topics such as Bach, opera, and conducting, he included a program called "The World of Jazz", which was telecast on 16 October 1955.

The show had its inane moments: toward the end Bernstein says, "Jazz used to advertise itself as 'hot'; now the heat is off. The jazz player has become a highly serious person. He may even be an intellectual. He tends to wear Ivy League clothes, have a crew cut, or wear horn-rimmed glasses." It also had its moments of insight as Bernstein wended his articulate and highly accessible way from variations on a theme by Mozart through jazz instruments and period styles. The program had an inestimable effect, now forgotten and even then underappreciated, on broadening the audience for jazz, a part of the upward spiral that began with the white middle-class attraction to West Coast jazz and would continue with fashionable college concerts, festivals, and government-sponsored international goodwill tours.

At the end of the show, to illustrate some of the style shifts in the history of jazz, Bernstein played excerpts of *Sweet Sue* from recorded versions by Bix Beiderbecke and Benny Goodman and then introduced what he considered to be an up-to-the-minute updating – "an advanced sophisticated art mainly for listening, full of influences of Bartók and Stravinsky, and very, very serious," he called it in his introduction – by bringing on a band made up of clarinet, flute, english horn, bass saxophone, bass, and drums to play an arrangement of *Sweet Sue* by one Danny Hurd. It was, needless to say, anticlimactic.

A few months later, when Columbia Records approached Bernstein to make an LP on jazz along the same lines as his television program but using its resources, both past and present, for illustrative material, one of the pieces that most clearly required revision was the post-Goodman version of *Sweet Sue*. George Avakian contacted the tenor saxophonist Teo Macero, a Juilliard graduate active in jazz-classical fusion experiments, to prepare both a swing arrangement – the Goodman recording used on the original show belonged to RCA Victor – and a modern arrangement. Macero's swing arrangement was accepted and eventually appeared on Bernstein's LP *What Is Jazz?* (Columbia CL919), played by the Don Butterfield

Sextet, with a tenor solo by Macero. But when Macero showed Bernstein his modern arrangement of it, Bernstein declared it "too lugubrious."

Macero prepared a second introduction, and Avakian brought in Davis to decide how to play it for the recording. Whether Davis chose Macero's first or second attempt is uncertain, but in any case all that survives of Macero's arrangement is an introductory tag lasting only a few seconds. Even less survives of the original melody known as *Sweet Sue*, for at the point when Macero's tag ends and one expects Davis to state some semblance of the melody, he launches instead into an improvisation that at no point refers directly to the melody. Coltrane follows, and Garland follows that, and the hoary old melody is never heard from. There is no chance whatever of its arising in the simultaneous improvisation by Davis and Coltrane that caps off the performance – Coltrane sounding timid, Davis taking charge, and the listener, even the stodgiest, dreaming he hears Bernstein in the control booth exclaim, "Far out!" while Philly Joe and the others try to hide their smiles.

All of You, Cole Porter's Hollywood hit for Fred Astaire just the year before, and *Round Midnight* (Monk's *Round about Midnight* with its title streamlined due to the new currency of the sung version) are something else again. *All of You* gets Davis's masterly treatment of the Jamal ballad style, the kind of integration into the quintet's style that he had been working toward for some time. It is played in Jamal's gentle, swinging tempo, with full value given to the rhythm players behind the horns, but the performance is a triumph of individual skills used to collective advantage. Davis pays unusual homage to Porter's melody at both the open and the close over a bobbing bass line by Chambers that mixes eighth-notes and rests; Coltrane is heard for the first time after Davis's solo, and at his entrance a new force from the rhythm section takes over as Chambers walks and Jones hits rim shots to close each bar.

All of You is one of Davis's finest ballad performances, but it has received less attention than it deserves because it was superseded immediately by *Round Midnight*, one of the most striking ballad performances in all of jazz. One notices first the symmetry of the arrangement, which presents three movements, the first and the third featuring Davis on muted trumpet playing variations on Monk's melody accompanied by Coltrane's obbligatos, the middle movement featuring Coltrane, introduced by a trumpet-saxophone fanfare. The middle movement doubles the tempo of the others, and Coltrane invents a beautiful melody for two choruses. On either side of it stand Davis's cooler tone poems. The ensemble passages are brief but effective, consisting of a variation of the familiar introduction and a fanfare to introduce tempo changes. Within the frame of the arrangement, the individual players all shine; they seem free to play and not at all fettered by the weight of the arrangement, the balance between the individual and the group marvelously maintained. That balance had grown with familiarity, but it went beyond that and was put in motion by Gil Evans, the arranger. Evans's role was not credited publicly until this title was reissued in 1973. The acknowledgement came as a surprise mainly because it came so irresponsibly and irremediably late, but was no surprise musically.

Since the working days of the short-lived Miles Davis nonet in 1948, Evans had eked out a living as a freelance arranger around New York. He worked for some radio shows, but the demand for original music on radio was waning fast, and he picked up some jobs in television, which was just coming into its own, but mostly he took whatever jobs came to him. He contributed supper club arrangements for popular singers such as Pearl Bailey, Tony Bennett, the actress Polly Bergen when she tried her hand at torch singing, and Johnny Mathis. Some of the work he did edged closer to jazz, such as his scores for the trumpeter Billy Butterfield, himself a freelancer surviving on studio work and records that used his pure tone in the saccharine context of mood music, and his arrangements for singers Helen Merrill and Peggy Lee, who had come up through the ranks of band singers before making it on their own. There was also a bit of work in jazz, for conservatory-influenced jazzmen such as Teddy Charles and Hal McKusick, and also for Benny Goodman and Gerry Mulligan, and three arrangements for Charlie Parker on Norman Granz's Clef label with the Dave Lambert Singers on *If I Love Again*, *Old Folks*, and *In the Still of the Night*. He was not languishing, but his activity was too diffuse, even with the nonet records coming out at intervals, to keep his name before the jazz public. He also had some bad luck; the Parker-Lambert recordings turned out to be, according to the critic Charles Fox, "the least individual and least successful pieces of writing Evans has done."

Still, one might have expected that more opportunities would come to him, no matter how effacing he tended to be. "As for jazz dates," Evans said later, "one reason I didn't do much was that nobody asked me." "Eight years after *Boplicity*, seven years after *Moon Dreams* – these figures are a disgrace to the world of jazz – Evans was commissioned to do a series of arrangements for a Miles Davis album," André Hodeir says, referring to the 1957 LP that for many years was thought to mark Evans's reunion with Davis. He continues: "In the meantime, everyone had forgotten who he was; jazz people don't give much thought to anyone who doesn't sing, play the trumpet, or lead a band. Gil's friends were a bit uneasy."

The turning point in Evans's fortunes came indirectly through his work for Helen Merrill, a fine ballad singer who failed to attract the audience she deserved in North America, although she had more success in the 1960s in Europe and especially in Japan (where she lived for several years before returning to New York in 1973). In the 1950s Merrill was featured for a while in the Earl Hines band, in which her husband, Aaron Sachs, played reeds, and her considerable potential as a singer won her a record contract with EmArcy, for which she made some excellent records, although she had to battle the management to get to make them on her own terms. Her first record for them, in 1954, featured the new-comer Clifford Brown playing obbligatos behind her, and a later record, made in July 1956, featured Gil Evans's arrangements. "That was only because Helen insisted," Evans says. "The a & r man [EmArcy's producer] didn't want me. I had a lot of trouble with him." Merrill not only insisted on using him, she also insisted on telling other people about him. One of the people she told was Miles Davis, whose quintet was touring in a concert package that summer that also included Merrill. She told Davis: "'I just finished this album with Gil Evans and, boy, you've got to use him.' Miles said, 'Well, yeah, I forgot about Gil; and I think I'll give him a call.' That's all he said," Merrill remembers, "and the rest is jazz history." The first step in that piece of jazz history, although almost no one knew it at the time, was Evans's arrangement of *Round Midnight* for the quintet on 10 September.

That fact that Evans was already involved in Davis's work in the fall of 1956 gives a new perspective on Davis's next recordings, which were also for Columbia but involved neither Evans nor the quintet. Instead, they involved two old col-leagues from the nonet, John Lewis and J.J. Johnson. Both Lewis and Johnson harbored ambitions to expand the horizons of jazz toward a new legitimacy by composing extended forms within the jazz idiom. They were by no means alone. David Amram, who had long worked in both symphonic and jazz music, explained how he and many others were beginning to approach the fusion of the two streams: "After working in both for so long I no longer saw a distinction, except the distinction that existed in other people's minds. There may be differences in terms of idioms, in approach and performance techniques, but ultimately it's all part of a world that expresses itself through a beautiful series of sounds. There was no reason I could not combine these sounds in terms of my life experience to make my own kind of music." Amram, Lewis, and Johnson belonged to a loose alliance of musicians trying to do just that, and their movement was gaining momentum at the end of the 1950s. Gunther Schuller, who now made his living as the principal horn in the Metropolitan Opera Orchestra, was the leading spokesman. He defined the movement's musical objectives as no less than the fusing of "the improvisational spontaneity and rhythmic vitality of jazz with the compositional procedures and techniques acquired in Western music during seven hundred years of musical development," and he coined the term for the fusion, "third stream music," implying the confluence of European and Afro-American tributaries. Its votaries were to have their most significant successes in the last half of the 1950s. Teo Macero and the trombonist Bill Russo were commissioned to write works for the New York Philharmonic, and a little later David Amram became the Philharmonic's composer in residence, all under the influential tutelage of Leonard Bernstein. In 1957, Brandeis University commissioned Schuller, Charles Mingus, George Russell, and the saxophonist Jimmy Giuffre to compose third stream works for their Festival of Arts. John Lewis was introducing fugues, rondos, and other European forms in a jazz context nightly with his Modern Jazz Quartet. J.J. Johnson, who had joined Columbia's roster of jazz talent, took up conservatory-influenced composition during an enforced layoff from jazz in 1952–3, when he lost his cabaret card, a sort of license to perform in New York clubs administered by the police department, because of drug charges.

In late 1956, he and Lewis were scheduled to record extended third stream compositions for Columbia with a brass and rhythm ensemble. Miles Davis was chosen as the principal soloist on both works. The details are as follows:

The Brass Ensemble of the Jazz and Classical Music Society
John Lewis, comp, arr; Gunther Schuller, cond; Miles Davis, Bernie Glow, Arthur Strutter, Joe Wilder, tpt; Jim Buffington, frh; Urbie Green, J.J. Johnson, tbn; Milt Hinton, b; Osie Johnson, dms; Dick Horowitz, tympani, perc. New York, 20 October 1956
Three Little Feelings (Columbia CL941; reissued on CBS [Fr] 62 637)

Same personnel except J.J. Johnson, comp, arr; Miles Davis, flugelhorn; omit Horowitz. New York, 23 October 1956
Jazz Suite for Brass (issued as above)

This music is virtually unknown to North American listeners. The original issue seems to have been a closely guarded secret, at least among jazz buffs, and there are apparently no commentaries and no reviews from North America. In a way, such neglect is a shame, because the music is ambitious and generally interesting, and because Davis and Johnson solo particularly well. Lewis's *Three Little Feelings* is the more successful of the two pieces. *Jazz Suite for Brass* suffers from sequences that seem unrelated, perhaps even left over from something else, notably at the beginning of the second movement and through most of the third. In all fairness, however, it should be noted that the English reviewer Max Harrison does not hear it that way at all. He says, "While the main thread is undoubtedly held by the soloists, the writing is everywhere precise in its intention, a genuine, if oblique, extension of Johnson's remarkable trombone playing." Harrison is especially enthusiastic about the first movement, on which it might be easier for other listeners to agree with him: "The rapid pace of the movement proper comes as a surprise, and dark mixtures of open and muted sound lead quickly to Davis's first contribution. He is heard on flugelhorn, and, in combination with the swift tempo, his melancholy creates an ambiguous feeling that is resolved by the extroversion of the composer's solo, which follows. Each improvises on the theme, thereby strengthening the movement's unity, and the ensemble is pointedly active behind them, not just accompanying but adding further perspective to their discoveries." The second movement provides a curious point of interest; its only soloist is Bernie Glow, who plays in a straight tone with emphatic vibrato, and the contrast between his feeling in this context and Davis's in the first movement provides an object lesson in the chasm between classical and jazz styles.

Three Little Feelings features Davis's open trumpet on the first and second movements and Johnson's trombone on the third. Of the first movement, a swinger, Harrison writes: "In the beginning three motives are announced, then piled on top of each other. Davis, on trumpet this time, improvises around one of them, a chromatic four-note figure. He sounds even more forsaken than in Johnson's [*Jazz Suite*], but is, of course, responding to the more emotional nature of the musical material. It is noteworthy that his acutely subjective art can fit into so deliberately organized a setting, but perhaps that is a commentary on both desire for freedom and desire for discipline." The second movement brings Davis even further into the foreground by reducing the role of the ensemble merely to sustaining chords behind him, in a ballad format. Another English critic, Ronald Atkins, notes the similarity between this movement and the later work of Davis with a large orchestra directed by Gil Evans. He says: "The second movement is on par with the outstanding Miles Davis–Gil Evans collaborations ... even though the backing might seem monochromatic by comparison. In what essentially is a ballad context, Davis is driven to excel himself and we must assume Lewis bears some responsibility for this." Atkins's point about the similarity can easily be taken further. The voicings behind Davis are remarkably similar to the voicings that Gil Evans was working on, although not as full-sounding in Lewis's arrangement as in Evans's because Evans's orchestras will be considerably larger and have more varied instrumentation. This impression of similarity cannot be dismissed as a kind of aural illusion, the result, say, of hearing Davis's familiar sound in front of a large orchestra, because the similarity in voicing is every bit as obvious in the third movement as well, where Johnson, not Davis, is the soloist.

It is ironic that the American audience, which was so quick to recognize the brilliance of the Miles Davis–Gil Evans collaborations, has never paid much attention to John Lewis's *Three Little Feelings*, its single most influential precursor. The gap is a disservice to Lewis as well as a missed opportunity. It is probably a consequence of the fairly rapid eclipse of the third stream as a movement, for it petered out by the mid-1960s. Its spirit survives in occasional orchestral works by those who were there when it bloomed, some of whom are now associated with the New England Conservatory in Boston, and by younger musicians such as

Anthony Braxton, Michael Gibbs, Allyn Ferguson, and Patrick Williams. However, it no longer has a recognized spokesman or an identifiable audience, two factors that discourage the record companies from keeping these and other recordings from the time in print.

Three days after the recordings with the Brass Ensemble, Davis was poised for the second of his marathon sessions with the quintet in the Prestige studios. The details are as follows:

Miles Davis Quintet
Miles Davis, tpt; John Coltrane, ts (except *My Funny Valentine*); Red Garland, pno; Paul Chambers, b; Philly Joe Jones, dms. New York, 26 October 1956
If I Were a Bell (Prestige LP 7129); *Well You Needn't* (Prestige LP 7200); *Round about Midnight* (Prestige LP 7150); *Half Nelson* (Prestige LP 7166); *You're My Everything, I Could Write a Book*, and *Oleo* (Prestige LP 7129); *Airegin, Tune up, When Lights Are Low, Blues by Five*, and *My Funny Valentine* (Prestige LP 7094)
Again, the issue numbers refer to the original issues titled *Relaxin'* (7129), *Cookin'* (7094), *Workin'* (7166), and *Steamin'* (7200), except for *Round about Midnight*, which first appeared on *Miles Davis and the Modern Jazz Giants* (7150), along with titles from the Christmas eve 1954 session.

In the five and a half months since the first Prestige marathon, the quintet have gone through some developments that become clear in the comparison. First, Coltrane is now generally included on the slow ballads. Earlier he had been asked to sit out; here he does so only on *My Funny Valentine*, a tune that came to bear Davis's signature from repeated playings over the years. "I played *My Funny Valentine* for a long time and didn't like it," he once said, "and all of a sudden it meant something." His audience certainly assumed it meant something to him when they heard this, his first, recording of it. On the other slow ballads, *Round about Midnight* (in Evans's arrangement again) and *You're My Everything*, the tempo doubles for Coltrane's turn, but he proves himself, as he had apparently proven himself to Davis's satisfaction in the intervening months, to be an effective ballad soloist.

Second, the rhythm section has become amazingly fluid, using all kinds of devices while in motion, regardless of tempo. They double tempos and halve them routinely on the ballads; Jones alone doubles his tempo behind Coltrane on *When Lights Are Low* while the others hold the original; Chambers walks throughout *Oleo* while the other rhythm players enter only for the bridge; and they play the gamut of tempos from the breakneck *Airegin* to the slow *My Funny Valentine* with no diminution of strength. Chambers is especially effective on his two solo turns, playing a showy arco solo on *Well You Needn't* and a pizzicato solo on *Blues by Five*, a head arrangement, that rivals Mingus's clarity and sounds more than a little like his choice of notes. By the fall of 1956, the prowess of this rhythm trio was widely recognized. They had recorded as a trio for Prestige, making an LP on which Garland introduced *If I Were a Bell* so effectively that Davis immediately added it to the quintet's repertoire, and musicians everywhere were buzzing about them. During a desultory set by the quintet at the Café Bohemia around this time, someone remarked that little seemed to be happening and Teddy Charles replied, "Watch the rhythm section. This is the best rhythm section in jazz, the hardest swinging rhythm section. Watch out when they loosen up."

In order to produce the quantity of music that Prestige needed from him, Davis was obviously digging deeply into his memory to come up with enough titles. The tunes he called at the two Prestige marathons make a kind of loose index of the music that he had worked on since arriving in New York. *Half Nelson* is one of the most venerable, dating from his first record date as a leader, in 1947, but Dizzy Gillespie's tunes, *Salt Peanuts* and *Woody'n You*, played at the first session, go back even farther, being among the most widely heard themes on 52nd Street when Davis arrived there. *Woody'n You* was added to Davis's recorded stock in 1952, the same year that he first recorded *Dear Old Stockholm*. *Tune up* first shows up in 1953, and so does Benny Carter's *When Lights Are low* (misidentified in Ira Gitler's notes for this session as *Just Squeeze Me*). *Four* was first recorded in 1954, and so were Sonny Rollins's contributions to his book, *Oleo* and *Airegin*. *In Your Own Sweet Way* and *Round Midnight* had entered his favor so forcibly that they were also recorded just weeks before their re-recording at the marathons. A few compositions destined to recur, notably *My Funny Valentine* and *If I Were a Bell*, get their first airing, and the sessions are rounded out by a list of pop songs apparently intended as fillers.

At least as interesting as what he dragged forward to play is what he left behind untouched. Whatever happened to the 1947 *Milestones*, recorded with *Half Nelson* and apparently forgotten along with his other originals of that day? What about the large repertoire he had played nightly with the Parker quintet: the Parker originals *Now's the Time*, *Ornithology*, *Chasin' the Bird*, *Scrapple from the Apple*, and so on, or the favored standards of the day, such as *My Old Flame* and *Embraceable You*? What of *Boplicity* and *Israel*, and the Dameron originals *Good Bait* and *Lady Bird*? Perhaps most surprising of all the omissions is Davis's fine blues *Down*, first recorded in 1951 and kept in the repertoire for a while but obviously forgotten when it might have been used to fill one of the blues slots at these sessions; instead they were filled by the head arrangements for *Blues by Five* and three renditions of *The Theme*. *Down* is not the only good original that might have made a reappearance; that list includes *Solar*, *Miles Ahead*, *Swing*

Spring, and lots of other titles. Davis's repertoire is always in flux, with favored entries eventually losing their place to newer ones. There seems to be no special structure to it, no pattern for what will be included and what will be omitted, and no highly conscious tinkering with it. Titles get added almost by chance, as *My Funny Valentine* suddenly took on meaning for Davis, and they get left off by chance too, as *Swing Spring* just never entered Davis's mind after it was recorded.

The rationale for Prestige's packaging of all these hours of music is a bizarre combination of business sense and discographical nonsense. *Cookin'* (LP 7094) came first, and promptly. It included a single slice of the last session, the last five titles in the order in which they were recorded except that the last two titles were reversed. It reached the market, perhaps as part of the contract terms, prior to Columbia's first album by the Davis quintet (although *Sweet Sue*, on Bernstein's *What Is Jazz?* LP, appeared before both of them). Since Davis tended to call the uptempo tunes toward the end of the marathon sessions, *Cookin'* is made up predominantly of hard swinging music played on the open trumpet, with a leaven of *My Funny Valentine* and the medium ballad *When Lights Are Low*. In selecting a predominance of fast, boppish tracks, Prestige was clearly aiming at the current market for neo-bop.

Columbia, which had proportionately much more neo-bop by the Davis quintet and much less ballad work, apparently had learned something about the métier of the quintet, and especially of Davis, because its first release, called *Round about Midnight* (CL949), made a judicious selection of the materials it was holding and came out with a predominantly lyrical program with each side ordered symmetrically as ballad-swinger-ballad (*Round Midnight*, *Ah-Leu-Cha*, and *All of You* on side 1, and *Bye Bye Blackbird*, *Tadd's Delight*, and *Dear Old Stockholm* on side 2).

Prestige probably learned from that selection, because its second selection from the marathons, *Relaxin'* (LP 7129), released the next year, presented a highly successful imbalance of two swingers (*Oleo*, *Woody'n You*) and four of the most attractive ballads (*If I Were a Bell*, *You're My Everything*, *I Could Write a Book*, and *It Could Happen to You*). That was followed only a few months later by *Workin'* (LP 7166), a selection of titles so strange that it suggests Prestige knew very well by then that Davis's records would sell adequately even without thoughtful programming; *Workin'* included all three versions of *The Theme*, counting the one called *Trane's Blues*, and the trio showcase *Ahmad's Blues*, with *Four* and *Half Nelson* and two good ballads (the ornate *It Never Entered My Mind*, and *In Your Own Sweet Way*). By the time it got around to packaging what was left over on *Steamin'* (LP 7200), in July 1961, Prestige had the dregs of the ballads (*Something I Dreamed Last Night* and *When I Fall In Love*), a frail waltz (*Diane*), and two reckless swingers (*Salt Peanuts* and *Well You Needn't*), with only *Surrey with a Fringe on Top*, a performance easy to underestimate because of the tune's dubious genealogy, drawn from the better half of the quintet's efforts.

Successive reissues have maintained the order and the mix of selections intact, and *Round about Midnight* has never been collected with the others. Almost everyone who listens to jazz has some or all of the Prestige packages in one or another of their releases, and one can only hope that the company will come to realize that to sell these performances again it must repackage and even do some selecting as well.

Davis's triumphs were not confined to the recording studio. Playing at the Café Bohemia when he was in New York, he nightly faced a huge poster of himself on the opposite wall, one of the gallery of jazz portraits that included Parker, Gillespie, Powell, and Roach and was the main attempt at decoration. He faced also a challenging contingent of musicians in the audience on most nights, including Mingus and the members of his first Jazz Workshop, who also worked at the club, Roach and Rollins from the Roach-Brown band, and Thelonious Monk. The shift of the jazz clubs away from Broadway and into Greenwich Village, where the Village Vanguard was also located, set the jazz musicians among some of the most creative young artists in all fields, for whom the Village was the hub of activity.

The garrets and studios of the Village were under unusual scrutiny at the time because the *New York Times* and other journals were touting a new wave in the arts in America, which they labeled the Beat Generation. Jack Kerouac, the novelist who surfaced as the new wave's leading spokesman, explained the label this way: "Beat means beatitude, not beat up. You *feel* this. You feel it in a beat, in jazz – real cool jazz or a good gutty rock number." Like all such labels, this one played down the individualism of the poets, novelists, and painters who were saddled with it and created a convenient fiction of uniform activity that was easier for outsiders to grasp. The Beats, according to their journalistic image, were amoral, apolitical bohemians who celebrated their freedom in quick sexual liaisons and spontaneous art works. Whatever the complex reality of creating art, the beatnik image fired the popular imagination. Jazz was part of it, and the Village was its setting. "Suddenly there were millions more people on earth, and they all seemed to be coming to Greenwich Village," said one habituée. Kerouac's novel *On the Road* was published by Viking Press in September 1957, crystallizing public awareness of the movement in swirling, eccentric prose that everyone who was anyone was reading – or pretending to read. The young artists who became closely identified with the movement, willingly or not, became celebrities. Kerouac was the lion, but the poets Gregory Corso and Philip Lamantia, the painter Larry Rivers, who also fancied himself something of a saxophonist, and many others were added attractions in the jazz clubs when they turned up in the audience. Kerouac was even booked into the Village Vanguard to 'play' regular sets, reading poetry with jazz accompaniment, the brainchild of the television talk show host Steve Allen, who was also a jazz piano player. Allen could not salvage Kerouac's performances, however, and neither could the good musicians with whom he shared the stand, among them Zoot Sims and Al Cohn. Throughout the engagement, Kerouac began each evening with faltering barely audible recitations that degenerated as the evening wore on into boozy, incoherent rants; on his better nights, he dispensed with the poetry and took up scat singing, including a faithful rendering of a Miles Davis solo that, according to one of Kerouac's biographers, "was entirely accurate, and something more than a simple imitation."

Not the least conspicuous member of the audience at the Vanguard or the Bohemia on many nights, though she was hardly a beatnik, was Baroness Pannonica de Koenigswarter-Rothschild, an English aristocrat known to the New York press as the Jazz Baroness and to the black musicians for whom she was something of a patron simply as Nica. For her, Horace Silver wrote *Nica's Dream*, Gigi Gryce wrote *Nica's Tempo*, and Thelonious Monk wrote *Pannonica*. The baroness had left her husband at his post in the French embassy in Mexico City in 1951 and moved with her daughter to the more thriving after-hours atmosphere of New York, where she lived in the fashionable Hotel Stanhope on Fifth Avenue. Her apartment became a hospitality suite for some of the greatest jazz players of the day, whom she treated generously. Monk was her closest friend among them, and through Monk she came to know the others, including Charlie Parker. When Parker died in her apartment, the *New York Mirror* bleated in its headline: "BOP KING DIES IN HEIRESS' FLAT." Most of her good works for the musicians were less conspicuous, but there was nothing inconspicuous about the baroness herself, whose attendance at a jazz club was usually signaled by the presence of her Bentley parked at the curb in front of it. Up to a point, she participated in their lifestyles as well as in their audiences. Her Bentley seemed to them neither more nor less exotic than Miles Davis's Mercedes-Benz, the first in a series of European thoroughbreds that he would own over the years. Hampton Hawes, who arrived in New York from Los Angeles that summer on the familiar rounds that addicted jazzmen were always making, recalled one incident: "Monk and his wife and Nica and I driving down Seventh Avenue in the Bentley at three or four in the morning – Monk feeling good, turning round to me to say, 'Look at me, man, I got a black bitch *and* a white bitch' – and Miles pulling alongside in the Mercedes, calling through the window in his little hoarse voice cut down by a throat operation, 'Want to race?' Nica nodding, then turning to tell us in her prim British tones: 'This time I believe I'm going to beat the motherfucker.'" These were heady times for jazz musicians.

The undercurrent for self-destruction persisted, and it was never far from the surface. Heroin addiction remained rampant. Hawes's summer in New York, for instance, ended with his hitting bottom again and finally committing himself to a narcotics hospital in Fort Worth, Texas. "Last thing I remember when the money was gone," Hawes wrote in his autobiography, "was sitting alone in Nica's Bentley in front of the Café Bohemia and Miles poking his head in with his sly grin and asking in his raspy voice, 'You cattin' with Nica?' And I'm mumbling, 'Yeah, cattin' with Nica,' trying to smile with my head on the thousand-dollar wood dashboard." For most of the jazz musicians, heroin remained an occupational hazard. The Miles Davis Quintet were no exception. While Davis himself remained straight, he was all alone in that respect. "His musicians, to a man, were still shooting up," according to J.C. Thomas, "at least in part due to the pervasive influence of Philly Joe Jones, who was to drugs that W.C. Fields was to booze." The addictions were taking a heavier and heavier toll on the quintet's performances, causing one or another of the musicians to be late almost every evening and sometimes to be absent for the whole night. Sometimes when they did show up, they might have been better not to.

John Coltrane was suffering most conspicuously, and on several nights he spent an entire set leaning against the piano, nodding. On one such night, a major record producer sat in the audience, expecting to sign Coltrane to a contract, but he left without even approaching him when he saw his condition. Ray Draper, the tuba player who recorded with Coltrane in 1960, remembers going to the Village Vanguard as a high school student in the mid-1950s and seeing Coltrane on the stand "disheveled, with his shirt collar dirty, buttons missing from his shirt, and his suit dirty and wrinkled." Draper told C.O. Simpkins that Coltrane seemed "locked in a struggle, playing only snatches of phrases and spitting out jumbles of notes. There would be long pauses of silence followed by brief spurts of more notes. Miles appeared angry with him." Between sets, Draper went downstairs to talk to the musicians: "John was sitting down, sick and uncommunicative. Two members of the quintet ran out to find him some drugs, after which he was a different person, talking and looking much better." Red Garland, who was in better control, paid the rent for his room only when it became absolutely essential for him to get a change of clothes. Hawes remembers, "He was always drawing money from the club so he could get his door unlocked, go back in his room to put on his clothes and go to work." With drugs using up so much of their incomes, setting aside money for food and rent was a constant, and nearly impossible, task for all the sidemen. In St. Louis, Coltrane and Paul Chambers shared a hotel room, as usual, but by the end of the engagement neither of them had any money to pay the bill, and they had to leave by the fire escape with their suitcases in hand.

No one was more aware of their problems than Davis, who faced them musically on the stand and managerially off it. He was also aware of the limits of his own power to solve their problems. "I just tell them if they work for me to regulate their habit," he says. "When they're tired of the trouble it takes to support a habit, they'll stop it if they have the strength. You can't *talk* a man out of a habit until he really *wants* to stop."

Davis's patience was far from inexhaustible and by the fall of 1956, Coltrane had succeeded in using up what there was of it. Davis warned him, and when Coltrane continued to dissipate, he brought in Sonny Rollins to replace him for an October date at the Café Bohemia. Part way through the engagement Davis relented, and both Coltrane and Rollins were in the band for a few nights. Paul Jeffrey, the tenor saxophonist, says, "I saw Coltrane at the Bohemia in late 1956, and this was one of the times Sonny Rollins and Trane both played with Miles. I knew Sonny's style, but Trane really surprised me. I'd always thought of Rollins as a great tenor virtuoso, but Coltrane more than held his own. He followed Sonny's melodic solos with some of the strangest, most convoluted harmonies and chord progressions I'd ever heard." Rollins's presence no doubt helped Coltrane to straighten himself out and play as well as he was capable of playing, but it was only temporary. For the last nights of the engagement, Rollins was Davis's only tenor player and Coltrane had returned to his mother's house in Philadelphia.

Immediately after the Bohemia date, Davis disbanded the quintet. He traveled without the others to Europe as a featured player in a touring concert package in November. Lester Young, another featured soloist on the tour, had no band of his own at the time, and he played his solo spots in front of the René Urtreger Trio, a French group. Davis also used Urtreger's trio for his spots. The other featured players were the Modern Jazz Quartet and the European orchestra of Kurt Edelhagen. This was Davis's second trip to Europe, seven and a half years after his appearance at the Paris Jazz Festival. This time he arrived as a leader, sharing top billing with Lester Young, a venerable figure although he was, at forty-five, a taciturn alcoholic of unpredictable musical prowess. The itinerary was good, taking in not only the cultural capitals Zurich and Paris but also Freiburg, Germany, a medieval city in the heart of the Black Forest. The distances were short enough to allow some leisure for sightseeing and other tourist activities – Davis bought a camera in Germany – and some hanging out with the growing community of expatriate jazzmen. The concerts were low-pressure affairs through which the musicians could coast if they chose to without ruffling their highly appreciative audiences. Private tapes of several of the concerts exist, but only one of them, in Freiburg, has been issued on record. The details are as follows:

Miles Davis and the René Urtreger Trio
Miles Davis, tpt; René Urtreger, pno; Pierre Michelot, b; Christian Garros, dms. The
Stadthalle, Freiburg, Germany, 12 November 1956
Tune up and *What's New*
(both on Unique Jazz UJ 14)

All Star Jam Session
Miles Davis, tpt; Lester Young, ts; Milt Jackson, vbs; John Lewis, pno; Percy Heath, b;
Connie Kay, dms.
How High the Moon (issued as above)

All Stars and the Kurt Edelhagen Orchestra
Davis; Young; Jackson; Heath; Kay; Conny Jackel, Hanne Wilfert, Rolfe Schnoebiegel,
Klaus Mitschele, Siegfried Achhammer, tpt; Otto Bredl, Heinz Hermannsdörfer, Werner
Betz, Helmut Hack, tbn; Franz von Klenck, Helmut Reinhardt, as; Paul Martin, Bubi Ader-
hold, ts; Helmut Brandt, Johnny Feigl, bs; Werner Drexler, pno; Kurt Edelhagen, cond
Lester Leaps In (issued as above)

Davis's exposure on the four titles on which he plays here amounts to slightly less
than twenty-four minutes, but his featured spot with the Urtreger Trio normally
included four titles instead of the two released on this recording. Alun Morgan,
the English critic, attended both concerts at Salle Pleyel in Paris, and he reports
that Davis played *Four*, *How Deep Is the Ocean*, *Tune up* and an unidentified
fourth title at both concerts. Morgan enthused over what he heard of Davis, but
perhaps he expected too little from him because Davis's important quintet recordings were not yet available. "He played brilliantly, surpassing in quality anything
which I had heard before," Morgan says. "His playing had the tonal richness and
melodic elegance of Bobby Hackett at his best combined with a highly personal
approach to improvisation." The Freiburg performance does indeed reveal some of
the remarkable facility Davis had shown in his recordings with the quintet, at
least on his solo features.

The other two titles at the Freiburg concert are loose improvisatory romps,
where the featured players are thrown together on stage to see what might happen. If nothing else, they document the decline of Lester Young, catching him
pathetically on *How High the Moon* as he solos at less than half the tempo of the
rhythm section and overstays his turn at the end when he cuts in to trade bars
with the other soloists. Young performed less and less frequently throughout the
rest of the 1950s, his great talent smothered by his apparent indifference not only
to music but to life, and he died in 1959.

The stay in Paris gave Davis and the others a chance to renew their acquaintance with the many bop musicians who had made their homes there. When Alun Morgan caught up with Davis in the audience at Club St. Germain, where Don Byas was appearing with the French pianist Raymond Fol and drummer Jean-Marie Ingrande, he found him at ease and accessible away from the pressures of the New York scene and the problems of his quintet sidemen. "Sitting there at the bar Miles was completely relaxed," Morgan writes. "He spoke slowly and with a deep, hoarse voice. A throat ailment had impaired his speech and for the same reason he wore a cravat instead of a tie." Later in the evening, Milt Jackson, Percy Heath, and Connie Kay arrived with expatriates Kenny Clarke, the MJQ's original drummer, and Bud Powell and his wife Buttercup. Powell, who suffered from schizophrenia, was recuperating. "Their delight at meeting Miles was obvious," Morgan says. "They pummeled each other good naturedly, arms were thrown around shoulders. Bud stood slightly apart and looked sad. The conversation flowed and laughter came easily. Later the hum of conversation was stilled. Someone said, 'Bud's going to play,' in a kind of shocked half-whisper; there was Bud up on the stand with Pierre Michelot and Alan Levitt. No one had noticed him leave the circle around the bar. All talking ceased as Bud went into a fast *Nice Work If You Can Get It* which began to degenerate into chaos before the end of the first chorus. A kind of paralysis seemed to have seized the pianist's hands and the more he tried to fight his way free the more inaccurate became his fingering. Four choruses and it was all over. Bud stood up quickly, bowed, mopped his face with a handkerchief and began his uncertain walk back to the bar ... It was an age before Buttercup led her husband back to the silent circle of embarrassed musicians. Miles broke the tension by flinging a comforting arm around Bud's shoulders. 'You know, man, you shouldn't try to play when you're juiced like that.' Within a few minutes the room was normal." Later that night, around 3 a.m., Morgan and his friends met Davis again, "strolling along the pavement with Sinatra-like nonchalance." He was looking for his hotel, the name of which he had forgotten.

Back in New York at the end of the month, Davis re-formed the quintet with Coltrane as the tenor saxophonist. Davis recognized better than anyone the strength of the combination of talents he had put together, notwithstanding the extramusical problems. "I always liked Coltrane," he said a few years later. "When he was with me the first time, people used to tell me to fire him. They said he wasn't playing anything. They used to tell me to get rid of Philly Joe Jones. I know what I want though. I also didn't understand this talk of Coltrane being difficult to understand. What he does, for example, is to play five notes of a chord and then keep changing it around, trying to see how many different ways it can sound. It's like explaining something five different ways. And that sound of his is connected with what he's doing with chords at any given time." Davis was equally generous about Philly Joe Jones, whom many observers considered to be the root of the personal problems in the quintet. Davis was willing to ignore the hassles – up to a point – because of Jones's talent as a drummer. "Look, I wouldn't care if he came up on the bandstand in his BVD's and with one arm, just so long as he was there," he told Nat Hentoff, in a widely quoted statement. "He's got the fire I want. There's nothing more terrible than playing with a dull rhythm section. Jazz has got to have *that thing*. No, I don't know how you get that thing. You have to be born with it. You can't even buy it. If you could buy it, they'd have it at the next Newport Festival." (A later version of this statement, also from Hentoff, replaces the sentence mocking the Newport festival by these words: "You have it or you don't. And no critic can put it into any words. It speaks in the music. It speaks for itself.") The two men who thus posed the greatest threat to the stability of the quintet, Coltrane and Jones, were also its necessary foils musically, providing the intensity and power that counterbalanced the lyricism of the other voices, especially Davis's.

The quintet began a series of engagements in December 1956 that would take them across the country on a two-month road trip. The first stop was Philadelphia, the hometown of three of the sidemen, in early December. (Some tapes of the quintet's club date on Saturday 8 December apparently exist, but they have not yet been issued publicly.) They probably moved on to Chicago over the Christmas season, Davis's regular stop at that time of the year. In January, they moved on to a club called Jazz City in Los Angeles. While there, the rhythm section moonlighted by recording with the alto saxophonist Art Pepper on a Contemporary album released under the title *Art Pepper Meets the Rhythm Section*. Two-thirds of the rhythm section, Chambers and Jones, also made some recordings with an avant-garde group led by the french horn player John Graas, called *Jazz Lab 2*, for Decca. Philly Joe Jones's entrepreneurial instinct went beyond merely making extra money in the recording studios during his stay in Los Angeles. Sy Johnson, a composer and arranger who was then in Los Angeles studying law, attended several evenings of the quintet's performances and indulged his hobby of photography. "I shot pictures by available light with my Leica whenever I could get close to the bandstand," Johnson says. "That in itself was unheard of in the 50s, and when I made some prints, Philly Joe undertook to sell them to the customers."

The extended stay at Jazz City was broken by a two-week interval at the Blackhawk in San Francisco. While there, the members of the quintet often turned up at an after-hours club called the Streets of Paris. Jerry Dodgion, the alto saxophonist, was particularly interested in the music of John Coltrane, which he was hearing live for the first time at the Blackhawk, but he could never get

Coltrane to play after hours. Whenever he invited him onto the stand, Coltrane replied, "Not right now, I'd rather listen." "That's what he did," Dodgion says, "for three nights straight."

Back at Jazz City in Los Angeles, Sy Johnson was surprised to find that Davis began seeking him out. "Miles sat down at my table late one night and began to talk about the Leica he got in Germany, and how much he liked it. He said he had the clerk set the shutter speed and aperture at the store when he bought the camera, and hadn't changed them since." From that night until the end of the engagement, Davis used Johnson as a buffer between himself and the other fans. "He would motion me into the kitchen of Jazz City with a nod, usually on the first intermission, when the club was crowded with people who wanted to talk to him. He'd stand with his back to the kitchen door, talking about his Mercedes, other players, women, and pointedly ignoring musicians and fans who wanted to say hello. They would wait patiently or try to say something over his shoulder, and finally drift away. I remember Benny Carter in line once, and murderous glances at me from some of the younger black players."

Davis was developing various ploys, apparently, to shield himself from his fans, who were increasing in numbers. Most often, of course, he was simply not around – when his sidemen went to an after-hours club, he went somewhere else. But on many occasions it was impossible for him to hide, and then he had to find some other way of keeping people at the distance he seemed to require. As often as not, he chose ways that were construed as rudeness, as with Sy Johnson. Another way, observed by Ross Russell, could be construed as arrogance. "Once in St. Louis he was standing on a corner after an autographing appearance at a record store, surrounded by sycophants, talking in low, barely audible tones," Russell says. "Suddenly an old acquaintance came hurrying up like a lost puppy to shout out an enthusiastic greeting. Miles froze the man with a penetrating look. Realizing that he had committed a serious gaffe, one that might cost him his status and wreck his career in jazz, the other had the presence of mind to instantly withdraw and walk slowly around the block. He then approached the group from a new angle and stood at its edge for some time. Finally Miles' eyes met his and there was the briefest of nods. The other had been restored to grace, but it had been a very near thing."

The same kind of imperiousness also surfaces around this time in some of Davis's statements to the press, which were usually only made out of a sense of obligation upon his arrival in a city where he had an engagement. He kept such meetings short, when he put up with them at all, but often the reporter went away with a bona fide pronouncement on the state of the art in jazz. In one such pronouncement, Davis blasted the style of jazz associated with California at the time. "You know what's wrong with the music on the Coast?" he asked, and he supplied his own answer: "Smog!" He went on to declare, "I've heard a lot of bad music coming from the Coast. Some of the arrangements are good but they die because there are no soloists. You've got to have a good rhythm section and you have to have guys who fit together. Maybe the climate has something to do with the guys playing the way they do. I know it makes my eyes water." Pronouncements such as these fed Davis's reputation as a controversial figure now that he was squarely in the public eye. It was not as if he had altered his behavior noticeably in order to gain the new notoriety. As Jackie McLean had said, "Miles was arrogant when his heels didn't point in the same direction." The difference was not so much in anything that he did but in the number of observers that he now had whenever he did anything.

Complaints about Davis's stage manner grew until they became a kind of critical obbligato to the music he made. Davis, sagely, has usually paid no attention at all to the complaints and gone about his business of making music, but on a few occasions when the obbligato has threatened to drown out the music altogether he has spoken up about it. "Some critic that didn't have nothing else to do started this crap about I don't announce numbers, I don't look at the audience, I don't bow or talk to people, I walk off the stage, and all that," he told Alex Hailey in the interview for *Playboy*. "Look, man, all I am is a trumpet player. I can do one thing – play my horn – and that's what's at the bottom of the whole mess. I ain't no entertainer, and ain't trying to be one. I am one thing, a musician. Most of what's said about me is lies in the first place." Faced with the same charges when he arrived in England for a tour in 1960, Davis used the same defense, simply denying the charges outright. "I don't know anyone," he told one reporter, "who would turn his back on the audience." During that evening's performance, Davis played part of the concert, as always, with his back to the audience. Part of the time that he did not have his back to the audience, he was nowhere to be seen, having left the stage, as usual, during some of the others' solos.

A few times, he has answered the criticisms more plausibly. "Everything I do, I got a reason," he says. "The reason I don't announce numbers is because it's not until the last instant I decide what's maybe the best thing to play next. Besides, if people don't recognize a number when I play it, what difference does it make?" Of course it makes no difference at all, except that performances of jazz have traditionally been presented with all the trappings of popular entertainment rather than of serious symphonic music, including patter from the stage. The absence of the small talk jars some of the more hidebound fans and critics. But, as Chris Albertson says, "We don't, after all, expect Rostropovich or Casadesus to warm up their audiences with small talk, and Miles Davis is as serious about his music as were Brahms and Schubert." In his own defense, Davis continues: "Why I sometimes walk off the stand is because when it's somebody else's turn to solo, I ain't going to stand up there and be detracting from him. What am I going to stand up there *for*? I ain't no model, and I don't sing or dance, and I damn sure ain't no Uncle Tom just to be up there grinning. Sometimes I go over by the piano or the drums and listen to what they're doing. But if I don't want to do that, I go in the wings and listen to the whole band until it's my next turn for my horn."

The unwritten code at a jazz performance calls for a player to remain in place following his own solo and absorb himself in the music that follows. In removing himself from the stage, Davis breaks part of the code conspicuously, but he does not break it completely, for he does not simply detach himself from the music. Robert Altschuler, the publicity director for Columbia Records, says, "I have been with him on several occasions when he left the stage during a performance. He either crouches or ambles to the side of the audience, and you realize that he is deeply concentrating on everything that his musicians are playing – he is digging his own band, digging it in a way a Miles Davis fan would. He simply becomes part of his own audience." Davis adds: "Then they claim I ignore the audience while I'm playing. Man, when I'm working, I know the people are out there. But when I'm playing, I'm worrying about making my horn sound right ... When I'm working, I'm concentrating. I bet you if I was a doctor sewing on some son of a bitch's heart, they wouldn't want me to talk."

He draws a closer analogy with classical musicians and other jazz musicians – white ones. "The average jazz musician today, if he's making it, is just as trained as classical musicians," he points out. "You ever see anybody go up bugging the classical musicians when they are on the job and trying to work? Even in jazz – you look at the white bandleaders – if they don't want anybody messing with them when they are working, you don't hear anybody squawking. It's just if a Negro is involved that there's something wrong with him. My troubles started when I learned to play the trumpet and hadn't learned to dance." Whether or not the code differs for white and black musicians, no musician of either color has ever defied the code the way Davis has.

Davis's stage manner has contributed mightily to his public image as the solitary, defiant black man. But his demeanor seems to have a much homelier foundation. "Basically Miles is very shy, that's the whole thing," says Dizzy Gillespie. "You know, I know him probably better than he knows himself. I was talking to his daughter Cheryl in St. Louis, and I said, 'Did you know that your father is really a very bashful man?' and she said, 'Yeah, I've always known that, but nobody else can dig it; he puts up that front to cover up the shyness.'" Nat Hentoff agrees: "Miles's way of coping with shyness is to affect fierceness. 'Like all of us,' a musician who has known him for many years explains, 'Miles has only a certain amount of energy, and he finds it difficult to meet new people. Rather than subject himself to what is for him a tiring discomfort, he tries to create so forbidding an image of himself that he won't even be bothered.'" In spite

Philly Joe Jones and Miles Davis (Raeburn Flerage, courtesy of *Down Beat*)

Miles Davis and Gil Evans (Columbia Records, courtesy of *Down Beat*)

John Coltrane and Thelonious Monk at the Five Spot, with drummer Shadow Wilson (Don Schlitten, courtesy of *Down Beat*)

of all the print his stage manner has engendered and all the psychologizing it has sparked, the best comment on it – perhaps the only one that need ever have been made – comes from Davis himself, from the mellower viewpoint of 1981. "I'm not being vain or anything, but that's the way I am," he said. "I play for myself and I play for musicians."

In April 1957, a little more than a month after the quintet had returned to New York from their West Coast stay, the drug problems of Coltrane and Jones were again causing professional problems that Davis found intolerable. He fired both of them. This time there was a note of finality to the firings, especially in Coltrane's case. Thelonious Monk, according to J.C. Thomas, walked in on the firing of Coltrane when he went backstage at the Café Bohemia between sets one night. As he approached the musicians' room, he saw Davis slap Coltrane and then punch him in the stomach. Coltrane, characteristically, took it passively, but Monk was outraged. "As much saxophone as you play," he shouted at Coltrane, "you don't have to take that. Why don't you come play with me?" Not long after, Coltrane joined Monk's quartet at the Five Spot and Sonny Rollins again took up the tenor saxophone chair in the Miles Davis Quintet.

All of Davis's problems that spring with the quintet's discipline and with his own public relations were more than counterbalanced by a musical project with Gil Evans that fired his enthusiasm more than anything he had worked on since his first project with Evans nine years earlier. This one was not altogether unlike that one, involving orchestral elements such as french horns and tubas in a distinctive jazz setting, but there could be no comparison in scope. The new project was far removed from the youthful experiments conceived in the grimy 55th Street basement. It involved a nineteen-piece orchestra, and it was backed by the corporate weight of Columbia Records. Planning by Davis and Evans had started in the fall of 1956, probably inspired at least initially by Davis's role as the featured soloist with the Brass Ensemble of the Jazz and Classical Music Society, but the final result went well beyond the concerns of the third stream movement, melding the styles of Davis and Evans so forcibly and so compatibly as to create an individuality all its own. Several critics immediately drew parallels with Duke Ellington's consummate orchestrations of the early 1940s. André Hodeir proclaimed, "After so many years the Ellington spirit has come into its own again, with a persuasive power it has never known since Ellington's own masterpieces of 1940. For the first time since then we are presented with a consistent approach to the full jazz band." The details are as follows:

Miles Davis with Gil Evans and His Orchestra
Miles Davis, flugelhorn; Bernie Glow, Ernie Royal, Louis Mucci, Taft Jordan, John Carisi, tpt; Frank Rehak, Jimmy Cleveland, Joe Bennett, tbn; Tom Mitchell, bass tbn; Willie Ruff, Tony Miranda or Jim Buffington, frh; Bill Barber, tba; Lee Konitz, as;

Danny Bank, bass clnt; Romeo Penque, Sid Cooper or Edwin Caine, flt, clnt; Paul Chambers, b; Arthur Taylor, dms; Gil Evans, arr, cond. New York, 6 May 1957
The Maids of Cadiz; *The Duke*
(both on Columbia CL 1041)

Same personnel and place, 10 May 1957
My Ship; *Miles Ahead*
(both issued as above)

Same personnel and place, 23 May 1957
New Rhumba; *Blues for Pablo*; *Springsville*
(all issued as above)

Same personnel and place, 27 May 1957
I Don't Wanna Be Kissed; *The Meaning of the Blues*; *Lament*
(all issued as above)

Davis and Evans's selection of melodies is astonishingly eclectic, ranging from compositions by jazz players with Brubeck's *The Duke*, Jamal's *New Rhumba*, John Carisi's *Springsville*, J.J. Johnson's *Lament*, Evans's own *Blues for Pablo*, and Davis's *Miles Ahead* (now credited also to Evans as co-composer), to theater songs with Delibes's *The Maids of Cadiz* and Kurt Weill's *My Ship*, and taking in even the trite pop ditty *I Don't Wanna Be Kissed*. Yet all these diverse sources come together in Evans's orchestrations as if they are brief movements in an extended suite, one melody giving way to the next almost imperceptibly in a linking orchestral passage. The themes of the ten identifiable melodies are, as Max Harrison puts it, "a series of miniature concertos for Davis," but the effect of Evans's orchestration is to turn them into "a continuous aural fresco whose connective resonance and authority gain strength with each addition."

So cohesive is the music, which was released under the title *Miles Ahead* (CL 1041) in the fall of 1957 and has never been out of print since, that there has been relatively little critical comment on the individual melodies themselves. The arranger Quincy Jones, speaking of Evans's ingenious arrangement of Brubeck's *The Duke*, says, "Gil put Duke into *The Duke*."

Hodeir, who wrote the original notes for the album, later singled out Evans's *Blues for Pablo*: "Gil Evans can write music, there is no doubt about that! I know of no other jazzman who can compare with him as a harmonizer and orchestrator, but he may not have quite come into his own as a composer. His own *Blues for Pablo* is the weakest piece on a record on which all the other themes chosen are unusually fine; but then perhaps it only seems so weak because it does not go with the rest of the pieces. It was originally meant to be recorded by Hal McKusick's small ensemble, and Evans was probably wrong to include it in a set where it was bound to be out of place." And yet, obviously, *Blues for Pablo's* provenance is no odder than any of the other themes, which come from all over the place. In his original notes for Columbia, Hodeir was enthusiastic about its arrangement, singling it out for the way in which "Evans breaks away here at a few points from the four-bar unit of construction and thus destroys the symmetrical form of the traditional blues, which is something that very few arrangers dare to do."

Hodeir's point about Evans's apparent weakness as a composer, which his criticism of *Blues for Pablo* seems to be in service of, raises the difficult issue of just where to draw the line between composing on the one hand and orchestrating and arranging on the other. Evans crosses that line and recrosses it freely in this music. As Whitney Balliett says, "Evans continually 'improvises' on the melodies in the ensemble passages and rarely presents them anywhere in straightforward fashion." His arrangements are, in a sense, compositions in their own right, as Charles Fox points out: "He establishes, one might say, a periphery of sound which acts as a container for his ideas, across which melodic lines are stretched, and which is disturbed by rhythmic devices. What he is striving for, perhaps, is a musical equivalent to James Joyce's theory of epiphanies, the awareness of an entire context of association and meaning existing within one clear image or (in the case of music) within one pattern or web of sound. It is ... action that has frozen into sound. The preoccupation may be reflected in the fact that Evans' work has largely been upon the plane of re-composition, the conversion of an existing tune into what is virtually a new and often much more exciting orchestral reality. It is, after all, a perfectly legitimate method of composing, analogous to the way a European composer uses folk-tunes or devises variations upon a predecessor's theme."

There is an extraordinary congruity between Evans's ensemble voice and Davis's solo voice, making a fusion in which it is almost impossible to separate the division of labor. "Gil has a way of voicing chords and using notes like nobody else," Davis says. "We work together great because he writes the way I'd like to write. In fact, years ago I used to do arrangements and give them to him to look over. He'd tell me my charts were too cluttered up, that I could get the same effect using fewer notes. Finally, I decided the best thing to do was let Gil do the writing. I'd just get together with him – sometimes not even in person, just on the phone – and outline what I wanted. And he always has such a complete feeling for what I mean that it comes out sounding exactly like what I had in mind." He put it more succinctly when he said, "I wouldn't have no other arranger but Gil Evans – we couldn't be much closer if he was my brother."

In turn, Evans lauds Davis's ability to exploit the tonal palette of the ensembles. "A big part of Miles's creative gift is the creation of sound," he says. "He arrived at a time when, because of the innovations of modern jazz, all new players had to find their own sound in relation to the new modes of expression. Miles, for example, couldn't play like Louis Armstrong because that sound would interfere with his thoughts. Miles had to start with almost no sound and then develop one as he went along – a sound suitable for the ideas he wanted to express. Finally, Miles had his own basic sound, which any player must develop. But many players keep this sound more or less constant. Any variation in their work comes in the actual selection of notes, their harmonic patterns, and their rhythmic usages. Miles, however, is aware of his complete surroundings and takes advantage of the wide range of sound possibilities that exist even in one's own basic sound. He can, in other words, create a particular sound for the existing context. The quality of a certain chord, its tension or lack of tension, can cause him to create a sound appropriate to it. He can put his own substance, his own flesh on a note and then put that note exactly where it belongs."

The collaboration could hardly have been more compatible. Even Davis conceded that he liked it. "I don't keep any of my records," he once said. "I can't stand to hear any of them after I've made them. The only ones I really like are the ones I just made with Gil Evans [*Miles Ahead*], the one I made with J.J. on by Blue Note date about four years ago [probably 20 April 1953], and a date I did with Charlie Parker."

Davis's own approval of the collaboration has been almost unanimously seconded. *Miles Ahead* was acclaimed immediately as a masterpiece of jazz orchestration, and it has held its place ever since. One of the few comments that was even mildly negative came in the *New Yorker* from Whitney Balliett, who conceded that the recording was "the most adventurous effort of its kind in a decade" and that "the playing throughout is impeccable," but found that, for his taste, the music lacked fiber, especially Davis's solos. "All the solos are by Davis, whose instrument sounds fogbound," he said. "Buried in all this port and velvet is Evans's revolutionary use, for such a large group, of structure, dynamics and harmony." He felt that the technical innovations were not sustaining enough in their own right: "There is, in fact, too much port and velvet, and Davis, a discreet, glancing performer, backslides in these surroundings into a moony, saccharine, and – in *My Ship* – downright dirge-like approach. The result is some of the coolest jazz ever uttered." Balliett's metaphor "port and velvet" was not unopposed, as Max Harrison picked it up and countered with a few metaphors of his own. "The scoring's effect is often that of light imprisoned in a bright mineral cave, its refinement such that at times the music flickers deliciously between existence and non-existence," Harrison wrote. "No matter how involved the textures, though, it is always possible to discover unifying factors as an altogether remarkable ear is in control, ruthlessly – and almost completely – eliminating clichés. Complaints that these Davis/Evans collaborations produced unrhythmic music were due to faulty hearing, and the widely quoted metaphorical description of the textures as 'port and velvet' is inept. Despite its richness, the orchestral fabric is constantly on the move, horizontally and vertically; it is unfortunate that some listeners cannot hear a music's pulse unless it is stated as a series of loud bangs."

Hodeir had some reservations, which he stated in an article published some time after he wrote the enthusiastic notes for the album. "I, for my part, wish that Evans's musical idiom took greater account of the blues spirit, and we may be sure that he himself would have liked to see his arrangements rehearsed as often as necessary and even performed publicly a few times before they were recorded. Now and then there are still a few rough spots, if not actual flaws, to be heard; a few solos were post-recorded – never a desirable procedure in any case – and it would have been well to replace one or two musicians (the flutist, for example, whose phrasing in *The Duke* shows that he simply did not understand the score). But even the sum of these reservations is of little weight compared with the amount of imagination, inspiration and sensibility that went into a record which, with all its faults, constitutes a remarkably successful achievement."

The release of *Miles Ahead* was greeted enthusiastically not only by reviewers but also by virtually all musicians and fans. Dizzy Gillespie, a musician far removed from port and velvet in most matters, said, "*Miles Ahead* is the greatest. I wore my first copy out inside three weeks so I went to Miles and said, 'Give me another copy of that dam record.' I tell you, everybody should own that album." For Tommy Flanagan, cryptically, "the *Miles Ahead* album was almost a copy of what Ahmad recorded with a trio." Art Pepper comments: "His [Evans's] writing for Miles on *Miles Ahead* to me was the most perfect thing I've ever heard done for a soloist with a band. Gil's understanding of Miles was perfect." And of Davis, Pepper adds: "His development has been phenomenal. I've listened to *Miles Ahead* by the hour and his warmth, choice of notes, and beautiful simplicity has touched my very soul." Few jazz recordings have met with, and sustained, the level of praise of this collaboration between Davis and Evans, which was the first of a series of splendid joint projects in these peak years.

While the *Miles Ahead* sessions were being recorded in the Columbia studios, Davis was again working at the Café Bohemia with his quintet, which now included Sonny Rollins and Arthur Taylor in place of John Coltrane and Philly Joe Jones. The new men seemed, at least on paper, fully adequate replacements, and both were at the peaks of their careers. Taylor was a steady, sensitive drummer, in some demand for recording sessions with pickup groups on such labels as Prestige and Riverside. Rollins had made a remarkable series of recordings for

Prestige in 1956, and the appearance of any new LP in his name was an event of more than passing interest. Nevertheless, the new men seemed to fit uneasily into the quintet, especially Rollins, and Davis never took this band into the recording studios, presumably because he reckoned that they had not gelled sufficiently. The only documents that survive are tapes of performances, of which a Saturday broadcast from the Bohemia has been issued on record. The details are as follows:

Miles Davis Quintet
Miles Davis, tpt; Sonny Rollins, ts; Red Garland, pno; Paul Chambers, b; Arthur Taylor, dms. Café Bohemia, New York, 13 July 1957
Four [*Four Squared*]; *Bye Bye Blackbird*; *It Never Entered My Mind*; *Walkin'* [*Roy's Nappin' Now*]
(all on Chakra 100)
Four Squared and *Roy's Nappin' Now* are the titles under which these tracks are listed on the record. Rollins does not play on *It Never Entered My Mind*.

All these titles except *Four* are incomplete. On *It Never Entered My Mind*, in the same Jamalesque arrangement that Coltrane sat out when it was first recorded for Prestige just as Rollins sits it out here, the missing material seems only to be the first four bars or so of Davis's introduction. The other two titles, however, are mere fragments, with *Walkin'* ending abruptly during Davis's opening solo, and *Bye Bye Blackbird* cut off early in Rollins's intriguing solo which sounds like Ben Webster playing bebop, after Davis has already soloed. On *Four*, the one complete performance, some idea of the developing group dynamics comes through, as Davis plays a cool, floating solo over the solid rhythm (in which Taylor's bass drum is overrecorded) and Rollins enters playing a hotter, busier solo after him. It affords a taste of what might have developed, but it is too little to do much more than whet one's appetite.

Later in the month the quintet appeared at the Great South Bay Jazz Festival in Great River, Long Island. Whitney Balliett, covering the festival for the *New Yorker*, mentions them only in passing, noting the presence of Rollins and Chambers among the sidemen and stating that their Sunday afternoon set "was notable for a languishing rendition by Davis playing a tightly muted trumpet, of *It Never Entered My Mind*."

Coltrane and the other members of the Thelonious Monk Quartet, which also included Wilbur Ware on bass and Shadow Wilson on drums, had taken up residence at the Five Spot for the summer, and they were suddenly the talk of the town. Monk had been unduly neglected for years, but a string of adventuresome recordings for Riverside was attracting attention to him, which would continue to grow over the next few years until he finally gained a measure of the respect with the fans that he had always been accorded by other musicians. The Five Spot engagement, which was eventually extended into the fall, made a perfect forum for his quartet, and Coltrane quickly developed into an ideal interpreter of Monk's beautifully quirky, idiosyncratic compositions. The Five Spot was packed throughout the summer, and one frequent visitor was Miles Davis. Joe Goldberg described the scene on one of those summer evenings: "A small, slim, graceful man, impeccably dressed in the continental style that was then a few years ahead of its time, leaned casually against the bar smoking a cigarette and listening to the music that Monk was making with one of his former employees. Everyone else in the audience – which was made up of collegians who at the time probably did not know who he was – was busy watching Miles Davis watch Monk." Davis could not help but notice that Coltrane was not only showing up regularly with Monk, and more or less on time (which was the best one could ever hope for from Monk, let alone Coltrane), but also that he was growing more confident with his restless, searching music as he conquered Monk's harmonic labrynths.

In September, Rollins quit the Miles Davis Quintet to form his own group. The time was ripe for him: his best recorded work had been in the company of rhythm trios rather than larger groups, playing his own repertoire. With the quintet, he had carried on playing Coltrane's parts in Davis's repertoire, and the comparisons of his playing with Coltrane's cropped up inevitably in the jazz press, leading to a lot of opinion-mongering which did neither saxophonist any good and fabricating a rivalry between the two men in which neither of them participated. For the rest of his career Rollins would work as a leader, often with just bass and drums accompanying him, and would continue to spell himself off with long periods of inactivity. To replace Rollins, Davis chose Bobby Jaspar, the Belgian flutist and tenor saxophonist who had been playing with J.J. Johnson off and on during the preceding year. Jaspar, at thirty-one the same age as Davis, had led his own quintet in France for several years, playing in a standard neo-bop framework in places such as Club St. Germain in Paris. A member of a patrician family that immersed itself in music and art, Jaspar had earned a university degree in chemistry before turning to music as a profession. In Paris, he met the expatriate singer Blossom Dearie, whom he married in 1955. The next year they moved to Greenwich Village, and Jaspar gained favorable notices wherever he played. His competence was hailed by the American jazz press as evidence that the present generation of European jazzmen had truly broken the barrier that until then had marked jazz as a music that could only be well played by Americans.

There were other changes in the quintet. Philly Joe Jones was back, replacing Art Taylor, but Jones's old running mate Red Garland was replaced by Tommy Flanagan. Paul Chambers remained on bass. Jaspar's tenure in the quintet lasted only about six weeks, and he may have been thought of by Davis as a temporary replacement from the beginning. No taped performances by this short-lived combination have come to light.

Whatever the conditions of Jaspar's appointment to the quintet, his term was inevitably limited by the availability of Julian (Cannonball) Adderley. Davis had begun talking to Adderley about the possibility of his joining the quintet during the summer, when Rollins was still his reed player. Adderley was then fronting his own quintet with his brother Nat Adderley, the cornetist, and had been doing so for over a year, since returning to New York after his summer of rave notices in 1955. Although he had quickly been accepted into the front rank of jazz musicians, he remained dissatisfied with the drawing power of his band, then earning $1,000 a week. "Nobody was really making it except for Miles, Chico [Hamilton] and Brubeck," he says. "I had gotten an offer from Dizzy to go with his small band. I was opposite Miles at the Bohemia, told him I was going to join Dizzy, and Miles asked me why I didn't join him. I told him he'd never asked me." It was not an opportunity that a shrewd assessor of talent such as Davis was likely to pass up. "Well, Miles kept talking to me for two or three months to come with him," Adderley says, "and when I finally decided to cut loose in October '57, I joined Miles. I figured I could learn more than with Dizzy. Not that Dizzy isn't a good teacher, but he played more commercially than Miles. Thank goodness I made the move that I did." He made no secret of his original motive in joining Davis. "I wanted to get the benefit of Miles's exposure rather than Miles's musical thing," he told Ira Gitler, but it was not long before the musical advantages outweighed the commercial advantages. "It was a commercial move but I noticed that Miles could do some things naturally that I had difficulty doing, and so we started finding out why, and it was easy, you know, more or less," he said. The main lesson showed in Adderley's ability to handle harmonics, and it served his purposes perfectly to learn his lessons while playing for larger audiences. For Davis, Adderley's presence restored to the quintet another perfect foil for his own more delicate, introverted sound. It was a pairing that could hardly be improved – except, perhaps, by the return of Coltrane.

The new quintet with Adderley made their debut in October in a concert package known as Jazz for Moderns which made a circuit around the United States and closed with a concert at Carnegie Hall the next month. Besides the Davis Quintet, the lineup included Helen Merrill, Gerry Mulligan's quartet, the Chico Hamilton Quintet, and two pop-jazz groups, the Australian Jazz Quintet and George Shearing's Sextet; at the Carnegie Hall finale, Shearing's group were replaced by an all-star swing group led by Lionel Hampton. Whitney Balliett's report singles out the new quintet for providing some of the few highlights of the evening: "The only indications that there was any life on-stage occurred during Hampton's performance, and during two of the four numbers by Davis's group, which included Julian Adderley on alto saxophone, Tommy Flanagan, Paul Chambers, and Philly Joe Jones. In *Walkin'* and *Night in Tunisia*, Davis, often a moody, hesitant performer, let loose a couple of belling solos that were spelled by some incisive drumming by Jones."

As soon as the tour ended, Davis traveled alone to Paris, where he was booked to play as a guest soloist for three weeks and to provide the soundtrack for a film entitled *Ascenseur pour l'échafaud* (released in Britain as *Lift to the Scaffold* and in North America as *Frantic*), directed by Louis Malle and starring Jeanne Moreau. French filmmakers had been experimenting with soundtracks by American jazz musicians for a few years and director Roger Vadim had come up with an impressive one earlier in the year when he had the Modern Jazz Quartet play John Lewis's score for his film *Sait-on jamais* (literally 'one never knows,' but released in English-speaking countries as *No Sun in Venice*). The experiments would continue for the next few years, notably with the Jazz Messengers' 1958 soundtrack for *Des Femmes disparaissent* (in English, *Girls Vanish*), directed by Edouard Molinaro. American filmmakers wasted little time catching on to the French trend, and for a few years at the end of the 1950s jazz musicians found themselves in some demand in the American film industry as well. Jazz figured prominently in, for example, Robert Wise's *I Want to Live*, a 1958 film with a soundtrack written by Johnny Mandel and featuring Gerry Mulligan, Art Farmer, Shelly Manne, and most of the other prominent West Coast players, and *Anatomy of a Murder*, a 1959 film by Otto Preminger with a soundtrack by Duke Ellington. Television went along too, notably in the soundtracks for hard-boiled private detectives such as *Peter Gunn*, an NBC series that began in 1958 with Henry Mancini's big band score played by the likes of Pete Candoli, Milt Bernhart, and Larry Bunker. The use of jazz and jazz-derived soundtracks became so predominant that jazz came to seem like the natural backdrop for high-speed chases, mass mayhem, and cold-blooded murder, because the films for which jazz players were enlisted were uniformly violent.

In *Ascenseur pour l'échafaud*, Davis's score accompanies a character named Julien as he murders his lover's husband and then is inadvertently trapped in an elevator while making his escape; it then accompanies a thief who steals Julien's car, goes joy-riding, and ends up killing a man with Julien's gun, with the result that Julien is arrested for the murder he did not commit after he emerges from the elevator the next morning. Fortunately, much of the music has a life of its own quite apart from the film which called it forth. The details are as follows:

Miles Davis Ensemble
Miles Davis, tpt; Barney Wilen, ts (on three tracks only); René Urtreger, pno; Pierre Michelot, b; Kenny Clarke, dms. Paris, 4 December 1957

Générique; L'assassinat de Carala; Sur l'autoroute; Julien dans l'ascenseur; Florence dans les Champs-Elysées; Dîner au motel; Evasion de Julien; Visite du vigile; Au bar du Petit Bac; Chez le photographe du motel
(all on Columbia CL 1268; reissued on Mercury [Netherlands] 6444 701)
Wilen is heard only on *Sur l'autoroute*, *Florence sur les Champs-Elysées*, and *Au bar du Petit Bac*; *Evasion de Julien* is a bass solo by Michelot; *Visite du vigile* is a duet by Michelot and Clarke; Urtreger does not play on these two tracks or on *Sur l'autoroute* and *Dîner au motel*.

Two of Davis's sidemen for the soundtrack recording, Urtreger and Michelot, were members of his backup trio on the tour with Lester Young and the Modern Jazz Quartet a little more than a year before. They are supplemented now by Bernard Wilen, known as Barney, a twenty-year-old tenor saxophonist already highly regarded in Paris, and by Kenny Clarke, whose uptempo brushwork figures prominently in the score.

The soundtrack preserves the edited version of the music recorded for it, keyed to the scenes of the film, rather than the masters from which the soundtrack was selected. Several of the titles are fragments, ending abruptly. The editing does some disservice to Wilen, who barely begins his solo on *Florence sur les Champs-Elysées* before he is cut off. But the tracks that end abruptly were probably never complete takes in the conventional sense, because of Davis's manner of scoring the film. Rather than devising a set of themes keyed to certain characters and elaborating them as the plot thickens – the normal compositional framework for film scores and one that John Lewis followed so ingeniously for *Sait-on jamais* that he ended up writing a suite that could be played thereafter in the MJQ's concerts – Davis viewed the film sequences for which he was to provide music, set the tempos and deployed the sidemen as he felt the scene demanded, and then improvised the soundtrack as the film sequence was replayed. It is a technique for film scoring that had probably never been used since the days of the silent films, when pianists and organists, Fats Waller among them, played live accompaniment to the films at every showing in the theater.

The entire soundtrack for *Ascenseur pour l'échafaud* was conceived and recorded in one sitting at a Paris radio studio after the day's broadcasting was finished. It is a tour de force in the art of improvising, and it shows as well as almost anything else Davis recorded the power and control he had over his art. Several of his solos have the unity of composed themes. On *Générique* and *Chez le photographe du motel*, his trumpet is distorted by the heavy-handed use of echo, but *Florence sur les Champs-Elysées* is a lush blues, *Au bar du Petit Bac* is a handsome simultaneous improvisation by Davis and Wilen (one of the simultaneous solo lines, probably Davis's, may have been added later by overdubbing), and *Dîner au motel*, is a muted trumpet solo accompanied by bass and drums that ranks with any of Davis's ballad solos for Prestige. On *Dîner au motel*, Davis's bell-like tone has an unusual wave motion, later explained as the result of a piece of loose skin from his chapped lip lodging in the mouthpiece. In spite of the stimulus for this music in the service of another medium, there is a great deal of it that deserves to be heard. The soundtrack recording won the Prix Louis Delluc the next year.

The soundtrack recording, though it forms the most interesting document to come out of Davis's Paris visit, was almost incidental in his busy three-week schedule. He started with a concert at the Olympia Theatre and continued with a three week stint at Club St. Germain, all with the same pickup band he used for the soundtrack recording. Michael Zwerin, the sometime trombone player who almost by accident played with Davis's nonet at the Royal Roost in 1948, was in Paris at the time "finding" himself (as he put it), and he kept tabs on some of Davis's public appearances. He was at the Olympia the first night, his sense of anticipation about the concert made all the keener by the fact that Urtreger's wife had spread the word among Zwerin's circle of friends that Davis had not yet shown up in Paris. "The Olympia Theatre was sold out that night, but by curtain time Miles' whereabouts were still a mystery," Zwerin recalled. "Finally the curtain went up, revealing Barney Wilen, René Urtreger, Pierre Michelot, and Kenny Clarke all set up. They started playing *Walkin'* and sounded fine. But no Miles Davis. Barney took a tenor solo, and as he was finishing, backing away from the microphone, Miles appeared from the wings and arrived at the mike without breaking stride, just in time to start playing – strong. It was an entrance worthy of Nijinsky" – or at least of Charlie Parker, who had occasionally choreographed similar entrances for himself in his younger days. Zwerin adds, "If his choreography was good, his playing was perfect that night."

Davis's Paris performances exposed a new audience to his stage manner and inevitably stirred up the controversy anew. André Hodeir, in his review of the concert, came down firmly on Davis's side. "He will not make concessions," Hodeir wrote. "When Miles cuts short the applause and moves efficiently from number to number, it's not from contempt of the public. On the contrary, he restores to the public its dignity by refusing it any concession in terms of choice of program or 'showmanship' on the part of himself and his musicians." Hodeir's point that Davis imposes his own recalcitrance upon his whole band proved true not only in Paris but elsewhere, somewhat to the chagrin of several American critics, who predicted that Davis's hiring of Julian Adderley, an effervescent showman with his own hands, was done partly as a concession to audience rapport. At no time did Adderley address Davis's audiences as long as he was in his band.

Zwerin also showed up in the audience at Club St. Germain nightly during Davis's first week there and occasionally during the other two weeks. One incident reported by Zwerin suggests that Davis was less than fully satisfied with his sidemen, although his displeasure did not seem to show in the music they made together. Zwerin says, "Once Wilen came over to me when I was sitting at the bar and said, 'You wouldn't believe what Miles said to me in the middle of my solo on the last tune. He said, 'Man, why don't you stop playing those awful notes?'" Zwerin was probably not nearly as surprised as Wilen expected him to be. After all, the only words Davis had said to him in Paris until then were, "Mike, you're putting on weight." Zwerin recalls that Wilen was not greatly upset by the insult: "Barney was a hot, confident young player at that time and, fortunately for him, was not inclined to paranoia. He thought it very funny and had just gone on playing." Davis's evaluation of his sidemen also became clear when the band made a television broadcast for Paris-TV, which is preserved on tape in some private collections. On Tadd Dameron's *Lady Bird*, Davis takes one and a half choruses for himself and allots Kenny Clarke one chorus alternating with the ensemble, but Wilen and Urtreger are given only half a chorus each.

Davis returned to New York in early December, and his quintet, with Adderley on saxophone, were installed again at the Café Bohemia, just as the Thelonious Monk Quartet with John Coltrane were finally ending their long engagement at the Five Spot. The tenor saxophonist Rocky Boyd had drifted onto the New York scene – he would play in Davis's quintet very briefly in 1962 before disappearing from jazz – and seems to have been acting as Davis's dogsbody, because Davis sent him over to the Five Spot with a message for Coltrane. He was to tell Coltrane that "a big, fat girl" from Boston (the description is C.O. Simpkins's), the thirteen- or fourteen-year-old daughter of a man who had hosted Davis and Coltrane when they played at Storyville in Boston, had arrived in New York in search of Coltrane. When Boyd passed along the message, Coltrane hid in the kitchen of the Five Spot and refused to appear on stage. Davis then had Boyd phone the girl's parents to come and get her.

The early progress of the Davis quintet with Adderley has not been documented on records or even apparently on private tapes of their performances. There is no reason whatever for suspecting that it was anything less than scintillating, given the talents of Davis and Adderley individually and their rapport with one another, all of which is abundantly documented starting just a few months later, in the spring of 1958. Still, Davis was restless, and the source of his disquiet had nothing whatever to do with Adderley's playing in the quintet but had something to do with Coltrane, whose work with Monk he had monitored carefully, however casual he tried to make it seem. Davis knew, as everyone else would soon know, that Coltrane had what Davis once called "*that thing*," the indefinable spirit that "speaks in the music." And he wanted it back in his band, where he could hear it every night and nurture it and take his own sustenance from it. Late in December, as Monk's quartet were wrapping up their engagement, Davis phoned Coltrane and said, "I want you back." And Coltrane paused a few seconds, and said, "All right." The Miles Davis Quintet thus gave way to the Miles Davis Sextet, perhaps the finest small band in the history of jazz.

8

Fran Dance
1958–9

If you place a guy in a spot where he has to do something else, other than what he can do, he can do *that*. He's got to have something that challenges his imagination, far above what he thinks he's going to play, and what it might lead into, and then above *that*, so he won't be fighting when things change. That's what I tell all my musicians; I tell them be ready to play what you know and play *above* what you know. Anything might happen above what you've been used to playing – you're ready to get into that, and above that, and take that out.   Miles Davis

John Coltrane rejoined Miles Davis's band late in December 1957, in time to play the Chicago engagement that was the customary stop for Davis's groups during the Christmas season. Red Garland also returned, and Philly Joe Jones had been reinstated earlier, and so at first the new sextet were just the original quintet with Julian Adderley added. But the new group were considerably more than the sum of their old parts, and the multiplier in the equation was Davis's search for a musical foundation that would unburden his music of what he had come to consider mere clutter. That search found a ready exponent in Coltrane, who also, surprisingly, became its most articulate spokesman in an article published in *Down Beat* in 1960. "On returning, ... I found Miles in the midst of another stage of his musical development," Coltrane explained. "There was one time in his past that he devoted to multichorded structures. He was interested in chords for their own sake. But now it seemed he was moving in the opposite direction to the use of fewer and fewer chord changes in songs. He used tunes with free-flowing lines and chordal direction. This approach allowed the soloist a choice of playing chordally (vertically) or melodically (horizontally)."

Davis's new development was gradual rather than revolutionary, the natural outgrowth of the direction he had begun with the harmonic clarity of the nonet, the use of space triggered by Ahmad Jamal, and the reductions found in Gil

Evans's orchestrations. It was also, according to the jazz educator Jerry Coker, a theoretical response to the maturation of any good improviser. Coker put it this way: "Imagine a student who has heard many recorded solos and knows all the possible chord scales and progressions. Perhaps he can even play indefinitely without playing a 'wrong' note, but he still has many choices to make in each phrase he decides to play, and chances are he isn't ready to make them. Some of the 'right' notes are 'righter' than others, and only observation and experience will eventually enable him to make better choices, and fewer choices too, since good improvisers usually acquire a sense for economy (deleting unnecessary pitches) as they mature. Miles Davis is today perhaps the most skillful in playing economically – stressing fewer, but well-chosen, notes and also making better use of rests, a very potent musical device."

The great improvisers in jazz, like the best artists in any other medium, have always learned to do what Coker here praises Davis for doing, manipulating the formal framework of their art in ways that often startle their audiences and always earn the admiration of lesser artists. Cecil Payne, the baritone saxophonist in Dizzy Gillespie's big band, watched it happening among the bop musicians. "Dizzy and Bird would be playing six or seven choruses – and every one would be different – and creating different sounds," Payne remembers. "See, Bird and Dizzy and Miles too developed to the stage where they could actually 'play.' What they were playing was free. You have groups that play 'free' music now, like the 'space' music or something like that. They're playing free. Actually Bird and Dizzy were playing free too. In their minds they were playing free. They didn't have any hangup about this chord or that chord. In their minds they were playing anything they could play, freely. But they were playing correct. I mean they were playing according to what the song they were playing to implied." The main difference between the great improvisers of the past and Miles Davis at this point in his development is that Davis took the next logical step and rationalized the harmonic basis for what Payne calls "playing free," and built it into the group dynamics of his band.

In Coltrane, Davis's explorations found not only a champion but also an adventuresome alter ego. "In fact, due to the direct and free-flowing lines in his music," Coltrane says in his *Down Beat* apologia, "I found it easy to apply the harmonic ideas that I had. I could stack up chords – say, on a C^7, I sometimes superimposed on an E^7, up to an F^7, down to an F. That way, I could play three chords on one. But on the other hand, if I wanted to, I could play melodically. Miles's music gave me plenty of freedom. It's a beautiful approach." As Coltrane settled into the new approach, he showed less and less tendency to play what he calls "melodically" and became a resolute experimentalist. "I was trying for a sweeping sound," he explained. "I started experimenting because I was striving for more individual development. I even tried long, rapid lines that Ira Gitler termed 'sheets of sound' at the time. But actually I was beginning to apply the three-on-one chord approach, and at that time the tendency was to play the entire scale of each chord. Therefore they were usually played fast and sometimes sounded like glisses. I found that there were a certain number of chord progressions to play in a given time, and sometimes what I played didn't work out in eighth notes, sixteenth notes, or triplets. I had to put the notes in uneven groups like fives and sevens in order to get them all in. I thought in groups of notes, not of one note at a time. I tried to place these groups on the accents and emphasize the strong beats – maybe on 2 here and on 4 over at the end. I would set up the line and drop groups of notes – a long line with accents dropped as I moved along."

Davis's music was the catalyst for Coltrane's conception, but he had been given a boost in that direction when he was playing in Thelonious Monk's band, and it came about because of Monk's uncanny intuition about harmony. Coltrane said, "Monk was one of the first to show me how to make two or three notes at a time on tenor. It's done by false fingerings and adjusting your lip. If everything goes right, you can get triads. Monk just looked at my horn and 'felt' the mechanics of what had to be done to get this effect." Naturally, Coltrane's experiments had their pitfalls. One of them came about because of the group accompaniment. "Sometimes what I was doing clashed harmonically with the piano – especially if the pianist wasn't familiar with what I was doing – so a lot of time I just strolled with bass and drums," Coltrane says. Another came about because audiences were not ready for what he was trying to accomplish. An English critic complained that his playing showed "a surfeit of passion at the expense of subtlety," and other listeners savaged his playing as incoherent, chaotic, illiterate, or worse.

Coltrane persisted, mainly because his work was understood and appreciated by the audience he considered most important – the other members of the sextet, especially Davis, who told Coltrane's critics, "He's been working on those arpeggios and playing chords that lead into chords, playing them fifty different ways and playing them all at once. He's beginning to leave more space except when he gets nervous." Davis also gave Coltrane the playing time he needed to pursue his experiments, which frequently led him to play at what might have appeared to other leaders to be unconscionable length. Adderley reports, "Once in a while, Miles might say, 'Why did you play so long, man?' and John would say, 'It took that long to get it all in.'"

At least as important to his development as the supportive setting of the sextet was the self-discipline he finally imposed on his private life. Coltrane was obsessive, a trait seen not only in his addictions to narcotics and alcohol but in many smaller ways as well, such as his gorging himself with sweets even when his teeth – not the least important physical equipment for a saxophonist – were constantly aching and rotting. But before Davis invited him back into the band in December 1957, he brought at least the most debilitating of his addictions into some semblance of control – apparently less than complete abstinence – through an obscure mystical experience, the details of which remain unknown although its effects are clear. In the notes for his album *A Love Supreme* (Impulse A-77), recorded in December 1964, Coltrane wrote: "During the year 1957, I experienced, by the grace of God, a spiritual awakening which was to lead me to a richer, fuller, more productive life. At that time, in gratitude, I humbly asked to be given the means and privilege to make others happy through music. I feel it has been granted through His grace." In the delicate balance he sought between sensuality and spirituality, Coltrane became a touchstone for the artistic temper of the time. John Clellon Holmes, trying hard to explain the Beat Generation to an eager public in 1958, said, "Nothing seems to satisfy or interest it but extremes, which, if they have included the criminality of narcotics, have also included the sanctity of monasteries." More than any individual directly associated with the Beat Generation, Coltrane embodied those extremes.

Through his conversion, the silent, diffident Coltrane found the conviction and determination to pursue his own star even against the refractory opposition of a large part of the jazz audience. He pursued it, as he did all the other things in his life, single-mindedly, and his long, turbulent solos with the sextet became part of a superb spectacle. On watching the sextet in action, Joe Goldberg remarks, "One speculated on how much of some men's personalities are released only in music: the quiet, pleasant Coltrane played fierce, slashing lines in direct opposition to the gentle, delicate phrases of the often blunt, arrogant Miles." The contrast in their musical and personal styles did not symbolize antipathy between the two men and was probably the source of their mutual respect. When Coltrane was listening to Davis soloing, Teo Macero remembers, "He'd smile like a little boy when Miles would play something he liked." Still, the path that Coltrane was taking, which would soon make him one of the supreme improvisers in the history of jazz, was a tortuous one, which could only be explored through what Hentoff calls "the sheer will to creativity of Coltrane on his better nights."

He was a notoriously late developer, and even then a painfully slow one. "With Miles, it took me around two and a half years, I think, before it started developing, taking the shape that it was going to take," he told Frank Kofsky. Davis was essential not only because he provided the musical approach that set it in motion but also because he was the most influential figure, the 'boss,' in jazz. "It was important for Coltrane to work with Miles," Hentoff says. "For one thing, of course, he received attention, with the Davis imprimatur legitimizing Coltrane for some of those who up to that point had considered Trane either incompetent or a charlatan or both. Miles, it was agreed by nearly all, could not and would not be conned musically. If he hired the man, the man must have something to say. That imprimatur also gave Coltrane confidence. Feeling set upon by the critics, he had passed a far more severe test by being considered worthy of a place in the Miles Davis band." Jimmy Heath, the tenor saxophonist, goes a step further: "At the time Coltrane was playing with Miles he worked just about every week and he practised more than anybody I ever met. So, if he didn't play better than anyone else he would have to be a dumb man. I think anybody who was a pretty good musician, who had the opportunities that Trane had, would get better."

With the striking dialectic of Davis and Coltrane in the sextet, Julian Adderley's presence might seem to be diminished, but there were few performances by the sextet that did not send the audience away buzzing about Adderley's prowess as well as, and often with flattering comparisons to, his front-line mates. Adderley's career after he left the sextet in 1959 has perhaps made it easier to underestimate his abilities, especially by contrast to Coltrane's career in the same period. Adderley's talent emerged as precociously as Coltrane's did methodically. He seems to have had his musical gifts intact from the moment he arrived in New York to play professionally, and in the fifteen years of his career after he left the sextet until his death in 1975 he seemed to many observers to be merely replaying what he had played before. His reach seldom – some might say never – exceeded his grasp, and he worked the rest of his career as a respected and popular, but not widely honored, figure. The shape that his career thus took, from an early creative peak that was consistently maintained but hardly rejuvenated afterward, is not at all unusual even for the major figures in jazz. It is much more commonplace than the multiple peaks of creativity in careers such as Duke Ellington's and Miles Davis's, or the fitful rise to brilliance in a career such as Coltrane's, and one can easily name great players – Louis Armstrong, Thelonious Monk, and Dizzy Gillespie among them – who achieved the heights of their abilities early and spent the rest of their careers at best approximating the powers of their early years.

One difference between Adderley and the others whose careers took a similar shape, apart from the obvious fact that his peak was not as salient historically as Armstrong's or Gillespie's or Monk's, is that while all of them, Adderley included, passed through long periods when their contributions were taken for granted, the others all eventually received their due in a thorough and broadly based revaluation that revived enthusiasm for their early music and elicited interest in their current music. Adderley, in contrast, died quite suddenly just before his forty-seventh birthday, and he had not yet received the revaluation he deserved. He was simply taken for granted at the time of his death and remains so today, notwithstanding the evidence of his brilliance on recordings not only with the sextet but also notably as the featured soloist in orchestrations by Gil Evans (reissued as Blue Note LA461-H2) and Ernie Wilkins (Riverside 377) and with numerous smaller combinations on Riverside and other labels. What the evidence shows, for those who bother to listen, is a remarkably facile, blues-oriented melodist with one of the richest, most expressive tones ever heard on an alto saxophone, an instrument that has had more than its share of articulate players in jazz but very few who rank with Adderley.

Adderley's period with the Miles Davis Sextet marked a time of some growth in his playing. "Miles taught me about chords, and Coltrane did too," he said later. "Coltrane knows more about chords than anyone. John knows exactly what he's doing; he's gone into the melodic aspect of chords. He may go 'out of the chord,' so-called, but not out of the pattern he's got in his mind." Occasionally Adderley's playing in the sextet reveals his debt to Coltrane, prompting Zita Carno, in an early article praising Coltrane's style, to remark: "Cannonball Adderley is by now classic proof that you can't play with Coltrane without being influenced by him." Adderley knew what Coltrane was doing harmonically beside him and shared in its inception to some extent, just as he expanded his range and his originality as a melodic player by learning from Davis on the other side. But most of all, finding himself in what might have become an intolerable position by playing nightly beside two of the greatest innovators in modern jazz, Adderley had the good sense to stake out his own ground and make a personal contribution to the music of the sextet that is hardly less central to it than the contributions of his more celebrated colleagues.

The first recordings made after the sextet were assembled were not by the working group but by a pickup quintet nominally led by Adderley with Davis as the second horn. They were made for Blue Note, with Davis participating by a special arrangement with Columbia, perhaps as a concession in order to release Adderley for future recordings with Davis on Columbia. The Blue Note session probably reflects the music made by Davis's quintet at the close of 1957, when Adderley was the only other front-line player. The details are as follows:

Julian Adderley and the All Stars
Miles Davis, tpt (except on *Dancing in the Dark*); Julian Adderley, as; Hank Jones, pno; Sam Jones, b; Art Blakey, dms. New York, 9 March 1958
Autumn Leaves; Somethin' Else; One for Daddy-o; Love for Sale; Dancing in the Dark (all on Blue Note 81595)

That Adderley was the leader of this session in name only is abundantly clear in the music that resulted, both in the allotment of solo space and in the choice of tunes. Davis states the melody alone on *Autumn Leaves* and *Love for Sale*, and he and Hank Jones, a superior accompanist who plays beautifully throughout this session, fashion a long, apparently extemporaneous movement at the end of

Autumn Leaves that ignores Adderley altogether. Adderley gets a more equal share on the two blues numbers, Davis's *Somethin' Else* and Nat Adderley's funky *One for Daddy-o*, and he finally gets the spotlight on *Dancing in the Dark*, in which he is the only solo voice. *Autumn Leaves*, a popular hit of the year before in an instrumental version featuring endless arpeggios by the cocktail pianist Roger Williams, gets an ornate arrangement in the style of Ahmad Jamal; Davis told Leonard Feather, who wrote the notes for the LP, "I got the idea for this treatment of *Autumn Leaves* listening to him." *Dancing in the Dark*, although it is Adderley's showcase, was also selected by Davis. "I made him play this because I remembered hearing Sarah Vaughan do it like this," Davis told Feather. Even on *One for Daddy-o*, the one number distinctly foreign to Davis's repertoire though it features a neat abstraction of the blues by Davis as well as a gorgeous traditional blues solo by Adderley, it is Davis's voice that breaks in at the end calling to Alfred Lion, the producer, in the control booth, "Is that what you wanted, Alfred?" Davis was clearly in charge, and even though this recording stands slightly apart from the magnificent music he made with his working band and with Gil Evans in these years, it nevertheless shares many of its best qualities.

The sextet finally made their recording debut in early April, in two recording sessions that left no doubt that Davis had assembled a great band. The details are as follows:

Miles Davis Sextet
Miles Davis, tpt; Julian Adderley, as; John Coltrane, ts; Red Garland, pno; Paul Chambers, b; Philly Joe Jones, dms. New York, 2 April 1958
Two Bass Hit; *Billy Boy* (rhythm trio only); *Straight No Chaser*; *Milestones*
(all on Columbia CL 1193)

Same personnel but omit Garland on *Sid's Ahead*; Davis plays piano and trumpet; same place; 3 April 1958
Dr. Jekyll [*Dr. Jackle*]; *Sid's Ahead* [*Walkin'*]
(both issued as above)
Dr. Jekyll is a misspelling (*pace* Robert Louis Stevenson) of Jackie McLean's title, *Dr. Jackle*.

With the expanded instrumentation from the quintet to the sextet, Davis makes strategic use of the instrumental combinations. Red Garland's role as a solo voice almost disappears, except for the trio track, *Billy Boy*, the American folk song that Ahmad Jamal rearranged into a swinging vehicle for piano players. Garland's version was only one of dozens being played at the time, which later prompted Jamal to complain, "I was stupid enough not to copyright the arrangement, and then Oscar Peterson did it, Red Garland did it, Ramsey Lewis did it, everybody did it, and I didn't get paid for it." Garland's only other solo turn is on *Straight No Chaser*, and everywhere else the space conventionally taken by the piano player is given to Paul Chambers on bass, who solos on every track except *Two Bass Hit* and *Milestones*.

The unusual emphasis on bass rather than piano as a solo voice rankled Garland, who walked out of the studio during the warm-up for *Sid's Ahead*, leaving Davis to double on piano and trumpet on the recorded version of this track. But the emphasis not only reflects Davis's displeasure with Garland; it also, more positively, reflects his delight in his bassist's development. Soon after these recordings were made, Davis told Nat Hentoff, "Paul Chambers ... has started to play a new way whereby he can solo and accompany himself at the same time – by using space well." How that polydexterity might translate into performance is hard to guess, but Chambers was given ample opportunity to show his wares both arco and pizzicato.

The solo orders take some unconventional turns, too. Adderley is the first soloist on *Milestones* and *Straight No Chaser*, followed by Davis and then by Coltrane, an order that exploits the stylistic contrasts among the three horns magnificently and also preserves the dynamics of the superseded quintet by allowing Coltrane to charge in behind Davis. On *Sid's Ahead* and *Two Bass Hit*, Coltrane opens the solo round, with Davis again interposed between the two reedmen on the former but not soloing at all on the latter. On *Dr. Jackle*, Davis solos first, exercising the traditional privilege of the leader in jazz bands, but the round of solos turns out to be another innovation, as Davis shares his final three twelve-bar choruses with Philly Joe Jones, and then Adderley and Coltrane trade choruses in their turn.

Probably a more challenging problem for Davis than alloting solo space for the expanded band was working out the ensembles. Only *Dr. Jackle* seems cluttered in the ensembles, and that impression probably comes not from the lines played by the horns so much as the quick tempo at which they are asked to play it, which prevents them from giving full value to each note. Otherwise the arrangements are very effective, even on the complex *Two Bass Hit*, where each horn takes charge of a counter-theme in a glorious small-band adaptation of John Lewis's composition. Equally noteworthy are Adderley's lead on the ensemble of *Straight No Chaser*, with the other horns playing tight dissonances under him, and the startling fanfare of *Milestones* from which Davis's translucent tone rises at the bridge.

But despite all the attention to solo orders and ensembles that went into these recordings, they succeed only because of the improvisations that sustain the moods of the ensembles and cohere both individually and collectively. Benny

Golson, who reviewed this album for *Jazz Review*, remarks that in *Two Bass Hit* "Coltrane enters into his solo moaning, screaming, squeezing, and seemingly projecting his very soul through the bell of the horn," and he adds: "I feel that this man is definitely blazing a new musical trail." Perhaps the best evidence of that new trail, in retrospect, occurs on *Straight No Chaser*, where Coltrane stacks up chords in breathless runs of eighth-notes and sixteenth-notes, a solo that makes a textbook demonstration of the "three-on-one" approach he discussed in his *Down Beat* article.

Golson and most other reviewers noted that Adderley's playing here shows Coltrane's influence, but that influence is more apparent than real at the point where most listeners think they hear it. In *Dr. Jackle*, the seams between the alternating choruses by the two players are almost indistinguishable, and there is momentary confusion on a first listening as to where Adderley leaves off and Coltrane begins, and vice versa. But the confusion does not seem to be caused by similarity of phrasing so much as by similarity of tone, as Adderley's full, rich tone on the alto almost seems to be aping Coltrane's tenor in the transitions. Coltrane's influence comes across more clearly on Adderley's solo on *Sid's Ahead*, a series of sweeping glissandi worthy of Coltrane at his best. The two reedmen are balanced by Davis's sure, spare trumpet, characterized by Golson as "a sound psychological approach in that he never plays too much." Golson adds, "He leaves me, always, wanting to hear more."

The power of the sextet is thus clearly demonstrated in their first recordings. Apart from *Dr. Jackle*'s flawed ensembles, each composition crystallizes various aspects of that power as a self-contained miniature. The intricate, ingenious arrangement of *Two Bass Hit*, which is worthy of Gil Evans, was almost certainly put together with only a few gestures by way of instruction for the reallocation of parts. For Ian Carr, the British trumpet player, it is *Straight No Chaser* that wins the accolades. "With Miles Davis, everything *counts*," Carr told Lee Underwood. "Everything must count, and every note must be accountable. If there's no reason for its being there, then it shouldn't be there. And he swings. For me, he swings more than any other trumpet player, more than almost anybody – just listen to his solo on *Straight No Chaser* on the *Milestones* album. No other trumpet player swings like that." Benny Golson points out, among the more arcane delights of this music, that Red Garland ends his solo on *Straight No Chaser* with "a beautiful harmonization of Miles's original solo on *Now's the Time*." He states flatly that *Straight No Chaser* is "the best track on the album."

At least as many people would choose *Milestones* as the best track. This new composition by Davis, which recycles the title he first used in 1947 – it was obviously too good a title to simply abandon – but otherwise bears no resemblance whatever to the earlier composition, contains a remarkable unity. Michel Legrand remarks, "I love the way they approach this melody – everything is for the melody; the chords are very simple, like a carpet on which all the music is based. In other words, the whole thing is not based on complexity, but on simplicity and purity." (It is juvenile, of course, to speak of any work of art as 'perfect,' but it is somehow irresistible to come right out and say – at least parenthetically – that *Milestones* seems to be a perfect jazz performance. Its components are a simple, memorable, highly original melody, followed by three individualistic explorations of the theme, each one as memorable as the theme itself, by Adderley, Davis, and Coltrane, all buoyed by the brash but sensitive rhythm section, and then the simple, unforgettable melody again. There is nothing more, it seems to me, that one might hope for or ask for in a jazz performance.)

Amazingly, *Milestones*, which appears to be simple, highly accessible, and above all swinging, also represents a structural innovation of great consequence not only for the music of Miles Davis but also for jazz in general. It is Davis's first completely successful composition based on scales rather than a repeated chord structure. James Lincoln Collier, in his history of jazz, describes its structure this way: "The ability to place his notes in unexpected places is Davis's strongest virtue. It colors his work everywhere. His masterwork in this respect is his *Milestones* ... It is made up of the simplest sort of eight-bar melody – little more than the segment of a scale, in fact – which is repeated and then followed by a bridge made out of a related eight-bar theme, also repeated. After the bridge, the theme is played once more. The point of it all lies in the bridge, where the rhythm goes into partial suspension. Miles stretches this passage out with notes falling farther and farther behind their proper places. Indeed, in the reprise of the theme at the end of the record he stretches the bridge so far out that he cannot fit it all in and has to cut it short." Collier adds: "It is built not on chord changes but on modes ... For Davis, who was already making a point of simplicity, they were a perfect vehicle. He was not the first to see what could be done with them, but he was the one who brought the idea to fruition. *Milestones* uses one mode on the main theme, then switches to a second mode for the bridge."

Collier correctly points out that Davis was not the first jazz player to promote a modal foundation for jazz compositions – that distinction probably belongs to George Russell. During one of Russell's enforced absences from jazz activity due to tuberculosis, he formalized his thinking in a dissertation called *The Lydian Concept of Tonal Organization*, first published in 1953 and required reading ever since for jazz scholars, but well before that Russell had tried to use modes in his writing. The first composition in jazz to use a modal organization is probably Russell's introduction to the Dizzy Gillespie orchestra's *Cubano Be*. "Diz had written a sketch which was mostly *Cubano Be*," Russell says. "His sketch was what later turned out to be the section of the piece called *Cubano Be* except that I wrote a long introduction to that which was at the time modal. I mean it wasn't based on any chords, which was an innovation in jazz because the modal period didn't really begin to happen until Miles popularized it in 1959. So that piece was written in 1947, and the whole concept of my introduction was modal, and then Dizzy's theme came in and we performed it."

Davis's contribution was not in discovering the innovation but in making it work. He was fully aware of the breakthrough he was making in *Milestones*, as its title indicates, and he described its advantages to Nat Hentoff at the time. "When you go this way," he said, "you can go on forever. You don't have to worry about changes and you can do more with the line. It becomes a challenge to see how melodically inventive you are. When you're based on chords, you know at the end of 32 bars that the chords have run out and there's nothing to do but repeat what you've just done – with variations. I think a movement in jazz is beginning away from the conventional string of chords, and a return to emphasis on melodic rather than harmonic variation. There will be fewer chords but infinite possibilities as to what to do with them." This was the innovation that Coltrane described when he spoke of Davis's "new stage of jazz development" and of his compositions with "free-flowing lines and chordal direction." Hentoff draws the conclusion from his discussion with Davis that "Davis thus predicts the development of both Coltrane and, to a lesser degree, the more extreme, more melodic, Ornette Coleman."

For the ordinary jazz listener, Davis's modal breakthrough is meaningful not for its formal musical properties or for its historical importance but for the gain in expression it allows the musicians, which in the hands of individuals of the caliber of Davis, Coltrane, and Adderley is heard and felt powerfully. In *Milestones* and in the other modal compositions that follow it in Davis's repertoire, there is no feeling of self-conscious experimentation and no implication that these musicians are revising the structural foundations of their art. In this regard, Davis contrasts strikingly with the proponents of third stream music and even with the humbler innovators in his old nonet, and also with the avant-garde or free form musicians soon to follow, all of whom spent more than a little energy talking about the uniqueness of their contributions rather than making their music.

After the *Milestones* recording session, Red Garland was replaced as the sextet's piano player. In the next few years, Garland would occasionally return to the group as a fill-in but his tenure as Davis's regular pianist, which had lasted two and a half years with a few interruptions, was over. Davis was not replacing Garland as a disciplinary measure but because he had found a new man who was already deeply involved in modal composition and improvisation. His name was Bill Evans, and few jazz musicians have ever presented so unprepossessing an appearance. Evans was pallid, with owlish glasses and lank hair that, even in the close-cropped Ivy League fashion he favored at the time, became disheveled in the drafts he caused when he turned his head. He was painfully shy and taciturn, and his personality seemed to be expressed perfectly in his posture at the piano, which was S-shaped, with his narrow shoulders hunched and his nose almost touching the keyboard. He joined the sextet with characteristic trepidation. He later said, "I felt the group to be composed of superhumans."

Among all of Davis's discoveries, none better demonstrates his prescience than Evans. Probably only Coltrane had a greater long-term impact on the music. Like Coltrane, Evans was a late-bloomer. Born and raised in Plainfield, New Jersey, a commuter community for New York, in 1929, he was still virtually unknown when he joined the sextet, although he had led a trio on a Riverside recording in 1956. Although he was raised within hailing distance of New York, his personal roots seemed to be oriented more toward the southeast: his parents retired to Florida, his older brother, a sometime musician who had allowed Evans to play piano in his semi-professional dance band as a teenager, settled in Baton Rouge, Louisiana, and Evans himself earned an undergraduate degree in music from Southeastern Louisiana College, about a two-hour drive from New Orleans.

After college, Evans held down jobs in several bands, starting in 1950 with the ill-starred Herbie Fields, with whom Davis had made his own recording debut five years earlier. While Evans's talent stirred almost no interest among jazz fans, other musicians often caught on to the values of his understated ruminations. It was the guitarist Mundell Lowe, with whom Evans had played in Louisiana, who first recommended him to Orrin Keepnews of Riverside Records. Evans kept up his music studies as much as time allowed while he was playing professionally, and he was enrolled at New York's Mannes School of Music when he joined Davis.

Evans's academic work brought him into close contact with George Russell, at first as a student but later as a colleague in the modal developments. Russell was almost as unknown as Evans in the late 1950s, but he began to get a few opportunities as the third stream movement crested, and he included Evans in them. Most notable was Russell's commission for the Brandeis University festival in 1957, entitled *All about Rosie*, which provided solo space for Evans, as did Russell's best-known recorded work of that period, *New York, N.Y.* (Decca DL 9216), recorded while Evans was a member of Davis's sextet. Through Russell and Gunther Schuller, Evans was also loosely associated as a sessional instructor with the School of Jazz in Lenox, Massachusetts, where the other two were on the faculty. If Russell was little better known to the general public than Evans, there was still a quantum difference in their status in New York's jazz community, where Russell's credentials went back several years, and it was almost certainly through Russell that Evans came to Miles Davis's attention.

Both Evans and Davis benefited. To the sextet, Evans brought a solo voice capable of holding its own with the three great hornmen, making it perhaps the greatest aggregation of soloists ever to play side by side in a working band. He also served as a third important researcher, with Davis and Coltrane, in the nightly nonverbal seminars for extending jazz's modal foundations. Davis's enthusiasm was, for him, effusive. "Boy, I've sure learned a lot from Bill Evans," he told Hentoff soon after Evans joined the band. "He plays the piano the way it should be played. He plays all kinds of scales, can play in 5/4, and all kinds of fantastic things. There's such a difference between him and Red Garland, whom I also like a lot. Red carries the rhythm but Bill underplays, and I like that better." Hentoff played Davis a recording by Oscar Peterson, and his critical comments crystalized his predilections about music in general and piano-playing in particular. "It's much prettier if you can get into it and hear the chord weaving in and out like Bill Evans and Red Garland could do – instead of being so heavy. Oscar is jazzy; he jazzes up the tune. And he sure has devices, like certain scale patterns, that he plays all the time." Davis continued: "Does he swing hard? I don't know what they mean when they say 'swing hard' anyway. Nearly everything he plays, he plays with the same degree of force. He leaves no holes for the rhythm section." Asked to compare Evans with Ahmad Jamal, Davis said, "Bill plays a little like that but he sounds wild when he does – all those little scales." From Davis this is high praise indeed, the first time in at least four years that he had found a piano player he could compare favorably to Jamal. To cap it all, he went on to say, "If I could play like Ahmad and Bill Evans combined with one hand, they could take the other off."

If Evans's effect on Davis was considerable, then Davis's effect on Evans was inestimable. By the close of 1958, at the end of his eight-month tenure as the sextet's pianist, Evans was recognized in *Down Beat*'s international survey of critics as the new star on piano, and the next year he began anew his career as the leader of a piano trio that would bring him two decades of critical and popular success matched by very few musicians in the history of jazz.

Evans had been with the sextet about five weeks when they broadcast from the Café Bohemia one Saturday in May, which is the first documentation of his work in the group. For some unknown reason, Julian Adderley was absent for the broadcast, reducing the group to a quintet. The details are as follows:

Miles Davis Quintet
Miles Davis, tpt; John Coltrane, ts; Bill Evans, pno; Paul Chambers, b; Philly Joe Jones, dms. Café Bohemia, New York, 17 May 1958
Four [*Four Plus One More*] (Chakra CH 100); *Bye Bye Blackbird* (unissued); *Walkin'* (unissued)

Only *Four* has been issued, and it is the least interesting of the three titles. It is another run-through of Davis's favorite set opener, with solos by Davis and Coltrane only. Coltrane's solo sounds awkward, and Davis re-enters playing the theme rather suddenly, as if cutting off Coltrane's attempt to begin another chorus. Evans is inconspicuous. On the other two titles, Evans solos after Davis and Coltrane mainly using soft-spoken single note lines with lots of rests. His playing is tentative, and on *Bye Bye Blackbird* it inevitably suffers by comparison with Red Garland's showy accompaniments in all the extant versions; *Bye Bye Blackbird* was a tune that Garland obviously loved to play. However, Davis's playing, probably in response to Evans's presence, finds him toying with the melody, a distinct departure from his usual verbatim statement; he interpolates snatches of Leonard Bernstein's *Maria* in two of his choruses, and in *Walkin'* as well as in *Bye Bye Blackbird* he sustains many of his choruses by repeating short phrases for as long as eight bars at a time. Apart from the slight changes in Davis's style, no particular concession is made to accommodate the new member of the band. The same three titles had also been called in his last broadcast from the Bohemia ten months earlier, when Sonny Rollins was a member of the quintet. The absence of *Milestones* and the other new entries in the repertoire seems a lost opportunity, but it might be explained by the absence of Adderley, whose presence in the ensembles was essential.

The drug problems among the sidemen apparently continued. "In a way, I suppose, I was a kind of stabilizing influence on the band," Adderley said later. "Two of the men he had – fine musicians – weren't exactly on time or dependable." Finally, in May, Philly Joe Jones left the band and Davis replaced him with Jimmy Cobb, a disciple of Jones who had been the drummer in Adderley's quintet before he broke it up to go with Davis. In letting Jones go after more than two and a half years, Davis knew that he was giving up Jones's extra, ineffable quality, which made him the most respected drummer of the day. Cobb was excellent, and he did most of the things that Jones could do on the drums, so that even expert listeners have sometimes been unable to identify which one of them is playing on some of the more obscure tapes from this period, but no one could pretend that Jimmy Cobb had whatever it was that Davis had called, speaking of Jones's drumming, "that *thing*." Because of the stature he had earned working for Davis, Jones could form his own band almost immediately and have it booked into Birdland and other major clubs, often with Red Garland playing piano for him. For Cobb, replacing the top drummer added pressure wherever the sextet played, but Cobb, a mature and sensible twenty-nine-year-old, worried more about sounding right than about taking on the ghost of Philly Joe. He was given a boost, perhaps unexpected, by Davis, who fended off the inevitable questions about his drummers with some tact. "Jimmy makes me play in a different way from Philly," he told a British reporter. "Everyone's got their own way of playing. Philly gets some things out of me that Jimmy doesn't but it's the same the other way. I play with the rhythm section."

Still, the two changes in the sextet's personnel in April and May forced some changes in emphasis. Adderley recalls that Davis's instinct was to play more ballads. "Especially when he started to use Bill Evans, Miles changed his style from very hard to a softer approach," he said. "Bill was brilliant in other areas, but he couldn't make the real hard things come off. Then Miles started writing new things and doing some of Ahmad's tunes. When Philly Joe left the band, Miles at first thought Jimmy Cobb wasn't exciting on fast tempos, and so we did less of those." The new emphasis was realized brilliantly in the first recording session by the sextet with Evans and Cobb, which took place just a few weeks after Cobb joined:

Miles Davis Sextet
Miles Davis, tpt; Julian Adderley, as (except on *Stella by Starlight*); John Coltrane, ts; Bill Evans, pno; Paul Chambers, b; Jimmy Cobb, dms. New York, 26 May 1958
Green Dolphin Street; *Fran Dance*; *Stella by Starlight*; *Love for Sale*
(first three titles on Columbia CL 1268; *Green Dolphin Street* and *Stella by Starlight* reissued [1973] on C32025; *Love for Sale* first issued 1975, reissued [1977] on JP 13811 and [1979] on 36278)
Fran Dance was identified as *Put Your Little Foot Right* out on the liner of Columbia CL 1268 but as *Fran Dance* on the label; subsequent recordings of the same composition identify it as *Fran Dance*.

The first three titles were released almost immediately as one side of an LP coupled with Davis's soundtrack for *Ascenseur pour l'échafaud* and won an immediate popular response with their delicate lyricism but intense swing.

This rare combination of elements carries over less thoroughly onto the fourth title, because *Love for Sale* was simply a head arrangement at a faster tempo designed to give the musicians a chance to cut loose after working through the tight, controlled arrangements of the other pieces. Evans told Sy Johnson, who wrote the liner notes for its belated release in 1975: "Paul Chambers and Jimmy Cobb were getting edgy having to hold back, and wanted to cook on something. Miles just turned and said *Love For Sale*, and kicked it off." The result is a straightforward romp in 4/4 time featuring long solos, without any of the orna- ments Adderley and Davis added to it in their Blue Note recording just ten weeks earlier. Evans's solo is a percussive essay with several tricks in the time, but all the others are just ebullient ad libs. Presumably the existence of the same title on the Blue Note recording led Columbia to withhold its release for seventeen years, but the two versions have little in common. The Columbia version also has little in common with the spirit and the form of the other three titles recorded on the same day, which are all thoughtful ballads.

Green Dolphin Street, best known in the annals of popular music because it became a hit after it was rejected for the background score of the 1947 movie by the same title starring Lana Turner and Van Heflin, ranks among the great ballad performances in jazz. Paul Chambers carries the entire arrangement by alternating a static eight-bar bass figure with eight bars of walking bass, creating successive currents of tension and release. Each of the soloists – Davis, Coltrane, Adderley, and Evans, in that order – must then cope with the alternating pulse in his own way. This tune was suggested by Adderley, and it is one of those rare discoveries that Ahmad Jamal then picked up from Davis's band rather than vice versa. But Jamal was not the only player who picked it up; Jimmy Heath recalls, "When Miles Davis started playing *Green Dolphin Street* everybody started playing it." For a while, it was as familiar in jazz clubs as *Salt Peanuts* had been ten years earlier.

Stella by Starlight gets a reverential, perhaps melodramatic, treatment, with Davis and Coltrane singing their roles as if performing an aria. The romanticism is blatant but not altogether ineffective, and this tune also became a favorite with jazz players.

The third piece, Davis's original *Fran Dance*, is based on a novelty dance number entitled *Put Your Little Foot Right out* which enjoined an earlier generation of Americans to form a circle on the dance floor and place one foot or the other in or out of the circle. Anyone old enough to remember the origin of *Fran Dance* might well have to face it with a supercilious grin, but fortunately few of Davis's listeners seemed to remember it and the tune was accepted in the form in which Davis presents it, as a haunting, romantic ballad. As such, it bears almost no resemblance to the original in mood, tone, or tempo, and little resemblance in melody, a fact that apparently occurred to Davis and his Columbia producers only after the notes for the original release were already printed, where it is identified by the novelty title.

The transformation of the source material into Davis's composition prompted Martin Williams to say, "Miles Davis, after all, can undertake some unspeakably mawkish material as *Some Day My Prince Will Come*, *Put Your Little Foot Right In* [sic] (which he calls *Fran Dance*), or *Spring is Here* and make it palatable by his intense involvement as he recomposes the melodies," and from that, Williams concludes: "In repertory, as in other obvious respects, Miles Davis's music often represents the triumph of an innate artistic sensibility over middlebrow taste." Williams's conclusion does not necessarily follow, of course. The banality of the lyrics or the dance steps associated with a particular melody does not in itself mean that the melody is also banal. Musicologists are just beginning to discover that American popular song has often obscured its artistry behind marketability, and most listeners can readily think of beautiful melodies with stupid lyrics. On at least one occasion, the transformation of a song has gone the other way, when Charlie Parker's *Now's the Time* was fitted with a lyric to become the boneheaded novelty dance called *The Hucklebuck*. By Williams's reasoning, whatever survives of Parker in *The Hucklebuck* must be mawkish, but clearly it is only what is added on to Parker that is mawkish, as Williams would no doubt agree. The appropriate conclusion, then, about Davis's ability at recomposition is not necessarily that it allows him to triumph over his "middlebrow taste" but that it reveals his ability to discern musical values beneath surfaces of such banality that most listeners miss them entirely.

Ironically, Davis's next recording venture was designed as an exercise in middlebrow taste. The record companies had discovered in the mid-1950s an untapped market for something they called mood music, an indefinable mélange somewhere between light classics and Hollywood production numbers. The original hit albums in the field, marketed by Capitol Records under the name of the television comedian Jackie Gleason and sometimes featuring the smooth cornet of Bobby Hackett, were apparently intended as boudoir music for the bourgeoisie, but when the marketing analysts discovered that the records were being played at reveille as well as at taps, and in the bathroom and kitchen as well as the bedroom, the race was on to supply a yawning populace with insipid soundtracks to accompany its most mundane activities. Into the gap rushed André Kostelanetz, Mantovani, Ray Conniff, and dozens of even less interesting orchestrators, with music not only to love by but also to eat by, drink by, and sleep by.

In 1957 Columbia imported the young Parisian arranger Michel Legrand to make a series of mood albums. The manager in charge of Legrand's projects may not have known that in addition to his successes as a songwriter and soundtrack arranger he was also a jazz piano player and an avid jazz buff. Certainly Legrand did nothing to tip his interest in jazz when he put together commercial albums with the titles *I Love Paris*, *Holiday in Rome*, *Vienna Holiday*, *Castles in Spain*, *Bonjour Paris*, and *Legrand in Rio*, all of which proved insipid enough to garner their share of the market and establish Legrand's name in the field. As his next excursion in mood music, he prevailed upon his producers at Columbia to let him make an album of jazz classics under the title *Legrand Jazz*. For the album, he enlisted a bandful of good jazzmen, including Davis, Coltrane, Evans, and Chambers from the sextet. The details are as follows:

Michel Legrand and His Orchestra
Miles Davis, tpt; Phil Woods, as (except on *Django*); John Coltrane, ts (except on *Django*); Jerome Richardson, bass clnt (except on *Django*); Herbie Mann, flt; Betty

Glamann, harp; Eddie Costa, vib; Barry Galbraith, gtr; Bill Evans, pno; Paul Chambers,
b; Kenny Dennis, dms; Michel Legrand, arr, cond. New York, 25 June 1958
Wild Man Blues; Round Midnight; Jitterbug Waltz; Django
(all on Columbia 1250; reissued on CBS [French] 62 637)
Davis does not play on the remaining titles of *Legrand Jazz* (Columbia 1250).

Legrand's concept was to embellish the familiar jazz melodies and the improvisations in a framework of orchestral textures, and he succeeds nicely. His writing
makes particularly interesting and unusual use – at least for jazz – of the vibraphone in the ensemble, where it functions almost exclusively as a rhythm instrument. Evans is prominent in the introduction to Fats Waller's *Jitterbug Waltz*, in
which he and Davis, Coltrane, Herbie Mann, and Phil Woods all play full
choruses. On *Round Midnight*, Davis states the melody except for the first
bridge, which is taken by Mann, and he solos throughout, playing many of the
same phrases as he did in his quintet's performance of Gil Evans's arrangement.
Django is also given over to Davis almost exclusively, as he first plays obbligatos
around John Lewis's beautiful theme, stated by the guitar, harp, and vibraphone,
and then as he solos over the backdrop provided by that same combination and by
Bill Evans.

For Legrand, meeting these musicians on their own ground proved to be a
bit daunting. "I loved the way Miles Davis and John Coltrane played," he told
J.C. Thomas, "but I was also a bit afraid. I wondered how they would react to
my arrangements. Miles didn't say anything, but John asked me, 'How do you
want me to play my solo?' I was amazed. All I could say was, 'John, play
exactly the way you feel after you listen to what's happening around you.'
When it came time for him to solo, he integrated himself thoroughly into my
arrangements without sacrificing one note of his own conception." Legrand's
point also holds for Davis, and as a result, while this music is slight it cannot
be dismissed as uninteresting. Legrand drew on the individualism of his musicians as well as on his stockpile of mood music devices to make a listenable
middle ground.

The session with Legrand began a busy summer of work for Davis. The main
event was the recording of George Gershwin's music for *Porgy and Bess* with Gil
Evans's arrangements, an undertaking that would require four separate studio
sessions with a large orchestra in July and August. At the same time the sextet
were booked in and around New York as well. One engagement, inevitably, took
the band to Newport, Rhode Island, for the Friday concert at the fourth annual
Newport Jazz Festival. It proved, if nothing else, that even this band could have
an ordinary outing. Their performance was recorded by Columbia, and four of the
six titles they played were released as one side of an LP six years later. The details
are as follows:

Miles Davis Sextet
Miles Davis, tpt; Julian Adderley, as; John Coltrane, ts; Bill Evans, pno; Paul Chambers,
b; Jimmy Cobb, dms. Newport, RI, 4 July 1958
*Ah-Leu-Cha; Straight No Chaser; Fran Dance; Two Bass Hit; Bye Bye Blackbird; The
Theme*
(first four titles on Columbia CL 2178; *Fran Dance* reissued [1973] on C 32025; fifth title
issued [1982] on C2-38262)
All issues of this material by Columbia incorrectly list Wynton Kelly as the piano player.

Although Davis included the relatively new *Fran Dance* in his Newport program,
the repertoire otherwise consists of old favorites, and here they sound a little the
worse for wear. The sextet's performance is substandard. Davis's most conspicuous contribution comes in tapping out overzealous tempos on all tunes, including
a breakneck tempo on *Ah-Leu-Cha* that reduces the ensemble to a shambles. The
playing is pretty well left up to Coltrane, who plays the only solo on *Two Bass
Hit*, as usual, and an incredibly long one on *Bye Bye Blackbird* (on which
Adderley is not heard at all) as well as taking his regular turn on all the others.

Davis's apparent lack of interest has been matched by Columbia's: it released
approximately two-thirds of it in 1964 and waited eighteen years before releasing
more; identified the piano player as Wynton Kelly when the announcement at
the festival, which occurs on the tape immediately following the part it mastered,
identifies him as Bill Evans; and stated on the 1973 reissue of *Fran Dance* that the
sextet shared the bill with Thelonious Monk and Pee Wee Russell, when in fact
they shared it with the Dave Brubeck Quartet. (Monk and Russell played
together at Newport five years later, in 1963, and some of the material they
played is coupled with the Davis sextet material from 1958 on Columbia CL
2178.)

The festival appearance worked well for Jimmy Cobb as well as for Coltrane,
but is otherwise quite undistinguished. *Down Beat's* review in its 7 August issue
was duly critical but chose to lay most of the blame in Coltrane's lap. "Unfortunately the group did not perform effectively," the review said. "Although Miles
continues to play with delicacy and infinite grace, his group's solidarity is hampered by the angry tenor of Coltrane. Backing himself into rhythmic corners of
flurries of notes, Coltrane sounded like the personification of motion-without-
progress in jazz. What is equally important, Coltrane's playing has apparently
influenced Adderley. The latter's playing indicated less concern for melodic structure than he has illustrated in the past ... With the exception of Miles' vital contribution, then, the group proved more confusing to listeners than educational."
These were complaints that Coltrane was to hear fairly often in the next few
years. In due course, he would impose greater consistency on his playing as he

became its master and the complaints would turn into almost universal praise, but now there were many nights when he communicated the search more than what it was that he sought, and the Newport festival of 1958 was one of these.

Maynard Ferguson often led his band opposite the sextet in clubs, and he recognized that Coltrane inevitably suffered by comparison to the other players on some nights. "In baseball, the more of a power hitter you are, the more often you miss, because you swing so hard," he explained. "I worked opposite Miles Davis when he had Cannonball and Coltrane, who admired each other very much. But Cannonball had the better average in the baseball sense. Because Coltrane was the *experimenter*. Maybe he had a minimal cult then, a tiny number of people starting to really love his music. And some that would resist it and then suddenly hear something in it. And it was a great education for me not to make judgements on people in the first ten hearings. Whereas some people make judgements on their *first* hearing." Coltrane always worked hard at his music; the same could not be said of his colleagues, and the festival concert was a performance at which Coltrane at least outworked the others.

The recording sessions for *Porgy and Bess* started on 22 July, but the day before the second of them took place, the sextet appeared in a Monday night engagement at the posh Plaza Hotel. The occasion was a command performance for the management at Columbia Records and its invited guests, to celebrate the jazz division's dominating position in the jazz market at a time when jazz was enjoying considerable popularity. The evening included, along with the sextet, sets by the Duke Ellington orchestra, Billie Holiday (a little less than a year before her death, and suffering), and Jimmy Rushing. Ellington and the vocalists appeared both before and after the sextet, which then had to work in a little clearing amid the orchestra's paraphernalia. The recording suffers from more than a few technical problems but the musicians were closer to the top of their form than they had been at Newport. The details are as follows:

Miles Davis Sextet
Miles Davis, tpt; Julian Adderley, as (except *My Funny Valentine* and *If I Were a Bell*); John Coltrane, ts (except *My Funny Valentine*); Bill Evans, pno; Paul Chambers, b; Jimmy Cobb, dms. Plaza Hotel, New York, 28 July 1958
Straight No Chaser; My Funny Valentine; If I Were a Bell; Oleo
(all on Columbia C 32470 [first issued 1973])
On the liner and label, the drummer is incorrectly listed as Philly Joe Jones, and *Straight No Chaser* is mistitled *Jazz at the Plaza*.

If Davis believed a few months earlier that Evans and Cobb were incapable of playing the hard swingers, he had obviously changed his mind by now. Both the

Plaza date and the Newport concert included fast pieces in proportions that were typical of his selections for sets prior to their joining the sextet. For Evans, the main concession is that *My Funny Valentine* has been turned into a feature for him to share with Davis. It gives him an opportunity to transform the simple melody in numerous complex variations, from his introduction unaided by the other rhythm players to his long, lyrical solo following Davis's. Evans receives some unnatural aid in taking the spotlight away from Davis on *My Funny Valentine* by the fact that Davis is under-recorded here, as he also is on *If I Were a Bell*. If the technical problems help Evans, however, they hinder Cobb; in making the technical adjustment to balance Davis, the engineers bring up Cobb's drums to the point where they are distracting. The best track, both technically and musically for the whole band, is *Straight No Chaser*, which, after an ensemble lapse where Adderley enters playing the lead before the other horns are ready, features long, facile solos by Davis, Coltrane, Adderley, and Evans, in that order. This title was probably the set closer at the Plaza even though it is placed at the beginning on the record, because it ends with a few bars of *The Theme* tagged onto it. But whatever the pleasures and the pressures of playing before the Columbia brass in an Edwardian setting that had never admitted jazz until then, for Davis they could only have been a momentary distraction from his real business at the time, which was taking place in Columbia's recording studios.

Porgy and Bess, the best-known American opera, was first produced in 1935, after nearly ten years of collaboration among George Gershwin, who wrote the music, DuBose Heyward, who wrote the libretto (based on his 1924 novel *Porgy*) and most of the lyrics, and Ira Gershwin, the lyricist for many of his brother's best-known songs, who helped Heyward with the lyrics. The thin plot revolves around a crippled black man who commits murder when he believes that he has lost his lover to another man, but most of the interest in the opera comes from its attempt at dramatizing the rich and colorful ghetto life of Catfish Row, a southern waterfront community. Gershwin's music self-consciously incorporates elements of black music – gospel, work songs, jazz – in a full-scale theatrical score. In 1958, *Porgy and Bess* was being produced as a motion picture directed by Otto Preminger and starring Robert McFerrin, Adele Addison, Sammy Davis Jr, and Pearl Bailey, and several record executives seized the occasion to commission jazz adaptations they could release amid the brouhaha that was certain to surround the release of the movie in 1959. *Porgy and Bess* offered a score that jazz players could potentially elucidate.

Jazz versions of Broadway musicals, movie and television themes, and the works of Tin Pan Alley songwriters had proven to be an unexpected boon to record companies in the wake of an enormously successful jazz version of some songs from the musical comedy *My Fair Lady* by the trio of André Previn, Leroy

Vinnegar, and Shelly Manne (*Shelly Manne and His Friends*, Contemporary C 3527), a best-seller on the pop charts for two years after its release in 1956. Jazz players – and pseudo-jazz players – had started cranking out versions of almost every imaginable score, from current Broadway hits such as *West Side Story* and *Li'l Abner*, to songbooks by Cole Porter and Harold Arlen, to the unpromising *Nutcracker Suite* and *Peter and the Wolf*, and even to school fight songs and national anthems.

Miles Davis and Gil Evans hardly needed the commercial boom to encourage Columbia's executives to finance their version of *Porgy and Bess* in high style because their collaboration on *Miles Ahead* left no doubts whatever about the commercial potential of further collaborations. Nevertheless, it must have done them no harm at all when they chose to work on Gershwin's score at such a commercially propitious moment. The details are as follows:

Miles Davis with Gil Evans and His Orchestra
Miles Davis, tpt, flugelhorn; Ernie Royal, Johnny Coles, Bernie Glow, Louis Mucci, tpt; Joe Bennett, Frank Rehak, Jimmy Cleveland, tbn; Dick Hixon, bass tbn; Willie Ruff, Julius Watkins, Gunther Schuller, frh; Bill Barber, tba; Julian Adderley, as; Phil Bodner (on 22 and 29 July), Jerome Richardson (on 4 and 14 August), Romeo Penque, flt; Danny Bank, bass clnt; Paul Chambers, b; Philly Joe Jones (on 22 July), Jimmy Cobb (on the other dates), dms; Gil Evans, arr, cond. New York, 22 July 1958
My Man's Gone Now; Gone Gone Gone; Gone
(all on Columbia CL 1274)

29 July 1958
Here Come de Honey Man; Bess You Is My Woman Now; It Ain't Necessarily So; Fisherman, Strawberry and Devil Crab
(all issued as above)

4 August 1958
Prayer (Oh Doctor Jesus); Bess Oh Where's My Bess; Buzzard Song
(all issued as above)

14 August 1958
Summertime; There's a Boat That's Leaving Soon for New York; I Loves You Porgy
(all issued as above)

Davis plays muted trumpet on *Here Come de Honey Man, Summertime*, and *I Loves You Porgy* and open flugelhorn on all other titles.

The extent to which Davis and Evans's *Porgy and Bess* is a recomposition of the original is truly remarkable; one can easily imagine the consternation of the Columbia executives when they realized – if they did – that moviegoers looking to this record for a recapitulation of the music they heard in the movie would discover, at most, a few scattered melodies and absolutely nothing else. Davis and Evans's work resembles the original opera no more than does Gershwin's own *Suite from Porgy and Bess* of 1936, perhaps even less.

The opera's most popular song – Gershwin always called it an aria – *I Got Plenty of Nuthin'*, is left out by Davis and Evans, as are several lesser numbers. A few are retained with their melodic lines more or less intact, especially *Summertime*, *It Ain't Necessarily So*, and *There's a Boat That's Leaving Soon for New York*, their melodies 'sung' by Davis quite faithfully over Evans's sonorous voicings. Others, notably *Bess You Is My Woman Now* and *My Man's Gone Now*, retain key phrases of the originals and build them into new songs. Still others are based on little more than the mood or the dramatic situation that Gershwin's music covered, as in the call-and-answer of *Prayer* and the dirge-like *Gone Gone Gone*.

Even more tangential in their relation to the original are *Fisherman, Strawberry, and Devil Crab*, apparently a free combination of elements suggested by Gershwin's *It Takes a Long Pull to Get There* and *Street Cries (Strawberry Woman, Crab Man)*, and *Here Come de Honey Man*, a march with a rapid crescendo and diminuendo suggesting a passing parade, perhaps inspired by the title of Gershwin's *They Pass by Singing*. One of the most effective pieces, *Buzzard Song*, which Davis later claimed sole credit for orchestrating, was not even used in the original production of *Porgy and Bess*. And the scintillating *Gone*, one of the most beautifully orchestrated drum features ever recorded and the showcase for which Philly Joe Jones was purposefully imported, has nothing at all to do with the music of George Gershwin but is Gil Evans's very own. Among the outpouring of jazz scores at the end of the 1950s and later, which were never more than jazzed-up versions of their Broadway or Hollywood originals, Davis and Evans's *Porgy and Bess* is a breed apart. It is a new score, with its own integrity, order, and action.

Davis's few comments on *Porgy and Bess*, all made during his interview with Nat Hentoff, which took place when the recording sessions for it were still very much on his mind, emphasize the recomposition from a different perspective by detailing the modal structure of Evans's score. Listening to the master tape that would later be released as *I Loves You Porgy*, Davis commented, "Hear that passage. We only used two chords for all of that. And in *Summertime* there is a long space where we don't change the chord at all. It just doesn't have to be cluttered up." Later on, he returned to the same theme. "When Gil wrote the arrangement of *I Loves You Porgy*, he only wrote a scale for me to play. No chords. And that other passage with two chords gives you a lot more freedom and space to hear things. I've been listening to Khachaturian carefully for six months now and the thing that intrigues me are all those different scales he uses. Bill Evans knows too what can be done with scales. All chords, after all, are relative to scales and certain chords make certain scales. I wrote a tune recently that's more a scale than a line. And I was going to write a ballad for Coltrane with just two chords." Davis's last comments almost certainly refer to his early efforts at composing the music he would record the following spring under the collective title *Kind of Blue*. For the time being, he was more interested in the state of the art. "Classical composers – some of them – have been writing this way for years, but jazz musicians seldom have," he said. "The music has gotten thick. Guys give me tunes and they're full of chords. I can't play them. You know, we play *My Funny Valentine* like with a scale all the way through."

Max Harrison, whose review of Gil Evans's music is probably the most comprehensive, stated flatly that "*Porgy and Bess* ... contains, at least in potential, the finest music Davis and Evans recorded together," singling out Davis's playing on *Prayer* and *My Man's Gone Now* as some of his most eloquent recorded work and Evans's orchestrations of *Fisherman, Strawberry and Devil Crab* and *Here Come de Honey Man* as "exquisite scoring." However, Harrison also expresses some reservations about the realization of Evans's charts for *Porgy and Bess*, stating that "the performances left even more to be desired than those of *Miles Ahead*."

Harrison's reservations apparently come not so much from his hearing of the recording as from the intelligence passed along to him by a member of Gil Evans's studio orchestra. In a personal letter to Harrison, this man, whom Harrison identifies only as "one of the musicians who played on the *Porgy and Bess* date," claims that Evans's charts were even more intricate and subtle than the recordings revealed, and that the members of the orchestra were prevented from realizing the full value of the charts because of the haste in which the sessions were conducted.

The musician's letter to Harrison is worth quoting at length not only because it documents his view but also because it offers an inside view of the recording sessions: "The crux of the matter is that Gil, on both sets of dates, did not rehearse carefully enough, as is evident already on *Miles Ahead*. I believe that this is mostly the result of the unfortunate conditions under which American recording is done. It is too costly for any project of more than average difficulty to be done well, unless the music in question is rehearsed before the date (which is illegal according to union rules), or has been previously performed. Under these, to say the least, less than ideal circumstances, both Miles and Gil have a too relaxed attitude about accomplishing the tasks they set themselves. In pieces which are scored as sensitively and as intricately as Gil's, it's a shame to let the performances cancel half of their effectiveness. Many details of scoring simply could not be – or at least were not – touched upon in the sessions I was on. Some things were left undone which I would not have let go. But, as I've indicated, the blame lies more with the conditions than the people. And I suppose one could say that it is remarkable that both LPs are as good as they are. If Gil were a better conductor it would also help: he sometimes confused the players. On the other hand, he is quite patient – perhaps too much so for his own good – and very pleasant to work for. Whatever excellence these recordings have I would attribute (apart from Gil's own magnificent scores, of course) primarily to the supreme abilities of some of the leading players, like Ernie Royal, Bill Barber, the very fine reed men (on all manner of flutes and bass clarinets), and in general the respect which all of us, in spite of what I've said above, have for Gil Evans."

This perspective on *Porgy and Bess* and also, incidentally, on *Miles Ahead* will stun legions of listeners, including many musicians, who have been struck by the subtlety and the intricacy of Evans's orchestrations in their received form. Whether Evans's charts can be executed with even more subtlety and intricacy will remain a moot contention until there are jazz repertory orchestras that perform scores such as Evans's *Porgy and Bess* publicly, rather than letting such flowerings of creative energy wither after a single performance in a studio.

If its performance is less than perfect, it nevertheless fuses sophisticated orchestrations and jazz substance so brilliantly that it is unmatched in the jazz canon. It found a large, appreciative audience as soon as it was released in 1959 and continues to find it today. Until 1971, when it was overtaken by *Bitches Brew*, an album of Davis's very different music of 1969, *Porgy and Bess* was his best-selling album.

After the summer's recording activities, the sextet returned to business as usual. Their tours to jazz clubs outside New York were eagerly anticipated and attended by capacity audiences. In Philadelphia, their usual venue was the Showboat, and Coltrane's hometown fans were enthusiastic supporters. Not the least enthusiastic were Earl and Carl Grubbs, cousins of his wife Naima and budding young saxophonists, who usually managed to get into the nightclub to hear him even though they were only sixteen and fourteen, respectively, in 1958. "Carl and I used to catch John at the Showboat here in Philadelphia, when he was playing with Miles," Earl remembers. "We were still teenagers, so we'd darken our mustaches to look older, and we'd get in most of the time. John would come over to our table and talk with us, and everybody else would wonder who we were and why he was talking with us. He used to do that a lot. He always took time to talk with us and show us things about his music and help us get our music down right."

Not all of Coltrane's visitors were so congenial. Jimmy Cobb remembers a near miss at the same club. "Coltrane and I were working at the Showboat in Philadelphia, and one night during intermission some guy came up to us and said, 'I'd like to see you both upstairs in the men's room.' I thought he was a faggot; I just said, 'So what?' Trane didn't say anything. Then the guy flashed a badge and said, 'Don't make a scene, I'm a narcotics officer.' We all went to the men's room, and he had us take off our shirts. He claimed some lady had told him we were on drugs. I showed him my arms and asked, 'Aren't they beautiful?' Then he looked at Coltrane's arms and said, 'What about those marks?' Trane looked sheepish and said, 'Those are birthmarks; I've had them as long as I can remember.' I almost cracked up, but Trane looked so boyishly innocent that the narcotics cop believed him, and he ended up letting both of us go."

A performance by the sextet at an unknown club sometime around the end of the summer has been preserved in private collections of tapes and shows what the jazz fans heard as part of a set on an ordinary working night. The three titles on tape are surprisingly familiar fare: *Walkin'* had been played by Davis's bands since 1954, and the two ballads, *All of You* and *Round Midnight*, were recorded at the same quintet session in 1956. To some extent, the perpetuation of the same old tunes was probably dictated by the fans, who, having bought the latest Miles Davis record, naturally expected to hear some of it played back to them, whether or not it had been recorded more than a year before and had been played for other fans in other cities scores of times. It was probably also a natural reaction for Davis and the others to perform material that was felt to be safe and comfortable. Most of the challenges for the sextet seemed to be left in the recording studio: in Gil Evans's scores, the 'new' ballads *Stella by Starlight* and *Green Dolphin Street*, the modal *Milestones*, and so on.

Each of the sidemen developed his own way of coping with the repetition of material. For Coltrane, of course, it was easy; he carried on with his restless search for new sonorities, leading him, for instance, to construct an impenetrable wall of eighth-notes on *Walkin'* that seemed to seal him off from the audience. For Adderley, besides studying Coltrane, there was the playful tinkering, as when he adds a new dissonance to the ensemble at the coda of *Walkin'* that gives it the sound of a train whistle. For Chambers, there was the challenge of humming along in unison with his bass solos, like some latter-day Major Holley or Slam Stewart, a gimmick first noticed in one of his solos at Newport and carried on in the clubs. For all of them, there was the challenge of playing *Round Midnight* with only the barest outline of Gil Evans's fatigued arrangement and all the notes altered a half-step here or an octave there. It was all in a night's work.

At least the rooms where they played changed – from night to night when they were playing concerts, and otherwise from week to week or from fortnight to fortnight. Sometimes they changed in a more irrevocable sense too, because jazz clubs have notoriously short existences and the sextet often went into a city after a year's absence to find that not only were they booked into a new club but that the available after-hours clubs were all new too. The clubs also changed when a competing club offered a better deal, a situation that very few other jazz bands ever experienced. A significant move had taken place in the spring of 1958, when Davis moved the sextet out of the Café Bohemia, where he had played regularly for over two and a half years, and into the Village Vanguard. The change took place just before Jimmy Cobb took over the drum chair, with the result that Cobb, who was with Davis for nearly five years, never played in the Bohemia. At the Vanguard, the sextet were usually paired with a soloist – often it was singer-pianist Blossom Dearie – or a small group.

No matter who shared the bill with them, the sextet's fans filled the room, a fact that was not easy to live with if one was in the other group. Jim Hall, the guitarist, remembers finding himself in that situation (although he may not remember Davis's drummer correctly): "I worked in a duo with Lee Konitz oppo-site Miles Davis at the Village Vanguard when he had Cannonball and Philly Joe Jones and Bill Evans, and the audience would listen to Miles as if they were in church, and then talk all the way through our set, which was about the way everything seemed to be going for me then."

By mid-1958, nearly everybody seemed to be listening attentively to Davis. David Amram, who paid Davis the compliment of adapting one of his phrases as a motif for his *Autobiography for Strings*, recalls an occasion when Dmitri Mitropolous inquired about Amram's activities and, upon finding out that Amram still worked at jazz sometimes, asked, "Who is the latest thing now, Dizzy Gilles-pie?" Amram told him no and named Sonny Rollins, John Coltrane, Bill Evans, and Miles Davis: "'Oh,' said Mitropolous, 'I've heard the music of Miles Davis, but I don't know much about the work of the other three. The only criticism I have of the jazz world is that every six months the heroes change.'"

Mitropolous chose his term well in including Davis among the "heroes." That was also the term being used by other people at the time. John Stevens, the English drummer, says, "A lot of things fall into place with Miles. Brilliant musi-cian, coupled with hipness, his image. That's why he's a culture hero. For his work and the way he's handled the system." He was certainly being looked on as something more than a trumpeter and jazz composer, and not only by the hipsters who had lionized Charlie Parker. Even *Life* magazine, the voice of the American bourgeoisie, knew about him; it named him along with a handful of black politi-cians, professionals, and businessmen as individuals who were advancing the prestige of black people in America at a time when the world was horrified by the news of racial violence in Little Rock, Arkansas. Miles Davis, the silent, sometimes sullen, recalcitrant, always uncompromising leader of the second generation of bebop revolutionaries, had become a bona fide celebrity.

The mystique surrounding him did not begin in 1958, and it did not peak then either. Its sources remain a mystery, but it was not cultivated by Davis; few stars in any performing art ever put less effort into their public relations. That too became part of the mystique, though it was nowhere near its essence. The mystique begins with a talent for making music that is at once self-communing and perfectly articulate, introverted yet highly accessible. George Goodman Jr sees the trumpet sound as the key to a more complex symbol: "To worshipful fans, from Hollywood to Antibes, the sound of Mr. Davis became the perfect signature for his personality, the style and substance of the new archetypal man of jazz. The trumpeter added a quality of elegance to Bird's image of raw authenticity, and it was embodied in the sound that fit him as perfectly as his finely tailored clothes." Those clothes, as almost everybody knows, would eventually win him recognition on the annual best-dressed lists, a piece of social frippery that he neither sought nor acknowledged. He exchanged his Mercedes for a Ferrari. The clothes and the cars were the conspicuous consumptions of a man who was almost invisible except when he was on the bandstand – occasionally glimpsed perhaps in a New York club, or thought to have been glimpsed there, and the whisper spread throughout the room. "All the money, cars, clothes, the bitches – all that was to match my ego," he told Don DeMicheal in 1969, in a *Rolling Stone* article. DeMicheal reported that Davis was no longer smoking, was driving a van, and was eating vegetables, which sounded more like the lifestyle of a *Rolling Stone* subscriber than of Miles Davis; the next time he was in the news he had smashed up his new Ferrari. The mystique kept on growing.

At the heart of Davis's lifestyle is financial security, which he grew up with in East St. Louis, surrendered for long enough in his early days of independence to learn how much he missed it, and regained with interest in the late 1950s. "When I first left home as a musician, I used to spend all I made, and when I went on dope, I got in debt," he said in his interview in *Playboy*. "But after I got enough sense to kick the habit, I started to make more than I needed to spend unless I was crazy or something." The greatest exponents of jazz were for several generations dealt rejection and borderline poverty, but Davis is a phenomenon. The mystique grew among his colleagues as well as his fans. "It came to the point where he made some money and invested it in blue chip stocks," Duke Jordan, his colleague in the Charlie Parker Quintet, says. "In other words, every time they turn the lights on in New Jersey, Miles is collecting some money. So that makes him independent, and once you're independent you can demand this and you can demand that." For Davis, more often than not, the demands are met.

Late in 1958, he was still living in an apartment on Tenth Avenue near 57th Street. The building housed other jazzmen as well, with John Lewis living on the same floor as Davis and Michael Zwerin on the floor below. The space was comfortable, and the decor was elegant. "The largest area in his apartment is the living room," Nat Hentoff wrote, describing the setting for his interview. "Like the other rooms, it is uncluttered. The furnishings have been carefully selected and are spare. Miles has a liking for 'good wood' and explains thereby why his *Down Beat* plaques – and even his Four Roses Award from the Randall's Island Festival – are all displayed. He has a good piano and an adequate nonstereo record player." Comfortable it may have been, but it was hardly the place to park a Ferrari, and he moved soon after into a large brownstone on West 77th Street near the Hudson River. The house is a converted Russian Orthodox church, with four storeys and a gymnasium in the basement. The decor, according to Sy Johnson, who went there to interview Davis in 1976, is based on "a circle-in-a-cube motif that is repeated throughout the house." Thus, the music room includes "a circular upholstered seat built around the wall, and a built-in piano overlooking the space." The liking for good wood is carried over into the new place, apparently, because Johnson adds, "Poll-winner plaques hung on the walls." One of Davis's favorite tales, which has now gone through a couple of variations, involves his answering the door when a repairman comes around and being mistaken for the butler.

The brownstone was not so much for him as for Frances Taylor, the Fran named in the title of his *Fran Dance*, whom he married at this time. A tall, elegant former dancer, Frances Taylor Davis was by all accounts even less interested in being in the public eye than her husband, although she let him talk her into posing for the cover photos on three of his albums in the 1960s. Her striking beauty and quiet dignity complemented Davis's image perfectly. As the decade drew to a close, everything that surrounded him seemed to complement his image perfectly. He could well afford to sit back a minute, look around, and say, "Now I got a pretty good portfolio of stock investments, and I got this house – it's worth into six figures, including everything in it ... Then I got my music, I got Frances, and I got my Ferrari." His only problems were the ones that go along with success, and they were beginning to mount up.

The most obvious problems came from within the sextet, where the success of the sidemen was making it feasible for them to strike out on their own. Julian Adderley had led his own band before joining, and Davis had sensibly let him take over some of the leader's duties with his sextet, thereby increasing his pay and expending some of his personal ambitions to the advantage of Davis's band. But by October he had reached the end of the term that he and Davis had informally agreed on when he joined. It took some doing by Davis and Harold Lovett, his manager, to keep Adderley in the band, but in the end they succeeded by appealing to Adderley's practical nature. Adderley explained: "I had planned when I joined him to stay with Miles about a year. But I stayed longer. Miles was getting more successful, and there was the business recession. I was functioning meanwhile as a kind of road manager – paying off the guys, collecting money." He stayed, somewhat uneasily and ever more restlessly, for another year.

Bill Evans presented a different case entirely. He had been earning excellent notices wherever the sextet played since he joined the band eight months before, but unlike Adderley he had been something of a nonentity when he joined, and neither he nor anyone else was certain that he was ready to make it on his own as a leader. He felt worn out by all the traveling and by the constant pressure of performing before crowds of Davis's fans. The other players, whose professional training had largely taken place on the road, seemed to have more stamina than he did. On more than a few occasions, too, he had heard rumblings from black fans and some black musicians about being a white man in a black band, and even though he knew that the rumblings did not mean anything – certainly not to Davis, who would have told him if they did – they still left him with a kind of hollow feeling. And then there was the heat he sometimes felt about his playing being too restrained on the faster pieces. Adderley said, "Although he loves Bill's work, Miles felt Bill didn't swing enough on things that weren't subdued." It was not something that Davis harped on – he seldom said anything about the music one way or the other – but it bothered Evans as much as if he did harp on it. After eight months, Evans said, "I felt exhausted in every way – physically, mentally and spiritually."

Evans decided to leave, regardless of what the future might hold, and he could not be dissuaded. His immediate plans were crystal clear; he intended to get some rest. He left the sextet in November and headed for his brother's house in Baton Rouge, where he rested and practiced away from the New York winter. After that, he returned to New York and went about the business of putting together his career as a leader. He would return to the Miles Davis Sextet one more time, for two days only, one in March and one in April, to participate in the recording sessions that would be the culmination of the great sextet. By that time, he was leading his own trio and by the end of 1959, when he settled on Scott LaFaro as his bassist and Paul Motian as his drummer, listeners everywhere started to take notice. James Lincoln Collier calls Evans "the piano player who has had the widest influence in jazz since 1960 or so."

In the two decades before Evans's sudden death in 1980, the relations between Evans and Davis were distant, as indeed they always had been, and perhaps a little cool. In 1969 *Rolling Stone* reported Davis as saying about Evans, "I liked the way he sounded. But he doesn't sound now like he did when he played with us.

He sounds white now." That was not a surprising sentiment from Davis at the time because he was making pronouncements on racial matters to the press fairly regularly, even though he had three white sidemen in his band. Between 1963 and 1971, Evans won three Grammy awards from the National Academy of Recording Arts and Sciences for the best jazz album of the year. At the 1971 awards ceremony Davis was also a nominee, and when Evans was announced as the winner, Davis and his table of guests left immediately. Asked by a television reporter if Davis's leaving should be taken as a slight, Evans just smiled and said that he knew Davis well enough to know that he had probably left because there was no longer any reason for him to stay.

Evans's comment showed an astute grasp of Davis's logic, but then, Evans had shown that grasp of his logic for years, in his music, which was always filled with the virtues that Davis extolled. His mature style blossomed during his months in Davis's sextet and came to full fruition almost immediately after he left it. Some of his critics complained that Evans had not only learned about music in Davis's band but had also learned his stage manners there. "Evans doesn't tell his listeners what he is playing, which is doubly rude: the composer is erased and the audience is made to feel unworthy of such information," Whitney Balliett complained, adding, "It's like a minister neglecting to reveal his chapter and verse." (Balliett's complaint about Evans refutes Davis's contention that the critics would not complain about his stage manner if he were a white man. Obviously they would.) For a student as apt as Bill Evans, even eight months was long enough to learn all manner of things in the Miles Davis Sextet.

For the sextet, Evans's departure coincided with a slowing down of Davis's modal experiments and finally, less than a year after he left, in their curtailment for several years. The main reason for that probably had nothing to do with Evans's quitting the band, as we shall see, but his resignation may have had a small effect on it. As Adderley said, comparing Evans to his successors, "His imagination is a little more vivid so that he tries more daring things." Davis's bands could not help but miss that quality as they went about putting in their night's work.

Davis immediately asked Red Garland to fill in until he could find the replacement he wanted for Evans, and Garland ended up staying for three months, until February, when he left to form his own trio. The sextet did not record in this period, but tapes of two engagements, one at the Spotlight Lounge in Washington, DC, and the other at an unidentified club, document the stylistic changes that followed. The tapes catch the sextet playing Sid's Ahead and Bye Bye Blackbird at the Spotlight, probably late in November, and yet another version of Bye Bye Blackbird (this one with Adderley sitting out) at the other club. Although Bye Bye Blackbird had been played countless times after Garland first left the band, none of Davis's pianists ever played it so well, or with such relish, as Garland did. Even the familiar tempo at which it was usually played, the standard Jamalesque groove, is accelerated considerably, as if in celebration of the return of a piano player who ponders less before he pounces. When the Miles Davis Sextet played in a concert package at Town Hall on the last Friday of November, in the company of bands led by Jimmy Giuffre, Gerry Mulligan, and Thelonious Monk, not only was Garland back but so also was Philly Joe Jones, and Davis celebrated their reunion in his band by letting them dust off *Billy Boy* as a trio feature.

The return of Garland solved Davis's major problem at the end of 1958, and Adderley's decision to carry on in the sextet for a while longer postponed that problem, but he still had to deal with Coltrane, who was even edgier than Adderley about striking out on his own. He was taking more than his share of criticism in reviews of the sextet's performances but he was aware that at least part of that criticism was because the reviewers and the fans turned out primarily to hear Davis and the popular Adderley. They had little inclination to try to understand what he was playing. However, everywhere they played there was a growing nucleus of listeners who were there specifically to hear him, and they sought him out between sets and sometimes even followed him from club to club. Even the unassuming Coltrane sometimes dared to think that there was an audience out there for a band of his own. His problem was in bringing himself to discuss making the break with Davis.

After more than three years together the early problems between them were long gone. Davis did not say much, of course, but Coltrane knew he was happy with the way he was playing. He let him play at length, and he no longer asked him to sit out on ballads; more often he asked Adderley, a very fine ballad player, to sit out instead. There were lots of little indications too. When Davis left the stand during the others' solos in clubs, he often sat with Naima Coltrane, who was there gently riding herd on her husband's activities between sets, and Davis had taken to ribbing Coltrane about his weight, which ballooned as his addiction to sweets was allowed free rein, but he was so concerned that he sold Coltrane some of his exercise equipment, including a punching bag, boxing gloves, and weight bars, with the promise that he would show him how to use it. Coltrane was naturally pleased to think that he met the approval of the man he had taken to calling "the teacher," but it certainly did not make matters easier for him now that he felt he should go out on his own.

When Coltrane got around to broaching the subject to Davis, Davis put him off by telling him that he was not yet ready for the problems of leading his own group. When he brought it up again and seemed adamant, Davis compromised by proposing that he stay with the sextet for the time being and begin a kind of apprenticeship for the business end of the job. Coltrane agreed, a little reluctantly at first, and Davis quickly made good on his end of the arrangement. In January, Harold Lovett took over Coltrane's financial affairs and immediately helped him negotiate a recording contract with Nesuhi Ertegun of Atlantic Records – he had been recording for Prestige as a leader for two and a half years – that would bring him a bonus of $7,000 annually. Lovett also set up a publishing company for Coltrane's music, called JOWCOL (for John William Coltrane). Davis then lined up Coltrane with Jack Whittemore, who would book Coltrane in the periods when the sextet were laying off. As a result, Coltrane was launched on what was really a double career.

Coltrane celebrated his independence promptly by recording for Atlantic on 15 January, with a quintet co-led by Milt Jackson. The session was fitted into his schedule hurriedly because he had to leave for Chicago soon after, where the sextet were booked into their usual venue, the Lounge at the Sutherland Hotel. In Chicago, Coltrane immediately recorded again, this time for Mercury in a quintet made up of the sidemen from Davis's band, nominally led by Adderley.

Coltrane's visit to Chicago was memorable in other ways. He was fitted for an eight-tooth upper front bridge when his teeth finally caved in under the constant assault of sweets. More important in the long run, one of his fans at the Sutherland introduced himself between sets one night as Pat Patrick, the baritone saxophonist in Sun Ra's experimental band. Coltrane was interested to hear of the changes that were moving a growing number of musicians in Chicago's jazz community, and Patrick arranged for him to meet Sun Ra. According to C.O. Simpkins, Coltrane confided to Sun Ra that he was deeply dissatisfied with his work in the sextet because it interfered with his own goals, and Sun Ra encouraged him to play further out with Davis and thus to stop trying to compartmentalize his development into the two separate aspects of his double career.

Coltrane's double career was not the strain it might have been because Davis, for the past year and a half, had grown more and more selective about the engagements he accepted. "I never work steady," he said in 1959. "I work enough to do what I want to do. I play music more for pleasure than for work." It was an artistically liberating regimen with more than a dash of good business sense. Since he was always in demand, he could refuse to play unless the price was right, and since he was not constantly in the public eye, he was in greater demand than ever. The regimen also helped the sidemen, who were well paid even playing less than a full schedule, because it gave them the chances they wanted to get out on their own. On one such occasion, both Adderley and Coltrane assembled bands to play in Birdland on a Monday night. The engagement became something of a watershed in Coltrane's progress and in the progress of the new free jazz that was suddenly finding adherents among many of the best young players arriving in New York. One of these was the tenor saxophonist Wayne Shorter from Newark.

Five years later, in 1964, Shorter would join Miles Davis's band and prove to be the catalyst for what would be Davis's best band since the sextet, but now, at twenty-six, he was relatively untried and he leapt at the chance to play in Birdland on Coltrane's one-night stand. "We had a rehearsal at his house, and that night we were playing," Shorter told Julie Coryell. "Opposite us was Cannonball with his brother Nat. Cannonball and Trane were working with Miles then, but they had time off and they split up and got different bands. Elvin Jones was on drums that night. It was historic; everybody realized it – we tore that place up. Ten years later, when I went to California, people were still talking about it – 'Yeah, we heard about it out here, that memorable Monday night at Birdland.' That's when Trane started playing all the new stuff he had written. It was a new wave."

There was indeed a new wave being felt in jazz in 1959. Coltrane was destined to be its patriarch, and the nucleus of his fans at all the performances of the Miles Davis Sextet comprised the leading edge of its audience. Coltrane's memorable nights away from the sextet only made him more uneasy about his role as a sideman.

Davis, as usual, was keenly aware of what was happening in jazz. In the first months of 1959 he spent many nights in the audience at jazz clubs, apparently keeping an eye out for the piano player who could replace Garland in his band. One of the young musicians he encountered was a young trumpeter named Freddie Hubbard, recently arrived in New York. Hubbard, who was working at Birdland, recalled the scene for Leonard Feather: "I was working there with Philly Joe, and I had my eyes closed, as I often do during a solo. I opened my eyes and there was Miles, and it scared me to death. I had tried for months to summon up the courage to speak to him, and he never said a word to me. So everyone asked him how he liked the way I played, and over the next couple of years he said things about me that were pretty cool, even though I didn't really have it together then."

Another young musician who caught Davis's eye was Josef Zawinul, a piano player from Austria who emigrated to the United States in January 1959, quit the Berklee School of Music almost before he started, and began working professionally, first in Maynard Ferguson's band and then as Dinah Washington's accompanist. Although it seems improbable, since Zawinul had arrived in the country only six or seven weeks earlier, Davis may have invited him to join the sextet as Garland's replacement. Zawinul told Conrad Silvert in 1978 that Davis had offered him an opportunity to record with him in 1959, but he declined because he felt that he was not ready. Nine years later, after a long stint as the piano player in Julian Adderley's quintet, Zawinul would record some remarkable music with Davis.

Davis finally chose as the sextet's new piano player Wynton Kelly, who joined the band in February. For Kelly, joining Davis was a break that was long overdue, not so much because he was old – he was twenty-eight – but because he had been playing professionally for a long time. He started working as a musician when he was twelve, and he was a veteran of all kinds of bar bands when he attracted attention in Dizzy Gillespie's short-lived big band of 1957. Born in Jamaica and raised in Brooklyn, Kelly is the first cousin of another Brooklyn pianist, Randy Weston, who is five years older. "He was already a fantastic pianist at the age of fifteen," Weston recalls. "He was a young genius."

Julian Adderley believed that Kelly's arrival in the sextet was a real advance because he combined the strengths of Red Garland and Bill Evans. "When Bill left, Miles hired Red again and got used to swinging so much that he later found Wynton Kelly, who does both the subdued things and the swingers very well," Adderley said, and he added: "Wynton is also the world's greatest accompanist for a soloist ... Wynton plays with the soloist all the time, with the chords you choose. He even anticipates your direction. Most accompanists try to lead you." Another of Kelly's early boosters was Bill Evans, who said, "When I first heard him in Dizzy's big band, his whole thing was so joyful and exuberant; nothing about it seemed calculated. And yet, with the clarity of the way he played, you know he had to put this together in a very carefully planned way – but the result was completely without calculation, there was just pure spirit shining through the conception." For many horn players, Kelly's ability as an accompanist made him their first choice for pickup groups in recording sessions. His tenure with Davis's bands would last more than four years.

The main activity of the sextet immediately after Kelly joined it involved him only peripherally and Bill Evans centrally. The occasion was the recording of five modal compositions eventually released together under the title *Kind of Blue*. They were recorded in two sessions, the first on 2 March and the second on 22 April, with a television appearance by Miles Davis and the Gil Evans Orchestra – the first public performance ever of the *Miles Ahead* material – interposed between them. Of the five compositions recorded in the *Kind of Blue* sessions, Wynton Kelly plays only on the first, *Freddie Freeloader*, and Bill Evans plays on all the others. *Kind of Blue* constitutes the culmination of the achievements of the great sextet of 1958–9, a stunning condensation of its strengths. Davis probably intended it to be a beginning, a new direction that would challenge his musicians and perhaps slake their urges to move on. *Kind of Blue* did provide a beginning, but only for other musicians, among them John Coltrane. For Davis, *Kind of Blue* seemed, under the circumstances, to be another major recording project, like the orchestration of *Porgy and Bess*, that was not followed up outside the studio. Five years would pass before he would try seriously to extend the direction in which it pointed, and by then almost all the circumstances were different. And so it became a culmination instead.

The project had been fomenting for some time. Davis's impetus is clear in all his talk of scales and chords, Khachaturian, musical space and clutter, which for more than a year had been his main musical preoccupation. The summer before, he told Nat Hentoff that he had written "a tune recently that's more a scale than a line"; he might have been describing the preliminary draft for any one of the compositions on *Kind of Blue*. Bill Evans, who had not been in close contact with Davis for four months and was away in Louisiana for part of that time, was also involved in the planning. Although Davis is listed as the sole composer of all five pieces, J.C. Thomas claims that Evans composed *Blue in Green* and *Flamenco Sketches*, and Thomas says that Evans once claimed credit for arranging all five. These claims were never amplified or corroborated, and Davis remains the credited composer, although clearly Evans was not invited to participate in the *Kind of Blue* sessions just for old time's sake. He was deeply, if unofficially, involved in them.

The details for the first of the two recording sessions are as follows:

Miles Davis Sextet
Miles Davis, tpt; Julian Adderley, as (except on *Blue in Green*); John Coltrane, ts; Wynton Kelly, pno (on *Freddie Freeloader*), Bill Evans, pno (on *So What* and *Blue in Green*); Paul Chambers, b; Jimmy Cobb, dms. New York, 2 March 1959
Freddie Freeloader; *So What*; *Blue in Green*
(all on Columbia 1355)

The music is best discussed along with its companion session on 22 April. Apart from the musical innovations taking place in the Columbia studio at this session, a homelier innovation appeared in the form of a new face in the control booth. It was Teo Macero, the tenor saxophonist and third stream composer, newly appointed at Columbia as a record producer. Before Macero's promotion, all of Davis's Columbia recordings were produced by George Avakian, although the producer was never listed as such on the albums. Afterward, almost all of Davis's massive output for Columbia would be produced by Macero (and after Macero's first two albums, producer credit would never again be omitted). Macero spent part of his apprenticeship at Columbia working on the post-recording production of the *Porgy and Bess* album, but with the *Kind of Blue* sessions he assumed full charge of production – whatever that may mean when Davis is the artist being recorded.

Macero did not entirely surrender his aspirations as a composer or as a player to become a producer, although his activities as a player at least were sharply curtailed. Macero points out that his active career as a musician was important in working effectively with Davis. "You can go along with an artist like Miles, and encourage him – these are new directions, these are new changes, this is something new that hasn't happened before," he told Gregg Hall. "You can be as current as he is because you've been going through the changes in a different way. I'm going through them as a composer, Miles as a composer-musician-performer." Macero's work with Davis has certainly been productive, which may speak volumes for having a Juilliard graduate with good professional credentials as a record producer, a position too often filled in the jazz field by a businessman who also happens to be a jazz fan. Macero certainly agrees, and probably Davis would too. Macero says, "He knows I have a great pair of ears and I'm looking out for his interests and he's looking out for mine, and it's nice. It's comfortable but, at the same time, it's very exciting because it's very creative." It has not always been smooth, but Macero's career got off to an auspicious start with *Kind of Blue*.

One month later, Miles Davis and Gil Evans performed the public debut of three titles from the *Miles Ahead* album of 1957, on the Robert Herridge Theater Show, a local New York television program on the arts. On the same program, Davis led a quintet in a performance of *So What* from the *Kind of Blue* session. The details are as follows:

Miles Davis Quintet
Miles Davis, tpt; John Coltrane, ts; Wynton Kelly, pno; Paul Chambers, b; Jimmy Cobb, dms. Robert Herridge Theater Show, New York, 2 April 1959
So What (issued [1975] on Beppo BEP 502)

Miles Davis with Gil Evans and His Orchestra
Miles Davis, tpt, flugelhorn; Ernie Royal, Clyde Reasinger, Louis Mucci, Johnny Coles, Emmett Berry, tpt; Frank Rehak, Jimmy Cleveland, Bill Elton, Rod Levitt, tbn; Julius Watkins, Bob Northern, frh; Bill Barber, tba; Romeo Penque, Eddie Caine, woodwinds, Danny Bank, bass clnt; John Coltrane, as; Paul Chambers, b; Jimmy Cobb, dms; unknown harp; Gil Evans, arr, cond
The Duke; Blues for Pablo; New Rhumba
(all issued as above)

When the film of the orchestral portion of this telecast was shown at the 1979 Newport Jazz Festival among other historically interesting clips of jazz performances, Whitney Balliett referred to it in his review as "a long, apathetic sequence showing Miles Davis playing *The Duke*, *Blues for Pablo*, and *New Rhumba* with Gil Evans's band." He was presumably criticizing the cinematography rather than the music, for the music itself is hardly apathetic. These arrangements are given a much more robust reading than they received on the rather muted, delicate versions of the definitive recordings of 1957. One can more readily separate the individual voicings that make up Evans's palette, with Bill Barber's tuba lines uncommonly clear, perhaps partly because of miking differences between the two productions. The difference in the performance of the arrangements reveals in Evans's music overtones of a more traditional big-band sound and again raises the issue of the awful waste when music of this caliber is stashed away in a bottom drawer instead of being reinterpreted in public performances.

The quintet's performance on the same show is notable as one of the rare occasions when a composition entered Davis's working repertoire immediately, *So What* having been played for the first time in the recording studio just a month earlier. The fact that Paul Chambers leaves out a phrase of his opening theme is the only obvious flaw created by its novelty. Coltrane plays magnificently. His tenor line – he played alto in the orchestra, something he had not done in public since his days with Gillespie in 1949–51 – suddenly sounds like the Coltrane of a few years hence, when he was at the height of his powers in the early 1960s. Near the beginning of his solo he improvises a sequence that he later developed into the melodic line for *Impressions*, one of his landmark compositions after leaving Davis's employ. The direct line from the *Kind of Blue* sessions to Coltrane's new music is thus neatly encapsulated.

Less than three weeks later, the sextet including Bill Evans reconvened to complete the recording of *Kind of Blue*. The details are as follows:

Miles Davis Sextet
Miles Davis, tpt; Julian Adderley, as; John Coltrane, ts; Bill Evans, pno; Paul Chambers, b; Jimmy Cobb, dms. New York, 22 April 1959
Flamenco Sketches; All Blues
(both on Columbia CL 1355)

Of all the *Kind of Blue* compositions, probably *Blue in Green* and *Flamenco Sketches* are the most difficult to appreciate on only a few hearings, and for similar reasons. The other compositions are sharply defined and immediately distinctive, but both *Blue in Green* and *Flamenco Sketches* are insinuating and calm; their themes are ripples whereas the others are waves. Their differentness, however, disappears after a few careful hearings, and they too fill their own distinctive space.

Blue in Green has what Evans, in his notes for the album, calls "a 10-measure circular form," without further explanation. The circularity is apparent, though only after listening with the kind of concentration needed to solve a conundrum, in the movement of the piece as a whole: it opens with Davis's muted trumpet exploring a theme, continues with Evans exploring a second theme, and then introduces Coltrane playing yet a third theme, but after that Evans returns with his earlier theme and Davis then closes as he opened. Each of the three players thus has his own scale to play, and only when the overall structure is understood do the three parts connect.

Flamenco Sketches is less puzzling (although for many years Columbia issued the LP with *Flamenco Sketches* identified as *All Blues* and vice versa, which made it much *more* puzzling). It is a slow blues constructed over a latinate beat that seems to be implied rather than stated. One reviewer, Ronald Atkins, notes that "few recordings exude so hushed an air of solemnity – a feeling arising as much from the absolute perfection of the solos as from the slow tempo."

The other three compositions draw the listener's attention more insistently. *Freddie Freeloader*, a more traditional blues than *Flamenco Sketches*, played in 4/4 time, gives Wynton Kelly a star turn for his only appearance. He fills in the spaces between the simple, singing lines played in unison by all three horns and takes the lead solo as well, in which he gets away with more than a few old-fashioned clichés amid the new sounds. While it is unjust to single out individual solos on an album loaded with excellent ones, Julian Adderley's marvelous blues on *Freddie Freeloader* stands out even in superior company.

The remaining two compositions, *All Blues* and *So What*, are purely and simply masterpieces. Max Harrison calls *All Blues* "a good example of primitive jazz serialism," which he explains this way: "Here, instead of a chord sequence, the improvisations are based on a series of five scales, that is, five selections of notes from the twelve available. Davis constructed fragmentary tone-rows which replace harmony in giving the music coherence." The ensemble structure builds up layers of sound, starting with a repeated trill by Evans, stepping up to sing-song cadence by the saxophones, and topping off with Davis's muted statement of the melody, all built on 6/8 rhythm. The solos that follow are of unequal duration, apparently dictated by each soloist's progress from scale to scale.

The most complicated work formally, *So What*, has also had the greatest currency among other jazz players, no doubt partly because Davis's band began playing it regularly from the very start, but also because of its infectious construction, in which Paul Chambers's ostinato, the unifying line throughout, is answered first by the piano and then by the horns. Martin Williams observes that *So What*, "in a sense restricted as well as free in its outline, asks the improviser to make his melody from one assigned Dorian mode for sixteen measures, then a half-step up for eight measures, then back to the first mode for the final eight measures." Jerry Coker, illustrating the point that Davis "didn't merely change *with* the times (with regard to style) but was largely – if not completely – *responsible* for most of the changes," explicates Davis's particular use of the Dorian scale, the mode that was the subject of George Russell's dissertation, observing that *So What* "introduced a voicing for the Dorian mode that is now often referred to as the *So What* voicing. Actually it is one voicing used in two different places in the mode, so that the keyboard player has two vertical chord sounds for each mode occurrence, with each using only available tones from the Dorian scale."

Coker's explanation is intended for musicians, but whatever else a general audience might take from it, it at least shows clearly a significant role that *So What* filled – and is still filling – in disseminating the use of modal structures among jazzmen. For the young players coming up in the years right after the recording of *So What*, formal instruction in the use of modes in jazz was simply unavailable. Young players struggling with *So What* eventually grasped its formal basis intuitively, and for the more thoughtful among them that was enough to start them working at extending it. Coker mentions McCoy Tyner, Herbie Hancock, Chick Corea, and Keith Jarrett among the prominent young piano players who make heavy use of its voicing in their own work. *So What*, and to some extent all the compositions on the *Kind of Blue* recording, provided informal lessons for jazz players emerging in the 1960s, but it did so only because of the masterful performance that introduced it to the public. It was a tune that young players felt they had to learn to play.

In any discussion of *Kind of Blue*, there is a temptation to belabor its formal aspects. While ignoring them is impossible, stressing them misrepresents the music and the intentions of the men who made it. Davis's major contribution to jazz form, of which *Kind of Blue* stands as the most influential example, involves a principled shift from the constraints of chordal organization to the different constraints of scalar organization. Instead of constructing melodies by selecting a few notes from each consecutive chord, Davis's music forced him and the other players to create melodies from a single scale for long stretches. In *So What*, only two scales are available in each cycle of thirty-two bars, forcing the improviser to find novel combinations by selecting notes from two sustained chords.

As a working musician, Davis showed no interest in the theoretical niceties of his innovation except as a means of relieving his music of the predictable chord progressions, creating an aural effect of lightness, and challenging his melodic ingenuity. Because his goals were functional rather than purely academic, he succeeded in bringing modal constructions fully into jazz where George Russell and others had not really succeeded despite years of diligent study. Davis's modal innovations have escaped entirely any allegations of obscurantism, formalism, ivory-towerism, and the like. On the contrary, the best of his modal compositions – *Milestones*, all of *Kind of Blue*, and some of Evans's recompositions on *Miles Ahead* and *Porgy and Bess* – met with an enthusiastic popular and critical response. His achievement was not merely in altering the formal basis of the music but in doing it in the service of some of the most affecting small-band and orchestral jazz ever played.

One of the most astute comments ever made about the *Kind of Blue* sessions came from Bill Evans. "We just really went in that day and did our thing," he told Lee Jeske twenty years later. In Evans's liner notes for the album, he says: "Miles conceived these settings only hours before the recording dates and arrived with sketches which indicated to the group what was to be played. Therefore, you will hear something close to pure spontaneity in these performances. The group had never played these pieces prior to the recordings and I think without exception the first complete performance of each was a 'take.'" That statement flatly contradicts J.C. Thomas's claim about Evans's role as a co-composer and jibes perfectly with everything we know about Davis's disdain for rehearsals and multiple takes. Valuing immediacy and spontaneity above polish and precision, Davis maintains that if a jazz musician were forced to respond to a situation he might otherwise have thought to be beyond his capacities, he might very well come up with an unexpected and stunning solution, perhaps even a moment of genius. "If you place a guy in a spot where he has to do something else, other than what he can do, ... he can do *that*," he told Leonard Feather. "He's got to have something that challenges his imagination, far above what he thinks he's going to play, and what it might lead into, and then above *that*, so he won't be fighting when things change."

Davis's belief in challenges lies behind his claim that "real" jazz records will have the "mistakes" left in them and also accounts for his disdain for rehearsing during the sextet years. Julian Adderley recalled, "As for rehearsals, we had maybe five in the two years I was there, two of them when I first joined the band. And the rehearsals were quite direct, like, 'Coltrane, show Cannonball how you do this. All right now, let's do it.' Occasionally, Miles would tell us something on the stand. 'Cannonball, you don't have to play *all* those notes. Just stay close to the sound of the melody. Those substitute chords sound funny.'" Adderley's five rehearsals in two years were a bonus that Bill Evans did not get during his eight months in the band. "We never had a rehearsal," he said. "Everything was done on the job. On the record dates, half or all of the material might be all new and had never been rehearsed before." Needless to say, that kind of regimen could work only with a cast of superior musicians. With the players in the sextet, especially on *Kind of Blue*, it worked magnificently.

The approach included potential pitfalls. If the group of musicians happened to be much larger than, say, six or seven, the lack of rehearsal time could be telling. It was also likely to pose problems for musicians who did not regularly work together or know one another's responses very well. Those problems cropped up two weeks after the second *Kind of Blue* session, on 4 and 5 May, when John Coltrane arrived at the Atlantic recording studios to make his second album under his new contract. The music he recorded was eventually released as *Giant Steps* (Atlantic 1311), and it is probably the first truly indispensable recording by Coltrane as a leader, so the method he used was hardly a complete failure. However, he arrived in the studio with a sheaf of completely fresh and unknown sketches for his compositions *Countdown* (based on Davis's *Tune up*), *Cousin Mary*, *Syeeda's Flute Song*, *Spiral*, and *Giant Steps*, all recorded in the two days, and several other pieces as well. He presented them, as Davis had done with him so many times before, to Tommy Flanagan, Paul Chambers, and Arthur Taylor.

As good as these musicians were, they found it impossible to handle all the material on such short notice. "As he explained to me, in this date he wanted to get a lot of things out of his system," Tommy Flanagan told Michael Ullmann. "He did a lot of songs with the same kind of chord progression as in *Giant Steps*. Some things didn't even appear on the record – we just couldn't play them. The tempos were too fast and we didn't have enough time to get it all down in one session." Then Flanagan reflected on the whole Davis-based process: "Why they like to do a whole album in one session I don't know. It almost kills you, to stay with that kind of playing – so intense – for eight hours a day. It takes a toll on you, unless you really know what you are doing. Trane knew what *he* was doing." Coltrane was also learning that there were other, perhaps better, ways of doing things than the ways that seemed to work so well for Miles Davis.

In the spring of 1959, Birdland revitalized its jazz policy after a period of wavering loyalties, and the Miles Davis Sextet moved in. Their engagement there is documented by a taped broadcast of *Bags' Groove*, which has not yet been released as a recording. (This performance has circulated among private collectors for many years mistakenly identified as *Walkin'*.) Its reappearance in Davis's repertoire for the first time since its extraordinary performance in the Christmas eve session of 1954 is almost certainly calculated to show off the strengths of Wynton Kelly. Although it is given an enthusiastic playing, it does not allow the sextet to show any of the subtlety of their recent recordings. It seems a little time-worn because it had been widely recorded after Davis's seminal recording of it, and it was also part of the Modern Jazz Quartet's working repertoire. Davis might better have started performing *Freddie Freeloader*, also within Kelly's métier, but unfortunately he never performed it beyond the studio walls.

Around the same time that Birdland reopened for jazz, an even more historic revival was attempted. The Apollo Theater in Harlem, for decades the most famous nightclub in uptown New York, was refurbished and reopened by some young black businessmen, in an attempt to revive its former glory. The revival did not work, but during the short lived reopening the Miles Davis Sextet were one of its headline attractions, in a jazz slate that also included Thelonious Monk, James Moody, Eddie Jefferson, Betty Carter, and comedienne Moms Mabley. The Apollo performances, as C.O. Simpkins recalls them, featured John Coltrane playing in a kind of extraterrestrial frenzy. On one occasion, Simpkins says, he "got down on his knees, throwing off the fire of his improvisation," and on another, he "closed his eyes and continued over the twenty minute time limit the Apollo set for each group." In Simpkins's description, everyone backstage except Miles Davis seems to have ended up in a comparable frenzy: "The lights were blinking. Curtains were going back and forth. The stage manager shouted to Miles, 'Go get him, man! Go get him! We runnin' over the show! Stop him!' but John kept on playing."

The sextet spent the first three weeks of June in San Francisco at the Black-hawk, receiving an enthusiastic review from Russ Wilson in the *Oakland Tribune*. Wilson singled out their performances of *Autumn Leaves*, *Two Bass Hit*, and *Billy Boy*, as well as "several new originals by Davis," among them "a still-untitled blues that starts and ends in 3/4 time" and "another that employs an Afro-Cuban beat," probably *All Blues* and *So What*, respectively. Wilson also broke the news of Coltrane's desire to move out on his own. "There's nothing definite yet," Coltrane told Wilson, "but I have been seriously thinking of it." Wilson went on to say, "Coltrane has informed Miles of this, and should the parting come, it will be amicable. Davis understands Coltrane's viewpoint and will not stand in his way." The article mentions that Coltrane's most likely successor in the band was Jimmy Heath. (Heath did become Coltrane's immediate successor, but only for two months and not until another year had passed.) Of Coltrane, Wilson notes, "In the last year or so he has come to be regarded as one of the most exciting and influential tenor saxophonists in jazz, a factor that figures in his thinking."

Not the least of Coltrane's successes during this year was an adulatory article entitled "The style of John Coltrane," by Zita Carno, in the October issue of the *Jazz Review*. "Coltrane seems to have the power to pull listeners right out of their chairs," Carno said. "I have noticed this terrific impact on the various rhythm sections he has played with; he pulls them right along and makes them cook, too." Carno's illustration drew on the sextet. "Say Miles Davis is the first soloist," she says. "Notice the rhythm section doesn't push. They are relaxed behind him. Now Coltrane takes over, and immediately something happens to the group: the rhythm section tightens up and plays harder. The bass becomes stronger and more forceful, as does the ride cymbal beat; even the piano comps differently. They can't help it – Coltrane is driving them ahead." What Carno had noticed was the stylistic contrast between Davis and Coltrane that Davis had built into the group sound almost from the beginning of Coltrane's tenure.

For all his restlessness, Coltrane remained with Davis long after their tour of the West Coast ended. He stayed mainly because he lacked confidence in his own drawing power as a leader and because he enjoyed the financial security of working for Davis. *Down Beat* reported that the sextet were paid $2,500 a week for their engagement at the Seville at the end of this tour.

Summer arrived and the sextet, barely back from their spring tour, set off on a round of festival appearances. One of these, in early August, took them to Chicago for the first Playboy Jazz Festival, sponsored by the phenomenally successful business conglomerate that started out as a magazine featuring naked women and trendy fiction, and expanded into nightclubs, health spas, television and film production, and much else. The jazz festival at Chicago Stadium was its latest venture. Coltrane chose to stay behind in New York, working at his own commitments, but if his decision upset Davis and the others it certainly did not show in the makeshift quintet's performance of *So What* that was broadcast from the festival. It is taken at a quicker pace than usual, a familiar change in Davis's live performances of his standard repertoire, but there is no impression of his carelessness in the quickening of the tempo, as there so often is in his other live performances, such as the Newport festival performance. Davis himself plays a long, ebullient, driving solo, and he is followed by a beautifully swinging statement by Adderley. Although the overrecorded drums threaten to drown out Wynton Kelly's solo, enough of it is recoverable to hear in it a sparkling, basic romp, and when the horns riff behind him in the last choruses he rises above them and earns a burst of spontaneous applause. The large, enthusiastic crowd may well be the key to what turns out to be a great live performance by the band, perhaps the best unissued performance from this period.

Near the end of August the band settled into Birdland. They were happy to be back in New York, but the long stint on the road in the spring and the summer traveling had taken their toll. Coltrane was back in the band, but he continued to complain about being there. Wayne Shorter, who was playing with Maynard Ferguson's big band opposite the sextet, listened every night to Coltrane's talk about starting his own band. At one point Coltrane told him, "You want to be with Miles? You got it. I'm finished doing the Miles gig." Davis seemed to be grumbling much of the time too, although that was probably less surprising. One night he left the stand while the rhythm trio were playing their feature and sat down at the musicians' table with Michael Zwerin. "Miles seemed annoyed," Zwerin says. "He said, 'What the hell is Paul doing with the time?' The time seemed pretty good to me, but I didn't comment." Things were not going very smoothly for Davis at the moment. And then the roof caved in.

On the night of 26 August, a Tuesday, the kind of muggy day you get in New York before the summer starts making its long transition into fall, Davis came up out of the basement jazz club with a woman at his side. She was young, and she was white. He walked with her to the curb where a taxi was waiting and watched her ride off in it. He glanced at his watch, and then he dug a cigarette out of his shirt pocket, but as soon as he got it lit the policeman who patrolled that part of Broadway strolled up and stopped in front of him.

"No loitering," he said. "Move along."

"I work here," Davis said with a glance. The cop was by Birdland every night. He knew who Davis was and what he was doing there.

The policeman told him move along again. He seemed to be dead serious.

Davis got serious too. "I'm not going nowhere – I'm just getting a breath of fresh air."

"Move!" he shouted.

"I'm trying to dry off, get some air. It's smokey down there ..."

The policeman said he would arrest him if he did not get moving right away, and Davis said, "Go ahead, lock me up." Broadway was crowded and several people gathered around them now, gawking.

The policeman stepped closer and said, "Are you goin' peaceful, or am I gonna put handcuffs on you?" He reached for Davis's wrist and Davis pulled it away; he reached for it again and Davis pushed his arm away. The cop moved in fast and grabbed his shoulders and somebody else came toward him out of the crowd, and after that everything was just a blur.

He was in a police station and blood was dripping onto his shirt, the way it does when you get a cut on the scalp. The policeman was holding him by the arm and the other man, the one who had hit him with the nightstick, was there too. He was a plainclothes policeman.

They had asked him who he wanted them to phone, and he gave them his home number, but now that things were coming clearer he knew he should have got Lovett and left Frances out of it, but the blood was oozing down his face onto his shirt and by the time they finished booking him on charges of disorderly conduct and assault, Frances Davis was there. She took one look at him and was nearly hysterical.

At the hospital with the police still standing around and his wife fretful beside him, a doctor put in ten stitches to close the gash in his head. Some reporters arrived and a press photographer came in after them. And then he was taken back to the station and kept there overnight. His arrest made the front pages of the New York papers the next day.

When Harold Lovett arrived in the morning to post bail he was livid. Miles Davis said little but he was livid too, now that the blur was clearing away. When a reporter asked him if it was true that the policeman dropped his nightstick and

Miles Davis Sextet listening to a playback in the studio; from left, Red Garland, Davis, Paul Chambers, and Julian Adderley (Columbia Records, courtesy of *Down Beat*)

Miles Davis recording *Porgy and Bess* (Don Hunstein, Columbia Records, courtesy of *Down Beat*)

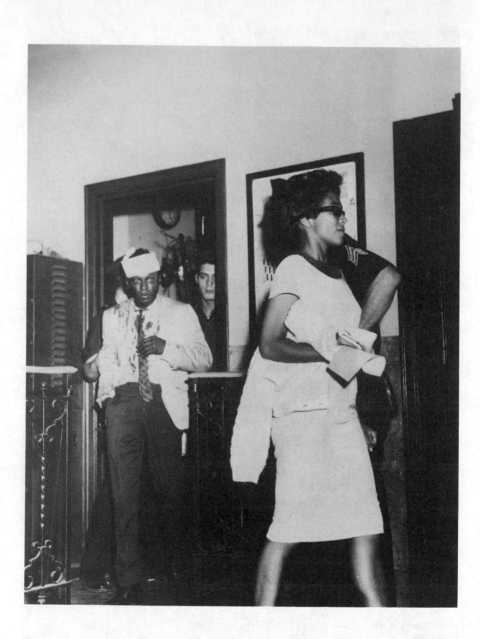

Miles Davis entering the police station after the Birdland incident (*New York Journal-American*, courtesy of *Down Beat*)

Davis had picked it up, he just pointed to the bandage on his head and said, "If I picked it up I wouldn't look like this."

That day a spokesman for the police department announced that Davis's cabaret card was revoked and until it was reinstated he was barred from working in New York clubs. Harold Lovett announced that Davis was suing the city for half a million dollars for illegal arrest. Those announcements made most of the front pages too. From then on, everything was in the hands of the courts and it looked as if it might take forever to get the whole thing settled. The newspaper accounts receded into the middle pages when they saw print at all.

In the cool world where Miles Davis was the undisputed champion, life went on pretty much as it always had. There were lots of whispers, naturally, and people who loved Davis's image more than his music saw the whole affair as another awesome act by their hero, taking on the whole NYPD, a real mystique-builder. Davis's closest associates, the men in his band, reacted the way jazzmen of their generation were expected to react. They went in and started the next set at Birdland without him, and they played their hearts out until closing time. Al Young, a novelist who went to Birdland that night to hear John Coltrane, came away thinking that Davis's absence had been a bonus for him. "Sure enough, there was Coltrane sounding totally different from the way he did on the latest recordings I'd gathered," he wrote. "It was the very night Miles Davis stepped outside between sets and got in an altercation with some cops about loitering. He had to be hospitalized. The band, winding up the evening without its leader, continued to smoke and burn until the very air crackled with flames scorching enough to warm the heart of even a plainclothes policeman. It was truly a Coltrane night."

In the larger world, the whole thing was forgotten almost as soon as the newspapers that reported it were thrown out. There were no editorials in the big dailies expounding on the right of a citizen to take a smoke break outside the place where he was working on a hot night, no law associations petitioning the revoking of a cabaret card because of a criminal charge that had not yet even come to court, no demonstrators marching to protest police brutality, and no riots in Harlem proclaiming the civil liberties of a distinguished member of the black minority. If the incident had happened five years later there might have been some response along those lines, and ten years later there might have been a whole program of responses along those lines, but this was 1959.

Davis's bitterness was undisguised. He stated immediately that the whole incident happened because the young woman he was escorting to the taxi was white.

The legal proceedings did nothing at all to assuage his bitterness either. His suit against the city had a reasonable legal basis but Davis was caught in a double bind with both the criminal charges hanging over his head and the police-controlled cabaret card revoked. (The constitutionality of the police issuing cabaret cards was strongly challenged at police commission hearings starting in late 1960 by a committee of entertainers and artists; as the committee piled up evidence of alleged irregularities in the issuing and withholding of the cards, police enforcement of card-holding slackened off and the city council finally abolished them altogether several years later.) In the end, Davis was enjoined by his lawyers to drop his suit altogether, evidently to fulfill his end of a plea bargain. On 24 October, almost two months after he had been hit on the head, a panel of three judges ruled that his arrest had been illegal and dismissed the charges against him.

The legal hassles ended around the time the gash on his head was fully healed, but the court's decision has not really had the same healing effect. Not surprisingly, he remains bitter. Also perhaps not surprisingly, he feels that he was attacked because he is a black man and that he was denied justice because he is a black man. Mary Lou Williams, the piano player who in her later years had a propensity for moralizing and spiritualizing, talked to Roland Baggenaes about the people she remembered from her days on 52nd Street, and when she came to Miles Davis she could not resist bringing his spiritual history up to date in her own peculiar terms. "Miles was terrific then," she said. "Miles was not like he is now. When I saw him in England he would try to be nice and everything, but, you know, something very bad happened to him when Birdland was open. Miles used to stand outside and he was beaten by the police and since that time he has been kind of – off. You know, I saw Miles in England and he just grabbed and hugged and kissed me, but I was afraid of him." Mary Lou Williams's impression of Davis is as unique as her impressions of dozens of other people; she seemed to see everyone with a singular eye. To her, Davis had withdrawn even further after the Birdland incident and had become vaguely threatening. But she was not the only one who saw that in him. Davis's idolators of the 1960s saw something of the same dark threat in his public image, and they took to calling him the "prince of darkness." Perhaps that is the image a man intends to leave people with when he drops ominous hints of malevolence, as Davis did when speaking to Joachim Berendt about the fate of the policeman involved in the Birdland incident. "The cop was killed, too," he said. "In a subway."

There can be little doubt that the incident remains for him an active ghost. When Sy Johnson interviewed Davis in 1976, seventeen long and eventful years after the incident, their conversation centered on music and musicians, but during a pause while they listened to a tape, completely out of the blue, there was a strange twist in the conversation:

"White people don't like me," Davis said. Johnson glanced over at him.

"'I mean, a policeman grabbed me around the neck.'

"'Why?'

"'"Cause I was black. I'm not gonna say what no white man wants me to say.'

"He reassured me, 'I'm talkin' 'bout a policeman – "Are you goin' peaceful, or am I gonna put handcuffs on you?" I'm supposed to say, "Yes, I'll go down peaceful"?'

"'That's what I would have said' [says Johnson, and after a pause:] 'Is it gonna be o.k.?'

"He shrugs."

The scars definitely seem to go deeper than his scalp.

The incident at Birdland affected his professional activities immediately following it. With his cabaret card revoked so that he could not work even if he wanted to, Davis absorbed himself in the legal battles being fought over him, keeping abreast of events whenever there were any new developments and suffering impatiently when there was nothing happening. The sextet ceased to exist at the end of September when Julian Adderley left, as he had said he would after two years. Coltrane did not leave immediately, although he always acted as if he wanted to, his vacillation continuing for another ten months. Wynton Kelly, Paul Chambers, and Jimmy Cobb remained too and stayed long after Coltrane finally left. So Davis still had the men he wanted, the ones he had brought along with him, two of them from the days of the quintet, another of them, Cobb, from the days of the great sextet with Bill Evans, and the other one, Kelly, though a relative newcomer, as close as anyone could be, as Adderley had said, to combining the talents of Evans and Red Garland. There was no lack of high-class manpower.

If there was something missing, it showed most conspicuously in Davis's lack of interest in expanding his music. For the next four years, he explored no new modal voicings, tried no new settings, and wrote almost no new music. To be sure, the Miles Davis Quintet remained one of the finest bands around, and Davis continued to play ballads as effectively as anyone ever had. But the rich promise of *Kind of Blue* remained largely unfulfilled, at least by Davis's bands. Most of Davis's career is impelled by his search for new plateaus, but between 1959 and 1964 he seemed content to remain on the plateau he was already on. In the same period, there were changes coming fast in jazz in general, and for the first and perhaps the only time in his career he would not only not direct those changes but he would not even appreciate them. It was a bitter irony for the man who said of his musicians, "He's got to have something that challenges his imagination, far above what he thinks he's going to play and what it might lead into, and then above *that*, so he won't be fighting when things change." As Martin Williams said, "*Kind of Blue* was an influential record both in and of itself and because it paralleled other, independently conceived, events in jazz. But for a while it seemed a rather isolated event for Davis himself – one might say that it was more immediately important to John Coltrane's development than to Davis, and for the next few years the repertory of ballads and standards was resumed to a great extent." For some four years – a relatively short time in so long and productive a career – there was a pause, and though it was highly creative in many ways, it was definitely out of character. For part of that time, one cannot even know for certain what Davis's music was like, because he entered the recording studios on only three days between April 1959, when he completed the second of the *Kind of Blue* sessions, and March 1961. For the time being, the apostle of change became the prince of darkness.

Bibliography

Adderley, Julian (Cannonball) "Paying dues: the education of a combo leader" *Jazz Review*. Reprinted in Martin Williams ed *Jazz Panorama* New York: Collier 1964

Albertson, Chris "The unmasking of Miles Davis" *Saturday Review* 27 November 1971

Amram, David *Vibrations* New York: Macmillan 1968

Anderson, Jervis "Harlem IV: Hard times and beyond" *New Yorker* 20 July 1981

Baggenaes, Roland "Duke Jordan" *Coda* October 1973

- "Interview with Mary Lou Williams" *Coda* July 1974

- "Red Rodney" *Coda* February 1976

- "Interview with Marc Levin" *Coda* March 1976

Balliett, Whitney *The Sound of Surprise* Harmondsworth: Penguin 1959

- *Dinosaurs in the Morning* Philadelphia: J.B. Lippincott 1962

- *Alec Wilder and His Friends* Boston: Houghton Mifflin 1974

- *Improvising: Sixteen Jazz Musicians and Their Art* New York: Oxford University Press 1977

- *Night Creature: A Journal of Jazz, 1975–80* New York: Oxford University Press 1981

Berendt, Joachim *The Jazz Book* St Albans, Herts: Paladin 1976

Berg, Chuck "Interview with Dexter Gordon" *Down Beat* 10 February 1977

Bernstein, Leonard *The Joy of Music* New York: Simon and Schuster 1959

Birnbaum, Larry "Ahmad Jamal" *Down Beat* March 1981

- "Eddie 'Cleanhead' Vinson" *Down Beat* October 1982

Bosworth, Patricia *Montgomery Clift* New York: Harcourt, Brace, Jovanovich 1978

Brown, Richard "Ah! Unh! Mr. Funk" *Down Beat* October 1979

Brown, Ron Review of *Miles Davis: Blue Moods* (America 30 AM 6051) *Jazz Journal* July 1972

Burns, Jim "Miles Davis: the early years" *Jazz Journal* January 1970

Butcher, Mike "Modern jazz: the bopsters and beyond" In Sinclair Traill ed *Concerning Jazz* London: Faber 1957

Carno, Zita "The style of John Coltrane" *Jazz Review* October and November 1959

Carr, Ian *Miles Davis: A Biography* New York: Morrow 1982

Chadbourne, Eugene "Heard and Seen: Miles Davis" *Coda* June 1973

Chilton, John *Billie's Blues* London: Quartet 1975

– *Who's Who of Jazz: Storyville to Swing Street* Revised Time-Life Records Special Edition 1979

Choice, Harriet "Miles Davis, solo: brews concocted and broods begotten" *Chicago Tribune* (Arts and Fun section) 20 January 1974

Coker, Jerry *The Jazz Idiom* Englewood Cliffs, NJ: Prentice-Hall 1975

Cole, Bill *Miles Davis: A Musical Biography* New York: Morrow 1974

Collier, James Lincoln *The Making of Jazz: A Comprehensive History* Boston: Houghton Mifflin 1978

Coltrane, John "Coltrane on Coltrane" *Down Beat* 29 September 1960

– Liner note *A Love Supreme* (Impulse A-77) 1964

Coryell, Julie, and Laura Friedman *Jazz-Rock Fusion: The People, the Music* New York: Delta 1978

Coss, Bill. Liner note *Miles Davis: Blue Moods* (Debut DEB-120) ca 1956

Crawford, Marc "Miles Davis: evil genius of jazz" *Ebony* 16 January 1961

Crosbie, Ian "Claude Thornhill" *Coda* October 1975

Crouch, Stanley. Liner note *Thelonious Monk at the Five Spot* (Milestone M-47043) 1977

Dance, Stanley *The World of Duke Ellington* London: Macmillan 1970

– *The World of Count Basie* New York: Scribner's 1980

Davis, Miles "Self-portrait of the artist" Columbia Records Biographical Service 26 November 1957

DeMicheal, Don "Miles Davis" *Rolling Stone* 27 December 1969

Dorough, Bob. Liner note *Yardbird Suite* (Bethlehem Records BCP-6023) 1976

Evans, Bill. Liner note *Miles Davis: Kind of Blue* (Columbia CL 1355) ca 1959

Feather, Leonard. Liner note *John Graas: Jazz Lab 2* (Decca DL 8478) ca 1957

– *Encyclopedia of Jazz* Revised. New York: Bonanza 1960

– *Encyclopedia of Jazz in the Sixties* New York: Bonanza 1966

– "The modulated world of Gil Evans" *Down Beat* 23 February 1967

– "Blindfold test: Miles Davis" *Down Beat*. Reprinted in Feather and Ira Gitler *Encyclopedia of Jazz in the Seventies* New York: Horizon 1976

– "Blindfold test: Michel Legrand" *Down Beat* 28 December 1967

– *From Satchmo to Miles* London: Quartet 1974

– *The Pleasures of Jazz* New York: Horizon 1976

– *The Passion for Jazz* New York: Horizon 1980

Feather, Leonard, and Ira Gitler *Encyclopedia of Jazz in the Seventies* New York: Horizon 1976

Feather, Leonard, and Conrad Silvert "Jazz world remembers Bird" *Down Beat* August 1980

Feather, Leonard, and Jack Tracy *Laughter from the Hip: The Lighter Side of Jazz* New York: DaCapo 1979 (first published 1963)

Fox, Charles "Gil Evans: experiment with texture" In Raymond Horricks ed *These Jazzmen of Our Time* London: Jazz Book Club 1960

– Liner note *Cannonball and Coltrane* (Mercury [Netherlands] 6336 319)

– *The Jazz Scene* London: Hamlyn 1972

Gardner, Mark. Review of *Miles Davis* (UAS 9952) *Jazz Journal* March 1972

Garland, Red "Memories of Miles" *Musician, Player and Listener* 41, March 1982

Getz, Stan. Album notes *Stan Getz* (Book-of-the-Month-Club Records BOMC 40-5510) 1980

Gifford, Barry, and Lawrence Lee *Jack's Book: An Oral Biography of Jack Kerouac* New York: St Martin's Press 1978

Gillespie, Dizzy, and Al Fraser *To Be or Not to Bop* New York: Doubleday 1979

Gitler, Ira. Liner note *Miles Davis and the Modern Jazz Giants* (Prestige LP 7150) ca 1957

– Liner note *Miles Davis: Collectors' Items* (Prestige LP 7044) ca 1957

– Liner note *Sonny Rollins First Recordings* (Prestige 7856) 1971

Gleason, Ralph J *Celebrating the Duke ... and Other Heroes* Boston: Little, Brown and Co 1975

Goddet, Laurent "Randy Weston interview" *Coda* 1 February 1978

Goldberg, Joe *Jazz Masters of the Fifties* New York: Macmillan 1956

Golson, Benny. Review of *Miles Davis: Milestones* (Columbia CL 1193) *Jazz Review* January 1959

Goode, Mort. Liner note *Basic Miles* (Columbia C 32025) 1973

Goodman, George, Jr "Miles Davis: 'I just pick up my horn and play.'" *New York Times* Sunday 28 June 1981

Gordon, Max *Live at the Village Vanguard* New York: St Martin's Press 1980

Gottlieb, William P. *The Golden Age of Jazz* New York: Simon and Schuster 1979

Grimes, Kitty *Jazz at Ronnie Scott's* London: Robert Hale 1979

Hailey, Alex "Playboy interview: Miles Davis" *Playboy* September 1962

Hakim, Sadik "My experiences with Bird and Prez" *Coda* 181, December 1981

Hall, Gregg "Miles: today's most influential contemporary musician" *Down Beat* 18 July 1974

– "Teo [Macero]: the man behind the scene" *Down Beat* 18 July 1974

Hamm, Charles *Yesterdays: Popular Song in America* New York: W.W. Norton 1979

Hammond, John, with Irving Townsend *John Hammond on Record* New York: Ridge Press 1977

Harrison, Max *A Jazz Retrospect* Boston: Crescendo 1976

Harrison, Max, Alun Morgan, Ronald Atkins, Michael James, and Jack Cooke *Modern Jazz: the Essential Records* London: Aquarius 1975

Hawes, Hampton, and Don Asher *Raise Up Off Me* New York: Coward, McCann and Geohegan 1974

Hentoff, Nat. Review of *Miles* (Prestige LP 7014) *Down Beat* 16 May 1956

– "Birth of the cool, parts 1 and 2" *Down Beat* 2 and 16 May 1957

– "An afternoon with Miles Davis" *Jazz Review* December 1958. Reprinted in Martin Williams ed *Jazz Panorama* New York: Collier 1964

– "Miles Davis: a story of Miles" *Esquire's World of Jazz* New York: Thomas Y. Crowell 1975 (from *Esquire* 1959)

– Liner note *The Piano Scene of Ahmad Jamal* (Epic LN 3631) ca 1961

– *Jazz Is* New York: Random House 1976

Hodeir, André *Jazz: Its Evolution and Essence* trans David Noakes. New York: Grove Press 1956

– *Toward Jazz* trans Noel Burch. London: The Jazz Book Club 1965

Hoefer, George "The birth of the cool" *Down Beat* 7 October 1965

– "Early Miles" *Down Beat* 6 April 1967

Holmes, John Clellon "The philosophy of the Beat Generation" *Esquire* 1958

Horricks, Raymond "Thelonious Monk" In *These Jazzmen of Our Time* London: The Jazz Book Club 1960

Jablonski, Edward "The making of *Porgy and Bess*" *New York Times Magazine* 19 October 1980

James, Michael *Miles Davis* New York: A.S. Barnes 1961

Jepsen, Jorgen Grunnet *A Discography of Miles Davis* Copenhagen: Karl Emil Knudsen 1969

Jeske, Lee "Bill Evans: trio master" *Down Beat* October 1979

– "Jimmy Knepper" *Down Beat*, August 1981

Jewell, Derek *Duke: A Portrait of Duke Ellington* New York: W.W. Norton 1980

Joans, Ted "Bird and the Beats" *Coda* 181, December 1981

Johnson, Sy. Liner note *Black Giants* (Columbia PG 33402) 1975

– "Miles" *Jazz Magazine* fall 1976

Katz, Dick "Miles Davis" *Jazz Review*. Reprinted in Martin Williams ed *Jazz Panorama* New York: Collier 1964

Kimball, Robert, and Alfred Simon *The Gershwins* New York: Bonanza 1973

Kofsky, Frank *Black Nationalism and the Revolution in Music* New York: Pathfinder 1970

Korall, Burt "Tal Farlow: Turning away from fame" *Down Beat* 22 February 1979

Lysted, Lars "Meet Benny Bailey" *Down Beat* 15 February 1973

McCall, Cheryl "Miles Davis" *Musician, Player and Listener* 41, March 1982

McDonough, Bob "Profile: Barrett Deems" *Down Beat* 5 October 1978

McRae, Barry. Review of *Early Miles* (Prestige PR 7674) *Jazz Journal* September 1975

Maher, Jack. Liner note *Miles Davis: Workin'* (Prestige 7166) ca 1957

Martin, John. Editorial *Jazz News* 1 October 1960

– "Miles out" *Jazz News* 1 October 1960

Martin, Terry. Review of *Miles Davis* (UAS 9952) *Down Beat* 22 June 1972

Meeker, David *Jazz in the Movies* New Rochelle, NY: Arlington House 1977

Mingus, Charles *Beneath the Underdog* ed Nel King. New York: Knopf 1971

Monk, Thelonious "What the performer thinks" *Esquire's World of Jazz* New York: Thomas Y. Crowell 1975

Moorhead, Arthur "Cedar Walton's major league play" *Down Beat* January 1981

Morgan, Alun "Miles Davis: Miles ahead" In Raymond Horricks ed *These Jazzmen of Our Time* London: The Jazz Book Club 1960

– Liner note *The Definitive Charlie Parker* Vol 4 (Metro Records 2356 087)

Morgenstern, Dan "Miles Davis" In George T. Simon et al *The Best of the Music Makers* New York: Doubleday 1979

Mulligan, Gerry. Liner note *The Complete Birth of the Cool* (Capitol M-11026) 1971

Nisenson, Eric *'Round about Midnight: A Portrait of Miles Davis* New York: Dial 1982

Nolan, Herb "Blindfold Test: Lenny White" *Down Beat* 14 March 1974

– "Helen Merrill" *Down Beat* 6 May 1976

O'Day, Anita, with George Eels *High Times Hard Times* New York: G.P. Putnam's Sons 1981

Pepper, Art, and Laurie Pepper *Straight Life: The Story of Art Pepper* New York: Schirmer 1979

Perla, Gene "Dave Liebman" *Coda* January 1974

Peterson, Owen. Letter *Jazz and Blues* March 1972

Porter, Bob "Talking with Teddy [Reig]" Album notes *Charlie Parker: The Complete Savoy Studio Sessions* (Savoy S5J 5500)

Priestley, Brian "Discography" Appendix C in Ian Carr *Miles Davis: A Biography* New York: Morrow 1982 pp 267–300

Primack, Brett "Drummers' colloquium III" *Down Beat* November 1979

Prince, Linda "Betty Carter: bebopper breathes fire" *Down Beat* 3 May 1979

Ramsey, Doug. Liner note *Julian Adderley: What I Mean* (Milestone M-47053) 1979

Reisner, Robert G. *Bird: The Legend of Charlie Parker* New York: Bonanza 1962

Renaud, Henri. Liner note *A Jazz Piano Anthology* (Columbia KG 32355) 1973

Rosenblum, Bob "Jimmy Heath" *Coda* June 1976

– Liner note *Chet Baker: Once upon a Summertime* (Artists House 9411) 1980

Ruppli, Michel "Discographie: Miles Davis" *Jazz Hot* February and March 1979

Russell, George *The Lydian Chromatic Concept of Tonal Organization* New York: Concept 1953

Russell, Ross "Bebop: Part III – Brass" *Record Changer* 1948–9. Reprinted in Martin Williams ed *The Art of Jazz* London: The Jazz Book Club 1962

– *Bird Lives! The High Life and Hard Times of Charlie (Yardbird) Parker* New York: Charterhouse 1973
– Liner note *Yardbird in Lotus Land* (Spotlite SPJ 123) 1975
Saal, Hubert "Jazz comes back!" *Newsweek* 8 August 1977
Saunders, Jimmy. Interview with Miles Davis *Playboy* April 1975
Shapiro, Nat, and Nat Hentoff *Hear Me Talkin' to Ya* New York: Dover 1955
Shaw, Arnold *The Street That Never Slept* New York: Coward, McCann and Geohegan 1971
Shera, Michael. Review of *Miles Davis-Tadd Dameron* (Columbia 34804) *Jazz Journal* April 1978
Silvert, Conrad "Herbie Hancock: revamping the present, creating the future" *Down Beat* 8 September 1977
– "Joe Zawinul: wayfaring genius" *Down Beat* 1 June 1978
Simmen, Johnny "George 'Big Nick' Nicholas" *Jazz Journal* September 1972
Simpkins, C.O. *Coltrane: A Biography* New York: Herndon House 1975
Smith, Bill "The Anthony Braxton interview" *Coda* April 1974
Spellman, A.B. *Black Music: Four Lives* (originally *Four Lives in the Bebop Business* 1966) New York: Schocken 1970
Stearns, Marshall W. *The Story of Jazz* New York: Oxford University Press 1956
Stern, Chip "Jack DeJohnette: South Side to Woodstock" *Down Beat* 2 November 1978
Stewart, Zan "Gil Evans" *Musician, Player and Listener* 39, January 1982
Sullivan, Patrick "Benny Bailey" *Jazz Journal* April 1977
Taylor, Arthur *Notes and Tones: Musician-to-Musician Interviews* New York: Perigee 1977
Taylor, J.R. Liner note *Charlie Parker Encores* (Savoy SJL 1107)
Thomas, J.C. *Chasin' the Trane* New York: Doubleday 1975
Traill, Sinclair "The Shelly Manne Story" *Jazz Journal International* August 1979
Tristano, Lennie. Liner note *Crosscurrents* (Capitol M-11060)
Ullmann, Michael *Jazz Lives* Washington, DC: New Republic Books 1980
Underwood, Lee "Profile: Ian Carr" *Down Beat* November 1979
– "Blindfold Test: Med Flory" *Down Beat* August 1980
Watts, Michael "Miles Davis" Ray Coleman ed *Today's Sound* London: Hamlyn 1973
White, Andrew. Liner note *John Coltrane: On A Misty Night* (Prestige P-24084) 1978
Wild, David. Review of *Miles Davis: Jazz at the Plaza* (Columbia C32 470) *Coda* March 1975
Wilder, Alec *American Popular Song: The Great Innovators, 1900–50* New York: Oxford University Press 1972
Williams, Martin *Where's the Melody?* New York: Minerva Books 1966
– *The Jazz Tradition* New York: New American Library 1970
Wilmer, Valerie *Jazz People* New York: Bobbs Merrill 1970

Wilson, John S. *Jazz: The Transition Years 1940–60* New York: Appleton-Century-Crofts 1966

Wilson, Russ. Review of Miles Davis Sextet at the Blackhawk *Oakland Tribune* 4 June 1959. Quoted in C.O. Simpkins *Coltrane: A Biography* New York: Herndon House 1975

Wisckol, Marty "Profile: Charles McPherson" *Down Beat* June 1981

Yanow, Scott "Columbia's Contemporary Masters Series" *Record Review* April 1978

– "Miles Davis: the later years" *Record Review* April 1978

Young, Al. Liner note *John Coltrane: Black Pearls* (Prestige P-24037) 1974

Zwerin, Michael "Miles Davis: a most curious friendship" *Down Beat* 10 March 1966

Index

Authors and composers are cited in parentheses following the titles of books and musical works, respectively.

Milestones 2:
The Music
and Times
of Miles Davis
Since 1960

Contents

Acknowledgments

It is my pleasure to acknowledge again the help and encouragement of Colette Copeland, Dale Dickson, Bernard Lecerf, Jan Lohmann, Dan Morgenstern, and Chuck Netley, and to thank Harald Bohne, Chris Chambers, Lewis Porter, and Frank Tirro publicly for the first time. I am grateful again to Jack Maher and Deborah Kelly of *Down Beat* for their help with the photographs, and especially to those who took the photographs that appear in this book. My thanks also go to John Parry for copy-editing, Will Rueter for designing, and Ron Schoeffel for editing. The index is dedicated to The Dog at Peppard. The book is dedicated to Sue, for all the usual reasons and then some.

No financial assistance was sought or received for the research and writing of *Milestones* I and II.

ABBREVIATIONS

The following standard abbreviations have been used in the discographical entries:

arr	arranger	gtr	guitar
as	alto saxophone	perc	percussion
b	bass	pno	piano
bs	baritone saxophone	ss	soprano saxophone
clnt	clarinet	tba	tuba
comp	composer	tbn	trombone
cond	conductor	tpt	trumpet
dms	drums	ts	tenor saxophone
flt	flute	vcl	vocal
frh	french horn	vib	vibraphone

PART THREE
PRINCE OF DARKNESS

I wish I was blacker than you.   Bud Powell to Miles Davis

9

Pfrancing
1960–2

Everything doesn't make me mad, angry. It takes a lot to make me angry enough. It's not that I'm angry, it's the way I speak. I don't *lie*, so it comes off like that.   Miles Davis

The promise of change was all around as the 1950s gave way to the 1960s, although it would have required a prophet to see the shape of things to come in the portents of the day. There was no such prophet, but many Americans in 1960 seemed willing to confer that title on their president-elect. His name was John F. Kennedy, at 44 the youngest man ever elected to the presidency, and he brought a new style into politics for these new times.

In his inaugural address on 20 January 1961, Kennedy proclaimed the new order in rhetoric that his immediate predecessors might have choked on. "Let the word go forth from this time and place, to friend and foe alike," he declared, "that the torch has been passed to a new generation of Americans, born in this century, tempered by war, disciplined by a hard and bitter peace, proud of our ancient heritage, and unwilling to permit the slow undoing of those human rights to which this nation has always been committed, and to which we are committed today at home and around the world." Kennedy's statement could almost stand as a clarion call to the political activists who would emerge not only in the United States but everywhere in the world by the middle years of the decade. It was closer to a prophecy than Kennedy himself would ever really know, because he was assassinated 34 months later, but it was also wrong in its details in a way that Kennedy could never possibly conceive.

The "new generation" was not the one "tempered by war" but the one conceived during and immediately after it, and "the torch" was not so much passed to it as seized by it. It was the generation of the 'baby boom,' the children born in the 1940s and early 1950s, who formed a new majority in all of the industrialized nations of the world and exercised their plebiscite with surprising power as they reached adolescence and early adulthood. By the time they reached the age of 30 – a birthday which, in their *Weltanschauung*, symbolized the age of hoary powerlessness – they revaluated virtually all their parents' values. Even as John F. Kennedy intoned the words of his inaugural address, they were pressing for more choice in education, which under the weight of their numbers became the fastest growing industry in the world. Still to come, though not far off, were confrontations on the folly of war for any putative principles, the incipient imperialism of foreign affairs, the covert elitism and racism of institutions, the sexism of traditional families, and much else besides. Their spokesmen were unelected and untitled, coming from the student ranks in the universities, the protest singers and poets in coffeehouses, the welfare workers in minority ghettos, and the international cadre of rock 'n' roll stars.

To anyone who could stir their imaginations, the new majority was willing to pay more than lip service. It was, above all, a generation of free spenders, raised in the relative peace and unbroken plenty of the post-war years. If the Great Depression still lurked neurotically in the minds of parents and caused them to extol the virtues of thrift and moderation, that only went to show how hopelessly antiquated the parents were. The new majority bought concert and movie tickets by the hundreds, books by the thousands, and records by the millions. It was a bonanza that promoters and publishers and record companies could not ignore, and their response soon made over large sectors of the economy until it seemed to serve under-30s only.

In the opening years of the new decade, Miles Davis seemed neither more aware of nor more responsive to the changes that were brewing than did any other jazzman his age. On 26 May 1959, he had turned 33. His altercation with the police outside Birdland that summer and its legal aftermath resulting in the dismissal of all charges on both sides merely hardened his veneer of cynicism about the world he never made. He was, for all that, riding a crest of popular and critical acclaim after the years of the first great quintet and the magnificent sextet. He seemed at first perfectly content to ride the crest. His supporting players from the great bands drifted away over the next few years, and replacing them with new sidemen who measured up to his exacting standards turned out to be a much harder task then it had ever been in the past. Because he was less than satisfied with the performances of many of his sidemen over the next four years, Davis spent even less time in the recording studios than he had in 1952, when his career was at its lowest ebb.

The first of the handful of studio recordings that he did make was with Gil Evans's orchestra, the *Sketches of Spain* sessions, and although it was a popular success it posed extraordinary technical problems, but a later one with Gil Evans from this same period, the *Quiet Nights* sessions, offered few technical challenges and turned out to be mediocre, an even more daunting result. Besides these, Davis made only two other LPs and a few isolated tracks in the studio, and Columbia Records was forced to record his live performances in order to keep its catalog up to date.

In his live performances, Davis often played less than he had a few years before, the result not only of his lack of interest in what his bands were doing but also of the acute pain he began suffering in his hip, a chronic ailment which in moments of crisis forced him to remove himself from the stand. His modal experiments with his sextet dimmed in their importance for his playing and for his band, and he seemed perfectly content to disengage himself from the formal innovations in jazz which John Coltrane and others took up in his stead. As for the other innovations coming into jazz at the time through the music of Ornette Coleman, Don Cherry, Cecil Taylor, and Eric Dolphy, Davis seemed positively hostile in his public pronouncements about them.

For Davis, these years were an interlude for discovering the resources that would lead him to his next great quintet, late in 1964. In the meantime, his music, when he chose to play it, perpetuated many of the strengths he had revealed so abundantly in the five years before. At its very best, whether with Gil Evans's orchestra or with his working quintet, it suffers hardly at all even in comparison to the music that went before it.

Davis made a last-ditch effort to dissuade Julian Adderley from leaving his band in September 1959 by offering him a guaranteed annual salary of $20,000, more money than Adderley could hope to make if he re-formed his own band. Adderley declined, choosing instead to resume his career as a leader alongside his brother Nat. He felt he had learned all he was going to with Davis, including some subtle lessons in leadership. "From a leader's viewpoint, I learned, by watching Miles, how to bring new material into a band without changing the style of the band," he said later. "And when it was necessary at times to change the style somewhat, Miles did it so subtly that no one knew about it." In fact, Adderley went on to become a popular leader without really changing his band's style from its basic blues-funk groove, although he started using an electric piano and bass in the late 1960s. He was confident that his band would succeed because of the exposure he had had with Davis. "I'd been getting inquiries from club owners about when I'd start my own band again because they kept noticing the response when my name was announced," he said. His band started off making $1,500 a week after he left Davis, compared to the $1,000 a week he had had difficulty commanding before he joined him.[1] Soon afterward, he had a string of successful records, first on the Riverside label and then on Capitol, depending largely on the pop-gospel compositions of Bobby Timmons, his first piano player, and Josef Zawinul, who replaced Timmons. His band became one of the biggest attractions in jazz for most of the decade.

With Adderley gone, Davis's band became a quintet again, with John Coltrane on tenor saxophone, Wynton Kelly on piano, Paul Chambers on bass, and Jimmy Cobb on drums. Coltrane could hardly muster more enthusiasm for playing Davis's music in their nightly routines than Davis himself could. He had declared his intention to become the leader of his own band repeatedly throughout 1959, and he would keep on doing so every time he spoke to the press or to other musicians. He stayed in Davis's band largely because he could not bring himself to set a date for his departure and stick to it, but his activities made it clear to everyone that he was more interested in his career outside the Davis Quintet, leading pickup groups on Atlantic recording sessions and in clubs on the quintet's night off. When the quintet made its tour of cities late in the year that would take it to Chicago for the usual Christmas engagement, Coltrane often stepped aside to let local saxophonists play in his place. At the Storyville Club in Boston, Rocky Boyd, one of Coltrane's admirers, often played as much as Coltrane did during the later sets of the night, and both of them played more than Davis did in those sets.[2] On returning in the new year to New York, where the quintet now worked regularly at the Village Vanguard instead of at Birdland, George Coleman played Coltrane's saxophone in some of the late sets.[3] Whether they knew it or not at the time, both Boyd and Coleman were auditioning for Coltrane's job.

Davis accidentally discovered that his career had reached a new plateau even if his music was, for the moment, standing still. In the marketing mentality of American culture, he had become the equivalent of a brand name. His name rather than his presence seemed to guarantee the success of the club engagements by his band, and he would sometimes play no more than eight bars of an opening melody before leaving the stand, or sit at the back of the club throughout an entire late-night set. Any carping about his absence was *lèse majesté*, and the complaints, for the time being, were few. Positive proof of Davis's stature surfaced in numerous glossy magazines in 1960, in the form of an advertisement for the Bell Telephone Company which showed a businessman in a hotel room talking on the phone, saying, "I was sitting here thinking of you while Miles played *My Funny Valentine* and I thought I'd call..." There was no need, of course, for further explanation.

Off the bandstand, Davis was less accessible than ever. Sy Johnson, who had moved to New York from Los Angeles, caught the quintet at the Village Vanguard and again photographed the group on the stand using available light. Where Davis had shown keen interest in Johnson's photographs of his band a few years earlier in Los Angeles, he now showed none at all. Instead, he approached Johnson and said, "I don't wancha takin' no more pitcha's, ya hear," and walked away. "He never said anything else," Johnson adds, "but he did frequently leave his trumpet on my table while he wandered around the club during solos by the rest of the band, and stub his cigarettes out in the ashtray."[4]

Max Gordon, the owner of the Vanguard, recalled another occasion when an avid fan of Davis was expected to feel privileged because Davis used his ashtray. "When Gary Giddins, the jazz critic, was fifteen, he used to spend the $2 allowance his father gave him to go to the Vanguard to hear Miles Davis on Sunday afternoon," Gordon wrote in *Live at the Village Vanguard*. "He'd come early, get a front seat. Miles was one of his jazz heroes. One Sunday, Miles, walking off the bandstand at the end of the first set, stopped to rub out his cigarette in the ashtray on Gary's table. 'Here, save it,' he said to Gary. 'Some day it's gonna be worth some money.'"[5]

If Davis approached his audiences, and his music, glibly when he played in jazz clubs, he certainly could not carry that over into the music he was recording in the Columbia studios. He was once again involved in a major project with Gil Evans, their third in three years, and even Davis feared that it was too ambitious. The music was later released, as *Sketches of Spain*, to the same popular acclaim as their earlier collaborations but a rather uneasy critical response, and it was recorded in two concentrated periods in the studios, the first in November 1959 and the second in March 1960.

The 1959 session provided most of the challenges for Davis and for the top studio men who comprised Evans's orchestra. The music they recorded, a single track lasting slightly more than sixteen minutes, was the adagio movement of Joaquin Rodrigo's *Concierto de Aranjuez for Guitar and Orchestra*, adapted for Davis's trumpet and flugelhorn. Davis first heard a recording of Rodrigo's *Concierto* earlier in the year in California. "After listening to it for a couple of weeks, I couldn't get it out of my mind," he says. When he played it for Evans in New York, they decided to adapt it for an album of Spanish themes. "As we usually do, we planned the program first by ourselves for about two months," Davis says. "I work out something, he takes it home and works on it some more; and then we figure out how we're going to do it. He can read my mind and I can read his."[6] Their score for the *Concierto* was so complex that the twenty-piece studio orchestra required eight sessions before producing the takes that were eventually released on the record.

Evans and Davis used the recording company's facilities, in effect, for protracted rehearsals, a practice that Davis would take up routinely by the end of the decade, when he began taking his working bands into the studio, recording several hours of music, and evaluating the results later. As a result, Columbia holds hundreds of hours of unissued material in its vaults that is unlikely to be issued as long as Davis is around to withhold his approval, and the first accumulation of rejected tape dates from the *Concierto* sessions. In 1959, it seemed a radical and probably expensive way of proceeding, and one that Teo Macero, Davis's producer, had to justify. "Who'd sit in a studio like I did for five sessions and hear a rehearsal?" he wondered, fifteen years later, and then he explained why he did it: "I knew there was something tangible there. Miles didn't show up for the first four sessions. He came and then he sat for the next two or three and I think most of the stuff came out of the last session. But you had to have some foresight. You had to have some understanding to say, 'Maybe it's tomorrow.' The experiment won't be completed until we finish. We don't really know, it's sort of a mixed-up jungle at the moment."[7]

Evans took charge of the sessions. Nat Hentoff attended one of them, on a Sunday probably just five days before the issued recording was made, and he noted that Evans "insists on hearing exactly what he has written," an observation that sharply contradicts those critics who claim that Evans is too easygoing when he conducts. Against pressures of time and grumblings of musicians, Evans persisted with the rehearsals until his score was finally mastered. "These look like flute parts we're playing," Ernie Royal, the lead trumpeter in the orchestra, complained. All the players found Evans's shifting, uneven tempos difficult. "To count at all," trombonist Frank Rehak said of one section, "you have to count four on every beat." Hall Overton, the classical composer who earlier in the year had scored some jazz arrangements of Thelonious Monk's music, was also in the studio on the Sunday that Hentoff was there. "This is the toughest notation I've ever seen in a jazz arrangement," Overton said. "It could have been written more easily for the players and the result would have been the same, but Gil has to have it exactly the way it happens in the piece." He added, "Fortunately, these guys are among the best readers in town." Later jazz adaptations of Rodrigo's first movement, notably by Laurindo Almeida with the Modern Jazz Quartet and by Jim Hall, have taken Overton's suggestion by simplifying the music, mainly using Rodrigo's melodies and tempos against a conventional jazz background, but they have missed entirely the rich textures that provide the substance of Evans's score. If Evans was undaunted by the difficulty of that score, Davis was not. "I always manage to put my foot in it," he said as he listened to yet another spoiled take at the Sunday session. "I always manage to try something I can't do. I'm going to call myself on the phone one day and tell myself to shut up."[8]

Then all the parts took shape, almost before anyone really expected them to. "All of a sudden," Macero said, "the last session comes and Miles plays and he plays straight through it and everything just sort of falls into place."[9] The details are as follows:

Miles Davis with Gil Evans and His Orchestra: Sketches of Spain
Miles Davis, tpt, flugelhorn; Ernie Royal, Bernie Glow, Taft Jordan, Louis Mucci, tpt; Dick Hixon, Frank Rehak, tbn; John Barrows, Jimmy Buffington, Earl Chapin, frh; James McAllister, tba; Albert Block, Eddie Caine, flt; Danny Bank, flt, bass clnt; Romeo Penque, oboe; Harold Feldman, oboe, bass clnt; Janet Putnam, harp; Paul Chambers, b; Jimmy Cobb, dms; Elvin Jones, perc; Gil Evans, arr, cond. New York, 20 November 1959
Concierto de Aranjuez
(Columbia CL 1480)

The complexity of Evans's score, from a listener's viewpoint, is reflected in the constant shift of textures throughout the sixteen minutes that the recording lasts. Its unity is a bit tentative, depending upon recurrences of Rodrigo's dominant melody, which is stated by Davis on flugelhorn right at the beginning (as it is stated by english horn in Rodrigo's original score), and then reinterpreted by him almost immediately (as by the guitar in the original). It is played by Davis as a highly personal lament, all of which occupies only the first quarter of the score; Rodrigo's melody returns to the foreground only in the last quarter, where it is played powerfully by the whole orchestra. In between, Davis plays in no less than four settings, all attractive in their own right but connected only by his unique sound, whether on open flugelhorn in the first half and coda, or on muted trumpet in the second half. Davis himself is the connecting thread, by design. "The thing I have to do now is make things connect, make them mean something in what I play around it," he said at the Sunday rehearsal.

It is a large responsibility, perhaps even too large. Davis and Evans's *Concierto* is likely to be heard by listeners who know it best as a medley of disparate pieces bounded by Rodrigo's melody. "That melody is so strong that the softer you play it, the stronger it gets, and the stronger you play it, the weaker it gets," Davis said at rehearsal, and Evans agreed, calling it a "distilled melody": "If you lay it on too hard, you don't have it."

That melody remains indelible because Davis states it and reinterprets it so strikingly at the start, separated by a beautiful interlude by a choir made up of trumpet, trombone, flute, and oboe. Much more than the melody echoes after a few listenings. In the middle of the score Davis plays a solo punctuated irregularly by trilled flutes and the harp. Immediately before and after, in two parts of Evans's score that are completely beyond Rodrigo, he plays the only segments that include anything resembling jazz rhythms. The second, with Davis playing muted, is underscored by a bass ostinato and carried along by the (sometimes slightly awkward) pulse of finger cymbals. The first has the syncopated rhythms of a walking bass and brushes on a snare drum.

The combined playing time of the two sections with quasi-jazz rhythms comes to less than four minutes, which may explain some of the coolness from the critics when the *Concierto* was released. Martin Williams said, "The recording is something of a curiosity and a failure, as I think a comparison with any good performance of the movement by a classical guitarist would confirm."[10] Max Harrison called it "a boring re-write" and "a strange miscalculation."[11] Even Rodrigo objected, according to Gil Evans. "There was only one version of it available then and now there's maybe fourteen," Evans pointed out in 1983. "The melody is so powerful. Rodrigo didn't like Miles' version of it but it brought him a lot of money in royalties. A *lot* of money."[12] Whether it is 'good' Rodrigo, or 'good' jazz, or even jazz at all can be debated endlessly. Most listeners seem to be as unconcerned about such matters as Davis and Evans apparently were, and they have kept the record in demand, and in print, ever since its release.

The remaining titles for Davis and Evans's collaboration on *Sketches of Spain* were more straightforward, but still very ambitious jazz orchestrations. They were recorded almost four months later in two sessions, after Davis returned from a tour of Boston, Chicago, and other cities with the quintet. Evans spent the interval listening to recordings of Spanish folk music and logged several hours in the library reading books on flamenco music, refining the bases of the other compositions and giving the next sessions a kind of scholarly diversity. The details are as follows:

Miles Davis with Gil Evans and His Orchestra: Sketches of Spain
Miles Davis, tpt, flugelhorn; Ernie Royal, Bernie Glow, Johnny Coles, tpt; Dick Hixon, Frank Rehak, tbn; Joe Singer, Tony Miranda, Jimmy Buffington, frh; Bill Barber, tba; Albert Block, Eddie Caine, Harold Feldman, flt; Romeo Penque, oboe; Danny Bank, bass clnt; Jack Knitzer, bassoon; Janet Putnam, harp; Paul Chambers, b; Jimmy Cobb, dms; Elvin Jones, perc; Gil Evans, arr, cond. New York, 10 March 1960
The Pan Piper; Song of Our Country
(*The Pan Piper* on Columbia CL 1480; *Song of Our Country* on Columbia KC2 36472 [1981])

Add Louis Mucci, tpt. Same place, 11 March 1960
Solea; Will o' the Wisp; Saeta
(all on Columbia CL 1480)
Song of Our Country was dated 11 March 1960 when it was issued in 1981, but the absence of Louis Mucci in the orchestra suggests that it was recorded the day before, as listed here.

The variety of orchestrations defies any concise description, and the success of the scores is mixed. *Song of Our Country*, which was not issued until 1981, stands apart from the rest musically. It opens with a full-bodied orchestral fanfare and closes with a suspended note by Davis, on flugelhorn, suggesting that it might have been written as a bridge between two of the other compositions in the original master plan, but, if so, that master plan is no longer reconstructable from the music available. The body of the piece is Davis's flugelhorn solo over orchestral figures, and it is much more in the spirit of Davis and Evans's *Miles Ahead* collaboration of 1957, and worthy of comparison with it in many ways.

Will o' the Wisp develops a theme from Manuel de Falla's ballet *El amor brujo*, thus resembling the *Concierto* in its provenance, but there is no resemblance in the result. However successful *Will o' the Wisp* may or may not be in adapting the original, on its own it fails rhythmically in its static seesaw of repeated orchestral figures, ending up as a kind of stiff-legged dance. *The Pan Piper* also includes a repetitive orchestral figure, representing the street cry of a vendor in the original folk recording which Evans adapted, but the repetition here is far from static, and over it Davis plays lyrically on muted trumpet; of Evans's orchestration, Davis said, "He made that orchestra sound like a big guitar."[13]

The remaining compositions, both credited to Evans but based on traditional Andalusian melodies, are masterful additions to the collaboration, notwithstanding Max Harrison's dismissal of them as "bogus flamenco."[14] *Solea* is indeed bogus flamenco, that is, flamenco adapted for a jazz soloist and orchestra, in which Davis plays an extended blues for twelve minutes over Evans's rich backgrounds. Davis's lament – *solea* is the generic term for a flamenco lament – sustains a single mood, in contrast to his caprices on *Concierto*, and the whole composition is powered by the two percussionists, used with a resourcefulness seldom given to percussion in Evans's arrangements. Throughout the entire composition, one of the drummers marks the flamenco rhythm on a snare drum and the other marks the 4/4 jazz rhythm on a ride cymbal. The two rhythmic pulses are felt alternately in a remarkably subtle exchange, the dominant flamenco rhythm subsiding imperceptibly until Davis and the orchestra are playing big band jazz in the middle section and then slipping as subtly back to flamenco by the end. The contending rhythms quite literally embody the musical forces at play throughout *Sketches of Spain* and counterbalance them brilliantly.

Saeta is no less successful, but on entirely different terms. It is essentially a three-minute exploration of a single scale by Davis, playing flugelhorn, supported all the while by nothing but a sustained chord from the woodwinds and the occasional march cadence of a snare drum. For Davis, it is an unflagging showcase of his taste and imagination, as he begins with a Spanish tinge in his phrases and a slight vibrato in his tone and builds an exotic blues solo in bent notes. His solo is framed by a march played as a crescendo at the opening and a diminuendo at the end, giving the aural effect of a parade approaching and stopping while Davis addresses it, and moving on when he is finished. The effect of the passing parade was used before this in Evans's *Here Come de Honey Man*, on *Porgy and Bess*, but without the emotive effect that it has here. The form is derived from an Andalusian procession through the streets on Good Friday which halts while a singer on a balcony directs her pain and remorse – *saeta* means 'arrow' – to the cross-bearing Christ. Davis's solo is raw in its emotion, and it seems all the more bitter and pained framed by the trite, business-like march cadence. Of the solo on *Saeta*, Martin Williams says, "Miles Davis plays with a stark, deeply felt communal anguish that jazz has not heard since King Oliver."[15]

In the previous collaborations of Davis and Evans, separating the parts from the whole proved almost impossible, and one could hardly avoid the conclusion that the whole was an unqualified success. In *Sketches of Spain*, the parts can be dealt with much more readily and almost require it. The success of the whole project is qualified, but among the parts *Solea* and *Saeta* are outstanding.

Later in the month, when Davis arrived in England on the first leg of a European tour, a reporter asked him if he enjoyed working with Evans's large orchestra. "I prefer to work with the quintet," he stated. "I like to hear the rhythm section."[16] His choice was clear no doubt because the arduous *Sketches of Spain* sessions remained so fresh in his mind. But some of his enthusiasm for the large-scale orchestral projects seemed to be gone for good.

So was some of Gil Evans's, although he did not realize it immediately. "You know, an arranger's job is kind of a loser's job, in a sense, because once you get paid for an arrangement, that's the end of it," he told Zan Stewart. "Like for the Miles Davis sides – *Miles Ahead*, *Porgy and Bess*, *Sketches of Spain* – I got paid and that's it. The people who wrote the original lines get the royalties. But at the time I never thought about it. I was having such a good time writing that music that it never dawned on me that years later I wouldn't be getting those checks in the mail."[17] Where Evans had composed only one title on each of the first two projects, on *Sketches of Spain* he is credited with three, *The Pan Piper*, *Saeta*, and *Solea* (as well as the belatedly released *Song of Our Country* from the same sessions). In 1983 he told Richard Cook, "I wised up when we did *Sketches of Spain* – those numbers credited to me are traditional tunes. You don't get royalties on public domain numbers."[18] Even so, he remained unlucky with royalties; he gave them to his first wife as alimony, and, according to Evans, by 1982 she had collected $240,000 on them.[19]

With *Sketches of Spain* finally completed, neither Davis nor Evans seemed anxious to return to the recording studio for a long time. For Davis, all recording, even with his quintet, was put off for a full year.

The studio sessions finished just in time for Davis to leave with his quintet for Europe. Coltrane presented a problem. He did not want to go on the tour, but instead of facing Davis with his decision he tried to recruit Wayne Shorter to take his place. "I had just gotten out of the army," Shorter says, "and one night Trane came over to Newark on his night off from Miles at Birdland. We had known each other, and Trane used to say to me, 'You're playing all that funny stuff like me ... all over the horn, funny.' Anyway, Trane then told me he wanted to leave Miles' group, and he told me, 'You can have the job if you want it.' He was giving me the gig for Miles! Anyway, he told me to call Miles, so I called him and said, 'Hello, I'm Wayne Shorter and I'm from Newark, New Jersey.' And you know Miles, he said in that voice, 'Who told you I needed a saxophone player?' And I said, 'Trane, John Coltrane,' Well, Miles says, 'If I need a saxophone player I'll get one.' Then we kind of measured each other to see who would hang up first."[20]

Norman Granz, who booked Davis's tour, advertised it as his "first extended European tour," with the emphasis, presumably, on "extended," since Davis had already played in and around Paris in 1949 and 1957 and in several European cities in 1956. As on all of Davis's European engagements, and indeed on those of all major American jazzmen, this one was well documented in unofficial tapings of the concerts, usually made informally by members of the audience but sometimes, judging by the quality of some of the tapes, taken directly from the sound system in the auditorium. For this tour, tapes of varying quality have turned up from the concerts in Paris (21 March), Stockholm (22), Copenhagen (24), and Scheveningen, a North Sea resort near The Hague (9 April). Two of the titles from the Stockholm concert were issued as recordings a few years later on a label called Bird Notes which has long since disappeared, and in 1979 a more generous sample of what the Davis Quintet played was issued on LP. The details are as follows:

Miles Davis Quintet in Stockholm and Scheveningen
Miles Davis, tpt; John Coltrane, ts; Wynton Kelly, pno; Paul Chambers, b; Jimmy Cobb, dms. Stockholm, 22 March 1960

Miles Davis (Columbia Records)

John Coltrane playing soprano saxophone (Lars Aastrom, courtesy of *Down Beat*)

Walkin'; All Blues
(both on Bird Notes; reissued in Europe on BYG 529608)
Both titles are incomplete; *All Blues* is mis-titled *Somethin' Else* on BYG.

Same personnel. Scheveningen, Holland, 9 April 1960
Green Dolphin Street; Walkin' / The Theme; So What; Round Midnight
(all on Unique Jazz UJ 19 [1979])
On aural evidence, *Round Midnight* is probably from a different concert from
the other titles; the recording is shrill, and the piano is out of tune.

The next few years include several recordings of live performances by
Davis's quintets made by Columbia with very good sound quality, but
none of them is as valuable as this one, documenting the final days of
Davis's veteran working band, even though its sound quality ranges
from good (on *Green Dolphin Street*) to awful (on *Round Midnight*). The
hours logged by the members of this band had not made them
complacent, at least not in these performances. Wynton Kelly, the
newest member, had joined the band in February 1959, more than a year
earlier, and Jimmy Cobb had joined a year before that; both Coltrane and
Paul Chambers had been with Davis since 1955, although Coltrane had
been removed from the band for a few intervals in that period. They play
together with an easy confidence that can bring out the best in each of
them.
    Even *Round Midnight*, in the familiar 1956 quintet arrangement by
Gil Evans, is enlivened by some new dissonances in the ensembles,
although this recording is diminished not only by its low fidelity but
also by an apparent splice after Coltrane's solo. *Walkin'*, even more
shopworn in Davis's repertoire, is saved from another stale recitation by
opening with Chambers's arco solo, which impels Davis into less
familiar territory for his own solo; in his last chorus Davis toys with a
childish jingle played in thirds for several bars, a surprising foreshadowing of his composition *Jean Pierre*, which became part of his repertoire
only in 1981.
    The other two titles, *Green Dolphin Street* and *So What*, are stunning
reworkings of two of Davis's most striking recordings with his sextet.
Both are played as unfettered romps in contrast to the carefully
controlled studio versions. On *Green Dolphin Street*, which lasts more
than twelve minutes, Davis constructs a hot solo that pulls apart the
familiar melody almost as thoroughly as do Coltrane's sheets of sound,

but *So What*, extended to seventeen and a half minutes in this performance, goes even further. Kelly, who had been asked to sit out on the original recording in favor of Bill Evans, fashions an ingenious solo in the style of Ahmad Jamal by sustaining the bass motif of the ensemble and building spare melodic phrases around it. On both *Green Dolphin Street* and *So What*, Coltrane plays long, intense, almost frenetic solos with enormous impact. He was by this time well launched on his career away from Davis's bands, and he was no longer holding back on his harmonic experiments when he played with Davis, as he had complained he was a year earlier. The spirit that would very soon bring him recognition as the most influential soloist of the time suffuses these live performances as clearly as it would his own recordings of *My Favorite Things* and *Equinox* for Atlantic later in the year. His solo on *So What* lasts nearly nine minutes and builds from an almost casual half-time vamp to a busy, moaning exploration that ranks with his best work.

Coltrane's playing with the quintet in Europe makes no compromises. He was restless and uneasy throughout the entire tour, making it clear to all the members of the band that he would rather be elsewhere, working on his own music on his own terms. His feelings hardly disrupted the others. All of them had watched him separate himself from their company and occasionally listened to his mild grumblings about needing to get out on his own. By now, they all openly wondered if he would ever get around to making the break he kept talking about, but in Europe they realized that he could not stay much longer. "All he had with him were his horns, an airlines bag, and a toilet kit," Cobb remembers. "He didn't really want to make the gig, but Miles talked him into it. He sat next to me on the bus, looking like he was ready to split at any time. He spent most of the time looking out the window and playing oriental-sounding scales on soprano [saxophone]."[21]

Soon after the quintet returned to the United States, Coltrane gave Davis two weeks' notice. He had done that before, of course, and had ended up staying, but this time there was a note of finality because he was already booked into the Jazz Gallery with his own quartet for nine weeks, beginning in May. After almost five years, his tenure in Miles Davis's bands was finished.

The break, when it finally came, proved far more traumatic for Davis than for Coltrane. Davis seemed unprepared despite all the signs that Coltrane was serious this time. He spent the next four years trying to find a suitable replacement, until the passing parade of saxophonists added up to a long list: Jimmy Heath, Sonny Stitt, Hank Mobley, Rocky

Boyd, Wayne Shorter (on a 1962 recording date), Frank Strozier, George Coleman, and Sam Rivers. None of them stayed long. Sonny Rollins, whom Davis had originally preferred to Coltrane and had enlisted as his replacement a couple of times, was not available, having retired from music yet again; this time he remained inactive for almost two years, until the fall of 1961.

Coltrane, who had for so long feared leaving the security of Davis's band, moved straight ahead. At the Jazz Gallery he received the same salary he was getting from Davis. His quartet there had Steve Kuhn on piano, Steve Davis on bass, and Pete LaRoca on drums, but after two weeks he replaced Kuhn with McCoy Tyner, thus finding almost at the beginning the piano player who would form the cornerstone for his working bands.[22] He played and recorded the music on which his reputation largely rests between the fall of 1961 and the end of 1964, in a series of brilliant recordings under his own leadership on Atlantic and Impulse. After that, his health began to deteriorate, and his music, though undeniably powerful, became so freighted with excesses that it became hard to understand and even harder to appreciate, seemingly requiring listeners to refer back to his music of 1960–4 for clarification. The difficulties posed by his later music hardly seemed to impose any burden on listeners who were paying attention at the time it was being made, when his earlier music was still fresh, and he found a large, almost idolatrous following among both musicians and fans until his early death in 1967.

The character of Coltrane's music undeniably changed after he left Davis, by degrees in the first few years and then by leaps. Soon after leaving he said, "I think I'm going to try to write for the horn from now on, just play around the horn and see what I can learn. All the time I was with Miles I didn't have anything to think about except myself so I stayed at the piano and [played] chords, chords, chords. I ended up playing them on my horn." His music eventually became less dense, especially when he played the soprano saxophone, and more melodic, but he explored modal frameworks until the last few years of his life, when he often chose freer forms. In 1965, he looked back on his years with Davis and noticed the similarities in his music. "I don't think it has changed basically – though I suppose I've grown a little musically," he said. "But then in some respects I think I might have been a little more inventive in those days."[23] With Davis, he had been forced to discover and integrate his own individuality in contexts determined by Davis. No one, before or since, rose so forcefully to that challenge.

The timing of Coltrane's quitting was unlucky for Davis not only because of the problem of finding a replacement. Coltrane's presence gave Davis's music an aura of experimentation, of restless searching for formal and harmonic expansions, that even the most unschooled listener could hardly miss. No matter that Coltrane's experiments originated with Davis and were, at least in the beginning, impelled by him; on the surface it was Coltrane, not Davis, who was the experimenter. That fact counted heavily on the tote board that jazz critics began drawing up in 1960.

Critics and fans suddenly took a vital interest in the search for new directions in jazz. Whether it was cause or effect, the central event of the new interest was the arrival in New York of two Los Angeles musicians named Ornette Coleman and Don Cherry. The hullabaloo surrounding their engagement at the Five Spot placed alto saxophonist Coleman and trumpeter Cherry at the center of the noisiest controversy in jazz since the "war of the moldy figs" fought over bebop in the 1940s, but this time the controversy had a much larger and more conspicuous battlefield because in the interim the jazz audience had expanded socially, culturally, and geographically.

It began innocently. John Lewis, doyen of the Modern Jazz Quarter (MJQ) and one of the most respected figures in jazz, was quoted in the *Jazz Review* in 1959 extolling the virtues of the two unknowns: "They're almost like twins; they play together like I've never heard anybody play together," he said. "It's not like any ensemble that I have ever heard, and I can't figure out what it's all about yet." From that germ, Coleman and Cherry's meteoric careers took shape.

Through Lewis's good graces, they were signed to a recording contract by Nesuhi Ertegun of Atlantic Records, the MJQ's recording company, and sent to the summer session at the School of Jazz in Lenox, Massachusetts, where Lewis was the director. Curiosity about the pair was further fuelled by Martin Williams's column on the School of Jazz in October's *Jazz Review*, of which he was co-editor, in which he wrote, "I honestly believe (not that I am alone or particularly original in believing it) that what Ornette Coleman is doing on alto will affect the whole character of jazz music profoundly and pervasively."

By the time Coleman and Cherry opened in New York in November for what would become a six-month engagement at the Five Spot, the critical artillery was already in place and the battle could begin in earnest. The music that Coleman and Cherry played, usually called "avant-garde" or "the new thing" at the time but perhaps more

appropriately called "free form," inspired passionate paeans and deri-
sive denunciations in about equal proportions and drew dozens of
names into the fray. For a short time, one counted one's friends in terms
of whether or not they shared one's opinion of Ornette Coleman.

Davis and Coltrane, like nearly all other jazz musicians, were
profoundly curious about the music, and both were frequent visitors at
the Five Spot, which was packed for weeks after the opening. Coltrane,
typically, watched Coleman with a wide-eyed but noncommital look
and said nothing; Davis watched too and even ventured onto the
bandstand at the Five Spot with him, but when he was asked directly for
his opinion, he issued a typically blunt judgment: "Hell, just listen to
what he writes and how he plays it," he said. "If you're talking
psychologically, the man is all screwed up inside."[24] That statement
was more than enough to relegate Miles Davis into the reactionary
faction in the hypersensitive critical climate of the moment.

Davis was not the only critic of Coleman and Cherry: virtually every
established jazzman who said anything at all expressed doubts about
their music. But very few had the temerity to say anything at all, and the
main reason for the silence was the enormous weight of articulate
opinion promoting their music as the "new thing." When Coleman took
the stage with his tiny white plastic alto saxophone and Cherry joined
him with his tinier pocket trumpet to play the rapid, daring, original
ensembles of Coleman's tunes – ensembles that cohered magically, but
seemed to have such a magical musical basis that even as astute a
listener as John Lewis could not figure out their theoretical underpin-
nings – they were hailed by a small but influential group as the
harbingers of the next step in the evolution of jazz. Not only John Lewis
and Gunther Schuller of the Lenox School, and Martin Williams and
Nat Hentoff of the *Jazz Review* spoke out, but notable figures beyond
the jazz world were convinced too. The Five Spot counted dozens of
artists among its Greenwich Village clientele when Coleman and
Cherry were playing, including Jackson Pollock, the patriarch of
modern American painting, and writers as different as LeRoi Jones (now
Amiri Baraka) and James Baldwin, among the leading young writers in
America, and Dorothy Kilgallen, the social columnist and television
panelist. Leonard Bernstein, the most prominent figure in American
music, was not only conspicuous in the audience; he was demonstrative
too. He sat in with Coleman's quartet, an act of more symbolic
significance than musical; one of the sidemen quietly told A.B.
Spellman, "He didn't really know what was going on."[25] Bernstein also,

on one memorable evening, leaped to his feet at the end of one set and declared that "this is the greatest thing that has ever happened in jazz" and that "Bird was nothing."

The display only hardened the suspicions of players like Randy Weston, who was booked opposite Coleman and Cherry that night, that the extravagant praise was nothing more than an attempt by the white establishment to foist their sensibility onto the development of jazz. Davis thought so too. Of Don Cherry, he said, "Anyone can tell that guy's not a trumpet player – it's just notes that come out, and every note he plays, he looks serious about, and people will go for it – especially white people. They go for anything. They want to be hipper than any other race, and they go for anything like that."[26]

Of Davis's turn on the bandstand with Coleman, Cherry says, "He wanted to try the pocket trumpet and he played practically all night." Davis even tried altering his musical conception to conform to theirs. Cherry recalls, "After I played, Miles said, 'You're the only mother I know who stops his solo right at the bridge.' And then he tried it."[27] Davis remained unconvinced that Coleman and Cherry offered anything worthwhile for the progress of jazz. And he saw no reason to alter his opinion a few years later, when he let Cherry sit in with his quintet for an evening.

Davis's outspoken criticism caused a few critics to wonder if his own success had not spoiled him and to evaluate his reaction as that of an established figure threatened by innovation. Davis insisted that he was only being honest where others were not. "People are so gullible," he told Leonard Feather, one critic who remained cool to Coleman's music. "They go for that – they go for something they don't know about ... because they feel it's not hip *not* to go for it. But if something sounds terrible, man, a person should have enough respect for his own mind to say it doesn't sound good. It doesn't to me, and I'm not going to listen to it, it doesn't sound any good."[28] Some other musicians were also willing to take a stand. "They're afraid to say it is nothing," Milt Jackson, Lewis's cohort in the MJQ, said. "There's no such thing as free form."

Looking back on the controversy more than two decades later, it is possible to sort out some home truths on both sides. Ornette Coleman and Don Cherry made music together that was eccentric and off-the-wall, and at its best, on a track like *Ramblin'* (on Atlantic 1327), it is full of feeling. It does not sound "terrible" at all; most jazz listeners would agree, at this late date, that it sounds beautiful. However, their music has only a tenuous formal framework, and it was never substantial enough to supplant the chordal and modal forms dominating jazz, as several commentators obviously thought it would. Coleman and Cherry played "melodically," in their terms, which meant that they responded spontaneously to one another's mannerisms, relatively unconstrained by the conventional formal guidelines of bars, chord progressions, choruses, scales, and the other musical trappings that comprise the shared, communal basis of Western tonal music.

In numerous statements, Coleman implied that the rudiments of his playing which everyone found so elusive were not essentially *musical* at all. "It seems impossible for Ornette Coleman to talk about music without soon using the word 'love'," Martin Williams wrote in his column from Lenox, "and when he plays one knows that, undeluded, it is love of man his music is talking about." "I just play life," Coleman said, "things that I encounter and experience." "There's a law to what I'm playing, but that law is a law that when you get tired of it, you can change it," he said later, and among the changeable elements he included tempo: "My music doesn't have any real time, no metric time. It has time, but not in the sense that you can time it. It's more like breathing, a natural, freer time." On the same point he said, "When you speak, the meaning itself gives the speed to the word. The same thing happens in music."[29] Assembled side by side, these statements emphasize the extramusical basis for Coleman's music, and its essential paradox. None of the activities he compares to his music is communal at all. Speaking happens with people taking turns, one after the other, and when two people try to speak simultaneously communication breaks down; breathing is done individually, without regard for the inhalation pattern of anyone else; experiences of life and love are felt and interpreted differently by different people, or at least will not be articulated similarly by them. But music usually takes place in groups and is a common expression by several individuals. It requires a shared body of "laws," and those laws can change only for the group, not for the individual. The logical conclusion of Coleman's pronouncements, if taken literally, would be musical anarchy, with the individual defying the group and standing apart from its expression.

Coleman's early history personifies that. In Fort Worth, Texas, where he was born in 1930 and lived until 1952, and in Los Angeles after that, Coleman sometimes earned a little money playing his tenor saxophone in rhythm and blues bands, but he was repeatedly excluded by jazz players whenever he attempted to play his alto saxophone with them. His fortunes took a turn only in 1958, when Don Cherry and a few other young musicians in Los Angeles got involved in trying to figure out what it was that Coleman was pursuing in his music. After repeated exposure, Cherry and the others, notably pianist Paul Bley, bassist Charlie Haden, and drummer Billy Higgins, managed to intuit so many of Coleman's mannerisms that they could play compatibly alongside him in his solipsistic flights. Cherry was the key, and by the time John Lewis heard them playing in Los Angeles he and Coleman had developed a rapport that was telepathic. Their music was beyond category, and they were playing together with utter conviction.

Their collaboration lasted a little longer than the Five Spot engagement, but the pressure of the critical controversy swirling around them and of the bloated expectations of a jazz revolution brought disruption. Soon afterward, Cherry went his own way, leaving Coleman on his own, as he had been when Cherry joined him. In the years since, Coleman has played and recorded very little, and while the aura of critical enthusiasm that surrounded him when he first became an international figure in jazz still gives a sense of occasion to his infrequent performances, he has probably never played as well or as convincingly as he did at the moment of his initial triumphs.

For all that, his influence has been and still is keenly felt. The avant-garde in jazz plays free form music in the terms that Coleman originally defined for it, either in tightly knit groups such as the Art Ensemble of Chicago and the World Saxophone Quartet, in which the members can comprehend and play off individual idiosyncrasies and at the same time develop and exploit group idiosyncrasies, or increasingly in solo performances by the likes of reedman Anthony Braxton and pianist Anthony Davis, where individual virtuosity can reign supreme without the fetters of group play.

Coleman and Cherry were not the first of the jazz avant-garde to emerge at the end of the 1950s, although their critical reception made them the most prominent. Cecil Taylor, a pianist from Boston, began being heard in New York fairly regularly in 1959, just before they arrived there, and Eric Dolphy, a reed and flute player from Los Angeles, joined Charles Mingus's band in 1960. One of Coleman's edicts said: "You can play flat in tune and sharp in tune," and Dolphy convinced most jazz listeners of the truth of that statement even if Coleman had left them unconvinced. Dolphy arrived in the public consciousness with an extraordinary individual voice on his several instruments, including flute and bass clarinet, but he was at his best on the alto saxophone, the instrument that Coleman favored. Dolphy's distinctiveness lay mainly in his use of tonality, which he altered with such fine control that his solos sometimes took on an eerie vocal quality. It was easy to recognize that he was 'playing flat' or 'playing sharp' in his solos, and just as easy to recognize that he was doing it in the service of his art. Where even Coleman's champions suspected that he not only would not play in a more conventional jazz framework but that he *could* not – a suspicion that Coleman would neither lay to rest nor confirm because he always refused to make the attempt – Dolphy left no doubt whatever about his musicianship. He could, and did, play in all manner of contexts from orchestral to bebop to free form, and he played as effectively and as distinctively in all of them.

Cecil Taylor had begun to find a few opportunities to display his rapid-fire, percussive, volcanic piano style when the fuss erupted over Coleman and Cherry in New York. His presence along with theirs at that moment naturally added to the critical impression that jazz was about to undergo the throes of revolution, the more so because Taylor had arrived from the opposite corner of the country, had never had any contact with the men from Los Angeles, and played equally eccentric jazz. Taylor's unique style seems to derive technically from jazz drummers rather than from other pianists, featuring an incredible outpouring of notes that mixes in a powerful thrumming of overtones. It is hard to imagine a piano style more antithetical to the one favored by Miles Davis in his bands, based on the harmonic niceties of men like Ahmad Jamal and Bill Evans, and Davis wasted little time in letting his feelings be known about Taylor's music. Symphony Sid Torin had started playing selections from Taylor's LP, produced by Nat Hentoff for Contemporary Records in 1958, on his radio show, prefacing the tracks, according to Taylor's bassist Buell Neidlinger, with remarks like: "This is a record by some gentlemen we understand have just escaped from Creedmore," a hospital for the criminally insane.[30] The publicity, and Hentoff's advocacy, helped to get Taylor occasional Monday night engagements at Birdland. Davis attended one of them along with Dizzy Gillespie, Sarah Vaughan, and Errol Garner. As Niedlinger remembers it, "Miles just laughed and split," but Taylor was left with a residue of more bitter memories: "Miles just cursed and walked out. Dizzy wandered in and out and kept making all kinds of remarks to Sarah, who was in a pretty vicious mood."[31] It was a hard baptism for the young piano player, and while he, unlike Coleman, persisted in developing his music publicly until he found, or developed, his audience, he has had little positive to say about his early detractors. Of one of them, he once said, "Miles Davis plays pretty well for a millionaire."[32]

Davis's involvement with the musicians who were emerging at the start of the 1960s comes as no surprise; he had always been aware of young musicians and new currents in jazz. More surprising is the apparent firmness of his stand on the side of the old order. He had been a member of the bebop revolution, the leader of the cool reaction to bebop and also, paradoxically, of the neo-bop reaction to cool, and then the leader in the modal reorganization of jazz structure. No one was in a better position to appreciate the inevitability of change. Now, he seemed determined to stake a claim for the status quo. Not content to watch and wait until the critical dust settled, as John Coltrane and others did, he waded in oblivious to the hypersensitivity of the time. When a supporter of Ornette Coleman declared that Art Blakey was "old-fashioned," Davis snapped, "If Art Blakey is old-fashioned, then I'm white." Against the enthusiasm of John Lewis and other spokesmen, Davis claimed he could not see any value in it at all. "What's so avant-garde?" he asked. "Lennie Tristano and Lee Konitz were creating ideas fifteen years ago that were stranger than any of these new things. But when they did it, it made sense."[33]

Once committed, he refused to revaluate, and for the first and only time in his career Davis was willing to stand aside and allow the innovations to proceed without him. It was remarkably out of character for him, and it did not last long, only during the short period when his own music seemed to stand still. Apart from these few years, his credo is well expressed in what he told Sy Johnson in 1976: "I got into music because I *love* it. I *still* love it. All kinds."[34] For the time being, he seemed to despise the kind of music known as the "new thing," and three or four years would pass before his own band responded to the newer, freer currents in jazz.

Davis's first choices to replace John Coltrane reflected his conservative mood. As soon as Coltrane left, Jimmy Heath was brought in. A tenor saxophonist and composer whose style was largely formed by the bebop revolution, Heath had just finished serving a fifteen-month term in the Lewisberg Penitentiary on a narcotics conviction when he joined Davis's band in the summer of 1960. He stayed in the quintet for about two months, playing engagements with them in Toronto and at the French Lick Jazz Festival, but after that, according to Bill Cole, Heath's parole board refused to let him travel beyond a ninety-mile radius of Philadelphia, his home town, and Davis, with another European tour set for the fall, was forced to find a replacement.[35] He invited Wayne Shorter, Coltrane's personal choice as his replacement, but Shorter was just settling in with Art Blakey's Jazz Messengers. "Miles called one time and asked Art if he could speak to me," Shorter recalls. "Art was saying 'He's trying to take my saxophone player,' and I told Miles that I felt an obligation to stay with Art. I didn't want to be one of those guys who just went from one band to another band every few months. Anyway, I stayed with Art for five years."[36]

In the end Davis hired Sonny Stitt, an alto saxophonist who doubled on tenor, another bebopper who had been Davis's bandmate with Billy Eckstine in 1946. Heath and Stitt were both solid and competent players, about the same age as Coltrane and Davis, but neither of them had shown any inclination to update their styles since their formative years. The spirit that Coltrane had brought to Davis's bands simply vanished.

Davis arrived in London on Friday, 23 September, to begin a round of concerts that would take him to the Gaumont Cinema, Hammersmith, in London (24 September), Colston Hall in Bristol (1 October), and Manchester (6 October). The leisurely pace of the English leg of the tour allowed him to spend some time sight-seeing, and he arrived with a small entourage that included his wife, Frances, who made a striking impression on every Fleet Street newsman who caught a glimpse of her, and Harold Lovett, his lawyer-manager.

Davis seemed completely unprepared for the hail of bad publicity in the tough London dailies covering his arrival. They played up his aloof stage manner, reiterating the old accounts of his turning his back on the audience and leaving the stage when his sidemen were soloing. That kind of notoriety was old hat to Davis, but the London tabloids added a sensational twist by implying that the reason for his unconventional behavior was hostility for white audiences. They also claimed that his entourage included a bodyguard and made it clear that this was a slight on British civility. "What do they think I am? A monster or something?" Davis asked John Martin, the editor of London's *Jazz News*. His treatment in the tabloids was, of course, no different from that routinely given to other visiting celebrities, but it had never before been dished out to a jazz musician.

He fared little better when the reporters turned their attention to his music. *Sketches of Spain* had just been released, and one reporter asked him if he thought that it was "really jazz." "I think so," Davis replied, and then he asked, "What do you think?" The reporter, it turned out, had never heard the record.

Davis provided fodder for controversy with his off-hand remarks to the press. "Some guy even said I didn't want to come here because I don't like the way Britishers speak," he complained to Martin. "I don't know who he was. He just came up to the stand one night and asked me. I said I didn't like the accent."[37] The remark, needless to say, kept the pot boiling on Fleet Street.

The publicity probably did him no harm at the box office. The concert at the Gaumont Cinema drew more than 7,500 fans. One of its reviewers complained that Davis was visible for no more than fifteen minutes.[38] While this was almost certainly an exaggeration, similar complaints would become familiar in the next few years.

The quintet's music with Sonny Stitt on saxophones survives, as expected, in private tapings from the Manchester concert and also from two concerts the following week on the continent, in Paris (11 October) and Stockholm (13 October). So far, only one title, *Walkin'*, has been issued on record, from the performance in Stockholm, and even it exists only on an obscure European label. The details are as follows:

Miles Davis Quintet
Miles Davis, tpt; Sonny Stitt, as, ts; Wynton Kelly, pno; Paul Chambers, b; Jimmy Cobb, dms. Konserthuset, Stockholm, 13 October 1960
If I Were a Bell; All of You; Walkin; All Blues; Theme
(*Walkin'* issued in Europe on Bird Notes; others unissued)
Stitt plays tenor saxophone on *If I Were a Bell* and *Walkin'*. No Blues and *Green Dolphin Street* also exist on tape, in incomplete versions, apparently from this concert.

Asked about sharing the front line with an alto saxophonist after so many years with a tenor man, Davis said, "I don't think about instruments. I pick a guy for what he can do. If I like the way he plays, then he's in."[39] When Stitt plays tenor, on *If I Were a Bell* and *Walkin'*, it is surprising to hear how much things stay the same. Stitt fills Coltrane's spaces in these familiar arrangements with fast, facile bebop solos, and everything else is unaltered. When he plays alto, the instrument on which he always seemed more comfortable, the spaces he fills are more lyrical than Coltrane's, with occasional runs and phrases invoking the ghost of Parker, and the whole band responds to the difference, most noticeably in the subdued, thoughtful reading of *All Blues* at this concert. There is an hour of interesting music in these extended concert performances and much more from the other sites in Europe; they will enhance the catalog when they are finally issued.

Soon after Davis and the quintet returned to the United States, they

Frances Taylor Davis and Miles Davis emplane for Europe, 1960
(KLM Royal Dutch Airlines photo)

Sonny Stitt and Miles Davis (Jim Marshall, courtesy of *Down Beat*)

began the round of club dates that would land them in Chicago for Christmas again. In Philadelphia, Davis became the go-between for a significant meeting between Elvin Jones and John Coltrane. Jones showed up at a club where the quintet were playing one night, and Davis passed along Coltrane's message that he wanted to hire him. Through exchanges of telephone numbers for which Davis served as the intermediary, Jones was able to join Coltrane in Denver a couple of weeks later, at first sharing drumming duties with Billy Higgins in Coltrane's quartet but soon taking over the drum chair.[40] Jones became a fixture in Coltrane's band, along with McCoy Tyner, staying with him from late 1960 until 1966 and providing the undercurrent for Coltrane's greatest work. The Coltrane Quartet, with Tyner, Jones, and initially Reggie Workman on bass but soon afterward, and for several years, Jimmy Garrison, moved almost immediately into the front rank of jazz. In *Down Beat*'s Critics Poll for 1961, Coltrane was named best tenor saxophonist and best "new star" on soprano saxophone, and his band were named best "new combo." Although Davis openly hoped that Coltrane would return to his band, he quashed any real chances of that when he brought him together with Jones, who proved to be the catalyst for Coltrane's success as a bandleader.

As generous as Davis could sometimes be with people, or at least with musicians, he seemed to spend much of his time practicing what Michael Zwerin once called "his famous salty-dog act." Anecdotes about Davis's mooning of the world circulated rapidly among his fans. When the advertising manager of *Down Beat* sent him the standard letter informing him that he had won a poll and suggesting that he take out a "thank you" ad in the magazine, Davis returned the letter with a circle around "thank you" and the words "fuck you" scrawled in the margin.[41] During his Christmas engagement at a Chicago club, Don DeMicheal, then newly appointed to *Down Beat*'s staff, suggested to Davis that he should present him with the 1960 Critics Poll plaque on the stage during a set, but Davis said, "You're not gonna plug that goddamned magazine on *my* bandstand. Give it to me at the bar."[42] Around this time Davis became a fearsome figure among the secretaries at Columbia, referring to them as "white bitches."[43] For a segment of his fans, each new anecdote added lustre to the mystique surrounding him.

So, of course, did his appearance on the list of best-dressed men in *Gentlemen's Quarterly* for 1961. Along with his Ferrari, his four-storey home near the Hudson, his beautiful wife, Frances, and the other women he sometimes escorted, the sartorial honor from *GQ*, which was followed two years later by a similar citation from *Playboy*, seemed to add a crowning touch, at least in the value system of most Americans raised in the 1950s.

All the accouterments of Davis's mystique were concentrated into an anecdote recounted by Joe Goldberg: "I chanced to be in Miles' white Ferrari when he was driving it up the West Side Highway at about 105 miles per hour. Frances got very frightened and asked him to slow down. Miles gave her the perfect Milesian reply, and I doubt that Brando, or Sinatra, or even Hemingway, could have said it better: 'I'm in here too.'"[44]

Max Gordon, who owned the Village Vanguard, felt the bite of his star attraction's lifestyle more keenly than most jazz club owners. Gordon also owned the fashionable Blue Angel in downtown Manhattan, and Davis became a regular customer. "Nights when Miles wasn't playing at the Vanguard he'd bring his current girl to The Blue Angel and order Piper Heidseick champagne," Gordon recalled. "One night I told the waiter to hand him the check. He tore it in two and sent the waiter back with this message: 'Tell your boss I'll never pay a check here. Tell him he's been underpaying me at the Vanguard for years. I gotta get even somehow.'"[45]

Any hard feelings that lingered among the critical fraternity as a result of Davis's position in the controversy over free jazz at the close of 1959 were pretty well dissipated by the start of 1961. For one thing, there was a critical reaction to free jazz, a kind of backlash, that left Ornette Coleman scuffling to find work soon after he closed at the Five Spot and led him to withdraw from active playing altogether during 1963–5, although several other players whose entries into the field were less meteoric than Coleman's continued to work fairly regularly and to show the way in freeing some of jazz's formal organization. For another thing, the jazz business was just beginning to feel the pinch of an economic recession. Unlike many other recessions that come and go in jazz history, the one just beginning in 1961 was destined to last for several years, until it touched almost everyone.

Jazz clubs closed frequently, as they always have and still do, but this time they were not replaced by new clubs a month or a year later. By 1965, when the recession bottomed out, it began to look like a permanent state of affairs. Looking back, it is easy to see that the recession involved a large swath of the entertainment industry, not just the jazz clubs. Many of the more fashionable supper clubs closed too (including Max Gordon's Blue Angel, in 1963), without replacements, as the whole concept of night-time entertainment underwent revision in America. But at the time, for those closest to the jazz business, its death looked real enough to cause some soul-searching.

The recession fed the backlash to free music, as more and more commentators looked around and noted that the empty clubs were featuring young players whose music seemed to be a lot more interesting to play than to hear. Stan Getz noticed that when he returned to the United States in 1961 after three years of living in Copenhagen and playing in Europe. "When we first got back, he was starry-eyed, happy, excited, and eager to hear what had been happening in the States during his absence," Getz's wife, Monica, told Don DeMicheal. "He eventually became disappointed at what he felt was a dead-end street of pretentious experimenting and repetitious self-indulging choruses – the more pretentious the music, the more ecstatic the hipsters. In fact, hipsters had seemed to become the larger part of the audience. Many true jazz aficionados had quit coming, being confused and bored. Only old friends like Miles and Diz gave him solace and hope and worried with him about the directions of jazz."[46] For Getz, as for Gillespie and Davis, the hard times to come were discomforting but not disastrous; many other musicians, including established players like Earl Hines, Gigi Gryce, Al Haig, and Tal Farlow, would be forced out of music altogether in the next few years.

Getz's quandary on first returning to the United States might have been resolved very simply if he had joined Miles Davis, who again found himself searching for a saxophonist for the quintet. Unfortunately, both men had worked too long as leaders for them to consider joining forces, even temporarily. Instead, Davis hired Hank Mobley, a solid journeyman whose best credentials stemmed from the neo-bop bands of the second half of the 1950s, when he played in the original Jazz Messengers of Art Blakey, moved out of that group with its pianist, Horace Silver, when he formed his own group, and ended the decade back with Blakey again.

Mobley's presence in Davis's quintet, while giving it a competent, experienced soloist, imported nothing new. In that sense, Mobley further diminished the probing, experimental cast of Davis's finest band only a few years earlier. While Julian Adderley remained unreplaced, Wynton Kelly had replaced Bill Evans and now Mobley was replacing Coltrane. The parallels in these two replacements were noted by Roger Cotterrell in the English magazine *Jazz Monthly*. "As Kelly is to Evans so, to some extent, Hank Mobley is to Coltrane," he wrote. "Mobley and

Kelly have certain points in common – primarily that they are both straightforward, fairly uncomplicated players who can usually be relied on to make a workmanlike job of a solo."[47]

Although Mobley lasted in the band for a year, Davis seems to have been less than enthusiastic about his playing the whole time. One night while Mobley soloed on the stand, Davis leaned over to Joe Goldberg and said, "Any night Sonny Rollins shows up with his horn, he's got a job."[48] When Goldberg told Coltrane about Davis's remark, Coltrane just smiled and gave it the most generous interpretation imaginable. "He'd hire Sonny, he'd hire me, he'd hire all of us, just to hear us play," Coltrane said. "He's got a lot of money, and he loves to listen to music."[49]

Davis did hire Coltrane, though only temporarily, when he finally got around to making a new studio recording in March 1961, his first in a year and the only one for another sixteen months. It was also his first with his working band for more than two years, since the final session of *Kind of Blue*, and it would be the only one with the working band for another two years. Nothing shows better Davis's disaffection for the work of his bands during this period, although he submitted the quintet to on-site recordings by Columbia at concerts and in clubs in the same period. It took three studio dates to complete the recording for the LP released as *Some Day My Prince Will Come*; only on the first does the working quintet appear on its own. On the next two, Davis brought Coltrane along with him, making the band a sextet for the album's title piece at the second session and replacing Mobley with Coltrane for one title at the third. The details are as follows:

Miles Davis Quintet: Some Day My Prince Will Come
Miles Davis, tpt; Hank Mobley, ts; Wynton Kelly, pno; Paul Chambers, b;
Jimmy Cobb, dms. New York, 7 March 1961
Drad-Dog; Pfrancing [No Blues]
(both on Columbia CL 1656)

Add John Coltrane, ts, on *Some Day My Prince Will Come*. 20 March 1961
Some Day My Prince Will Come; Old Folks
(on Columbia CL 1656)

John Coltrane replaces Mobley on *Teo*; Philly Joe Jones replaces Cobb on *Blues No. 2*. 21 March 1961

Teo [Neo]; I Thought about You; Blues No. 2
(first two titles on Columbia CL 1656; *Blues No. 2* on Columbia 36278 [released 1979])
Drad-Dog is mistitled *Drag-Dog* in most references, from Jepsen on, but appears as *Drad-Dog* on both the liner and label; *Pfrancing* was issued under the title *No Blues* in subsequent recordings of live performances; *Teo* was issued under the title *Neo* in a subsequent recording.

These recording sessions are a puzzling mixture of carefully controlled, rehearsed pieces (*Pfrancing, Some Day My Prince Will Come, Old Folks, I Thought about You*) and extemporaneous head arrangements (*Drad-Dog, Teo, Blues No. 2*). Some of the puzzles will probably disappear when the whole session is finally collated; there is certainly more music from it in the vaults, and some of the issued titles are merely excerpts.

Davis seems to have used his studio time partly to work out some new ideas, as he had done for *Concierto de Aranjuez* and would do routinely a few years later. *Drad-Dog* and *Teo*, in particular, seem to be the result of editing longer takes. *Teo* catches Davis playing with a Spanish tinge, very much in the style of *Sketches of Spain*, and Coltrane follows him with a tinge that drifts eastward toward, say, Lebanon as he goes, but the whole piece seems poorly defined and incomplete. *Drad-Dog* seems even more obviously a paste-and-scissors job. Notwithstanding its boppish (but so far unexplained) title, it is a quiet ballad, without an identifiable melody – an improvisation with a theme unstated or deleted – and it stops without really ending.

These tracks show the imprint of Teo Macero, Davis's producer at Columbia for the previous two years and for many years to come. They are not the first; *Porgy and Bess*, on which Macero worked in post-production, apparently includes some post-recorded solos by Davis, and *Concierto de Aranjuez* seems to be spliced together from two or three different takes, its continuous flow an aural illusion. Now, on *Drad-Dog* and perhaps on *Teo*, Macero seems to have taken a further step, not only pasting together disparate parts, but actually selecting a part of the whole to stand alone.

The first hint about the rest of the music made at these sessions came to light in 1979, with the release of *Blues No. 2*, an extemporaneous blues at a lively tempo that spotlights the muscular drumming of Philly Joe Jones, a guest in the studio that day who sat in behind Jimmy Cobb's drums. Jones trades four-bar breaks with Davis and later follows solo choruses by Davis and Mobley with a solo of his own, but he is hardly less conspicuous when he is supporting the other players, and this performance is a belated reminder of the strength he added to Davis's bands as a regular sideman from 1955 to 1958.

The real interest of these sessions, however, comes from the set pieces that Davis introduced into the band's repertoire. *Pfrancing*, a wonderfully evocative title capturing references to Frances Davis and to a whole semantic field taking in prancing, dancing, and frantic, all of which suit it nicely, quickly became a nightly fixture under the more prosaic title *No Blues*, with its call-and-answer theme abbreviated to only a couple of bars and its tempo almost doubled. Here, at its first airing, Davis's call is echoed by Mobley in alternating bars three times, and the ensemble is stretched out for another six bars holding the last note of the call. The twelve-bar ensemble thus forms a memorable little ditty to frame the round of solos, where in later versions it is never more than a few perfunctory bars before the solos.

Old Folks is a tightly muted standard ballad very much in the style of Davis's affecting ballads for Prestige a few years earlier, and worthy of comparison to them, while *Some Day My Prince Will Come*, a waltz sung by Snow White in Walt Disney's first animated feature in 1937 (re-released in movie theatres with great acclaim in 1958), is another masterly conversion of unlikely material by Davis along the lines of *Fran Dance/Put Your Little Foot Right out* and a worthy addition to the line of lilting ballads that includes not only *Fran Dance* but also *Round Midnight, All of You, Green Dolphin Street*, and *If I Were a Bell*. Those bright ballads, conceived by Davis out of elements he heard in the work of Ahmad Jamal, were – and still are – the basis for Davis's appeal to listeners whose tastes were formed by singers like Frank Sinatra, Peggy Lee, and Sarah Vaughan, and *Some Day My Prince Will Come*, true to form, found a wide audience. It did so, needless to say, without pandering in any way.

Davis plays the original melody with more than a little respect, but his tone is ambiguous and leaves no doubt that the coming of the prince might not be such a wonderful thing. Mobley and Kelly solo after Davis, and then Davis returns to play the melody again, just as he would at the finish of a regular quintet performance, only instead of closing he sets the stage for Coltrane's explosive solo, a brawny dismembering of the fragile melody that somehow manages to be lyrical. The performance evokes the powerful interplay that Davis and Coltrane worked on for so many years, and although it is something of a postscript to those brilliant years it maintains the same high style.

When the LP was released a few months later, more than a few heads turned at the sight of the portrait of a doe-eyed woman with a Mona Lisa smile that graced its front cover. The model, it turned out, was Frances Davis. "I just got to thinking that as many albums as Negroes buy, I hadn't ever seen a Negro girl on a major album cover unless she was the artist," Davis told Alex Hailey in an interview for *Playboy* magazine. "There wasn't any harm meant – they just automatically thought about a white model and ordered one. It was my album, and I'm Frances's prince, so I suggested they use her for a model, and they did it."[50] Davis himself appeared in a black-and-white photograph on the back cover, in place of the usual liner notes, which he had been trying to get rid of for some time. "I've been trying to get Irving [Townsend, Columbia's chief of production] for years to put out these albums with no notes," Davis told Ralph J. Gleason, in an oft-quoted statement. "There's nothing to say about the music. Don't write about the music. The music speaks for itself." The back cover of *Some Day My Prince Will Come* simply named the six musicians, listed the titles played and their playing times, but gave no clue to the deployment of the tenor saxophonists on the various tracks.

With or without liner notes, Davis's albums were automatic best sellers in the jazz field and had been for some time. Columbia's biggest problem in these years was to persuade him to record often enough to keep it supplied with new albums for the marketplace. Finally, Columbia decided that if Davis would not come to it, it would go to him, and it began recording him in live performances a month after the studio sessions for *Some Day My Prince Will Come* were completed.

The quintet were scheduled to make a tour of jazz clubs in several cities that would include two weeks at the Blackhawk in San Francisco, a well-known and long-lived club, as jazz clubs go, where the previous year Riverside Records had made a successful on-the-spot recording of Thelonious Monk. For Davis's engagement there, Columbia set up recording facilities in an adjoining bar and added hours of material from Davis to its stock. These live performances were the first Davis ever knowingly made for later release on record, the extensive collection of his earlier performances, including those from Newport and the Plaza Hotel in 1958 later issued on Columbia, having all been taped incidentally, sometimes surreptitiously. That circumstance made Davis's sidemen more than a little self-conscious, according to Ralph J.

Gleason, the jazz columnist for the *San Francisco Chronicle*, whom Davis told, "They're all worried about making records with me," and then he added: "And I'm just standing here, minding my own business, being my own sweet self." But Davis was not unaffected by it either, and he kept checking on the sound quality the engineers were getting next door, or he dispatched Wynton Kelly to check on it, on the nights when recordings were being made. One result is that Davis plays long, generous solos on all the titles recorded, something that he was not always inclined to do during a regular night's work at a jazz club in these years.

When the recording equipment was not in place, he ran true to form at the Blackhawk, seldom playing the last set of the evening and never playing the Sunday matinée set. The Blackhawk, as Gleason describes it, was obviously a club where Davis felt relaxed and where he apparently knew that his absences from the stand when his sidemen were working would not cause problems for him. The owner simply shrugged, "I should complain, as long as the people come."[51] When he was avoiding the bandstand, Davis was not avoiding the people; he signed autographs and answered questions, usually with a word or two, and wandered around the club freely. He did not join the other members of his band at Jimbo's Bop City, the after-hours club where they went almost nightly after their 2 a.m. closing at the Blackhawk.[52] Instead, he got some sleep and spent the daytime hours visiting friends in the area. Gleason, a nonsmoking, nondrinking diabetic whose voluminous jazz journalism was always infectiously enthusiastic, discovered that Davis's easy manner around the Blackhawk did not mean that he had mellowed in any way. "Once he told me he had been past my house that afternoon en route to Dave Brubeck's," Gleason said. "'Why didn't you stop in?' I asked in a stereotyped social response. 'What for?' he answered with shattering frankness."[53]

His easy manner did, however, mean that Columbia could capture some good playing from him at the Blackhawk, and the amount of music it added to its catalog was considerable, as it had hoped. So far the music from the Blackhawk recordings comes to almost 112 minutes, with, surely, much more to come. The details are as follows:

Miles Davis Quintet: At the Blackhawk
Miles Davis, tpt; Hank Mobley, ts; Wynton Kelly, pno; Paul Chambers, b; Jimmy Cobb, dms. The Blackhawk, San Francisco, 14 April 1961
Walkin'; Bye Bye Blackbird; All of You; No Blues; Bye Bye [The Theme] (all on Columbia CL 1669)

Same personnel, same place, 15 April 1961
Well You Needn't; Fran Dance; So What; Oleo; If I Were a Bell; Neo [Teo]
(all on Columbia CL 1670)

Same personnel, same place, 21 April 1961
Green Dolphin Street
(on Columbia 13811 [1977])

Same personnel, same place, 22 April 1961
Round Midnight
(on Columbia KC2 36472 [1981])
Hank Mobley does not play on *All of You* and *If I Were a Bell*; Columbia CL 1669 also includes Wynton Kelly, unaccompanied, playing *Love I've Found You*; both *Walkin'* and *Round Midnight* are followed by a few bars of *The Theme* tagged on to the end, and *So What* is followed by a few bars of *No Blues*.

While Davis plays at great length on these performances, Mobley gets to play much less. Not only does he sit out on *All of You* and *If I Were a Bell*, where Davis had occasionally asked other tenor saxophonists to sit out in the past, but he also does not solo on *No Blues, Bye Bye,* and *Well You Needn't*, where the saxophonist, under ordinary circumstances, would be expected to solo. Mobley's solos were apparently edited out, but Wynton Kelly's solos are preserved on every track. On *Well You Needn't*, Mobley's solo may be missing because he did not know this Monk composition, as his ragged playing in the ensemble suggests.

Generally, the performances are interesting verions of mainly familiar fare in Davis's repertoire, noticeably freer and more expansive than the original studio versions. Davis makes allusions to other pieces, playing snatches of *Bye Bye Blackbird* in the first chorus of his improvisation in *So What* and a few bars of *I Get a Kick out of You* in his solo on *If I Were a Bell*, something he does very infrequently in his studio solos. Two of the compositions recorded only a month earlier have been added to the working repertoire, another relatively unusual occurrence, and both are retitled – *Pfrancing* as *No Blues*, and *Teo* and *Neo* – even though the originals were not yet available and Davis could have easily standardized the titles on the two releases if he had wanted to. The second of these new pieces, *Neo*, receives a performance far superior to the one in the studio a month earlier, which was tentative and ill-defined. Here, after a slightly awkward opening bar by Wynton Kelly (who is obviously reading from the lead sheet), the rhythm section finds its way much more confidently, and both Kelly and Davis end up taking two long solos.

When the two LPs of this material were released together in the fall, they were packaged identically except for the color of the print on the front covers, which was nearly illegible on the black background of the cover photo. The near-identity of the two packages caused no end of confusion among buyers, who had to discern the words *Friday Night* on one and *Saturday Night* on the other. The cover photo again featured Frances Davis, this time looking worried behind the shadowy figure of her husband, in what looks like a still from an old Hollywood melodrama.

A little less than a month after the Blackhawk engagement, Columbia recorded Davis again in a live performance, this time in New York, with his quintet and the Gil Evans Orchestra at Carnegie Hall. The concert was a benefit for the Africa Relief Foundation, and, true to the temper of the times, the sidewalks outside Carnegie Hall were picketed by protesters carrying placards declaring "AFRICA FOR THE AFRICANS" and "FREEDOM NOW." The Africa Relief Foundation, a nonprofit organization raising funds for goods to be sent to Tanganyika and Zanzibar (later united as Tanzania), was viewed by the picketers as a tool for perpetuating colonialism.

Davis and the other musicians began the concert unaware of the political controversy out on the streets, but they soon learned about it. As Davis finished stating the melody of *Some Day My Prince Will Come*, the third composition on the program, Max Roach and another protester walked to the stage carrying placards and sat on the edge holding them up to the audience. Davis faltered and then stopped playing and walked into the wings. Roach and the other man were finally persuaded to leave the hall. After a long interval, with the audience at first restless and then almost ready to give up hope, Davis returned and, without a word, kicked off the opening bars of *No Blues* with the quintet.

When a reporter for the *New York Post* asked Davis about the incident he snapped, "I don't know what Max was doing. Ask *him*." Roach offered this explanation: "I was told some things about the Foundation that I thought Miles should know. Some people tried to contact him but they couldn't get to him. I went on stage because I wanted Miles to be aware of these things."[54] Roach spent much of the rest of the decade as an activist in black nationalist and civil rights causes, playing jazz and recording infrequently. His most ambitious record was the *Freedom*

Now Suite (recorded in 1960 for Candid, reissued in 1980 as Columbia 36390), its title bearing a reminder of the placard he carried onto the Carnegie Hall stage at Davis's concert.

Musically, if not politically, Davis's Carnegie Hall concert was unblemished. It was an enormously ambitious undertaking, and the reviews were unanimously enthusiastic. The recording, released about a year later, somehow misses the impact that the concert, by all accounts, had. One cause of the discrepancy may be the imperfect balance of the sound recording, but another cause, perhaps more significant, is the heavy editing of the master tape. The recording recapitulates the concert only very indirectly, and the transformation from concert to record remains a second-rate document of one of Davis's greatest critical successes. The details are as follows:

Miles Davis at Carnegie Hall. New York, 19 May 1961
Miles Davis Quintet: Miles Davis, tpt; Hank Mobley, ts; Wynton Kelly, pno; Paul Chambers, b; Jimmy Cobb, dms
Gil Evans Orchestra: Ernie Royal, Bernie Glow, Johnny Coles, Louis Mucci, tpt; Jimmy Knepper, Dick Hixon, Frank Rehak, tbn; Julius Watkins, Paul Ingraham, Bob Swisshelm, frh; Bill Barber, tba; Romeo Penque, Jerome Richardson, Eddie Caine, Bob Tricarico, Danny Bank, woodwinds; Janet Putnam, harp; Paul Chambers, b; Jimmy Cobb, dms; Bob Rosengarden, perc; Gil Evans, arr, cond
Orchestral introduction (orch); *So What* (quintet and orch at beginning); *Spring Is Here* (Davis, Kelly, and orch); *No Blues* (quintet); *Oleo* (quintet); *Some Day My Prince Will Come* (Davis, Kelly, Chambers, Cobb); *The Meaning of the Blues* (orch); *Lament* (orch); *New Rhumba* (orch)
(all on Columbia CL 1812)
The version of *New Rhumba* on the record may have been recorded later and spliced in; some discographies list the re-recording date as 27 July 1962, but by then this record had been released (Priestley 1982).

The concert, insofar as it can be reconstructed, included several additional compositions and also presented them in a different order, with longer versions of *No Blues* and perhaps some of the other quintet performances. No tape of the concert has shown up in private collections, no program was distributed on the occasion, and, as usual, no announcements were made from the stage, so that the members of the audience, including the professional reviewers, were uncertain of some of the titles played, but the critics' descriptions were fuller than they might otherwise have been because of the significance of the event itself, and those descriptions along with what can be gleaned from the record allow a tentative reconstruction. The critics' accounts do not, of course, completely agree. Describing Davis's stage manner, John S. Wilson, writing in the *New York Times*, says, "Although he has often been charged with treating his audiences disdainfully, he not only smiled on a couple of occasions but acknowledged applause with a quick glance over the footlights and a slight nod of his head."[55] Whitney Balliett, however, reviewing the same concert in the *New Yorker*, says, "Davis never lets his audiences know that he knows that they're there; he neither speaks to them nor looks at them nor even plays to them."[56] Balliett's and Wilson's accounts of the music played, along with that of George T. Simon in the *Herald Tribune*,[57] suggest the following program, in this order:

Orchestral introduction (orch)
So What (quintet and orch at beginning)
Spring Is Here (Davis, Kelly, and orch)
Someday My Prince Will Come (quintet)
No Blues (quintet)
The Meaning of the Blues (orch)
Lament (orch)
New Rhumba (orch)

Oleo (quintet)
perhaps *All Blues* (quintet)
Saeta (Davis and orch)
Solea (Davis and orch)
Concierto de Aranjuez (Davis and orch)

The listing of *All Blues* is nothing more than a guess based on Simon's description of the piece as "a groovy, middle-tempoed blues." The other titles are quite firm, and the order shown cannot be far off, although there might have been an additional quintet title.

Some Day My Prince Will Come includes little more than a recitation of the melody by Davis, which may be all he played before he was distracted by Roach's protest, but the truncated version as it stands hardly fits Simon's description as "a passionately swinging waltz."

The issued version of *No Blues* lasts almost twelve minutes, but its climax has been deleted in spite of Simon's praise for it as "a fast blues climaxed by exciting two-bar challenges between Davis and drummer Jimmy Cobb," one of the highlights of the concert.

Some justifications for doctoring the original tape so heavily are not hard to guess. One was to improve the quality of the sound, which would also account for the post-concert re-recording of *New Rhumba*, spliced into the master tape in place of the version played at the concert. Some of the high frequencies of the orchestral playing are fuzzy in *The Meaning of the Blues* and *Lament*, played here as a continuous suite with *New Rhumba*, as they were in the original recording on *Miles Ahead* (1957), and on *New Rhumba* they might conceivably have been worse. Another reason was to fit the material onto a single LP. Not only were double-album sets rare at the time (although the Blackhawk sessions came out on two LPs), but *Saeta*, *Solea*, and the *Concierto* were probably felt to be too recently recorded, with *Sketches of Spain* only two years old. However, *Some Day My Prince Will Come* was only one year old and was released in the new, but brief, concert version. But however cogent Davis and Teo Macero's reasons might have seemed for altering the tape of the Carnegie Hall concert, one has to second-guess their validity. From the tape of a magnificent concert, Columbia managed to release a moderately interesting LP. The LP might have been commensurate with the concert if it had retained the integrity of the original program and allowed the immediacy of the playing to compensate for the extra length of some of the compositions and the imperfect sound.

The LP that resulted has its merits. Chief among them is a driving version of *So What*, the playing of the quintet clearly invigorated by the setting. Among its delights is the aggressive drumming of Jimmy Cobb, sounding less docile than he had become in recent outings and, in fact, more like Philly Joe Jones, whose style he favored when he first replaced Jones in Davis's bands. *So What* also includes Hank Mobley's best solo on any recording he made while he was in the Miles Davis Quintet, a confident, inventive solo that holds together from start to finish.

The only new writing in the concert, apart from the orchestral introduction which lasts just under a minute, is *Spring Is Here*, a beautiful voicing by Gil Evans for Davis's reading of the ballad. Although the entrance of Wynton Kelly (or perhaps Evans, on piano) as Davis's accompanist on the last chorus where the orchestra is expected suggests that the arrangement was not quite finished when the concert day arrived, the rest of the arrangement is a good example of Evans's ability to create motion with wind instruments, leaving the rhythm instruments in secondary roles. The harmonization of Evans's arrangement was shaped by Bill Evans's recording of *Spring Is Here* with his piano trio (on Riverside RLP 12-315),[58] and out of that sketch Gil Evans built an arrangement for a twenty-one-piece orchestra that sounds hardly less compact than the trio version. Gil Evans's *Spring Is Here* exists only in this concert version, and that alone almost vindicates the release of the LP in its received form, if justification is really needed.

After this spurt of well-documented activity in the spring of 1961 – in the studio making *Some Day My Prince Will Come* in March, at the Blackhawk in April, and at Carnegie Hall in May – Davis went through another long period, lasting more than a year, of relative inactivity, from which no permanent transcripts of his playing survive. He stayed close to New York, working sporadically with Gil Evans on a new project for Columbia, their fourth. He worked occasionally with the quintet, but the tenor saxophone chair remained unsettled. Hank Mobley stayed for a while, without getting much gratification from the job or giving much enthusiasm to it. Rocky Boyd replaced Mobley late in 1961, and soon after that he vanished.[59] One of the more mysterious figures in an art form peopled by them, Boyd had been on the fringes of the jazz world for a couple of years, occasionally seen in the company of John Coltrane, notably on a couple of Coltrane's visits to Boston, which may be Boyd's home city. In 1961, Boyd seemed prepared to make a breakthrough in New York. He led a quintet with Kinney Dorham at the Jazz Gallery in the spring and made a recording as a leader with a group that included Dorham, pianist Walter Bishop, who had recommended him for the record date, bassist Ron Carter, and drummer Pete LaRoca (reissued under Dorham's name in 1974 on Muse 5053). The record reveals Boyd as a competent, apparently confident, tenor player who has learned several lessons from Coltrane, and it gives a promising start for a relative newcomer, but there is nothing else. During his time with Miles Davis, no records were made and no tapes of their club dates have turned up. Early in 1962, Boyd left New York as a member of Philly Joe Jones's quintet, and he has seldom played publicly since.

Davis played frequently at the Village Vanguard, and at his request the performer who shared the bill with him was Shirley Horn, the singer-pianist from Washington, DC, whose first record impressed him immensely. But he had little enthusiasm for his night's work. Joe Goldberg described his laconic performance on a Sunday afternoon around this time. "From various parts of the room, the members of the group walked casually toward the bandstand," Goldberg wrote. "Davis materialized from a dark corner of the room where he had been talking to the small son of his bassist Paul Chambers. Resplendent in a tight white suit and green sportshirt, he strolled to the piano and, cigarette in mouth, played a few chords. A waiter handed him his trumpet. He stepped to the microphone, without any perceptible word to the other musicians, assumed the familiar introvert stance, horn pointed toward the floor, and began to play *Some Day My Prince Will Come*. The tight sound that prompted British theater critic Kenneth Tynan to refer to him as a musical lonely-hearts club was heard briefly ... and the audience applauded wildly. By the time the applause had subsided, Davis was off the stand."[60]

For many members of the audience, even a brief appearance was enough; it was hardly new to his more experienced fans, although Davis had usually played at least a full chorus before moving to the back corner of the room in years past. Some fans inevitably complained. Davis's absence had been easier to tolerate when Coltrane was left on the bandstand in his stead, but Hank Mobley or Rocky Boyd could scarcely make up the difference, as Davis himself knew too well.

As Davis's performances became more offhand, more people began resenting him. They could hardly be expected to know, because neither Davis nor anyone who knew him ever talked about it, that he was suffering physically most of the time now, from pains that shot through his joints and left him numb and aching, especially in his left leg. He refused to show it, neither wincing when the pain hit nor limping when his hip stiffened. Instead, he played a few notes and stood in the shadows behind the audience, leaving them to draw whatever conclusions they pleased.

The pains were nothing new to Davis – only their severity was. For several years an arthritic knuckle had been visible on his right hand, the hand used to manipulate the valves of the trumpet; that knuckle was the most obvious sign of his affliction and would remain the only one until about 1981, when, returning to performing after a long layoff, every part of him, from his sunken cheeks to his shuffling gait, showed his pain. But that was almost two decades away, and in the meantime he kept up a stoic facade, as he had, in fact, from his adolescence on. For his disease was not recent. It is called "sickle-cell anemia," a congenital disease that afflicts members of the black race only, and he was born with it. When Davis first felt its effects in his joints, mildly, as a youngster, he started the lifelong pattern of working out in a gymnasium. "The reason I started doing it was to make my legs stronger," he said,[61] and his legs, at the hip joints, were most seriously affected. Exercise of the kind Davis has always done – skipping rope, punching bags, shadow boxing – speeds the circulation of the blood and thus may postpone the severity of the sickle-cell symptoms.

Davis's case is described medically as "mild," but he has felt pain for years. He is not alone. In the United States, one black baby in 400 suffers from it, and for many of those, the disease is acute, not mild, causing destruction of red blood cells, jaundice, and critical pains in the abdomen, back, and bones and leading to stunted or slow growth and usually early death. One American black in 10 carries the recessive gene for the disease.[62] In equatorial Africa, where it originated, the figures are probably much higher.

The disfiguring symptoms are caused by a physical mutation visible only under a microscope. Some red blood cells, normally saucer-shaped, are crescent-shaped, like "sickles" in the description of the rural Illinois doctor who identified the disease in 1904 and gave it the name that has stuck to it ever since. The sickling effect, in turn, results from defective hemoglobin, the protein in red blood cells responsible for carrying oxygen to all parts of the body, which lacks one of the hundreds of amino acids that do the work. The disease affects black people exclusively because the missing amino acid proved in some undetermined way to be a defense against malaria. After hundreds of generations in equatorial Africa, carriers of the sickle-shaped cell increased because they survived malaria epidemics, but away from malaria-infested environments, the defective cell becomes not only dysfunctional but also a crippler and a killer in its own right.

The elongated blood cells tend to become trapped in the small blood vessels of the body, blocking the flow of blood and causing local death due to oxygen deficiencies. In acutely affected children, the high concentration of defective cells affects both vital organs and joints, but in mild cases the cells affect joints mainly, especially the upper arm and hip, causing arthritis.[63] By 1962, when Miles Davis turned 36, the deterioration of his hip joints and other parts of his body was so advanced that he felt some pain all the time.

His music inevitably began to show the effects. He finally returned to the Columbia studios in late July 1962, more than sixteen months after his last studio date. Instead of returning with his quintet, which still did not include a regular saxophonist, he was back with Gil Evans and a large orchestra, but this time the result, perhaps predictably given the highly commercial impetus that lay behind the music, was something of a shambles. The recording that finally resulted was called *Quiet Nights*, and it attempted to cover the current craze for a Brazilian samba form called the bossa nova. Stan Getz started the trend with an album called *Jazz Samba* (on Verve) recorded in February, in which he and acoustic guitarist Charlie Byrd introduced some beautiful melodies by a Brazilian songwriter named Antonio Carlos Jobim. The album became an instant success, and in a branch of the music industry where successes of any kind were suddenly few and far between the race was on in several quarters to cover the same territory. Dozens of jazz-samba LPs were produced in the next months, none of them more successful than Getz's own; Getz even scored popular hits with an instrumental version of Jobim's *Desafinado* from the first album and a vocal version of *The Girl from Ipanema*, sung by Astrud Gilberto and including Jobim on piano, from *Getz/Gilberto* (Verve v-8545), his fourth bossa nova LP in a little more than a year and perhaps the best of them all. *Time* magazine reported at the beginning of 1963 that there were at least forty bossa nova albums on the market.[64]

Miles Davis and Gil Evans's entry into bossa nova began soon after Getz's first album was released, but they never completed the LP, and it was released, incomplete, only after another year had passed. It amounted to less than twenty-one minutes of almost motionless music filled out with another six minutes by Davis and rhythm trio. Compounding the half-hearted music of *Quiet Nights* were anonymous liner notes apologizing gratuitously for "Miles the man and Miles the dedicated and instinctive musician" – apologizing for his stage manner and the infrequency of his recordings – and claiming, with bald chicanery, that *Quiet Nights* "has been three years in the making, and is most likely the first 'Bossa Nova' music recorded in the country." It was not the first by several months; it was not the best by an even wider margin. The details are as follows:

Miles Davis with the Gil Evans Orchestra: Quiet Nights
Miles Davis, tpt; Steve Lacy, ss; other members of the orchestra unidentified;
Gil Evans, arr, cond. New York, 27 July 1962
Corcovado [*Quiet Nights/Slow Samba*]; *Aos pes da Cruz* [*Slow Samba*]
(both on Columbia CL 2106)

Similar personnel, same place, 13 August 1962
Song #1; *Wait till You See Her*
(both on Columbia CL 2106)

Some discographies list *New Rhumba* on the July session and give its issue details as *Miles Davis at Carnegie Hall* (Columbia CL 1812), but Brian Priestley (1982) notes that this LP was issued before the July recording date.

The music lacks the bright lyricism that gave bossa nova its charm and made it interesting in other hands, especially Stan Getz's. The arrangements seem to be little more than sketches, and they are played without any real conviction. *Song #1* builds a dramatic setting quite effectively, but its foreground remains empty. *Aos pes da Cruz* finds Davis noodling over an indiscriminate hum from the orchestra. Even *Corcovado*, one of Jobim's most striking melodies, falls flat in the brief, dirge-like treatment it gets here. On the issued take, *Corcovado*'s length is doubled by splicing onto it an alternate take of *Aos pes da Cruz*, and while the splicing is done so cleverly as to seem almost seamless the expedient adds nothing. The LP is mood music with no discernible mood, and neither Davis nor Evans was satisfied.

Before they could return to the studio for the remaining session, which would be no more successful, Davis and Evans collaborated on another, even stranger, recording project for Columbia. The managers, searching for a gimmick to bolster sales in their jazz department, came up with the idea of putting together a Christmas jazz album and commissioned their leading jazz artists to contribute one track each. Davis, understandably nonplussed, finally found a solution of sorts. He and Evans had spent some hours listening to an LP of winsome, jazzy vocals by a man named Bob Dorough. The LP, entitled *Devil May Care* (reissued in 1976 as *Yardbird Suite*, Bethlehem BCP-6023), had been around since 1957. It attracted a small but enthusiastic coterie of listeners at the time, and Davis first heard it by chance while visiting a friend. He liked it well enough to borrow it and play it for Evans. Its showiest tune is *Charles Yardbird Parker Was His Name*, Dorough's vocalization of *Yardbird Suite*, but it also includes a clever original called *Devil May Care* and several offbeat ballads, notably Hoagy Carmichael's *Baltimore Oriole* and Duke Ellington's *I Don't Mind*. The whole thing is sung and played with the kind of whimsical originality that, then as now, either wins over its listeners immediately or leaves them cold.

Davis was won over, and when he was faced with the necessity of coming up with a Christmas song he tracked down Dorough, then living in California, and called him up. Dorough, who had spent years on the fringe of the jazz and entertainment worlds in New York, Paris, and now Los Angeles, supporting himself by doing musical odd jobs in the long wait between club dates, could hardly believe – or readily understand – the gravelly voice at the other end of the line talking about Christmas carols in July. He remembers Davis exasperatedly asking, "What the fuck am I supposed to play for them? *White Christmas?*"[65]

He enjoined Dorough to write a song for him called *Blue Xmas*, and Dorough arrived in New York in August with an outline for that song and a couple of others under his arm for a date with Davis at the Columbia studio. The details are as follows:

Miles Davis with Bob Dorough
Miles Davis, tpt; Frank Rehak, tbn; Wayne Shorter, ts; Paul Chambers, b;
Jimmy Cobb, dms; William Correa (Willie Bobo), bongos; Bob Dorough, vcl;
Gil Evans, arr. New York, 21 August 1962.
Blue Xmas (To Whom It May Concern); Nothing Like You
(Blue Xmas on Columbia CL 1893, reissued on CBS [Fr] 62637; *Nothing Like You* on Columbia CL 2732 [1967])

Omit Dorough. Same place, 23 August 1962
Devil May Care
(on CBS [Fr] 62637 and Columbia C 32035 [1973])
A few notes on piano, by either Dorough or Evans, are heard at the beginning of *Blue Xmas.*

The small band assembled to play Evans's arrangements of Dorough's tunes includes Frank Rehak, a solid studio musician and capable jazz player who often played in Evans's studio orchestras; William Correa, known a little better by his stage name, Willie Bobo, who was probably the percussionist in the *Quiet Nights* band; and Wayne Shorter, still committed to Blakey's Jazz Messengers, who filled in because Davis's working band lacked a saxophonist. (Wynton Kelly's absence is not unusual, because Evans's arrangements for Davis had never included a piano.)

Blue Xmas is handsomely arranged, with effective ensemble voicings for the three horns and the bongos, obbligatos by Davis around Dorough's vocal, and a full solo chorus for Shorter that is worthy of, and indeed all but indistinguishable from, Coltrane. All of this can hardly hide the fact that *Blue Xmas* is an almost unsingable muddle of sophomoric cynicism. Dorough, an effective, quirky singer well versed in handling unusual lyrics, is stymied by couplets like these:

It's a time when the greedy
Give a dime to the needy ...
Lots of hungry, homeless children in your own backyards
While you're very, very, very busy addressing twenty
    zillion Christmas cards ...

(Dorough does not have to bear full blame for the lyric; Davis is listed as the co-composer.) Most seriously, the dark sentiments of the song simply ring false when intoned in Dorough's huckleberry talking-singing style.

Nothing Like You, the other new song he brought with him, is more in his line. Subtitled *An Extravagant Love Song* when Dorough finally got a chance to record it on his own in 1976 (on his own label, Laissez-Faire 2), the lyric, by Dorough's occasional collaborator Fran Landesman, piles up praise for the lover ("Nothing like you has ever been seen before / Nothing like you existed in days of yore...") until it amasses a heap of euphoria. In Evans's arrangement, Dorough sings from start to finish over chords held by the three horns, with no instrumental breaks at all. The brief recording made an unexpected, and unexplained, appearance as a filler at the end of an LP by Davis's 1967 quintet (*Sorcerer*), a context so alien to its high spirits that it has furrowed listeners' brows ever since.

The most successful use of Dorough's music by Davis and Evans came on *Devil May Care*, the bright song from Dorough's Bethlehem LP which, unluckily for Dorough, dispenses with his lyric altogether and is played as a straight, uptempo instrumental. Dorough's original arrangement had featured a trumpeter prominently, and Evans's arrangement capitalizes on that by turning it into a real romp for Davis, who plays variations on the melody, and also for Shorter, who sounds completely confident on his chorus as Davis's saxophonists seldom had since Coltrane.

More than two months passed before Davis and Evans returned to the studios to continue their work on *Quiet Nights*, but in the interim, almost incredibly, they had done nothing at all to strengthen the concept they were working on, and the results were, if anything, even more insipid. The details are as follows:

Miles Davis with the Gil Evans Orchestra: Quiet Nights
Miles Davis, tpt; orchestra unidentified except for Ernie Royal, tpt; Frank
Rehak, tbn; Jimmy Buffington, John Barrows, frh; Janet Putnam, harp; Jimmy
Cobb, dms. New York, 6 November 1962
Once Upon a Summertime; Song #2
(both on Columbia CL 2106)
Most discographies list Elvin Jones, perc, but similarities between the bongo
playing on *Nothing Like You* (recorded August 1962) and on *Once Upon a
Summertime* suggest that the player could be William Correa.

Song #2 consists of a twelve-bar phrase, which is repeated by the
orchestra several times, and Davis, sounding small on muted trumpet,
playing the same phrase once; the whole performance lasts about one
and a half minutes. *Once Upon a Summertime* somehow fails to
become bossa nova at all in Evans's arrangement, and the bongo player
heard patting away behind the orchestra seems to be playing a different
arrangement from the others. (Two years later Evans tried again with
Once Upon a Summertime, including it among his arrangements for
vocalist Astrud Gilberto on a Verve pop album [v-8643]; Gilberto, who
scored some bossa nova hits with Stan Getz by projecting innocence in a
frail, off-key voice, projects little more than sour notes on Evans's
arrangement.)
   Quiet Nights was far from finished in any real sense, but Davis and
Evans gave up on it. They did not return to the studios either to revise or
extend or augment what they had already recorded. They would
probably have forgotten it completely if Columbia had not released it
the following year.
   The critical response was predictable. Leonard Feather placed the
blame for its release squarely on the company; "Columbia, despairing of
ever luring Davis and Evans back into a studio together," he wrote,
"scraped the bottom of its corporate barrel and came up with an LP called
Quiet Nights."[66] Others saw in it all the worst tendencies of their work
together. It "exposed the partnership's weaknesses," Max Harrison
said,[67] and Martin Williams made the same point less tersely: "Evans
has frequently provided a fascinating and effective setting for Davis's
improvisations. On the other hand, it seems to me that Evans does not
utilize the rhythmic idiom of modern jazz. And in his approach there is
the implicit danger that one may end up providing only a succession of
beefed-up, quasi-impressionist color-harmonies and background for

Davis's horn, a danger which is fully encountered in some selections of the languid Davis-Evans LP called *Quiet Nights*."[68] Williams's criticism seems to lay the blame unfairly on Evans, and both he and Harrison imply that the very existence of *Quiet Nights* somehow tarnishes the previous collaborations, but regardless of the details their overall impression was unanimously seconded.

"They should have never released it. It was just half an album," Evans said, and then, typically, he qualified even that mild complaint: "But I guess they had to."[69] Davis was not so mild. He refused to talk to Teo Macero for two and a half years. When Gregg Hall asked him why, he said: "'Cause he fucked up *Quiet Nights* ... In the studio he was busy looking at the score, saying, 'Jesus, you use these chords.' I said, 'Man, just record it and don't worry about no chords.' You know what I mean, instead of looking at the score, he should have just brought out the sound. He fucked it up." Davis complained to Goddard Lieberson, Columbia's president, but he backed off when Lieberson asked him if he wanted Macero fired.[70]

Macero continued producing for Columbia, including some of Davis's records. "I was working on his projects as if he were walking in the door every day," Macero says. "Records just kept coming out. I was sending him the records, but if I got a response or not was immaterial. I didn't care because I knew they were right and I knew he would like them."[71] But for the time being, Macero had little contact with Davis's projects. From the time of the second session for *Quiet Nights*, in November 1962, until late in October 1966, a period only two weeks less than four years, Davis recorded only three titles – one afternoon's work – in Columbia's New York studios, where Macero was stationed. In the same period, Columbia released five LPs by Miles Davis's bands, and CBS affiliates in Germany and Japan released two more, but apart from those three tracks – about half an LP – all the music was recorded either at live performances or in Columbia's Los Angeles studios. Macero is credited as producer on three of the seven LPs.

Davis's inability to turn out recordings that came close to the level he had maintained since he first signed with Columbia in 1955 was now obvious. Since the pair of LPs that had been put together from the Blackhawk engagement, Columbia had offered Davis's fans only the disappointing edition of the Carnegie Hall concert, one track of Christmas humbug, and some motionless bossa nova. Stretched out over a period of two years, those releases provided little sustenance for Davis's following. His personal appearances, which continued to be lethargic and became even more infrequent, gave them even less. Inured by success and bothered by pain, Davis seemed indifferent to fans and foes alike. At the beginning of 1963, the year in which Davis would turn 37, he appeared to be ready to assume the mantle of elder statesman, along with Dizzy Gillespie, Thelonious Monk, and his other mentors from the bebop revolution, or perhaps even to join Sonny Rollins in premature semi-retirement.

As it turned out, he did neither. His resolve to keep on playing at the head of his own working band beat back his indifference when he faced what might have been the final crisis. His rhythm section, the only stable element in his band for the past two years, quit the quintet together at the close of 1962. By then, their departure seemed little more than a formality. Because of the sporadic bookings with Davis, they had already set themselves up as the Wynton Kelly Trio for some club dates and record sessions. They simply decided to stop being a splinter group and work full-time as the Wynton Kelly Trio, sometimes collaborating with guitarist Wes Montgomery in bookings where they received equal billing. As a trio, they were well known, well established, and very good – much better, in fact, than they appeared to be in most of their recent work with Davis, which had been suffused by stale familiarity.

For Davis, their departure compounded his immediate problems. Now he needed to recruit not merely a saxophonist, as he had almost semi-annually since Coltrane's departure in 1961, but a whole band. More than that, their resignations finally severed the links with the bands with which he had made his finest music. All three men had been associated with him for so long that their presence was taken for granted, not only by the fans but by Davis. Faced with deteriorating health and, at least as crucial, with the kind of complacency born of commercial success – which seemed to cling to him even when he was giving less than his best efforts – he might easily have coasted, headlining concert packages with other 'all stars' when he chose to and devising recording projects with Gil Evans and others.

Instead, he set about rebuilding his band. It would not be easy, starting from scratch, and it would not be fast, but in less than two years he would be leading a new band in a new style that many observers would laud as a rival for his quintet and sextet of the 1950s. Certainly it would be the best small band in the land. In the interim, he had to shake off his complacency and go through a period unlike any he had been through since 1954–5, a period of actively scouting young musicians, aggressively recruiting them for his band, even when it caused some friction with his old colleagues such as Jackie McLean and Art Blakey, and firing men who did not have the mettle he was looking for. It proved an effective antidote for everything that ailed him, as piece by piece, musician by musician, he inched toward the new order, in his band and in his music.

10

So Near, So Far
1963–4

Art forms require [father figures] just as much as people do, usually opting for
innovators who are also guardians of tradition, creative yet holding a watching
brief for the past. Louis Armstrong was the first, then Duke Ellington ... To
suggest that Miles Davis has now taken over – from Ellington more than
anybody else – will stir up protest, but only from jazz fans who are blind to both
his innate conservatism and his revolutionary fervour.   Charles Fox

The defection of the rhythm trio at the end of 1962 seemed to catch
Davis by surprise. They had given their notice – had in fact indicated
that they were planning to leave together months before – and he had
ignored it, assuming they would show up to work with him now just as
they had so many times before. Partly to give them more work, he had
accepted several bookings in eastern cities for January and in California
for February, March, and April, starting at the Blackhawk in San
Francisco.

When the commitments had to be fulfilled he found himself without
a band. He failed to appear for the first engagement, a weekend booking
in Philadelphia, and the promoter sued him for expenses, eventually
winning a settlement of $8,000. He canceled the next engagement in
Detroit at the last minute, and the promoter there also launched a suit
for expenses. He tried to persuade the rhythm section to return for a
concert in St. Louis, and he showed up for it himself, claiming that it
was the absence of Wynton Kelly and Paul Chambers that forced him to
cancel, but the promoters there launched a suit against him too.

As the opening date for his engagement at the Blackhawk neared, he
faced the fact that he would never be able to coax the rhythm trio to
rejoin him, and he telephoned the owner just a few days before the date

to postpone the opening by a week. Davis then got down to the real business of trying to assemble a new band.

Ironically, the saxophone chair was the only one more or less settled. For a club date in New York at the end of the year, Davis had used a young alto player named Frank Strozier, a brilliant technician whose style derived from Charlie Parker's, although Strozier was conversant with everything after Parker as well. He invited him to join the band for the California tour, making a start on the recruiting job.

Davis soon discovered that in hiring Strozier he had tapped a small network of able, young musicians who hailed from Memphis, Tennessee. Strozier eagerly recommended a piano player, Harold Mabern, a high-school friend who had left Memphis with him for Chicago in 1954, when Strozier was 17 and Mabern 18, played beside him there in a band called MJT+3, organized by Walter Perkins, a Chicago drummer, and moved to New York with him in 1959.

The new bassist came highly recommended by everyone Davis asked. He was Ron Carter, a Detroiter like Paul Chambers. Carter had earned a bachelor's degree from the Eastman School of Music in Rochester, New York, and arrived in New York to take his master's degree from the Manhattan School of Music in 1960–1. He kept busy working as a freelancer in pit bands and orchestras as well as jazz groups. He had toured Europe for three weeks with Julian Adderley's band, primarily as the accompanist for Adderley's regular bassist, Sam Jones, when he played a cello feature. After graduating in June 1961, he gained attention playing with Randy Weston, Herbie Mann, Bobby Timmons, and Thelonious Monk.

Carter was working regularly at the Half Note in a quartet led by Art Farmer and Jim Hall, with Ben Riley on drums, when Davis approached him. Carter turned him down because he felt committed to Farmer and Hall, but Davis went to Farmer and persuaded him to let Carter join his band that night at the New York try-out. "It was the most important turning-point of my career," Carter told Louis-Victor Mialy, "and maybe of my life." Like Strozier, he was 25 when he joined Davis's band in the first months of 1963.

Davis surrounded himself not only with a complement of new men, but with men who were more than a decade younger than he was. It was a striking change of direction for him. For the New York try-out of the new band before heading west, Davis borrowed Jackie McLean's drummer, a 17-year-old whiz kid from Boston named Tony Williams. Williams could not join Davis for the West Coast tour because of his commitments with McLean, but Davis knew that Williams was the drummer he wanted for his band.

During the try-out, Davis expanded the band to a sextet, adding tenor saxophonist George Coleman, who had been playing regularly with organist Wild Bill Davis in one of the many organ-tenor duos that had found favor in bars at the time. Coleman, who had played John Coltrane's tenor in some late-night sets by Davis's bands a few years before, was less polished than Strozier and Carter, and more emotive, playing ebullient jazz with a heavy tone that could hold its own night after night alongside a Hammond organ. He also was part of the Memphis connection, having attended high school with Strozier and Mabern, who probably recommended him to Davis. He eventually found favor with Davis as they never did, outlasting both of them in Davis's band. (Two other members of the Memphis group were trumpeter Booker Little, one year younger than Strozier, and pianist Phineas Newborn, five years older; their continuing presence in jazz might have elevated Memphis as a modern jazz breeding ground comparable to Detroit a decade earlier, but Little died of uremia in 1961 when he was 23 and Newborn was hampered by psychiatric problems that prevented him from working regularly and fulfilling his enormous potential.)

When Davis reached California, he recruited Frank Butler, a Los Angeles freelancer, as his drummer. With so many changes after such a lengthy period of relative stability, Davis found the adjustments hard to take. He felt uncomfortable soloing over Mabern's accompaniment. He also felt uneasy about extending the solo space to accommodate the extra horn. "I think what he really wanted was a quintet," Coleman told Andrew Sussman, "'cause he used to always complain about the lengthy solos. And what he would do, he'd say (in a whisper), 'Hey, Frank, go tell George he's playin' too long'; and then he'd come to me and say the same thing – 'Tell Frank he's playin' too long.'"[1] Under these circumstances, the sextet could not last very long.

Near the end of the Los Angeles engagement, Davis was scheduled to record in the Columbia studios, but he used only Ron Carter and Frank Butler at the recording session. George Coleman turned up on a title issued several years later and probably played on the other titles which are so far unissued and unidentified. (At the end of *Summer Night*, Davis is heard saying, "I'm gonna play another one, Teo, but I want to hear that one first"; the session almost certainly included versions of *Seven Steps to Heaven* and *Joshua*.)

Mabern was replaced at the recording session and the final Los Angeles club date by Victor Feldman, an English pianist who also plays vibraphone and drums. Feldman had first earned a reputation with a few American jazz fans during the war, when he was not yet a teenager, as the drummer in a band led by his older brothers at his father's London pub. The band attracted all kinds of servicemen posted in England, including alto saxophonist Art Pepper, who sat in with it every time he could get leave. Feldman moved to the United States in 1955, when he was 21, and made a strong impression on several people, including Davis, as a piano player and vibist. "Why does everyone here apologize for British musicians?" Davis asked John Martin in 1960. "You can play jazz in Britain. You've got some good men here ... Victor Feldman, he's good. I told Cannonball [Adderley] to get him. He's playing with Cannonball right now."[2] Feldman played in Adderley's band until 1961, including the European tour with Ron Carter in the band, and then moved to Los Angeles where he has worked ever since on film scoring and studio work with only occasional forays into jazz.

One of these forays, perhaps the most auspicious of Feldman's career, was in Columbia's Hollywood studios with Miles Davis. Davis not only used him as his piano player at the Los Angeles sessions, but also solicited two compositions from him, *Seven Steps to Heaven* and *Joshua*, which he added immediately to the working repertoire. If he was hoping to lure Feldman away from Hollywood and back into the jazz life, he was disappointed, but in Feldman's playing for the recording session and in his contributions to the repertoire Davis proved his point about Feldman's ability. The details are as follows:

Miles Davis with Victor Feldman: Seven Steps to Heaven
Miles Davis, tpt; George Coleman, ts (on *So Near So Far*); Victor Feldman, pno; Ron Carter, b; Frank Butler, dms. Los Angeles, 16 April 1963
I Fall in Love Too Easily; Baby Won't You Please Come Home; So Near So Far; Basin Street Blues
(*So Near So Far* is on Columbia KC2 36472 [1981]; the other three titles are on Columbia CL 2051.)

Same personnel, without Coleman. Same place, 17 April 1963
Summer Night
(on *Quiet Nights*, Columbia CL 2106)
The second session probably includes unissued versions of *Joshua* and *Seven Steps to Heaven* as well.

While Davis's band has the appearance of an all-star group, he obviously recognized its limitations when the results were in. Only the slow ballads were released at the time. Anything played faster than a medium tempo was re-recorded a month later in New York with a different piano player and drummer, and the New York versions of *So Near So Far*, *Joshua*, and *Seven Steps to Heaven* were coupled with the Hollywood ballads *I Fall in Love Too Easily*, *Baby Won't You Please Come Home*, and *Basin Street Blues* to make up the LP *Seven Steps to Heaven* (Columbia CL 2051).

Another of the Hollywood ballads, *Summer Night*, filled out the second side of *Quiet Nights*; it is a haunting ballad and a superb example of Davis's ability to evoke a quiet mood, but its inclusion on *Quiet Nights* could not rescue that LP from the critical blast. *I Fall in Love Too Easily* seeks the same quiet mood less successfully, with Davis's pauses in the melody line interrupting the flow of melody and leaving the impression of formlessness.

Baby Won't You Please Come Home and *Basin Street Blues* are much more successful. Davis reached back into the history of American song for these titles, both composed by black songwriters in the early decades of the century. *Baby Won't You Please Come Home*, credited to Clarence Williams, a controversial figure in early jazz who allegedly took advantage of Bessie Smith and other black performers by shaving their royalties and laying claim to their songs, is played as a languid ballad that shifts into a lilting blues after Davis's introduction of the melody. *Basin Street Blues*, written by Spencer Williams (no relation to Clarence), was part of the standard repertoire of New Orleans bands in the earliest days of jazz history and subsequently passed into the repertoires of revival bands. Traditionally, it was played as a medium-tempo paean to the city that the musicians had left behind them when they moved north along the Mississippi:

Basin Street is the street
Where the élite always meet
In New Orleans
My land of dreams ...

Davis plays it as a kind of requiem, slow and mournful, emphasizing the element of nostalgia which in traditional versions exists only as an undertone. His deliberate, wispy tone makes a striking reinterpretation of the content of the original song.

Of the remaining titles recorded in Hollywood only *So Near So Far* has been released, belatedly. Compared to the version re-recorded in New York and released with these ballads, the Hollywood version is much more straightforward but by no means inferior.

Davis's working sextet on his California tour, with Strozier on alto and Mabern on piano, was destined to go unrecorded. As soon as he returned to New York, Davis quickly set about assembling yet another new band. Only George Coleman and Ron Carter kept their places.

Young Tony Williams came in as the drummer. "When Miles asked me to play with him, it felt like the most natural thing in the world for me," Williams said. "I was prepared. I knew all of his music. I had studied everything he had done up to that point. I felt deep down that I was without question the best drummer for the job."[3] Davis agreed, and from the very beginning of their association he worked with Williams closely, as he had with Philly Joe Jones at the beginning of their association almost ten years earlier. "I made Tony play his bass drum, because he didn't play it at all," he told Arthur Taylor, another former drummer in Davis's band who published a volume of "musician-to-musician" interviews years later. "And he didn't play his sock cymbals, so I started him on the sock cymbals. I made him play the bass drum even, and all the rest he had."[4]

Besides his remarkable technique, Williams brought into the band an infectious enthusiasm for life in general and for Davis's music in particular. It shone through in his playing and seemed to move everyone on both sides of the bandstand. He made his tastes known to everyone, and they included a boundless affection for the music on *Milestones*, the first LP Davis made with his great sextet of 1958. "That's a smoking record," Williams said. "That's the definitive jazz album. If you want to know what jazz is, listen to that album. That has all you'd ever want to hear. It embodies the spirit of everyone who plays jazz."[5] The music on the *Milestones* LP had been set aside by Davis by the time Williams joined his band, and Davis's composition *Milestones* had never been included in his working repertoire, even though it is among his most interesting and memorable compositions. Now, with Williams's enthusiasm urging him on, Davis finally began playing *Milestones* in public. Its resuscitation would be only one of the first, and the most obvious, signs of Williams's influence. There would soon be more, and in all of them Williams would serve his new bandleader superbly. "The first music I fell in love with was the music that Miles Davis wrote," he told Julie Coryell. "I just heard other things in that music and liked it." Some

Victor Feldman (Bernie Senensky)

Miles Davis with Ron Carter and Tony Williams (Don Schlitten, courtesy of *Down Beat*)

Tony Williams with Miles Davis (Heye Wessenbergh, courtesy of *Down Beat*)

of those "other things" had been hidden in Davis's music for the past few years, but they would not stay hidden for long with Williams around.

Davis in turn became an indefatigable champion of his new, young drummer. "Tony Williams can swing and play his ass off," Davis told Don DeMicheal. "Tony Williams is a motherfucker ... I don't think there's a drummer alive can do what Tony Williams can do ... Tony plays to the sound, and what he plays to the sound is real slick shit. He might play a different tempo for each sound."[6]

Williams was only a few years older than Miles Davis's sons. He was born in Boston in 1945, and his father was Tillmon Williams, a jazz saxophonist who stayed close to Boston throughout his career. When Tony was only 10, his father set up a drum set for him in the attic, showed him a few rudiments, and watched as the boy outgrew his home-made lessons almost immediately. Luckily, a superb jazz drummer, Alan Dawson, lived just a couple of blocks away, and Tillmon Williams often played with Dawson in bands around the city. The elder Williams dropped around and asked Dawson to start teaching his son, but Dawson had never done any teaching or even thought about doing any and appeared reluctant. Williams asked him to listen to the boy. "He took me up to the attic where Tony, who was eleven but looked about nine, was seated behind this set of drums," Dawson remembers. "Tillmon picked up his horn to blow, and this baby started to cook, playing beautiful time and fills. Believe it or not, this youngster had good time, good taste, and good feeling – everything but chops."[7]

Dawson became his teacher and, incidentally, launched himself on a new career, eventually joining the faculty of Boston's prestigious Berklee School of Music. Under Dawson's tutelage, his first student's natural gifts flourished. Williams began playing publicly in Boston a few years later, and in 1962, when he was 17, he moved to New York as the drummer in Jackie McLean's band. From the beginning, Williams showed little patience with the traditional timekeeping aspect of the drummer's role, preferring instead to let his feeling for the mood or melody of the piece guide the tempo. That approach would have been highly unconventional, an abberation even, just a few years earlier, but Williams's tastes were partly shaped during the first burst of free form playing, and in Boston, the home of Cecil Taylor, Sam Rivers, and other early free form players as well as the seat of the progressive New England Conservatory, Williams felt the effects of the freeing of form and incorporated it into his style almost subconsciously.

For a lot of older musicians, Williams's style caused havoc, but for Davis, himself an amateur drummer, it was a perfect challenge. "A lot of musicians can't play with him," Davis told Arthur Taylor, "because they're used to playing on the first beat and he accents on the second and third beats if you're in 4/4 time. Sometimes he might accent on any beat. And he might play 5/4 time for a while, and you've ... got to know about rhythms and the feel of different rhythms in order to play with him, because he might haul off and do anything rhythmically. If you don't have any knowledge of time and different time changes, he'll lose you."[8]

Williams's ability and his unquenchable enthusiasm pervaded Davis's performances from the beginning, and Davis's admiration for what he was doing sometimes made it hard to tell who was leading whom in the band. Summing up Williams's contribution years later, Barry McRae wrote: "Never before had a percussionist exerted so much personal influence on the overall sound of a Davis group. Philly Joe Jones had never been a boring back-room boy but his role had been to provide colouration in the ensemble and rhythmic impetus to the solo voices. This he had done brilliantly without ever moving out of the rhythm section ... In musical terms [Williams] had become a powerful voice on equal footing with the horns but more significantly he had introduced an intensity that spoke of the avant garde movement in a way that Davis and his sidemen had previously avoided almost consciously."[9] He was only the first of Davis's young sidemen who would import the influence of the new wave, sometimes subtly and sometimes not so subtly, into his band.

Davis's new piano player was Herbie Hancock, a Chicagoan who had just turned 23 when he was hired. Davis had met him a year earlier, not long before Wynton Kelly announced that he was quitting his band, but if Davis was impressed by Hancock's playing at that first meeting he did not show it by renewing his acquaintance when Kelly left. The meeting had taken place at Davis's house when trumpeter Donald Byrd arrived one evening with Hancock in tow and introduced him as his new piano player. Hancock had come to New York as a member of Byrd's band early in 1961 and had played regularly with him ever since without attracting much attention from reviewers. At their first meeting, Davis asked him to play something and Hancock sat down and played a ballad. Afterwards, Davis said to Byrd, "He's got a nice touch."

More than a year later, in May 1963, Hancock was surprised by a telephone call from Davis asking him to come over to his house.

Hancock later described the events of the next three days to Leonard Feather in *From Satchmo to Miles*. He spent them rehearsing Davis's repertoire with George Coleman, Ron Carter, and Tony Williams, while Davis apparently listened to them on the house intercom. Only on the third day did Davis join the group and then only briefly, but at the end of the day he reappeared to tell them to go the Columbia studios the next day. Hancock told Feather: "I said, 'Wait a minute – what? I thought you were auditioning ... Does that mean I'm in the group or what?' He said, "You're making the record, ain't you?'"[10] Hancock became a mainstay of Davis's working band for the next five years.

The new Miles Davis Quintet assembled at the Columbia studios to complete the recordings begun in California. The details are as follows:

Miles Davis Quintet: Seven Steps to Heaven
Miles Davis, tpt; George Coleman, ts; Herbie Hancock, pno; Ron Carter, b; Tony Williams, dms. New York, 14 May 1963
Seven Steps to Heaven; So Near So Far; Joshua
(all on Columbia CL 2051)

The recording session is marked by brisk, confident playing for the most part, making a good debut for the new band and a strong portent of even better playing to come. The one noticeable lapse comes on *So Near So Far*, which has been almost completely reworked from the arrangement recorded in Hollywood. The original version was played in 4/4 time with the song-like melody played by the trumpet and tenor in unison, where this version is played in 6/8 time with Davis's statement of the melody accompanied by Coleman's arpeggios. In the opening ensemble, Coleman sounds ill at ease, and his arpeggios come out like awkward practice scales; the closing ensemble, following solos by Davis, Coleman, and Hancock, corrects the problem, suggesting that another take might have been all that was needed to bring this title up to the standard of the rest of the session. However, this take preserves Hancock's most effective solo of the day, an easy recitation in block chords which Davis had long favored in his pianists.

Joshua, Victor Feldman's composition, and *Seven Steps to Heaven*, by Feldman and Davis, introduce two new modal pieces into Davis's book, and both also entered the working repertoire immediately. *Joshua* sounds vaguely like a reorganization of the vamp from *So What*, and *Seven Steps to Heaven* recalls the declamatory opening of *Milestones*, but both are distinctive in their details and make welcome additions to the repertoire. The arrangements make good use of the new talent surrounding Davis. Both are introduced by a line from Carter, and on *Joshua* Hancock's piano cues the repetitive theme, while on *Seven Steps to Heaven* Williams's drums play fills around the simple, seven-note theme stated by trumpet, tenor, and bass. Davis leaves no doubt about his feelings for his young sidemen, alloting Hancock a solo on all titles, and giving Williams a prominence that he had not allowed his drummer in studio recordings since the days of Philly Joe Jones. Williams even gets a solo chorus on *Seven Steps to Heaven*, and although he is less adventurous on both his solo and his accompaniment than he would be when he settled into the band, this playing is solid enough to serve notice that an important new drummer was emerging.

Davis knew the potential of his new band and filled his calendar with concert and club engagements. During one of the band's first stints, at the Showboat in Philadelphia, while New York suffered the first of a series of 'brown-outs,' a widespread electrical failure that dimmed the lights, stopped elevators, and made walking in the city more perilous than it was in ordinary night-time circumstances, Teo Macero escaped the city by organizing an impromptu excursion to Philadelphia with some friends to give them a preview of the new band.[11] For the young sidemen, Macero's cheering from a stage-side table in a distant club bolstered confidence, and perhaps even Davis took some heart from it.

Soon afterward, Columbia released *Quiet Nights*, and Davis blamed Macero. He refused to enter Columbia's studios at all for the rest of 1963 and all of 1964, a period of twenty-two months. Columbia was forced, as it had been in 1961, to set up its recording equipment at Davis's performances in order to keep its catalog current. As a result, there is no lack of material by the new band on record, but there is a lack of the kind of careful material, including new compositions and new arrangements, that Davis reserved for his studio sessions. The full schedule of playing dates did nothing to help Davis's health, which continued to deteriorate alarmingly, to the point where at times he could not bend his joints or walk at all immediately after rising from sleep. The few people who were close enough to know about his health problems – his wife, his manager, and his sidemen – knew that some attempt would soon have to be made to correct his condition.

The quintet's major projects for the summer involved jazz festivals, which were springing up all over the world as the flagship festival at Newport moved into its ninth successful year. Davis had the quintet booked to play both the festival at Antibes, France, in July and the one at

Monterey, California, in August, and the round of engagements on the club circuit helped the band pull together. One stop was Davis's home territory, St. Louis, and a part of a set played there was later released on record. The details are as follows:

Miles Davis Quintet: In St. Louis
Miles Davis, tpt; George Coleman, ts (except *I Thought about You*); Herbie Hancock, pno; Ron Carter, b; Tony Williams, dms. Jazz Villa, St. Louis, June 1963
I Thought about You; All Blues / The Theme; Seven Steps to Heaven
(all on VGM 0003 [1981])
I Thought about You is apparently missing the first eight bars of the melody; *Seven Steps to Heaven* is missing the opening theme.

This unexpected half-hour of music preserved from the first days of the new quintet is interesting mainly for the obvious enjoyment the sidemen were finding in playing together. On *I Thought about You*, the slow ballad recorded by Davis in 1961 and now brought into the working repertoire, Hancock and Carter are featured in consecutive solos that sound at times like a duo instead, so rich is the comping of one for the other. On *All Blues*, Williams obviously relishes playing the 6/8 meter, especially behind Coleman's long and lively solo, which Williams propels uninhibitedly. On *Seven Steps to Heaven*, both Coleman and Hancock fool with the tempo, which has accelerated considerably from the recorded version of a month before, as is usual in Davis's club performances; Coleman and Hancock both halve the tempo at unexpected moments, and Carter and Williams scramble behind them to keep pace.

The next month the quintet were in France, where they played a concert in Paris on 25 July and starred in the Jazz Festival at Antibes from 26 to 31 July. They were recorded in action at the festival, this time officially rather than informally as in St. Louis.

The Antibes recording was produced by the French corporate arm of Columbia's mother company, CBS, from the transcription of the French national radio-televsion network. Since the mid-1950s, industries had been expanding internationally at an alarming rate, creating multinational giants beyond the purview of governments and far removed from individual consumers. CBS, long a dominant corporation in the American entertainment industry, with branches in motion pictures, radio, and television as well as records, was expanding by the mid-1960s not only into publishing and other areas in the United States, but also into the global entertainment industry, in France, Germany, and Japan, where it eventually linked up with Sony, itself a multinational corporation.

For Columbia in New York, French CBS's record of Davis at Antibes represented one of the first realizations that its recording artists had become multinational properties too. For Davis, recording in France maintained his resolution to stay out of the New York studios. While the record produced by French CBS was released almost simultaneously by Columbia, later recordings of Davis by CBS branches in Germany and Japan would be completely independent, even when the recordings were mastered from tapes produced in the United States. Davis's shift from Columbia's roll of exclusive recording artists to a multinational property was an insignificant ripple in the global shift of economic power.

For jazz fans, the much more important fact was that French CBS caught Davis and his quintet in a brilliant performance at Antibes, a sparkling Mediterranean resort town in the region of the Riviera. The details are as follows:

Miles Davis Quintet: At Antibes
Miles Davis, tpt; George Coleman, ts; Herbie Hancock, pno; Ron Carter, b; Tony Williams, dms. Festival du Jazz, Antibes, 26–31 July 1963
Autumn Leaves; Milestones; Joshua; All of You; Walkin'
(all on CBS [Fr] 62390 and on Columbia CL 2183)
The CBS release was titled *Miles à Antibes*, the Columbia release *Miles Davis in Europe*. Transcriptions of ten more titles by the Davis Quintet at Antibes exist but have not yet been issued.

In every respect, this release seemed newsworthy for jazz fans. French CBS managed to pack a little more than an hour of music onto the two sides of the LP, so that even its most trivial aspect was a revelation to North American listeners, accustomed to fewer than forty minutes per LP. For those who could get hold of the French pressing, the sound seemed cleaner than they were accustomed to on American pressings of the day. The whole package went a long way toward redressing the twenty-seven minutes of torpid music presented on *Quiet Nights*. Here was a renewal of spirit in Davis's music. Even the working repertoire had been expanded. Besides Davis's perennials, *All of You* (first recorded in 1958, and played frequently ever since) and *Walkin'* (first recorded in

1954, and played nightly ever since), there were the new *Joshua* (recorded two months earlier and not till then issued) and two startling resuscitations: *Autumn Leaves* (recorded by Davis in a band nominally led by Julian Adderley in 1958) and *Milestones* (recorded by the sextet in 1958, and never brought into the working repertoire until this time).

Milestones seemed especially welcome, as one of Davis's finest compositions, neglected by him for more than five years while several other musicians, notably Bill Evans in a trio arrangement (on Milestone 47002) and Gerald Wilson in a big band arrangement (on Pacific Jazz PJ-61), had kept on exploring its modal beauties. Tony Williams was by no means alone in counting it among his favorite compositions, and at the first familiar notes of its fanfare the audience at Antibes burst into applause, a reaction that dozens of Davis's fans shared when they put this record on their turntables a few months afterward.

The recording also clearly established George Coleman as Davis's most effective saxophonist since Coltrane. Coleman shows none of Coltrane's inclinations for teasing apart the formal structure of a song as he plays it, but at his best he comes close to conveying the impression of raw power that Coltrane had, bringing back into Davis's band the basic contrast between the two horns. Coleman also sustains long solos that are seldom repetitive and always swing.

But the essential revelation of this record was the dominance of the new and virtually unknown drummer, Tony Williams. He used his brushes sensitively behind Davis on the two ballads, *Autumn Leaves* and *All of You*, but he clearly preferred the sticks, switching to them as soon as Davis had finished playing and sticking with them until he returned to play the out-chorus. On the faster tempos of *Milestones* and *Joshua*, he chattered along behind the soloists filling all the spaces musically and sometimes threatening to take charge altogether if the soloist did not rise above his level. On the swinger, *Walkin'*, Williams simply thundered along, pushing the other players until they seemingly had to clear out of his way for an extended drum solo, a rare enough occurrence in Davis's music, and removing himself temporarily to allow Coleman and Ron Carter enough room for a duet. The Antibes LP was not Williams's recording debut, but it provided the first revelation of his power.

Williams could make Davis forget his physical suffering and play at close to the top of his form again, as he showed at Antibes, especially in his busy solo on *Milestones* that suggests he was as pleased as everyone else to find himself working over that old composition again. As soon as

Davis heard the tapes from Antibes he knew that his opinion of Williams's talents would very soon be widely shared. "When the test pressings of this album ... reached Miles, he almost wore them out," Ralph J. Gleason wrote in the liner notes for the American release. "It was not a happy time for him in many ways, but these test pressings made it better. I can think of no higher compliment than to point out that Miles called from Los Angeles one morning just to play a passage over several times in which Tony Williams did something particularly exciting."[12] The record met with great critical success, winning kudos as the jazz album of the year in *Jazz Magazine* and other citations when it was released in 1964.

Williams quickly became the most conspicuous young jazzman around. Later that summer, at the Monterey Jazz Festival in California, the Davis quintet were waiting for their scheduled appearance when one of the bands booked for the previous day showed up without a drummer. The band consisted of guitarist Elmer Snowden, 63 and all but forgotten apart from the fact that he had led a band in the 1920s that the young Duke Ellington had taken over, and bassist Pops Foster, 71, and someone suggested, presumably in jest, that Tony Williams should fill in. "He was seventeen and he had never heard of either Elmer Snowden or Pops Foster," Ralph J. Gleason reported some years later, "but he played with them that afternoon and, since Tony is now – and was even when he was seventeen – a musical genius, the result was spectacular. It was one of the finest moments of that whole Monterey festival."[13]

The festival came at the beginning of an extended stay in California for Davis in the fall of 1963. He spent his time working with Gil Evans on the score for a play called *Time of the Barracuda*, starring Laurence Harvey and Elaine Stritch. "Miles and I went to a hotel in L.A., on the Strip, called Chateau Marmont, an old time movie star place," Evans said. "We moved in – we each took as suite and we had two pianos, one in his suite and one in mine. He'd come to my place and we'd play things and I'd go to his and we'd play things. We worked on it for quite a while, a couple of weeks every day. Concentrated – with the script."[14] Harvey came in and consulted with them, and so did the author and director. Davis and Evans finished the score, a suite cued to the script with pieces lasting from forty-five seconds to four minutes, and recorded it at Columbia's Hollywood studio, probably produced by Irving Townsend, with an orchestra comprised of three french horns, bass trombone, three flutes, and rhythm.

Then the problems began. The San Francisco opening was postponed when the musicians' union ruled out the taped score and required a pit band. Then Harvey, a gifted classical actor and notorious misogynist, and Stritch began feuding. The play folded. "Columbia still has the tape," Evans said, and then he shrugged, "It will come out some day."

Evans has recorded some themes from *Time of the Barracuda* on his infrequent LPs. So far the only hints of the collaboration are his 1964 recording of *Barracuda*, a jazz waltz (Verve v6-8838) and *Flute Song* (Verve v6-8555), both credited to Evans alone, and *Hotel Me* (also Verve v6-8555, and recorded again in 1971 on Artists House 14), credited to both Davis and Evans. *Hotel Me* is based on a wicked striptease vamp that Evans says he took from Otis Spann's comping on a Muddy Waters record. On Evans's 1964 recording the vamp is sustained by drummer Elvin Jones and two of Davis's bassists, Ron Carter and his predecessor, Paul Chambers; the most prominent solo voice is Evans's piano, but other voices rise intermittently from the trilled background, notably the bass clarinet of Eric Dolphy. The 1971 recording, a much less effective orchestration, is dominated by a baritone saxophone, either Howard Johnson or Trevor Koehler, and includes a ragged ensemble passage based on Davis's original, and unissued, solo.

Columbia has kept the original tape in its vaults, apparently fearing another fiasco after *Quiet Nights*. For Davis and Evans, *Time of the Barracuda* added another frustrating experience to their collaborations. From then on, they would work together only sporadically, with little conviction. Few of their projects would ever be completed, and none would rival the ambitions or the standards of their earlier work.

In November 1963, President Kennedy was shot and killed in a motorcade going through the streets of Dallas, Texas. The act sent shock waves throughout the world as a first reaction, and it gave breadth and depth to the dissatisfaction with established political and social mores among the young. In the United States and all the industrialized countries of the West, many young adults began advocating political ideals for alternative societies and in some cases undertaking political acts against the status quo for their causes. Political unrest and civil disobedience became part of the maturation rite for the rest of the decade.

Among jazzmen the assassinated president had earned a measure of respect for raising issues involving race relations, and even the most apolitical among them usually found something admirable in the sense of style that he brought to his office. As it happened, one of the last official acts that Kennedy performed was to sign an executive order pardoning pianist Hampton Hawes, who had spent five years in prison for heroin addiction and was expected to spend many more. Hawes returned home to Los Angeles and began playing at a club on Sunset Boulevard, and one of his first visitors was Miles Davis. "He dropped by," Hawes remembered in his autobiography, "threw his arms around me, and said in his husky voice, 'Did they make a faggot out of you?' I said, 'No, but I learned to mop and cook.'"[15]

Presidential politics came under fire in 1964, after Kennedy's vice-president, Lyndon B. Johnson, was elected to the White House on the strength of his association with the Kennedy administration. Johnson almost immediately undertook a massive build-up of men and material in Vietnam, a tiny country in southeast Asia of which most Americans had never heard. Vietnam was locked in a civil war with ideological overtones, as the communist north battled the republican south. The south had originally been supported by France, which had a colonial tie with Vietnam, and China responded by backing the north, but when the intervention threatened to alter the remote civil war into an international conflict, France backed off. In a fateful move, the implications of which became clear only a few years after his death, Kennedy moved American men and materials into the gap left by France, and Johnson then supervised a massive build-up of American troops in Vietnam.

For the rest of the decade, American participation in Vietnam's civil war became the focal point of mass protests and civil disobedience in the United States, as American youth challenged traditional authority. In 1964, the cataclysm was still to come, but the seeds of protest were visible enough to inspire a mock campaign in the jazz world by nominating Dizzy Gillespie for president. As the fantasy of "Dizzy for President" captured the popular imagination, Miles Davis's name inevitably came into it. The satirist Dick Gregory suggested, "How about Miles Davis for Secretary of State?" But Dizzy Gillespie replied, "Miles Davis has offered to serve as Minister of the Treasury, but I've persuaded him to head the CIA instead."[16] The mockery of the political system implied in the campaign was a harbinger of much tougher and much more serious protests soon to follow.

Inside the jazz world, meanwhile, Davis's renewed energy with his young sidemen practically restored him to his position of dominance. Following the release of *Miles Davis in Europe* in 1964, he found himself back on top in most of the polls, including *Down Beat*'s International Jazz Critics poll, ahead of Gillespie, Clark Terry, Art Farmer, and Louis Armstrong, who placed behind him in that order, and his youthful band ranked second, behind Thelonious Monk's quartet featuring tenor saxophonist Charlie Rouse and ahead of Coltrane's band and the Modern Jazz Quartet.

For all that, he still refused to enter the studios in order to record with his band, and Columbia was again forced to capture his music in a live performance early in 1964. The concerts took place at Philharmonic Hall in New York, part of the new Lincoln Center for the Performing Arts, with Teo Macero ensconced in the control booth supervising the sound quality.

True to the temper of the time, the occasion had a political motive. The concerts were benefits to support voter registration drives in the southern states of Louisiana and Mississippi, where generations of black people had never exercised their franchise, either out of ignorance of the registration process or, equally likely, out of fear of reprisals from the local white community. Now, in 1964, just over a century after the Emancipation Proclamation, teams of student-workers and liberal activists were engaged in locating unregistered blacks, who sometimes formed a majority in their local polls, schooling them in the registration process, and encouraging them to turn out to vote. All of this was undertaken at considerable risk, and the registration workers, usually middle-class college students from northeastern states, became targets of abuse and sometimes assault from the hidebound conservatives in the areas. Davis's concerts at Philharmonic Hall, to provide funds for the registration drives, were sponsored by the National Association for the Advancement of Colored People (NAACP), the traditional organizer of black political action, and two upstart organizations, the Congress of Racial Equality (CORE) and the Student Nonviolent Coordinating Committee (SNCC), which were aggressive, youth-dominated groups that threatened to supplant the established NAACP in leading the fight for racial equality.

Davis, as expected, neither acknowledged the political motive of his concerts directly nor observed it in any overt way, choosing instead to use the occasion to run through his regular repertoire in rapid succession. Out of the concerts, Columbia eventually mastered two LPs, the first (CL 2306) released a few months later and the second (CL 2306) a year later. The details are as follows:

Miles Davis Quintet at Philharmonic Hall
Miles Davis, tpt; George Coleman, ts; Herbie Hancock, pno; Ron Carter, b; Tony Williams, dms. Philharmonic Hall, New York, 12 February 1964

So What; Walkin'
(both on Columbia CL 2453)
All of You/The Theme (inc.); *Stella by Starlight; All Blues; My Funny
Valentine; I Thought about You*
(all on Columbia CL 2306)
Four; Seven Steps to Heaven; Joshua/Go Go [theme and announcement];
There Is No Greater Love/Go Go [theme and announcement]
(all on Columbia CL 2453)

Years after these LPs were released, a *Down Beat* reviewer referred to the
second one, entitled *'Four' and More* (CL 2453) as "one of the certifiably
classic live jazz LPs."[17] Certainly they offer a great deal to listen to,
preserving almost two hours of music and showing the quintet off in
long elaborations – the shortest running almost eight minutes – of some
familiar themes. Only *Stella by Starlight* is in any sense unfamiliar,
having finally found a place in the working repertoire after its studio
recording in 1958, no doubt because, as with *Milestones* and *Autumn
Leaves*, Davis was pressed by his young sidemen to play publicly the
music they had admired on his records a few years earlier.

Stella by Starlight gives Herbie Hancock the starring role in a long,
musing solo that spotlights his delicate touch on the keyboard and also
his highly inventive lyricism, which recall Bill Evans's style in the
sextet five years earlier. (Hancock's solo is interrupted momentarily
near the end by a ripple of applause marking Davis's return to the stage
from the wings, where he had shared a bottle of wine with the
announcer, Mort Fega.) Hancock's confidence shines through the
evening, and so does Coleman's; both take long solos on every title,
filling in the long spells while Davis wandered in the wings and
ultimately copping the solo honors with their work.

The chief impression of Ron Carter and Tony Williams, neither of
whom had shown any lack of confidence in their playing in the past and
were certainly not going to start on this night, is one of incredible speed
and endurance. All the uptempo pieces are played at almost the same
blinding speed, a result of the acceleration Davis imposes on his music
in a direct relation to the frequency with which he plays it in public, and
most of the fastest pieces are collated side-by-side on the second LP,
'Four' and More, rather than in the order in which they were played at
the concerts. Listening to *So What, Walkin', Joshua, Four*, and *Seven
Steps to Heaven* in succession, as they come up on the LP, is exhausting
for the listener, let alone for Carter and Williams, who sustain a tempo

that must be close to the physical limits of bass plucking and drumming throughout. For listeners to the LPs, as opposed to spectators at the concert, the acceleration of tempo seems mindless, reducing the individual features of compositions as different as *So What* and *Four* to a kind of sameness, and one might as well be listening to *Walkin'*, Davis's standard fast-tempo number for years, five times in succession for all the difference it makes.

The tempos do not faze the musicians, who respond to the exigencies of the moment with remarkable ease. On *Joshua*, Carter and Williams lead Hancock and Coleman through a series of stop-time intervals, and on *Seven Steps to Heaven* Davis leads the band into an improvised coda, but neither these spontaneities nor any others, and there are several, lead to even momentary confusion. The Davis Quintet had cohered in less than a year together into a strong unit. In that respect, they seemed already to be the equal of Davis's great bands in the second half of the 1950s. The comparison faltered, really, only with respect to solo strength, with Davis himself taking fewer chances in his own playing, and Hancock and Coleman still searching for their individual voices. Davis, presumably, would summon up his resources when the time was right, and the Philharmonic Hall concerts boded well not only for Hancock's future but also for Coleman's. Coleman had established his ability to swing hard, but at the Philharmonic he is no less effective soloing on the ballad *I Thought about You*, playing variations on the melody as interesting as any ballad improvisations of the evening. Although on the ballads the tempo always rises to medium when Coleman's turn comes, he shows signs of developing his ballad style to complement his other strengths.

Unfortunately, Coleman chose to cut off his development in the well-publicized setting of the Miles Davis Quintet. He quit in the spring, a few months after the Philharmonic concert. Carter quit around the same time, but only temporarily and for entirely different reasons. As a New York freelancer, he found himself in demand often enough that he could give up the traveling he was forced to do as a member of the quintet. Carter reconsidered his decision after an interval of playing the mixed bag that freelancers were called for and rejoined Davis's band in time for the summer tour.

Coleman did not return. Ever since, almost every time a fan sidles up to him in a jazz club, he has had to face the question of why he quit. It is not a question that he finds easy to answer, and over the years he has amalgamated several possible answers into one. "Miles was ill during that time – a lot of times he wouldn't make the gigs and it was frustrating," he told Andrew Sussman in 1980. "I would be standin' out front and a lot of people thought *I* was Miles Davis, if you can believe *that*. And I used to stand out front and make a gig some nights after the first set, 'cause he would split – 'cause he was hurtin', you know. His hip was botherin' him – and so there was a lot of pressure on me, and sometimes the money would be late and I'd get it in a check and have to try to get it cashed, so I really got tired of it; so I just decided to leave."

Musically, Coleman always seemed to feel that he was the odd man in Davis's band. Five years older than Hancock and ten years older than Williams, Coleman had set his style by the time he joined the band, but he found that something extra was expected of him. "I began to take more chances, play things that I didn't know how I was going to come out of, whereas before I was always a careful player – always strictly tryin' to play the changes no matter what," he said. "Maybe not succeeding all the time, but always trying. With Miles I began to stretch out a little bit, play some different stuff. He left it more spontaneous – in a creative sense."[18] The difference between Coleman's playing when he joined and that when he left is clearly shown in his original recording of *So Near So Far* and almost everything he played at the Philharmonic concert. He became more adventurous, and he remained so to some extent after leaving Davis, but he never realized the full potential implied at that concert. That discrepancy almost certainly accounts for the persistent question about his leaving, or at least for the fans' expectation that his answer will be worth asking for. Of all the reasons he has given from time to time, the most convincing one involves the direction the music was taking. "He says he left Miles Davis because the band was heading into areas he wasn't convinced about," reviewer Mike Hennessy wrote in *Jazz Journal*.[19]

Both Hancock and Williams kept close tabs on the freer forms of Ornette Coleman, Cecil Taylor, and Eric Dolphy. Those forms were, after all, among the main currents of their formative years, as they had not been for Coleman, and they made their strongest impact on jazz just when Hancock and Williams arrived in New York to begin their professional careers. In Hancock's playing the influence of Taylor and the others is hard to pinpoint, because he works mostly in the harmonically complex but carefully controlled métier of Bill Evans, but he was completely open to innovations of all kinds and felt comfortable in almost any context. His favorite job before joining Davis was a short-lived but influential engagement under the leadership of Dolphy.

In Williams's playing the influence of the free form players is more obvious, as he ranges freely over his drum set apparently unfettered by anything but the limits of his imagination.

Within a few years, Hancock's and Williams's association with Davis would be used routinely by advocates of the avant-garde as evidence that Davis's attacks on Cecil Taylor and the others were hypocritical; Davis was encouraging Hancock and Williams to incorporate freer elements into his band even as he was making the attacks. A.B. Spellman quotes one advocate saying: "When Miles first heard Cecil, back in the 50s, he put him down, right? Well, it's an interesting thing that Miles's present piano player, Herbie Hancock, is trying to go in Cecil's direction, because he thinks that's where the music has to go. And the musicians dig Cecil. Miles's drummer, Tony Williams, does. Tony would rather play with Cecil than with Miles. That would sound strange, wouldn't it? But it's a fact."[20] Fact or not, it had enough credence to be spoken aloud without anyone rushing in to debunk it.

Davis nonetheless kept up his frontal assault on the new music whenever he was cornered for an opinion. Eric Dolphy's playing drew one of his most caustic comments: "He plays like somebody was standing on his foot." The line appeared in *Down Beat* on 13 June 1964, as part of Leonard Feather's blindfold test, and it had the kind of audacity that made it stick in people's minds, whether they were outraged or delighted by it. It was still fresh when news of Dolphy's sudden death broke on 29 June. Dolphy died just nine days after his 36th birthday from a heart attack brought on by an undiagnosed diabetic condition. He left behind a fairly rich discography of works recorded mainly in the four-year span from 1960. The best of his recordings were made with bands led by either John Coltrane or Charles Mingus, and he had made such a strong impression touring Europe with Mingus's band in 1964 that he had decided to try his fortunes there. He died in Berlin.

The elegies following his death naturally drew attention to Dolphy's openness, his easy nature, and his romanticism, all of which shone through in his playing, and amid all the praise Davis's comment lingered like a bad odor. David Baker, the jazz educator who has transcribed several of Davis's improvisations, tried to explain it away by saying, "I really believe very strongly that when Miles uses language like that, that's a language of endearment."[21] Almost no one ever believed that Davis sincerely held such a low opinion of Dolphy's playing, and the rumor circulated that Davis had been trying to hire Dolphy when Dolphy chose instead to join Mingus for the European tour.[22]

If Dolphy seemed an unlikely choice for Davis's band in light of

Davis's public views of the avant-garde, he was certainly no more unlikely than the man who finally replaced George Coleman. He was Sam Rivers, a tenor saxophonist who had moved to Boston at the age of 17 to study at the New England Conservatory and by 1964, when he was 34, had made a formidable reputation in Boston jazz circles but almost none beyond them. Tony Williams pleaded Rivers's case to Davis whenever he got the chance, playing him tapes and lauding his ability. But when Coleman quit, Davis automatically thought first of Wayne Shorter. Shorter had been made the musical director of the Jazz Messengers and felt more committed than ever to Art Blakey. In the end, Davis told Williams to go ahead and bring in Rivers for the spring tour of American clubs that the band were making before heading to Japan for a month of concerts.

Williams located Rivers touring with T-Bone Walker, the old blues shouter, and sent him a telegram saying: "Come to New York, George split. Miles want you to join his group."[23] Rivers arrived in time to spend some hours learning Davis's repertoire with the help of Hancock and Williams before starting the American leg of the tour.

Just before the quintet embarked for Japan, Ron Carter rejoined them at a Birdland engagement. Davis was apparently uneasy about Rivers's playing already, but he had no hope of changing saxophonists at such a late date.

A selection from one of the Japanese concerts, at Kosei Nenkin Hall in Tokyo, has been issued on record. It was produced by Japanese CBS-Sony with characteristic attention to sound reproduction and packaging. It is the only record issued that documents the six-month tenure of Rivers in the Miles Davis Quintet. The details are as follows:

Miles Davis Quintet in Tokyo
Miles Davis, tpt; Sam Rivers, ts; Herbie Hancock, pno; Ron Carter, b; Tony Williams, dms. Kosei Nenkin Hall, Tokyo, 14 July 1964
If I Were a Bell; My Funny Valentine; So What; Walkin'; All of You/The Theme
(all on CBS-Sony [Jap] SONX 60064R)

Even playing this familiar repertoire – all but one of these titles had been recorded at the Philharmonic Hall concert earlier in the year, and all but one had been recorded at the Blackhawk more than three years earlier – this band sounds subtly different. In Japan they were tuxedoed and cosseted, and, perhaps not coincidentally, their music came out careful and considered. The tempos are not accelerated noticeably, and the tenor and piano solos are not distended, perhaps because Davis, on his best behavior for his first exposure to a lucrative new audience, remained onstage all evening.

The subdued jazz they played obviously suited Hancock perfectly. He muses through all his solos and introductions, playing delicate, spare phrases. On the bullish *Walkin'* he slows the tempo to a near stop during his solo, and on *My Funny Valentine*, which gets its finest performance of any of the dozens that Davis has recorded, he stops the rhythm altogether and plays an unaccompanied solo. The mood of the performance works equally well for Davis, although the sound of his muted trumpet on *If I Were a Bell* and *All of You* has a noticeable burr. He is involved enough to take equal time on his solos, and on the ballads he returns after the others not merely to close out the piece but to work out another solo.

Rivers is much less involved, contributing very little to the ensembles, not even the usual saxophone vamp on *So What*. He comes to life only in his solos, which are tidy and compact. For the first time, Davis appears alongside a saxophonist who does not routinely draw on the bebop arsenal of fast runs and broad-toned repetitions in the lower registers, although Rivers's solos here are decidedly within the bebop context. Rivers nudges his solos from a conservative reworking of the melody toward phrases that alter the tonal center of notes. His solos on *If I Were a Bell* and *All of You* take on a vocal quality, which has the same source as Eric Dolphy's style but does not resemble his sound. Rivers's tone is thinner and reedier than the tone favored by bop-influenced players, and for the first time Davis's band lacks the basic contrast between the 'soft' trumpet and the 'hard' tenor. Whatever contrast Davis and Rivers might have generated tonally is lost in any case because Rivers, unlike every other saxophonist Davis has employed, does not rush in immediately after Davis's solos but enters after a pause.

Most of the changes in the quintet's style are positive, or at least have the virtue of novelty. Very few are determined by Rivers's presence. Davis's involvement, his equal participation in the solo sequence, and his care in selecting tempos and limiting the others' solo space all seem unlikely to be responses to Rivers's presence. Perhaps Hancock's liberties with tempo and phrasing are indirectly linked to Rivers, as a response to his freer conception, but some development along these lines was inevitable. Rivers brings to the group a truly distinctive solo voice on saxophone, the most distinctive since Coltrane, and Davis's involvement may well come out of a need, conscious or not, to assert and hold onto his own ground. Rivers's apparent reluctance to participate in the familiar group dynamics, or perhaps his inability to do so because of his natural tone, altered the sound of the band more than anything else, and that might have proven positive in the long run if Davis had been willing to work out the new balance with Rivers. But he was not. By the time the quintet returned to the United States, Davis had given Rivers his notice and was once again searching for a tenor saxophonist.

Rivers left the quintet in August and carried on his highly individualistic course in jazz. The exposure with Davis, though brief and poorly documented, did him no harm. He made his very first recordings as a leader the following year, when he was already 35, on an exclusive contract with Blue Note. He returned to Boston University as a composition major, worked with Cecil Taylor regularly in the last three years of the decade, and in 1971 opened a studio in Manhattan where he fostered the development and dissemination of free form music. Although he never became widely heard or much recorded, he influenced the young experimenters of the 1970s more directly than many musicians who had those advantages.

Looking back on his tenure in Davis's band, Rivers maintains simply that their music was incompatible. "Miles was doing things that were ... pretty straight," he says. "I was there, but I was somewhere else too. I guess it sounds funny, but I was already ahead of that. I kept stretching out and playing really long solos, and that's probably why I didn't last."[24] His incompatibility does not show on the Tokyo recordings, where he is reined in, but eventually it should be documented when further recordings, from Japan or elsewhere, become available.

More than the music, Rivers seemed to find the lifestyle as a member of the Miles Davis Quintet stifling. Essentially it involved traveling with a set band, playing a set repertoire, and working within chordal and modal forms. He had never done those things for any significant period in his life, and now that he was edging into middle age he was reluctant to start. If they were the traditional lot of jazz musicians, and the source of whatever security they had, they still could not tempt him as they might others. "I believe that the musicians who went through Miles's bands were just as impressed with his lifestyle as they were with his music," he told Michael Ullmann. "So if you want to achieve that kind of lifestyle, there's certain things you have to do with the music. You're

[not] going to have it while playing at the frontiers of the music."[25] Rivers has never had it, and apparently he does not miss it.

Earlier in the summer, while the quintet were in Japan, Wayne Shorter had resigned from the Jazz Messengers after five years. He took the summer off, resting and writing music. He gave some thought to leading a band of his own and spent some time talking about it with some of his friends, but he soon abandoned the idea. "I saw that it meant a lot of work and growing old fast," he said, " a hard way to go."[26] When Davis and his sidemen landed in Los Angeles from Japan they apparently did not know that Shorter was available, because Davis prepared to play a series of engagements in California with just his rhythm trio. Rivers maintains that Art Blakey still posed a stumbling block between Shorter and the Davis band. In Rivers's version, Davis and Blakey arranged to trade tenor players but Rivers spoiled the deal by backing out. "I just decided I didn't want to go into any more bebop," he said. "I was already past bebop."[27] Whatever the circumstances, Davis faced the prospect of playing his West Coast dates with Hancock, Carter, and Williams backing him.

It was not a situation that he relished or that he was prepared to accept easily. Shorter soon found himself under some pressure. First he received a call from Jack Whittemore, Davis's agent, explaining that Davis and the others were scheduled to open at the Hollywood Bowl and did not have a saxophonist. Whittemore asked Shorter to phone Davis. He hardly had time to ponder the call because his telephone kept ringing. He remembers: "Ron, Herbie and Tony would call me and talk to me and say, 'Hey, man. Why don't you come on the band? Come on, man. Come on, man.' That's Tony, right? And Herbie used to say, 'Well, I think the opportunity is wide open,' and Ron would say, 'It's all right with me, strictly all right.'" Finally, Shorter decided that he would call Davis and at least listen to what he was offering. "I called Miles then," he told James Liska, "and he picked up the phone and said, 'Wayne, come on out.' Like he was expecting my call, you know? Like it had all been set up. I went and got a tuxedo made, and they flew me out first class. I joined and we opened at the Hollywood Bowl playing *Joshua*. And we had no rehearsal. Miles had said in the dressing room, 'Do you know my music?' And I said, 'Yeah.' He said, 'Oh-oh.' Then we went on. For six years."[28]

11

Circle
1964–8

Coleman Hawkins once told me not to play with anybody old because they'll be hard to bend to the way you want them to play ... I don't tell them what to do, I just *suggest* something and if they don't like it they'll suggest something else. Say, we can do this *and* this. Or they'll know what I mean and add something to it that makes it better.   Miles Davis

"It's quality that makes the music good," Miles Davis once told Don DeMicheal. "If you get the right guys to play the right thing at the right time, you got everything you need."[1] When he added Wayne Shorter to the quintet that already included Herbie Hancock, Ron Carter, and Tony Williams, Davis closed the circle. Surrounded by the young sidemen, he produced four solid years of exploratory small band jazz.

Shorter was the catalyst. He had been John Coltrane's personal choice to replace him in Davis's band as early as 1959, and his instinct, when Shorter finally joined five years after that, proved unerring. Coltrane was originally impressed by the confident young saxophonist when he began turning up at informal playing sessions while he was still a major in music education at New York University, and he grew more impressed when Shorter came into Manhattan on weekend leaves after he was drafted into the army to serve in the army band at Fort Dix.

Picking Shorter out of the crowd of aspiring young jazz musicians was not difficult for Coltrane or anybody else. He arrived already equipped with that indefinable quality that had marked Sonny Rollins ten years earlier among his adolescent peers in Harlem. Shorter was born in 1933 in Newark, New Jersey, across the Hudson River from Manhattan. One of his contemporaries in Newark was LeRoi Jones, the poet and playwright (later known as Amiri Baraka), and although Jones and Shorter were raised in distant neighborhoods and attended different schools, Jones knew a lot about Shorter. He recalled Shorter's stature among Newark teenagers in a profile for the *Jazz Review* in 1959, when Shorter had just finished his stint in the army and was still largely unknown. Jones attempted to define "the kind of aura he cast even as an adolescent, maybe because we were all adolescents ... but I think not. I think Wayne carries that aura around him like an expensive Chester-field. Talking to him one senses immediately this air of 'invincibility'. Hearing him play, one is convinced that it is no mere air."[2]

Testing himself alongside Coltrane and others as an undergraduate gave Shorter more self-assurance, and he used the two-year stint in the army band not only to hone his playing skills but also to develop his composing ability. He was a member of Maynard Ferguson's sextet when Jones wrote about him, but he stayed only briefly in that band, and when Coltrane's recommendation to Davis was thwarted because Davis persuaded Coltrane to stay with him he joined the Jazz Messengers, forming one of Art Blakey's most formidable front lines with the young trumpeter Lee Morgan. He never developed into the flaming free former that Jones, and perhaps Coltrane too, seem to have anticipated. With Blakey he played and wrote music that carried on Blakey's neo-bop style, extending it somewhat but basically staying within the category. By the time he joined Davis he was as ready to bend the traditional categories as were his colleagues in the band, both in his playing and in his writing.

With Davis as with Blakey, and indeed with the musical associations he formed after leaving Davis, Shorter experimented *with* form rather than *without* form, as a kind of experimenting traditionalist or a progressive conservative. He has never really abandoned the lesson he learned from Coltrane in his youth. "You know, when you're into something, like John, you may make a lot of fluffs and clinkers, but that's in it, too," he told Jones between sets at Birdland. "All that stuff counts. If you're really doing something, you can't be safe. You've just got to blow, and try to take care of some business some way."[3] Because he respects form but needs to take risks with it, Shorter's career looks like a paradox among the jazzmen of his generation: he is a 'tough' or 'difficult' player who has always performed to fairly large, catholic audiences. Shorter has worked throughout his conspicuous career almost inconspicuously, inspiring neither fan clubs nor cults, as a featured player and composer but never a star attraction. His role in the resurgence of the Miles Davis Quintet in 1964–8 (and after that) is crucial, but it is never more than equal to that of the other sidemen.

No other period in Miles Davis's music presents so orderly an appearance. Its key documents are six studio recordings made and released at more or less regular intervals over three years: *E.S.P.* (recorded early in 1965), *Miles Smiles* (1966), *Sorcerer* and *Nefertiti* (both 1967), and *Miles in the Sky* and *Filles de Kilimanjaro* (both 1968). But the period encompasses much more. The last two LPs were selected from a vast store of studio recordings Davis made at the time, some released several years later and much unreleased to this day; most of that music points ahead to the next period of his development rather than substantiating this one. There are also a number of live recordings made early in this period that catch Davis and the quintet reworking the old repertoire rather than working out the entirely new one introduced on the studio recordings. And there are even more intervals of relative inactivity for the quintet than usual, the result of Davis's health deteriorating to the critical point. With enforced absences from performing come increased activity on orchestral projects with Gil Evans, each one destined to be aborted or stillborn. Those that got as far as the recording studio remain there still, in Columbia's vaults, and a whole sub-theme of these years thus remains completely unknown.

With all this diversity, the six studio recordings stand as the touchstones of the period. For reviewers and fans alike, they belong at or very near the apex of Davis's achievements as a jazz musician. The critical consensus is simply stated by Harvey Pekar, in a 1976 article in *Coda*: "When Shorter joined him ... Miles embarked on a new era of exploration that rivaled his 1955–9 period."[4] Ironically, the significance of the quintet's music and its consistent excellence were not widely appreciated at the time, by fans or reviewers. The critics formed their consensus after a gap of several years, not surprising in most art forms but a startling contrast with Davis's earlier peak period, when his music won both the large audiences and the critical plaudits that have stuck with it ever since.

The delayed reaction was partly inherent in the music itself. It demanded new perceptions from its audience and thus required a period of acclimatization before it could be fully accepted. But those demands would not, under ordinary circumstances, have been so great as to require all the time the listeners took. The main reason lay in the times.

Put simply, almost no one was listening. Davis continued to fill concert halls and jazz clubs all over the world, just as he had for almost a decade and would do later. His new records sold well, with only a slight and hardly worrisome falling off in sales compared to his new releases of a few years earlier. But he was almost alone in holding his place with the fans. John Coltrane did too, Thelonious Monk probably could have if he had wanted to, and the Modern Jazz Quartet continued to thrive in Europe, but in general it was a bleak time for jazz.

"Jazz is dead" became a catchword. It was seriously debated in the jazz periodicals, complete with learned-sounding arguments that the music had exhausted itself in the rapid evolution since the turn of the century. Among the most reactionary elements of the jazz audience, as we have seen, the catchword was reinterpreted as: "Ornette and Cecil have killed jazz." However it was phrased, what it really meant was that the audience for jazz was disappearing fast. So too, naturally, were the musicians. At some point or other during the 1960s, Kenny Drew, Art Farmer, Johnny Griffin, Dexter Gordon, Arthur Taylor, Mal Waldron, and many others moved to Europe, Helen Merrill moved to Japan, Randy Weston to Morocco – an exodus in search of a small but loyal audience. Dozens of others disappeared, sometimes irretrievably, into carpentry, sign painting, selling, counselling, teaching, and any other jobs they could find; Eddie (Lockjaw) Davis became a booking agent at the Shaw Artists Corporation, usually with rock bands for clients. Others stayed in music but not in jazz; Hampton Hawes spent these years playing ballads for stockbrokers and their secretaries from 5 to 9 p.m. in a San Francisco bar, and many jazz musicians counted him lucky. Red Garland went home to his father's house in Dallas and sat out the whole decade, playing only occasional weekends at local bars.

In the jazz world, everything seemed to go wrong. "All the clubs were closing and none of the musicians were working," Garland told Len Lyons when he finally returned to jazz in 1978, and he added: "I thought jazz was finished."[5] He was not alone. "The clubs were beginning to hurt," Hawes complained. "The kids were jamming the rock halls and the older people were staying home watching TV. Maybe they found they couldn't pat their feet to our music anymore. Big-drawing names like Miles and John Coltrane were breaking out of the thirty-two-bar chord-oriented structure and into free expression – or 'avant-garde' or 'outside', whatever tag you want to stick on it – charging the owners so much they had to raise the covers and minimums."[6] The complaints of Hawes and the other jazzmen made a long list, and if none of them went far into the heart of the matter all of them had some bearing on it.

Davis complained too, but it was all relative. Max Gordon, the owner of the Village Vanguard, takes some pride in his attempts to hold the line on the fee he had to pay Davis. In one of Gordon's vignettes, probably from around this time, Davis demanded the impossible sum of $6,000 for a week at the Vanguard, and Gordon had no choice but to turn him down. The next day he received a call from Jack Whittemore, saying: "Miles called, said he saw you yesterday ... He said something about a week in May, that you got a week in May open. Right?"

"'Right.'

"'He sounded interested. Maybe I can get him to take it.'

"'How much money?' I asked.

"'Forty-five hundred.'

"'I paid him thirty-five hundred last time.'

"'Miles said forty-five.'

"'Thirty-five,' I screamed.

"'Make it forty and I'll talk to him.'

"'Talk to him. Talk to the bastard. And wrap it up, Jack.'

The next day Gordon found a message on his answering box saying: "You got him for forty – OK?"[7] For Davis and his young sidemen the "death of jazz" had less credibility than it did for many others.

Even so, Davis's fees looked significant only beside the fees commanded by other jazzmen. Performers outside jazz were suddenly commanding stipends unimaginable just a few years earlier. In North America and every other industrialized society, the economies of the 1960s began to show the effects of an inflationary spiral sharp enough to disabuse every citizen of the delusion that prices and wages were fixed things; whereas in the previous decade prices and wages had inched upward almost imperceptibly, now they began to shoot up in annual and semi-annual bursts, and by the time the 1970s arrived they increased in quarterly or monthly bursts. Even with the popular consciousness of inflation in the marketplace, the money paid to star attractions and to "superstars" – a brand-new word for a brand-new phenomenon – seemed astounding, and record-setting grosses were reported in the press with numbing regularity.

Both the swelling prices paid to popular performers and the dwindling audience for jazz and other serious music reflected a new balance of power.At its leading edge were four improbable iconoclasts from Liverpool who called themselves the Beatles. Their first hit records, starting in 1962, were as easy to disparage as most of the pop music of the preceding decade, their lyrics as preoccupied with holding hands, dancing with only one partner, and pledging undying love. That made it easy to overlook the careless charm in their early records and consign them to the pop wastebasket that would come to be known as "bubble-gum music," inanities strung together for "teeny boppers," the new majority. But their music was everywhere, and sooner or later the most hardened critic had to recognize its growing preoccupation with themes such as hypocrisy, self-deception, and loneliness, often expressed in small ironies and neat images.

And the Beatles were not alone. The list of pop songwriters capable of touching a serious theme grew rapidly – Harry Chapin, Bob Dylan, Phil Ochs, Joni Mitchell, Randy Newman, and many others. They harked back not to their pop predecessors such as Jerry Lee Lewis, Bill Haley, and Elvis Presley, purveyors of doggerel notwithstanding the necromancy that surrounds them two decades later, but to Woody Guthrie and the Weavers, the self-styled 'folk' singers of the American labor movement.

The new sophistication of the songs soon found performers of more than ordinary gifts. Singers, not surprisingly, came first, as people such as Paul McCartney, Joan Baez, Art Garfunkel, and James Taylor could span octaves without losing tone or abandoning key. Instrumentalists followed soon after: arranger Sly Stone, organist Garth Hudson, and guitarists – guitars were suddenly everywhere – Keith Richard, Eric Clapton, Jimi Hendrix, Robbie Robertson, Carlos Santana. To all these was added a fringe of performers whose particular gifts seemed strictly limited but whose performances were elevated well beyond those limits, such as Arlo Guthrie, Woody's son, the mild-mannered folkie whose *Alice's Restaurant* dismembered the Vietnam war and reigns as the satirical masterpiece of a satirical era; and Janis Joplin, the vulnerable ruffian who transliterated Willie Mae (Big Mama) Thornton's spirit and some of her style into pop music.

All these elements amounted to a pop explosion, not only in gate receipts and fans per household and concerts per capita but also – unpredictably and astonishingly – in quality. Originally directed to teenagers, already the booming majority, the pop culture found their older brothers and sisters receptive too and spread from there to their uncles and aunts and – like, what a turn-off, man – to their parents. Teenage styles spread like ink on a blotter. Before long, lawyers were wearing colored dress shirts, stockbrokers were wearing flared cuffs on their pinstripes, chartered accountants were wearing blue denims, and professors were wearing ponytails. And most of them were buying the Beatles' records, attending Simon and Garfunkel's concerts, and picking out basic chords on guitars.

Jazz was not alone in losing its audience. Drama withered, trying unsuccessfully to relocate its audience by relaxing its mores on language, nudity, and almost everything else. Musical comedies played to half-empty halls except when they incorporated rock 'n' roll plots, as in *Bye Bye Birdie* and *Grease*, or became topical, as in *Hair*. Symphony orchestras commissioned rococo arrangements of melodies by the Beatles and the other hitmakers for pop recitals. Jazz musicians also tried to adapt to the pop cult by laying pop melodies like a thin veneer over their improvisations. Duke Ellington, in the sixth decade of his life and the fourth decade as America's most self-reliant composer, arranged and recorded some Beatles' tunes to help pay for the upkeep of his orchestra.

Miles Davis's music, for the time being, betrayed no special awareness of the pressures of the pop explosion. His managers at Columbia knew better than to propose anything that sounded like a compromise to him, and, besides, he continued to hold his own – for the time being, and with a slight but perceptible slippage – in the changing marketplace. His autonomy would be respected as long as the Columbia executives who had grown up with him in the organization kept their places and would be questioned only later in the decade when new managers, especially Clive Davis, rose through the ranks to reassert Columbia's dominance in what was, in effect, a new billion-dollar entertainment industry. When that happened, Davis would react not by importing a rock veneer into his music but by altering its very substance. Until then, he piloted his new quintet through a period of growth and change that was internal to the group rather than directed at the changing tastes of the world beyond jazz music.

The internal growth and change were not, of course, unaffected by what was happening outside. They were also guided and inspired by the predilections of his sidemen, entirely appropriate to their youth. In September 1964, when the circle was closed by Shorter's joining, Davis was 38, but Shorter was 30, Hancock 24, Carter 27, and Williams 18. The sidemen carried the confidence that seemed endemic to the under-thirties of the day, and Davis gave them something close to a full share in determining the quintet's direction.

Years later, Ron Carter described the participatory democracy that changed the quintet's direction this way: "Sixty per cent of this was the band taking a new direction and 40% was Miles recognizing this, and, while not being able to predict it would go a certain way, understanding that it was definitely taking a turn. I think he was happy to take a back seat and be an inspiration but not hold the reins too tight, and give the horses their head knowing that it would work out all right."[8] There could be no standing still.

The young sidemen worked together easily and developed an unusual rapport. Davis was soon drawn into it. Contrary to his dark public image, he appeared to his band, Carter told Louis-Victor Mialy, "warm, friendly, open – happy to offer, to share his experience with you, always willing to lend you money or even borrow it for you, always ready to invite you for lunch or dinner, always anxious to show you the good note, the best note to play, to advise you about your problems. I have only superlatives for the man."[9] The others shared his feelings.

The band thrived on the confidence that they were peers on their instruments and ranked among the best players around. They were as willing to challenge one another on the bandstand as Davis had been with his great sextet in the recording studio, and for much the same reason: the challenges might lead to stunning solutions and new directions.

The new directions took a while to assert themselves. In a busy fall schedule that included a sojourn in California and a tour of European capitals, Shorter and the others played Davis's time-worn repertoire. The first of their performances to find its way onto record came soon after Shorter made his debut at the Hollywood Bowl, on Steve Allen's television show from Los Angeles. The details are as follows:

Miles Davis Quintet on The Steve Allen Show
Miles Davis, tpt; Wayne Shorter, ts; Herbie Hancock, pno; Ron Carter, b; Tony Williams, dms. The Steve Allen Show, Los Angeles, September 1964
No Blues
(Teppa 76)
The opening theme is missing from this recording.

Beneath the obscure sound of this unauthorized recording, apparently taken from the impoverished sound system of a home television set, the quintet romp through *No Blues* sounding not much different from any of the other quintet versions of years past. Only Hancock stands out, not so much in his note-filled solo as in his comping for Davis and Shorter, in which he picks up their phrases and tosses them back at them. Many clearer examples of Hancock's growing skill as an accompanist follow this one.

The European tour that followed took them to Berlin (25 September), Paris (1 October), Stockholm (3), Copenhagen (4), and other cities, including Barcelona, and again resulted in an LP issued by a CBS subsidiary, just as Davis's most recent trips to Japan and to France had. This time the producer was German CBS. The details are as follows:

Miles Davis Quintet in Berlin
Miles Davis, tpt; Wayne Shorter, ts; Herbie Hancock, pno; Ron Carter, b; Tony
Williams, dms. Philharmonic Hall, Berlin, 25 September 1964
Milestones; Autumn Leaves; So What; Walkin' / The Theme
(all on CBS [G] 62976)

Three of these four titles were recorded at Antibes more than a year
earlier, with George Coleman in the quintet. The differences between
the performances are subtle, and probably only noteworthy in the light
of what was to come. Certainly Tony Williams does not come close to
his outstanding performance at Antibes; on *Milestones* he enters a
couple of bars late at the beginning and somehow never seems to catch
up. But Wayne Shorter adds an adventurous voice, whether compared to
Coleman or to his own playing with the Jazz Messengers. The elements
of his style, deliberately or not, invite comparisons: the dry tone of
Coltrane, the short, choppy phrases of Jackie McLean, and the sliding
onto and away from the tonal centers of notes of Dolphy. They converge
into an approach that is ultimately his alone.

Herbie Hancock, more surprisingly, alters his role almost completely.
His calm, unruffled solos never beg attention, and yet he quietly
dominates much of the music. On *Milestones* and *Walkin'* he slows the
tempo by degrees to a complete stop before revving it up again to its
original pace, an audacious move that belies the quiet surface of his
solos. In support of other soloists, especially on *Autumn Leaves* and
Walkin', he plays much less than comping pianists were expected to,
instead chipping in dissonant splashes of chords at irregular intervals
and punctuating the soloists' statements like a percussionist rather
than providing a running commentary on them as pianists had done not
only in bebop but also in every older style of jazz. He thus liberates the
ensemble from the steady progression of chords and breaks away from
the pianist's traditional role in much the same way that drummers were
breaking away from their time-keeping role. Although it seemed a
radical departure, it was dictated in the first place by Hancock's
befuddlement with Davis's music. "Herbie wanted to quit when he first
got with me," Davis told Gregg Hall. "He said it didn't seem like there
was enough music for him to play. I said, 'Well, then, lay back,
motherfucker. You just told yourself what to do.' He would play for a
while and could not keep it up and sometimes it just seemed like there
wasn't anything for him to do."[10] Hancock's solution to his dilemma
made an influential precedent for a host of young pianists then coming
into jazz.

By the time the quintet reached Barcelona near the end of the tour, they welcomed some free time to behave like tourists. For Davis, it was an opportunity to seek out some of the Spanish music that he had hybridized in *Sketches of Spain*. He and Ron Carter headed into the Catalan backwaters of the city and found a restaurant far from the tourist paths. "I don't speak Spanish and Miles hardly speaks at all," Carter said later, "but there was no communication problem. I took the waiter by the arm and went back to the kitchen to see what was available. I suppose they could have thrown us out. But the staff seemed flattered at our interest. The result was an incredible fish dinner, followed by two hours of beautiful flamenco."[11] Whether or not the occasion reinforced Davis's feeling for flamenco, it definitely aroused his feeling for fish. A few years later, when he took up cooking, he made bouillabaisse one of his specialties.

Soon after the quintet returned to the United States, again to California, which Davis had been using as his home base as often as New York for a year and a half, they began working on a new studio recording, the first in almost two years. The LP that resulted, called *E.S.P.*, would be an eye-opener, the first of the series of LPs that would reveal the new balance of the quintet as none of their live performances, before or after, ever did. In that new balance, Tony Williams was to be the kinetic force, the hub of action, and, inevitably, the attention-getter. "The dense, complex, polyrhythmic textures of his best performances are wonders in themselves," Martin Williams commented, "yet they are always in motion, always swing, are always responsive to the soloist and the ensemble, and are never interfering or distracting. And for his splashing, complex cymbal work alone, Williams belongs among the great drummers in jazz history."[12]

Williams's drumming forced the rest of the players to react. Hancock told Conrad Silvert: "The difference between what Miles had been playing before the quintet crystallized and what we played was incredible. Like, Tony was introducing rhythms I had never even heard. I think what made the band unique was the interplay of the rhythm section, the way the ball passed around ... and at the same times Miles and Wayne floated on top of the ever-revolving rhythm section sound. And just the way Tony mixed up the roles of different parts of the drums – the focus might be on a snare drum, or another time on the bass drum, or it might be totally the cymbals without any other parts of the drums."[13]

Because of his power, Williams could not be missed, and it is easy to undervalue the contributions of the others in what developed. "I'm inclined to think that the band was important for all of us to grow in," Ron Carter points out, adding: "It is also true that we had all kind of decided on our kind of groove before we joined the band. Obviously Miles saw that we had something to offer before we joined, or he wouldn't have asked us. It's clear that he wasn't picking a bunch of total beginners in concept and technique."[14]

Carter was probably the most secure player in terms of technique among the young sidemen, a fact that seems vitally important for someone faced with holding his ground nightly alongside Williams's drumming dervish. Carter did just that, holding his ground, and the combination was stronger than either of its parts. "When Miles Davis had Ron Carter and Tony Williams," Michael Moore, another technically excellent bassist, observed, "Carter was the anchor, and Williams tended to rush the beat. That created tension, and tension creates excitement."[15]

Hancock enhances that tension with his percussive colorations in the ensembles, but in his solos he more often seems to bring it under control by dictating the pace to the others. His response to the powerful duo is to speak softly in their company, the antithesis of the most obvious or expected response, and in doing so he reserves his own personal space where he might otherwise have simply been swallowed up.

The rhythm section, in any consensus, rival any other ever assembled in a working band. They have persisted remarkably, lasting long after all three players finished their tenure with Davis, so that they remain a set group for recording sessions and occasional tours more than twenty years after Davis first put them together. In 1983, Carter told Lee Jeske: "We have found – and I will speak for them at this point – that we seem to make the most incredible music with the least amount of effort with each other. And the camaraderie that's involved – this is our twentieth year of playing together – both on and off the bandstand has sustained itself, and I'm sure that it plays a big role in our respect and our response to each other's musical talents and our ability to sacrifice our personal needs, musically, to make that music go in the direction that it's going, without input."[16]

As for Davis, he stirred up his own creative energy with the new quintet. Perhaps his response really was, as Carter later said, 60 per cent reaction to the creative juices unleashed by his young sidemen and 40 per cent rediscovery of his own resources, but, when all else is said and done, the direction taken by his new quintet was truly new only to the young sidemen themselves and not at all new to him. For him, the new music was a return to the principles he had already asserted brilliantly

Wayne Shorter (Bernie Senensky)

Ron Carter (Bernie Senensky)

in *Kind of Blue*, almost six years earlier. He reasserted his belief in the modal basis for jazz composition and improvisation, presided over the development of a whole repertoire of original compositions, and reclaimed his position in, as Martin Williams put it, "the advance guard of the period."

There can be no doubt that his imprint was on everything the band produced. "He was the only bandleader who paid his personnel not to practise at home," Shorter says, "so as to avoid the polish that makes even some improvised music sound boring. He always wanted it fresh."[17]

That gambit had been easier for Davis to enforce a few years earlier, when he could simply show up at the recording studio with a completely new set of sketches and compositions for his band to play. Now, in the new band, he was only one of the composers; all five members would contribute, and Shorter in particular made several key contributions. "Herbie, Wayne or Tony will write something," Davis told Arthur Taylor, "then I'll take it and spread it out or space it, or add some more chords, or change a couple of phrases, or write a bass line to it, or change the tempo of it, and that's the way we record."[18] On the first LP he claimed credit as co-composer for his efforts, but thereafter the pieces were credited individually to the sidemen. Several of the very best compositions, in any case, are Davis's own. After marking time for a few years, Davis was rejuvenated.

The first studio recordings took place in Hollywood, under the supervision of Irving Townsend. The details are as follows:

Miles Davis Quintet: E.S.P.
Miles Davis, tpt; Wayne Shorter, ts; Herbie Hancock, pno; Ron Carter, b; Tony Williams, dms. Los Angeles, 20 January 1965
E.S.P.; R.J.
(both on Columbia CL 2350)

Same personnel. Same place, 21 January 1965
Eighty-One; Little One
(both on Columbia CL 2350)

Same personnel. Same place, 22 January 1965
Iris; Agitation; Mood
(all on Columbia CL 2350)
Most discographies list an unissued drum solo by Tony Williams recorded on 22 January, but it is probably the one spliced onto the beginning of *Agitation*.

It is hard to imagine music more unlike, say, *Some Day My Prince Will Come*, the "ofay Disneyland tune" (as Hampton Hawes once called it) which was Davis's hit between *Kind of Blue* and these recordings. Some of the new pieces seem anti-melodic, especially the three by Carter: *Eighty-One* (written with Davis), *R.J.* (dedicated to Ralph J. Gleason), and *Mood*. On *Eighty-One*, the trumpet and the tenor saxophone state melodic phrases with long pauses in between, as if to disguise any melodic coherence. On *Little One*, by Hancock and Davis, Shorter opens with a single phrase, Davis plays the next one, and then they repeat them in turn, again breaking up the traditional coherence of melody.

Agitation, by Davis, *E.S.P.*, by Shorter and Davis, and *Iris*, by Shorter, preserve the melodic line in the opening and closing, although they are "simple in structure and sparse melodically[,] containing relatively few notes," as Harvey Pekar noted in his overview.[19] Even these take liberties with conventional structures, as *Agitation* opens with a drum solo, and all of them shift freely in tempos. Time signatures also move around: *Eighty-One* is basically in 6/8 time but shifts to 4/4 time for parts of the solos, and *Little One* opens and closes as a pulseless mood piece but shifts surprisingly into 3/4 time for the solos.

The music is, as Scott Yanow says, "a total break from the past,"[20] and James Lincoln Collier described Davis's stylistic departures this way: "His playing is thoroughly modal, often interrupted by tempoless stretches. He is inflecting his line with a lot of half-valving and often intentionally letting notes fall off pitch, as if he were mocking his own music. He is using the upper register more. The delicacy and interest in note placement that characterized his work previously is less in evidence, and, at times, as, for example, in *Iris* on *E.S.P.*, his line is filled with vast, empty phrases, like wind in a ruined cathedral."[21]

For Davis's perennial fans, *E.S.P.* served notice not only of a change in direction but also of an about-face in his stated position on Ornette Coleman and the other exponents of freer forms. That change was also implied in the title, *E.S.P.*, which seemed to reflect the cliché current among both the adherents and the detractors of free forms, that the only way bands would play unstructured music together was through extrasensory perception or mental telepathy. Davis offered his listeners music held together by less rigid structural principles than he had formerly used, and he was showing off a new, young band capable of suffusing each piece with a remarkable unity. If they were not exactly appealing to ESP, they were nevertheless giving up the familiar hallmarks of melody and tempo in favor of the much more elusive notions of mood and atmosphere. And *E.S.P.* was only the beginning, though a remarkable one. The next step, however, took almost twenty-two months, as other matters intervened.

In the spring of 1965, Davis's hip ailment hindered his mobility and kept him in constant pain. Thrombosis in the joint had caused the left socket to deteriorate, and the only chance of his continuing to walk unaided was through an operation to replace the dead socket. The surgery and its complications laid Davis up for seven months and kept the quintet inactive all that time. It may have been scheduled for earlier in the year than April, perhaps closer to the end of January, when *E.S.P.* was concluded, but Davis's general health forced his doctors to postpone the operation. "A doctor went to check my blood pressure and he said, Where is it? Do you *have* any blood? Really?" Davis told Cheryl McCall. "He told me to eat some bread so I could get my strength up and have my blood. I had to have a five hour operation and I needed strength for that."[22] The first operation on 14 April replaced the hip ball with a graft from Davis's shin. Davis allowed three months for recovery and booked an engagement at the Village Vanguard in August, but as the date approached he remained hurting and nearly immobile. The bone graft had failed, and in August he went through a second operation to replace the joint with a plastic one. He would not be ready to resume performing until November.

In the meantime, *E.S.P.* was released. If its contents were largely unexpected, its cover at least carried a familar theme. It again depicted Frances Taylor Davis, this time with Davis peering up at her from a chaise longue. It was the third of his covers that she had graced, in alternate years since 1961, and the last. The marriage had become troubled, and it would gradually dissolve, ending in divorce after nine years.

The young sidemen kept busy during the layoff, playing on several recording dates and in pickup bands. All of them took studio calls, and Carter especially was in demand for all kinds of jingles, pit bands, and studio dates, so much so that he occasionally missed Davis's engagements outside New York during his remaining three years with the band. They also played together as often as they could, thus reinforcing the bonds that worked so well for Davis's music. Usually Tony Williams instigated their reunions. On his own debut LP as a leader (*Spring*, Blue Note BLP-4216), recorded in August, he hired Shorter and Hancock. His friend Sam Rivers, also recording for Blue Note at the time, used Carter and Williams on *Fuchsia Swing Song* (BN-4184) and Hancock and Carter on *Contours* (ST-84206). Williams booked a trio engagement at a small club in Boston for Shorter, Carter, and himself, where they collectively worked on free improvisations.[23] When Davis reassembled them, they resumed their work with him without any preliminary rehearsals.

Davis made his return to performing in the week beginning Tuesday, 16 November, at the Village Vanguard. His appearance was eagerly anticipated after the seven-month absence and the cancellation during the summer. Dan Morgenstern, who covered the opening night for *Down Beat*, reported that "the long lines of people waiting outside – not a common sight on today's night-club scene – testified to Davis's drawing power, and the music more than justified the turnout."[24] Ron Carter could not break a commitment and was replaced by Reggie Workman. That change caused no problems. Workman, originally from Philadelphia, had worked with Coltrane in his first bands and had played alongside Shorter in the Jazz Messengers in Shorter's final years with that group. After that, he stuck close to New York rather than traveling regularly with bands, but his reputation among musicians as a power bassist capable of fitting into any context has always been formidable. (When Mal Waldron, long domiciled in Europe, signed a recording contract with the Munich firm ENJA in the early 1970s, he stipulated that the company provide him with an opportunity to record in New York with Workman as his bassist.) The quintet, with Workman filling in, played excellently by all accounts.

If the audiences found little diminution of Davis's music, Max Gordon found none at all in his business acumen. "Miles always liked to get $1,000 front money before he'd open," Gordon recalled. "If I didn't have it, he might open, but after the first set opening night, he'd come to me and, scanning the crowd, whisper, 'Don't forget the grand if you want me to come in tomorrow night.'"[25] Michael Zwerin, part of the audience on the first weekend, recalled that Davis "had been sick and hadn't played much in about six months, so he sounded a little weak," but that was no drawback. "I would rather listen to a weak Miles," he added, "than a strong almost anybody else – especially the way he plays a ballad ... He blew *Old Folks*, and a young girl sitting near me said softly, 'He opens up melodies like a flower.'"[26] Davis had recorded *Old Folks* in 1961 on *Some Day My Prince Will Come* and had seldom played it since.

The rest of his repertoire for this engagement and the tour that followed was similarly retrospective, consisting of ballads and Davis's old standbys. Morgenstern caught the quintet playing *Round Midnight*, *If I Were a Bell*, *When I Fall in Love*, *I Thought about You*, *Four*, *So What*, *All Blues*, *The Theme*, and "a spontaneous blues, on which Davis dug deeply to roots, toying with phrases from *Royal Garden Blues* and *Easy Rider*."

The Vanguard comeback, like other comebacks by Davis to follow, was not just an exploratory engagement for testing himself physically and musically, but a full-fledged return to work. It was followed by an engagement at the Showboat in Philadelphia in early December and, immediately after that, by two weeks, from 21 December until 2 January, at the Plugged Nickel in Davis's traditional Yuletide stopover, Chicago. The engagement at the Plugged Nickel aroused even more excitement than the one at the Vanguard, the local demand having been whetted by Davis's canceling three previous engagements scheduled during the year, the most recent in mid-October. Ron Carter had resumed his place in the band, and Davis had updated the repertoire by adding *Agitation*, the first of the quintet's new music to enter the working book.

Davis's high spirits at the Plugged Nickel showed when he agreed to let a teenaged saxophonist sit in with the band, perhaps through the intermediacy of Hancock, a native Chicagoan who knew many of the local musicians. As it happened, the young saxophonist never summoned the courage to take the stand. "I was seventeen or eighteen when a friend of mine set it up for me to sit in with Miles," John Klemmer recalled several years later, "and I just sat there, kept on drinking and holding on to my horn. I never got up. I just tripped out on the idea that Miles was gonna let me."[27] Klemmer moved to California a few years later as a soloist with the Don Ellis orchestra and gained some prominence fusing jazz forms with rock elements in the early 1970s.

Adding to the hubbub at the Plugged Nickel was the presence of Teo Macero and a flotilla of mobile recording facilities hired by Columbia. Davis's long absence from performing coincided with an equally lengthy absence from recording, and Columbia was having little success getting a commitment from him for a return to its studios. It moved in to record the first three nights of his engagement. Ironically, the enormous quantity of music it taped then lay in its vaults until Japanese CBS-Sony mastered two LPs from it in 1976; Columbia finally reissued the Japanese masters as a double album in North America in 1982. The music issued so far hardly makes a dent in the tapes, even though only the second and third nights' performances are apparently suitable in quality, the first night presumably given over to setting up and attuning the recording equipment. With typical assiduity, the Japanese producers listed the recorded materials, set by set, from which their LPS are selected, providing not only an indication of what will eventually be issued but also a document of Davis's repertoire at the time. The details are as follows:

Miles Davis Quintet at the Plugged Nickel
Miles Davis, tpt; Wayne Shorter, ts; Herbie Hancock, pno; Ron Carter, b; Tony Williams, dms. The Plugged Nickel, Chicago, 22 December 1965
Set 1: *If I Were a Bell; Stella by Starlight; Walkin'; I Fall in Love Too Easily*
Set 2: *My Funny Valentine; Four; When I Fall in Love; Agitation; Round Midnight; Milestones/The Theme*
Set 3: *All of You; Oleo; I Fall in Love Too Easily; No Blues; I Thought about You/The Theme*
(*Round Midnight* on CBS-Sony [Jap] 25 AP 291)

Same personnel. Same place, 23 December 1965
Set 1: *If I Were a Bell; Stella by Starlight; Walkin'; I Fall in Love Too Easily/ The Theme*
Set 2: *All of You; Agitation; My Funny Valentine; On Green Dolphin Street; So What/The Theme*
Set 3: *When I Fall in Love, Milestones; Autumn Leaves; I Fall in Love Too Easily; No Blues/The Theme*
Set 4: *Stella by Starlight; All Blues; Yesterdays/The Theme*
(*Stella by Starlight* [set 1], *All Blues, Yesterdays/The Theme* on CBS-Sony [Jap] 25 AP 291; *Walkin', Agitation, On Green Dolphin Street, So What/The Theme* on CBS-Sony [Jap] 25 AP 1)
All titles issued by CBS-Sony are included on Columbia C2 38266 (1982).

Judging by the typical length of the issued titles, Columbia holds enough material from the Plugged Nickel for five or six more LPS. Except for *Yesterdays*, which Davis recorded in 1952 and had never played since, the titles are, of course, familiar, but the music itself contains many innovations when compared to the last live performance recorded by the quintet, twenty-six months earlier in Berlin. It represents a much more decisive departure from the bebop conventions or, put positively, a much more fluid approach to matters of form and phrasing.

Shorter especially seems uninterested in developing melodic variants of the themes. His solos create sound effects, altering tonality and breaking phrases unexpectedly, so much so that when he reins himself in with occasional references to the original melody he makes the melody itself sound incongruous. On *Agitation*, in his first chorus he leads Hancock into a wild pursuit that ends with the usually calm Hancock unleashing a flurry of Taylor-made runs.

All the music is amazingly fluid: tempos and time signatures alter continually, harmonies in the ensembles shift constantly, familiar breaks such as the one on *Round Midnight* between Davis and Shorter become raunchy, and solos turn suddenly into simultaneous improvisations – by Shorter and Williams on *So What* and by Shorter and Davis on *Yesterdays/The Theme*. Nothing at all in this music seems fixed, and, at its best, on *All Blues* and *Yesterdays/The Theme* (both, one notes, from the same set, from which another title, perhaps of comparable quality, remains unissued), the listener gets the thrill of a musical giant slalom where every turn is completely different from the ones before it. The performance, or as much of it as we have so far, seems to be a textbook example of Davis's feeling for leadership, notwithstanding the six months of independent activity by the players. "I give them their heads," Davis told Don DeMicheal, "but I try to tell them what sounds best. I tell them to always be prepared for the unexpected – if it's going out, it might go out more, an extended ending might keep on going."[28]

He now had musicians who were more than willing to "go out more" and to "keep on going." Their six-month recess from the quintet while Davis recuperated clinched that. During that time each of them had become involved with more of the music being played in New York than they otherwise could have. The atmosphere had calmed down by degrees since 1960. Conspicuous opportunities for playing the new music were rare, and livelihoods for those who played it were tentative, but the jazz business was depressed everywhere and so were all the performing arts; the new men hardly needed to feel paranoid or resentful about their poverty when it seemed to be a general condition. In 1960 it had been possible to see the new music as a kind of graft, or perhaps a parasite, on the jazz scene; by 1965, that view had become implausible. The new music remained. It had survived the period of vituperation, and, more important, it had survived a period of critical and popular neglect. And it had taken root.

John Coltrane's conspicuous support, recording with people such as Archie Shepp, Pharaoh Sanders, and Rashied Ali and occasionally adding them to his band increased their credibility with the general audience, and so did his own increasingly free music. The proponents of the new music not only carried on with it but their numbers increased, and they continued to work at their music with the same conviction as any other school of musicians, or perhaps more.

Ornette Coleman reappeared, after an almost complete withdrawal from performing in public that lasted from 1962 well into 1965. He was back, but without Don Cherry, usually playing only with a bassist and a drummer. Cherry, along with a host of new musicians, including Albert Ayler and Marion Brown, was in Europe, where a small but fervid audience for their music developed in France, the Netherlands, Germany, and Scandinavia. Coleman's biggest success since his Five Spot engagement came in November 1965, when he toured Scandinavia with bassist David Izenzon and drummer Charles Moffett. Coleman and almost everyone else involved in jazz were amazed when Coleman's recording of part of a concert in Stockholm, *At the Golden Circle, Vol. 1* (Blue Note BST 84224), was named best album in *Down Beat*'s Jazz Critics Poll for 1966, edging out Davis's *E.S.P.*, the two LPs being not so different from one another in spirit as anyone could have predicted.

Elsewhere in the same poll, Davis's sharp return to form since 1963 and his continuing explorations with the new quintet since 1964, despite the layoffs, were rewarded with wins both for the top small band and for the top trumpeter.

The comeback was cut off abruptly. On the last day of January 1966 Davis was hospitalized again, this time with a liver inflammation. The disorder probably originated as another symptom of the oxygen deficiency caused by the sickle cells, but it was certainly aggravated by liquor. Davis, whose struggle to withdraw from heroin was twelve years in the past, was forced to give up alcohol. "What could be any worse than whiskey?" he asked Cheryl McCall. "It's got my liver all fucked up."[29] Giving up alcohol was no great problem – he would do it, as Mark Twain did tobacco, several times over the next years – but sitting around recuperating for another three months proved harder. On a Monday night in the middle of March, he slipped out to a club called Slug's and sat in with a band led by trumpeter Lonnie Hillyer and saxophonist Charles McPherson, two young Detroiters who had apprenticed with Charles Mingus's band and were trying to put a band of their own together. Soon after, he reassembled the quintet and started back to work.

Again, the comeback tour made no concessions to his health. It included a month-long swing along the West Coast and then a return to the east for the summer. Ron Carter refused to make the western tour, as he usually did in the years to come; in his place, Davis took Richard Davis, the versatile virtuoso who turned up on dozens of recordings and was considered by many musicians to be the best modern bassist of all, and not only in jazz. Included in the itinerary were some college concerts, one at Portland State College in Oregon (on 21 May) and another at Stanford University in California (on 22 May); the one at Stanford was the final concert sponsored by the student union in a series called Jazz Year, a program designed to improve economic conditions for jazz players. After more then twenty-five years of playing his music in jazz clubs, Davis found the college concerts a relief in every respect, and he was not reluctant to say so. "I make more in one night on a college date than you pay me in a week," he once told Max Gordon. "And I don't have to take all that shit! ... I can't stand the whole fuckin' scene. The cats comin' around, the bullshit, the intermissions. I hate intermissions. And you lookin' sore because I ain't up on the bandstand. And the people! 'Play *Bye Bye Blackbird*!' Shit! I don't drink now. I work out in Stillman's Gym four hours a day. I used to have to come down every night. Down to your plantation. Now I come when I want to come. On a college concert I do two short sets and I'm through. I don't have to hang around, listen to a lot of bullshit!"[30]

Whatever attractions the night-life surrounding a club date had once held for him were curtailed by his health problems, at least for the time being. He turned 40 just four days after the Stanford concert, but he spent his birthday playing in another jazz club, Shelly's Manne-Hole, owned by the drummer, in Los Angeles. For working jazzmen, there was really no way to avoid clubs altogether, and the quintet played there from 24 May until 5 June.

Not all the concert dates were a distinct improvement on the club dates anyway. After closing at Shelly's Manne-Hole, the quintet played a one-night stand in San Diego under excruciating circumstances. The details were supplied by Gil Evans, who was in California rehearsing and performing with an orchestra he assembled for the Monterey Jazz Festival and some other California engagements. Evans traveled with Davis to the San diego concert. "This was in a great big ballroom they had converted into a supper club, and the acoustics were terrible," Evans told Leonard Feather in an interview for *Down Beat*. "They had the group down on the floor, maybe ten feet from the stage, on a little platform, with no shell. I asked the woman who owns the club why they weren't playing on the stage, and she said, 'Well, I like to have them down in front of the people, because the people like to see the emotional expressions on their faces.' The whole thing looked like a set for a Hollywood movie." Evans added, "The piano was absolutely impossible – an old, worn-out grand piano – so that all the important things that Herbie Hancock played were almost completely lost."[31]

Evans's California orchestra was the first he had assembled without Davis since 1961, when he fronted a short-lived orchestra, and for the first time in his career he was playing piano in the band. He had enlisted a good lineup, including tenor saxophonist Billy Harper, tuba player Howard Johnson, and drummer Elvin Jones. After their debut at the Monterey Festival, they played at Shelly's Manne-Hole and were recorded playing concerts at both UCLA and Costa Mesa. Evans seemed ready to embark on his career as a full-time bandleader, but for several reasons – bad recording conditions, a strung-out trumpet player, lack of rehearsal time, and so on – none of this music recorded in California was issued on record. One of the sixteen compositions he arranged for his California orchestra, *Freedom Jazz Dance* by saxophonist Eddie Harris, showed up a few months later in a version by the Miles Davis Quintet, probably an unacknowledged adaptation of Evans's arrangement, but otherwise the music he played in California disappeared without a trace.

Both in California and in New York, Evans and Davis continued working together. They had never ceased doing so, although the last public evidence of their collaborations, the *Quiet Nights* arrangements, was now four years old. Whenever Evans listened to Davis with the quintet, his mind was partly on the orchestrations he might devise for him, and he heard lots of possibilities in Davis's work at the San Diego concert. "When he played *All of You*," he told Feather, "he got the most delicate type of sound – his muted sound – you notice the tremendous power behind the horn, even though it is muted. More often than not, when people play with mutes, everything sounds relaxed, but with Miles there's an extraordinary tension; he went past that quiet feeling and into a thing where it just floated. That's what we have to develop on our next album. I want to write accompaniments for just that particular kind of sound."[32]

With Davis's enforced layoffs from performing in the previous year, the two men spent more time than usual working out ideas. They had several projects half-formed with many more to come, and that was perhaps part of their problem.

Back on the east coast for the summer, the quintet appeared at the

Newport Jazz Festival on 4 July, Independence Day. They played *All Blues* and *Stella by Starlight*, both firmly established as favorites by Davis now, although he had ignored them for years after his original recordings of them. *Stella by Starlight* provided a particularly effective showcase for Ron Carter, who had emerged as one of the best supporting players and remained unsung because he so seldom took a solo.

The Newport Festival had become an institution since it began in 1955, when Miles Davis had scored one of the festival's most conspicuous artistic triumphs, but it was suffering growing pains. It had diversified to the point where Davis branded it, to the delight of almost everyone, "a supermarket." In an effort to keep the crowds during the years of the jazz recession, George Wein added the Newport Folk Festival in 1963, capitalizing on the enthusiasm for folk-pop and folk-rock among the young audience. By 1966 the town of Newport was overrun by campers and partygoers at festival time, and Wein added an opera festival that year, hoping to give the crowds a leaven of highbrows. The additional genre only lengthened the party season at the Newport spa. "It takes only one trip to the Newport Jazz Festival – the gentry in the front row with their martini shakers, the sailors squatting in the back, their heads between their knees, upchucking their beer – to remember what a weird mixture is Miles Davis' world," wrote Murray Kempton in the *New York Post.* "Was ever anything in America at once so fashionable and so squalid?"[33]

Jazz would eventually outlast folk music and opera as the festival feature, but the burghers of Newport were growing impatient with the fashionable squalor Wein was planting in their community every summer.

The Miles Davis Quintet finally returned to the Columbia studios in October, this time in New York with Teo Macero in the control room. In the long interim, both Herbie Hancock and Tony Williams had signed recording contracts with Blue Note, and their releases for Davis's recordings had to be negotiated. The resulting LP, titled, lugubriously, *Miles Smiles*, showed even greater cohesion than *E.S.P.* In his 1978 article, Scott Yanow declared it "the essential quintet album from this period." The details are as follows:

Miles Davis Quintet: Miles Smiles
Miles Davis, tpt; Wayne Shorter, ts; Herbie Hancock, pno; Ron Carter, b; Tony Williams, dms. New York, 24 October 1966
Circle; Orbits; Dolores; Freedom Jazz Dance
(all on Columbia CL 2601)

Same personnel. Same place, 25 October 1966
Ginger Bread Boy; Footprints
(both on Columbia CL 2601)
Freedom Jazz Dance is probably arranged by Gil Evans or in collaboration with
Evans.

Any description of the music contained on *Miles Smiles* is bound to be
couched in contradictions, for the music includes a ballad that is not a
song (*Circle*), an unforgettable melody that mimics semi-articulate
speech (*Dolores*), and two funk-gospel pieces that are not funky
(*Freedom Jazz Dance, Ginger Bread Boy*). Even more obviously than
most Miles Davis LPs, this one consists of previously unrehearsed
music; several of the ensembles are rough, especially the closing theme
of *Dolores*, in which Davis and Shorter seem to tempt one another by
playing fragments that leave the other player stranded, and *Freedom
Jazz Dance* where Davis makes a false start. Hancock plays as if his
piano were a horn; on *Orbits, Dolores,* and *Ginger Bread Boy* he is silent
in all ensembles and during Davis's and Shorter's solos, entering as the
third soloist and then, on all three tracks, fashioning his solo out of
single-note lines played by the right hand only.

Notwithstanding the contradictions, *Miles Smiles* is the most consistently interesting album by Miles Davis since *Kind of Blue.* The rough
ensembles matter less than they otherwise might because the compositions are played as multi-part simultaneous improvisations rather than
set ensembles followed by individual solos. Partly, this realignment of
traditional form seems a natural development from Tony Williams's
refusal to be subjugated, and it was implicit from the beginning but only
burst into the open here. Williams is everywhere, including many places
where jazz listeners least expect to hear him. On *Freedom Jazz Dance,*
his rhythm is not metrical but builds around an uneven drum roll. He
marks the time with his high-hat, and the dance rhythm pervades the
track almost in spite of Williams, sustained by Hancock and Carter.

Hancock's reduction of the piano to a single-note instrument in the
treble clef follows from the modality of the writing. When the
harmonies are not pre-set, there is nothing for a comping piano player to
feed to the other players and Hancock eliminates the left hand not only
when the others are soloing but also when he is.

The unity of the pieces and thus their coherence, those elements that
Davis and many others complained about in free form playing by lesser
bands than this one, fall almost by default to Carter, and he responds

brilliantly. On *Footprints* he carries the 6/4 riff throughout the length of the piece, altering tempo and occasionally playing a variant or inserting a bar of 4/4 time but never for a moment letting the time signature slip. He is simply indispensable.

Regardless of these liberties with form, the music on *Miles Smiles* is hardly less accessible to bop-bred listeners than Davis's earlier work. Only *Orbits*, one of three Shorter compositions and the shortest track on the LP, seems to keep its structural secrets hidden after repeated listening. Douglas Clark's explanation that "it is made up almost entirely of minor seconds and perfect fourths, orbiting around its tonal centre (c)" and that it "is dodecaphonic (but not serial)"[34] does not help much for anyone trying to figure out how the solos by Davis, Shorter, and Hancock, all apparently unrelated in mood, style, and melody, are expected to work together. Otherwise Shorter's compositions on this LP, *Footprints* and *Dolores*, are memorable pieces that passed quickly into the repertoires of other bands. They consist of brief, melodic catch-phrases – the entire written portion of *Dolores* lasts no more than eight bars – that get repeated arbitrarily in the opening and closing ensembles. The point of the catch-phrase is to encode the scale that is available to the improviser, but the quality that distinguishes both *Footprints* and *Dolores* is the clarity of the mood that the catch-phrase also encodes. Shorter's compositions thus direct the improviser not only to the form (the scale) but also to the content (the mood) with only a few deft strokes. They do not present a melody in the conventional sense of a paragraph of ordered musical phrases and clauses; that presentation is left to the improviser.

Traditional forms, specifically the twelve-bar blues and the thirty-two-bar song dominant in jazz for decades, provide no precedents for Shorter's modal compositions. They have slightly more influence on Davis's *Circle*, which is decidedly a ballad (by any definition) although not exactly a song (by the formal definition). Davis's tightly muted exposition of the melody over conventional rhythm accompaniment – Hancock comping, Williams using brushes – relates *Circle* to the long line of ballads Davis has recorded since 1948, but is formally weird, consisting of a twenty-two-bar statement with no discernible bridge. The recorded version also catches Shorter playing a more conventional ballad solo than he usually played in Davis's band, as if to guarantee that Davis's oldest fans would find a point of reference.

More surprising are the two blues-based numbers in the gospel-funk style, *Freedom Jazz Dance* by Eddie Harris, the Chicago saxophonist who was experimenting with electric instruments and attracting some rock fans, and *Ginger Bread Boy* by Davis's old friend Jimmy Heath, the saxophonist who was now mainly occupied writing charts for Julian Adderley, Herbie Mann, and others. ("When people like that record an album that sells twenty or thirty thousand copies," Heath told Valerie Wilmer, "that's a nice little taste to come in out of the mails when you're not working."[35]) Both compositions were originally built on chord progressions with strong blues melodies, but Davis strips them down and distends them so that the blues seem to be ejaculated like steam from a geyser. The homely phrases of the originals are bandied about and permuted over and over again by all five players so that they are never quite set aside and never quite in focus. For the listener, the music presents both the conventional and the unexpected not by moving between one pole and the other but by straddling the poles.

Much of *Miles Smiles* balances that same tension between the old and the new. It seemed an automatic choice when it was cited as record of the year in *Down Beat*'s readers' poll in 1967.

Davis's health continued to nag him until he was forced to make some adjustments. He took the quintet into the Village Vanguard early in 1967, but he eased the physical strain of the engagement by playing three consecutive weekends rather than a straight week, beginning on 20 January. He also eased the playing load on himself by expanding the band into a sextet. The sixth man was Joe Henderson, a tenor saxophonist who gained his first professional experience in Detroit. Although he was a few years younger than Shorter – he would turn thirty later in the spring – his background was very similar. He too had put in time with the US army band, serving from 1960 to 1962, and he came into Davis's band after playing a year and a half with Horace Silver's quintet, a band that worked in the same neo-bop style as Art Blakey's Jazz Messengers. Henderson had a warmer, more robust tone than Shorter, his debt more to Sonny Rollins than to Coltrane, but he too was a transitional player capable of moving with self-assurance from bebop to freer forms when he improvised.

So far, Henderson's tenure in Davis's band remains undocumented, but in addition to his weekends at the Vanguard he remained with the band for a tour of fifteen cities in February and March, in a concert package called the World Series of Jazz. The other headliners included Count Basie and his orchestra, Sonny Stitt, Billy Eckstine, and, in keeping with the mood of the time, a South African folk singer named Miriam Makeba and a political satirist named Dick Davy. The promoter of the tour, Teddy Powell, told *Down Beat*, "The receipts are greater from my jazz promotions than my rock-and-roll shows."[36] The hardest of jazz's hard times appeared to be over.

Around this time, possibly beginning with the weekend performances at the Village Vanguard, Davis began playing his nightclub sets and concerts in a single, unbroken continuum. The change was radical but in retrospect seems a straightforward response to the dictates of his new music. Having abandoned prescribed bar sequences for explorations of mood, some of them determined by successions of scales, Davis began to segue from scale to scale even when the scales belonged formally to different compositions. The changes of mood associated with different compositions evolved in the transitions, as did changes of tempo, time signature, scale, and the rest, but just as the structural elements had become increasingly fluid, so too had the mood, almost by definition, being ineffable or at least less effable than structure. The quintet's performances, at their best, became improvised suites organized around a few common themes instead of a sequence of unconnected melodies.

It was an audacious move, but it represented a small step from Davis's usual practice in his performances for more than a decade, when he gave the downbeat and started the next number as soon as the applause for the previous number had begun. That old practice always roused the ire of fans who expected their applause to be acknowledged, but the new practice left them with no intervals for applause at all as the music rolled inexorably onward.

"The things of music you just finish," Davis told Don DeMicheal in 1969, when questioned about his continuous sets. "When you play, you carry them through till you think they're finished or until the rhythm dictates it's finished and then you do something else. But you also connect what you finished with what you're going to do next. So it doesn't sound like a pattern. So when you learn that, you got a good band, and when your band learns that, it's a good band."[37]

Davis's precedent, like the other precedents he set with his controversial stage manner, won hardly any converts among other musicians. One who followed his lead was Max Roach. Charles Tolliver, Roach's trumpeter for the last two years of the decade and, incidentally, one of the few trumpet players whose style seemed completely uninfluenced by Davis, explained that "you can create a concert-type thing in a club" with continuous sets. "A lot of times you want to connect different songs," he told Valerie Wilmer, "and applause in between is a waste of time. Miles is the first person who started doing it, and Max does it too.

It really keeps you on your toes, because the musicians who are working with you know all the things that you're going to do, but they don't know in which order you're going to play them."[38] Even Roach and Tolliver did not persist, and the practice of playing continuous sets remains an idiosyncrasy of Davis's performances.

In April, Davis moved with the quintet to the West Coast, alternating his home base as he had done for four years. This time, the stay lasted five weeks. Joe Henderson left the band, and Ron Carter took another leave. For the first concert on the tour, at the University of California in Berkeley, Davis borrowed bassist Albert Stinson from the John Handy Quintet, San Franscico's top jazz group. The Berkeley concert, in the hotbed of student activism, also featured the Modern Jazz Quartet and Gerald Wilson's big band, an aggregation of California studio musicians. Originally scheduled for the outdoor Hearst Greek Theater, rainstorms forced the concert inside to the Harmon Gymnasium, which was packed with 8,000 wet fans. Russ Wilson, covering the event for *Down Beat*, provided what was probably the first notice of Davis's uninterrupted recitals in describing "an electrifying set that continued for 62 minutes, almost without pause." He listed the elements of the medley in order as *Agitation*, *Ginger Bread Boy*, *Round Midnight*, *So What*, *Walkin'*, and *The Theme*, a sequence of familiar titles except for *Ginger Bread Boy*. The concert included a public display of feeling so rare that Wilson could hardly leave it out: "So superb was drummer Tony Williams' playing on *So What* that Davis, after ending his monumental solo, walked over and patted him on the back."[39]

For the rest of the West Coast engagements, the quintet was completed by bassist Charles (Buster) Williams, a 25-year-old from New Jersey who had earned his reputation with the Jazz Crusaders, a California band directed by drummer Stix Hooper. Davis first heard about Williams from Hampton Hawes the previous summer. Hawes's tale of Davis's first exposure to the talented young bassist, as he told it to Harvey Siders, remains one of the great nonsequiturs in the history of talent scouting. "I had told Miles, 'There's a young cat in Los Angeles named Buster Williams who can really play.' Miles said, 'Can he really play?' And I said, 'Yeah, he can play.' I was playing one night," Hawes continued, "and Miles was there, and Buster came up and played so good, Miles threw up on his pants. And that's the truth."[40] Talent like that apparently could not be denied, and the Davis Quintet, with Buster Williams on bass, moved into a San Francisco club called the Both/And for the middle two weeks of April.

Hawes was a member of the audience at the Both/And. He was still playing solo cocktail piano in the early evenings and keeping his parole officer happy, if not himself, by doing it. Davis's opening night gave Hawes's spirits such a boost that he later described it, with slight variations, both to Harvey Siders and in his memoirs. "Miles looked at me in my sharp suit and said, 'Where you playin'?' figuring at 9:30 I must be going to work instead of coming." Hawes told him about his "sad gig" and then found a seat in the audience to listen. "They were really doing something," Hawes said, "and ... I walked over to the stand and I said to Herbie, 'Get up, get off the piano.'" He continues: "I wound up in the middle of a tune with Miles' band wondering, what the fuck am I doing up here. Finished the tune and afterwards asked Miles, 'Was it cool?' He said, 'You're a crazy motherfucker. It was beautiful.'" Hawes added, "Now *that*'s all that counts, as long as you mean it."[41]

Hawes escaped the tedium of his 5-to-9 job in the fall of 1967, when he left San Francisco on a catch-as-catch-can global tour that restored some of his confidence and revived some of his reputation. As jazz music in general came on better times, so did Hawes, and he worked productively, though shifting indecisively between milder-mannered bop than he had formerly played and amplified, rock-based music, until 1977, when, at the age of 48, he died of a massive stroke.

The Davis Quintet moved on to Seattle, into a club called the Penthouse, and then in early May to Los Angeles, where they again recorded in Columbia's Hollywood studios. As had happened a few years earlier on the recordings for *Seven Steps to Heaven*, Davis was dissatisfied with the recordings made in Hollywood and chose to re-record the material when he returned to New York a week later. This time he rejected all the Hollywood takes in favor of the New York ones, and so far only one of them has come to light. The details are as follows:

Miles Davis Quintet with Buster Williams
Miles Davis, tpt; Wayne Shorter, ts; Herbie Hancock, pno; Buster Williams, b; Tony Williams, dms. Los Angeles, 9 May 1967
Limbo
(on *Directions*, Columbia KC2 36472)

Shorter's theme for *Limbo* is not particularly attractive, simply a unison run by the trumpet and saxophone up the minor scale and back down it. It suggests motion but goes nowhere, always ending up at the same place, thus making a fair definition of its title. On both the Hollywood and the subsequent New York versions, Hancock is all but nonexistent until he plays his one-handed solo. The main difference in the two versions, apart from the greater length of Davis's and Shorter's solos on the later version, is Tony Williams, who is torrential throughout the New York version but plays the Hollywood one as if handcuffed, giving it a calmer – or 'laid-back,' as the California buzz-word might put it – surface.

Limbo's re-recording took place just a week later, with Ron Carter back in the band, at the sessions for the LP Sorcerer. The details are as follows:

Miles Davis Quintet: Sorcerer
Miles Davis, tpt; Wayne Shorter, ts; Herbie Hancock, pno; Ron Carter, b; Tony Williams, dms. New York, 16 May 1967
Limbo; Vonetta
(both on Columbia CL 2732)

Same personnel. Same place, 17 May 1967
Masqualero; The Sorcerer
(both on Columbia CL 2732)

Same personnel, except Miles Davis does not play on Pee Wee. Same place, 24 May 1967
Prince of Darkness; Pee Wee
(both on Columbia CL 2732)

None of these titles is composed by Davis; Shorter contributes four (Limbo, Vonetta, Prince of Darkness, and Masqualero), Hancock the title piece (The Sorcerer), and Williams the one on which Davis is unaccountably absent (Pee Wee).

On Pee Wee, where the young sidemen are left to their own devices and one might have expected an excursion into the further reaches of free forms, they turned out instead a slow, undistinguished ballad, warmly played by Shorter as Hancock comps behind him; it is easily the most conservative music on the LP.

Vonetta and Prince of Darkness, also ballads, are more interesting. Prince of Darkness begins as a medium fast ballad and continues as such for Davis's long, lyrical solo; then the tempo varies behind both Shorter and Hancock, and the final statement of the theme ends up, perhaps unintentionally, faster than the opening statement.

Vonetta shows a masterly use of the quintet's resources. Essentially a medium ballad, Davis plays a lyrical solo following Hancock's introduction, and Shorter and Hancock preserve his mood in their solos. Carter's walking bass line buoys the solos, making *Vonetta* a ballad performance worthy of comparison to *Circle*. But it is more than a stunning ballad because of Williams, who sustains an undercurrent of quasi-military rolls on his snare drum in the background. The effect is strange and tense, as if the peaceful mood of the ballad might be ripped apart at any moment. The contrasting elements work so impeccably that they seem to be a carefully calculated device, but they came about spontaneously. As Hancock recalled several years later, Williams used the drum roll because Davis turned to him as they were about to record *Vonetta* and said, "Play a *Rat Patrol* sound."[42]

Masqualero, with a Spanish tinge that is almost a bolero and almost a flamenco, in an uncategorizable time signature, and *The Sorcerer*, a medium uptempo number that strains Davis and Shorter by requiring them to solo in alternating eight-bar fragments, vary the pace of the LP. *The Sorcerer* is dedicated to Davis and named for him, "because," Hancock says, "Miles *is* a sorcerer. His whole attitude, the way he is, is kind of mysterious. I know him well but there's still a kind of musical mystique about him. His music sounds like witchcraft. There are times I don't know where his music comes from. It doesn't sound like he's doing it. It sounds like it's coming from somewhere else."[43]

After listening to the piece called *The Sorcerer* on a blindfold test presided over by Leonard Feather, trumpeter Bobby Bryant complained, "The sameness which is occurring on [Davis's] recent records I don't like," and added: "The guys around him are very exciting; they are inventive enough, and certainly a great deal of energy goes into their performances. If it were not for that amount of energy, especially in the case of the drummer, they would really sort of fall flat."[44] No doubt Bryant's complaint stems in part from a nostalgia for the music played a decade earlier, but his observation about the "sameness" picks out a real problem in some of the recordings the quintet made. With the composed themes so concise, amounting to only a few bars, they must perforce be brilliantly constructed to be effective. Nondescript themes, as in *Limbo* and *Pee Wee*, and on *Orbits* from *Miles Smiles*, slip past without asserting any distinctive mood, leaving behind only an expanse of improvisation on minor scales – the sound that Collier characterized as "vast, empty phrases, like wind in a ruined cathedral."

The problem is not inherent in the conception itself. themes for modal improvisation can be longer and more fully explicated, as Davis demonstrated with *All Blues* and *So What*, and they can also be succinct and still effective, as Shorter demonstrated with *Vonetta*, *Dolores*, and *Footprints* and Davis with *Agitation*. The problem arises when they are short and easy, as some are on the *Sorcerer* LP.

The cover of the *Sorcerer* LP featured a striking profile of a black woman. Although few observers could have identified the woman in 1967, when the cover first appeared in record stores, four or five years later she had become one of the best-known young actresses around. She was Cicely Tyson, one of Davis's companions at the time and eventually his fourth wife, marrying him in 1981 when their relationship outlasted an intervening marriage. "I have a thing about helping black women, you know," Davis told Gregg Hall, "because when I was using dope it was costing me a couple of grand a day and I used to take bitches' money. So when I stopped to clean up, I got mad at *Playboy* and I wouldn't accept their poll because they didn't have no black women in their magazine, you know. So I started putting them on my covers. So I put Cicely's picture on my record. It went all around the world." In the same interview, he claimed to have "taught her a lot of stuff" about acting as well. "I taught her about eyes," he said. "You see, black people's eyes are so wide anyway, so I told her not to open her eyes too much. She had a habit of overacting. I taught her to be subtle, you know, and when it comes time to use some volume, she'd know it." He even did some dramatic writing for her. "I wrote a little thing for her," he told Hall. "It was outtasight! Man, it had her subconscience [*sic*] talking to her and her looking at it and doing something else. It was outtasight!!"[45] So far, the playlet has remained out of sight for Tyson's public.

As Davis prepared for an unusually busy summer and fall schedule that would find him recording and performing more frequently than he had done for years, he and Gil Evans continued their sporadic collaborations on several projects. One of these, certainly the one that aroused the interest of jazz fans, was a bigger band that Davis and Evans were hoping to use as a working band in club and concert dates. "I believe that Miles now is going to have a big band," Evans told Leonard Feather in an interview the summer before. "He would like to, and he is about ready. The time is right. Not an enormous band but about a dozen men. We could work out a library together. It wouldn't be that difficult to book him with a band. He could play at the Vanguard, at Shelly Manne's, or in the place where I heard him the other evening, in San Diego." Evans hastened to add that the band was not intended to replace the quintet.

"Of course when I say it's time for him to have a big band," he added, "that's no reflection on the quintet. They're all wonderful musicians."

Evans's conception of the big band scores was derived partly from what he heard in the quintet: "If Miles could get a band to play the kind of accompaniment he gets from that combo – a sort of orchestral parallel to what happens in the combo – it would be really sensational. If Miles just had a few horns doing the equivalent of what Herbie does, he'd have a fantastic band."[46] Most fans reading Evans's description agreed wholeheartedly. But nothing ever came of it. When Davis and Evans finally recorded together the next year, making some tapes for Columbia that have never been issued, it was with a much larger orchestra.

Years later, Evans suggested in an interview with Zan Stewart that the working big band collapsed because he and Davis could not find financial backing, but he also implied that their collaborations at the time were impeded by Davis's arthritic joints as well. "Sometimes I'd be up at his place," Evans said, "and we'd be working on something, because for a while there we were out to do something but it never materialized on account of the money, and he'd be sitting at the piano, trying to play some chords and he'd say, 'Oh, ouch, ouch, ouch!!' It was agony for him to try and play those chords."[47]

Davis and Evans were also trying to put together the material for a studio project, their first in almost five years. "We have so many new numbers half-finished now," Evans told Feather. "In fact, I don't even know how much music we've got. I talked to Miles just the other day, and we decided to put all the music together and get going on another album as soon as we can." Pressed for details about the music already prepared, Evans became vague, saying that they were "just some songs. Not necessarily standards. It's hard to say what we're going to come up with, but we've written a couple of tunes."[48] None of their efforts from late 1962 to early 1968 received performances, either in public or in the recording studio.

Meanwhile, Ron Carter and Tony Williams, with youth on their side, used some of their time off to dig deeply into yet another musical direction. On 26 May 1967, they appeared at Carnegie Hall accompanying the third-stream pianist and composer Charles Bell. Bell's ensemble also included Richard Davis, a bassist gifted, as Carter was, in both symphonic and jazz music, and guitarist Les Spann, who was added to the ensemble for the premiere of Bell's *Second Quintet: Brother Malcolm*, dedicated to Malcolm X, the charismatic spokesman for black nationalism who had been assassinated in 1965.

For both Davis and his sidemen, most outside activities ended in June, when the quintet spent no less than four days in the Columbia studios recording more original compositions written by the sidemen. The material from the first three days was released soon after on an LP titled *Nefertiti*, and it falls clearly within the domain already charted in the previous three LPs made in the studio. The details are as follows:

Miles Davis Quintet: Nefertiti
Miles Davis, tpt; Wayne Shorter, ts; Herbie Hancock, pno; Ron Carter, b; Tony Williams, dms. New York, 7 June 1967
Nefertiti
(on Columbia CS 9594)

Same personnel. Same place, 19 June 1967
Fall; Pinocchio; Riot
(all on Columbia CS 9594)

Same personnel. Same place, 22 June 1967
Madness; Hand Jive
(both on Columbia CS 9594)
The 19 June session is produced by Howard A. Roberts; the other two by Teo Macero.

If the *Sorcerer* LP contained some perfunctory writing and playing, *Nefertiti* resumes the careful innovations of *Miles Smiles* and rivals the earlier LP as a showcase of this quintet's achievement. Davis solos magnificently on the open horn throughout, capturing the broad tone and the grace of his playing on *Porgy and Bess* and *Kind of Blue*; he solos especially effectively on Hancock's *Madness* and on Shorter's *Fall* and *Pinocchio*. *Hand Jive*, by Williams, and *Riot*, by Hancock, are relatively simple exercises, the former a sequence of solos over a steadily accelerating tempo, the latter a short but tidy theme with surprisingly short, but also tidy, solos.

The most conspicuous strengths seem to flow directly from Shorter's contributions, not only – not even principally – as a soloist but as a composer. His three themes, *Nefertiti*, *Fall*, and *Pinocchio*, float over the restless rhythms of Carter and Williams and the occasional bright splashes of Hancock. Their composed phrases, usually played in unison by Davis and Shorter, are wafted aloft by the rhythmic cushion even though they seem detached from its intensity. Shorter's own solos for the first time show a parallel detachment, as Davis's often had. So conspicuous a transformation drew many notices. "Once the hardest of hard bop tenors, Shorter had softened his strident sound, simplified his ideas and abandoned the harmonic structures of the jazz mainstream in exchange for a greater use of scales and subtle coloristic effects," Bob Blumenthal wrote in *Rolling Stone* some years later. "His twisting, haunting compositions were becoming statements in themselves instead of mere frames for solos. All three Shorter tunes on *Nefertiti* use melodic repetition to an unprecedented extent and, as interpreted by the great Davis quintet, ... became hypnotic messengers of something new."[49]

On *Pinocchio*, formally the simplest of the three Shorter compositions, the short theme recurs at the breaks between each of the soloists (Davis, Shorter, and Hancock) as well as at the open and close. On *Fall*, a beautiful ballad exploiting Davis's lyricism in an ode to autumn, Shorter's melody recurs sporadically, but entirely naturally, all through the piece – before, during, and after all the improvised statements – and simultaneously inspires and determines the improvisations.

Nefertiti goes a step further: it includes no solos in any conventional sense. Instead, Davis and Shorter repeat the mournful theme over and over again throughout the long track (almost eight minutes). Yet both in feeling and in fact, the composition remains rich in spontaneity; improvisation is in a sense constant, not only in the play of the rhythm section but even in the theme statements by the horns, which repeat the same basic scale again and again with different nuances each time. It is a remarkable conception, demanding free interplay and controlled license, and one that could be carried off successfully only by players who are gifted individualists and devoted collectivists. Because of this striking performance, Shorter's composition became an instant postbop classic.

With *Nefertiti* and his other two compositions on the *Nefertiti* LP, Shorter took a giant step into the forefront of the jazz of the 1960s in the unanimous view of critics and musicians. One of the musicians who took special notice was Josef Zawinul, Julian Adderley's pianist and composer-arranger, who was busy at the time inventing new uses for electronics in the gospel-funk writing that had sustained Adderley's quintet for several years. "I heard *Nefertiti*," Zawinul said, "and that's when I felt Wayne was the guy I should do something with. He had the new thinking."[50] Together, Zawinul and Shorter would direct some of the most enterprising permutations in the music of the 1970s with their band called Weather Report.

The Davis quintet's later recording session that same month resembles the music of *Nefertiti*, although none of the three compositions by Shorter measures up to any of the three recorded earlier. Presumably for that reason, these tracks were not released until 1976, when they appeared as one side of an LP titled *Water Babies*. The details are as follows:

Miles Davis Quintet: Water Babies
Miles Davis, tpt; Wayne Shorter, ts, ss (on *Sweet Pea*); Herbie Hancock, pno; Ron Carter, b; Tony Williams, dms. New York, June 1967
Water Babies; Capricorn; Sweet Pea
(all on Columbia PC 34396 [1976])

The three pieces strike moods and hold them: *Water Babies* is lazy and carefree, *Capricorn* mysterious, and *Sweet Pea* ruminative. Of *Sweet Pea*, Douglas Clark observes: "The melody had apparently been with Shorter for some time because it appears at more than double the tempo, at the end of his solo on *Madness* from *Nefertiti*."[51] (The uncertainty of the recording date for *Sweet Pea* apparently gave Clark the impression that Shorter had been saving the theme for a while, but the recording dates for *Madness* and *Sweet Pea* may have been within days of one another.)

Shorter records on soprano saxophone for the first time on *Sweet Pea*, and dozens of other reedmen soon followed him by doubling on the 'straight' horn. The soprano had a history of neglect among woodwind players. Among jazz players, it seemed for decades to be the exclusive property of Sidney Bechet, the old New Orleans nonpareil who spent most of his career in Paris. Bechet used it in preference to the clarinet as his main instrument because it gave him enough amplitude to drown out brass players, and a few of Bechet's admirers from Johnny Hodges to Bob Wilber had picked it up occasionally as a second instrument, more in homage to the old master than as a serious alternative.

The soprano carried the stigma of being hard to play in tune. It came into favor among younger players in the late 1960s by a circuitous route. Steve Lacy had been playing the soprano in Dixieland bands when the avant-garde players became conspicuous in 1959–60, and Lacy, a thoroughly uncategorizable New Yorker, joined them in lofts and clubs almost immediately. The soprano was the only horn he owned, and so exotic was it at the time that most of the younger musicians, including other reed players, had to ask him what it was when he took it out of its case. One of the most curious, naturally, was John Coltrane, who promptly got one of his own in 1960 and began playing it soon after in club dates and on records. As Coltrane became the supreme influence in the jazz of the day, the soprano's star rose as well, until virtually every saxophonist under 40 had one. The horn – a fatter, shinier clarinet – quickly became commonplace. "The outcast in the saxophone family," as Humphrey Lyttleton called it in a chapter on Bechet,[52] was an outcast no more. In 1969, *Down Beat* added a category for soprano saxophonists to its polls. Ever since Shorter unveiled his soprano in the recording studio in 1967, every one of Davis's saxophonists – and there have been many – has doubled on that instrument.

A few days after the *Water Babies* recording session, on 2 July, the quintet shared the stage at Newport with a typically cluttered bill that also listed the Bill Evans Trio, the Max Roach Quintet, Sonny Rollins, the Woody Herman orchestra, singer Marilyn Maye, and a rock band with some slim jazz credentials called the Blues Project. The stage was also literally cluttered because the small bands had to work around the set-up for Herman's orchestra rather than taking the time to rearrange the stage for each group. Ira Gitler recalls "Tony Williams playing on Don Lamond's drum set, the wood chips behind the drummer's spot making that part of the stage look like a sawmill."[53] For Davis and his sidemen, the Newport concert was only the first of several dates in 1967 that would be promoted by George Wein; plans were under way for the quintet to join a package Wein was taking to Europe in the fall.

On 17 July, John Coltrane died. He had been playing in public infrequently for the previous five months, but he explained his relative isolation with a variety of excuses, saying that he was tired of playing in nightclubs or that he was busy working on new music. In fact, he was suffering from cancer of the liver. On the day before his death, with the pain so intense he could no longer bear it, he drove himself to a hospital and checked in. The news of his death numbed the jazz world as nothing had since Charlie Parker's death twelve years earlier. For younger musicians, Coltrane's death became one of those iconic events that stays vividly in the mind. "I was coming back from the midwest with Ray Bryant when they announced that John Coltrane had died," drummer Ronald Shannon Jackson remembers. "It seemed like something had burst my bubble – all the feelings I had for music ... When he died, it just took a lot out of me."[54] Jackson quit music abruptly and only returned as a full-time professional several years later.

At the moment of Coltrane's death, the black neighborhood of

Newark was in turmoil, with riots and fires and looting. It was the start of America's long, hot summers, as the black population grew impatient with the slow advances of the civil rights legislation and demonstrated its unrest in open rebellion in the ghetto streets of almost every major city. Malcolm X was dead and Martin Luther King would be assassinated the next year, and John Coltrane's music, as searing, outspoken, and powerful as the man himself was taciturn and meek, captured the rhetoric of human dignity and human aspiration as forcefully as Malcolm's writings or King's preachings. Deborah D'Amico, in an elegy for Coltrane (quoted in full by J.C. Thomas), wrote:

we are lucky, I suppose,
that they let you blow at all
their love is gold
that turns to dollars

yours streamed from your mouth
as free as air,
as rare as free[55]

By the time of his death at the age of 40, Coltrane "had passed," as Whitney Balliett put it, "from mere musician to messiah."[56] Just as the jazz world was showing signs of recovery after years of recession, Coltrane's death took away one of its most inspirational figures.

Two of the other inspirational figures, Miles Davis and Dizzy Gillespie, took their bands into the Village Gate for the entire month of August. It was pairing that kept the crowds lined up outside the Greenwich Village club for the entire engagement, and those who managed to get a seat in the muggy downstairs room for a complete set heard an encapsulated history of the changes in jazz in the two decades since the 1940s, when Gillespie was the bop guru of 52nd Street and Davis was his star pupil. Gillespie's quintet, with James Moody on tenor saxophone, clung to their bebop roots and played some of the repertoire (Con Alma, Night in Tunisia, I Can't Get Started, and so on) that Gillespie had played for years. Gillespie's fervor was infectious, and his band played energetically enough behind him, but Miles Davis's young quintet sometimes seemed to overflow with energy. On some of their non-stop sets, familiar themes dissolved before listeners could identify them, and the entire set turned into explorations of completely unfamiliar themes, forms, and balances. Listeners could hardly help but draw comparisons even though the musics were by now different enough to defy comparison.

One night the audience at the Village Gate included Sugar Ray Robinson, the former welterweight and middleweight boxing champion, and Archie Moore, the former light-heavyweight champion. Out of it came a situation that Gillespie likes to cite as proof for his theory that Davis suffers from abject shyness. "Now, Miles is a big fight fan," Gillespie points out, "so one would think that introducing the fighters from the stage would have been his moment ... Anyhow, Miles, whose band was on the stand, came over to me and said, 'Hey, Sugar Ray and Archie Moore are here.' I said, 'So?' and he said, 'Well, won't you introduce them when you go on?' I said, 'Hell, you're on now. You introduce them. You've got it!' But he didn't introduce them. He left it to me."[57]

Davis's and Gillespie's bands again shared a stage four days after they closed at the Village Gate, on 1 September, when they played at the Laurel International Jazz Festival in Maryland, yet another addition to the summer jazz festival circuit. In the parade of musicians playing that night, which included Herman's orchestra, organist Jimmy Smith, and singer Etta Jones, was Gary Bartz, a young saxophonist born and raised in nearby Baltimore who had just made his first LP. Three years later, Bartz would become a member of Davis's band.

The difficult climate for any music that could not attract a teenaged following became clear when George Wein organized the benefit concert to aid the Metropolitan Opera Orchestra. The activist climate on civil rights issues also came clear. Wein lined up Miles Davis and Duke Ellington, whose bands could fill the posh Met facilities at the Lincoln Center, and, while both agreed and ended up performing, Davis found the decision far from easy. "We gave a benefit for the Metropolitan Opera band," he said later, "and they don't even hire Negroes. And I was gonna tell Duke not to do it, but I told George, 'Now, George, you make sure they hire some Negroes.' But a Negro player told me they get their white cousins and all that bullshit in line to play with them. That's some sad shit."[58] Despite the inroads in the civil rights struggle in the 1960s, symphonic music remained a white preserve in 1967. Ortiz M. Walton, in his book *Music: Black, White and Blue*, points out that he was one of only two blacks employed full-time by any of the five major symphony orchestras in the United States until 1969,[59] when several black musicians including bassist Arthur Davis, a conservatory-trained musician whose best exposure had been with John Coltrane's band, brought a civil suit against the New York Philharmonic. Miles Davis and a lot of other musicians were well aware of the inequities long before the suit brought the facts into the public consciousness.

From 19 October until 12 November 1967, the Miles Davis Quintet played concerts in Europe as part of a touring package known as Newport Jazz Festival in Europe. Wein organized the tour, and the complex of sponsors, musicians, itineraries, and locales made it perhaps the most complicated movement of performing artists ever undertaken. Wein had lined up Pan-American Airlines and the US Department of Commerce as sponsors, thus underwriting his own expenses and ensuring first-class travel for the musicians by attracting public and private funds, a flair that Wein has exploited ever since he began promoting the Newport Jazz Festival for the Lorillard Tobacco Company. For the London leg of the tour, 23–29 October, he tied in his musicians with an ongoing concert series called Jazz Expo '67, named after the enormously successful world fair, Expo '67, in Montreal that summer. Wein's line-up of musicians performed in various combinations, with some groups leaving for the next city as other groups were arriving.

The musicians, both in sheer numbers and in the temperaments involved, made an awesome lot: besides Miles Davis and his four sidemen, they included Thelonious Monk, with an octet featuring Ray Copeland, Jimmy Cleveland, Johnny Griffin, Phil Woods, and Charlie Rouse; Sarah Vaughan accompanied by the Bob James Trio; vibraphonist Gary Burton's quartet with guitarist Larry Coryell; a bevy of guitarists of all ages and styles: George Benson, Buddy Guy, Jim Hall, Barney Kessel, and Elmer Snowden; Archie Shepp's avant-garde quintet, with two trombonists, Roswell Rudd and Grachan Moncur III, and drummer Beaver Harris; Clark Terry; and the Newport All Stars, featuring Ruby Braff, Buddy Tate, and, on piano, George Wein. Most promoters might have balked at the prospect of having any two of Davis, Monk, Shepp, or Braff on a tour, let alone all of them, and the tour itself was neither brief nor sedentary. In the span of about four weeks, they mounted concerts in more than twenty cities in Ireland, England, Finland, Denmark, Sweden, Germany, Holland, Belgium, Switzerland, Italy, France, and Spain. Several of the concerts were taped, including Davis's concerts in London (29 October), Stockholm (31), Karlsruhe, Germany (1 November), Copenhagen (2), Berlin (4), and Paris (6), but none of them has yet been made public.

Relations between Davis and Wein, not surprisingly, have often been strained and have sometimes erupted into recriminations, the first coming at the end of this tour. Both are hard-nosed businessmen, but Wein is blustery and extroverted where Davis is taciturn and introverted, and the combination seldom mixes smoothly. For all that, as the top performer and the top promoter in jazz, they are practically forced to respect one another – sometimes grudgingly, at least on Davis's part – and they have often argued bitterly. Their negotiations about money, beginning with this tour, are hard fought and usually end with Davis getting what he considers his due. "He pays enough money and everything," Davis once conceded.[60] But Wein, with his promoter's instinct, apparently believes that if he has to pay Davis top money he can take his consolation by announcing the terms to the press and getting some publicity for his concerts from the news. It is a practice that rankles Davis. "I think George Wein is unfair," he told Don DeMicheal. "I'm on his tour, but I think he's using me. I wrote him a letter and told him. He tells other people how much I make. He kinda glorifies that, y'know."[61]

Davis's complaints on this tour began with the fitness regimen he was trying to keep up while traveling in Europe. He had stopped drinking because of his liver ailment, but the reason he gave to Arthur Taylor, who interviewed him a few weeks after the tour ended, overlooked his health problems entirely. "When you do one-nighters, like we did in Europe," he said, "and you drink every time you eat, you wind up feeling real tired before a concert. You get up early in the morning ... You might have a hangover and it carries on, and you won't be able to think right." The regimen was also supposed to include regular workouts, but Davis figured that Wein prevented him from doing that: "The only thing I asked George was, 'Wherever we go, try to find a gymnasium in the town so I'll have something to do.' He didn't do it. I figured he'd take care of it himself, but he had those in-between guys, the middlemen, who didn't think it was important. But to me it was important. I guess they thought it was a joke."[62] The afternoons of inactivity nagged at Davis throughout the tour.

His consolation came from the concerts themselves. "I had a nice time in Europe because the band played good," he told Taylor. "The band plays pretty good sometimes." Listeners everywhere agreed. Valerie Wilmer, covering the concert at London's Hammersmith Odeon, in which the Davis quintet were billed, as they often were throughout the tour, with Archie Shepp's quintet, called it "a concert that had everyone standing on their ear." She reported that Davis's continuous recital included *Round Midnight* and four or five other melodies; at the concert four days later in Copenhagen, Davis included *Round Midnight*, *Masqualero* (from the *Sorcerer* LP), and *No Blues* in his recital. "In spite of all his pretensions to the contrary," Wilmer added, "Davis is by dint of both sound and appearance the master showman." She also recognized the crucial role of Tony Williams behind Davis's solos. "He's loud, sure, but Miles likes it that way because it spurs him into moments of starkly screaming beauty," she said. "The excruciating cry of the Davis horn owes more than a little to Williams. The music was bittersweet perfection."[63]

The coupling of Davis's quintet with Archie Shepp's indicates recognition by the promoters of Davis's recent alliance with freer jazz, a recognition not nearly as widespread as it should have been, perhaps because most jazz fans and many reviewers were still smitten with Davis's earlier records and had not caught up to him in the interval. To someone like Wilmer, of course, the coupling just seemed natural. It may or may not have seemed so natural to Davis, so recently an outspoken critic of the avant-garde. He continued to demonstrate his umbrage publicly. At one concert Davis asked Shepp to join his band on stage and then, according to Barry McRae, "stormed off because Shepp had hogged the solo limelight, playing music with which he had little sympathy."[64]

When the tour reached Barcelona on its last leg, Wein, according to Davis, "tried to slip in two extra concerts and told me he'd pay my room rent. I called him and said, 'George, if we're doing an extra concert, give me more money.' And guess what he said: 'Man, like I don't have no bread.' So how you going to talk business like that?" One of Davis's periodic complaints about Wein is that he affects jazz slang when talking to musicians instead of using business terms. It always succeeds in rousing Davis's ire. In Barcelona, Davis replied, "If you don't have no bread, get somebody else, 'cause I'm leaving." "When it gets so you feel like you're being taken advantage of," Davis told Arthur Taylor, "it's best to leave, because he's not treating you like a man." Davis took the next flight back to the United States. Wein immediately told reporters that Davis had left without giving notice to anyone, including his musicians, who played at the Barcelona concert as the Wayne Shorter Quartet. Davis maintained that he had told Wein at the airport that he was leaving. "Oh yeah, George stopped a check because I didn't play in Spain," Davis added. "I was there for two days. So now I'm suing him for what he said. For always dropping all the weight on me."[65] As on other occasions, recriminations and hard feelings flew back and forth and then were forgotten by both parties, until the time came to enter into a new business deal.

As soon as the quintet reassembled in New York, Davis started putting in hours with them in the recording studio, a sharp reversal of his infrequent visits to Columbia's studios for several years and a practice that he would continue long after he disbanded his good young quintet. Many of the recording sessions were decidedly experimental, recorded rehearsals rather than performances, and they show Davis searching for ways of incorporating new elements into his music. The new elements derive mainly from rock and soul music, but at this stage they are relatively mild effects and not at all the full-fledged incursions that would show up in his music with *In A Silent Way* and *Bitches Brew* a little more than a year later. They point in that direction, undeniably, but they consist of electronic instruments, either electric piano played by Hancock or electric guitar played by a guest sideman, overlaid on the style of the regular quintet. Later, after the quintet disbanded, the fusion of jazz and rock-funk-soul elements became part of the fabric of the music.

Of all the music recorded from December to March, only one title was released at the time. Seven more titles were held until 1979 or 1981 and then compiled along with unreleased material from other periods in two collections of Davis's music put out during his years of temporary retirement. These seven titles show clearly that Davis's development of his fusion style was much more gradual than anyone suspected at the time. The remaining unreleased music from this period, which is voluminous if not monumental, will probably not contain many surprises, after the samples from so many different dates spread over these months.

Davis's first attempt at finding richer textures for his music left him bitter. He added a young guitarist, Joe Beck, to the quintet for some recording sessions in December and worked out some arrangements for the altered instrumentation, probably enlisting Gil Evans's aid, but he was dissatisfied with the results. Two titles from these sessions were issued belatedly, and the details are as follows:

Miles Davis Quintet + Joe Beck
Miles Davis, tpt, chimes; Wayne Shorter, ts; Herbie Hancock, celeste; Joe Beck, gtr; Ron Carter, b; Tony Williams, dms; probably Gil Evans, co-arr. New York, 4 December 1967
Circle in the Round
(on *Circle in the Round*, Columbia 36278 [1979])

Same personnel; Hancock plays electric piano. Same place, 28 December 1967
Water on the Pond
(on *Directions*, Columbia KC2 36472 [1981])

Beck was just outgrowing his reputation in the New York musicians' community as a guitar prodigy. He was 22 now, but he had been in recording studios almost continuously for four years. He was a new breed; traditionally, studio musicians had come from the ranks of experienced pros who had paid their dues in symphonies and road bands. Beck arrived from Philadelphia fresh out of high school and fell into studio work. "I was the only guy in my age group that could play at the time in New York," he told Julie Coryell. "It just happened that there was a bunch of guys doing jingles who were starting out at the same time I was. It was a very special time, and I don't think it could ever occur for a kid again." After about a year he was in steady demand as an arranger as well as a player, and, in his version, he fell into arranging commercials by accident too. "A guy approached me in a bar and asked me to do a demo for a jingle," he recalled. "I said okay because he said he had a budget of $250, and I figured I'd play all the parts myself and take the $250 and split, which I did; but they bought it for thousands of dollars. I ended up doing hundreds and hundreds of commercials for every conceivable instrumentation, and they paid me very well to learn how to arrange."[66] Although Beck credits good luck, he had risen to the top in one of the most brutally competitive music markets anywhere, and it was his precocious talent that saw him through. On his studio rounds he inevitably got to know Ron Carter, who may have recommended him to Davis, but Beck also had a reputation in jazz circles from playing in Gary McFarland's studio orchestras and in bands led by Paul Winter, Jeremy Steig, and Chico Hamilton; he worked with Gil Evans a few months before Davis hired him and continued working with him whenever Evans assembled a band until 1970.

On *Circle in the Round*, Beck settles into a steady repetitive drone that maintains the 12/8 time signature all through and functions solely for keeping the time. The rambling, twenty-six-minute track rides along on Beck's rhythmic groove, giving a foretaste of the fusion style to come. Beck's presence frees Carter from his usual time-keeping and allows him to take a short solo, a rarity in his studio recordings with the quintet. Hancock's celeste allows his typical chordal colors to reverberate, something he would accomplish more facilely on the Fender Rhodes piano in later sessions. While the track is interesting as a foreshadowing of fusion, it is flawed by several abrupt transitions (possibly splices) and by a series of false endings. Musically, its interest resides almost exclusively in Davis's solo choruses on open trumpet – he reappears to solo five times, probably through the dubious magic of splicing – and over the background guitar his playing takes on some of the timbre and the lyricism of his solos over Gil Evans's orchestrations.

Water on the Pond is more of an entity: a simple, self-contained medium-tempo ballad based on a rhythm maintained by Beck and Carter, with good solos by Davis on muted trumpet and Shorter on tenor saxophone. This track marks Hancock's recording debut on electric piano and apparently also his first attempt at playing an electronic keyboard, and he is predictably cautious, asserting himself only mildly when Davis stops the rhythm and plays over Hancock's and Beck's fills.

Hancock's debut on Fender Rhodes piano came about as one of Davis's calculated surprises. When Hancock arrived in the studio that morning, Davis pointed him toward the piano already set up in the corner. Josef Zawinul had been playing an electric piano nightly in Julian Adderley's band, and Davis was fascinated by it. "Miles came to see me and checked it out," Zawinul says, "and then he got an electric piano for Herbie Hancock."[67] Hancock, too, was smitten and spent long hours working on his technique. The instrument would soon alter Davis's music in several ways. "My playing of the electric piano ... gave the music plenty of bottom," Hancock says, "and when the individual band members became more aware of the Rhodes, their writing began to change as a result, and in a subtle way the rhythms began to change."[68] At the time of the recordings with Joe Beck, those changes were still a long way off.

Beck's presence marks the beginning of Davis's long search for richer textures in his music. In the dynamics established by the working quintet, Tony Williams had been mainly responsible for the density – what Davis and the others call "bottom" – while the others kept up an austere surface. Now he wanted to enrich the density of his music by augmenting Williams's drumming with more varied timbres in the rhythm. He has Hancock comping on celeste and electric piano and himself striking the chimes, but the key addition was expected to come from the arranged ostinato of the guitar. The changes are not completely successful. Although the textures on *Circle in the Round* and *Water on the Pond* are altered from those of the quintet's performances, they are not richer. Davis considered the sessions a failure, and he laid the blame squarely on Beck. "I was so mad, they gave me a royalty check and I didn't even look at it," he told Martin Williams at a recording session a month later, when he brought in George Benson to play guitar. Williams reported then that "Davis was still smarting from the experience of a previous session when an otherwise capable studio guitarist had failed him miserably."[69]

It is impossible to know, of course, what Davis expected of Beck, but on the aural evidence of the two tracks released so far the failing – if it can be called that, when the tracks offer so many points of interest – seems to rest partly with Tony Williams as well as with Beck. Beck plays his parts mechanically, without departing from his arranged lines, but Williams allows him to take over the rhythms completely and loses his identity in the restraint he imposes on himself. He seems intent on keeping out of Beck's way instead of sharing in the new dynamics of the augmented band. His dissatisfaction is almost audible in the stilted drumming on these tracks.

Davis blamed Beck, and he attributed much of the problem to the pigmentation of Beck's skin. "When whites play with Negroes and can't play the music, it's a form of Jim Crow to me," Davis told George Benson within ear-shot of Martin Williams. "Studio musicians – they're supposed to know what's going on in our music, too. One, two, three, four – anybody can do that. And if you don't do it, they don't believe the beat is still there."[70]

Before Davis could line up a new guitar player he spent more hours in the recording studios with the quintet, allowing Hancock to work on the electric piano. So far, only an excerpt of these sessions has been issued. The details are as follows:

Miles Davis Quintet
Miles Davis, tpt; Wayne Shorter, ts; Herbie Hancock, electric pno; Ron Carter, b; Tony Williams, dms. New York, 11 January 1968
Fun
(on *Directions*, Columbia KC2 36472)

As its title implies, *Fun* is merely an out-take, a four-minute slice in which Davis plays a few notes at the beginning and then fails to return after Shorter's solo.

Davis added George Benson to the quintet for a series of recording sessions in the next two months. A gifted natural musician, Benson earned his first dollar from music at the age of four, singing on street corners in Pittsburgh. He started picking out tunes on electric guitar three years later, when his stepfather retrieved his old instrument from a pawn shop and brought it home. "I remember sitting with my ear pressed up against the amplifier all night long until I fell asleep," he told Julie Coryell, "and that sound has been with me from that day to this."[71] He left home to tour with organist Jack McDuff when he was 18 and began recording on his own for producer Creed Taylor at 21. He was only a week away from his 25th birthday at his final session with Davis's band, and he was already a highly adaptable guitarist (and singer). He still had to wait a few years before scoring the blockbuster successes that people such as Taylor considered inevitable for him. Those came in the 1970s, notably with a 1976 LP called *Breezin'* (Warner Brothers BS 2919), a million-selling record – 'platinum' in industry argot – in a style best described as middle-of-the-road jazz-rock-soul-funk. When he went into the studio with Davis, his successes were modest and had come mainly in jazz. The details are as follows:

Miles Davis Quintet + George Benson
Miles Davis, tpt; Wayne Shorter, ts; Herbie Hancock, pno; George Benson, gtr (except on *Teo's Bag*); Ron Carter, b; Tony Williams, dms; Gil Evans, co-arr. New York, 16 January 1968
untitled composition; *Paraphernalia*; *Teo's Bag*
(untitled composition unissued; *Paraphernalia* on *Miles in the Sky*, Columbia CS 9628; *Teo's Bag* on *Circle in the Round*, Columbia 36278)

Same personnel; Benson on *Side Car II* only. Same place, 13 February 1968
Side Car I; *Side Car II*
(both on Columbia 36278)

Same personnel, including Benson. Same place, 15 March 1968
Sanctuary
(on Columbia 36278)

Evans's participation has never been credited or acknowledged, but Martin Williams attended the January session seeking fodder for his *Stereo Review* column, and when Evans showed up he explained, "I midwifed a couple of these pieces."[72] He spent the day in the studio, occasionally answering Davis's summons to clear up points in his arrangement.

The first two hours of the January session, called for 10 a.m. and under way by 10.30, were spent on an untitled composition by Hancock arranged by Evans. The band played sixteen takes before Davis was satisfied, and even then his satisfaction was apparently relative, because the track has not yet been released. Williams reported the progress through the takes in some detail, watching Davis and Shorter integrate their phrasing of the "rolling melody" as Hancock advised Benson: "Some of these are chords. Some are just sounds." Tony Williams worked out his part without the guidance of a score, "feeling his way into it," Williams wrote, "in a highly personal manner": "He began with a bit of history, an old-fashioned, regular *ching-de-ching* cymbal beat. By the second or third run-through, he was trying a conservative latin rhythm, executed chiefly with wire brushes on his snare drum. But within a few more tries, his part had become a complex whirl of cymbal, snare and tom-tom patterns and accents, although there was no question of where the beat, the basic 1-2-3-4, was falling."[73]

As the flawed takes piled up, Macero was reminded of the very first band that Davis formed with Gil Evans as arranger. "That line is hard," he said. "It reminds me of those things Miles did for Capitol. Remember them? But this is much freer, of course." After the sixteenth take, Macero announced that Martin Williams considered it a good one, to which Davis replied from the studio, "What the fuck has Martin got to do with it?" But after the playback, he said, "That's all right, Teo."

Shorter's *Paraphernalia* followed and took shape more quickly. Williams watched the sidemen consult with one another over the score and work out its details as Davis sat back, seemingly disinterested. "His presence is authoritative and puts his sidemen on their mettle, and he knows it," Williams commented. "But when the moment is ready for a decision, he makes one. 'Wayne, you don't play the 3/4 bars, and the last 4/4 bar is cut out.'"[74]

Williams left the session after *Paraphernalia*, and Benson apparently did too, leaving the quintet to run through a head arrangement later released as *Teo's Bag*, setting a quick tempo for solos by Davis, Shorter, and an otherwise silent Hancock. The track probably took only a little longer from inception to recording than its actual playing time (almost six minutes) and was tacked on to the end of the reel of tape to fill out the day's work, but it was released before the still-nameless piece with the careful arrangement that occupied most of the session. "That's hard work — making records," Davis told Williams. Made harder, no doubt, when the results of the work are issued so unpredictably.

Paraphernalia was the first music released from any of these sessions, appearing later in the year on *Miles in the Sky* with three quintet tracks and thus finding a place in one of the key documents of the period. The addition of Benson appeared at the time to be a minor whim, and it was more than ten years before the extent of Benson's work with the band became clear. His presence makes little real difference to the quintet's style, certainly less difference than Beck's had made, because all the other players, including Tony Williams, are uninhibited by his presence. *Paraphernalia* is a moody exploration of a minor mode with a very subdued solo by Benson following Davis's and Shorter's solos and a displaced acoustic solo by Hancock following the final statement of the theme. Benson conspires effectively with Hancock and Carter to create the effervescent rhythm line that makes the descending scale of the theme sound strangely doleful.

Davis later told Arthur Taylor that he added Benson for this title because "I wanted to hear the bass line a little stronger." He explained: "If you can hear a bass line, then any note in a sound that you play can be heard, because you have the bottom. We change the bass line quite a bit on all the songs we play. It varies. So I figured if I wrote a bass line, we could vary it so that it would have a sound a little larger than a five-piece group. By using the electric piano [*sic*] and having Herbie play the bass line and the chords with the guitar and Ron also playing with him in the same register, I thought it would sound good. It came out all right. It was a nice sound."[75]

Davis's predilections with the bottom of his music were no mere dalliance. His conception of the fusion to come goes through several phases that thicken the rhythmic density of his music until, finally, in his 1972–5 band, there is virtually nothing left but rhythmic textures.

With Benson, he was less single-minded about the guitar's rhythmic purpose than he would later become. On *Sanctuary* at the March session, the rhythm is largely implied. Benson adds nothing to it and is almost undetectable except for chipping in an occasional chord. Williams, too, is inconspicuous apart from some scattered percussion effects, including a creaky door sound that disrupts the mood. The composition, by Shorter, is a melancholy ballad, played with full respect for its melody and, except for the creaky door, its mood. It will reappear in a definitive version sixteen months later, as part of the *Bitches Brew* LP, but this earlier, unexpected recording of it, a more straightforward jazz version, is as full of feeling. Any comparison between the two is certain to find advocates for the first version in spite of the obvious merits of the later. The differences between them provide a graphic illustration of the changes that Davis was about to make in his music.

George Benson and Joe Beck were only the first indications of those modifications.

The remaining title recorded with Benson in the band, *Side Car*, is a complex composition by Davis. The two released takes suggest that it proved too difficult to execute in the studio time allotted to it. Its theme is stated in unison eighth notes by Davis and Shorter at a fast tempo, with staccato bursts that give it a singsong quality. Shorter struggles with his part in the ensemble, especially in the second version, and on the first manages only a very methodical solo in a strangely thin tone. For Davis, it is an ambitious piece of writing in a period when he tended to leave adventurous composition to the other members of his band.

Later in March, Davis and the quintet spent several hours recording with a large orchestra under Gil Evans's direction. Finally one of the collaborations between Davis and Evans seemed to be coming to fruition.

Evans's charts, as usual, challenged even the experienced pros he had assembled for the studio call. Howard Johnson, Evans's first choice as a tuba player since 1966, told Lee Jeske how he came to learn how to follow one of Evans's directions at these sessions and also, incidentally, supplied one of the few hints of what was played. "There were things Gil requested of me that no one ever asked me to do before and I didn't know how to do some of them," he said. "He used to use the phrase 'a light sound', and I didn't know what he meant by that for years. One time we were in the studio with Miles Davis' quintet and a large orchestra, and there was one part that was very difficult. It wasn't so difficult to play, but I'm not a great reader; I had to play the line with Ron Carter, and it was pretty high up. He was playing with his bow, and we had to be in tune, and the pressure was really *on*. I wasn't sure of myself so I pulled back a lot, and when I heard it back, because I was scared, it was really light sounding and just right. And Gil said, 'Yeah, that's the sound I mean,' very calmly. And it really blew me away because I hadn't heard it myself before. I never duplicated it again on that date, but I learned how to play that way then.'[76]

Most other details remain unknown because none of this material has ever been released, although a few of them might be inferred from the music presented in concert by Davis and Evans a month later, which was also recorded and remains unreleased. These studio dates may have been intended primarily as rehearsals for the upcoming concert, and for Evans it must have seemed like progress just to get as far as a studio appointment and a concert with one of his projects with Davis.

Several of those projects were already gathering dust in Davis's music room. In January Davis had told Arthur Taylor that he and Evans had "been working on something for about three years," but he still could not predict how it might turn out. He showed Taylor some "little sketches," played some phrases from them on the piano, and explained: "We write, and then we take out everything we don't like, and what's left is what we record."[77] Since 1962, the process of taking out "everything we don't like" had left them with almost nothing at all.

They were not getting much help from Columbia's managers, who believed they were doing all they could to unleash the creative energies that had produced *Porgy and Bess*, Davis's best-selling LP. Columbia's most recent proposal to Davis and Evans was to make a jazz version of the score of *Dr. Dolittle*, a 20th Century Fox film directed by Richard Fleischer. The movie, a musical for children about an eccentric old dandy, played by Rex Harrison, who consorts with strange animals and Samantha Eggar, was released in 1967 and perished because of miscasting and – believe it or not – a thoroughly forgettable score. Davis and Evans took Columbia's suggestion seriously enough to listen to the score, and Davis seemed generous to fault in telling Taylor that "*Dr. Dolittle* has about three songs in it that are worth something, but the rest have to be rebuilt." Columbia eventually released a mildly jazzed-up version of *Dr. Dolittle* (cs 9615) by the Dixieland piano player Joe Bushkin, with orchestrations by Billy Byers. Davis and Evans's *Dr. Dolittle* project, predictably and perhaps mercifully, was never completed, like all their projects at that time except for the score of *Time of the Barracuda* and the studio rehearsals for their concert, which went into Columbia's vaults.

The concert was in California, at the second Jazz Festival of the University of California at Berkeley, where the quintet had played the year before when rainstorms forced them to move indoors instead of playing in the Greek Theater. This year, with an eighteen-piece orchestra to accommodate in addition to the quintet, the weather was kinder. The concert was described in a *Down Beat* report filed by Sammy Mitchell.

Davis and Evans appeared in the final performance of the first evening, following Cecil Taylor and Carmen McRae. They used a format similar to their Carnegie Hall concert of 1961, the only other one they had ever presented, with the quintet playing part and then holding their places as featured players with the orchestra for the remainder. But the quintet played most of the concert on their own and the orchestra participated in only three compositions. Mitchell cited as the major "disappointment" "the sparseness, in quantity, of this new collaboration between Evans and Davis."[78]

The quintet, with bassist Marshall Hawkins filling in for Ron Carter, who again stayed in New York, offered extended versions of some of their best recent works; only *Round Midnight* is brought forward from Davis's standard repertoire of a few years earlier, transformed into a duet by Davis and Hancock. The orchestral repertoire was entirely new. The details are as follows:

Miles Davis Quintet with the Gil Evans Orchestra
Miles Davis, tpt; Wayne Shorter, ts; Herbie Hancock, pno; Marshall Hawkins, b; Tony Williams, dms. Greek Theater, Berkeley, California, 19 April 1968
Agitation; Footprints; Nefertiti; Round Midnight (Davis, Hancock only);
Ginger Bread Boy
(all unissued)

Gil Evans, arr, cond; Davis; Shorter; Hancock; Hawkins; Williams; Esther Mayhan, Arthur Frantz, frh; Howard Johnson, tba; Dick Houlgate, Bob Richards, bassoon; Anthony Ortega, flt, ss; John Mayhan, flt, bass clnt; Joe Skufca, oboe, english horn; Herb Bushler, gtr, el b; John Morrell, gtr, mandolin; Jeff Kaplan, gtr; Suzanna England, harp; Tommy Vig, marimba, perc
untitled raga; *You Make Me Feel Like a Natural Woman; Antigua*
(all unissued)
The order of performance at the concert is as shown except that *Ginger Bread Boy* was played by the quintet between *You Make Me Feel Like a Natural Woman* and *Antigua*.

In his report, Mitchell likens the quintet's performances, except for *Round Midnight*, to the evening's earlier appearance by Cecil Taylor, which he called "atonal lightning" and "dissonant thunder," and he makes no bones about preferring Carmen McRae's intervening set to both of them. He complains about Davis's technique, described as "unsteady as a drunk on the fast runs" of *Footprints* and as "fog-drenched" on *Nefertiti*. On the orchestral numbers, obviously much more to his taste, he had no such complaints, and of the untitled raga he says, "Davis' lines were long manicured fingers that reached and expertly flexed inside the silken glove of Evans' subdued orchestration." The raga effect was simulated by a combination of mandolin, electric guitar, and steel guitar, with the marimba carrying the 5/4 time.

Antigua, by Shorter, featured duets by Davis and Shorter over the orchestra's quiet colors. "All good stuff," Mitchell states, "beautifully backed." Of Evans, he declares: "This showing punched no holes in his reputation as a supreme orchestrator. He is the Boswell to Davis' Johnson: illustrating journeys, underlining anecdotes, revealing Davis' personality in full."[79] One can only wonder, even if the performances preserved on tape turn out to be less exquisite separated from the atmosphere of the Greek Theater, why they have been withheld so long.

Back in New York in May, Davis took up where he had left off before the orchestral preparations intervened. He took the quintet into the recording studios and recorded three tracks which, with *Paraphernalia* from a January session, comprised his next LP. The details are as follows:

Miles Davis Quintet: Miles in the Sky
Miles Davis, tpt; Wayne Shorter, ts; Herbie Hancock, pno; Ron Carter, b; Tony Williams, dms. New York, 15 May 1968
Country Son
(on Columbia CS 9628)

Same personnel. Same place, 16 May 1968
Black Comedy
(on Columbia CS 9628)

Same personnel; Hancock plays electric piano. Same place, 17 May 1968
Stuff
(on Columbia CS 9628)

Reviewers of *Miles in the Sky* sensed that something in Davis's music was changing, although they had some difficulty saying what it was. Lawrence Kart, writing in *Down Beat*, said, "This record ... shows the effect of the Coleman-Coltrane revolution even as Miles denies it, for their assault on the popular song has pushed Miles along the only path that seems open to him, an increasingly ironic detachment from sentiment and prettiness."[80] In *Coda*, Harvey Pekar wrote: "The general character of Miles' music seems to change beginning with *Miles in the Sky*. On it he and his sidemen generally play more aggressively and are less interested in improvising lyrically."[81] And yet, in terms of aggressiveness, Tony Williams is hardly more cyclonic here than he was on the three previous LPs, and, in terms of lyricism, Davis and Hancock allow themselves no fewer quiet moments. Change was in the wind, all right, but it does not seem attributable to the Coleman-Coltrane elements or the disavowal of lyricism. Those aspects belonged equally to *Nefertiti* and *Sorcerer*. For the most part, *Miles in the Sky* belongs with them in the style that developed soon after Shorter joined the band and adds very little that is significant to it.

What is new exists in hints, especially on *Stuff* and *Country Son*, both written by Davis. *Stuff* locks Hancock into a little rock vamp on the electric piano and stifles – or at least tries – Williams into boogaloo rhythms that are infectious, toe-tapping, and trite. For Williams, the cadences seem ridiculously easy, and he executes them with a dutiful clarity as long as he can hold himself to them. For Hancock, the vamp may or may not be absurdly easy – it sounds as if it should be – but in either case he is willing to stick with it all the way. In doing so, he gives one of the first indications of the adaptability that in the next decade would permit him to court and find considerable pop fame.

Country Son, a more interesting composition, moves each soloist in turn through a meditative section, a funky rhythm, and a 4/4 striptease shuffle, except in the opening played by Davis, which has no rhythmic developments at all, suggesting that several minutes of the opening have been deleted. Again, Hancock provides a clue to the change that is brewing. In his solo he repeatedly comes up with little funk phrases that sound alien to his style. In the context of the whole LP, they are easily overlooked, and even the more conspicuous amplified vamp and the jolting drums of *Stuff* seem little more than unusual devices. They take on significance in the larger context afforded by the piecemeal release of other material from this period, and still more in the light of Davis's directions after disbanding the quintet, only a few months later.

Those months were spent in the familiar summer rounds of concerts and club engagements, made busier because they had to be fitted into the new regimen of regular recording sessions. In June, the quintet spent the first week at the Showboat in Philadelphia, returned to New York to put in three days recording tracks for their next album, and then left immediately for Minneapolis, where they played a concert at the Tyrone Guthrie Theatre on the same bill as the singer-pianist Mose Allison. Davis squeezed in a short holiday in London, where among other activities he took in a few sets by the Bill Evans trio at Ronnie Scott's jazz club. Back home, the two jazz festivals of the summer – Newport was not on the itinerary, probably because of the stand-off between Davis and Wein following the European tour – brought the quintet together with a baffling mélange of talent, as usual. At the

Randall's Island Festival, Davis and his sidemen shared the first night with Dizzy Gillespie, Ahmad Jamal, organist Shirley Scott, singers Irene Reid and Jimmy Witherspoon, and a comedian named Irwin C. Watson; if the promoters hoped to provide something for every taste they apparently succeeded, because the first-night attendance numbered almost 20,000. In early September, at the second annual Laurel International Jazz Festival in Maryland, they appeared along with Count Basie's orchestra and singer Joe Williams, the Horace Silver Quintet, and, again, Dizzy Gillespie. In between the two festivals, Gillespie was again their nightly companion as his band and Davis's shared the billing at the Village Gate in July. In early August, the quintet played at Count Basie's jazz club in Harlem, where Davis introduced his new bass player, David Holland, still jet-lagged from his flight from England. As if the regularly scheduled quintet engagements were not enough for the rejuvenated Davis, he then joined Max Roach's band at Count Basie's for a weekend in August, making a rare appearance as a guest soloist.

All the activity kept him from completing the LP started in June, but as soon as his schedule eased off in September he returned to finish it. The LP, called *Filles de Kilimanjaro*, is transitional not only in its style, as *Miles in the Sky* also was, but in its personnel. Davis had used the summer activities to break in replacements for Herbie Hancock and Ron Carter, who moved out on their own after more than five years with Davis. By the time of the September recording session, the replacements, Chick Corea and David Holland, fit easily into the concept of the recording begun by their predecessors. The details are as follows:

Miles Davis Quintet: Filles de Kilimanjaro
Miles Davis, tpt; Wayne Shorter, ts; Herbie Hancock, el pno; Ron Carter, b; Tony Williams, dms; Gil Evans, co-comp, arr. New York, 19 June 1968
Petits machins (*Little Stuff*)
(on Columbia CS 9750)

Same personnel. Same place, 20 June 1968
Tout de suite
(on Columbia CS 9750)

Same personnel. Same place, 21 June 1968
Filles de Kilimanjaro (*Girls of Kilimanjaro*)
(on Columbia CS 9750)

Chick Corea, acoustic pno, replaces Hancock; David Holland, el b, replaces
Carter. Same place, 24 September 1968
Frelon brun (Brown Hornet); Mademoiselle Mabry (Miss Mabry)
(both on Columbia CS 9750)
Most discographies, following the liner information on CS 9750, list Corea and
Holland on *Petits machins* in June and Hancock and Carter on *Frelon brun* in
September; however, Holland did not arrive in the United States until August.

Filles de Kilimanjaro presents more elaborate melodic lines than the
quintet had been working on for a couple of years, the palpable effect of
Gil Evans's participation as a composer as well as arranger.

   Tout de suite opens and closes as a ballad and features Hancock's
electric piano throughout. The keening line of the ballad gives way,
inexplicably, to improvisations in free, unsyncopated time – perhaps
intended as the allegro movement of the suite indicated punningly in
the title. Hancock both starts and ends the solo round with Davis and
Shorter in between. *Filles de Kilimanjaro*, a swaying 5/4 tune, has a
strong folk feeling in its written opening, and the time signature is
preserved throughout but the original melody is not reprised at the
close, the piece ending instead with a long coda in which Davis and
Hancock exchange phrases of irregular length. *Mademoiselle Mabry* is
all melody, in a sense. Chick Corea plays its long and complex lines at
the beginning and then repeats them over and over as Davis and Shorter
superimpose variations; by the time Corea's solo turn arrives, the
melody has been repeated so often that it lingers strongly behind his
variations. *Petits machins* sounds almost like a bebop riff, an astonishing sound to hear in Davis's music at this late date, but the connection is
quickly erased by the soloing, which again seems dissociated from the
written opening except when Shorter, like a latter-day Thelonious
Monk, revives its strains to parody them, and again the opening riff is
not repeated at the close. The bop overtones are thus fleeting. They are
more emphatic in a recording of this composition retitled *Eleven* by Gil
Evans and his orchestra around 1972 (on *Svengali*, Atlantic SD 1643) and
in a recording by Johnny Coles, a sometime sideman with Evans, under
its original title (on *Katumbo [Dance]*, Mainstream MRL 346). Neither of
the later recordings abandons the riff so quickly or submerges it so
thoroughly in the improvisations.

   Petits machins, Tout de suite, and *Filles de Kilimanjaro* seem in one
respect to be the apogee of the quintet's development in the four years
after Shorter came along to complete its tight circle. Where the best

pieces on *Miles Smiles* and *Nefertiti* found the quintet using minimal structures in favor of exploring a common mood, the best pieces on *Filles de Kilimajaro* take the further step of releasing the players from the strictures of a common mood as well. The composer's mood is set as strongly here as it was on, say, *Footprints* or *Circle*, but there it was dominant because it was not only established in the theme but also carried over into the solos. Here it dominates only in the sense that it comes first – it precedes the solo statements temporally – but it is not retained. Just as tempos, bar lines, and harmonies had become flexible elements in the quintet's music, now mood is no longer fixed. Listeners must discover the unity of the pieces instead of just locating it, as viewers must discover the unity in a painting with several simultaneous perspectives. The problems caused by requiring such active listening were relieved somewhat by the strength of the composed themes and the sometimes brilliant interplay of the veteran combination that the quintet had become. Listeners did not seem to find *Filles de Kilimanjaro* abstruse when it was released in 1969; *Down Beat*'s readers voted it best record of the year.

Once again, Gil Evans's role – this time a central one – went uncredited and unacknowledged by Davis and Columbia. The first hints of his involvement came three or four years later, with the new versions of *Petits machins/Eleven* recorded by Evans and Coles citing the composers as Evans and Davis in the small print on the label. On Davis's LP, *Petits machins* and all other compositions are credited solely to Davis. In 1977, nine years later, Dan Morgenstern's column in *Jazz Journal International* carried the following notice: "It is not common knowledge that the *Filles de Kilimanjaro* date was largely written and arranged by Gil."[82] Evans had been willing to let decades go by without claiming credit for arranging Davis's 1956 recording of *Round Midnight*, but something stirred him to make public his involvement in *Filles de Kilimanjaro*. He showed something less than temerity in doing so, granting himself no more than a credit line in small print and a single sentence in an English jazz magazine, but at least he put the information into the public domain. After so many years of frustrated projects, unissued recordings, and uncredited arrangements with Davis, he finally seemed to be growing restless by the end of the 1960s.

"I was domesticated," he told Zan Stewart, "I spent all my time with my family. I only got a band together because I was tired of sitting at the piano for thirty years trying to find different ways to voice a minor 7th chord."[83] He formed a band of his own in 1970, at the age of 58, and kept it together more or less steadily for the first time since 1961. In between, he had contented himself with bringing together some players for a weekend engagement whenever the opportunity came his way and with assembling an orchestra for a few weeks in 1967 and a few days in 1968 in California, but he would spend the 1970s developing some projects of his own.

His projects with Miles Davis continued. By now they were part of the way of life for both men, but the new projects had much the same failure rate as the old ones – which might also have become part of their way of life. Neither of them considered simply putting an end to the unproductive collaborations. They were the bond between them. "Oh yeah," Evans says, "he's family to me."[84]

Just as the music of *Filles de Kilimanjaro* served notice of Davis's changing conception and introduced some new personnel in his quintet, so its cover, more circuitously, indicated a couple of other changes, one in the slogan "Directions in music by Miles Davis" printed above the title and the other in the cover photograph.

The photograph, a full-face portrait of a woman with a three-quarter portrait superimposed, probably obscures the face of Betty Mabry, the namesake for *Mademoiselle Mabry*, an aspiring young soul singer. Davis had been divorced from Frances Taylor in February; the divorce was a formality because they had been living apart for some time. Davis's most frequent companion for two years had been Cicely Tyson until Mabry came along. She was 23, and a voluble young beauty who had done some modeling, managed a rock club, and written some soul songs, including one called *Uptown* that was recorded by the Chambers Brothers. She moved among some of the top stars of the rock world and had no qualms about chiding Davis for playing unamplified music without a boogaloo beat. "Miles was dazzled," according to Eric Nisenson in *'Round About Midnight: A Portrait of Miles Davis.*[85]

They were married on 30 September 1968, in Gary, Indiana. Davis and his quintet were playing in Chicago at the Plugged Nickel when he arranged a private wedding to be attended by his brother and sister, their families, and a few close friends. It quickly became public knowledge, because Mabry told a *Down Beat* reporter all about it. "He called me from Chicago and said, 'Sweetcakes, get your stuff together and come to Chicago, we're getting married,'" she told the reporter, and then she announced this pledge: "One of the sexiest men alive is Miles Dewey Davis. We're going to be married forever, because I'm in love and Mr. Davis can do no wrong as far as I'm concerned. He's experienced in all facets of life, has terrific taste in everything, loves only the best, and has taught me many things. I was never really a jazz fan because I lean mostly to rhythm and blues and pop, but Miles's *Sketches of Spain* and *Kind of Blue* really sock it to me. But Miles is the teacher, so I'm going to be cool, stay in the background, and back up my man."[86]

Their marriage lasted little more than a year, although the divorce took three years. Their friendship has been more abiding, and so has Mabry's influence. Davis's listening habits soon reflected her tastes, and still do, and some of the pop and funk elements she exposed him to began to show up in his music, filtered through his sensibility. "Betty would influence Miles musically perhaps more than any of his previous women," Nisenson points out.[87] In the aftermath of their tempestuous marriage, Leonard Feather asked Davis why he got married if he did not believe in families, and Davis replied, "Because they asked me. Every woman I ever married asked me."[88]

The slogan "Directions in music by Miles Davis" was repeated on his next LP, *In a Silent Way*, and then was dropped. The message it was intended to convey, Davis told Don DeMicheal, was a personal declaration of independence: "It means I tell everybody what to do. If I don't tell 'em, I ask 'em. It's my date, y'understand? And I've got to say yes or no. Been doing it for years, and I got tired of seeing 'Produced by this person or that person.' When I'm on a date, I'm usually supervising everything."[89]

Teo Macero, who had been listed in the credits of Davis's LPS starting with *Some Day My Prince Will Come*, the third he produced for him, was now restored to favor after taking the brunt of his wrath for releasing *Quiet Nights*, but Davis intended the new slogan to proclaim – to Macero and everyone else – where the real power in the control room rested. Little or nothing of this message came across, of course, in the slogan itself, and many listeners assumed that Columbia, in displaying it, was simply absolving itself from responsibility for the contents of the enclosed recordings, which had been going through some radical changes and were about to go through many more. Those listeners were wrong: neither Columbia's managers nor Macero were disinterested bystanders in the directions that Davis's music had started to take.

The "directions" flaunted on the LP covers were already a source of bafflement and concern as well as admiration for at least one of Davis's old cronies. Dizzy Gillespie, having spent two consecutive summers alongside Davis's quintet at the Village Gate, told Leonard Feather, "Miles should be commended for going off in a completely new direction. He's just as brave as shit ... I don't think I got that much guts. Sometimes I find myself playing those same old licks I used to play, till I get stale as a motherfuck."[90] He was more baffled than appreciative when Feather played him some of Davis's new music on a blindfold test. "It reminded me so much of Ornette Coleman," he said,[91] but because he knew it was Davis he was willing to concede that it had redeeming qualities, even if he could not figure out what they were. "The guy is such a fantastic musician that I know he has something in mind, whatever it is," he said. "I know he knows what he's doing, so he must be doing something that I can't get to yet."

Backstage one night at the Village Gate, Davis brought in a tape of his most recent recording session. "He played some of it for me," Gillespie told Feather, "and he said, 'How do you like that shit?' I said, 'What is it?' and he said, 'You know what it is; same shit you've been playing all the time,' and I said, 'Have I?' I said, 'Look, I'm going to come by your house and spend several hours and you're going to explain to me what that is.'"[92] A few years later Davis grumbled, "Dizzy asks me to teach him. I say, 'Yeah, come by. I'll show you everything we're doin'. It'll be my pleasure.' And he don't come by."[93] By then, Gillespie may have despaired of ever catching up with Davis's directions.

As soon as Davis disbanded the quintet that had been his workshop for so many innovations since 1964 and had supplied the impetus for them in the first place, the new directions came fast. Sometimes, later on, they seemed to come faster than the speed of sound, but for the next year they brought new life not only to Davis's music but to jazz as a whole.

Miles Davis and Gil Evans (Alan S. Flood, courtesy of *Down Beat*)

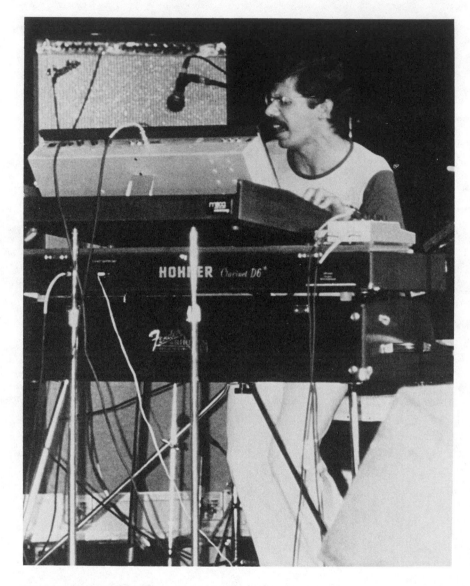

Chick Corea (Bernie Senensky)

12

Miles Runs the Voodoo Down
1968–9

I was telling Herbie the other day: 'We're not going to play the blues anymore. Let the white folks have the blues. They got 'em, so they can keep 'em. Play something else.' Miles Davis

In 1968 Miles Davis faced some inevitable changes. In the spring he turned 42, an age when most jazz musicians are content to replay the style they developed in their peak years. The opportunity – and the inclination – to do just that had presented itself in the early years of the decade, but somehow he had risen above the temptation and hired the young men who first pushed him and then followed him along a course of radical change. Now those young men were entering their own peak years and all of them were restless. They had spoken among themselves about moving out on their own, and finally Herbie Hancock and Ron Carter had taken the daunting step of speaking to Davis about quitting the quintet. The others would follow them soon enough: Tony Williams would leave at the end of the year, and Wayne Shorter would leave in 1970. Those changes were inevitable and so, really, were the changes in his music.

Davis's health, for the time being, was better than it had been for years, and his energy made him as restless as his sidemen. The hours he spent in the recording studio, adding instruments to the ensemble, plugging in amplifiers, reworking arrangements, were the most visible sign. Nothing he heard in the jazz being played around him seemed to provide the clues for what he wanted to hear from his own band. "You can't find a musician who plays anything different," he complained to Arthur Taylor at the start of the year. "They all copy off each other. If I were starting out again, I wouldn't listen to records. I very seldom listen to jazz records, because they all do the same thing. I only listen to guys who are original, like Ahmad Jamal and Duke Ellington, guys like Dizzy Gillespie, Sonny Rollins and Coltrane."[1] More often he listened to records that were not jazz. The day before Taylor interviewed him he had spent some hours listening to *Threnody for the Victims of Hiroshima* by the Polish composer Penderecki.

He was also listening to music categorized at the time as "acid rock," the harsh, dissonant, caterwauling amplifications that were at the leading edge of the rock movement. Tony Williams, who just a few years earlier was credited with infiltrating Davis's music with free-form effects from Ornette Coleman and Cecil Taylor, had transferred some of his boundless enthusiasm to the proponents of acid rock, and before long Davis would speak knowledgeably, and reverentially, about the music of Jimi Hendrix, among others. It would take Davis a few years to incorporate the effects into his music, but the negative lesson from what he heard around him was clear enough: the changes in his music would not be derived from anything in jazz.

He was not the only jazz musician looking beyond jazz for the sources of change. If Ornette Coleman and John Coltrane cast their shadows on the best music of the quintet that was now dissolving, there was never any doubt whatsoever that they were only shadows, never substance, in his music. He accepted their influence only on his own terms. From now on, the shadows of Coleman and Coltrane would recede ever further into the background. For the next year another saxophonist would cast his shadow faintly on Davis's music. His name was Charles Lloyd, and compared to Coleman and Coltrane he was a saxophonist of modest gifts. His influence in jazz was so brief that it is almost entirely forgotten already, and it had much less to do with the music than with its reception. While Lloyd's influence was still fresh, in 1968–9, Davis made two LPS and several individual cuts (with many more still unreleased) that were iconoclastic but popular, and influential but controversial. The two LPS, *In a Silent Way* and *Bitches Brew*, stimulated discussion and debate – and record sales – as few other records have in jazz history.

In 1967–8, Charles Lloyd was a phenomenon. He had played regularly in Chico Hamilton's band starting in 1961, when he was 23, and he moved on into Julian Adderley's band for several months in 1964–5, without attracting any unusual attention from either critics or fans to his soft-spoken style on the flute and tenor saxophone. Then in 1966 he formed his own quartet with three young unknowns: pianist Keith

Jarrett, who was 21, bassist Ron McClure, 25, and drummer Jack DeJohnette, 24. They played at the Monterey Jazz Festival that September and received enthusiastic reviews for their bright, driving performance. As a result, Lloyd was profiled in *Harper's* magazine in an article by Eric Larrabee that focused on the plight of a younger jazz musician searching for an audience when times were tough in jazz. He was also named as the tenor saxophonist deserving wider recognition in *Down Beat*'s poll of critics that year.

The wider recognition soon came. Almost by accident, the Charles Lloyd Quartet were invited to play one set on a trial basis at the Fillmore Auditorium in San Francisco, the top rock emporium in the world, and to the surprise of everyone they won a standing ovation from the teenaged audience and were called back for several encores. The event was trumpeted far and wide by the press and the public relations men serving the new youth industry. Charles Lloyd was suddenly 'in.' A live recording by the Lloyd Quartet at the Fillmore a few months later, in early 1967, called *Love-In* (Atlantic SD 1481), became a strong seller in the jazz field and beyond. Lloyd received notices in *Time* and several other magazines, including *Billboard*, which called his quartet "the first psychedelic jazz group," and added, as if by way of explanation, "It really relates to the nostalgia of the war-baby generation." Whatever that might mean, it was couched firmly in the argot of the day – which Lloyd himself spoke fluently. "I play love vibrations," he told the *Time* interviewer. "Love, totality – like bringing everyone together in a joyous dance."[2] With that, the Charles Lloyd Quartet crossed the psychological barriers that had until then kept all but an eccentric fringe of a vast audience of music-consumers away from jazz.

Lloyd's success was a revelation. Almost no one in jazz had really believed that it was possible for jazzmen to play directly to that audience. Certainly several people had been working at siphoning off part of that young audience. Herbie Hancock was one of them. In his independent recordings as a leader for Blue Note records, he spoke of "the concept that there is a type of music in between jazz and rock. It has elements of both but retains and builds on its own identity. Its jazz elements include improvisation and it's like rock in that it emphasizes particular kinds of rhythmic patterns to work off of."[3] In Hancock's recordings such as *Maiden Voyage* (Blue Note BST 84195) and *Speak Like a Child* (BST 84279), the idea of a possible jazz-rock fusion emerges cautiously in some tracks, but generally the rhythms remain mild-mannered and more squarely in the jazz mainstream than the ones

Hancock was playing with in Davis's quintet nightly, and Hancock's piano playing remains more firmly rooted in Bill Evans's delicate lyricism than it often was with Davis. Hancock played music that approximated his description of the fusion on Davis's *Stuff*, recorded for *Miles in the Sky* in May 1968, with its boogaloo drumming and amplified vamp. Just a few days before that, Hancock had recorded *Country Son* with Davis and included in his solo peculiar little melodic touches quite unlike his usual phrasing. When *Country Son* was first released, the most that almost any listener might have noticed was that those phrases sounded unlike Hancock, but within a few years almost every listener could have gone a step further and pointed out that they sounded a great deal like Keith Jarrett. The echo of Jarrett in Hancock's solo on *Country Son* is unmistakeable. Jarrett was then almost unknown, but Hancock was only one of the many jazz musicians listening to him. Probably Miles Davis was too. Actually, they were listening to Charles Loyd, his leader, and inevitably hearing Jarrett as well. And they were listening because Lloyd was the man who had made the breakthrough.

Surprisingly, Lloyd does not seem to have tried very hard, or very consciously, to fuse elements of jazz and rock. He seems to have done little more than hire young men who had grown up in the baby boom generation and let them play their own styles. Keith Jarrett could spin bright, stylish melodies seemingly endlessly, and his technique was as accomplished as his melodies were attractive. When the spotlight fell on the Charles Lloyd Quartet, he thrived, being named the piano player deserving wider recognition by *Down Beat*'s critics in 1967 and going on to become one of the leading lights of jazz in the 1970s. Jack DeJohnette took only a little more time to rise into the top rank of jazz drummers. He propelled Lloyd's music with the drive of a rock drummer, and his work in the group made the most obvious compromises with teenaged tastes, but it soon became evident that his talents were far from exhausted by that style. He was named the drummer deserving wider recognition by the *Down Beat* critics in 1970, after he left Lloyd and joined Miles Davis's band, and from there he too went on to become a respected drummer and bandleader in jazz.

Both became much more conspicuous figures in jazz than their leader. Soon after making the breakthrough at the Fillmore, Charles Lloyd began to devote more of his time to practicing and teaching trans-cendental meditation in California. By 1971, although he was still occasionally active in music, he was almost completely forgotten by the fans who vote in *Down Beat*'s Readers Poll, many of whom no doubt first became interested in jazz because of his *Love-In* LP.

The breakthrough itself, although fewer and fewer observers would correctly credit (or blame) Lloyd for it, continued to reverberate. One of the movements it stirred up resulted in attempts by largely rock-trained musicians to add some sophistication to their music by using jazz instrumentation, big band devices, and instrumental solos. The first and most successful was Blood, Sweat and Tears, a nine-piece band started in 1968 that included Lew Soloff, later lead trumpeter in the Thad Jones–Mel Lewis orchestra, among its founding members. Blood, Sweat and Tears had three hit records in 1969, and other groups patterned along the same lines soon followed, including Chase, led by former Woody Herman trumpeter Bill Chase, and others such as Chicago and Lighthouse with more remote jazz connections.

A more abiding movement came from within, when dozens of jazz musicians began to notice the possibilities of importing rock elements into their music. When it first gained momentum, in the early 1970s, the movement looked like a stampede. Part of the rush was caused by jazzmen hoping to storm in and make a quick killing as many rock superstars had been doing for a decade, with little regard for their own artistic integrity or for the values of jazz. A few succeeded, but their success soon wore out, as pop fads always do. Some returned to jazz, playing not much differently than they had before, and several others disappeared from music, as last year's hitmakers are expected to in the pop culture. While the amplified compromises of fusion music looked like a majority in the early 1970s and seemed to threaten to become the mainstream, by now enough time has passed for one to look back and notice its diminution, until it looks more like a footnote in the history of jazz.

A few other jazzmen took an entirely different stance. They examined popular music skeptically and disdainfully, but they found in it some genuine sources of energy and inspiration for their music; what they imported remains in their music. One of these was Miles Davis. Ironically, neither his music nor his image seemed suited to fusion superstardom. George Avakian, writing the liner note for Charles Loyd's *Love-In* in 1967, quotes an anonymous rock promoter extolling the virtues of Lloyd for younger fans. "Who else is there?" the promoter asks, and he then answers his own question: "Either you get someone old enough to be their father, or a bunch of angry guys pouring frustration, protest and hate messages out of their horns. That's not the message these kids want to hear."[4] Whether they wanted to hear it or not, Davis was about to give them some protest, and perhaps some frustration and hate too. And it would come from a man old enough to be their father. And if it was not exactly for teenagers, it certainly found an audience among the twenty- and thirty-year olds, to say nothing of the older jazz buffs, some of whom hated it and some of whom did not, but almost all of whom listened to it, at least once.

The dissolution of the quintet allowed Davis to move another step in the direction of fusion by hiring replacements who were – or would become, under his tutelage – more comfortable with amplified instruments. At the time, the change seemed accidental, and Davis probably would have been just as happy to have kept his old band. "It may have been Miles was into electronic music," recalled Ron Carter, who was not into electronic music himself. "It may have been Herbie was into electronic music. It may have been any of these factors. I was leaving the band and we all had talked about leaving. Maybe Miles felt that if he couldn't find guys who carry on the tradition we had set up playing acoustically, he could find a whole different kind of sound from guys who maybe didn't play as well but had enough electronic interests and the control to be able to contribute to his new band."[5] Whatever the reasons, Carter and Hancock were leaving, but Davis would not let them go completely. In effect, they only quit his traveling band. They would join him in the recording studio on several occasions in the next few years. They became members of Davis's studio stock company.

Hancock had found the complexity of the quintet's music harder to come to terms with in the last few years, and his own music on Blue Note reflects his preference for simpler, more straightforward music. "We were always trying to create something new," he told a reporter from *Newsweek*. "It became more and more difficult. Like trying to make conversation never using any words you used before. Miles would say: 'Don't ever play anything straight.' When it worked it was magic. But the music kept getting further and further out and more complex."[6] Davis saw him growing uneasy with the quintet's direction. "Herbie wanted to quit...," he told Jimmy Saunders, "because once in Chicago, he said, 'Miles, sometimes I feel like it just ain't nothing to play.' And I said, 'Then just don't play nothing.' He's a great musician, man, and he knows what's happening. But you can't be a nice guy. He's a nice guy. But me, I ain't nice. I don't care if you don't like me – as long as you can play."[7] The turning point for Hancock was the LP he made for Blue Note titled *Speak Like a Child*. "You know, it's funny," he told Julie Coryell, "when I did that record I knew that was the sound I wanted for my own band. That's when I knew I was going to switch from Miles."[8] The sound consisted of an acoustic piano trio (Hancock, Carter, drummer Mickey Roker) with accompanying colors supplied by a trio of wind instruments (Thad Jones, flugelhorn; Peter Phillips, bass trombone; Jerry Dodgion, alto flute). "Miles suggested a couple of things," he said; "I think he suggested the bass trombone."[9]

Hancock left the quintet in August, soon after *Speak Like a Child* was released. In his first years on his own, he maintained the sextet format of *Speak Like a Child*, using two brass and one reed plus rhythm, but his music quickly divested itself of its conservatism and emulated Davis's movement to more electronics, including a synthesizer, and more percussion, until 1976, when Hancock occasionally returned to acoustic piano and the jazz style he played in the 1960s.

The new piano player, Chick Corea, was just a year younger than Hancock. Davis's attention was drawn to Corea by Tony Williams, who knew him from his Boston days. Corea was playing in Stan Getz's band when Davis first heard him, but by the time he got the call to join Davis he was working as Sarah Vaughan's accompanist. Corea, like Williams, had started in music very young and had been playing professionally most of his life, under the tutelage of a father who was a professional musician. Armando Corea was a jazz trumpeter and arranger around Boston, and he encouraged his son to play several instruments, including drums, trumpet, and vibraphone as well as piano. Davis was delighted by Corea's versatility. "He can play anything he wants to play," he told Sy Johnson, "just like me. He's a music-*lover*, you know."[10]

Beginning with his tenure in Davis's band, Corea became a conspicuous figure in jazz, playing an enormous range of styles from jazz-rock to acoustic duets and free form, all with considerable, and obvious, zeal. His enthusiasm also delighted Davis. "We used to talk about music until late every night," he said.[11]

Until he joined Davis's band, he had never played electric piano and was not certain that he wanted to. "At first, Miles kind of pushed the Fender piano in front of me against my will," he told Conrad Silvert, "and I resisted. But then I started liking it, especially being able to turn up the volume and combat the drummer."[12] His resistance resulted not only from Davis's insistence but also from his dislike for the 'feel' of the instrument. "At first I didn't like it very well because mechanically it's a far inferior instrument to a regular acoustic piano," he told Julie

Coryell. "It still is, but I enjoyed being able to play at a louder volume, mainly so that I could play more comfortably with the volume level of drummers like Tony Williams and other young drummers who were putting out in those days. After that I started liking the timbres of the electric piano and other electronic keyboards and just naturally began using them in my playing, my compositions, and my groups."[13] (The same year that Coryell's book appeared, a very similar dialogue with Corea, except for the point about the Rhodes's mechanical inferiority, was used in advertisements for Rhodes Keyboard Instruments. Asked when he started playing a Rhodes electric piano, Corea replies: "When I started with Miles Davis. We were in a studio, and Miles pointed to this electric piano and said, 'Play it.' I didn't like it." "Didn't like it?" the interviewer asks, and Corea replies: "Not because of the instrument. I just didn't like being told what to do. No musician does. But when I started concentrating on the Rhodes, I came to appreciate all it could do...")

As soon as Corea adjusted to the electric keyboard, he began using it more often than the acoustic piano, and his rapport with Davis, like his facility with the Rhodes, seems to have been almost instantaneous. "We play by sound," Davis said. "I mean I'll give Chick a chord and the sound I want from the chord. He knows I'm musically intelligent enough to give him that. If I don't give him the sound and the approach, he can't play it the way I want to hear it. But there're so many variations on the sound I give him that he's got to get the sound first."[14] Corea's talents were fully exposed during the club and concert engagements the band played during his two-year tenure, but in the recording sessions released at the time he usually found himself alongside one or more other keyboard players where his individual contributions were hard to appreciate.

When Ron Carter left the quintet late in July, Davis hired Miroslav Vitous, a 21-year-old Czech whom he first heard playing with the Bob Brookmeyer–Clark Terry Quintet.[15] Vitous, who later formed the cooperative band called Weather Report along with Wayne Shorter and Joe Zawinul, filled in temporarily while Davis awaited the arrival from England of David Holland, a lanky 22-year-old whom Davis had literally hired off the stage at Ronnie Scott's in June. "Fairytale, wasn't it?" Scott said afterward. "Miles coming in and picking up David Holland like you pick up a girl."[16]

Holland had just finished his final year at the Guildhall School of Music and had taken a job in the band backing singer Elaine Delmar at

Ronnie Scott's for July. "In my last year at college," Holland told Bill Smith in *Coda* magazine, "I was quite active in London. I was doing recordings, some studio work, I was at college, then playing with [John] Surman, and I took a month at the Ronnie Scott club because Bill Evans was going to be there, with Eddie Gomez and Jack DeJohnette, and I had a gig in a supporting band backing a singer. During the last week that Bill was there, Miles came into the club, to see Bill and Jack ... and offered me the job, and that was the beginning of the whole thing."[17]

Davis may have shown up in London because Evans or DeJohnette knew he was looking for a bassist and tipped him off about the talented unknown in the backing band. Whether the recruiting job was by design or by accident, it soon entered jazz folklore. "One night the word went round, 'Miles Davis is in the club,'" John Marshall, the drummer in the backing band recalls. "We did our first set, and Bill went on and we were just going on again when Dave said, '*Miles Davis has offered me the gig,*' and I said, 'Oh really?' and sat down at the drums. But it turned out to be true." And then Marshall adds, "If Miles wants you he doesn't care what color or nationality you are. And his track record is incredible – he can just put bands together. He just *knows.*"[18]

Davis phoned Holland at the end of July to confirm the hiring and gave him four days to get to New York for the band's opening at Count Basie's club in Harlem where they were playing for two weeks. "I always wanted to come to America," he said, a few weeks later, still slightly dazed, "but I never dreamed it would be this way." He was barely off the plane before he was playing his first set. "Miles is incredible," he told Leonard Feather. "I feel such strength flowing from him – he's the kind of man that only comes along once in a generation. It's awe-inspiring being around him and these other great players – I feel like I've entered an institution of higher learning. Miles likes to move from one tune to another, without pausing, so we never know what's going to happen next. You've got to be ready to move wherever he goes – usually he'll play an opening phrase that gives just a hint of the next number."[19]

Holland's resilience was quickly tested in other ways as well. Less than seven weeks after arriving in New York, he recorded the final two tracks of the *Filles de Kilimanjaro* LP, and the day after that, on 25 September, the quintet opened a four-day engagement at the Plugged Nickel in Chicago. From there, they went on to play concert and club engagements in California, including a concert at the University of California in Los Angeles, where Leonard Feather inquired about the new bassist. "Miles was so happy," Feather reported, "that he couldn't even put on his surly act for me. 'How about that Dave?' he said backstage ... 'Ain't he a bitch?'"[20] The new band seemed to be shaping up superbly, even in the critical eyes of its leader.

Nevertheless, soon after returning to New York, Davis augmented the working quintet with the two defectors from the old quintet for his next studio session. The recordings, released in 1976 on the LP *Water Babies* along with the old quintet's work from June 1967, extend the stock company concept begun when he added Joe Beck and George Benson earlier. The idea of mixing in various other players with his working sidemen obviously caught his fancy, because he stuck with it every time he made studio recordings for the next four years. The details are as follows:

Miles Davis Ensemble: Water Babies
Miles Davis, tpt; Wayne Shorter, ss (on *Two Faced*), ts (on both titles); Chick Corea, Herbie Hancock, el pno; Ron Carter, David Holland, b; Tony Williams, dms. New York, November 1968
Two Faced; Dual Mr. Tillman Anthony
(both on Columbia PC 34396 [1976])

Considering the extra players added to the ensemble, the music is surprisingly delicate. Hancock and Corea prove to be fully compatible sharing the same instrumental space, as they would again some eight years later when they began presenting duo concerts on acoustic pianos. Here, both play electric pianos, but their roles are clearly defined. Hancock contributes to the bottom on both pieces. On *Two Faced* he plays infrequent chords that punctuate the others' phrases, as he had done with Davis for so many years, and on *Dual Mr. Tillman Anthony* he repeats the staccato rhythmic figure that is the unifying thread of the piece with one of the bass players. Corea ventures more freely, improvising harmonies and feeding the soloists, in the more traditional piano role. He solos on *Dual Mr. Tillman Anthony*, and he and Hancock exchange phrases as simultaneous, but very polite, soloists on *Two Faced*.

The role of the two bassists is harder to divine. One bassist, probably Carter, plays very prominently throughout *Two Faced*, essentially carrying the theme of the piece with a phrase that recurs strategically throughout, and on *Dual Mr. Tillman Anthony* one bassist, again probably Carter, repeats the rhythmic pattern with Hancock all the way through. Through all of this, the second bassist is undetectable, and

Wayne Shorter (Bernie Senensky)

Josef Zawinul (Bernie Senensky)

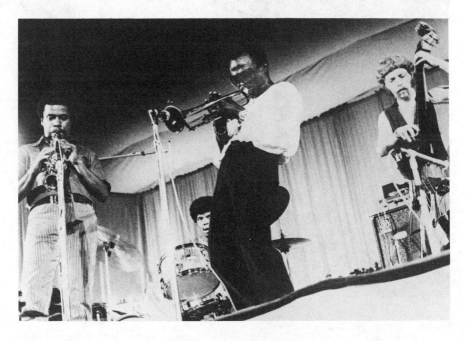

Miles Davis with Wayne Shorter, Jack DeJohnette, and David Holland
(Trombert, courtesy of *Down Beat*)

whatever space he was supposed to fill cannot be determined from the results. The music is notably high-spirited – relaxed, unfettered, rhythmic, and accomplished – as *In a Silent Way*, with an enlarged stock company, would also be. It obviously leaves a lot to the individual players' discretion. "It's almost aleatory," Ron Carter would say a few years later,[21] and the rewards when the individual players are in such good form radiate from the music.

With the stock company concept justified at least to his own satisfaction, Davis made the move that added a vital dimension to it for the next fifteen months. He invited Josef Zawinul, the Viennese emigré who spoke and acted more 'American' than many natives of New York, his home for nine years, to join the stock company and, as an afterthought, to bring along some music to the recording studio. "Miles called me up one day in the morning," Zawinul told Ray Townley, "and told me to come down to the recording studio at one o'clock. I said fine. After about a minute, he called me back and told me to bring some music."[22]

As it happened, Zawinul had plenty of music stockpiled from a winter he had spent in Vienna in 1966–7 renewing his ties with the family he had left behind him eight years before, when he boarded a steamer from France at the end of 1958 and set sail for the United States. The chance to rest and relax in Vienna came about when he was invited there to serve as a judge at the International Jazz Competition, but the reprieve from the nightly round of jazz clubs soon weighed heavily on him and the best outlet he found was composing. An inveterate composer even when he was working long hours in jazz clubs, he poured all his energies into the task that winter and returned with no fewer than ten charts in his luggage, including *In a Silent Way*, *Directions*, *Early Man*, *Orange Lady*, *Pharaoh's Dance*, and *Double Image*, all of which would find their way onto recordings by either Davis's company or Zawinul's groups or, often, both and would take their place among the hallmarks of the jazz of the early 1970s.

While the number of compositions was unusual for Zawinul or anyone else to write in such a short time, their success was no surprise. Zawinul was already as well established a composer as he was a pianist; any listener who had been paying attention for the previous six or seven years knew something of his accomplishments in both areas. Those who kept a scholarly eye on jazz developments in Europe knew about him long before that.

Zawinul was born in Vienna in 1932 and raised and educated there during the Nazi occupation. He finished his schooling and began working as a professional piano player during the Allied occupation. When the Allies quartered the city in the post-war armistice, Zawinul's family home was in the Russian sector, a geographical accident that prevented him from emigrating as early as he had hoped but did not prevent him from listening to jazz on the military radio stations or watching movies in the adjacent American quarter. George Shearing and Errol Garner, he told Julie Coryell, made the earliest impact on his playing.

Starting in 1952, when he was 20, he played professionally, often as the leader of his own trio. In 1958, he won a scholarship to the Berklee School of Music in Boston and set sail for America, with no intention of studying when he arrived. Almost 27, he was determined to succeed as a jazz pianist in New York. He had been in the city only a few weeks when Maynard Ferguson recruited him into his band for a Birdland engagement, and then Zawinul joined a band led by Slide Hampton, Ferguson's featured trombonist, and kept on playing.

Only a few months after his arrival, probably while he was still with Hampton's band, Zawinul made his first American recording for a label called Strand Records, one of a group of fly-by-night companies known collectively at the time as 'supermarket labels,' because they packaged ridiculously cheap records by generally obscure musicians and displayed them on racks near the check-out counters at supermarkets hoping to catch the eye of impulse buyers on their way home with the week's milk and eggs. On the racks among such gems as *Mediterranean Cruise with Los Españoles* and *Explosive Vocal Percussion with Myra March*, *To You with Love* by the Joe Zawinul Trio (Strand SLS 1007) looked neither more nor less promising in 1959. It was, however, superior to most of Strand's offerings and certainly much better than it needed to be for the supermarket rack. It shows Zawinul with his Shearing and Garner roots well behind him and in debt much more manifestly to Red Garland and Ahmad Jamal. Zawinul, in the company of bassist Ben Tucker, drummer Frankie Dunlap, and bongo player Ray Barretto, plays *Love for Sale, Squeeze Me*, and *It Might As Well Be Spring* from the common Jamal-Davis list of standards along with seven other ballads, all neatly arranged for easy listening. He sometimes slips in one of the patented little blues doodles that soon made his style readily identifiable.

Davis was aware of him almost from his first public performance in the United States because Zawinul was playing in Ferguson's band opposite the Davis sextet at Birdland in August 1959, when Davis was involved in the altercation with the police that led to his arrest.

Davis kept tabs on Zawinul's progress after he joined Julian Adderley's quintet in 1961, a job he held until 1970. With Adderley, Zawinul made numerous national and international tours, recorded often, and played many kinds of music. Although Adderley's band made and kept their reputation playing jazz with a blues and gospel tinge, Zawinul co-composed (with William Fischer) *Experience in E*, a symphony for Adderley's quintet and symphony orchestra, and played and composed jazz themes celebrating the civil rights movement (*Walk Tall, Country Preacher*, for the Reverend Jesse Jackson), ballads, bebop, and much more. The Adderley quintet's recording of Zawinul's *Mercy, Mercy, Mercy* in 1967 became a hit single in the pop field. On it, Zawinul played the Fender-Rhodes piano, and if it was not the first time the instrument had been used on a jazz recording it was certainly the first time it had been used so conspicuously. It gave a new respectability to electronic keyboards. It prompted Davis's visit to Zawinul's apartment to tinker around with his Fender-Rhodes, and then he ordered one for Hancock to play on *Water on the Pond* that December. He may also have learned about Zawinul's pile of charts on that visit.

Zawinul was already one of the most interesting composers and players around when he answered the call to join Davis's company in the recording studios, and his presence on the recordings of the next fifteen months gave the kind of edge to Davis's talents that Gil Evans had given them ten years before and had somehow failed to give them since. At 36, he was older than everyone else in the company except Davis, although he was only one year older than Wayne Shorter. Along with his compositions, he brought experience and unflappable confidence into the studio sessions.

Those qualities almost guaranteed that he would never be content, as Gil Evans had been, to lend his talents to Davis's music obsequiously. He used the experience to develop his own approach. "Not from the music," he told Ray Townley, "but from the way Miles handled a recording session I learned a whole lot. They had the tapes running constantly, not to lose certain things. The best things are usually happening when you just get together and try this shit, you know. Miles is a leader, but in such a relaxed way that you never feel like someone is trying to tell you something. There was very little talking going on. It was more just the vibes."[23] In the 1970s, when he entered his forties, Josef Zawinul, the pink-complexioned, balding immigrant, his clear, dark eyes peering out from behind a wall of massed keyboards, would rival Davis as the leader of the fusion movement.

Zawinul first appeared in Davis's recording ensemble in late November on some sessions from which four titles were released belatedly. On the evidence of what has been released so far, Davis clearly wanted Zawinul more for the music he brought along than as a player, although the music seemed to be an afterthought when the invitation was extended. Two of the three titles are Zawinul's, but his contribution to the playing consists solely of adding depth to the rhythms by playing bass notes on the beat on acoustic piano. Were it not for his name on the personnel lists, a listener might never guess he was there. The details are as follows:

Miles Davis Ensemble
Miles Davis, tpt; Wayne Shorter, ts; Chick Corea, Herbie Hancock, el pno; Josef Zawinul, pno; David Holland, b; Tony Williams, dms. New York, 25 November 1968
Splash
(on *Circle in the Round*, Columbia 36278 [1979])

Shorter plays ss; Holland plays el b; Jack DeJohnette, dms, replaces Tony Williams. Same place, 27 November 1968
Directions (take 1); *Directions* (take 2); *Ascent*
(all on *Directions*, Columbia KC2 36472 [1981])

Davis's *Splash* shows his growing fascination with rhythm as the main component for his music. It is organized around the repetition of eight-bar segments at medium tempo, in 5/4 time, with two-bar rests. The soloist constructs his improvisation over as many of these consecutive ten-bar patterns as he chooses, either filling the rests with breaks, as Davis invariably does, or stopping with the rhythm, as Shorter, to good effect, sometimes does. Davis's trumpet playing sounds strangely uneasy with the format, especially considering he wrote it, and he is bothered by sour notes near the beginning of his solo.

Zawinul's *Ascent*, a tone poem similar in its intention to his *In a Silent Way* and *Orange Lady*, fails to find a consistent mood on this playing and remains vague and undefined throughout; it is a failure endemic to this form of composition, which sets up a quiet mood and then seeks to embellish it with sound effects. With no rhythmic pulse to carry the piece, anything less than a concentrated effort by the principal players stalls the implied movement and ends up giving the impression of motionlessness, and the dominant effect is tedium. The success of later recordings of tone poems by Zawinul and Davis elevated the form to the status held by ballads in other jazz genres, but *Ascent*, in this version, would not have provided much incentive for others to take it up.

Zawinul's *Directions*, a pulsating swinger that Zawinul was already playing in Adderley's band, is here revealed in its first, but far from its last, version by Davis. *Directions* became Davis's set-opener almost immediately, and snatches of it occurred in live recordings by Davis's bands long before these studio recordings were issued. *Directions* later became the set-closer for Zawinul and Shorter after they formed Weather Report in 1971, making it one of the most conspicuous strains of the fusion movement. Its appeal is obvious in these recordings. Drummer DeJohnette swats out the 4/4 beats, and his muscular pulse is reinforced by Zawinul and Holland, while the horns play the quick ascent and descent of the theme. The issuing of two takes, a rare event after so many years of Davis's insistence on recording in a single take, indicates how deliberate was his quest for new effects. The two takes show a clear development: on the second, a unison introduction has been added to set off the theme, which then seems to explode following the quieter opening. But the rhythm is much more crisp and the solos are more effective on the first take, suggesting that between the two issued takes there was a long, tiring process of change. Since, by all accounts, the tapes were running continuously throughout Davis's recording sessions, that process of change might someday be documented.

None of these tracks ends with anything that could be called an arranged ending, not even a reprise of the theme. Davis was obviously already planning to 'compose' the final releases from pieces recorded at various times in the studio. His use of post-production splicing, editing, and overdubbing, aided and abetted by Teo Macero, became significant in Davis's releases from this time on, in an increasing degree that at its more extreme did not always, or perhaps often, have happy results. Davis was by no means alone in his reliance on post-production devices, although he was one of very few artists in jazz to pick them up, and he remains to this day the jazzman who took those devices to the greatest extremes. An influential precedent for heavy post-production reworking came in 1967, when the Beatles announced that they would no longer perform in public but would exist solely as recording artists. (A few years before that, Glenn Gould, one of the world's leading concert pianists, had made the same decision.) The Beatles then released *Sgt. Pepper's Lonely Hearts Club Band*, a magnificent pop album by any standards. Its success had conspicuous consequences for the recording business: the Beatles' producer, George Martin, became something of a celebrity in his own right, tagged the "fifth Beatle," and the use of post-production devices was considered to be vindicated in the frenetic quest for hits that has always been the main objective of the pop industry. The fact that those devices contributed very little to the quality of *Sgt. Pepper* got lost in the rush.

In jazz, extensive use of post-production editing hardly outlasted the heyday of fusion music, and even then it was practiced only on a few dozen recording artists in the genre (Davis, Hancock, Donald Byrd, Weather Report, and some others) and by a few 'slick' labels such as CTI, a New York company owned by Verve's former producer Creed Taylor, which routinely added solos and extra rhythm to its releases.

Any discussion of the legitimacy of post-production devices ultimately raises the issue of whether a recording can be an art object in itself, with its own esthetics determined by the manipulation of sounds and textures by a composer-producer – or perhaps by a team of composer-producers that includes the musicians who made the inventory of sounds to be manipulated – or whether a recording is only a means of documenting a performance, which is the true art object and the source of whatever esthetic pleasure the recording can convey.

This controversy has never arisen about other 'packaging' media for art forms, but both possibilities are found. On the one hand, publishers and printers might make novels and poems harder or easier to read and enjoy, but they can scarcely alter or pre-empt the esthetics of the performance – the novel or the poem – they are conveying; printers and publishers, by the nature of their medium, must be artisans not artists. On the other hand, film is a "director's medium" precisely because it can be used to document an actor's performance in the purest sense only by making the most prosaic and boring use of the medium – by, say, training a camera on a stage and making a visual record of a stage play; its most effective use requires heavy post-production editing, elevating the director from artisan to artist.

Sound recording developed primarily to freeze performances in time, as does print, and only later developed the technological flexibility – first mastering onto tape, then multi-tracking, and then 'hot-house' sound effects (pitch manipulation, wah-wah, fuzz-wah, and the rest) – to afford a producer the kind of scope required to 'create' a performance in a workshop, as does a film director. Recordings of classical symphonic music can probably never rely heavily on post-production tinkering and be taken seriously, so revered is symphonic music as a performer's art, and recordings of pop music might well be fabricated entirely in a workshop, because pop artists are so little respected as performers (and so highly regarded as icons) that their audiences often drown out the sound from the stage anyway.

Jazz music has been a highly individualized performer's medium throughout most of its history, and traditionally any post-production alteration with esthetic (as opposed to acoustic) purposes of an arrangement by Duke Ellington, or an ensemble by the Modern Jazz Quartet, or a solo by Charlie Parker would have led jazz fans to dismiss the recording as flawed and unworthy of attention. Those standards seemed to be breaking down in the 1970s. Neither Macero nor Davis seems to have had any qualms at all about what they were doing to Davis's music, and the post-production finalizing became part of their studio routine. "We don't stop the tape machines like we used to do in the old days – they run until the group stops playing," Macero told Chris Albertson. "Then we go back, listen, and decide between us what should be tacked to what – it becomes a search-and-find routine, and finally it's all there, it's just a matter of putting it all together."[24] Many jazz fans accepted recordings at least partly created in the editing room with the same equanimity Macero and Davis showed in producing them.

The period did not last long, but it subsided because of changing tastes rather than popular protests, and the use of post-production devices in jazz recording is likely to arise again as long as listeners show the same tolerance. The music of Miles Davis that was recorded and released in the first half of the 1970s exacts a toll on the listeners' patience and confidence. We now have the takes of *Splash*, *Ascent*, and *Directions*, flawed perhaps but unspliced, because they were released later, on the 1979 and 1981 LPs (neither produced by Macero), after the post-production excesses had become passé, but we get their counterparts released 1969–75 in fragments, with a piece of one spliced onto a piece of another and a solo from one superimposed on another. It is sometimes impossible to know if we are listening to the music of Miles Davis, the trumpeter, or of Davis-Macero, the composer-producer.

Jack DeJohnette's presence in Davis's ensemble with Zawinul and the others for the recording of *Directions* and *Ascent* marked another change in the working band. Tony Williams had handed in his notice with Hancock and Carter but stayed reluctantly for three more months at Davis's request. He told Lee Underwood: "His music was changing. I was a low man on the totem pole, too, and I felt it. He wasn't offering me anything better, and he was talking about using two drummers, which I couldn't see happening. When Herbie left, I figured it was my time, too. Better for me to jump then and make all my mistakes while I was young."[25] He was unbelievably young, still a few weeks away from his 23rd birthday, but he was already a veteran after five and a half years in Davis's band. Since May 1963, when the rejuvenation of his music began, the only drummer besides Williams to play behind Davis was Max Roach, on the weekend at Count Basie's when Davis had sat in with Roach's band.

Finally Davis had to find a replacement, not only because Williams was demanding that he do so but also because Davis's thirteen-concert tour of Japan, scheduled to begin on 6 January, was being held up by Japanese immigration authorities, and Williams was thought to be one of the causes. According to a news item in *Down Beat*, Japanese officials had been reluctant to grant visas to touring American jazzmen since 1967, when several touring drummers were arrested and convicted; Williams had been in some unspecified trouble in Japan.

The tour was finally cancelled even though the promoters had already sold all 2,400 tickets for the opening concert in Tokyo. "They had us on tenterhooks right up to the end," Jack Whittemore, Davis's manager, announced. "The Japanese promoters kept cabling us that things looked 'favorable,' but the visas never came through. When we got the final refusal, the only explanation given was 'personal reasons.'"[26] By then, Davis had replaced Williams with DeJohnette.

For Williams, the release gave him the freedom to fulfill his first ambition. "I knew I was going to leave someday and get my own band," he told Lee Underwood. "Even before joining him, I had dreamed of being what he is. I looked up and saw stars, and I wanted to be a star too. I wanted to be a bandleader. I wanted to make my own music." He felt he had postponed that ambition long enough. "Miles is a very strong personality," he said. "He has definite ideas about what he wants. Therefore, you live in *his* world. Living in somebody else's world is not easy. I was subject to his whims and desires and caprices. It took me a long time to realize that and to get out of it."[27]

He rejoined Davis a few times as a member of his studio stock company but most of his energies were devoted to his own trio, called Lifetime, which he formed in February 1969, three months after leaving

Davis's band. Lifetime's brand of fusion, marked by high-amplitude energy and Williams's shouted vocals, attracted some attention from promoters and record executives but excited less attention from fans. Nothing that Lifetime played on its own found anything close to the success, in either the short or the long run, that its members had while playing in Davis's stock company. For Williams, whose raw talents shone so brilliantly from the moment he was seen playing publicly, the first years as a leader after leaving Davis were successful, but much less so than Hancock's were and Shorter's would be, and less even than Carter's, when he led a non-fusion jazz band between his busy outings as a freelancer.

Williams regained some of his stature among jazz drummers in the second half of the 1970s, when he joined forces with a small and mutable nucleus of star players for record dates, concerts and festivals, and sometimes tours, especially when his rhythm section mates were Herbie Hancock and Ron Carter.

Williams's replacement, Jack DeJohnette, had become peripatetic since leaving Charles Lloyd's group late in 1967, after two years, when Lloyd had elected to curtail his touring activities. His exposure with Lloyd and with Stan Getz in early 1968, with Bill Evans on a European tour in the summer, and with Jackie McLean and Getz again in the fall built his reputation quickly. He was playing with McLean's band when Davis started scouting him, as Tony Williams had been six years before. "Miles started to come around to hear Jackie to hear me," DeJohnette says. "Jackie said to me, 'You're going to be Miles' next drummer, and I know, because I always get the drummers first.'" Then Davis managed to persuade Williams to stay with him, and DeJohnette waited impatiently for his turn. When the opening came, he applied directly. "I had just quit Stan Getz," he told Chip Stern, "when Dave Holland called me and said that Tony had just quit to form Lifetime. So I called Miles, we haggled about price, and I joined them for a gig the next week in Rochester."[28]

The rock-flavored studio recordings of *Ascent* and *Directions* took place soon after, but DeJohnette found the live performances more taxing. "That band was a lot more avant garde than people were ready to admit," he says. He stayed with Davis for two and a half years, supplying his bands with the rock-solid, showy beat that Davis's fans had grown accustomed to with Williams, who was three years younger, but playing a much less unbridled style. DeJohnette's style seemed much more like an updating of Philly Joe Jones's than a perpetuation of Williams's.

Davis's recordings with the growing stock company had so far remained unissued, even though they had been going on since December 1967, when guitarist Joe Beck had joined the quintet in the studio. Starting with some sessions in February 1969, all that began to change. These sessions would be issued, not only because Columbia needed a new release from Davis for its fall catalog but also because the music finally came together in a strong amalgam of talents, so that even though it was novel in approach and style, there could be no mistaking its merits. The novelty preoccupied the fans and critics at the time of its release more than its merits, largely because the long buildup to this music had all gone unheard.

The February recording band were made up of familiar names except for the guitarist, John McLaughlin. He was completely unknown beyond a small coterie of musicians in England, and he was only slightly better known when the recordings were issued a few months later. His presence among the others in the stock company, as it turned out, was as big a surprise to him as it was to the fans who bought the new LP, *In a Silent Way*, on its release. McLaughlin had been in the United States for only a few weeks when the first session took place. He arrived to join Tony Williams's trio, Lifetime, which also included the organist Larry Young. He was 26, and his background as a musician in England was probably more diverse than almost any American player could have had at the time, including classical piano studies, dance bands, professional Dixieland, avant-garde jazz, and highly amplified rock. He came to Williams's attention, and probably Davis's too, through David Holland, who loaned Williams a tape of McLaughlin's playing and extolled his playing to anyone who would listen.

McLaughlin's introduction to New York musicians came in December, when he joined Williams and Young in Lifetime at Count Basie's club. "After thirty seconds of his first solo," said Larry Coryell, then considered to be the most promising young guitarist, "I turned to my wife and said, 'This is the best guitar player I've ever heard in my life.'" Coryell was not the only musician who was impressed by what he heard. "That night," he recalled, "everybody was there – everybody from Cannonball's group; I think Miles was there; Dave Holland – and we were all totally knocked out by that fantastic debut of John."[29] Davis immediately invited him into the recording studios with his stock company. "I found myself after two days in the same recording studio as Miles Davis," he told Julie Coryell, "and I was nervous simply because this man had lived inside of my imagination, inside my record player for so many years."[30]

Many listeners hearing McLaughlin on *In a Silent Way* for the first time assumed that he had been conscripted from the rock ranks, and even those who learned something about his background thought of him as a rock musician. As the fusion movement spread, someone with McLaughlin's credentials would be less anomalous, but at the time his presence aroused curiosity. "I didn't use John as a rock player but for special effects," Davis explained to Don DeMicheal. "John's no more a rock guitar player than I'm a rock trumpet player."[31] Those "special effects" were, however, largely rock effects. The full range of his capabilities would take longer to expose, because his most conspicuous work for the first two years in the United States came on records with Davis, and he played fusion music nightly with Lifetime, but there he had a chance to expand. "While I was recording and playing with Miles," he says, "I was working with Tony Williams's Lifetime, which was a completely new form and which I felt very happy about. It was a new direction which I was really a contributor toward, and this constrasted working with Miles, where I wasn't a contributor except under his own terms. This was fine, because his own terms were very educational to me – so I had the best of both worlds."[32]

In February, Davis brought McLaughlin into the studio with an aggregation that included Zawinul, whose composition *In a Silent Way* would provide the title for the LP and also its centerpiece, and a group of musicians from his past and present working quintets. The details are as follows:

Miles Davis Ensemble: In a Silent Way
Miles Davis, tpt; Wayne Shorter, ss; Chick Corea, Herbie Hancock, el pno; Josef Zawinul, el pno, org; John McLaughlin, gtr; David Holland, b; Tony Williams, dms. New York, 18 February 1969
SHHH/Peaceful
(on Columbia CS 9875)

Same personnel. Same place, 20 February 1969
In a Silent Way; It's about That Time
(both on Columbia CS 9875)
Zawinul plays electric piano on *In a Silent Way* and organ on the other titles.

These recordings shocked the jazz critics and many fans late in 1969. The effect was calculated. "This one will scare the shit out of them," Davis told Don Heckman just before their release, and he insisted that

Heckman listen to some of the mixed tapes over the telephone while a Columbia engineer dutifully played them at the other end.[33]

Compared to the music to come, it is hardly shocking. It seems, in retrospect, to be Davis's valedictory to the careful, lyrical trumpet playing that had brought him such adulation in the 1950s. At the time, no one could guess that what would follow would make it look relatively conservative, but it is beautifully lyrical when compared with both what followed and what came before.

Davis's admonition to his working quintet of a few years earlier, that they should never play anything "straight," has obviously been withdrawn. There is a great deal of straight playing here, with tempos and time signatures sustained throughout each segment, harmonic roles well defined, and, above all, melodies grasped and refined. Listeners whose attention was not completely distracted by the unfamiliar electronics that form the background discovered in *In a Silent Way* a reaffirmation of Davis's venerable musical values. The context is, of course, entirely different. "The music here is static harmonically," Harvey Pekar points out. "It depends for interest on the inventiveness of the soloists and the contrapuntal and textural blend that the players can create while improvising simultaneously."[34] In those respects, it is perhaps not so different after all from the music of the Davis quintet that preceded it. But it is more tightly organized.

Almost nothing is left to chance. Tony Williams is reined in most obviously. He is silent on *In a Silent Way*, and on both *SHHH/Peaceful* and *It's about That Time* he maintains a metronomic pulse, the former on cymbals and the latter on snare, that is bright, elastic, and ingenious but never spontaneous or impulsive, the other characteristics usually associated with Williams's drumming in Davis's bands. Corea, Hancock, and McLaughlin meld their tones into a remarkably self-effacing blend. All contribute sparingly, sensitive to the amount of space that the others require, and collectively they build a rhythmic-harmonic cushion in which individual contributions count for very little. On *SHHH/Peaceful*, they share two interludes on either side of Shorter's solo that amount to pauses in the motion of the piece rather than solos of any conventional sort.

Zawinul stands apart from the others. His organ drone is the principal accompaniment for Davis's solos on *SHHH/Peaceful*, which state the theme at the open and close of the extended recording, and on *It's about That Time* his organ joins Holland's bass in stating the pattern of the quicker, second theme that recurs throughout. On *In a Silent Way*, he states his own indelible melody first, on electric piano, before Shorter enters to restate it on soprane saxophone and Davis and Shorter state it a third time in unison. Those three separate interpretations of the melody comprise the complete take of *In a Silent Way*; there are no solos, no variants, and no developments, but Zawinul's tone poem, a melody that magically finds a sound parallel to silence, insinuates itself into the memory more powerfully than the two lilting, assertive ballads.

Almost as distracting as the amplified undercurrents of this music when it was first released was its form. The LP presents two sidelong tracks, entitled *SHHH/Peaceful* and *In a Silent Way/It's about That Time*, as unbroken twelve-inch expanses of vinyl. Davis had been playing his concert and club performances as single, unbroken sets for years, but his recordings had taken the conventional shape that jazz records had always taken. The appearance of the new record was novel, and so was its organization. Each side was selected from music recorded in a three-hour studio session, with some splicing and other manipulation to make the finished issue. *SHHH/Peaceful* contains a single theme, notwithstanding its double title, and could possibly even be a continuous take on the aural evidence, although it probably is not. *In a Silent Way/It's about That Time* leaves no doubt at all about its provenance. It opens with the quiet strains of *In a Silent Way*, which lasts four minutes and twelve seconds, and then swings into *It's about That Time* as soon as the last reverberation of the electric pianos has faded; after about eleven and a half minutes, and no more than a second or two of real silence, *In a Silent Way* returns, in exactly the same take that had opened the side. It may be the only instance in the history of the recording industry when record buyers were sold the same take of a piece twice on the same record, but Davis's orchestration of Zawinul's striking melody not only works well as an entity but also works well as a frame for Davis's *It's about That Time*, and no one complained about the duplication.

Viewed in the line of development of Davis's experiments with the studio stock company since late 1967, the LP appears as a culmination. The two sessions managed to balance the ensemble and control the colors of the instruments, many of them relatively new in Davis's musical concept. The rock elements in the drumming and in the electric pianos and guitar were mild importations, and the contcxt remains essentially jazz. Davis was bringing all these features into his studio work of the past year and a half, and they finally came together strongly. But none of the developmental work had been released, or would be for several years, and *In a Silent Way* appeared not as a culmination at all but as an abrupt shift. Its polish and precision made it appear remarkably mature, and Davis was hailed as the prime mover in the fusion movement by a public that could not know – had no way of knowing – that the concept did not spring fully grown one day in February 1969, or that several others hands, including Hancock, Zawinul, Williams, and others, had worked patiently along with him in developing it.

In format and intention, the studio sessions were collaborations that Davis presided over and directed, but the released material, beginning with *In a Silent Way*, not only listed Davis most prominently and failed to mention the cooperative system behind the music, but also unabashedly listed Davis as composer on some themes rumored to have been developed in the studio by Corea, Zawinul, Shorter, and the others. It was a practice that predictably drew some comment from the others, especially Zawinul. "We were already playing new things with Cannonball's band," he pointed out ten years later. "We played *In a Silent Way* two years before I gave it to Miles to record."[35]

Zawinul received full credit for composing *In a Silent Way*, but Davis transformed it in the studio. McLaughlin says, "He has a genius for bringing out in musicians what they want to do which corresponds to what he wants. *In a Silent Way* is a perfect example. When Joe Zawinul brought it in originally, there were many more chords. What Miles did was to throw out the entire chord sheet. He took Joe's melody and turned it into something that was far from what we'd been rehearsing in the studio. He made that piece into something of lasting beauty."[36]

That kind of credit to Davis did not sit comfortably with Zawinul, although he was willing to concede that his composition was altered by Davis. "I cut it later myself," he said, referring to his 1970 recording on Atlantic (SD 1579), "and I played on my album the whole version like I wrote it originally. Miles only played the last part ... Miles stayed on the tonic, while I on my recording changed the bass notes."[37] Those bass lines were the chief difference McLaughlin noted between the written version and the version Davis recorded, but Zawinul claimed that Davis later restored much of the original score by overdubbing. "Well, Miles was doing something different, but you've got to consider one thing," he told Larry Birnbaum. "On this first album, *In a Silent Way*, he had a lot of bass lines added on and they were my bass lines. I put them on there, to give it a certain feeling."[38]

When he could be persuaded to say anything at all on the subject, Davis seemed willing enough to credit Zawinul. In the brief notes that

Davis wrote for Zawinul's 1970 Atlantic LP, he said, "Zawinul is extending some thoughts that we've both had for years. And probably the thoughts that most so-called now musicians have not yet been able to express." To that, in a postscript longer than the note itself, he added: "In order to write this type of music, you have to be *free inside of yourself* and be Joe Zawinul with two beige kids, a black wife, two pianos, from Vienna, a Cancer, and cliché-free."[39] For those who saw the tribute and realized how rare it was from Davis, the short statement implied a mountain of praise for Zawinul's contribution.

The other players were never as vocal as Zawinul in claiming credit for themselves because of Davis's mastery over the collaborative process. "Miles directed," John McLaughlin said, "and without that, it wouldn't be what it is, that's for sure." Asked directly by Lee Jeske about Davis's pre-empting credit for arranging and composing several themes that should have been credited to Corea or Zawinul, McLaughlin said, "It happened to me too with certain things – you make a suggestion and then it's rearranged in form. But I can only give credit to Miles because he puts a print on it that's particularly him and particularly whole."[40] Certainly Teo Macero, from the vantage point of the control booth, agreed wholeheartedly. "That influence was so potent and so strong every time they went in there that [they] couldn't afford to screw around," he told Gregg Hall, "and, in fact, none of the musicians do. When they're in the studio it's like god coming – oh, oh, oh, here he comes. They stop talking, they tend to business and they listen, and when he stops, they stop. When he tells the drummer to play, the drummer plays. When he tells the guitar players to play, they play and they play until he stops them. This is a fact, not hearsay; I've seen it ... They got more out of him than they have given to him. He is the teacher. He's the one who's sort of pulling the string. He's the professor. He's the god that they look up to and they never disagreed, to my knowledge, in the studio. If they did, they got a goddam drumstick over their head and I've seen that happen too."[41] Every one of the players involved in *In a Silent Way* absorbed the lessons thoroughly enough to become a leader in the fusion movement.

If Davis was hoping to attract the attention of rock fans and rock musicians, at least those who took their music seriously, in attempting the fusion, he succeeded. *In a Silent Way* was received by at least a small group outside jazz as expressing what Davis called "the thoughts that most so-called now musicians have not yet been able to express." What he may not have been fully aware of was the extent to which some of his previous music was already being listened to by some of the better popular musicians. Joni Mitchell, a songwriter who eventually tried to incorporate some jazz elements into her music, admitted that "*Nefertiti* and *In a Silent Way* became my all time favorite records in just any field of music. They were my private music; that was what I loved to put on and listen to – for many years now. Somehow or other I kept that quite separate from my own music, I only thought of it as something sacred and unattainable." Mitchell did not try using Davis's concept in her own work for several years, until 1979, when she recorded an album of jazz vocals based on melodies by Charles Mingus, who had died at the beginning of the year. By then, she had grasped some of Davis's methods as had few of his contemporaries in jazz. "Miles always gave very little direction, as I understand," she said. "It was just 'Play it. If you don't know the chord there, don't play there,' and that system served him well. It was a natural editing system. It created a lot of space and a lot of tension, because everybody had to be incredibly alert and trust their ears. And I think that's why I loved that music as much as I did, because it seemed very alert and *very* sensual and very unwritten."[42] She applied those methods and made a musically interesting fusion of jazz elements in pop that is in some ways the pop counterpart of the neat fusion of elements in jazz represented in *In a Silent Way*.

With all the recording activity by augmented personnel, Davis still kept up his full schedule of performances with his working quintet, now made up of Wayne Shorter, Chick Corea, David Holland, and Jack DeJohnette. Their summer round of festivals included concerts on both nights of the Antibes Jazz Festival, 25 and 26 July, and one night at the Monterey Jazz Festival in late August, almost half the globe away. Reviews of the new quintet were as effusive as they had been for the old one. "The group is an intellectual experience," Harvey Siders wrote in his review of the Monterey performance. "Miles and his alter ego, Wayne Shorter, are gravitating ever closer to a free Nirvana, basing their improvisations on arbitrary scales and/or modes, rendering all conventional frames of reference obsolete. Tempos change and moods shift almost subliminally. The rhythm section follows with an uncanny instinct." Siders adds, ominously, "He left many of his listeners behind."[43] The disaffection of a segment of the jazz audience had barely begun; it would grow in the years ahead.

Siders's account of the live performance implies that the music was a direct descendant of the previous quintet. Certainly it had the same spirit, perpetuating the spontaneous solutions that Davis had long required of his sidemen as the current studio sessions, with their protracted rehearsals and assigned roles, no longer did. No recordings by this quintet have been issued. In the studio, they always shared the floor with guest players, and Columbia, holding what they considered a superabundance of Davis's studio sessions, felt no need to add to it by recording his concerts. "The live stuff really should have been gotten on tape," Corea says, "because that's when the band was burning ... That quintet developed some really beautiful improvised stuff. We would do two or three pieces that were just strung together, one right after another for the whole concert, and we would make this wonderful, wonderful composition."[44]

Corea holds a cache of tapes accumulated on its tours, and several performances exist in other private collections. Notable among them is the concert recorded by Radio-diffusion, France, at Antibes (26 July), which catches the quintet moving glibly through several themes. Two of them, *Spanish Key* and *Sanctuary*, were not recorded in their approved versions until a month later, for *Bitches Brew*, and the performance of music prior to its recording date probably has no precedent in Davis's career. For the first time Davis was spending hours with his band rehearsing; they were working on new themes all the time in Columbia's studios and were ready to play them outside the studio. *Directions* opens the concert, and it too was completely unknown to the audience. By the time Davis's 1968 recording of it was released in 1981, it was well known in a 1972 version by Weather Report (on *Live in Tokyo*, CBS-Sony [Jap] sopj 12-13-xr, and edited to one-fifth its length on *I Sing the Body Electric*, Columbia kc 31352) and indirectly from Davis's concert recordings of 1970 (where it was never named). The other themes invoked at Antibes are *Masqualero* and *Nefertiti*, both recorded in 1968, and *I Fall in Love Too Easily*, first recorded by Davis in 1963 and played frequently since but hardly one of his signature ballads. The burst of studio activity led him to eradicate the familiar repertoire he had clung to since the 1950s – *Walkin'*, *So What*, *My Funny Valentine*, *Stella by Starlight*, *Green Dolphin Street*, and all the others. They clung to him, too, and he continually fielded requests for them. Occasionally in the next year he gave in and played a request, but after that he never played them again, much to the consternation of his oldest fans.

The concert tapes reveal the talents of Corea, Holland, and DeJohnette as the studio recordings never do. There their individuality was subjugated to the augmented rhythm sections that formed the purée of fusion music. Here, they function as individuals always have in small-band jazz: they toy with time signatures, comp for soloists, and construct solos of their own. Corea plays the Fender-Rhodes piano with Zildjian instincts and Steinway dexterity; few electric piano players – and there would soon be dozens of them – succeeded so well in imprinting their own voices onto its circuitry. Holland plays electronically too but switches to the old upright bass whenever his solo turns come around, and in the ensembles and his solos – that is, on both electric and acoustic instruments – he shows the nimble technique that made him stand out on the Soho stage when Davis recruited him. DeJohnette proves harder to admire, perhaps because he has to combat the echoes of Williams that linger in Davis's music. Williams played tough, but DeJohnette sounds tougher as a basic 4/4 drummer hitting cymbal splashes on every beat. In Davis's band even more than in Charles Lloyd's, he sticks to the beat single-mindedly, as no other drummer of Davis's did until Al Foster, his successor. Together, the new rhythm team leave no doubts about the underlying pulse in Davis's music, which had become a more fluid element with the previous quintet. Now the beat became the only fixed point, and, in the bands that succeeded it, it often became the whole point. Before that happened there was a lot to listen to, but so far none of it is available. Corea says, "With Miles I hope they release everything I've ever done with him. I only remember going into the studio quite often and hardly hearing anything."[45]

With all his recordings and concerts in 1969, Davis cut a large swath in the jazz world. The activity was reflected in all the polls and awards by which a small segment of the audience makes its opinions and impressions known. In *Down Beat*'s poll of its readers, Davis was conspicuous even for someone who had dominated several categories for decades. He was named top trumpeter ahead of Gillespie, Clark Terry, and Freddie Hubbard; his quintet was named top small band ahead of Elvin Jones's, the Modern Jazz Quartet, and Gary Burton's; he was named Jazzman of the Year as well, over Buddy Rich and Duke Ellington; and three of his LPs were cited among the top eleven: *Filles de Kilimanjaro* was first, *In a Silent Way*, although released so late in the year that it had not made its full impact, was third, and *Miles in the Sky* was eleventh.

With those honors and many others to show for his year's work, both Davis and Columbia should have felt satisfied. Instead, Davis found himself under increasing pressure from Columbia to plunge further into the youth market.

The pressure was not exactly new to him, but lately it had become more intense. *In a Silent Way*, with its creative and tasteful use of rock elements, represented Davis's first serious response. If it seemed a blantant compromise to a few purist fans and critics, most saw it as a strikingly innovative and artistically successful use of new instruments and new textures in jazz. It caught the attention of jazz fans as no other LP by Davis had for almost a decade, and of a small but significant segment of the rock audience, the ones willing to stretch their imaginations and raise their sights.

The broader response still fell short. "It didn't sell well at all," Teo Macero said. "It sold 80–90,000 units."[46] That figure was excellent for jazz sales, but it only whetted Columbia's appetite when it was thinking in terms of hundreds of thousands of sales. Its perspective was shaped by its enormously successful popular music division, where aggressive recruiting and promoting had vaulted Columbia into the forefront of the teenage music market.

The man credited for Columbia's surge was Clive Davis, a Columbia lawyer who became vice-president and general manager in 1966 and hoisted himself into the presidency soon afterward. Under Davis, Columbia's image was transformed from the safe, familial face that had long made it the General Motors of the record industry, with a safe, familial roster that included Mitch Miller singalongs, Andy Williams, and the Ray Conniff Singers, to the showcase for the baby boom counterculture, with recording stars such as Bob Dylan, Donovan, Janis Joplin, Simon and Garfunkel, the Byrds, Sly Stone, and Carlos Santana, each of whom could sell a million new records for the company annually with a little luck and a lot of promotion.

Clive Davis's transformation of Columbia started as a make-it-or-break-it risk for the hustling young executive. "If a revolution came," he declared in his memoir of his Columbia days, *Clive: Inside the Record Business*, "it would require new faces and new minds, not a cosmetic job by past masters."[47] As a corporate philosophy, Davis's view posed a threat to every officer in the company; the "new faces and new minds" he was looking for were not confined to the roster of recording stars. More than a few of his peers in the executive suite expected him to self-destruct when he started lighting the fuses for the "revolution," and more than a few hoped he would when the shrapnel spilled over into their departments.

The marketing department was one of the first to feel the impact; Davis recalls that the introduction of the new young personnel he placed in marketing put "some radical thinkers" into the department, a description that hardly does justice to the impact in the corporate corridors of mutton-chopped dropouts with hair down their backs.

Columbia, and Davis, thrived. For Davis it was a mission. He hopped planes to the farthest reaches and threw open the doors of his paneled office in order to hear a new group that someone somewhere had tipped him about; he negotiated contracts and listened to unmastered tapes; he was a president in shirt-sleeves, who had the gall to make million-dollar decisions guided by his gut reaction to music made for, and often by, people more than two decades younger than he.

At the end of 1968 and beginning of 1969, he made some decisions that aggrandized even his impressive portfolio. He signed a newly formed band called Blood, Sweat and Tears, and then he signed a band called Chicago. Both groups played rock, but it was musically literate rock compared to almost all the successful bands of the day. It was, in the perception of almost everyone, rock with a jazz bias, and although the jazz elements were milder in both groups than the rock elements were in *In a Silent Way*, they were sufficient to separate the bands from the main currents of commercial rock and thus to make their signing a heavy risk.

The risk turned into a windfall profit. In 1969, both bands scored huge hits with pop singles and best-selling LPs. Their releases on Columbia diverted the pop currents and left most of the competition high and dry. If he was not before, Davis certainly was now the champion of the fastest waters.

His successes with pop music that flirted with jazz strengthened his resolve to get Columbia's jazz division moving at a pace that came closer to matching the other divisions. It was already, of course, healthy, with an incomparable vaultful of classic jazz from Bessie Smith to Thelonious Monk and a current roster, admittedly sparser and aging after several years of retrenchment during the bad times, that included Charles Mingus, Stan Getz, and Bill Evans as well as Miles Davis. But Clive Davis was not inclined to compare his jazz division to those of other companies; he compared it instead to the other divisions at Columbia, and he was thoroughly dissatisfied. "I am very eager to allow Columbia to be used by the most forward-looking American jazz artists, to explore what kind of synergy can come out of jazz and rock," he told Chris Albertson in 1971. "What do the jazz giants, the leading figures of today, have to say? What is their reaction to the fact that, in attempting to fuse jazz and rock, Chicago and Blood, Sweat and Tears have reached millions of people all over the world while they, without such an attempt, only reach a few thousand with their music?"[48]

The target of many of Davis's pleas to broaden the musical ground was Miles Davis. That seemed to contradict his principle about "seeking new faces and new minds, not a cosmetic job done by past masters," but Clive Davis knew about Miles Davis's gift for self-renewal – Miles Davis had never allowed himself to be pegged a "past master" anyway – and he may also have sensed that the real fusion, if it were to happen, would require a masterly musician. One thing he never wavered on was Davis's ability to reach a larger audience. "When I took over the Presidency of Columbia," he said, "he was one of the company's mainstays. His albums *Sketches of Spain, Kind of Blue* and *Porgy and Bess* were landmarks. But his sales in recent years had fallen off; he sold between forty and fifty thousand albums now – he'd once sold more than a hundred thousand, sometimes a hundred and fifty thousand."[49] Those were the credentials that convinced Clive Davis that he already had the right man under contract.

His program for Miles Davis's breakthrough went well beyond his recording activities. "I suggested that he play the Fillmore – or places like it – if he wanted to reach a larger audience and raise sales. Youth was ready for Miles Davis, but he had to play where they went for their music." Miles Davis was infuriated by the suggestion. After fourteen years with Columbia, years when his records made with complete autonomy had won honors and compiled sales figures undreamed of for any other jazz artist, he was not likely to accede to the suggestions – or the dictates, as he saw them – of a Columbia executive who had been around for only four or five years. Clive Davis felt his fury when he pressed the suggestion by telephone. "He wasn't going to play for 'those fucking long-haired white kids,'" he was told. "He would be 'ripped off'; Bill Graham [owner of the Fillmore] wouldn't pay him enough *money*. The audience would be prejudiced because he was black. And furthermore, if the head of Columbia was espousing this, he wanted off the 'fucking label.' And he hung up on me."

Soon afterward, Clive Davis received a telegram stating that Miles Davis would make no more records for Columbia and demanding that he be released immediately. The day after that, Jack Whittemore called and offered him a chance to back down from his position and patch up the affair, but he did not take it. "Miles's manager called the next day," Clive Davis recalled. "Wow, Miles was really heated up! What in the world had I said to him? I told him what had happened and I added that I was *still* convinced we had the same objective. Young audiences were getting into sophisticated fusions of jazz and rock; they could easily get into Miles – but they had to be exposed to him. The way to do it was for him to play Fillmore. I added that I had nothing to apologize for; I wasn't giving Miles his release."[50]

Détente was obviously impossible. What had so far been a private disagreement between the president of Columbia and the leading jazz artist became public and grew nastier.

Several New York newspapers and the wire services they feed carried stories announcing that after almost fifteen years Miles Davis would leave Columbia for Motown Records, a Detroit-based company founded by Berry Gordy that rose to prominence on the strength of soul hits by Diana Ross and the Supremes, Smokey Robinson and the Miracles, the Four Tops, and other groups. Motown was revered by many jazz musicians as well as pop singers as a corporation that epitomized black initiative. (The bloom did not last long; reservations were soon being voiced, as when Elvin Jones, in 1971, told Arthur Taylor: "Motown Records is supposed to be a black company – well, I know that it is not. Maybe originally Berry Gordy conceived the idea, but the time has long since passed where he has anything at all to do with that company other than being a front-office man. I think it probably belongs to the Bank of America ... I'm sure it's not controlled by the finances of Negroes. It's controlled by the established finances who control everything."[51] Whatever the facts about Motown's corporate control, the perception of its 'blackness' that made it an ideal in the 1960s faded in the cynicism of the 1970s.) Whether or not Davis discussed his move seriously with Gordy or others at Motown has never been corroborated. His reason for making the move, according to the newspaper accounts, had nothing to do with his artistic autonomy, a reason that might have raised some eyebrows among those who knew that Motown's output had a homogeneous rhythm-and-blues veneer, called the 'Motown sound,' widely attributed to Gordy's overwhelming influence in its studios. Instead, according to Davis, he was leaving because Columbia exploited its black artists.

Now it was Clive Davis's turn to be infuriated. He made an angry denial and demanded a public retraction from Davis. The retraction, predictably, never came. "Clive asked me why I had said that," Davis told Albertson several months later, when the furor had died down, "and I said, 'Was I telling a lie, Clive? If you can say I'm a liar, I'll retract that statement.' You see, all those records I have made with them have been a bitch, and they come out being rich behind all this token shit." Davis began referring to himself as "the company nigger."

"You would think he's not grateful," Clive Davis said when Albertson passed along Davis's remarks, "but I just know he is. I'm not sure that it's his mind he speaks; I'm not sure that he doesn't tell people what they want to hear, because it takes a certain amount of research before you go off making such statements. I do mentally treat him differently, not because he's black – we have a tremendous number of black artists – but because he's unique among people, and you expect the unexpected from Miles Davis."[52]

Not only did Miles Davis not retract his statement, but he repeated it several times in the years to come, well aware that he had hit a corporate nerve. "I think they're the saddest record company in the world," he told Gregg Hall in 1974, long after he had resettled comfortably into Columbia's roster, "But the greatest ... They don't do nothin' for niggers – nothing!"[53]

Clive Davis could not respond publicly to that statement because by then he had been ousted at Columbia after being charged with procuring narcotics for his recording stars; the charges were eventually dismissed – with much less publicity than when they were laid – and he started his own record company, Arista, which gained some prominence in the second half of the decade for its avant-garde jazz division under producer Michael Cuscuna. Had he still been at Columbia, he probably would have responded to Davis's charges with the same mixture of bitterness and resignation he showed earlier. "It bothers me," he told Albertson, "because I think we have really done a tremendous amount to be creative along with him, and we work very closely with him so that we make sure he sells not only to jazz audiences and to contemporary rock audiences, but to rhythm and blues audiences as well."[54] He connects, as he apparently always connected, the idea of "being creative along with him" with expanding his audience from jazz into rock and rhythm and blues.

When Miles Davis announced his imminent departure from Columbia, the reality of that departure was closer to fantasy than fact, for reasons that had nothing to do with artistic autonomy, race prejudice, incompatibility, or anything else that impinged on the creative process. The plain fact was that Davis's finances were bound to Columbia almost inextricably. Clive Davis knew that; Miles Davis's threat to leave, he said, "both disturbed and amused" him – disturbed him that he would consider it and amused him that he would think it could be accomplished so easily. "In the process of becoming a star in the jazz world," Davis wrote in his memoirs, "he'd acquired some expensive habits: exotic cars, beautiful women, high-fashion clothes, unusual homes. He's also gotten in the habit of calling Columbia regularly for advances."[55]

Miles Davis took the financial arrangements for granted. "The Internal Revenue Service is always after me," he told Albertson, "but I just send their bills on to Clive. I got one for $39,000, but he took care of it." "Miles Davis is treated very well by Columbia Records," Clive Davis said. "I think he's really appreciative of it too – we don't get Internal Revenue bills from Chicago or Blood, Sweat and Tears."[56]

Columbia's decision to subsidize Davis with advances against his future earnings was made before Clive Davis got there, but he perpetuated it. In his version of the high finances of modern record production, "fifty thousand albums barely takes you out of red ink," and he adds: "We began to give Miles additional money each time he recorded an album; we weren't making any money at all." As Davis's sales hovered around 50,000 throughout most of the 1960s, a period when most jazz artists would have been delighted by sales of 10,000, the advances and tax payments became a sizable investment by Columbia on future sales or, looked at from the opposite direction, a nearly perpetual bond on Davis's career. "Miles nonetheless called constantly to ask for more," Davis says. "He has a raspy, low voice – a fiery whisper that conveys heat over the telephone while you are straining to find out how much money he wants. He is spell-binding, and he can talk. After a while, the money business got to be sort of a joke. For Miles called often – sometimes urgently – and I had to figure out each time if he was serious. Walter Dean [Columbia's head of business affairs] got some of his calls too – fortunately – and he handled them well; sometimes he spent *hours* on the phone listening to that hoarse, almost demonic voice and dodging its monetary thrusts."[57] Despite his well-publicized threat to leave Columbia, Miles Davis had been too successful too often with his "monetary thrusts" for it to consider releasing him.

The facts are clear: after publicly repudiating Clive Davis's suggestion, Miles Davis's music became increasingly hybridized, soon finding the broader audience that would fill the largest rock concert halls. The interpretation of these facts is not so clear. Many jazz critics and fans made the obvious interpretation that Davis bowed to pressure from Columbia. Bill Cole, in his 1974 biography, stated that Davis "relented," and he concluded: "Miles Davis became a household word at the expense of his own creativity and the intrinsic value of his whole band."[58] That interpretation finds little credence among other commentators. Dan Morgenstern, in his book *Jazz People*, dismissed the notion altogether, saying: "Critics who think his recent direction, which has brought him closer to rock and soul music than to their idea of what jazz should be, is the result of record-company persuasion simply demonstrate their ignorance. Miles is his own man; his need to be up-to-date, to change, to move on, is not dictated by outside pressure but by inner needs."[59] Teo Macero, closer to the situation than almost anyone else, agreed. "He has never been bound by convention," he pointed out.[60] Sonny Rollins, normally as taciturn as Davis himself, also rose to his defense. "He was always a resourceful musician who was able to use whatever was around for his own sound," Rollins pointed out. "He doesn't like to be typecast, so what you would call his rock period was very natural ... The music had gotten to a standstill insofar as a lot of guys were playing clichés other people had done over and over again. The music that Miles was playing was perfectly compatible with the guys that were coming up at that time, like Billy Cobham, John McLaughlin and Chick Corea, and I'm sure he was a hero figure to them."[61] Rollins's point about Davis changing his music in order to find the idiom of the young players makes sense for a man who filled his bands with young musicians rather than men of his own jazz generation, and it is a point that Gil Evans later used to explain a parallel change in direction for his own music.

Davis had been flirting with disparate musical elements for two years, so that his new emphasis was not the complete turnaround it once seemed. Now he moved into fusion music in earnest.

In August, Davis assembled his stock company with several new faces to record the music that would be released six months later under the title *Bitches Brew*. The two-record set proved commercially successful probably beyond even Clive Davis's hopes, selling 400,000 copies in its first year and going on eventually to sell more than 500,000. But *Bitches Brew* takes the fusion music only one small step beyond *In a Silent Way*, recorded six months earlier. Like *In a Silent Way*, *Bitches Brew* presents a transitional conception of music, the difference being that the fusion elements of *Bitches Brew* are more robust, especially in the density of the percussion. The details are as follows:

Miles Davis Ensemble: Bitches Brew
Miles Davis, tpt; Wayne Shorter, ss; Chick Corea, el pno; David Holland, b;
Jack DeJohnette, dms; Jim Riley, bongo. New York, 19 August 1969
Sanctuary
(on Columbia CS 9996)

Miles Davis, el tpt; Wayne Shorter, ss; Benny Maupin, bass clnt; Chick Corea, Josef Zawinul, el pno; John McLaughlin, el gtr; Harvey Brooks, el b; David Holland, b; Jack DeJohnette, Lenny White, Charles Alias, dms; Jim Riley, perc, dms. Same place, Same date
Bitches Brew
(on Columbia CS 9996)

Add Larry Young, el pno. Same place, 20 August 1969
Spanish Key
(on Columbia CS 9996)

Omit Zawinul, Davis plays trumpet. Same place, Same date
Miles Runs the Voodoo Down
(on Columbia CS 9996)

Add Zawinul, el pno; Shorter plays ts and ss on *Pharaoh's Dance*; omit Davis and Shorter on *John McLaughlin*. Same place, 21 August 1969
Pharaoh's Dance; John McLaughlin
(on Columbia CS 9996)

"It was really free," said drummer Lenny White, describing to Julie Coryell the process that ended up as *Bitches Brew*. "Miles would say play and he'd play something, then he'd say stop. Then he'd say, now, Benny Maupin, you play something and we'd be playing and he'd say, stop. There weren't any real roles. There was a sketch and everybody would play to the sketch for a minute or however long the sketch was, eight or twelve bars. There would be a tonal center and the rest was left up to everybody else. He got all these people who were great improvisers and put them together. We all played and there was just a blend; it was like a palette of a lot of different colors. Everybody was adding a lot of different things. For that time it was really different. To this day it still is."[62]

Lenny White was 20 when he joined the small battalion of drummers to make *Bitches Brew*, an art student at the New York Institute of Technology who played drums to pay his way through college. He had worked with Jackie McLean before and after DeJohnette worked with him, and his presence in McLean's band caused a lot of half-serious comment about Davis automatically recruiting him, as he had Williams and DeJohnette before him. For three days in August it came true. White was playing with another drummer, Rashied Ali, when a friend of Davis's introduced himself and took White's telephone number, and a few days after that White received a call from the same man inviting him to join the recording ensemble.

Benny Maupin, who went on after *Bitches Brew* to play his bass clarinet in Herbie Hancock's fusion bands for several years, joined the stock company for *Bitches Brew* with no more preparation. "It came about as a result of Jack DeJohnette talking to Miles about me," he told Elliot Meadow in *Down Beat*. "Jack was in the group at the time and Miles was considering hiring me but that never happened. However, I did make *Bitches Brew* and I'm sure that exposure helped me."[63]

The large number of players and the unfamiliarity of several of them with Davis's methods caused some problems that show in the finished LP, notwithstanding the scrupulous editing that turned at least nine hours of studio time into a little more than an hour and a half of music. The LP includes many stretches in which nothing happens apart from the constant burble of the dense rhythmic mélange. Zawinul's *Pharaoh's Dance* suffers most noticeably, in a performance that never seems to come into focus over the chugging beat of the drums and grows more diffuse throughout its unconscionable length (20 minutes and 7 seconds); almost the entire second half of that length is a colorless rhythmic ramble. Davis's *Bitches Brew*, even longer (27 minutes), is more successful, with interludes of echoing trumpet electronics at the beginning, middle, and end separating a brighter theme, but, again, much of the second half is turned over to what sound like background rumblings. The track titled *John McLaughlin*, although credited to Davis as composer, is just a slice of tape from the intervals between takes that catches McLaughlin, Maupin, and one of the pianists, probably Corea, bouncing ideas off one another while the rest of the ensemble (minus Davis and Shorter) keep up a steady beat. (The title of the short piece flattered McLaughlin when he saw it. "That was the biggest surprise to me," he said. "I mean, I saw it on the record. I was shocked, really shocked."[64])

These long rhythmic passages may or may not have delighted Davis's new fans who bought the record in such numbers, but they predictably left his old fans unmoved. "To me jazz has to stimulate [and] this is not necessarily stimulating," Clark Terry said, when Leonard Feather played him the track called *Bitches Brew*. "It's something to listen to as far as new sounds are concerned, but it could just as easily have been background for a scene in a jungle movie ... an Australian setting with the foo birds running around and the kangaroos making love to each other." And then he added, appeasingly, "I'm not necessarily putting it down; it's different."[65]

Still, the rhythmic passages do not fill the recording; far from it. There is, in what is left over, a great deal for jazz fans to listen to once they adjust themselves to the new textures, dense rhythms, and amplified instruments. When *Bitches Brew* was first released, the shock of all that was new on it definitely impeded any broadly based appreciation of what it had to offer for jazz listeners, but in a few years – with denser rhythms clouding Davis's music and electronics becoming common-place – the LP became easier to hear somehow; that fact alone may account for its continuing sales long after the initial burst of sales had died down, a commercial history very different from pop albums.

Jazz fans who returned to it after a pause found a haunting modal ballad, Shorter's *Sanctuary* (in which Shorter is heard only in the background, playing the melody behind Davis's dominating trumpet). The ballad develops from almost complete silence, as Davis and Corea alone play the theme, to high intensity as the rhythm trio builds relentlessly to a climax; like so much else on this LP, the development is repeated twice in its entirety, as if Davis were afraid that his listeners might not be capable of figuring out his formal devices if he played them only once, but this time the repetition avoids the undirected rhythmic intervals.

Spanish Key, composed by Davis, may be the most completely successful track, considered as an orchestration of diverse elements capable of sustaining interest from start to finish. Its organization, typically loose but no more so than most of the music played by Davis's previous quintet, offers two recurring and apparently unrelated themes. The first, played repeatedly by Davis and referred to obliquely by both Shorter and Maupin in their solos, is an ascending run of one bar with the last note held through a second bar. The other, played in the bass clef, is a quick rise and fall that momentarily freezes the thumping drums. The first theme, as the tonal center of the piece, is readily available and recurs continually, but the second theme, as a kind of rhythmic sub-theme, recurs irregularly and infrequently; when it does it alleviates the percussive pulse remarkably. One of the pianists, probably Zawinul on the aural evidence, determines the occurrences of the sub-theme, and the same player also dominates the sequences in which the guitar and pianos intermingle without superimposed horns. *Spanish Key* also features a beautifully clear-toned, unamplified solo by Davis, but it is the piano player in the background who seems to hold the piece together so effectively.

Notwithstanding its silly title, *Miles Runs the Voodoo Down*, another memorable theme by Davis, inspires the best solos on the LP, with good ones from Shorter and McLaughlin and a splendid one from Davis. It sound like an exotic dance except for a turbulent, but brief, explosion of percussion near the end, and the theme cajoles the players into fashioning rich and melodic variations. Davis's solos on *Miles Runs the Voodoo Down* and *Spanish Key* alone should have vindicated the LP for most of his fans.

All of Davis's solos follow the canon of jazz improvisation established, in jazz legend, when Louis Armstrong first overpowered an ensemble and superimposed his own inventions on collective improvisations. Davis stands apart, "the soloist," as Barry McRae wrote in *Jazz Journal*, "showcased by the seemingly dense backgrounds he had chosen."[66] The other soloists do not stand apart in the same sense. Shorter enters into his solos unobtrusively, slowly rising out of the backgrounds, and McLaughlin hardly rises at all, so that his solos always seem to be shared with one or more of the piano players. The group remain an ensemble in the root sense of the word.

The separateness of Davis from the others was felt physically as the music was being made. "On *Bitches Brew* Miles wasn't even playing that much," Zawinul told Larry Birnbaum. "Miles was inside the booth with Teo Macero and he just came steppin' out here and there and played a couple of notes, but mainly he just let us play. It was Chick and me playing and Wayne was back there with Benny Maupin. We had this music, man, and we played and we rehearsed and we put things together."[67] The new collectivism of fusion music, a throwback to the old collectivism of New Orleans jazz bands but one that seemed separated from it by millennia instead of decades, was one more adjustment that listeners were expected to make.

"We were better off when 'Miles smiled,'" said one of his fans, who rued the day Davis left bebop behind but had managed, finally, to tolerate his modal music. Now he and hundreds of others faced moving another giant step, and many of them balked. "This was probably one of the most controversial records and jazz personalities of the past century," Clark Terry said two years after it was released, and he shook his head remembering the reactions Davis provoked with it: "The way he's been ostracized and criticized – and probably rightly so ..."[68]

Not all of Davis's peers reacted negatively. A few noticed that *Bitches Brew* did not in any way pander to teenaged tastes. It was probably more unlike anything that rock fans had ever heard than it was unlike what jazz fans were used to. It caught the public ear but was resolutely in

Miles Davis's – not Clive Davis's – own idiom. "The value of what Miles is doing now," Herbie Hancock said, "is that he is, in effect, setting up a criterion of excellence in the direction of rock that nobody else has achieved, in terms of instrumental efficiency, interaction, and all of those things that just hadn't happened too much in rock before."[69] Shelly Manne, the drummer who learned his trade on 52nd Street when Davis was learning his and later helped transliterate Davis's 'cool' experiments into the West Coast sound, agreed. "The performer can't concern himself with bending to play something he thinks people will like," he told Leonard Feather, "because by doing that he's subconsciously killing his own creative powers. He has to play what he feels, and just hope it will be liked ... Miles Davis did that and his latest LP sold close to a quarter of a million."[70]

Miles Davis, of course, needed no lectures on the value of pursuing his own star. In 1968, when he was feeling the pressure from Columbia's managers, he told Feather: "Anybody can make a record and try to do something new, to sell, but to me a record is more than something new, and I don't care how much it sells. You have to capture some feeling – you can't just play like a fucking machine ... You are what you are, no matter what you do. I can be loud and no good, soft and no good, in 7/8 and no good. You can be black and no good, white and no good ... A guy like Bobby Hackett plays what he plays with feeling, and you can put him into any kind of thing and he'll do it."[71] In the final analysis, perhaps the most important aspect of *In a Silent Way* and *Bitches Brew* is that they both manage, in no uncertain terms, "to capture some feeling."

Soon after recording *Bitches Brew*, Davis made his peace with Clive Davis. He called him and said he would consent to play at the Fillmore East, Bill Graham's New York counterpart of his San Francisco Fillmore (which now became "Fillmore West"). Clive Davis immediately proposed billing the Davis quintet with Laura Nyro, one of his favorite young rock ballad singers on the Columbia label. They were given equal billing, but in the show business pecking order there was no doubt about their ranking on the night of the concert: Davis opened the show and Nyro closed it. For Miles Davis, one of the greatest players in jazz for two decades, opening for youngsters with few musical credentials turned out to be a situation he had to live with as long as he made forays into their territory.

Instead of arousing his outrage and causing a further disruption of his relations with Columbia's president, the Fillmore billing filled him with anticipation and led him to make yet another peace offering. "A week before the Fillmore East concert...," Clive Davis recalls, "a package arrived at my hotel one day containing black and gray striped flared pants, a black and gray striped vest and a long-sleeved black silk shirt. A note from Miles asked if I would wear the outfit to the first performance. 'I want you to look special,' Miles wrote. I was very touched. It wasn't a typical outfit for me, but everyone needs a change of style now and then; and so I took it to a clothing store for a fitting. Miles played a beautiful set that night, and he was terribly pleased to see me in the outfit. We posed for pictures, which eventually appeared on the cover of *Cashbox*."[72]

And with that, Miles Davis crossed the invisible, but once impregnable, barrier between jazz and rock audiences. He also absorbed another lesson in humility that would become commonplace for him in the years ahead. "During the first Fillmore concert, some of Laura's girlish fans had trouble getting into him,"[73] Clive Davis says. So would the fans of Crosby, Stills, Nash and Young, and The Band, and Santana, and many of the other bands for whom he would open at the Fillmore and elsewhere. But Davis seems never to have considered that he might have been out of his natural element. Instead, he was determined to conquer the new world.

PART FOUR
PANGAEA

In a whirl of thighs
Jazz concert dollies
Cool us Miles
Warm eyed
Beneath the sleek
Cheek to cheek
Explosive
Like the music

Norman Humphreys *Concert* (1970)

13

Funky Tonk
1969–71

One thing about Miles and his music, in working with Miles, you can experiment as much as you wish. You can take his music, you can cut it up, you can put the filters in, you can do anything you want to as long as he knows who it is. I mean, he's not going to let just anyone do it.   Teo Macero

The dark underside of the bright ideals of the 1960s cast its shadow gloomily as the decade came to a close. It was not that those ideals were inverted into cynicism, at least not right away. The cynicism was held in abeyance for a few more years, closer to 1974, when President Richard Nixon resigned his office before he could be impeached for improprieties that had helped him score a landslide victory in the presidential campaign of 1972, and it did not set in irrevocably until the second half of the decade, when a long economic recession caused the piecemeal dismantling of many of the social, cultural, and educational programs that had been erected in response to those ideals. But by 1970 no one could carry his or her ideals with utter conviction any longer; no one could pretend that the world would become a fairer, freer place simply by willing it to be so, or even by marching and singing and demonstrating against the inequities and the injustices. "You gotta sing *loud*, if you wanna end wars and stuff," Arlo Guthrie had declared in *Alice's Restaurant*, but by the end of the decade the singing had grown faint.

No single event crystallized the growing gloom more powerfully than a demonstration at Ohio's Kent State University in America's heartland early in May 1970, which ended with National Guardsmen firing their m-1s into the crowd of about 500 unarmed students protesting President Nixon's decision to move troops into Cambodia and further escalate America's undeclared war in southeast Asia. Four students, two men and two women, aged 19 and 20, no different in most ways from thousands of other bright, middle-class achievers who populate universities all over the world, were killed on the grassy knolls of the campus, and people everywhere were numb with disbelief.

The Kent State students were counted as four more victims of the Vietnam War. By now, even the diminishing group favorably disposed to the American presence in Vietnam – the 'hawks,' as opposed to the 'doves' – had to admit the terrible toll that that war was taking on Americans. The number of young people maimed and dismembered and killed in combat was appalling, but the body counts really had to go beyond that. The war was reviled and despised not only, or even principally, by the young people but by many older people as well, enough of them altogether to form a sizable minority at odds with civic authority. Opposition to the war had spread even to the troops already in Vietnam, to the extent that some percentage of the long casualty lists was routinely attributed to sending dispirited and demoralized troops into combat.

For many of those troops, coming home took its own toll. Many young men and women had embarked for Vietnam in the same spirit in which their fathers had embarked for Korea and for Europe one or two decades before them, but the Vietnam veterans returned to find no ticker-tape parades or hometown celebrations but only quiet relief from parents and sullen disinterest from some of their peers; they soon discovered that in putting their lives on the line against an elusive foe they had earned no more respect from their peers, and often much less, than had their classmates who had dodged the draft and were living in napalm-free self-exile in Toronto or Amsterdam or Stockholm. That realization, dawning while the horrors of war still invaded their sleep, wounded many of the young people whose limbs were unscathed.

By the end of the decade, almost no American escaped some deep personal torment as a result of Vietnam. Miles Davis's sons, Gregory and Miles, both attained draft age as the buildup of American troops under presidents Kennedy and Johnson grew deadly serious. By 1969, Gregory, the elder of the two, had been discharged from the army. Davis introduced him to Don DeMicheal in Chicago in the fall, where father and son were honing their boxing skills in a gym. "'Greg won three [boxing] titles while he was in the Army,' says the young man's obviously proud father. 'Plays drums too.'"[1] But his sons were suffering, and Davis blamed the system. In 1970, he told an interviewer from *Zygote* magazine: "There's so much graft and shit, you wouldn't believe the shit going down with dope. The dope goes in and the judges know about the dope, so subsequently the dope comes up to Harlem and the Spanish people. Both of my sons are hooked because there's nothing else for them to do. There's nothing for them to go to school for 'cause they're gonna get fucked over by the system."[2] Ten years later he was more guarded when he spoke to Cheryl McCall. "They took my son," he told her, "fucked *him* up in the war. I don't even want to say which son."[3]

The war was the main issue, but hundreds of other issues, great and small, percolated into public consciousness, and few of them failed to show a dark side. Another one that touched Miles Davis, at least indirectly, was the government's response to sickle cell anemia, the disease that hobbled Davis and hundreds of other black Americans. In 1970, Senator John V. Tunney of California declared: "It is fair to say, and research figures prove the fact, that if sickle cell anemia afflicted white people, we would have made a commitment long ago to end this disease."[4] Tunney sponsored the National Sickle Cell Anemia Act declaring the condition "a targeted disease for concentrated research" and quickly won executive approval for allocating several thousand dollars to research.

When the act reached the Senate, it presented senators from urban districts with an apple-pie issue, and they tripped over one another to broadcast their approval to their black constituents by upping the ante. By the time the act cleared the Senate in 1972, it carried allocations of $25 million in federal research grants for 1973, $40 million for 1974, and $50 million for 1975.

What the politicians apparently never considered was that sickle cell anemia, a genetic disease, has no foreseeable cure – no vaccine or serum can eliminate sickle-shaped blood cells without eliminating normal blood cells too. The research investment might improve palliative treatment for the sufferers, but the only way to eliminate the disease is by blood-typing the black population and counseling carriers against producing offspring.

When teams of counselors set up clinics in the ghettos with federal funds and began dispensing their advice to one out of every ten blacks – potentially affecting one black couple in five – against raising a family, the outcry was predictable. "I can't tell any of my patients not to have children because of sickle cell anemia," said one black, female obstetrician. "Most of them regard birth control as a white plot against black people. I'm not certain they're wrong."[5]

The talk of genocide, long a topic that concerned black intellectuals, quickly drowned out any talk there might have been about government largesse in sickle cell research, adding its bitter taste to the brewing cynicism. "I don't know about the world," Davis said, "you can see it's already fucked up. They're still practicing genocide with the black people, nobody ever says anything about that, they always talk about the Jews. They never talk about the black people getting fucked up."[6]

For jazz, the social movements of the 1960s brought an unexpected bonus when dozens of universities and other institutions recognized "black studies" — history, sociology, arts, including music, and other facets of the participation of Afro-Americans in the world — and devised curricula and programs. Jazz had been held in low esteem by educated blacks as well as educated whites for most of its history, until it moved into the cultural citadels as the keystone of black studies and acquired an air of institutional legitimacy that was long overdue. Dozens of jazz artists were appointed to teaching posts, among them David Baker, Billy Byers, Jerry Coker, Richard Davis, Alan Dawson, John LaPorta, Ralph McDonald, Jackie McLean, Bob Northern, George Russell, Bill Russo, Billy Taylor, and Cecil Taylor. Miles Davis had his chance to join them. "They asked me did I want to be dean of Howard University's music department," he announced, and then he reported his predictable answer. "Hell, no! See, I don't think like that, man. I don't like them bourgeois niggers. That's why they're rebelling at Howard. For a long time they wouldn't even have jazz concerts on the campus of Howard University."[7] A few years later, asked about Howard University's offer by Gregg Hall, he was less bellicose about his reason for rejecting it. "I can't do that shit," he said, "I teach my musicians."[8]

Davis had grown jaded about using jazz, or at least about using *his* jazz, for social purposes. Recalling the benefit he had played for voter registration drives in 1964, he said in 1981, "I just did one concert. It was a double concert, but I'm not going that way again. I think the government should take care of their own people."[9] Now he had other, less idealistic goals.

"I could put together the greatest rock and roll band you ever heard," he boasted to Don DeMicheal late in 1969,[10] after *Bitches Brew* had been recorded but still months before it was released. During the first five years of the 1970s, he seemed to be trying to make good on his boast, although, naturally, there was always something *sui generis* in his music and it never convincingly stood as "rock and roll" anyway. Neither did the music inspired by and sometimes dedicated to Miles

Davis that many other jazz musicians were playing for the next six or seven years. But if the music that came to be called jazz-rock fusion was never really rock it seemed to many listeners in the jazz community to be not quite jazz either.

The conventional labels had seldom seemed so imprecise, and Davis deplored all of them. "I don't like the word 'rock' and all that shit," he said, just a few minutes after boasting about putting together "the greatest rock and roll band you ever heard," and rock was not the only one: "'Jazz' is an Uncle Tom word," he added; "it's a white folks' word."[11] A few years later, he declared, "There's no such thing as 'bebop.' It's a white man's word to sell black music."[12] And he was quoted in *Melody Maker* saying: "Rock is a white man's word. Blues is a white man's word. Jazz is a white man's word." Davis's diatribes were hardly surprising when he was playing music that defied those labels, and even less so when he had always maintained that music should not be discussed, even when it was more readily categorizable.

Whatever else it was, fusion music was undeniably an assault on a mass audience, and the audience materialized en masse as soon as *Bitches Brew* was released. Davis kept silent about the ulterior motive in his plunge into fusion music, but others did not. Herbie Hancock, only 29 at the end of the decade but already an established jazzman after his years with Davis had made him a poll winner and a conspicuous name in the field, admitted that his own fusion music, which would be the most lucrative of all in the short run, began as a search for the masses when his musical ideals clouded over. "I started thinking of the great masters I know – Miles Davis, Charlie Parker, John Coltrane, those guys to me, more than anybody else, seem to be the giants of my era – I'm none of those guys, or anywhere near them," he told Leonard Feather in *The Pleasures of Jazz*, "so I might as well forget trying to be in that category. Forget trying to be another genius or legend in my own time. Once I got the idea of becoming a legend or genius out of my head, then I felt satisfied in just making some nice music and making people happy."[13]

Hancock's greatest commercial success, a 1974 LP called *Headhunters* that had almost nothing to do with jazz, sold more than 500,000 copies in a few months, but Hancock had been building toward that commercial peak for four years. Along the way, he was yoked into concert bills as the opener for acts like the Pointer Sisters, a rock-gospel trio, and ingenuously observing to the press that the most gratification he ever hoped to get out of his music was a standing ovation like the one he had seen the Pointer Sisters get. Even before *Headhunters* was released, the Pointer Sisters had fallen in popular esteem to the point where they would have been happy to find themselves opening for Hancock, and by the time *Headhunters* completed its quick heist they were no longer filling the biggest rooms in Las Vegas. Perhaps their decline helped Hancock appreciate how fickle were the hands that gave adoring ovations, because soon after *Headhunters* he resumed displaying his delicate touch on acoustic piano on records and in concerts, something that many listeners assumed he had forgotten entirely after his years of synthesized fuzz-wah. He has done so regularly ever since, in an all-star jazz band called VSOP, duets with Chick Corea, and other outings. At the same time, he has carried on recording funk.

Davis's history in fusion music misses both the commercial highs and the artistic lows of Hancock's, but not by much. In the sixteen months following the *Bitches Brew* sessions, Davis put himself through an extraordinarily productive period, even by the standards of his own highly productive career. He recorded so often that Columbia's managers, who a few years earlier were trying to cajole him into the recording studios, shook their heads in despair at the prospect of mastering his enormous backlog. He led his working band, still comprised of some talented young individuals despite the changes in personnel, through a dizzy round of concert and club engagements, some of them at the large rock emporiums favored by Clive Davis, and he proliferated his recording backlog by getting Columbia to tape his performances at Fillmore West, Fillmore East, the Isle of Wight Pop Festival, and at a club in Washington, DC. (His music from this period is also documented on an unauthorized recording of a performance at Philharmonic Hall.)

As if that were not enough, he also became what is known, in agentry circles, as a "more visible personality," appearing at Columbia's publicity bashes, on televison talk shows as a non-talking guest, and at other 'image-making' functions. With it came a new image ready to be made. Gone was the Italianate wardrobe, the pinstripes and patent leather elevator shoes that were his cachet for *Gentleman's Quarterly*, and in their place came buckskin jackets with fringes, embroidered dashikis, and clogs or boots with three-inch heels. The new look did not arrive suddenly. It came by degrees in the late 1960s, and by the end of the decade Davis was a trend-setter in the anarchic fashion show of those times just as he had been in the charcoal-grey button-down days a decade earlier. Some fans mourned the change, and one of them was his daughter Cheryl. "I loved it when he used to dress so cute in those suits," she told David Breskin, "when I was a teenager. Those Italian suits. Polka-dot ties. Those cute suits. Oh, he was so cute."[14] The difference in style was obvious, but the effect remained the same. Davis's audiences had always included a fringe of idolators who were just as interested in what he wore as in what he played, and his new look just kept them coming.

The differences in his music were greater. After making his reputation as a master of melody with the experimental nonet at the end of the 1940s and the great quintet and sextet of the 1950s, and then moving on to become an ingenious manipulator of harmonies with the modal and tone-centered compositions of the long-lived quintet of the 1960s, Davis moved now to highlight percussion. He had given the piano player less and less to play in ensembles for years now, and he reached a point where some of his recording contingents omit the piano player; in his next phase, beginning in 1972, he would form his working band with two guitarists and no piano player at all. His trumpet playing usually rides above the rhythmic current, but more and more, especially in the live performances, it is reduced to only a few notes, often with heavy electronic inflections; in the next phase of his development, he plays the trumpet even less and often abandons it for the organ or piano. These aspects of his music become dominant later, when he settles into the fiercely percussive style, but they are already broad tendencies in the flood of recordings that followed *Bitches Brew*.

That outpouring is remarkably diverse, spanning a stylistic range that occasionally approaches the control he exercised over *In a Silent Way* or seems to be lurching out of control altogether, a kind of wild ride impelled by flailed drums. While the diverse range is perceptible in the music that has been made available, the character of the music remains far from clear. Several hours of it have been issued, but probably scores of hours have not been. Compounding the problem, most of the music released is obscured by splicing, overdubbing, tape loops, and other post-production devices. The live performances show the heavy hand of editing no less than the studio recordings. Many of the recordings obviously combine fragments of several different recording sessions or concert sets that might someday be unscrambled by issuing complete takes or continuous performances. In the meantime, the character of the music remains nebulous and the discographical puzzles are legion. Davis's most prolific months in an incredibly productive career have so far left his listeners with some strangely unrewarding music.

Those months came perilously close to being snuffed out before they got underway. On the night of 10 October 1969, Davis was sitting in his Ferrari in Brooklyn in the small hours of the morning with a woman named Marguerite Eskridge when he looked out his window and saw a man with a pistol pointed at him. The man fired, shattering the window and grazing Davis. "I don't know what it was all about," Davis told Cheryl McCall. "The agency knew, 'cause they were having an agency war. I didn't know it. I was talking to Marguerite. If she had gotten out of the car she'd have got killed. But I had just kissed her in the car, you know? And I look around and this guy is staring at me, and I said *shit* this is [it]."[15]

In the aftermath, police investigators searched Davis's car and said they found marijuana. He was arrested, but the charges were later dismissed for lack of evidence.[16] It was his first arrest since the Birdland incident in August 1959.

Davis denies any knowledge of the gunman's motives, but no one, not even Davis, has ever suggested that he might have been a mistaken or innocent target. Lunatics are not completely unknown on the streets of Brooklyn, and a black man in a white Ferrari might make as conspicuous a target as anyone else for someone in search of a target, but this gunman had an accomplice driving his car, and the notion of lunatics traveling in pairs strains credulity. He was not the near-victim of a crime of passion either. Asked if he thought the gunman might be the woman's husband, he replied, "I don't mess with married women."[17] Davis's explanation that he was caught in "an agency war" might account for the fact that the gunman missed him from point-blank range, if the shooting was intended only as an underworld warning. He had recently signed a marketing deal with a black-owned public relations firm called New Wave Communications after complaining about Columbia's and Jack Whittemore's work on his behalf, with unknown repercussions.

Rumors of Davis's associations with underworld figures have occasionally surfaced throughout his career, sometimes encouraged by Davis himself. When his interview with Sy Johnson was interrupted by a telephone call, Davis identified his caller as "one of my old gangster buddies."[18] Art Pepper, the alto saxophonist who spent several years in San Quentin and other prisons for crimes related to narcotics, admired Davis for allegedly defying the underworld, especially for informing on narcotics peddlers – "burning connections" in Pepper's jailyard argot. "Miles Davis is basically a good person and that's why his playing is so beautiful and pure," Pepper says in *Straight Life*. "This is my own thinking and the older I get the more I believe I'm correct in my views ...

He's tried to give an appearance of being something he's not. I've heard that he's broken a television set when he didn't like something that was said on TV, that he's burnt connections, been really a bastard with women, and come on as a racist. The connections probably deserve to be burnt; they were assholes, animals, guys that would burn you: give you bad stuff and charge you too much, people that would turn you in to the cops if they got busted. Most of the women that hang around jazz musicians are phonies. And as for his prejudice, ... that's what he feels he should be like. He's caught up in the way the country is, the way people are, and he figures that's the easiest way to go."[19] For someone like Pepper, who lost more than he won in his battles with both the underworld and the police, the rumors about Davis, a clear winner, increased his esteem almost boundlessly.

The shooting incident launched new rumors, which probably gave the incident its dénouement. Joachim Berendt reported: "Miles set a reward of $10,000 for the capture of the two assailants. Nobody collected the reward, but a few weeks later the two gangsters were mysteriously shot."[20]

Just a few days after the shooting, Davis was playing music again, appearing with his quintet at the restored Apollo Theater on a bill titled Midnight Concert in Harlem. The concert also featured Bill Evans, Herbie Hancock, Donald Byrd, Milford Graves, and the Thad Jones–Mel Lewis orchestra, all part of an international fund-raising campaign for a jazz center in Harlem.

A week later, the quintet left for Europe on a two-week tour of nine cities. The tour began in Milan with two concerts (on 26 October), and moved to Rome (27), Vienna (31), London (1 November) and Ronnie Scott's club (2), Paris for two concerts (3), Copenhagen (4), Stockholm (5), Berlin (7), and Rotterdam (9). Despite the crowded schedule, Davis somehow found time to circulate in some of the cities. After finishing his London concert, he turned up in the audience in Ronnie Scott's club, where he was scheduled to play the next night. The entr'acte at Scott's was Professor Irwin Corey, an American comedian who played a crazy genius in his act. Scott, an enthusiastic raconteur, told Kitty Grime, "Miles came in with a whole entourage – girl friends, barber, lawyer, shoe shine boy, you know. And they all sat down front. And he had these huge wrap-around sunglasses on. And Corey suddenly bent down and whipped the glasses off Miles and put them on. And said, 'No wonder you're smiling – everyone looks black.'"[21]

Davis was treated almost as irreverently when he phoned Jack

Whittemore from Paris during the same tour. "I needed a few albums, a cut of my latest record," he told Max Gordon. "Friends, critics, broads wanted one. So I called up Jack in New York. 'Call CBS,' I told him, 'and tell 'em to call Paris and have their wholesaler here deliver a dozen albums to me in my hotel.' So what do you think Jack said to me? 'Who do you think you are, Frank Sinatra?'" Davis was not amused. "I'm getting rid of that bastard," he told Gordon. "What's Sinatra got I haven't got?"[22] For Whittemore, Davis's agent for some fifteen years, Davis's threat to change agents was nothing new, and a few more years passed before the change was made.

Back in the United States, Davis kept up the pace. The quintet played at the Garden State Jazz Festival in Holmdel, New Jersey. Chris Albertson, covering the Festival for *Down Beat*, filed a report filled with superlatives about their non-stop performance. "Davis and Wayne Shorter expressed themselves eloquently," Albertson wrote, "stepping to the back of the huge stage between chill-provoking solos as the rhythm section exploded in a pulsating orgasm of hip sounds, pianist Chick Corea embroidering electrical embellishments that lent a tinge of rock to this memorable piece. During the second minute of the tumultuous ovation that followed, the young lady seated behind me was still gasping, 'Oh God, oh God, oh God.' Her reaction was understandable. She had just witnessed contemporary jazz at its peak of perfection."[23]

Audience reactions were not always so effusive. When the quintet moved into the Plugged Nickel in Chicago, Don DeMicheal listened impatiently to the grumblings of a longtime Davis fan who shared the elbow space at the bar with him, and the grumblings were only silenced when Davis brought forward some of his old familiar titles – *Walkin'*, and especially *Stella by Starlight*, which Davis played, according to DeMicheal, "much as he has for the last several years – with an inner pain that touched the heart."[24] It was probably the last time he made that concession.

The Plugged Nickel engagement was followed by a week at the Colonial Tavern in Toronto, 1–6 December, and it turned into an especially notable engagement for local fans who watched Davis's public audition of Toronto guitarist Sonny Greenwich. "One day I got a phone call," Greenwich told Mark Miller in *Jazz in Canada*. "I had seen Miles before in New York, but I'd never spoken to him. He'd never heard me play; he'd heard *of* me, I guess, through Wayne and the guys. I just got a call one morning. 'Sonny? ... Miles.' You know, with his voice? I thought somebody was joking." Greenwich, then in the most active phase of his playing career, has emerged sporadically and unpredictably to display fervid improvisations that evoke memories of Coltrane.

During his week with Davis's band Greenwich continually wrestled with sound problems from his cheap amplifier, but he held his own on the stand and Davis discovered off the stand that he was a boxing fan as well. At the end of the week Davis invited him to join the band, but Greenwich, who had had immigration problems a year before when he played a week-long stint at the Village Vanguard, was skeptical. "I told him he'd have problems getting a lawyer to get me down there," Greenwich recalled. "He said he could do it. But nothing ... I didn't hear from him."[25] Greenwich slipped back into his silent ways, and he has broken his silence less frequently in the years since, barely often enough to fuel the legend that surrounds his playing.

After the week in Toronto, Davis and his sidemen finally took some time off. What was a Christmas break for most of them was a more decisive break for Wayne Shorter, who ended his long tenure in the working band. His departure at the end of 1969, after five and a half years, ended the musical associations that Davis had formed in the 1960s. Shorter had no alternative plans, quitting mainly just to settle down for a while. "I spent the next year moving all over New York, getting a family started and basically doing no music," Shorter says.[26] He played on two of Davis's recording sessions early in the new year, and he recorded an album of gentle, impressionistic music for Blue Note in August (*Odyssey of Iska*, BST-84363), but mainly he was content to compose and practice out of earshot of audiences.

He grew restless only months later, and then he made a significant move. "At the end of 1970 Joe [Zawinul] and I got on the phone – he wasn't with Cannonball anymore – and talked about starting something up together rather than doing it individually," he says. Their band was called Weather Report, and Miroslav Vitous joined them as co-leader but left after two years. Several bassists, drummers, and percussionists have completed the personnel over the years. They signed a recording contract with Columbia, made a couple of innovative recordings in their first two years, and then progressively diluted their jazz content in favor of funk, becoming one of the conspicuous commercial successes as the fusion peaked. By the end of the decade, they had increased the jazz content in concerts and, less noticeably, on records, and kept going strong.

Shorter's replacement in Davis's band was Steve Grossman, a

Brooklynite who turned 19 in January 1970, soon after he joined. Grossman is white, an unremarkable fact except that Davis seemed preoccupied with racial stereotypes in music at the time. "It's social music," Davis said of rock in a long interview with Don DeMicheal for *Rolling Stone* that took place while he was playing at the Plugged Nickel, and then he launched into a diatribe on music and race. "There's two kinds – white and black, and those bourgeois spades are trying to sound white and the whites are trying to sound colored. It's embarrassing. It's like me wearing a dress. Blood, Sweat and Tears is embarrassing to me ... They try to sing black and talk white."[27]

"I can tell a white group just from the sound, don't have to see them," he added, repeating a claim that had occasionally been made by jazz musicians for years without ever being substantiated. Leonard Feather's blindfold tests, a regular feature of *Down Beat* for decades, have piled up several instances where a jazz musician casually labeled an unidentified record racially and was wrong. Sometimes Feather deliberately tested a musician on his perceptions of race when he was known to have made claims on the topic. Roy Eldridge was the first, and he failed miserably at it in the 1950s, but of course his failure did not lay the issue to rest. Davis, too, had made several wrong guesses on various blindfold tests. Listening to a record by Buddy Colette, Davis said, "All those white tenor players sound alike to me," and more than a decade later he labeled Sun Ra's Arkestra a "white" band.[28]

Davis's version of the myth is not segregationist. "You got to have a mixed group – one has one thing, and the other has another," he told DeMicheal. "For me, a group has to be mixed. To get swing, you have to have some black guys in there." Davis, of course, often included white players in his band from the time he chose Lee Konitz for his nonet in 1948, with Bill Evans in 1958, Chick Corea and David Holland in 1968, and now Steve Grossman, and he had the long association with Gil Evans as well as more recent ones with Josef Zawinul and John McLaughlin. Few musicians should have been in a better position to realize that the racial stereotyping was nonsense. Earlier in the interview with DeMicheal, he praised the drumming of Buddy Rich, but he now said: "See, white guys can only play at a certain tempo. They can play here [taps finger], but they can't play here [slightly faster tapping] or here [faster tapping] ... For me, if I listen to a white group, they got to have some spades in there for me to like them in more than one tempo. Spades got that thing – they can tighten it up."[29]

Davis's remarks have no real bearing on his music or on his recruiting;

in practice, he continued to select his sidemen by choosing the best musicians for the job. But his remarks were well publicized when the interview was published, and they no doubt helped to perpetuate the ignorance and the hatred that fastens itself to racial stereotyping within jazz and beyond it. If exactly the same remarks had been made by a white jazz musician and published in *Rolling Stone*, the outrage of fans and critics – both black and white – would have been deafening, and rightly so.

Around the time that Grossman replaced Shorter, Davis added another musician to his working band, making it a sextet. He was Airto Moreira, a 29-year-old Brazilian percussionist. Moreira, who later went by his first name only as Brazilian soccer stars and other celebrities do, had emigrated to the United States in 1967, arriving in California, where he hoped to establish his reputation in jazz as he had already done at home. During his first year, he saw two concerts by Davis in California and made up his mind that he would someday play in his band. After the second concert, he managed to make his way backstage to Davis's dressing room door, where he stood and, in faltering, almost incomprehensible English, attempted to explain to Davis his admiration for his music and his ambition to join his band. After a few minutes of the monologue, Davis, perplexed and perhaps embarrassed by the flowery sentiments, said, "So what?" and closed the door in his face.

Moreira had better luck after he moved to New York in 1969. He was befriended by Walter Booker, the bassist in Cannonball Adderley's band, and through Booker he met and played with Adderley, Zawinul, and others. In Brazil, Moreira played drums as well as congas, bongos, and maracas, but his first chances to play in New York were on the latin percussion instruments only. Davis had already used Don Alias and Jim Riley as percussionists on some recording sessions, and late in 1969 he asked Moreira, probably on Zawinul's recommendation, to show up for a recording session. For the next two years, Moreira worked for Davis.

With his highly visible role in Davis's working band, the use of percussion in jazz underwent a dramatic increase. Dozens of bands began using a percussionist, a term that denoted a non-drumming percussion player or a person who played any number of percussion instruments other than the conventional drum kit. Moreira, encouraged by Davis, led the way for percussionists to proliferate their instruments. To the expected congas, bongos, and maracas, Moreira added instruments at a wild rate, until by the time he left Davis he counted 32 different noise-makers. He described some of them in an interview with

Lee Underwood: the berimbau, a single string with a movable gourd as a resonator capable of making a non-electronic wah-wah sound; the cabacas, a gourd wrapped with beads that slide against its surface when it is turned; the reco-reco, a bamboo stick with ridges that resonate when stroked with a stick; the ganza, a metal tube with pebbles inside, in various sizes to make various pitches; and all sorts of other exotic devices, most completely unknown to jazz audiences, plus a few not so exotic, such as the wooden soles of clog shoes, then fashionable, which Moreira banged together like non-resonating cymbals.

In Davis's live performances, Moreira made a spectacular show, sitting onstage on a blanket with his array of noise-makers spread out around him. Even Davis was impressed. After his solos he often crouched down beside Moreira's blanket and stared intently at his every move. Moreira's impact on the jazz world was enormous. As more percussionists appeared, percussion, as Moreira put it, "became an instrument instead of just background," and *Down Beat* responded by adding percussion as a category in its polls in 1974. It was a category that Moreira automatically won year after year.

Moreira, trained as a drummer, did not arrive in the United States with his talents as a percussionist fully formed or even clearly defined. He had to teach himself how to use most of his unconventional instruments, and the only useful lessons he ever received, he has said many times, came from Miles Davis. "He was the most profound influence that I ever had in my career," he told Underwood, "meeting him and listening to the very little he had to say. He once came to me and said, 'Don't *bang*. Just play.' That's all, 'Don't *bang*. Just play.'" Those imperatives turned into a long learning experience. "When I asked him, 'What do you mean, don't bang, just play?' he said, '*You* figure that out,'" Moreira remembers. "He was a beautiful guy, and a nice guy, too, but I was terrified for the first month."[30]

Moreira described to Dan Morgenstern what happened after that. "At first I didn't understand what he meant, and then I realized that he wanted me to hear the music and *then* play some sounds. So then I'd listen and not play at all, and then he came to me after a few concerts and said [imitating Miles's voice]: 'Play, man – play more!' So then I'd start to play more, but in the right places, and then I really got into the thing of listening to the music and picking up the right instrument at the right time and playing the right sound. Miles doesn't say very much, but when you understand him, everything he says means a lot."[31] Moreira's contribution to Davis's music, apart from the long solo spots that he was allotted in concert performances while the rest of the band retreated to the wings, was felt rather than heard. He added another layer to the growing density of the bottom, the undertone of Davis's music that was becoming its focus.

Davis's crowded performing schedule was matched by an equally crowded recording schedule, and Columbia was growing concerned about the amount of material it now held. "When we met [around 1966], he felt underpaid and was producing relatively few albums," Clive Davis recalls. "After that, we had trouble slowing him down. He started recording three albums a year, sometimes right on top of each other. He would call Bruce Lundvall [head of marketing], Bob Altschuler (another jazz aficionado) [head of publicity], or myself and play long passages. Then he'd want *that* album released, despite his backlog. If we had just had a release in December, he'd record an album in January and want it out immediately. And we'd protest, saying that the December one needed time for sales and exposure. Then he'd call in March telling us to forget the January album – he had a new one."[32]

Beginning with *Bitches Brew*, all of Davis's records on Columbia except two (*Jack Johnson* and *On the Corner*) until 1981 were issued as double albums, called 'twofers' (from the advertising claim, never literally true, that one was buying "two for the price of one"). Even so, the music that was released represents only a fraction of what was recorded, consisting of one or two titles from several dates and a staggering assortment of bands, the permutations and combinations of Davis's stock company. But the increased production, marketed in the more expensive twofers and sold to a larger audience in the wake of *Bitches Brew*, still did not succeed in balancing Davis's accounts with Columbia, at least not during Clive Davis's term of office. "At no time did Miles ever fully recoup his advances," Davis says. "Yet our relationship remained warm because I dealt with his financial problems on the assumption that he was good for Columbia in the long run, both on commercial and cultural levels."[33] If he hoped that increasing his production would eventually free him from the company, he was stymied, and he has remained with them ever since.

The first recording session following the *Bitches Brew* sessions took place in November and introduced Steve Grossman and Airto Moreira, among others, into the ensemble. The first significant issue, amounting to nearly half an hour, was held until 1974, when it appeared on the *Big Fun* LP, but a hint (2 minutes and 42 seconds) was issued in France the year before as a 45-rpm bonus in a three-album boxed anthology, *The*

Essential Miles Davis (CBS [Fr] S66310); the B side of the 45-rpm gave a hint, the only one so far, of the music from a session nine days later. The details are as follows:

Miles Davis Ensemble
Miles Davis, tpt; Steve Grossman, ss; Benny Maupin, bass clnt; Herbie Hancock, Chick Corea, el pno; John McLaughlin, gtr; Harvey Brooks, el b; Billy Cobham, dms; Airto Moreira, perc; Khalil Balakrishna, Bihari Sharma, sitar, tamboura. New York, 19 November 1969
Great Expectations [*Great Expectations/Orange Lady*]; *Great Expectations* (45 rpm)
(first version on Columbia PG 32866; second on CBS [Fr] 4927)

Omit Corea; add Josef Zawinul, Larry Young, el pno, and Ron Carter, b. Same place, 28 November 1969
The Little Blue Frog (45 rpm)
(on CBS [Fr] 4927B)
Orange Lady, composed by Zawinul, comprises the second half of the long version of *Great Expectations*.

Great Expectations consists of a single phrase repeated over and over by Davis, sometimes with Grossman's soprano and Maupin's bass clarinet playing in unison, as the percussion ensemble, eight men strong and laced with the exotic sounds of Indian instruments, rumbles and roars underneath. The point of the exercise is apparently to stimulate the rhythm players because the melodic surface is unrelieved, and perhaps purposeful, monotony. Although it is hard to be certain when the music consists only of a simple, repeated refrain, the short version of *Great Expectations* from France does not sound like an excerpt from the longer version but instead seems to be another slice of the master tape.

Davis's use of the sitar in this and later sessions reflects the discovery of Eastern music and also of Eastern cuisine, dress, and especially mysticism that took place in the late 1960s. The new interest made Ravi Shankar, the sitar virtuoso, a cult figure who played his music in packed bars and concert halls and inspired George Harrison of the Beatles and other rock guitarists to take up the instrument. Harrison's sitar accompaniment on *Norwegian Wood* in 1966 and the next year on *Within You without You* on the influential *Sgt. Pepper's Lonely Hearts Club Band* LP gave rise to a fashionable affectation in the pop music of the day, and Davis was one of the few who followed the lead in jazz. For

Davis, the Eastern instruments came along opportunely as he was searching for more varied percussion colors.

The second half of the long version of *Great Expectations*, separated audibly by a pause but not visually by the usual band of vinyl, is Zawinul's beautiful theme, *Orange Lady*. Davis allows himself to embellish the theme, but the musical elements are otherwise much the same as for *Great Expectations*, the main difference coming from Zawinul's writing, which attracts attention to itself as Davis's theme never does. Zawinul was surprisingly philosophical about being uncredited. He simply said, "There was some kind of mess up with the titles, so it was not mentioned it was my tune." By the time Davis's version was released, *Orange Lady* had already appeared on the inaugural Weather Report LP of 1971 (Columbia C 30661), in a version incomparably more subtle and graceful than Davis's.

As with much of Davis's work of this period, the music itself is often less interesting than the process involved in making it. Davis was experimenting, trying to control musical elements complex both in their diversity and in their provenance. The experiments seldom failed to reward the musicians. "The unifying spirit was Miles," said Billy Cobham. "He brought together a lot of musicians from different parts of the world and then would scream at them in a soft whisper, 'I want you to do this! No, don't play, play this, don't play,' that kind of thing, and out of it came this concoction, this brew. I mean, it was like he was stirring a big, black pot of notes."[34]

Cobham's presence in the studio when DeJohnette was Davis's drummer in the working band underlines his different intentions in the two settings. As a jazz drummer, DeJohnette gave Davis the solid backing for his quintet's improvisations, but Cobham, a self-taught drummer born in Panama and raised there and in Brooklyn, brought a broad, uncategorizable background and helped make some broad, uncategorizable music. At the time of these recordings, Cobham played regularly with the fusion band Dreams. Davis once suggested that he should join his band, and Cobham was willing. "I really loved to play with him," he told Brian Priestley; "I *never* had any hassles with that cat over *nothing*. Sometimes just being in his presence can really cool you out – he doesn't have to say anything. You know, it's not like I consider him a god or anything, but there's a charisma or something about the cat that I wish there were words for."[35] But Davis did not renew his suggestion, and Cobham played with him only in the studio.

Besides the hours he spent in Columbia's studios, Davis also began spending some of his time at functions designed to circulate his name more widely. He visited a recording session by Laura Nyro, one of Columbia's best-selling young ballad writer-singers and a special favorite of Clive Davis's, where he was encouraged to play as a guest star in her backing band, but after listening to the arrangements he decided that there was no space for him to play.[36] He also donned his tuxedo to attend a formal party for the singer Janis Joplin, hosted by Clive Davis to "offset ... some of the more scruffy stories" about the hard-living diva of rock.[37] Miles Davis found himself among many of the other luminaries of the Columbia roster: Tony Bennett, Bob Dylan, Laura Nyro, Johnny and Edgar Winter, among others, as well as Earl Wilson and Leonard Lyons, show business columnists in New York newspapers.

He was probably more in his element being interviewed by Dwike Mitchell, the pianist in the Mitchell-Ruff Duo, for the soundtrack of a film documentary called *The Legacy of the Drum*, with music by Dizzy Gillespie and the Duo.

The recordings with large ensembles continued in January and early February, at some sessions with Wayne Shorter back in the ensemble. The details are as follows:

Miles Davis Ensemble
Miles Davis, tpt; Wayne Shorter, ss; Benny Maupin, bass clnt; Chick Corea, el pno; Josef Zawinul, el pno, org; David Holland, b; Harvey Brooks, el b; Billy Cobham, Jack DeJohnette, dms; Airto Moreira, perc; Khalil Balakrishna, sitar. New York, 27 January 1970
Lonely Fire; Guinnevere
(*Lonely Fire* on *Big Fun*, Columbia PG 32866; *Guinnevere* on *Circle in the Round*, Columbia 30278 [1979])

Omit Maupin, Brooks; add John McLaughlin, el gtr. Same place, 6 February 1970
Gemini/Double Image
(on *Live-Evil*, Columbia 30954)

Lonely Fire, by Davis, opens as an anticipatory, pulseless call, repeated over and over by Davis, and then alternately by Davis and Shorter, like a soundtrack for a suspense movie, except the suspense is never resolved. After some eleven minutes, with the listener's patience sorely taxed, and perhaps the musicians' too, David Holland introduces an insistent bass riff that carries along the rhythm and breaks open the musical stalemate; Davis solos, and then Shorter, and then Corea and Zawinul together. During this nine-minute sequence, before the band returns to the monochromatic suspense motif for the final minute, *Lonely Fire* cruises along with some of the infectious drive and plain-spoken joy of *It's about That Time.*

The other two recordings from the same time have more in common with its suspenseful phase than with its looser segment. *Guinnevere,* based on a ballad by David Crosby, the lead singer of the Byrds who had just joined three other lead singers from other bands to form a 'supergroup' called Crosby, Stills, Nash and Young, lacks the lyric of the original, a love song to the first lady of King Arthur's Round Table, and gains only a plodding beat; Davis occasionally directs a few notes outside the repeated melody statement, but the only real relief from the repetition comes in an incongruous passage dominated by the whining sitar and some jungle percussion.

Gemini/Double Image, a medley of Zawinul compositions, yokes the two themes together almost imperceptibly and recites them repetitively, again without any solos, over a backdrop dominated from beginning to end by John McLaughlin's guitar accents, in a milder imitation of Jimi Hendrix, the lefthanded rocker who used his guitar as a lightning rod.

All this music, which fills more than three-quarters of an hour in the form in which it is issued, pares down the music into its simplest components – the beat is constant or nonexistent, the tonal centres are narrow, and the melodies are repeated single phrases – as if Davis were struggling to maintain control of his unwieldy ensemble.

Immediately after, at least in the sequence of events reconstructible from the music released to date, Davis began recording with smaller groups, although he continued to form recording bands rather than merely calling in his working band. The reduced ensemble helped to free his music somewhat and allow the individuals more room to play. The details are as follows:

Miles Davis Ensemble
Miles Davis, tpt; Wayne Shorter, ss; Benny Maupin, bass clnt; John McLaughlin, gtr; David Holland, b; Billy Cobham, dms. New York, 17 February 1970
Duran
(on *Directions,* Columbia KC2 36472)

Miles Davis, tpt; Steve Grossman, ss; John McLaughlin, gtr; David Holland, b; Jack DeJohnette, dms. New York, 27 February 1970
Willie Nelson
(on *Directions,* Columbia KC2 36472)

Same personnel. Same place, 3 March 1970
Go Ahead John
(on *Big Fun*, Columbia PG 32866)

Duran might have given Davis the hit that Clive Davis thought he needed if it had been released at the time instead of eleven years later. It uses the fusion vocabulary more blatantly than anything he had recorded so far, with a simple bass riff providing the unity of the piece and brash chords from the guitar punctuating the easy rhythm. It is no more sophisticated, and no less accessible to teenaged audiences, than most of the hits of Blood, Sweat and Tears. Davis plays an electrified funk solo, McLaughlin an acid solo, Maupin and Shorter a helter-skelter duet, and Cobham a bumptious interval; judicious editing of any of these pieces onto two sides of a 45-rpm single might have sent the kids scurrying.

If it had been released at the time, it would have had a different title. *Duran* refers to Roberto Duran, the welterweight boxing champion from Panama, Cobham's native land, who rode roughshod over other welterweights in the late 1970s, earning the epithet *manos de piedra* ('hands of stone'). But Davis's use of Duran's name was not clearly an homage when it appeared on the 1981 release: in 1979 Duran had defeated Sugar Ray Leonard, an American hero in the 1976 Olympics whose image was as pristine as Duran's was nasty, but in their 1980 rematch Duran walked away from Leonard in the middle of the eighth round, conceding his championship for reasons that never really stood up to scrutiny. As a boxing fan, Davis might have named his tune *Duran* either to honor the 1979 champion with fists of stone or to deride the 1980 pug with feet of clay; if the latter, Davis probably intended the title to be a critical comment on his little rock ditty of years before.

For *Willie Nelson* there can be no doubt about Davis's intentions in naming the piece for the rough-voiced middle-aged country balladeer. Soon after it was released in 1981 Davis told Cheryl McCall, "I *love* the way Willie sings; the way he phrases is great. He phrases sometimes like I do."[38] The next year he proved his fanship by detouring to Las Vegas and visiting Nelson backstage at Caesar's Palace, where according to rumor the two of them wrote a country song called *Expect Me Around*,[39] and after that Davis continued his tour wearing a cap with "Willie Nelson" emblazoned on its crest.

The piece bearing Nelson's name seems somewhat less than idolatrous. It consists of a stretch of music that catches the pianoless quintet working over an uptempo riff, but, despite its liveliness and Holland's amazingly supple accompaniment behind McLaughlin's solo, it is a head arrangement of no special distinction, lacking a beginning and an end (though credited to Davis as the composer).

Go Ahead John, with exactly the same band in the studio four days later, includes more interesting moments, although it was obviously composed in the editing room. Its first eleven minutes and its closing four and a half minutes resemble Willie Nelson as a head arrangement built on a riff, with the riff sustained this time by McLaughlin's steady wah-wah in the background. Spliced into it is an unrelated theme that opens with two minutes of a slow blues unaccompanied except for occasional notes from Holland; Davis's blues solo becomes a duet with himself by overdubbing, and then builds into a quintet performance lasting ten more minutes. The overdubbing effect is made by super-imposing part of Davis's solo on other parts of it, in what Teo Macero calls a "recording loop." "You hear the two parts and it's only two parts, but the two parts become four and they become eight parts," Macero told Gregg Hall. "This was done over in the editing room and it just adds something to the music ... I called [Davis] in and I said, 'Come in, I think we've got something you'll like. We'll try it on and if you like it you've got it.' He came in and flipped out. He said it was one of the greatest things he ever heard."[40] In spite of the gimmickry, the blues segment manages to state some old verities in a new context, and state them powerfully. Most jazz listeners can hope that someday Go Ahead John will be unscrambled and re-presented to them as, among other things, an unhurried blues by Davis accompanied only by Holland.

On the night of 3 March, Davis again ran afoul of the law. He was sitting in his red Ferrari with an unidentified woman in a no-standing zone on Central Park South when a patrolman approached to ask him to move, noticed that the car had no inspection sticker, and asked Davis for his license and registration. Davis, wearing a turban, a sheepskin coat, and cobra-skin pants, began rummaging through a handbag and exposed a pair of brass knuckles. The patrolman booked him on charges of carrying a deadly weapon and driving an unlicensed, unregistered, and uninspected vehicle. The next day he was fined $100 for being an unlicenced driver and cleared of the other charges.[41]

A week later, Davis and his working band again appeared at the Fillmore East. Davis's band played the opening set at a concert that featured the Steve Miller Band – "how's that for noblesse oblige?" James Isaacs remarked – and Crosby, Stills, Nash and Young. The concert realized one of Davis's fears about entering the rock circuit. "The audience, at least in my section," Isaacs reported, "nattered incessantly, passed contraband and generally ignored Miles and his cohorts throughout their open-ended fusion set."[42] Soon after, Davis rebuked the quality of the musicians who topped him on the bill in his forays into the rock world. "In rock groups the guys know so little about harmonies," he complained to an interviewer for *Zygote* magazine. "It's a shame because they don't study. They deal in visual appearance and loudness, and in sex ... All the jazz musicians can play in any school of music because they have the knowledge. It's usually the rock musicians that don't have a musical background. They just pick up on something. They just play a regular triad kind of sound."[43] Some rock musicians were willing to concede that point. A few years later, the manager of an English band called the Clash refused an interview with a music magazine by stating: "We know nothing about music. If you want to know about music, ask Miles Davis or somebody like that. We're all trying to find out what it is."[44] Despite Davis's disillusionment with the company he kept at the Fillmore, both in the audience and on the stage, he kept on playing the Fillmores and other rock halls.

Davis's enlarged circuit exposed him not only to the teenaged audience but also to America's bourgeoisie when he began appearing on Nielsen-rated national network television shows. He and his band performed on the televised Grammy Awards show for 1970 from Alice Tully Hall in the Lincoln Center, as one of the music acts that broke up the seemingly endless parade of recording personalities being presented with awards. The show barely missed televising a spontaneous news happening when its host, Merv Griffin, a singer with swing bands in the 1940s now grown roly-poly and ingratiating as the host of a televison talk show, broke protocol and rushed up to Davis after his short piece, grasping his hand and directing a supercilious comment into the television camera. "Merv Griffin is embarrassing to me," Davis told Chris Albertson a year later, still smarting from the incident; "I felt like yanking off his arm."[45]

Davis knew that the large, middle-class, middle-aged audiences courted by Griffin and the other talk show hosts made no real contact with his music and that the hosts themselves were incapable of bridging the gap. "The trouble with those cats," as he put it, "is that they all try to come off to those middle-aged white bitches."

Aggressive promoting by Columbia nevertheless got him several spots on the talk show circuit, which had become the prized promotional vehicle for publishers and movie distributors as well as record companies. Once or twice a year from 1970 until 1972, by which time either Davis could stand it no more or the mass audiences could no longer tolerate even a few minutes of his increasingly percussive music, Davis appeared before millions of television viewers late at night, decorously garbed as he pointed his trumpet at the floor and squeezed out a few tortured notes, a taciturn mystery man who acknowledged neither the audience nor the smiling host.

After the Grammy show incident, he never consented to appear on Griffin's show, but he made his brief appearances with Johnny Carson, Dick Cavett, and Steve Allen. He explained his refusal to talk on the talk shows this way to Albertson: "Dick Cavett and Johnny Carson don't know what to say to anybody black, unless there's some black bitch and she's all over them. It's so awkward for them because they know all the white facial expressions, but they're not hip to black expressions, and – God knows – they're not hip to Chinese expressions. You see, they've seen all the white expressions like fear, sex, revenge, and white actors imitate other white actors when they express emotions, but they don't know how black people react. Dick Cavett is quiet now when a black cat is talking to him, because he doesn't know if the expression on his face means 'I'm going to kick your ass,' or if 'Right on' means he's going to throw a right hand punch. So, rather than embarrass them and myself, I just play on those shows and tell them not to say anything to me – I have nothing to say to them anyway."[46]

He was less philosophical about it all when he told Don DeMicheal, "I can't be on none of those television shows, 'cause I'd have to tell Johnny Carson, 'You're a sad motherfucker.' That's the only way I could put it. If I did that, right away they'd be telling me, 'You're cursing.' But that's the only way I can say it."

Davis's revulsion eventually included even Steve Allen, television's original talk show host in the 1950s whose feeling for jazz made his *Tonight* show the only regular showplace for jazz groups on the commercial networks. Allen had turned his talents to songwriting and other less public forums but returned to television hosting for a while in the late 1960s. "I was supposed to be on Steve Allen's show," Davis said, "but I sent him a telegram telling him he was too white, his secretary was too white, his audience was too white. And he wanted me to play for scale! Shit. I can't be standing there in front of all those middle-aged white broads – and all of them got maids. I can't be associated with that kind of shit. I got a maid myself. See, whatever they're trying to do, they're trying to get those middle-aged white bitches to watch it."[47] But Davis kept appearing sporadically for a couple of years, probably because his managers felt it was good for his image.

In between his celebrity turns, Davis took another small ensemble into the Columbia studios to record music for the soundtrack of a feature film called *Jack Johnson*. Although the film, with unconventional cinematography and controversial subject matter, stood little chance of finding a mass audience, it is an unequivocal artistic success. Director William Cayton turned scant and often flawed photographic resources into a coherent and dramatic documentary, juxtaposing still photos, boxing footage, and newsreels to evoke the life and times of the first black heavyweight champion (1908–15) from the early years of the century until his death in 1946. Teo Macero, credited as musical director for the film as well as producer for the LP, patched together snippets of Davis's music to accompany the shifting images. If the music was unspecified for the visual images at its inception – and there is no feeling that Davis tailored his improvisations to the finished film, as he had to Louis Malle's *Ascenseur pour l'échafaud* in 1957 – Macero's marriage of music to image brought them together ingeniously. The music forms a legato undercurrent for the film, quickening its still images and smoothing its stroboscopic motions.

In its own right the music on the LP, which bends the literal meaning in proclaiming itself the "original soundtrack recording," makes a self-contained continuum of shifting moods. The editor's hand is always evident, and the LP poses so many discographical puzzles that the music on it may never be identified in all its parts, but it is for all that one of the more effective, and certainly one of the more listenable, pastiches composed by Davis-Macero. The details are as follows:

Miles Davis Ensemble: Jack Johnson
Miles Davis, tpt; Steve Grossman, ss; Herbie Hancock, el pno, organ, probably synthesizer; John McLaughlin, probably Sonny Sharrock, el gtr; Michael Henderson, b; Billy Cobham, dms. New York, 7 April 1970
Yesternow

Same personnel. Same place, date uncertain, but probably the same or similar
Right Off
(both on Columbia s 30455)
The recording date for *Right Off* was originally given as 11 November 1971, but Davis and his band were in Europe on that date; Ruppli silently emends the

date by bringing it forward a year, to 11 November 1970, putting the second session, with its identical personnel and similar music, seven full months after the first. Besides the music from these sessions, the LP includes some music from other sources. *Yesternow* incorporates one and a half minutes of *SHHH/ Peaceful* (18 February 1969), starting at 12:30, and 1 minute and 40 seconds of Miles Davis and a large orchestra at the end. The orchestral sequence also includes a 12-second recitation by Brock Peters, the actor who speaks Jack Johnson's lines on the film soundtrack.

The two sides of the *Jack Johnson* LP consist essentially of two different fusion riffs, the one on *Yesternow* a quiet, suspenseful phrase and the one on *Right Off* a rocking medium-uptempo phrase, with interpolated material interrupting the basic riffs or altering their tempo. Because of the editing-composing process, one can seldom trust one's ears about the music. Sonny Sharrock is listed as the second guitarist because he told Valerie Wilmer that he heard himself on the recordings; neither the personnel nor the recording dates were listed on the LP itself, and Sharrock was not included in the information that Columbia eventually gave out. "I am on the *Jack Johnson* album on the *Yesternow* side, near the end," Sharrock said. "I'm soloing using an echoplex. My solo was mixed down low under Miles."[48] The second guitar is indeed heard momentarily late in *Yesternow* (at 22:30), but a second guitar is heard much more prominently near the end of *Right Off* for several minutes (beginning at 20:44 and showing up throughout Hancock's organ solo and Grossman's soprano solo for the next four minutes). The second guitar in those instances may be Sharrock's, or an overdubbing of McLaughlin. Similarly, a second bass is heard clearly in *Yesternow* (in the seventh minute). The synthesizer parts, probably contributed by Hancock, are concentrated in the second half of *Yesternow*, following the interpolation of *SHHH/Peaceful*, and showing up off and on until the end, when the fragment of Davis and the orchestra breaks in.

Davis's selection of musicians for the soundtrack includes only Grossman from his working band. The others make an unpredictable mix, with Hancock, McLaughlin, and Cobham all at various stages of the fusion crossover, Sharrock a Coltrane-based free former, and Michael Henderson, who in five months would join Davis's working band, a funk bassist from Stevie Wonder's backup band.

Davis kept a tight rein on the disparate elements. "On *Jack Johnson*, Miles instructed almost everybody individually about what he really wanted from them," Cobham recalls. "He tried to show me, physically, what he wanted." In a later interview, he emphasized that Davis's attempt to take over his drum set did not irk him. "And it was *not* in an obnoxious way," he told Brian Priestley, "it was not meant to degrade. I always felt that he always got the most out of the cats that worked with him because everybody loved him, if only for the musician that he is and what he stands for." Cobham even found Davis accommodating when he did not follow his instructions: "He said, like in *Jack Johnson* [hoarse whisper], 'I want this and I want that' and I said, 'Oh yeah? o.k.' and I didn't do it the way he wanted me to do it, and then he just left me alone. He sorta knew just when to let me be, because maybe he felt he was beating a dead horse, you know. But yet when I heard the record, man – if you can't make the adjustment to him, he will adjust to you quite naturally."[49]

Davis directed the musicians almost wordlessly. "It was nice to play with him without having him speak to you verbally," Cobham told Gregg Hall, "because you could learn so much from what he said through his instrument. It's another way of communicating. And one of Miles's major attributes is that he knows how to do that first nature, rather than second nature."[50]

Three days after the *Yesternow* session, Davis flew to San Francisco with his working band to play a concert at the Fillmore West. David Holland was absent, and Michael Henderson filled in for him, the studio sessions apparently serving as his audition. The concert was recorded – Davis's first live recording since his engagement at the Plugged Nickel in 1965 – and released as a double album totalling eighty minutes by Japanese CBS-Sony in 1973. The details are as follows:

Miles Davis Sextet: at Fillmore West
Miles Davis, tpt; Steve Grossman, ss; Chick Corea, el pno; Michael Henderson, el b; Jack DeJohnette, dms; Airto Moreira, perc. Fillmore West, San Francisco, 10 April 1970
Black Beauty I [medley includes *Directions*]; *Black Beauty II* [medley includes *Sanctuary*]; *Black Beauty III* [medley includes *Bitches Brew*]; *Black Beauty IV* [medley includes *Spanish Key*]
(all on CBS-Sony [Jap] SOPJ 39–40)

The sound quality is mediocre, and the playing includes very few moments of distinction. Davis apparently had some reservations about releasing this material on record, but the liner insert (in Japanese) attempts to vindicate the release by arguing that he was seldom satisfied with any of his records. With this one, he had good reason to be dissatisfied. Steve Grossman shows up particularly poorly, especially on the first two sides, with a nervous downpour of notes that is narrow in range and unimaginative. The long, continuous, apparently unedited concert ends with desultory applause.

The main value of the record is in documenting Davis's format for his live performances, using the repertoire of his most recent recordings exclusively, something he had never done before. Many of the themes that surface in the medley had not yet been released in their studio versions, and the only familiar old strain comes at the very end when Davis plays four notes of *The Theme* as a signal to his sidemen to wind up the proceedings.

The themes that do appear are sometimes difficult to identify – so difficult, in fact, that they are unidentified on this recording and all the live recordings to come, appearing instead under cover terms (in this case, *Black Beauty* i–iv) credited to Davis as composer (even though Zawinul and Shorter composed some of them). They are introduced obliquely, by a few notes by Davis or a few repetitions of the bass riff or the rhythm motif, any of which are sufficient to lock the players into the tonal center of that theme for the indeterminate period during which it serves as the improvisational base. The format is loaded with risks. It can inspire creative bridges and emotive playing melded into a spontaneous suite or degenerate into a babble of voices bogged down in search of the musical means to get from one theme to the next.

Although Davis was already experimenting with bands that did not include a piano in the studio and would eventually form his working band without one, he remained convinced enough of the piano's role in his music to expand the band by adding a second pianist. Keith Jarrett, who turned 25 around the time he joined Davis's band in May, now shared the keyboards with Corea at Davis's concerts. He had successfully used two (or more) keyboardists in several of his recordings, notably *In a Silent Way* and *Bitches Brew*, and now used them in his live performances for the first time. The pairing of Corea and Jarrett could hardly be expected to last very long, when both were emerging as leaders in their own right, but Davis got them to stretch out their overlapping terms in his band for four months.

Corea was already considering moving out of Davis's band with David Holland and forming his own band, but he postponed his departure until after the summer round of concerts. Jarrett had been leading his own trio, with Charlie Haden on bass and Paul Motian on drums, since leaving Charles Lloyd's band at the end of 1968, and he kept the band together, expanding them to a quartet with the addition of reedman Dewey Redman, while he played regularly in Davis's band.

Jarrett's quartet lasted for several years after he left Davis, when he began splitting his time between working with his quartet and playing solo piano concerts. The concerts became the touchstone of his reputation, as he spun out continuous melodies with dazzling displays of taste and control. Jarrett's solo concerts, preserved in great numbers on the Munich label ECM from 1973 on, comprise some of the brightest moments in the jazz of the time, and they are as thoroughly individual, consistently swinging and harmonically inventive as any jazz piano music past or present. Toward the close of the 1970s, buoyed by the success of his piano recitals, Jarrett grew more ambitious, producing unwieldy orchestrations that seemed to satisfy his drive to create music beyond category but also seemed, even to listeners predisposed toward his music, designed to satisfy an audience of one.

Even before Jarrett's ambitions led him away from the jazz mainstream, he seemed to be undervalued by part of the jazz audience. One complaint was that his piano performances often lacked intensity and ended up being easy recitals that hid as many of his gifts as they revealed. More often, the complaints centered on his stage manner and had the same nitpicking illegitimacy as the ones that dogged Miles Davis's career for so long. Like Davis, Jarrett presents himself to his audience as a brittle, arrogant character. He occasionally interrupts his performances to lecture audiences on their coughing, or plays a brief, and loose, adaptation of Mozart as the entire second half of a concert for jazz listeners, or refuses to play at all because of some flaw in the piano imperceptible to all but himself. Critics offended by Jarrett's arrogance as a performer have easily found more extraneous aspects to criticize in his extravagant body movements on the piano bench and his adamant opinions about almost everything. As Jarrett became better known in the mid-1970s, such criticisms often appeared to hinder the appreciation for his achievement, a body of solo piano music that celebrates, as he put it, "one artist creating sponteneously something which is governed by the atmosphere, the audience, the place (both the room and the geographical location), the instrument; all these being channelled consciously through the artist so that everyone's efforts are equally rewarded."

Almost forgotten by the time he reached the height of his success a few years after leaving Davis's band was the fact that a younger, more flexible Jarrett had so recently been willing to bend one of his most adamantly held opinions in order to play beside Davis. Jarrett despises electronic instruments and considers his solo concerts to be part of "an anti-electric-music crusade.""Electricity goes through all of us," he declared in 1973, "and is not to be relegated to wires."[51] His view probably had a salutary effect by encouraging other young players to impose some restraint on the use of electronics in jazz, which became such a fad in the early 1970s that it threatened to supplant deeper musical values, but for the year and a half that Jarrett stayed with Davis he played electric keyboards exclusively. "If I wanted to play with him, which I didn't mind the idea of at the time, I wasn't going to be able to change his music to suit me," he told Ted O'Reilly. "I did it with that knowledge so I was not upset about it."[52]

He later told Julie Coryell that Davis had been asking him to join his band for a few years, but that he had resisted his offers only partly because he would have to play electronic keyboards. "Actually, more than the electric thing," he said, "I couldn't stand his preceding band and I wondered if I could do anything, if I could save anything, and if I couldn't, I'd leave right away." And then he added, "It turned out very well because the whole band kind of changed around the time I joined." In fact, the band remained intact for four months after Jarrett joined, and even then only three of the six members changed, Corea, of course, among them. The only attraction Jarrett found in the band, he says, was Davis himself. "With Miles, fortunately, I liked his playing throughout the change of personnel he had," he said. "The time I had heard the band that made me feel bad about it, the only person who I thought was playing music at all was Miles. So I realized that, if I would play with the band, at least I would have that camaraderie with him, that I could trust his playing and maybe he could trust mine." He shrugs off his compromise with electronics, saying, "the music wouldn't sound like anything at all with acoustic instruments ... But I knew it was temporary and I told him it was temporary."[53]

Jarrett's stay was temporary, but it was not brief, and it was the prelude to his rise to prominence. "I just put him at the piano and let him go," Davis told Leonard Feather, and then he added: "Keith wasn't playing the piano like that before he joined me."[54]

Jarrett joined Davis's recording ensemble for two sessions, one in May and the other still undated; only one title from each date has been released. The details are as follows:

Miles Davis Ensemble
Miles Davis, tpt; Benny Maupin, bass clnt; Keith Jarrett, el pno; John McLaughlin, gtr; Jack DeJohnette, dms; Airto Moreira, perc. New York, 21 May 1970
Konda
(on *Directions*, Columbia KC2 36472)

Miles Davis, tpt; Steve Grossman, ss; Keith Jarrett, Herbie Hancock, keyboards; John McLaughlin, gtr; Michael Henderson, b; Billy Cobham, dms; Airto Moreira, perc. New York, 1970
Honky Tonk
(on *Get up with It*, Columbia C33237)

Neither piece resolves into a well-defined concept, and neither makes any special use of Jarrett's presence in the ensemble. *Konda* attempts to work out an arrangement for a written unison passage by Davis and Maupin played over a non-jazz rhythm in which Moreira's plucked berimbau is conspicuous. The attempt fails, ending up in a non-swinging oriental dance cadence, and DeJohnette enters for the first time about halfway through, leading the rhythm players into a conventional funk sequence unrelated to the preceding part.

   Honky Tonk is more interesting, as an attempt to get a group of jazz sophisticates – the same band that recorded the *Jack Johnson* soundtrack, with Jarrett and Moreira added – to play the unsophisticated funk of a bar band from, say, Chicago's South Side so that Davis can play a low-down blues over it. "I listen to James Brown and those little bands on the South Side," Davis told Don DeMicheal. "They swing their asses off. No bullshit."[55] Davis's band, intentionally or not, makes a wry abstraction of the whole idea, like a troop of models striking poses against a Skid Row backdrop.

   Leonard Feather used *Honky Tonk* on a couple of blindfold tests and found a consensus. Ron Carter conceded that "this leaves a lot to the players' own discretion and levels of musicianship ... and that will work if the players involved are all at the same level." But, he said, "It seems that the levels of the players involved are very different." He added: "It seems that ... the basic rhythm – the percussion, the guitar player and the keyboard – are all playing at random, and, for me, at a loss of something that's really quality."[56] That remark seconded the opinion of trumpeter Blue Mitchell in an earlier test: "It doesn't sound like a composition; it just sounds like somebody blowing ... trying to kill some time till the set's over." And he added: "I hope it ain't anybody I know."[57]

Both *Honky Tonk* and *Konda* simply fade out when the length of vinyl allotted for them on their belated releases is filled.

In a unique event replete with symbolic significance, Davis joined somebody else's recording ensemble on 29 May, when Flying Dutchman Records brought together jazz musicians from all eras to pay homage to Louis Armstrong, recording a vocal album called *Louis and His Friends* that would be released on his 70th birthday on 4 July. Besides Davis, the friends included Eddie Condon, Ornette Coleman, Bobby Hackett, and a dozen others.[58] The collected ensemble sang *We Shall Overcome*, the anthem of popular protest in the 1960s, behind Armstrong's lead, giving Davis his first discographical entry as a vocalist. His voice in the chorus went undetected, making his vocal debut less than auspicious, but the gesture counted more.

The feelings between Armstrong and Davis, the two dominating trumpeters in jazz's historical oligarchy, had always been surprisingly congenial considering their differences in age, style, and attitude. On the few occasions when Davis has said anything about Armstrong, he has been full of praise. "You know you can't play anything on a horn that Louis hasn't played – I mean even modern," he told Nat Hentoff in 1958. "I love his approach to the trumpet; he never sounds bad. He plays on the beat and you can't miss when you play on the beat – with feeling. That's another phrase for swing."[59] He was almost as effusive with Alex Hailey, in the *Playboy* interview of 1962, when he said: "I love Pops, I love the way he sings, the way he plays – everything he does, except when he says something against modern jazz music. He ought to realize that he was a pioneer, too." Around the time that Davis gave this mild rebuke to Armstrong for scorning bebop, he himself was publicly scoffing the avant-garde styles of Ornette Coleman, Don Cherry, and Cecil Taylor, but the parallel apparently did not strike him. His comment about Armstrong's disdain for bebop led him to recall an early meeting, probably around 1950, when Davis was in his early twenties and Armstrong in his late forties. "A long time ago," he said, "I was at Bop City, and he came in and told me he liked my playing. I don't know if he would even remember it, but I remember how good it felt to have him say it."[60]

Apart from their mutual admiration, the two men have almost nothing in common apart from the instrument they play, and no two figures in the rapid evolution of jazz make such an instructive contrast. Some of the rich implications were drawn by Leonard Feather in his book *From Satchmo to Miles*, a title that in itself evokes a universe of fascinating diversity for jazz listeners. "Miles' personality has built a mystique around him and has contributed to the hold he has on the public," Feather began. "The irony lies in the fact that three or four decades ago Louis Armstrong, whose attitudes were antithetical to Davis' in almost every conceivable way, also owed his commercial achievements in large measure to his personality. Armstrong, accepted first by musicians as the supreme instrumentalist, later reached the masses by being, onstage, exactly what they wanted him to be. Davis, after gaining similar in-group acceptance, went on to acquire his material luxuries, and massive income tax problems, by doing precisely the opposite: defying the public to like him, insisting that he be accepted solely for the instrinsic value of his music."[61]

Jazz musicians separated by stylistic chasms have occasionally managed to collaborate effectively: one thinks of Sidney Bechet and Martial Solal, Pee Wee Russell and Thelonious Monk, Duke Ellington (as pianist) and Charles Mingus, and a few others. Davis and Armstrong might have found a common ground playing ballads together in the 1950s – indeed, the thought of that missed opportunity might be enough to make some grown-up jazz fans weep – but by 1970 the most that anyone could wish for would be to have Davis singing inaudibly in Armstrong's chorus. A year later Armstrong died, while Davis was engrossed in exploring his electronic frontier.

Early in June, Davis assembled his aggregation in the studio to record some curious little miniatures written by Davis and arranged by the Brazilian multi-instrumentalist Hermeto Pascoal, an old colleague of Airto Moreira's who had been his co-leader in a Brazilian band called Quarteto Novo. The details are as follows:

Miles Davis Ensemble with Hermeto Pascoal
Miles Davis, tpt; Steve Grossman, ss; Chick Corea, Herbie Hancock, Keith Jarrett, keyboards; Ron Carter, b; Jack DeJohnette, dms; Airto Moreira, perc; Hermeto Pascoal, voice. New York, 3 June 1970
Selim; Nem Um Talvez [Selim]
(both on *Live-Evil*, Columbia G 30954)
Selim and *Nem Um Talvez* are different takes of the same composition.

Miles Davis, tpt; Steve Grossman, ss; Chick Corea, Herbie Hancock, Keith
Jarrett, keyboards; Hermeto Pascoal, el pno, whistling; John McLaughlin, gtr;
David Holland, b; Jack DeJohnette, dms; Airto Moreira, perc. New York, June
1970
Little Church
(on *Live-Evil*, Columbia G 30954)

Davis's melodies are little set pieces played slowly by the ensemble,
which forms an instrumental choir. In the mastering, the other players
are mixed low beneath Davis's trumpet, which is distorted electronically, and Pascoal, who moans the melody on *Selim/Nem Um Talvez* and
whistles it on *Little Church*. Both melodies are doleful, unrelieved by
rhythmic pulse or harmonic variety. The title *Selim*, which is 'Miles'
backwards, somehow seems appropriate for the monochromatic dirge
that it represents.

As dirges, *Selim* and *Little Church* work better than *Nem Um Talvez*,
because *Nem Um Talvez* adds Moreira playing a pitter-pat percussion
line that has the effect, roughly, of a tap dancer in a funeral procession. If
Moreira's role on *Nem Um Talvez* was a miscalculation, it was probably
emphasized by the release of these short, strange pieces of petrified
melody on the LP called *Live-Evil*, where they stand among long, mostly
live performances of heavily amplified fusion music.

A few days later, Davis played an engagement at the Fillmore East
again, with both Chick Corea and Keith Jarrett in his band. Columbia
recorded the concerts on four consecutive nights, from Thursday to
Saturday, and released the edited materials – each evening reduced to
one side of a record – as quickly as possible, hoping to catch the tide that
was carrying *Bitches Brew* into six-figure sales. Helped along no doubt
by the name of the rock palace in its title, *Miles Davis at the Fillmore*
became another big seller. The details are as follows:

Miles Davis Septet: at Fillmore East
Miles Davis, tpt; Steve Grossman, ss; Chick Corea, el pno; Keith Jarrett, org;
David Holland, b; Jack DeJohnette, dms; Airto Moreira, perc. The Fillmore
East, New York, 17 June 1970
Wednesday Miles [medley includes *Directions*, *Miles Runs the Voodoo Down*,
Bitches Brew, *The Theme*, and other titles]
(on Columbia G 30038)

Same personnel, same place, 18 June 1970
Thursday Miles [medley includes *Directions*, *Pharaoh's Dance*, probably

Milestones, It's about That Time, The Theme, and others]
(on Columbia G 30038)

Same personnel, same place, 19 June 1970
Friday Miles [medley includes *Pharaoh's Dance, I Fall in Love Too Easily, Sanctuary, Bitches Brew, Miles Runs the Voodoo Down, The Theme*]
(on Columbia G 30038)

Same personnel, same place, 20 June 1970
Saturday Miles [medley includes *I Fall in Love Too Easily, Sanctuary, Bitches Brew, Miles Runs the Voodoo Down, The Theme*, and other titles]
(on Columbia G 30038)
Medley identifications are by Nils Winther-Rasmussen and Jan Lohmann; few of the identified themes are complete performances from the concerts.

Compared to the relatively orderly performances on *Bitches Brew*, the music that attracted most of the young fans to the Fillmore, these concerts presented Davis's new fans with fleeting allusions to dozens of themes and restless inventions of wholly new music. The presentation had nothing in common with any other rock or pop concerts, which attract their audiences mainly on the expectation that the performers will reprise their greatest hits, current or recently past, allowing the audience the noisome delight of recognition.

Davis's music for these concerts, in a real sense, did not exist before he played it, leaving the audience little or nothing to recognize, even for those listeners who knew every phrase on *Bitches Brew*. For fans willing or able to alter their concept of how concerts worked, Davis's were bright and flashy happenings. Dave Liebman, a 24-year-old saxophonist just beginning his professional career with a fusion band called Ten Wheel Drive, had no trouble altering his concept, and he could hardly contain his enthusiasm. "I saw him at the Fillmore, man, with Keith Jarrett and Chick Corea, the first time they ever played together, on organ and electric piano," he said. "I mean they didn't even know each other, know what I mean? And Miles is sittin' there playing right in the middle of it. You know? 'cause he likes the unpredictability."[62]

The unpredictability is preserved on the recordings, and perhaps even enhanced. The editing needed to reduce an hour or more of performing to less than half that length on record takes the hard course of condensing the entire performance by snipping and splicing parts from here and there rather than selecting a continuous sequence containing highlights. The editing strategy probably gives a truer sense of being there, although its compression taxes the listener's concentration even more than actually being there ever would.

The few critics who have looked back on Davis's music of the 1970s all hear in the *Fillmore* recording the seeds of many of the properties yet to come. "On balance, the Davis concert at *Fillmore* is an artistic triumph," wrote Barry McRae in *Jazz Journal*, "but the frantic, electronic ending to *Thursday Miles* and the ludicrous opening of *Saturday Miles* bode badly for the immediate future."[63] Scott Yanow concluded that "too much of this set is consumed by endless 'battles' between Chick Corea on electric piano and Keith Jarrett on organ. *At Fillmore* has several other faults that would be present on Davis's future albums: overlength, an occasional lack of direction, and poor editing." But he adds: "Still, there are moments."[64]

Davis's band toured the United States playing rock halls with the band Santana, led by (and named for) guitarist Devadip Carlos Santana. Davis eventually adjusted to his new milieu, feeling comfortable playing as an opening act and performing in front of noisy teenagers. "The audiences didn't always know how to deal with him," Clive Davis reported, but " he has a sense of arrogance about him that speaks out to an audience."[65]

Some musicians caught on more quickly. Santana was one of the first, as Davis's tour companion and Columbia stablemate. Davis began attending Santana's concerts, talking to his musicians backstage, and showing a keen interest in Santana's *Abraxis* LP in all phases of its production. "Back when Miles used to come hear us every night at the Fillmore East," Santana says, "I began to realize that maybe – just maybe – we had something important to say." The main lesson that Santana learned from Davis was the same one that hundreds of jazz musicians had learned over the years. "Through Miles Davis, I learned about the use of space between the phrases," Santana told Lee Underwood in a *Down Beat* interview. "Silence gives people time to absorb the music. Otherwise you sound like a machine gun."[66]

The young musician who fascinated Davis most of all was Jimi Hendrix, the powerful guitarist who overlaid screaming electronics on a basic blues style he had learned when he played in the backup bands of Little Richard and the Isley Brothers. Hendrix was a particular favorite of Betty Mabry, and Davis soon shared her enthusiasm. As he had always done, he passed along his enthusiasm to Gil Evans, and Evans, whose music seemed worlds removed from Hendrix's, became as rapt as

Davis. "I bought all his records and I realized what a good songwriter he was," Evans said. "He was the kind of person who'd write a song every time something would happen to him. A true songwriter."[67] Davis was more impressed by the high-volume, electronic theatrics of Hendrix's guitar sound, and he began searching for a guitarist who could bring that sound into his band. Dominique Gaumont, one of the guitarists who later filled that role, recalled that Hendrix's LP *Band of Gypsies* "traumatized Miles."[68] Although Hendrix's music had blues roots and used improvisation, he never aspired to play jazz and made no conscious efforts to fuse his music with jazz. The respect he gained among some members of the jazz audience, which crested with his election to *Down Beat*'s Hall of Fame in 1970, seemed a spontaneous response to his strikingly distinctive style. "Hendrix, as a guitarist, was an innovator," Evans said. "He set the tone for guitar." As fusion blurred the hidebound categories, Hendrix's originality hoisted him to a status he neither sought nor exploited in what was, to him, an alien genre.

The fusion of jazz with rock, soul, funk, and other pop elements was itself perceived as an alien genre by much of the jazz world, including some of the younger musicians. "Miles is a beautiful cat and I love him, but he's gone off in a strange direction," Freddie Hubbard told Leonard Feather. "Now that I'm getting my shit together, Miles is gonna have to change. As far out as he's gone now, it sounds like a bunch of noise. Not so long ago a lot of young trumpeters were following Miles; now they're trying to play what I'm playing."[69] Those were bold words, but the challenge they implied fizzled out. A few years later Hubbard too began dabbling in fusion, at least on record, and for several years he bobbed back and forth between commercial funk and modal jazz so capriciously that it was hard to guess where his convictions lay.

If Davis's involvement in fusion had an uncertain effect on jazz, there can be no doubt that it had a salutary effect on the rock audience. Whitney Balliett points out: "People tend to get locked into the music they grow up on; whatever comes later is threatening and foreign, and whatever came before is quaint. This insularity is particularly true of the first rock generation, which, with unwise revolutionary fervor, slammed the door on the past. But jazz musicians like Miles Davis and Buddy Rich and Joe Zawinul and Gil Evans have chipped away at the kids' armor, and, from all reports, they are beginning to pay attention."[70] Pianist Ramsey Lewis saw Davis's use of rock elements as the key to expanding the vocabulary of jazz. "It was not until the late sixties when Miles Davis gave his stamp of approval by incorporating some of these

Jimi Hendrix (courtesy of *Down Beat*)

Paul Simon, Clive Davis, and Miles Davis at the Anti-Defamation League luncheon, 1971 (Clive Davis personal collection, courtesy of Helen Merrill)

ideas into his albums that musicians accepted the fact that rock rhythms and influences other than the traditional ones could be integrated with jazz," Lewis wrote in his preface to Julie Coryell and Laura Friedman's *Jazz-Rock Fusion*. "Now with Miles's blessing, it was no longer taboo to venture beyond the traditionally accepted structures, harmonies and rhythms." Lewis added: "Davis extended the harmonic concept, employed polyrhythmic patterns, added electronic instruments and devices to his trumpet along with his highly unique and creative ability, and set the pace for what has come to be known as fusion music."[71]

Coryell's book also included a jazz-rocker's parody of the Lord's Prayer by guitarist Larry Coryell that said, in part, "Our Father, who art a cross between Miles Davis, John Coltrane, and Jimi Hendrix, hallowed be thy name ... And lead us not into disco, but deliver us from commercialism."[72] In spite of Coryell's petition against commercialism, one of the forces that fostered fusion was purely commercial, and many observers saw *Bitches Brew* more as a commercial coup than a musical one. In the immediate aftermath, numerous jazz musicians seemed prepared to pursue their commercial quarry as far into the pop side of the fusion as the audience deemed saleable, and many attempts at fusion music in the first half of the 1970s are grab-bags of rock excesses, unworthy of serious attention except as period pieces.

As Davis's backstage involvement with Santana and others developed, he still remained curiously aloof. In the summer of 1970, New York newspapers made considerable to-do about rumors that Davis would play as a guest soloist with Cream, a supergroup comprised of three top British rock musicians, guitarist Eric Clapton, bassist Jack Bruce, and drummer Ginger Baker, at the Randall's Island Festival. The rumors were quashed at the last moment, after considerable publicity, when Davis announced that he would play only with his own band at the festival. "I don't want to be a white man," Davis told reporters, in a circuitous answer to their question about playing with Cream. "Rock is a white man's word."[73]

He also avoided a meeting with Jimi Hendrix, under strange circumstances. Betty Mabry held a party for Hendrix at Davis's house in 1969, and the guest showed up but the host did not. Eric Nisenson says: "Miles, who hated parties, especially ones for men in his home, conveniently arranged to be working at a late recording session and never showed up at all. However, he left a score for Hendrix to look at, and called him from the recording studio. Unfortunately, Hendrix could not read music, but the two had a lively musical discussion anyway." Davis's absence proved fateful for his marriage; according to Nisenson, Mabry and Hendrix began seeing one another regularly.[74]

Davis resisted meeting the rockers on their own terms, musically and socially, but he became more involved with their audiences. On 29 August 1970, he played for a gigantic crowd, variously estimated from 100,000 to 400,000, on a 165-acre farm near East Afton on the Isle of Wight, off the south coast of England. The Isle of Wight Festival was an attempt to replicate the rock "happening" of the previous summer at Woodstock, New York, which had attracted 500,000 fans in a similar setting. There the size of the crowd had been totally unexpected, and the inadequate food supplies, toilets, and other amenities were further complicated by downpours of rain that turned the farmland into a quagmire, but the vast crowd kept its high spirits and turned the four-day festival into one of the signal events in the baby boom hagiography. Reports trumpeted the camaraderie that prevailed over the awful conditions; "Woodstock nation" was held up as a symbol of the peace-loving citizenry fostered by the ideals of the 1960s. The Isle of Wight Festival, blessed by fair weather, brought teenagers from all over the world who filled the rolling fields in front of the scaffolded bandstand like stalks of wheat. Besides Davis's sextet, the lineup included a contingent of rock and pop stars including Jimi Hendrix, Sly and the Family Stone, David Bromberg, Leonard Cohen, Kris Kristofferson, Procol Harum, and Ten Years After. A tightly edited sampling of Davis's performance, amounting to seventeen and a half minutes, was released a few years later with selections by other featured performers at the Isle of Wight and some from the Atlanta Pop Festival in a three-LP package called *The First Great Rock Festivals of the Seventies*. The details are as follows:

Miles Davis Septet at the Isle of Wight Festival
Miles Davis, tpt; Gary Bartz, as, ss; Chick Corea, pno; Keith Jarrett, org; David Holland, b; Jack DeJohnette, dms; Airto Moreira; perc. Isle of Wight, England, 29 August 1970
Call It Anythin' [medley includes *It's about That Time, Spanish Key, The Theme*, and other titles]
(on Columbia G3x30808)

The medley, in the form preserved on record, is heavily percussive, with especially forceful electric bass by David Holland often leading the assault. The Isle of Wight performance marks the first appearance on record of Gary Bartz with Davis's band, replacing Steve Grossman. Grossman's contributions to Davis's concerts seldom survived the transition onto records; on the *Fillmore* LP, his presence is almost undetectable. Bartz fares little better on the Isle of Wight recording, being heard mainly in a brief solo near the beginning, but long enough to make a more aggressive and more melodic impression.

When the music issued from Davis's festival performance offers little to interest jazz listeners, the band's experience of playing before hordes of young people in an open field affected the musicians powerfully. Airto Moreira later cited it, in the interview with Lee Underwood for *Down Beat*, as the turning point in his career. "They covered all the mountains and the hills," he recalled.

It was like an ocean of human beings everywhere. They were all young people in the sun, and everybody was crazy and happy, drinking wine, tripping on acid and laughing to be alive. We started playing and everybody started liking it. They got into the music more and more. We were improvising, of course, and everything was *burning*, man. Then one guy dropped out. As the music played, another guy dropped out, and then another, until everybody had stopped but me. I was playing *cuica*, the 'talking drum'. All of a sudden I was playing by myself. And there were 400,000 people out there waiting for me to play. Miles was standing on my right side holding his trumpet, looking into my face. 'Play!' So I started to play a solo on the *cuica*. Never before in Europe had they ever heard this drum that talks and squeaks and laughs and cries. I played, and played more, and I got into something really strong. And I was cooking, man! One guy in front stretched his arms over his head and began to sway in time to the rhythm, and then another guy and another guy and another guy. And then *everybody* started to wave their arms like that in rhythm. I looked out and there were 400,000 people swaying together like waves in the ocean. 'Wow!' I thought. 'What is this? ... Me, by myself, doing this ... and playing with Miles Davis!' That was the turning point in my career. I could communicate to 400,000 people – 400,000 people *in Europe*! If I could do that then, I knew I could do that anytime, anywhere.[75]

Most reviews of the festival simply passed over the Davis band's performance, listing their presence among all the other acts and dwelling on the huge, polyglot crowd that camped out in the farmer's field. Only *Melody Maker*, Britain's pop music newsmagazine, took much notice of Davis, and the gist of its comment was bafflement at

Davis's aloof stage manner. The notice brought a swift rebuke from Davis by long-distance telephone from Milan. According to Leonard Feather, Davis told *Melody Maker*'s editor: "What kind of man can call me 'arrogant'? I know where you're at. You shouldn't be a critic. You are a white man looking for white excitement, but there are more subtle forms of excitement."[76] He went from there to blast the whole world of rock music.

Davis's riposte seemed as far out of character as did his appearances at Columbia's publicity luncheons and on television talk shows. For decades, he had maintained a stony silence about his critical notices. In 1962, in the *Playboy* interview, he had stated his view on critics clearly. "I don't pay no attention to what critics say about me, the good or the bad," he told Alex Hailey. "The toughest critic I got, and the only one I worry about, is myself. My music has to get past me and I'm too vain to play anything I think is bad."[77] Now, as he courted rock stardom, he gave up the pretence and was willing to take on the critics.

Whenever he talked to jazz writers, he made a point of letting them know that he held the rock world in low esteem. "We're not a rock band," he told Dan Morgenstern. "Some people get that idea because we've amplified, but with amplification, we can be heard and we can hear each other ... Our music changes every month."[78] But those changes all seemed to be taking him in the same direction, and he began to fit in more easily with the company he kept at the Fillmores, the Isle of Wight, and elsewhere.

In the aftermath of the Isle of Wight Festival, while Davis and his band were making a short tour of Europe, Jimi Hendrix settled into London for a series of playing engagements. Hendrix's two most recent LPs had failed to become best sellers, and although he was only 28 he was feeling the strain. In the accelerated grimace of the pop culture, one was not allowed a modest success after a bonanza without arousing a chorus of whispers among managers, bookers, record executives, and the trade magazines. Davis had been involved in one of the plans for reviving Hendrix's appeal. "You know they came to me to reorganize Hendrix's band," Davis told Gregg Hall.[79] Producer Alan Douglas had tried to bring Davis and Hendrix together in the recording studio earlier in the year, but one or the other had repeatedly backed off, coming up with an excuse to cancel the date. Finally, Davis had demanded $50,000 as his share in the collaboration and Douglas ended the negotiations. Instead, Douglas turned to Gil Evans, and plans got underway for an album. "Jimi would just play the guitar and I was to write the charts," Evans reported. "Alan had played Jimi a couple of the Miles albums that I had written for and he liked them."

Hendrix was expected to return to New York for his first meeting with Evans, but he died in London three days earlier, choking on his vomit when he was unable to wake himself after a night of drinking capped by sleeping pills. "Nobody ever told him not to mix barbiturates and alcohol," Evans told Zan Stewart. "Funny, you'd have thought the word would have gotten around because some famous people have died like that: Dorothy Kilgallen, Tommy Dorsey. It's a loser."[80] Evans carried on with the orchestrations of Hendrix's music on his own, becoming the greybeard of the fusion camp when the LP, *The Gil Evans Orchestra Plays the Music of Jimi Hendrix* (RCA CPL1-0667), appeared in 1974.

Hendrix's body was returned to Seattle, his home, for a spontaneous but well-publicized wake. Davis, who had grieved privately when Parker and John Coltrane, his chief mentor and his greatest pupil respectively, were buried, attended the funeral at the Greenwood Cemetery in Seattle on 1 October, his presence publicized by an Associated Press wirephoto.

As soon as Davis's band returned from the European tour, Chick Corea and David Holland resigned. They shared some ideas about music that they felt were stifled as long as they were playing Davis's music. "We were buddies in Miles's band," Corea explained, "and shared a liking for acoustic music, forms not based on the usual influences. We were listening to people like Stockhausen, John Cage, Ornette Coleman, Paul Bley, Messiaen and Varese."[81] "We both wanted to leave the group," says Holland. "I didn't feel there was anything more to be done with Miles, for my own taste, for what I wanted to do."[82]

In spite of all the changes in Davis's music during Corea's and Holland's tenure, both felt that it had not changed enough to suit them. "The premise on which Miles' music is built is still largely the old-fashioned one of a soloist and a rhythm section," Holland said. "I feel that the most positive direction for him to take now would be to go into the concept of playing a supporting role, as well as a supported one, and into more interaction between the players on a somewhat subtler level."[83] Corea agreed, at least as far as saying that Davis's music changed very little. "To me Miles's playing didn't change that much," he said. "He was essentially playing similar ways, only the music around him had changed."

Still, neither of them could deny the large-scale transformation of Davis's concept, if not of his soloing, in the transitional band of which

they were members. "It's interesting in retrospect," Corea acknowledged to Kitty Grime. "Miles is a good example because his music is
very well documented on record. But, like any musician that's moving
on, it's always in a period of transition. Like, when I came with the band,
it was the *Nefertiti* period with Wayne and Herbie and so on. Then the
electric elements got added to the band, and Miles had some ideas about
some rock rhythms that he wanted to play, and the music gradually
tended towards that. Until, at the end of my stay with the band, the
music was very heavily rock-oriented." Corea also observed the
transition in a later stage, after he left the band. "About a month after I
left the band, I heard the group. It was playing some very, very strong
rock music, but very creative, very nice. So that was a whole trip that's
still moving."[84]

Corea and Holland immediately formed a trio with drummer-
percussionist Barry Altschul and tried out at the Village Vanguard. One
of the spectators was the young reedman Anthony Braxton, who had
already been discussing with Corea the directions in music in which he
was interested. "When I first met him," Braxton says of Corea, "he was
fixing to quit Miles because Miles was doing more commercial music.
Chick was interested in more contemporary kinds of music, with more
open forms. Another use of language."[85] Braxton joined the group, to
form a high-minded quartet called Circle that lasted until 1972. After
Circle, Corea formed his own band called Return to Forever and began
playing rock-influenced jazz again, but relying on more subtle, or at
least more subdued, effects than were being used by either Davis's band
or Weather Report. Braxton, Holland, and Altschul often played
together afterward in concerts and on records in free form settings and
became stalwarts, along with Sam Rivers, Oliver Lake, Kenny Wheeler,
and the members of the Art Ensemble of Chicago, in the revitalized
avant-garde of the 1970s that formed a strong counter-trend to the
thickening fusion movement.

Davis already had Keith Jarrett on hand to replace Corea. He briefly
brought in Miroslav Vitous to play bass, as he had in 1968, but Vitous
left to become a founding member of Weather Report, and Davis hired
Michael Henderson, whom he had often conscripted for his recording
ensembles to give the patented funk bottom to some of his records.
Henderson was the bassist in Stevie Wonder's soul band and had
apprenticed with Aretha Franklin and the Motown lineup. He became
the first, but not the last, funk musician to join Davis's working band,
and his hiring marked a decisive change in Davis's live performances. It

also, incidentally, earned Davis the enmity of Stevie Wonder, the top-selling black pop singer of the day. "Stevie Wonder, now there's a sad motherfucker," Davis told Gregg Hall. "He thinks I stole Michael Henderson from him, but Michael came to me. I never did anybody like that in my life."[86]

Henderson had just turned 19 when he joined, and he stayed five years. Throughout, he gave Davis's audiences the kind of show they had come to expect from the backup bands of pop stars, and Davis apparently valued his contribution to the band even when his youth and his onstage style made things difficult. Davis described the problems for Sy Johnson: "Michael fartin' around, showin' off, not being a group player. He'll do that shit two nights and I'll tell him, 'Michael, you been fuckin' around for two days. Settle down!' And he'll say, 'I knew you were gonna say that!' And I'll say, 'Man, bitches make you act funny.'"[87]

With Gary Bartz replacing Steve Grossman on reeds in the summer, Henderson replacing Holland, and Jarrett taking over solely on keyboards in the fall, Davis's band ended the year with a revamped look. The changes were not as significant stylistically as they might have been or as they would be in later personnel changes, notwithstanding the loss in jazz virtuosity from changing the bassists. DeJohnette and Moreira remained from the band that had begun the year, and the other changes balanced the gains and losses. Bartz was, if anything, a more willing soloist than Grossman, standing apart from the ensemble more, as Davis also did. Jarrett, left to his own devices now, could range more freely away from the organ, but with Davis he remained, as Corea also had, essentially an ensemble player.

The burst of recording activity that had begun near the end of 1967 and kept Davis and his coterie of musicians busy almost constantly in the studios began to peter out in the spring of 1970. Apparently satisfied that he had worked out most of the problems he faced in fusing electronics and funk rhythms with his music, and perhaps deterred from the extra musical activity by Columbia's distress about his overproduction, Davis settled back into the more familiar routine of earlier years. He had recorded several times with various groups from January to May, but since then his only studio appearance – the only one to come to light in Columbia's releases so far – was the minor session with Hermeto Pascoal. His other recordings for the year were live performances at the Fillmores and the Isle of Wight festival. So far, no studio recordings by the band with Bartz and Jarrett have turned up at all, even though that band stayed together for more than a year.

Columbia recorded the new band extensively during an engagement at a Washington club called the Cellar Door in December, but after several nights of taping Davis was dissatisfied with their performances. "Miles was looking for an element he hadn't quite nailed down," according to Mort Goode, in a promotional newsletter printed on the inner sleeve of some Columbia LPs, including Davis's *Live-Evil*, the LP on which excerpts of the Cellar Door performances were eventually issued. "Now it was Saturday morning," Goode continues. "And the thought came clear. 'Let's get John McLaughlin down from New York. For tonight.' Phone calls. To friends. To acquaintances. Seeking John. Locating him at last. 'Come on down. The first set is at 9:00.' The first set began without McLaughlin. He hadn't arrived in time. Came in halfway through. Unpacked. Set up. Fitted in as though he had been there forever." The addition of McLaughlin, in Goode's view, represents "Miles' instinct for the right touch, his understanding of talent, his ability to make use of it brilliantly."[88]

The tapes of the evening's performance with McLaughlin in the band were then added to the pool of tapes from the other nights, "an original working pile of thirty reels," according to Teo Macero. Davis and Macero then selected "ten to fifteen" of the reels and made what Macero calls a "distillation" for the *Live-Evil* LP, where they were collated with the short studio tracks involving Hermeto Pascoal. "The album is partly live, and it has an ethereal evil, where the mind is clouded and all these things are happening," Macero told Chris Albertson, before the LP was released. "It's like a wild dream."[89] The music from which Davis and Macero concocted the "wild dream" has never been released in unedited versions, and its character remains unclear. The details, such as they are, are as follows:

Miles Davis Sextet, plus John McLaughlin: Live-Evil
Miles Davis, tpt; Gary Bartz, as, ss; Keith Jarrett, pno, el pno; John McLaughlin (19 December only), gtr; Michael Henderson, el b; Jack DeJohnette, dms; Airto Moreira, perc. The Cellar Door, Washington, DC, probably 16–19 December 1970
Sivad; What I Say; Funky Tonk; Inamorata and Narration by Conrad Roberts (all on *Live-Evil*, Columbia G30954)

Whatever the purpose might have been in editing the tapes, it had nothing to do with making the performances more coherent. All the live tracks on *Live-Evil* involve ear-wrenching shifts of mood and tempo, most of them caused by splicing.

Gary Bartz's contributions emerge from the chaos unusually effectively. he dominates the first third of *Funky Tonk* and the first half of *What I Say* with solos that sound as if they have been preserved whole, and he proves more assertive than either Steve Grossman or Wayne Shorter in the same situation. Like Shorter prior to 1969, Bartz liked to develop a melodic idea rather than play with effects fed to him by the rhythm section, as both Shorter in his final year and Grossman had contented themselves with. Both *Funky Tonk* and *What I Say* swing wildly throughout Bartz's solos, but both tracks continue long after Bartz grows silent, and both lapse into ambivalent, unfocused passages in his wake.

Funky Tonk later springs to life again during an unaccompanied solo by Keith Jarrett on electric piano, in which he builds momentum until he is playing a sort of psychedelic fugue, providing one of the best interludes on the LP and one of the few effective examples of his work on the amplified instrument anywhere. According to Mort Goode, Jarrett's wild invention sprang partly from a malfunction in the piano: "The electric piano wasn't functioning perfectly [and] Keith Jarrett had to improvise around the mechanical problems. The improvisation brought forth the Far East sound, the feeling of gamelin music."[90]

Davis's use of a wah-wah trumpet effect also drew a favorable notice from at least one critic. Barry McRae, writing about Davis's rock music in *Jazz Journal* in 1972, cited Davis's reverberations on *Funky Tonk* as "his excellent solo in this genre" and went on to say: "His now strong commitment to rock music has become more aesthetically credible and throughout *Live-Evil* he matches his surroundings with artificially assisted sound in a way that is both apt and compatible."[91]

Out of the astounding variety of sounds spliced together to make *Live-Evil*, then, it is possible for listeners to isolate bright moments for Bartz, Jarrett, and Davis, but the dominant impression is the befuddling variety itself. *Sivad* – 'Davis' spelled backwards – perhaps shows it most of all, as it moves from Davis's amplified sound over an insistent beat into a pretty ballad introduced by Jarrett as a feature for Davis's muted horn and finally into a slow blues by McLaughlin. All three phases are well defined in their own right, but the transition from one to the next is abrupt and disquieting. The listener must puzzle through three unrelated themes under one title on an LP that includes also *Selim* and *Nem Um Talvez*, the same theme under two different titles.

Live-Evil seems to have purged Davis's impulse to compose his music almost entirely in the editing room. His music had been heavily edited before and would continue to be for the next two years, but never again would some thirty reels of tape be reduced to a little more than 100 minutes of playing time. For Macero, the hefty editing jobs on Davis's music provided a challenge that he accepted eagerly. "The music needs to be played with," he contended, and he saw his post-production duties with Davis as a vote of confidence from the man who a few years before had rejected his services altogether. "Both of us have learned from the things we've done together," he told Gregg Hall. "I learned from the standpoint of editing, shifting the compositions around so that the front becomes the back, the back becomes the middle, the middle something else. It's a creative process being a producer with Miles. In fact, it's more of a creative process than it is with any other artist. You have to know something about music. You really need to be a composer, because for a lot of it he relies on you and your judgement."[92] What the manipulations contributed to the performances that served as the raw material can be known only when some of the unedited reels of tape finally become available.

Around the time of McLaughlin's guest appearance at the Cellar Door, Davis asked McLaughlin to quit Tony Williams's Lifetime and tour with him. After giving some thought to the proposition, McLaughlin turned him down. "I had too much music invested in Lifetime," McLaughlin told Lee Jeske more than a decade later. "I had a freedom there that was irreplaceable. But when I started chafing at the bit in Lifetime, it was Miles who suggested that I put my own band together."[93] That happened a few months later, when McLaughlin formed his Mahavishnu Orchestra, an electronic quintet that quickly joined Zawinul and Shorter's Weather Report, Corea's Return to Forever, and Hancock's Mwandishi among the most popular bands in the fusion movement, along with the bands of Davis, whose touch was obvious in the music that all of them played.

Although Davis could not persuade McLaughlin to join his band, he was now convinced that he needed a guitarist, and he began keeping a watchful eye out for the right player. It would take him more than a year to find one, and then his choice would move his music further from its jazz roots. In the meantime, his sextet remained intact throughout 1971 except for Airto Moreira, who defected to join Corea and then strike out on his own, in a band featuring the vocals of his wife, Flora Purim. Moreira's replacement was James Foreman, who became better known as Mtume, a congas player who made sparing use of the more exotic rattling and scraping devices Moreira had introduced but later added a synthesizer to Davis's ever-increasing percussion backdrop.

Although Davis's band remained strong in individual jazz talents, he seemed no more satisfied with it than he had at the Cellar Door. He carried on playing his full complement of concert and club appearances, but he neither recorded any of those performances nor took the band into the studio. The lack of activity may also have had an extramusical cause, for Davis's hip ailment was again causing him pain. The only documents of this band's work after the Cellar Door engagement at the end of 1970 are private tapings, which are relatively copious because the itinerary included a busy European tour in the fall, and one unauthorized record of a concert performance late in the year in New York.

If Davis remained unconvinced about his band's prowess, the jazz audiences did not. *Down Beat*'s readers voted him Jazzman of the Year for the derring-do of his fusion experiments in the poll results announced at the end of 1971 and also gave first place to both his touring band, with Weather Report second and Herbie Hancock third, and to his trumpet work, ranking him ahead of Freddie Hubbard and Dizzy Gillespie. His LPs of the previous twelve months also placed well in the popularity poll, with *Jack Johnson* third behind Zawinul and Shorter's debut LP *Weather Report*, a strikingly original fusion with a delicate edge, and Duke Ellington's *New Orleans Suite*. Significantly, Davis's *Live at Fillmore* LP, more representative of his current music than *Jack Johnson*, placed only ninth; that low ranking was an early harbinger of the jazz fans' growing dissatisfaction with Davis's further dilutions of the jazz element in his music. His 1971 awards looked pretty much like a continuation of his career-long mastery of the poll system, but they would turn out to be his last significant showing for the entire decade.

His itinerary for 1971 had been partitioned geographically with unusual neatness: he spent most of the spring around Los Angeles, the summer in New York, and the fall in Europe.

The Los Angeles sojourn began with a concert at the immense Hollywood Bowl, where Davis's sextet opened the concert for the main attraction, a countrified rock 'n' roll band called The Band. One of the most musicianly rock groups of the day, The Band, a quintet comprised of Levon Helm, from Arkansas, and Robbie Robertson, Garth Hudson, Richard Manuel, and Rick Danko, from Ontario, first gained recognition as Bob Dylan's backup band and then attracted a discerning audience with their own understated songs. Their music was, even to the most catholic tastes, leagues apart from Davis's.

Predictably, The Band, according to Leonard Feather, "was wildly received; Miles, opening the show, played continuously for 15 minutes and walked off to tepid applause."[94] The press notices reflected the same mismatch of tastes. "The critics wiped [Davis] out in the papers the following morning," Morgan Ames reported. But Ames, in his liner note for *Miles at Fillmore*, claims that Davis's reception at the Hollywood Bowl was at least more tolerant than many observers believed. "In amphitheaters as large as the Hollywood Bowl," Ames explains, "a roaring ovation can sound like a polite coming-together-of-hands, unless you listen closely and look around you. I did. Hippies were on one side of us, non-descripts were behind, a black couple was on the other side. Front-to-back it was a happily received evening. People liked what Miles was about, even if they couldn't grasp his free-form display. They felt his honest effort, his adventure, his openness, and they took him in without asking why."[95]

Davis faced crowds more conversant with his music when he moved into Shelly's Manne-Hole with his band for a week. He earned $4,000, the largest fee that Shelly Manne had paid since opening the club in 1960, but Davis's band sold out most of its sets all week and gave Manne's club a much-needed boost. Davis was well aware of the Manne-Hole's precarious finances when he accepted the booking. "I worked Shelly's just to help keep the place open," he told Leonard Feather. "I lost about ten pounds in that motherfucker. I made $4,000 a week there, but I went in weighing 139 and came out weighing 129."[96] Manne recognized the gesture by Davis. "Everyone puts him down, and sure, he has his faults," he told Harvey Siders. "But he also took care of business. The back room would be full of friends and hangers-on, but Miles would keep checking his watch, and when the next set was supposed to begin, he'd say, 'Okay, let's go.' And one Saturday night, when there was a tremendous crowd waiting to get in, Miles actually split the last set in order to play an extra one."[97]

Among the friends crowding into the musicians' room night after night were dozens of other musicians. They turned out in unusual numbers nowadays wherever Davis was playing, and the Manne-Hole hosted jazz players all week long. Their interest was precipitated by rumors of his defection from jazz, which preceded him wherever he traveled. "I had to go and see if it was true what the guys on the street were saying," J.J. Johnson said, and, on finding out it was indeed "true," Johnson could only give his assent: "It's out there, what he's doing. But I approve. Listen, Miles is doing his natural thing, he's just putting it in today's setting, on his own terms. If you put Miles and his new group in the studio and record them on separate mikes and then you cut the band track and you just played the trumpet track, you know what you'd have? The same old Miles. What's new is the frame of reference."[93]

Most musicians reacted the same way, usually betraying more than a little bafflement at the sound of Davis's band but finding some reassurances in Davis's own sound. "If he ever plays something that I don't enjoy," Maynard Ferguson said, "I tend to wait and think, well, pretty soon I'll probably *hear* him, because he is also in his directions a believer in change. Otherwise he'd still be doing nineteen-piece versions of *Sketches of Spain* or pretty tunes with a mute." And Beaver Harris, the avant-garde drummer, said: "Miles Davis – whatever he's doing, you can bet he's advanced. He's played with all the advanced players in the world, and now he's dealing with the advanced electronics of the world. But he's still playing Miles Davis."[99] Art Pepper, the alto saxophonist whose return in 1971 after years of wasting away in prisons turned into one of the highlights of jazz in the 1970s, could hardly help comparing what he heard from Davis on his return with the seminal works of a decade earlier. "Yeah, I loved all those things," he told Hal Hill, referring to the collaborations with Gil Evans, "but now Miles has gone way beyond that, and some people don't like him at all. Miles has eliminated the space that I liked about him before," said Pepper, and then hastily added, "but now the space is even greater, every note is like a gem, he has reached the epitome of music."[100] A lot of musicians were thinking aloud about Davis's music, and many of them seemed to be covering any doubts they had with a layer of tact. No one wanted to be a 'moldy fig' or a reactionary as the jazz world faced some new directions.

Davis's fans mixed curious regulars, some of them recalling two decades of his changing music, with a new breed attracted by *Bitches Brew*, and there would always be enough of both to fill a hall or a club even after many critics and musicians began expressing their doubts more openly. Shelly Manne counted on that when he paid Davis the record-high stipend and earned a reprieve for his jazz club. But Manne's business acumen backfired when he booked Davis a year later. The new owners of the building that housed the Manne-Hole built a recording studio adjacent to the club, and Davis's music not only could not save the club this time but inadvertently closed it. "The studio, unbeknown to us, had an echo chamber right above our club," Manne told Sinclair Traill, "but they told me everything was fine. They were going to renew our lease, they loved having us there. So I figured everything was O.K. until one day right out of the blue [they] served us with an eviction notice! Thirty days to vacate because the music, especially with groups such as Miles Davis, was feeding into the echo chamber and lousing up their recordings. They said they had done a record the night before and it had screwed up the whole record because Miles's music had infiltrated the echo chamber."[101] The Manne-Hole closed early in September 1972.

After his week at the Manne-Hole in the spring of 1971, Davis, feeling fatigued and complaining about his weight loss from the constant performing, turned down an engagement in Boston and stayed in Los Angeles for several weeks, as he often had since the 1960s. His residence there, as usual, was the Chateau Marmont on Sunset Boulevard, described by Leonard Feather as a "fading relic of the old Hollywood." He spent his days, according to Feather, working out at a gym with "his own personal trainer and watching baseball on the black and white television set at the Marmont with his "lissome girlfriend."[102]

Davis's divorce from Betty Mabry became official in the third year of their marriage, although they had not been living together for some time. Their relationship had been stormy, but they remained friendly. Mabry launched her singing career under her married name, Betty Davis, and she sought her ex-husband's advice on her recording ventures, including his active participation on one track of her 1975 LP (Island ILPS 9392), a song called *You and I*, written by Mabry, with Davis credited as "director" and Gil Evans as arranger and conductor of the brass backing.

Soon after the divorce she scored a modest success with her first LP, entitled *They Say I'm Different* (Just Sunshine Records 3500). Her songs, all written by her, explore the familiar blues-soul-pop themes of broken hearts, unfaithful lovers, and spent emotions in straightforward, if sometimes strained, lyrics. In *Your Mama Wants You Back*, she sings:

Can you hear your mama callin'?
She's a-callin' you on the phone.
Can you hear your mama cryin'?
A girl said you weren't at home.

Occasionally she breaks away from the safer pop territory for more unorthodox subjects, as when she roughs up her clear, girlish timbre in *He Was a Big Freak* to deliver such lines as: "I used to beat him with a turquoise chain; ... He used to laugh when I'd make him cry." Fans who imagined that her ex-husband might be the target of these barbs could also imagine that Miles Davis framed a musical reply to her when, a few years later, he titled on of his themes *Back Seat Betty*. But Eric Nisenson asked Davis about *He Was a Big Freak* and Davis said: "Well *she* was the biggest freak I ever met, but the song wasn't about me, it was about Hendrix. I'm a big freak myself, but I don't want anybody beating me with a lavender whip."[103]

Davis returned to New York in May 1971 and immediately led his band into a club called the Gaslight for a five-night stand. Once again he was kept busy in a social whirl of promotional events by Columbia. At Clive Davis's urging, he attended a party at Tavern-on-the-Green celebrating the end of a week of SRO concerts at Carnegie Hall by Chicago. Most of Columbia's stars dutifully turned out, including Stevie Wonder, to honor the seven young Chicagoans who had found the crest of the commercial wave in orchestrated rock. Says Clive Davis, "They were star-struck at meeting Miles and Stevie and were knocked out by the entire evening."[104]

Davis also attended a luncheon of the Anti-Defamation League at the Waldorf-Astoria, where Clive Davis was presented with the League's Man of the Year award. "It was not a typical scene for Miles," Clive Davis recalled, "but he viewed it as a personal responsibility and sat with me, Paul Simon, André Kostelanetz and others on the dais."[105] As much as anything else, the occasion was probably an object lesson for Davis as he watched the man he had once accused of racism receive the highest honor from a respected civil rights organization.

The summer rounds again included the Newport Jazz Festival, which Davis's band played on 5 July, a Monday. The parade of bands at the concert seemed dizzying in its variety. The concert opened with a quintet led by Gene Ammons and Sonny Stitt; those two reedmen had been Davis's closest friends in Billy Eckstine's band in 1946 and were still playing the swing-inflected bebop that they had all played then. Two other bands were working in Davis's more recent directions: one of them, Soft Machine, a short-lived group looking for the commercial potential in jazz-rock, and the other, Weather Report, gathering momentum for a long life playing not only jazz-rock but, in their turns, funk-rock and disco-rock and, occasionally, jazz as well. Davis's touch was evident all afternoon.

The European tour in the fall of 1971 looked like a hit-and-run affair, with concerts in twelve cities in three weeks. Some taped performances exist in private collections from the concerts in Zurich (22 October), Paris (23), Brussels (26), Paris again (27), Rotterdam (29), Belgrade (3 November), Vienna (5), Berlin (6), Uppsala (7), Copenhagen (8), Oslo (9), Cologne (12), and Festival Hall, London (13). Jack DeJohnette had left the band in the summer to form his own fusion band, called Compost, and although they started with the obvious advantage of a Columbia recording contract they struggled to find an audience and steady work; they were destined not to join the long line of successful bands spawned by Davis's stock company. DeJohnette returned to Davis's band whenever their schedules permitted in the next months, but on the European tour Davis tried out Leon Chancler.

Davis put his European tour into the context of his performing schedule for Leonard Feather, in *From Satchmo to Miles*. "I got a tour in Europe," he said. "I'll make about $300,000 on it. Then I won't work again until the spring and I'll make a spring tour. No more week here and three weeks off and a week there. I'm through with that shit." When Feather asked how he expected to keep his band together through the long periods of inactivity, he replied, "I can always get a group. The men I need I can keep on salary while I'm laying off."[106] Noting Davis's indifferent attitude about performing, Feather concluded that the light schedule amounted to "a policy of semi-retirement." Feather must have been aware also that Davis's recording activities had become even lighter, practically nonexistent. He predicted that Davis schedule might well become "almost total inactivity" before much longer. Feather's remarks, which appeared in print in 1972, proved to be prophetic, and Feather was one of the few observers not completely surprised when Davis limped along in something that might be described as semi-retirement from 1972 to 1975 and then retired fully for more than five years after that.

At least one other observer noted in retrospect that Davis seemed less than fully involved with the music of his band at his European performances. "In his London concerts in November 1971," Barry McRae wrote in *Jazz Journal* in 1975, "we began to hear too much of the hot declamatory outburst and less of the natural lyricism. The Davis who had swept along with the rock sounds had become bogged down by them. His use of wah-wah trumpet was less effective and, of all things, it lacked the rhythmic subtlety that had always seemed the trumpeter's birthright. This could be construed as moving back into the ensemble but the outcome was strangulation, not inspiration."[107]

On 26 November 1971, less than two weeks after returning from Europe, Davis and his band performed a concert at Philharmonic Hall in New York. Don Alias was added to the band, and Jack DeJohnette returned for the concert, which proved to be the last gasp for the working band with Keith Jarrett and Gary Bartz, and, for that matter, the last gasp until 1981 for a band of Davis's in which a majority of the sidemen were schooled in jazz.

The concert drew more than the usual advance publicity when Davis telephoned Jack Whittemore from Paris a month before and told him to spend half of his fee buying tickets for the concert and to distribute them among young people who could not afford them. "Miles has never done anything like this before," Whittemore told Chris Albertson, "but nothing he does surprises me." For Whittemore, the main problem was "how to go about distributing more than $2,000 worth of free tickets to the right people."[108] Davis's largesse came as a response to his new awareness of his stature in the black community, where his broader, younger audience of recent years saw him not so much a musician as a hero. "I like when a black boy says, 'Oohh, there's Miles Davis,' like they did with Joe Louis," he told Gregg Hall in 1974, recalling an incident at a concert in the American south around this time. "Some cats did me like that in Greensboro. They said, 'Man, we sure glad you came down here.' That thrilled me more than anything that happened to me that year."[109] For his concert at the Philharmonic, he was hoping that some of those youngsters could be in his audience.

The concert was taped privately and later released in part as an unauthorized LP proclaiming itself a "special limited anniversary issue for collectors." The details are as follows:

Miles Davis Septet at Philharmonic Hall
Miles Davis, tpt; Gary Bartz, as, ss; Keith Jarrett, el pno, org; Michael Henderson, b; Jack DeJohnette, dms; Don Alias, James Foreman, perc. Philharmonic Hall, New York, 26 November 1971
Bwongo [medley: *Directions, Sivad, What I Say*]; *Ananka* [medley: *What I Say* (cont), *Sanctuary, Miles Runs the Voodoo Down, Yesternow*]
(both on Session 123)
Identification of the medleys is by Jan Lohmann.

The final ten minutes of the recording, identified as the *Yesternow* theme from the *Jack Johnson* LP, features Davis's incantatory amplified sounds over percussive accents and Bartz's down-home blues on the alto saxophone over the same percussive accents, making a stylish conclusion to the record. Almost everything that precedes it – and the record logs a generous forty-seven minutes of the concert – highlights a percussive barrage that overwhelms the music and in effect becomes the music.

One of the regrets about this band's lack of recordings arises from the interest in Keith Jarrett's work, but on this recording (and on the European concerts as well) Jarrett goes largely unheard, his ensemble contributions swallowed up in the percussion and his solo efforts, on this record no more than one minute of electric piano on *Directions*, lost in the mix. Long before Jarrett took off on his own singular course, Davis had relegated him to the backdrop in his band, a missed opportunity for Davis's music as well as Jarrett's.

In relegating him so, Davis obviously implied no disrespect. After all, he had now relegated himself in the same way.

14

Sivad Selim
1972–5

Alone

for Miles Davis

A friend told me
He'd risen above jazz.
I leave him there.
    Michael S. Harper

As the wall of percussion moved out of the background of Miles Davis's music and into the foreground, numerous critics, fans, and musicians began to balk at the direction his electronic experiments were taking. They had been laying back for three years, waiting to see what he would do, and stifling their doubts because Davis had led the way so often before. That period of grace was now over.

Davis chose musicians with diverse backgrounds to replace the jazzmen of his last band, and their limitations seemed obvious to the jazz audience even if they successfully filled the roles Davis assigned them. His studio recordings of the period, as they came out at irregular intervals, laid bare those limitations, and, because the recording ensembles sometimes imported musicians of proven abilities, the new LPs seemed proof positive that the limitations lay not so much in the music's execution as in its conception. Either way, the band's failings were pinned on Davis.

The recordings of the period showed much more diversity than Davis's critics seemed willing to concede, but their common element was a bumptious, domineering rhythm. *On the Corner* (issued in 1972) sounded like a crass attempt at funk; in the words of a reviewer in *Coda,* it presented "nameless, faceless go-go music." *In Concert* (1973), recorded live at Philharmonic Hall, preserved remarkably little of Davis's trumpet playing and perhaps even less of his guiding hand. *Get Up with It* (1974) featured long, listless rambles and little else, with Davis playing sustained chords on an organ most of the time. *Dark Magus*, *Pangaea*, and *Agharta*, all concert performances released after Davis retired in 1975, showed more spunk in the onstage give-and-take but not much more definition. Davis repeatedly expressed his admiration for James Brown and Karlheinz Stockhausen, musicians so far removed from one another that they seemed irreconcilable, but Davis's bona fide masterworks of this period, easily overlooked in the musical morass, drew on both sources: *Rated X* (recorded in 1972, released in 1974) unleashes seven minutes of distilled tension in an idiom that defies category, and the *Maiysha/Jack Johnson* segments of *Agharta*, a 1975 Japanese concert performance, magically bring into focus the musical forces over which many thought Davis had lost control.

He seemed to be struggling for control physically as well as musically. His arthritic hip kept him in constant pain and forced him to abandon his regimen in the gym. He had more run-ins with the police, leading to a variety of charges, including alleged narcotics and weapons offenses. The abstinences of a few years earlier were replaced by indulgences. He drank more heavily, perhaps hoping to kill the pain, but succeeded only in aggravating a peptic ulcer. He began receiving injections of morphine in order to keep moving. And, in the end, he collapsed and stayed down for a long time.

Until the collapse, Davis swaggered through his public appearances, conducting his bombastic rhythm sections autocratically onstage and damning both his old peers and his young disciples offstage. But the tumult of his life and his music could not drown out the chorus of critics.

"Maybe he's doing it sincerely," Clark Terry told Leonard Feather, "but I do know that it's a much more lucrative development for him. I happen to know that there was a period when in spite of all his many possessions – investments, home, car – there was a period when he needed to bolster these: he really needed to get into a higher financial bracket. And there was an opportunity for him to get into this kind of thing, and he took the opportunity to jump out and do it."[1] Betty Carter lumped Davis with Herbie Hancock and Donald Byrd as a musician abusing his talent. "He did the same thing, for money," she said. "It's all about money ... They have a 'reasonable' excuse for the why of what they're doing, but the only excuse is money."[2] John Hammond, long associated with Columbia, agreed: "The musicians who are selling out voluntarily are succumbing to the worst instincts of the capitalist system," he said, and he added, "For Miles Davis, who was a real original, to be putting out crap – repetitious crap – that's a disgrace."[3] "Miles Davis is a consummate blues player," Archie Shepp commented, but then he felt the need to qualify that remark: "I don't mean what he's playing now; what he's playing now impresses me as something very antithetical to the blues. It depresses me when I hear formerly good blues players in a certain context merely pandering their artifacts for money's sake, for commerciality, because they cheapen the genuine product."[4]

Overlooked in these criticisms were the facts that Davis's music was not commercially successful, at least not by the standards he had set with *Bitches Brew*, and was no more readily accessible as soul music than as jazz. It was a different species, or perhaps several of them.

Other commentators rose to Davis's defence. "Miles isn't up there to please everybody, or anybody," Herbie Hancock said. "He's there to be honest, that's all; and he has to be taken for what he is."[5] Cecil Taylor explained to Nat Hentoff the difference in Davis's musical orientation that seemed to be disorienting his critics. "As Miles Davis's European technical facility becomes sparser," Taylor said, "his comment from the Negro folk tradition becomes more incisive. He's been an important innovator in form in jazz, but again not out of theory, but out of what he hears and lives."[6]

What Davis was hearing – and apparently living – had changed, as Taylor notes, but it was not so much "Negro folk" music as black pop music, and not in any sense a "tradition" but only the most current samples. Dave Liebman, who played reeds and flutes in the band for much of this period, told Gene Perla: "Every time I've been with him on the road or at his house, I've never heard a tape in the machine – and there's always something on – that is older than a few days or a week. He doesn't listen to anything that's in the past, of his own music ... I've never heard him listen to anybody else's music, except maybe a particular track of Sly [Stone] or James Brown. Of the music the group is doing, he won't even listen to a tape of two weeks ago. That's already old to him. So when you see that in him, it's really understandable why, to me, the music has moved in another direction."[7] Gil Evans, who was making similar, though less radical, changes in the rhythms of his infrequent music, stated simply, "Jazz has always used the rhythm of the time, whatever people danced to."[8]

Davis's most direct incursion into what he saw as the musical space charted by Sly Stone, James Brown, and the rhythm bands of Chicago's South Side, the studio recordings released as *On the Corner*, was scheduled for the Columbia studios early in 1972, but it had to be postponed when Davis was rushed to the hospital suffering from gallstones in April.

The sessions finally took place around June, after a long layoff, and when the music was released in November it got a harsher reception than anything Davis had ever recorded. Reviewers savaged it, and many fans ignored it. Most of Davis's Columbia LPs have stayed in print continuously, but inexpensive copies of *On the Corner* were available in delete bins at record stores within sixteen months of its release.

Everything about the LP seemed blatant. Its cover, inside and out, was festooned with ghetto caricatures by cartoonist Corky McCoy: prostitutes, gays, activist, winos, and dealers. Apart from them there was only (as Jérome Reese described it) "une grande photo du beau Miles en star 'sexy'." None of the other musicians was identified. And, it turned out, both the cover design and the missing credits were Davis's brainchild. "I didn't put those names on *On the Corner* specially for that reason, so now the critics have to say, 'What's this instrument, and what's this?'" Davis explained to Michael Watts. "I told them not to put any instrumentation on ... I'm not even gonna put my picture on albums anymore. Pictures are dead, man. You close your eyes and you're there." Watts asked him what would appear on future covers and was shown a stack of cartoons. "Things like that, man," Davis said.[9] Mark Zanger, in an overview of Davis's music of this period in *The Real Paper*, commented: "The album is best seen, rather than heard, as Miles's manifesto."[10]

The instrumentation varies from track to track, and the music probably comes from several sessions in and around June. Tentative lists of personnel, all slightly different, have appeared in at least four different sources, indicating a befuddling parade of musicians through the studios, and the music gives those players few opportunities to identify themselves. The details are as follows, with the collective personnel listed first and the instrumental breakdown for the titles listed separately:

Miles Davis Ensemble: On the Corner
collective personnel: Miles Davis, el tpt; Dave Liebman or Carlos Garnett, ss, ts; Benny Maupin, bass clnt; Chick Corea, el pno; Herbie Hancock and/or Harold I. Williams, el pno, synthesizer; David Creamer, el gtr; Colin Walcott,

sitar; Michael Henderson, b; Jack DeJohnette and/or Billy Hart, dms; Badal Roy, tabla; Don Alias and/or James Mtume Foreman, congas, perc. probably June 1972

Davis; Liebman; el pno; synthesizer; Creamer; Henderson; dms; congas; perc
On the Corner; New York Girl; Thinkin' One Thing and Doin' Another; Vote for Miles
(all on Columbia KC 31906)

Davis; Garnett; other instruments as for *New York Girl*
Helen Butte
(on Columbia KC 31906)

Davis; synthesizer; Walcott; Henderson; dms; Roy; congas; perc
Black Satin
(on Columbia KC 31906)

Omit Davis; add Garnett, ss, and Creamer; other instruments as for *Black Satin*
Mr. Freedom X
(on Columbia KC 31906)

Garnett, ss; Maupin; el pno; org (perhaps Davis); Henderson; dms; perc
One and One
(on Columbia KC 31906)
Some discographies list John McLaughlin, el gtr, in addition to, or instead of Creamer.

The music, notwithstanding the changes in personnel and instrumentation, humps along on electric discharges, like a man walking barefoot on a field of broken egg shells. Stan Getz heard the first three titles, which form a continuous track, as part of a blindfold test with Dan Morgenstern and commented: "Is that a Miles offering? If that's Miles, where is Miles? He was directing. It sounded like they were gathering at the elephant graveyard. I didn't hear any elephants screech, though." And then he grew serious: "That music is worthless. It means nothing; there is no form, no content, and it barely swings. The soloists are playing a half tone above and a half tone below so it'll sound modern, but there's nothing to build on or anything logical – nothing."[11]

The feeling of monotony arises from the simple harmonic foundation of each piece, what Clark Terry called "the one-chord modal bag." Ron Brown, reviewing the LP for *Jazz Journal*, said, "It sounds merely as if the band had selected a chord and decided to worry hell out of it for three-quarters of an hour. Also the solos are practically nonexistent; Miles wanders over to spit a hasty note into the rhythmic wodge every now and again, like he did on his last visit to London."[12] Terry viewed the simple harmonies as a cynical expedient in Davis's search for a mass audience: "Miles is smart enough to put something where they can reach it on their own level. If they're not hip enough to know what's happening ... they're going to grasp whatever is simple enough for them to cop. And the simple thing for them to cop happens to be that one-chord modal bag that is so fashionable."[13]

Terry surmised correctly that Davis had a specific audience in mind. Davis told Michael Watts in *Melody Maker*, "I don't care who buys the records as long as they get to the black people so I will be remembered when I die. I'm not playing for any white people, man. I wanna hear a black guy say, 'Yeah, I dig Miles Davis.'"[14] That admission added insult to injury. Bill Cole, in his biography of Davis, called *On the Corner* "an insult to the intellect of the people."[15] Brown concluded his review by saying, "I'd like to think that nobody could be so easily pleased as to dig this record to any extent." But Davis was not willing to concede that *On the Corner* was a miscalculation. Questioned about it, he became defensive, as when Sy Johnson told him he was having trouble "following the music" with the extra rhythm players. "You can't understand me 'cause you're not me," Davis said. "In the second place, you're not black. You don't understand my rhythms. We're two totally different people. That's almost an insult to say you don't understand."[16]

Davis's apparent reluctance to play his trumpet also drew comments from the reviewers. Beginning with *On the Corner*, he seemed content to play few notes and short interludes. When Watts asked him about it he said, "Because you have technique you don't have to use it. You use it when you feel like it. I mean, you can run, but if you can walk you walk, right? You do what you gotta do. It's called good taste. I play whatever comes into my black head, man."[17]

The only other music to be released from these June sessions, a long piece that filled one side of the *Big Fun* LP two years later, shares some of the main characteristics. The details are as follows:

Miles Davis Ensemble: Big Fun
Miles Davis, el tpt; Sonny Fortune, ss, flt; Carlos Garnett, ss; Benny Maupin, bass clnt; Lonnie Liston Smith, el pno; Harold I. Williams, synthesizer;

Michael Henderson, b; Al Foster, Billy Hart, dms; Badal Roy, tabla; James
Mtume Foreman, perc. New York, 12 June 1972
Ife
(Columbia PG 32866)

The music moves along over a simple, repeated bass riff, its progress
charted mainly by the percussionists, whose interplay seems somewhat
less jittery than it is on *On the Corner*. The rhythm is suspended
altogether in the last third while Davis muses over sustained organ
chords; this section gives a foretaste of the style that Mark Zanger
would call "pseudo-trance music" when it appeared in abundance on
the 1974 LP *Get Up with It*.

In these June studio sessions, Davis used seventeen different sidemen
in various combinations. Many were unknown and untried, members of
a loosely knit contingent of young musicians who gravitated to New
York with high aspirations, enormous self-confidence, and unpredictable talents. Davis had regularly recruited his sidemen after hearing
them play publicly with other bands, but now he began looking for them
before they had a chance to establish their reputations beyond their own
circle of acquaintances. He relied on people such as Herbie Hancock, Gil
Evans, Sonny Rollins, and a few others, including friends of friends, to
relay the names of youngsters heard by chance in a loft jam session or on
a one-night stand. Usually he phoned the potential recruit himself and
told him to appear in the recording studio at an appointed hour; on one
memorable occasion in 1974 he would tell two new recruits to meet him
onstage at Carnegie Hall during a concert.

The parade of players did nothing to stabilize the conception Davis
was working on in his music. Only bassist Michael Henderson and
percussionist James Mtume Foreman were retained from the working
band of the previous year. To replace Gary Bartz on reeds, he had brought
three different musicians into the recording studio in June. Although
Dave Liebman became his first choice for the next two and a half years,
he also used both of the others, Carlos Garnett and Sonny Fortune, from
time to time. All three were relatively experienced, although only a
little better known than most of the other sidemen. Garnett, born in
Panama in 1939, had played in rock bands in the 1960s before joining
Freddie Hubbard and Art Blakey. Fortune, a Philadelphian, was a year
older; he had played for years in local bar bands before going on the road
with Mongo Santamaria's band and was a regular member of McCoy
Tyner's quartet when he first recorded with Davis. Liebman, from
Brooklyn, was first noticed in Ten Wheel Drive, a jazz-rock band in the

shadow of Blood, Sweat and Tears in 1970, when he was 24, and he was playing regularly in Elvin Jones's quintet, where he shared the front line with Steve Grossman, when he first recorded with Davis. Davis's sporadic playing schedule required him to keep all three on call, because between his playing dates they were busy with other commitments, often with bands they led themselves.

He often used Jack DeJohnette as the drummer in his studio ensembles, but DeJohnette was also working as a leader. For *Ife*, he borrowed Billy Hart from Hancock's band, whose talents were well known to Davis. Hart recalled their first meeting. "One time I was working with Herbie at the Vanguard, and after the set I sat down at one of those chairs next to the drums," he said. "I was soaking wet. I guess the music had been satisfying. I'm sitting there dripping. I couldn't even open my eyes. Suddenly I heard this voice in my ear – 'You played your ass off.' I looked up and it was Miles. He startled me. The very next thing he said was, 'You know, sometimes you can play behind the beat, and that shit swings. And sometimes you can play on top of the beat, and *that* shit swings. But sometimes you can play right over the beat, and *that shit swings.*'"[18]

The second drummer on *Ife* was Al Foster, an athletic-looking young man with a ready smile. He was just starting to work professionally, and the recorded evidence of *Ife* reveals nothing about his ability, but he became Davis's regular drummer not only in the band of 1972–5 but also in the new band formed in 1981, after Davis's emergence from retirement, making his association with Davis the most enduring of any sideman. Compared with the pyrotechnical fireworks of Philly Joe Jones, Tony Williams, and DeJohnette, Foster is an elemental player whose main strengths are in setting up a rhythmic pattern and sustaining it for long stretches. None of the other personnel changes reveals as tellingly Davis's changed conception. From the beginning, he instructed Foster, according to Dominique Gaumont, to "copy the simplicity of Buddy Miles,"[19] Hendrix's drummer on *Band of Gypsies*, and Foster has done that, with muscular ease, ever since.

Foster joined Henderson and Foreman in the rhythm section of the working band, and they were its only fixtures. Either Liebman, Garnett, or Fortune was usually available to fill the reedman's spot when Davis accepted performing engagements, and the other players were recruited as he needed them. Davis no longer maintained a working band, for the first time in years, but he had a pool of players on which he could draw. Many musicians came into the band as unknowns and remained unheralded both with Davis and afterward. The pattern broke the spell of Davis's reputation as a star-maker.

The band had a built-in instability, and several critics began to question the abilities of some of the sidemen. Asked by Harriet Choice how he knew what musician was right for his band, Davis retorted, "The same way I know what girl I want to screw."[20] To many jazz fans, that recruiting policy seemed much less selective than it had once been. Dave Liebman, who was, with Sonny Fortune, probably the best jazz player associated with Davis in this period, suggested that Davis's critics were looking for talents in the sidemen that they were never intended to have. "Miles has picked these people to achieve the sound that he wants," he said. "Some are not experienced in jazz. This band is made up of so many different elements that only a few of the cats have swung in the jazz thing for a long period of their musical life. The other cats are coming out of funk or something different."[21]

Davis himself seemed content with the challenge of adjusting to the youthful mix of disparate backgrounds he had put together. "I'm 48," he told Sy Johnson. "I never feel that shit. I'm not vain. As long as I'm not draggin' the musicians I'm with – and I pick the best ones I can find, that are available to me – then I figure I'm pretty alright. That's the way *I* judge."[22]

For all that, the young sidemen treated him as a grey eminence. When Johnson arrived to interview Davis, he passed Al Foster and Michael Henderson in the foyer and said, "I'm off to see the master." "Do you call him that too?" Foster asked. "Some of the guys in the band call him the master." Davis once complained facetiously, "They think I'm their father! [They say,] 'We don't see *you* fuck around on the road.' I say, 'I told you I used to have a bitch for every night I went to work, and one night I went to work and all seven of them were there.' Shit!! *That*'s why I don't fuck around."[23]

On the Corner fell far short of Davis's commercial expectations, but he saw that not as a failure of the musicians or the music itself. He blamed his manager and Columbia. He replaced Harold Lovett, his manager for seventeen years, with Neil Reshen. He renewed his feud with Columbia, this time over its apparent failure to sell *On the Corner* in black neighborhoods. "You know," he told Michael Watts, "I will make $500,000 in a year, but I will do it for $5 if my music would get to the black people, and Columbia couldn't get the albums into Harlem ... That's what I'm told by the vice-president. He don't talk to me on the phone for nothing."

While Watts interviewed him, they were listening to tapes that Watts described as "the next step from his *On the Corner* music." "I've been up for three days writing this fucking music," he complained, "and Columbia ain't going to sell it, anyway. They sell all the pretty, little faggot-looking white boys, that's their thing. I just got an offer from Motown for this new album." He claimed that he was being taken for granted at Columbia. "When I make a record and it sounds good, they say, 'Well, that's Miles.' Y'know, it's supposed to sound good. That's why I'm leaving Columbia, man, I'm not going to give them this latest album ... I'll erase it ... I told Clive [Davis]. Sent a telegram, told him he should get a black – he should use his sources all over the country to get a black man who thinks black to sell the music to black people, 'cos the white people seem to know about it ... I been exploited for ten years, man."

When Watts called Bob Altschuler at Columbia to check the story, Altschuler told him calmly that Davis could not terminate his contract. "This is his way of pressuring Columbia," he said. "We talk to him every day. He needs reassurance."[24]

A few weeks after his June studio dates, Davis was involved in controversy at the Newport Jazz Festival, now transplanted from the Rhode Island resort to New York. He was listed as the featured performer at afternoon and evening concerts in Carnegie Hall on 4 July, but did not appear. In his place Freddie Hubbard led a quartet, sharing the bill with Sonny Rollins's quartet. Davis had warned the New York newspapers that he had no intention of showing up and supplied them with the kind of caustic comments that gave the festival some sensational publicity. He was not offered enough money, he said, and he had never agreed to play the concerts in the first place. Besides, in his opinion the festival catered to older styles by booking musicians such as Dizzy Gillespie and Sarah Vaughan.

His comments brought a sharp rebuke from Mary Lou Williams. "You know what evil is?" she asked Roland Baggenaes. "What Miles just did ... If you and I know someone, well, we could talk about him but to say it in the paper like that – that's very bad. Selfishness and bitterness will make you evil ... He can stop bookings of those people." As for Davis's claim that he was playing more current music, Williams said: "I hear what he's playing, he's playing practically the same style he always has played. But he's got the modern thing in back of him, the guys who make the noise ... Listen to his tone, listen to his chord changes and you'll hear it. So Miles Davis really has no reason to say anything about Dizzy Gillespie or Sarah Vaughan."[25]

If Vaughan heard about his remark, she was apparently not upset enough to say anything publicly, and Gillespie remained magnanimous when Leonard Feather gave him the chance to respond by asking for a comment on Davis's fusion music. "Whether it'll last, what he's doing now, that's not up to me to judge," he said. "Time alone judges that, so I just sit here and wait until – well, if he's hooked that far out in front, wait for time to catch up with it ... The guy's a master, so I wouldn't come out and say that I don't like what he's doing now." And then he slyly added, "Besides it would be out of line. Could the King of England criticize the King of France?"[26]

Davis's refusal to appear at the Newport Festival in what would have been his first concert date in months set in motion some speculation about whether or not the fee was the real issue, as he had claimed. Whitney Balliett, in his review of the festival for the *New Yorker*, suggested that "the real reason may have been fear, for he has played little in recent months, and a trumpeter's chops, if not used, can deteriorate in a week."[27] But Davis had spent several hours in the recording studio in the weeks leading up to the festival. The studio work was planned partly as preparation for his return to performing, both to restore his embouchure and to assemble a new band. Rather than the embouchure, it was probably the failure to fashion a working unit from the passing parade in the studio that kept him off the Carnegie Hall stage.

He kept trying. On 7 July, just three days after he was to have played at the festival, he led another group into the recording studios. The personnel remains unknown, and the only music released from the session came out on a 45-rpm single for the teenage market. The scant details are as follows:

Miles Davis Ensemble: Molester
Miles Davis, el tpt; rest of personnel similar to *Ife*. New York, 7 July 1972
Molester, part 1; part 2
(Columbia 4-45709 [45 rpm])

The release of *Molester* on 45 rpm inaugurates a set of releases of Davis's music for the pop market, probably as Columbia's response to Davis's charges that it was not marketing his music properly. In the instances to come, the 45-rpm release is usually a slice of music from an LP currently in preparation and can safely be ignored in favor of the longer LP versions in charting Davis's music. *Molester* so far has shown up exclusively on the 45-rpm release.

Its title may ironically commemorate Davis's latest run-in with the police. Just two days after he recorded it, he was arrested and charged with "unlawful imprisonment and menacing" of a woman named Lita Merker at his house. The woman accused Davis of shouting insults at her and preventing her from leaving. The arresting officer reported no evidence of assault. Davis pleaded not guilty, and the case was adjourned to 22 August.[28] Privately, Davis maintained that the incident started as an argument between his girl friend and Merker, whom he had known as a neighbor for several years, and that it ended out of court with apologies all round.

By September, he had gathered more players for his working band and returned to the studio with them. Carlos Garnett was probably the reed player at this recording date, but he is not heard on the music that has been issued so far. With Davis playing keyboards more than trumpet, the recording ensemble became a rhythm band, and they produced, in *Rated X*, one of Davis's most striking percussion pieces. The details are as follows:

Miles Davis Ensemble: Get Up with It
Miles Davis, org (on *Rated X*), el tpt, el pno (on *Billy Preston*); Cedric Lawson, el pno (on *Rated X*), org (on *Billy Preston*); Reggie Lucas, gtr; Khalil Balakrishna, sitar; Michael Henderson, b; Al Foster, dms; Badal Roy, tabla; James Mtume Foreman, perc. New York, September 1972
Rated X; *Billy Preston*
(both on Columbia C 33237 [1974])

Billy Preston, dedicated to the veteran soul musician who had been imported by the Beatles to lend some weight to their final album, *Let It Be*, belongs to the genre of *On the Corner*, with layers of wah-wah modulations from the trumpet, guitar, and organ reverberating through the hefty rhythmic bottom.

Rated X, however, bursts out of the confines of Davis's current conception. It defies category – certainly not jazz by any known standard, and at least as far removed from soul-funk-rock pop music, yet made from components of both. Davis pits himself on the organ against the bumptious rhythm band. He plays sustained, two-fisted chords that sound like a soap opera soundtrack in the unaccompanied opening. Then the rhythm starts fretting beneath him. Whenever the rhythm threatens to become the focal point it is stopped abruptly; it is cut off for a few seconds at a time, irregularly, isolating the awful drone of the organ. The mood is strangely menacing, with the rhythm band boogying like dancers at a high school sock hop while the Prince of Darkness looms over them like the grim reaper. It is taut, unpleasant music, and it could do nothing to revive the interest of jazz fans in what Davis was pursuing, but it is also a simple, audacious concept with great integrity and power. And it is Davis's most conspicuous success in adapting the values of European avant-garde composers, especially Karlheinz Stockhausen.

Davis occasionally cited Stockhausen in his terse and mostly unenlightening comments to interviewers seeking an explanation for his music, and in 1980 he was joined by the German composer in Columbia's recording studios in a collaboration that is still unissued. The best information on the unlikely pairing, and on the role of a young English cellist-composer named Paul Buckmaster, who also joined them on the 1980 studio date, comes from Ian Carr in *Miles Davis: A Critical Biography*. According to Carr, Davis first met Buckmaster on his English tour in 1969, when he was played a tape of a Buckmaster composition featuring bass and drums distorted electronically to create moods. "Definitely space music," Buckmaster told Carr. Davis was so impressed that he kept up his sporadic acquaintance on subsequent tours. In 1972, Davis summoned him by phone to New York in order to work on some new music. Buckmaster stayed with Davis for about six weeks in May and June, when Davis was working on the music for *On the Corner*, and he was present in the studio when that music was recorded. As Carr puts it, "It is ironical that after his discussions with Paul Buckmaster, and after his immersion in the music of Stockhausen, Miles should have produced an album so alien to the European tradition."[29] But Buckmaster's influence, if not immediate, became clearer with the recording of *Rated X* and soon began to show up in many smaller ways.

Carr reports that Buckmaster spent hours during his stay at Davis's practicing Bach's cello suites, often under the critical gaze of his host. Soon Bach's name also began to crop up in Davis's conversation, as in his description of unconventional melodic organization for Sy Johnson. "I think it's time people changed where they put the melody," he said. "The melody can be in the bass, or a drum sound, or just a sound. I may write something around a bass line. I may write something around a rhythm ... I always place the rhythm so it can be played three or four different ways. It's always three rhythms within one, and you can get some other ones in there too." And then he looked quizzically at Johnson, a well-schooled composer in his own right, and asked, "Do you know what I mean? It's almost like Bach. You know how Bach wrote."[30]

Buckmaster brought Davis a recording of Stockhausen's *Mixtur* and *Telemusik*, Carr says, and for the next days Davis's house reverberated with the strains of Stockhausen's electronic recomposition of symphonic orchestrations. Davis also bought several cassettes of Stockhausen's music to play in his Lamborghini.

The effect of Davis's study of Stockhausen could not be repressed for long. He passed along some of the cassettes to Gil Evans, as he had Rodrigo's *Concierto* and his other enthusiasms over the years. For Davis, the discovery of Stockhausen and the avant-garde European composers must have seemed like a vindication of the post-production composing he had been doing with Teo Macero for at least four years, and also of the reorganization of conventional musical values – harmonically, melodically, and now rhythmically – that had attracted him ever since the days of his 1949 nonet. *Rated X*, Davis's own "space music," shows Stockhausen's influence compositionally, but his influence would soon show, more tangentially, in Davis's concert format as well.

On 10 September, just a few days after the recording of *Billy Preston* and *Rated X*, Davis led his working band onstage at the Ann Arbor Blues and Jazz Festival in Michigan. "Miles Davis was to end the festival, but instead he began the night's festivities," Bill Smith wrote in a *Coda* photostory. "ZAAAPPPP ... just like that. Dressed in his finest silks and satins, the Prince of Darkness simply overpowered everything. Incredible." Smith then posed a question that other members of the audience were thinking: "Why does it sound so crappy on his last three records?"[31]

The records Smith refers to are *At Fillmore*, *Live-Evil*, and *On the Corner*. Certainly one reason they seemed less satisfying to most fans than Davis's live performances was because they lacked the physical presence of Davis, a charismatic performer now no less than in his tailored days of ballad musings. Ralph J. Gleason offered a novel theory to account for the discrepancy. "The kind of music Miles Davis plays now," he contended, "stretches the capability of stereo to its limit and finds it failing. There is more sound here than stereo can handle on record ... I have heard Miles's band ... and the effect was overwhelming. So overwhelming that in retrospect the stereo records he has made sound pallid by comparison, even granting the ordinary distance between live and recorded performances."[32] The difference in feeling between his records and his performances seemed to mark another reversal from the late 1950s and early 1960s, when Davis seemed sometimes to save the band's peaks of originality for the studio, in recordings such as *Milestones* and *Kind of Blue*, while he continued to play the well-worn repertoire – *Round Midnight, Bye Bye Blackbird, Four*, and the rest – on their nightly round of club dates.

Dave Liebman, who was gaining recognition as a jazz saxophonist in work he was doing outside Davis's band, became something of an apologist for Davis with members of the jazz audience. "This band is a combination of almost all the free elements that have been used in the last ten years, the avant garde elements of music [which are] the free association of ideas, and the thing that rock has brought to the music which is the steady vamp bassline or rhythm to work off of," he told Gene Perla. "It's a combination of those two things with all the other elements taken out here and there from jazz: the use of lyricism, straight ahead – like Miles will play a really pretty melody once in a while, quiet everybody down, and it'll be just him playing alone sometimes. It seems to me that he's using all the things he's gone through in little packages almost." He saw Davis less as a leader in the time-honored sense than as a spontaneous composer. "It's like a concerto where you have your adagio and allegro sections," he continued. "Now he's manipulating the controls in a way more than he did when he was playing the straight jazz thing. It's like one long piece or suite every time we play. Within it there is always the texture of drums, then the quiet latin thing, then the psychedelic thing. It goes through maybe five, six or seven moods."[33] Again, the convergence of Davis's goals with avant-garde European composition becomes clear, but transformed into a jazz-derived format in which composition is spontaneous and improvised.

Little of the live vitality of Davis's band was preserved in the recording, later in the month, of a Philharmonic Hall concert. The four-sided Columbia release relied less heavily on extensive editing and fanciful remixing than other recent releases of live performances, but the new band members were undeniably less talented jazz players than their predecessors on the *Fillmore* and *Live-Evil* performances, and the new LP did little or nothing to assuage jazz listeners, who again found themselves greeted by Corky McCoy's caricatures on the package. The details are as follows:

Miles Davis Nine: In Concert
Miles Davis, tpt, probably org; Carlos Garnett, ss; Cedric Lawson, el
keyboards, synthesizer; Reggie Lucas, el gtr; Khalil Balakrishna, sitar; Michael
Henderson, b; Al Foster, dms; Badal Roy, tabla; James Mtume Foreman, perc.
Philharmonic Hall, New York, 29 September 1972
side 1 [medley includes *Rated X*]; side 2 [medley includes *Black Satin*]; side 3;
side 4
(all on *In Concert*, Columbia KG 32092)

The reviewer for *Coda* concluded: "*In Concert* exudes more vitality on
any one of its four sides than the sapless *On the Corner* could muster in
any one bar ... Its vitality is probably a direct result of Miles Davis's
continuous participation in the music, although it may also be
connected to the fact that there are fewer drummers this time."

Throughout its hour and a half playing time, there are several
attractive moments. Side 1 closes with a lush ballad by Davis and
Garnett; side 2 is dominated by *Black Satin*, from the previous LP,
exploited here for its interesting melody, in a context where melody is
rare. Side 4 includes a funereal blues by Davis over a one-bar motif
carried by the bass and organ.

Much of the rest seems unexceptional. On side 3, Henderson repeats
three notes on his bass with scarcely a variation for almost fifteen
minutes, which is, as the *Coda* reviewer notes, "pure torpor." Side 1
meanders through multiple moods and tempos so rapidly that none of
them makes a point. Side 4 includes a hard rock number featuring
Reggie Lucas that depersonalizes Hendrix's sound woefully. "Almost
everything sounds like something that Miles has recorded before," one
reviewer said, "but little of it is identifiable and its parts seem more or
less interchangeable."

John Toner, reviewing the LP in *Jazz and Blues Journal*, gloomily
concluded of Davis: "He has always consciously attempted to simplify
the lines of his music to allow freedom of expression, but this time he
has created a prison rather than open musical spaces. Davis has got
nothing but the cluttered and static form which he once professed to
hate so much." And Scott Yanow, in *Record Review*, wrote: "Up until
1972, it could be truthfully stated that every Miles Davis album was
worth owning. *On the Corner* and *Live at the Philharmonic* are
exceptions."[34]

Davis continued touring with his new band in October, playing at
Paul's Mall in Boston and at a club in Denver. In between, he was

scheduled to play a concert at Painters Mill Theater, but the concert was cancelled, *Down Beat* reported, due to lack of advance ticket sales.[35]

In the early morning hours of 21 October, after returning to New York from his concert in Denver, Davis ran his Lamborghini into a concrete island and broke both his ankles. "I was cruising, y'know, but I was still up from that gig in Denver," he told Michael Watts. "I musta hypnotized myself 'cos I went right up fast ... I was only doing about thirty miles an hour. I ran up on an island. I was just tired." During the long layoff while his ankles were encased in casts, Davis tried to deal lightly with the accident. "I'm all right," he told one reporter. "I'll just have to stop buying those little cars."[36] And to another he said, "I fucked the car up, but it wasn't a mess. I got a new one. A Ferrari."[37] He was immobilized for two and a half months, and when he returned to playing he still had to hoist himself around on crutches with the ankles swathed in walking casts. More serious in the long run were the strain that the casts placed on his deteriorating hip joint and the debilitating effect on his general health of the enforced inactivity.

While he was sitting idle, the jazz periodicals published their year-end poll results for 1972, and Davis, coming off a year in which he was largely inactive in the first four months and completely inactive in the last two, with only a controversial LP and concerts by an untried band in between, fared poorly. The *Down Beat* poll of international critics placed his band fourth, after the Dixieland collective called the World's Greatest Jazz Band, Ornette Coleman, and the Modern Jazz Quartet. *Down Beat*'s readers' poll showed his band seventh; the top three places went to bands spawned by Davis's fusion experiments of 1969–70: Weather Report, John McLaughlin's Mahavishnu, and Chick Corea, and the next three were the MJQ, McCoy Tyner, and the World's Greatest Jazz Band. *On the Corner* was left off all the lists of new albums, although *Jazz Journal* listed two Prestige twofers of Davis's 1954–6 music (seventh and eighth) among the best reissues. Most telling was his fall from grace among the trumpeters, possibly his worst showing in twenty-five years. The *Down Beat* critics placed him fifth, after Dizzy Gillespie, Clark Terry, Don Cherry, and Roy Eldridge; the *Down Beat* readers made him a distant second behind Freddie Hubbard.

The *Down Beat* editorial accompanying the readers' poll results noted Davis's poor showing and commented: "It's Miles who opened the door for most of these younger players [who supplanted him]." If that was intended to console Davis by putting him in the role of patriarch, Davis soon showed that he was feeling anything but patriarchal toward his former protégés. In interviews, he unloaded venomous views. Of Hubbard, his replacement not only in the top spot in the readers' poll but also at Newport in New York, he said, "He don't have no ideas and no talent. All he does is run up and down the scales. I used to teach Freddie ... Man, he doesn't have any imagination. If you don't have no imagination, then you don't have no talent, right?"[38] Of Weather Report, he concluded, simply, "Foggy. It's foggy." Wayne Shorter, so long his right-hand man, was blasted gratuitously for what seemed to be sexual rather than musical misdemeanors. "He fell in love, man," Davis told Jimmy Saunders in *Playboy*. "He started playing pretty, syrupy music. Ain't no fire there no more ... You can't come, then fight or play. You can't do it. *I* don't. When I get ready to come, I come [laughs]. But I do not come and play." Of Josef Zawinul, who had complained that his contribution to Davis's early fusion music remained largely unacknowledged, Davis said, "Zawinul is like Sly and Mingus. They write things and they fall in love with them. You know what I mean? I don't write things for myself. I write for my band. When you write things for yourself, your ego takes over."[39] Herbie Hancock, who remained in closer contact with Davis than most of the others, almost escaped Davis's venom altogther. "Herbie tries to be too intellectual," Davis told Gregg Hall for *Down Beat*. "He needs to be edited." And then he added, "But he's the only one out there."[40]

The younger players were not the only ones to feel Davis's bitter mood. He had unloaded on Dizzy Gillespie and Sarah Vaughan in his defence of his cancellation at Newport, and now he maligned Max Roach, whom he would describe a few years later as "my best friend." "When I was with Bird," he told Michael Watts, "Fats Navarro used to say I played too fast all the time, but I couldn't swing with Max Roach 'cos he couldn't swing."[41] As an attempt to revise the history of bebop, the comment is simply ludicrous.

It was probably during the enforced idleness following his accident that Davis recorded *Red China Blues*, one of the anomalies of his recorded works. A conventional down-home blues gussied up with riffs by a brass section, *Red China Blues* is devoid of the imprint of Davis. It appears to be an attempt to break into the middle-of-the-road music market served by FM-radio. The details are as follows:

Miles Davis Ensemble: Get Up with It
Miles Davis, el tpt; unidentified brass section arranged by Wade Marcus; Wally Chambers, harmonica; Cornell Dupree, gtr; Michael Henderson, b; Al Foster,

Bernard Purdee, dms; James Mtume Foreman, congas; rhythm arranged by
Billy Jackson. New York, possibly early 1973
Red China Blues
(on Columbia C 33238)
The date is controversial; Priestley lists it as "possibly January 1973," Ruppli
as "June 1974." An excerpt was released on 45 rpm (3-10110) backed by an
excerpt from *Maiysha* (recorded 19 June 1974).

The dominant sound comes from the amplified harmonica; Davis
contributes only a few notes, mixed into the background. Horace Silver,
on hearing the piece in a blindfold test with Leonard Feather, simply
said, "It ain't my particular cup of tea, to tell the truth. I wouldn't
venture forth to buy it. I doubt if it was given to me that I'd play it." So
alien was its sound from anything Silver recognized that he mistakenly
took it to be part of Davis's new direction, and he was willing to be
charitable under the circumstances: "We all have to open our minds,
stretch forth, take chances and venture out musically to try to arrive at
something new and different, and he's doing it – and I give him credit for
that."[42] But *Red China Blues* stands apart from Davis's music in this
period or any other. Far from being venturesome or new or different, it is
just a blatant attempt to win friends, something Davis otherwise never
felt impelled to do in his music. It lacks all conviction.

In January 1973, Davis re-formed his band with Dave Liebman on
reeds and flutes for a new round of concerts. The reviews were
devastating. In Montreal on 24 January, John Orysik called it "a most
unusual concert": "The percussion section, Mtume in particular, was
the only highlight. Miles distorted everything he played and I couldn't
hear Dave Liebman for the overamplification of the other instruments.
Most distressing to hear Miles, I wish I'd stayed home."[43] The concert
was sold out, and so were two concerts on 28 January at the Guthrie
Theatre in Minneapolis, but the reviews from Minneapolis were even
worse. "The critics' views were unanimous – Davis stunk up the joint!"
Ron Johnson reported in *Coda*. "The sound was loud, almost cacophony, and there were just very few occasional approaches to jazz
music. It was probably the worst jazz concert in Guthrie history."[44]

On returning to New York, Davis took his band into the recording
studio for rehearsals, with producers and engineers present and tape
running. They spent all day on 13 February in the studio and probably
other days around the same time, but so far none of the music has been
issued. Dave Liebman described the process: "We go into the recording

studio there's no, like, take one. Light goes on, they miss it [the beginning], they miss it. [Davis] is aware of the light, but it's, you know, no cutting, no outtakes, nothing like that. Just play. Rehearse on tape." The extra hours of exposure to one another were absolutely crucial to the band members because of the way Davis was letting the music evolve. "I mean there *are* some melodies," Liebman confessed, "and they're made up on the gig and after a few nights we play the same thing and I say, 'All right, that's a new melody, I got to get something that goes with it.' It's totally improvised and loose."[45]

Davis again ran afoul of the law. He was arrested early in the morning of 23 February and charged with possession of cocaine and a .25-caliber automatic pistol. Davis and an unidentified woman were apparently trying to arouse someone in his house to let them in when neighbors called the police to investigate the commotion. Police found a purse thrown behind a bush containing three packets of cocaine and the loaded pistol. Davis spent the night in jail and was charged in the morning. On 1 March, he was fined $1,000 for possession of a deadly weapon, but the cocaine charge was dropped for insufficient evidence.

After all the run-ins, several offices of the New York Police Department had files on Davis. His home address and his automobile license plates appeared on the police blotter often enough that few narcotics officers or patrolmen needed special instructions on receiving a late-night complaint.

Davis's Ferrari was temporarily inactive because of the walking casts he wore, but otherwise his driving attracted police attention regularly. "I did that shit once in front of a brother; I did one of those things that only a Ferrari can do," Davis told David Breskin. "He stopped me and said, 'God*damn*, Miles, why do you do that shit?' I said, 'What would *you* do if you had this motherfucker?' And he said, 'Okay, go ahead.'"

"The white cops, they all know me by now," he added. "Mother-fuckers say, 'Oh, that's just *him*.'"[46] On their house calls, the police entered the dim sanctum of the brownstone to find the once-stylish decor going to seed. Davis admitted three interviewers—Harriet Choice, Sy Johnson, and Michael Watts—to his home, and all of them described the music blaring from the speaker system, television sets flickering in dark corners, and pieces of the expensive wardrobe strewn about. He complained to the interviewers that he felt isolated and alone—"Dizzy asks me to teach him. I say, 'Yeah, come by' ... And he don't come by"—but he seemed to be surrounded by people and activity. His gofers, male or female, emerged at the first hoarse shout, on call night and day to give him a rubdown or run an errand. He spent hours on the telephone, calling his sister and his acquaintances on the slightest pretext, often playing them tapes by long distance. Once he carried a tape to Sly Stone's apartment that he thought Stone should hear. "I took a gun over there one day and put it right to his head," Davis told Gregg Hall. "I said, 'Man, sit down, we *will* listen to this!'" And then he laughed and added, "Of course there were no bullets in it."[47]

Davis's life seemed more orderly when he was on the road, ensconced in hotel suites. He made another personnel change in his band for a pair of concerts in western Canada, in Edmonton on 29 March and Calgary on 1 April 1973. He replaced Cedric Lawson on keyboards with Lonnie Liston Smith, who had played keyboards for him on the recording of *Ife* almost a year before, but instead of transporting the Fender-Rhodes electric piano, Davis took along a Yamaha organ for Liston to play. The rest of the band remained intact, with Liebman, Reggie Lucas, Balakrishna, Henderson, Foster, Mtume, and Badal Roy.

It was a rare occurrence for Davis's concerts during this period to find a sympathetic reviewer, but *Coda* magazine assigned the task to Eugene Chadbourne, the free-form guitarist then based in Calgary. Chadbourne approached Davis's new music with an open mind, much as he approached his own spontaneous performances, and filed a report far removed from the perfunctory dismissal accorded to Davis by most reviewers at the time. His account is one of the few that capture in prose the elements that Davis was unabashedly promulgating.[48]

Chadbourne duly noted the disaffection of most of the audience, from Davis's older fans – one of whom spent the intermission yelling, "Where's Dizzy?" – to the rock fans who did not return after intermission. But Chadbourne waxed enthusiastically about the percussive elements that were driving others away. "As far as percussion sections go," he said, "this is IT. The blending of congas and tablas, with Al Foster's rough-and-ready, runaround drumming in back of it, has to be one of the most inspiring sound arrangements Miles has come up with ... Everything is rhythm! The electric guitar chops away, often sounding like an African log drum. Henderson's bass work is percussive, often resembling the sound of a wet finger rubbed against the top of a conga drum. The organ fills up any spaces in the music like hot, melted wax poured onto cheesecloth. The music has been called amelodic, and it might be – but somehow you find yourself humming along to it. Sound, pure sound and sensation, are the main components." He compared Davis as an innovator with the Art Ensemble of Chicago and Ornette

Coleman, noting that his music now had similar "aspects," but he added that "it is still Miles' thing, an approach to sound that no one has attempted before."

Noting that Liebman seemed to have difficulty finding space for himself in the ensemble, as other critics would also note, Chadbourne sought an explanation from Liebman. "You don't get the same feedback, with the rhythm responding to everything you do," Liebman told him. "You are sort of playing *over* it, almost beside the point. Like a vocalist singing over a bunch of horns. It's really a pattern behind you." Chadbourne contrasted Liebman's and Davis's voices in the ensemble this way: "Whenever Miles played, the music was not a pattern at all — there was response, encouragement from the group, and small, subtle examples of give-and-take. But with Liebman — nothing. His winding, sonorous sax warbled over a glass wall." Chadbourne's own explanation for the problems Davis's reedmen were having was that "this music may be so personal to Miles that no one else can find his own voice in it."

Davis himself seemed to be enjoying the performance immensely, notwithstanding the fetters that remained from his automobile accident more than five months earlier. Chadbourne described him "hobbling around on a walking cast with two shiny metal crutches, sitting on a high black stool, his feet surrounded with mute, wah-wah pedal, a hundred different wires ... Constantly signalling, conducting, cueing, waving his crutches around like grotesque batons."

Chadbourne also offered an insight into the critical and popular outrage that so often greeted Davis's music. "If you don't like Miles," he said, "you'll hate this new music, because his career can be summed up as a struggle to tone down his arrogance into terms an audience can feel comfortable with. His new music is pure arrogance. It's like coming home and finding Miles there, his fancy feet up on your favorite chair."

Lonnie Liston Smith's tenure with Davis's working band began and ended with this brief western tour. Although he was a veteran member of bands such as Art Blakey's and Rahsaan Roland Kirk's, Smith had trouble fitting into Davis's ensemble. At the concerts, Chadbourne noted, "Several times Miles, perhaps dissatisfied at the sound of the organ, limped over to the instrument to demonstrate what he wanted." Smith's problems were not unexpected, because he was, in effect, learning to play his instrument on the bandstand. When Davis called to offer him the job, Smith assumed that he would be playing electric piano. "[I] haven't played the organ since college," he told Chadbourne, in an interview published in *Coda* nine months after the concert, "and there is a wah-wah pedal, and this thing, it isn't exactly a moog but it's like one, and I've never used any of that stuff either. So it's all new."

Smith's job was made all the more difficult because Davis's ideas about what he wanted from the organ, as well as from the electric piano, were so specific by now that only Davis himself could supply them. After trying Smith, Davis stopped carrying a keyboard player in the band, and he spent as much of his performances playing keyboards as trumpet.

Smith remained undaunted. "It's a gas playing with Miles," he said. "The first thing I realized was, he's really serious about this stuff! That knocked me out, the way he's really into it. I heard him on that wah-wah pedal doing some amazing things, and I thought, well, I'll try that too. We can still all learn from Miles, that's what I mean. He's a master. Other people are growing – we are all growing – we'll be the Tranes and the Birds and the Miles of the future, but he's it right now."[49] A few years later, Gregg Hall passed along some of Smith's flattering remarks to Davis, and Davis said, "Oh yeah, I taught him a lot of shit."[50]

Smith left the band at the same time as the exotic percussionists Balakrishna and Roy, and Davis added a rhythm guitarist, Pete Cosey, to the band. Cosey, a stolid, Buddha-like figure, sat almost motionless on the stage during Davis's performances for the next two years, strumming out chords that melded into the rhythmic bottom of the music. The percussion elements grew even denser.

Davis had been playing keyboard instruments in the recording studio for some time and had occasionally played them in performances even when he carried a keyboard player in the band. Now, he became the band's only keyboard player. "Well, I only play to get the idea how it's supposed to go but it always turns out that my piano playing – I hate that word 'better' but it brings out the band, and doesn't clutter too much either," he told Michael Watts. "When I play piano in my band, they swing. When my piano player plays they swing sometimes but they don't swing all the time. I don't worry about anything 'cos I have Reggie [Lucas], y'know, the rhythm swings, but you have to watch a musician and anticipate it."[51] About his organ playing, he was more modest. "I can't play it the way I want it," he told Sy Johnson. "I know guys who can show their technique and all that stuff. I just play it for Dave [Liebman, when he is soloing] and difficult little sounds and shit. Reggie can play the same things [on guitar] that I can play. I taught him to make the same sounds."[52]

Davis's critics were aware of his limitations as an organist. "About the best thing that one can say about Miles's organ playing is that sometimes it works out like a delicate Japanese wash," Mark Zanger commented. "At its worst it sounds like daytime TV. Miles on organ reveals what most great instrumentalists reveal on secondary instruments: intellectual concepts stripped of the technique that would grab one emotionally."[53]

The attention to keyboards shifted Davis's attention even further from the trumpet, which he had been playing much less in concerts and on recordings both in the sense that he used it less frequently and that when he did use it he played very few notes. Woody Shaw, a forceful young trumpeter just reaching maturity as a jazz soloist in the early 1970s, speculated: "He's a little older now, and I guess he's sort of tired of blowing his lips away, which you do on trumpet."[54] Others, Davis among them, saw the sparse trumpet calls as a response to the "pure sound and sensation" aesthetic of his music. Charles Fox commented that Davis's "cluster of notes ... struck the ear like separate images, the conception pointilliste instead of linear."[55] Liebman agreed that Davis's parsimony was the best method for coping with the rhythms. "Using short rhythms, playing one note, dit-dit, and letting them [the rhythm section] have it," Liebman explained, was one of the lessons he was learning from Davis. "When the rhythm section is happening, he hardly plays. He'll play the least and yet most. Also, it's not quite stage presence, but it's a way of drawing the powers that are up there and dispersing them ... It's a much more compositional thing than I had thought of. Where is it going? It's not just going to the end of the tune because there's no such thing as that any more."[56]

The first public appearances of the reorganized band took place in California. They played in Los Angeles at the Dorothy Chandler Pavilion as part of a week-long program sponsored by Columbia Records to promote the breaking down of barriers between musical categories. Clive Davis was behind it, and his enthusiasm for a project so close to Miles Davis's expressed wish suggests again that the two men were listening to one another. Columbia assembled its artists from different genres in threes for the concerts, with the profits turned over to charity. The night before Davis appeared, McLaughlin's Mahavishnu Orchestra had shared the stage with Loudon Wainwright III, a folk-cum-novelty singer, and Anthony Newman, from classical music. Davis's band appeared alongside Earth, Wind and Fire, a rock band, and Ramsey Lewis, the pianist.

Davis's California tour also included concerts at the Santa Monica Auditorium and back in Los Angeles at the Shrine Auditorium, with Nina Simone sharing the bill. A ten-minute segment of one of these concerts was filmed for a television–FM radio simulcast on a public network series called "Midnight Special." The film clip opens abruptly with a rollicking rhythm sequence and follows the musicians in their detached machinations through two mood changes as the concert ends. Compared with conventional clips in the series, Davis's band seem to be engrossed in surrealistic music-making.

Davis spent much of the second half of 1973 playing in Europe on two separate tours, his first since October 1971 because of his health. Although he had resumed touring, he still suffered from various ailments. He wheezed slightly from the nodes on his larynx which had grown back – they had probably never been completely removed – since the operation that inadvertently altered his voice in 1956; he suffered from stomach aches and occasional vomiting from an ulcer, which was especially aggravated by liquor; and he still walked stiffly because of the arthritic hip, which had grown much more painful after the strain of wearing casts on his ankles.

The first tour, in July, took him on a round of jazz festivals in Pescara and Verona, Italy, and Montreux, Switzerland, and to London for a concert at the Rainbow. Ron Brown, reviewing the London concert for *Jazz Journal*, saw some advances in the way Davis had unified his young band: "He's managed to whip his line-up ... into an exciting, swirling rhythmic unit, as recognizable as a Miles Davis 'sound' as were the quintets with Coltrane and Shorter." But Brown, like most other reviewers, regretted Davis's almost complete withdrawal from soloing. "The amazing and almost heart-breaking crunch lies in the fact that Miles himself hardly plays at all," he said. "He spits a strangled bleep into the action every couple of minutes, and we're left with an efficient backdrop with nothing to back up." The result, he said, was "a Miles Davis concert that had everything but a substantial helping of Miles Davis."[57]

Before returning to Europe in the fall, Davis and his band again spent several hours in the recording studios. On at least one of these sessions, Davis did not show up at all. After everyone else was assembled and set up, ready to play, he phoned Teo Macero to tell him he would not be coming, and Macero got Davis's permission to tape some music by the sidemen, with Liebman on flute. Liebman began leading the band through something he calls *Slow Vamp* when Macero interrupted them with the message, "Miles says play a lot. Do something." He had apparently been listening on the telephone from the control booth and decided to let the band add more hours to Columbia's huge accumulation of his music, even in his absence. Asked by a reporter whether he had played well on the occasion, Liebman said, "It was *out*, y'know, but I don't know. Miles got it. I'll hear it. It was out. It could be good, it may have come out great. I don't know."[58] So far nothing has been released under the title *Slow Vamp*, and none of Davis's releases credits Liebman as composer, but parts of the session may turn up spliced into other titles – may already have turned up – in the cut-and-paste process.

Liebman's flute is heard fairly prominently on a track called *Calypso Frelimo*, which fills one side of the *Get Up with It* LP almost to overflowing. At thirty-two minutes, it runs very close to the limits of microgroove technology. The details are as follows:

Miles Davis Ensemble: Get Up with It
Miles Davis, tpt, org, pno; Dave Liebman, flt; John Stobblefield, ss; Pete Cosey, Reggie Lucas, gtr; Michael Henderson, b; Al Foster, dms; James Mtume Foreman, conga. New York, possibly September 1973
Calypso Frelimo
(on Columbia C 33238)
Two sides of a 45-rpm single (4-45946), *Big Fun* and *Holly-Wood*, were recorded in September 1973, possibly at the same sessions as *Calypso Frelimo*; the excerpt *Big Fun* is not related to the music on the LP *Big Fun* (Columbia PG 32866), although both were released in early 1974.

Calypso Frelimo is divided into three parts. It opens as a frantic exercise for the rhythm team, with Davis on electric trumpet, Liebman on flute, Davis again, and Stobblefield on soprano saxophone taking turns playing above the wall of rhythm. Then the rhythm stops abruptly after Stobblefield's contribution (the only time he is heard) and resolves into an eerie stasis, the only motion at the beginning supplied by a recurring bass riff; as the rhythm players re-enter one by one, Liebman's flute and Davis's trumpet again take turns playing above them. Then the rhythm rises again, making a long crescendo back to the frantic pace of the opening. The only unifying element is a two-bar calypso phrase stated by Davis on organ near the beginning of each of the three parts and heard at unpredictable intervals throughout. Davis's organ and trumpet overlap in several places, indicating overdubbing, and the whole piece was probably composed in the editing room.

As a composition, *Calypso Frelimo* simply seems disjointed. The calypso phrase is too sporadic to give the listener a focal point, and probably too insignificant for that in such a long exposition. Yet Davis apparently pinned his hopes on this track making a breakthrough. "My next thing, *Calypso*, will set a new direction," he told Gregg Hall in 1974. "The entire record will be one track."[59] He changed his mind, or was talked into changing it, about filling both sides of an LP with it – surely he was not considering filling four sides with it, although most of his LPS were now twofers – and even as an overlong single side its rudimentary melody and one-chord harmony are spread thin.

The return trip to Europe lasted three weeks and sent Davis and his band on a taxing itinerary to Malmo (24 October), Stockholm (27), Copenhagen (29), Berlin (1 November), Bologna (10), and Paris (15), with two concerts in many of the cities. Davis was in excruciating pain from his hip, and it was probably near the beginning of this tour, perhaps in Malmo or Stockholm, that he received an injection of morphine to kill the pain. Davis told Cheryl McCall: "A doctor told me in Sweden – *he shot me right in the leg* – he said I know how many girls want to come over here and give you a *shot*. I said fuck that if I don't feel better. He said tomorrow you'll feel better, or the next day."[60] Davis continued the tour feeling more comfortable than he had for a long time, but he began to rely on more injections to keep going. The pain-relieving benefit of morphine exacts a well-known price from the user, not only because it induces a dependency, as do all products of the poppy seed, but also because it dulls the sensation of pain without altering the cause of the pain in any way. When Davis collapsed in 1975, he blamed the morphine for preventing him from realizing how far his health had declined.

The year-end poll results for 1973 again revealed that Davis was losing his grip on the segment of the audience that bothered to vote. *Down Beat*'s critics' poll named Dizzy Gillespie top trumpeter and Jon Faddis, a 20-year-old very much in Gillespie's mold, top new trumpeter. The readers' poll named Freddie Hubbard, for the second year in a row, ahead of Davis. For Davis, that result may have seemed especially ominous because Columbia had just signed Hubbard to a long-term contract. Hubbard certainly saw it that way and so, according to him, did Columbia's executives. "When I first went there in 1973," Hubbard told Steve Bloom, "this is what they told me: 'We're gonna make you the number one trumpet player at Columbia because Miles isn't playing.'"[61] Hubbard made eight albums for Columbia in the next seven years and then moved to Fantasy Records.

If Davis felt any pressure from Columbia's hiring of Hubbard or his poor notices, he did nothing to alter the course of his music or his influences. He listened to Stockhausen, but more often he listened to black pop performers. Harriet Choice entered his inner sanctum for an interview and spent most of her time studying the decor – "Miles' records, plaques, art, trinkets, various musical instruments, and huge plastic plants" – while Davis wailed away on a drum set to a loud James Brown tape that repeated over and over again. Davis wore a black patch over his eye but the co-habitants of his house, two young women named Loretta and Ruby, assured Choice that there was nothing wrong with his eye. "He just likes to wear the patch sometimes. He's got a bunch of different ones," Ruby shouted over the din of the drums.[62]

The influence of Stockhausen, as Davis finally assimilated it, showed more in his approach than in his technique or composing. Certainly Stockhausen's influence is felt more directly in the work of younger jazz musicians, especially Anthony Braxton and the later work of Keith Jarrett. For Davis, two years older than Stockhausen, the German composer's example seems mainly to have reinforced his conviction that conventional form – the beginning, middle, and end prescribed by Aristotle – is an artificial limitation. Stockhausen has expounded a theory of "process compositions," the basic notion that "what one hears in music is only an excerpt, what I call a window, in an unlimited time." He derided conventional form, the converse of process composition, in an interview with John Diliberto: "Though sometimes a composer is pounding on the table like Beethoven at the beginning of the *Fifth Symphony* and gives the impression of 'Now I start,' or when they hit the last two chords five times or more to say, 'Now I really stop, are you aware of this?,' still this is fake because he could have started before and he could've gone on if he had wanted to because the basic truth in every spirit is that there is nothing like limited time. To present a work of art with a particular beginning and end, and to reinforce the impression is only an illusion. It is one proposition of an excerpt of time, the timeless time."[63]

Davis shared that basic concept and had incorporated it years earlier into records that splice tapes made months or even years apart and concert performances that move imperceptibly from one musical nonsequitur to another. Encouraged by Stockhausen's example, he now declared: "I'm through with playing from eight bars to eight bars. I always write in a circle. I never end a song. It just keeps going. The public likes starts, confusions, and happy endings."[64] But the elements of their music could hardly have less in common. For Stockhausen they are symphonic components filtered through acoustic devices, and 'found' sounds such as short-wave bands. For Davis they are the trappings of black pop music, arranged densely and amplified deafeningly.

"You know what he listens to at home, man?" Liebman asked an interviewer. "You think he listens to what those traditionalists always hounding him to listen to, classical, even *jazz*? Shit, he's into the same kind of stuff guys our age are into – rock and roll, man, whatever, Sly, James Brown, Hendrix, *music*, man. He absorbs what is around. He *is* what's happening."[65]

Davis seemed inclined to agree. "I'm 48 but so what?" he told Jimmy Saunders. "Am I supposed to stop growing?" To Harriet Choice he said: "I'm never into anything *new*. What's the evolution? In music, you take out what you don't like any more, and what's left is what you like. And you've got to keep doing that." He was willing even to recall his early development to point out how it matched his current temper. "I looked at all the other trumpet players, the way they held their horns, the way they fingered the horn," he said. "And I paid attention to how each would play a different phrase. Seventeen different trumpet players are going to play the same phrase seventeen different ways. You've got to eliminate some of it. But you've got to see all the possibilities."[66]

This process of elimination threatened to resolve into nothing at all. He claimed that he was working toward performances in which nothing happened. "We might get up there and just hold hands," he said. "We have rehearsals, like a five-hour rehearsal of nonreaction ... Like, if I say, 'Ba-bop-ba-ba-ba,' you don't say, 'Bop.' You don't do that. You don't say nothing."[67] And again, "Yes only means something after you've said no. We had a five-hour rehearsal one day, and I gave the band a certain rhythm and told them to stay there. Not to react. To let me do all that. Afterwards, they said, 'Thanks, Miles.'"[68] Liebman was apparently describing one such rehearsal when he said, "Even playing E^b for four hours, which is what we did most of the time, even within the context of that very limited area and beat, and four guitars and an amazing amount of sound – even within that I was able to discern the subtleties of Miles's playing."[69] And what of the other band members? Liebman said nothing, but Davis said, "My ego only needs a good rhythm section. I mean, my band now, man, they have so much fine energy and I got to bring it out of them or it don't work."[70]

As for jazz, Davis no longer liked even to hear the word, which he considered racist. "It's a white man's word," he told Hubert Saal in

Newsweek.[71] So, in his view, was almost every other word that had been applied to a musical category. "I don't play rock. Rock is a white word," he railed. "And I don't like the word jazz because *jazz* is a nigger word that white folks dropped on us. We just play *Black.* We play what the day recommends ... You don't play 1955 music or that straight crap like *My Funny Valentine.*" When Harriet Choice asked him about playing jazz, he scoffed, "Don't use that word with me. That's an Uncle Tom word. Clues for white folks in theaters and the dine-and-dance places. They know what they're going to get, except with my band or Chick's or Herbie's. Otherwise it's the same old shit." Choice pointed out that his audience, and Hancock's and Corea's too, were largely white, whereas Sonny Stitt and Gene Ammons drew black audiences, but he just scoffed again. "They draw the pimps and all that shit," he said. "The young blacks don't have enough money to see Herbie and Chick. You gonna print that?"[72]

In the band's performances, the jazz elements became secondary, and accidental. "The jazz swing," Liebman told Gene Perla, "happens completely spontaneously. None of our songs are planned that way. There are a few times that it presents itself, mostly between Al and Michael, the bass and drums. Sometimes between Al and Mtume, like they'll kind of signal each other in a way and swing out. There have been a few times that they have been unbelievable, the lift that it gives to the music. Miles gets so excited he suddenly gets a whole different personality. He'll start to move around a lot. One time it happened we were playing a funky thing and suddenly it went into 4/4 double time. He took the mute out, threw it off the stage, and started burning eighth notes. It was incredible, really a lift." But it remained far from the core of Davis's music. "That doesn't seem to be near the main sound of the band," Liebman added, " and I think this is due largely to the people who are playing and the way Miles has picked these people to achieve the sound that he wants."[73]

The performances had turned into a process, with no pre-set sequences and few replicable patterns. Davis conducted the process with a kind of mephistophelian glee. "I could make the cats in my band play by just looking at them," he told Julie Coryell. "I'd look at them and not say anything. They'd wait and watch. Finally, I'd say, 'Mother-fucker, will you get down!'"[74] He no longer left the stage when the band were playing, but spent most of the evening at stage center, facing Foster's drum set, occasionally inclining his head or raising his hand, and sometimes sweeping his hand grandly to stop the rhythm dead. For the sidemen, the conducting style became an advanced test in interpreting body language. "He doesn't tell you how to play," Liebman explained. "I mean, he'll sometimes get very general, conceptual about it. He doesn't say, 'You gotta play the first bars with me, then skip four' – you know, like a *head* – no such thing. You gotta be able to *read* Miles. That's the thing. And that's one of the things he judges musicians on: the ability to translate what *Miles* wants ... Nothing is ever said. You know? It's totally physical movement. And sometimes not even overt physical movement, it's just a vibration you get if you study the man and if you're – you know – aware. That's all. With Miles, part of the playing is the watching. That's playing, you dig? You gotta know what's happening, and everybody does, all the people that are there."[75]

In spite of his waning health, Davis performed more frequently than he had for years, putting on display not only his latest transmutation of the music but also some new idiosyncrasies in his stage manner. At the end of 1973 he played a concert at Carnegie Hall; "he was forty minutes late, he spat on the stage a few times, and his trumpet, some said, was lost in the electrics," Choice reported.[76]

In January 1974, he embarked on a tour that would conclude with another concert at Carnegie Hall on 30 March. The first stop was supposed to be the Outremont Theatre in Montreal, but the concert was cancelled because, according to a rumor reported in *Coda*, he decided to attend the heavyweight championship bout between George Foreman and Joe Frazier that night.[77] So the first stop was Massey Hall in Toronto on 27 January. The reviewers, predictably by now, were torn between the power and conviction of the rhythms and the inscrutability of their succession. "Miles' attitude toward the world of listeners ... seems to say, 'Here it is. You need the music more than it needs you, so take it like it is or split,'" Alan Offstein wrote in *Coda*, and then he added, "Plenty of people did split from Massey Hall after the first set; however, a sizeable portion stayed on and dug the music of a still-reigning master of jazz."[78] In the *Toronto Star* Peter Goddard noted: "Davis kept his own contributions last night to a minimum of notes, even if they seemed to have been wrenched, screaming, from his electronically amplified trumpet ... Davis constantly goaded and coaxed his players last night, keeping his back turned on the audience much of the night."[79]

As at the Carnegie Hall concert the month before, he started about forty minutes late and projected a stream of spit toward the drums. The spitting, apparently an unconscious habit, was all the more noticeable because Davis removed his robin's-egg-blue cashmere jacket and placed it neatly beside the pedestal for Foster's drums, where it absorbed more than a little of his spit as the evening wore on.

From Toronto, the band traveled to Chicago for a 1 February concert, Davis first appearance there in three years, and to Minneapolis, where they played two concerts at the Tyrone Guthrie Theatre on 5 February. In San Francisco later in the month, they settled into the Keystone Korner for two weeks, playing a rare nightclub engagement. The sound level in the small club was deafening, but Ralph J. Gleason, for one, not only learned to live with it but found it the main source of strength in the music. "In a nightclub the sound completely surrounds you," he wrote in *Rolling Stone.* "The bass produces tones you can feel in the air around you and in the pit of your stomach. The synthesizer, the guitars, the wah-wah effects of Miles's trumpet, all combine to deluge you in sound from all corners of the room. But the bottom pulse, which is really at the same time a kind of melody of different tones, keeps the emotional feeling building and carrying you along so that at the end of a set you are emotionally exhausted but exhilarated, out of breath but not tired."[80]

Gleason's reaction was evidently shared by the Japanese producers of Davis's *Pangaea* LP, a 1975 performance with the same rhythm team, because they included on the liner this piece of advice: "We suggest that you play this record at highest possible volume in order to fully appreciate the sound of Miles Davis."

When the band returned to New York at the end of March for the closing Carnegie Hall concert, Davis's spittle was finally brought to his attention. Sy Johnson had attended the concert with Thad Jones, where they sat in the third row. "Thad got so upset that you kept spitting on the stage that he left," Johnson told Davis. "He kept saying, 'Miles shouldn't spit on stage at Carnegie Hall.' And finally he said, 'I'm sorry, Sy, but if he spits one more time I'm gonna have to go!' And you spit, and he went." Davis looked embarrassed and said, "Didn't he know I just got over pneumonia?"[81] But he brought the habit under control soon afterward.

The Carnegie Hall concert was recorded by Columbia and released in Japan on CBS-Sony in 1977 as *Dark Magus.* The performance is comparable in most respects to the other concerts from this tour (of which the Massey Hall concert is preserved in a low-fidelity tape in some private collections). The presentation at Carnegie Hall, described by Noë, began with the house lights on: "Musicians began setting up nonchalantly and Miles strolls on *ever* casually, making the whole thing look like a sound check. All of a sudden, without obvious reason, Miles starts to play, and the band follows with a wall of heavily larded rhythm. It seems he is trying to make it look as if it didn't matter when he started, it was all his whim." To that, Liebman responded, "It *is* his whim ... That's the thing! ... Miles can do that and have three thousand musicians follow him. Right? So what I learned in that respect from Miles was to be able to watch him and be on his case – which I am, 'cause I don't *play* a lot. I'm the only one in the band who doesn't do something all the time. Miles, when he's not doin' something, he's directing, so I'm the only cat that's standing there, keeping his cool. Sometimes I'll hear something to play. Or sometimes *he'll* call *me* in. In other words, my gig is to follow him."[82]

While this extraordinarily complex process was unfolding at Carnegie Hall, Davis auditioned two musicians who had never played with him. Whatever the intended effect on his music, in the end the impact was negligible. The music was already so dense, and the roles of the regular members, who had been together almost a year, were so tightly circumscribed, that a listener would hardly know that two extra players had been added to the ensemble. But Davis's audacity in adding them is the stuff that legends are built on. Liebman says, "What he was doing – which he often does at big kinda gigs like that – is change the shit up, by doing something totally out. Totally unexpected. I mean, we had been a band together on the road for a year ... And then, suddenly, a *live* date, New York city, Carnegie Hall, the cat pulls two cats who never even *saw* each other. I mean, you gotta say, 'Is the man mad or is he – he's either mad or extremely subtle.'"[83] The details are as follows:

Miles Davis Ensemble: Dark Magus
Miles Davis, tpt, org; Dave Liebman, ts, ss; Reggie Lucas, Pete Cosey, gtr; Michael Henderson, b; Al Foster, dms; James Mtume Foreman, perc. Carnegie Hall, New York, 30 March 1974
Moja; Wili
(both on CBS-Sony 40 AP 741-2)

Add Azar Lawrence, ts; Dominique Gaumont, gtr
Tatu [ends with *Calypso Frelimo*]; *NNE*
(both on CBS-Sony 40 AP 741-2)
Davis plays trumpet on *Moja* and trumpet and organ on the other titles.

This music is distinguished by a long ballad sequence introduced by Liebman and sustained by Lucas and Davis in the second half of *Moja*, and by a short blues by Davis near the end of *NNE*.

The unexpected guests, saxophonist Azar Lawrence and guitarist Dominique Gaumont, make their presences felt somewhat in *Tatu*, where Gaumont follows Lucas's solo with a long, nebulous passage muddied by heavy use of the fuzz-wah, and Lawrence skirmishes briefly with Liebman in a duet and then plays a choppy, disjointed solo. As Noë remarked, they "seemed to be following different orders than those the band were picking up on" – through no fault of their own, he might have added.

Azar Lawrence, who was just 20 when he auditioned at Carnegie Hall, was the most highly regarded young saxophonist around. From Los Angeles, he arrived in New York the year before to join Elvin Jones's band when Liebman left it for Davis's, but he switched to McCoy Tyner's quartet a few weeks later and was still playing with that band when he appeared with Davis. *Esquire* magazine, in an article profiling the young people it considered to be future leaders in business, law, and the arts, had singled out Lawrence as the rising star in jazz just before his audition. That early promise remains largely unfulfilled; after his Carnegie Hall audition, Lawrence returned to Tyner's band for a while, and he occasionally played as a competent sideman, but seldom as a leader, since then.

If Davis was hoping to rouse Liebman's competitive instinct by bringing Lawrence onstage, he certainly succeeded. "Azar Lawrence played with Miles for the first time at this concert, and Miles didn't keep him for one minute longer," his fellow auditioner, Gaumont, said, and he added, "Liebman, on the other hand, took care of himself very well; he was very attentive."

Gaumont himself, though the recorded evidence scarcely suggests that he fared any better, was hired and stayed with the band for the rest of the year, apart from a brief return to his home in Paris. He harbored no illusions about Davis's motive for bringing him onstage, because he was completely unknown to jazz audiences not only in America but also in France. "Miles had no need of me," he admitted, "but he wanted to make Lucas flip [*faire flipper Lucas*]."[84] Lucas, Gaumont says, wanted a raise, and Gaumont's presence was Davis's way of telling him that he was not indispensable.

For Gaumont, it seemed an unbelievable break. He had attended both of Davis's concerts at the Olympia Theatre in Paris just four months before and become star-struck. "That's the guy I'm going to play with," he told himself, and through a complex chain of acquaintances that started with Oliver Lake, the St. Louis reedman who, like many other free-form jazzmen at the time, was living in Paris, got an introduction to Pete Cosey, who in turn introduced him to Al Foster. Foster, whom Gaumont calls "truly *la crème* among men," took him in when he arrived in New York from Paris and twice played Davis a demonstration tape by Gaumont over the telephone. The tape had Gaumont playing with the Black Artists Group, a Paris coalition of St. Louis avant-garde players including Lester Bowie, Charles Bobo Shaw, and Lake. Davis was impressed enough to tell Foster to bring Gaumont over to meet him, and one week later he met him for the second time, on the Carnegie Hall stage. Gaumont had been in the United States exactly two weeks on the night of the concert. He was 18.

Gaumont attributes whatever success he had at his audition to his briefing at the Olympia concerts. "I had seen what Miles did in Paris at the two concerts I went to," he told an interviewer for *Jazz Hot*, "and since I'm a child of music I could play with them." Davis was no doubt attracted by Gaumont's rough approximations of Jimi Hendrix, his main influence. He had first heard Hendrix's records two years before he journeyed to the United States and the impact was greater than Davis's. He said, "After I discovered Hendrix at fifteen, I still had another year of school, but I spent the year in my basement practising the guitar like a madman."

More than anyone else, Gaumont exemplifies Davis's predilection for sidemen who were relatively unschooled and unsophisticated. "I teach my musicians," he told Gregg Hall. "I taught my drummer everything he knows about playing drums. I play drums myself. I'm teaching a young boy now that I have in the band. His name is Dominique. He's about nineteen and he's from Bahia. He's a baddd motherfucker. He's like Hendrix. I have to show him the different chords. You know, Hendrix never did learn any chords."[85] Though his tenure with Davis was short and, as we shall see, not always pleasant, Gaumont concedes that he learned a great deal. "It was Miles who helped me understand, when at the beginning I considered his methods less valid than Hendrix's," he said. "In playing with him, I learned the differences of phrasing, tempos, and silences."[86]

"So Miles had me on his hands," Gaumont said later. "Two days after the concert his office called me with a firm offer of employment and said they would arrange to get my working permit. We then went on a tour across the country. Every night was different ... That's how Miles is, never the same, he has such power."

In May, Columbia released the first new LP by Davis in eight months, and it pinned some hopes on the LP recouping some of the listeners who had passed up *On the Corner* and *In Concert*. It was called *Big Fun* (PG 32866), and it again featured Corky McCoy's cover caricatures, this time somewhat subdued. Each of its four sides was filled with a single composition recorded a few years earlier. The most recent music was *Ife* (recorded 12 June 1972), with three of the men in the current band (Henderson, Foster, Mtume) among its eleven players; the other sides were *Great Expectations* (19 November 1969), *Lonely Fire* (27 January 1970), and *Go Ahead John* (30 March 1970), with more recognizable names among the studio stock companies such as Wayne Shorter, Chick Corea, Herbie Hancock, and Josef Zawinul. The selection seemed a calculated move by Columbia to strengthen Davis's recent showings with his comparatively anonymous sidemen, but Teo Macero told Gregg Hall that he had been actively working on these releases for years. "*Big Fun* didn't just happen overnight," he said. "That thing has been brewing for a long time. There has been trial and error in the editing room, trial and error in the studio. There are a lot of things that have been done since then that haven't come out. But this one has been [produced] over a period of at least three years. Some of it went back – I was just looking at the sheet today – to 1969 ... Five years later, and I'm just now putting it together. I'm telling you, it's like a composition."[87]

Most reviewers, and also those listeners who were still paying attention, were relieved to discover its relatively lyrical bias, especially on *Great Expectations* (which turns into Zawinul's *Orange Lady*, unannounced, as its second half) and *Lonely Fire*, but the LP fell far short of Columbia's commercial expectations. Davis did not share those expectations at all. When Gregg Hall, interviewing him around the time of its release, told him that Columbia thought it would be "bigger than *Bitches Brew*," Davis, dumbfounded, replied, "How??? I did *Big Fun* years ago."[88]

Davis then told Hall about his expectations for *Calypso Frelimo*, the most recent music that he and Macero were working on, which he hoped would eventually come out as a whole LP. Sometime between then and its December release, Davis changed his mind about issuing so lengthy a version, and one factor in that decision was Davis's subsequent recording of another long composition that he was anxious to release as quickly as possible. The new piece was titled *He Loved Him Madly*, and it appeared on *Get Up with It* (Columbia KG 33236), the

December release, as an overlong single side, as did *Calypso Frelimo*; the remaining sides of the double album were filled out by the evocative *Rated X*, the jejune *Red China Blues*, the 1970 *Honky Tonk* with Keith Jarrett in the band, and some other short pieces.

He Loved Him Madly eulogized the death of Duke Ellington on 24 May 1974. Although Davis and Ellington had had very little personal contact – surprisingly little, considering that their careers among the leaders of jazz had overlapped for 25 years – Davis was deeply moved by Ellington's death, and within days he assembled his working band in the studio to record his memorial. The details are as follows:

Miles Davis Octet: Get Up with It
Miles Davis, tpt, org; Dave Liebman, flt; Reggie Lucas, Pete Cosey, Dominique Gaumont, gtr; Michael Henderson, b; Al Foster, dms; James Mtume Foreman, conga. New York, probably 27 May 1974
He Loved Him Madly
(on Columbia KG 33236)

There can be no doubt that this music is deeply felt. Whether it succeeds in matching the feelings to the man whose death evoked them is a separate question, and one that would be debated hotly. It is a dirge, carried by long, motionless organ chords, with occasional drum rolls as punctuation and long, spacey interludes by guitar, flute, and trumpet that add color to the organ drone without distracting the listener from it. The organ dominates, although it seems more appropriate as a background for a spoken elegy or perhaps for a musical allusion to Ellington's style. The anticipation that something will arise to fill the empty foreground is the listener's main response on the first listening, but the foreknowledge that it never comes affects further listenings. *He Loved Him Madly* thus reduces to a passionately understated individual response to Ellington's death. At that level, it is articulate enough, even affecting, but as a composition it is too monochromatic to justify its half-hour length.

If Davis misjudged the length, he nevertheless fully intended it to be nothing more or less than the highly personal, almost private, statement of his feelings that it is. His original title for it was *He Loved Us Madly*, according to Sy Johnson, and that title obviously designates Ellington. The published title, *He Loved Him Madly*, connotes Ellington but designates Davis, a subtle shift of emphasis that is more appropriate for the music.

In spite of its apparent simplicity, the elegy aroused Davis to revive his arranging skills, which had not only been set aside but had become antithetical to his music since 1971. "We really rehearsed!" Gaumont reported. "Miles sat at the piano and showed Al and me the melodic line of *He Loved Him Madly*." But Gaumont was not convinced by the result. "It's not my favorite," he added; "I find it's the sort of thing you listen to only once."[89]

Sy Johnson was scheduled to interview Davis on the morning of the recording, but when the interview had to be postponed Macero suggested instead that Johnson drop into the studio for the end of the recording session. When he arrived, "the control room was full of thick Spanish funereal music and solemn men filling out w-4 forms ... Miles came out of the studio wearing a big jaunty hat, looking pinched and tired beneath it. He leaned on the console for a few minutes, lost in the music. Then, smiling wanly and touching a few hands, he slipped out the door." As Johnson listened to the playback, he noted that "the band sounded sure of itself on the slow, treacly tempo. I was sorry I hadn't seen them record it."[90]

Davis's elegy for Ellington pays homage to him not as a direct influence but as a man who followed his own star and enriched the jazz spectrum enormously. Although Ellington was easily the most honored and respected jazz figure of all, Davis felt that he did not receive his due. "The public completely ignored Duke," he told Julie Coryell. "He was a great man. I'd put him and Stravinsky in the same category. He was trying to teach everybody something."[91] When *Down Beat* solicited tributes from people all over the world to commemorate Ellington's death, Davis offered the one that has become the most widely quoted: "I think all the musicians in jazz should get together on a certain day and get down on their knees to thank Duke."[92] *He Loved Him Madly* attempts to transform that sentiment into music.

How well it succeeds became a minor controversy. Even Jérôme Reese, whose assessment of Davis's "electronic" music is seldom critical, notes that on *Get Up with It* Davis's "sonority tends to deteriorate," and from that he concludes that "Miles is fatigued and his 'personal problems' are becoming a handicap for his music."[93] Barry Tepperman, reviewing the LP for *Coda*, labeled it "identifiably personal, rhythmically involved background music, compressing the limitations of his [Davis's] horn to their ultimate closure, with absolutely nothing to project it into consciousness." As for *He Loved Him Madly*, Tepperman states: "The only vague interest in this bonsai album comes in an artistically absurd dedication 'For Duke'."[94] Poles apart, Burnett

James listed *Get Up with It* among the best records of 1975 in the year-end tabulation for *Jazz Journal*, specifically because *He Loved Him Madly* "remains the finest and most profound tribute in music yet paid to Duke."[95] That opinion fanned the flames that had been raging through *Jazz Journal*'s letters section, where readers had hotly expressed their opinions on the matter for the past months.

Ralph J. Gleason, writing in *Rolling Stone*, saw the controversy as a positive sign of Davis's integrity, which had occasionally been impugned on the evidence of *On the Corner* and *Red China Blues*. "The greatest single thing about Miles Davis is that he does not stand still," Gleason wrote. "He is forever being born. And like all his other artistic kin, as he changes, leaves behind one style or mode and enters another, he gains new adherents and loses old ones ... It is a tribute to artists like that when the pages of publications steam from the anger of thwarted fans. It is a measure of their artistic value and integrity."[96]

In August, Davis replaced Dave Liebman in the working band with Sonny Fortune, and while Fortune was finishing his commitment to the Buddy Rich orchestra he replaced Liebman on a recording session in June on one of the pieces that would fill out the *Get Up with It* LP. The details are as follows:

Miles Davis Ensemble: Get Up with It
Miles Davis, tpt, org; Sonny Fortune, flt; Reggie Lucas, Pete Cosey, Dominique Gaumont, gtr; Michael Henderson, b; Al Foster, dms; James Mtume Foreman, perc. New York, 19 June 1974
Maiysha
(on Columbia KG 33236)

Omit Fortune and Gaumont. 20 June 1974
Mtume
(on Columbia KG 33236)

Mtume is a rhythmic ramble with layered wah-wahs from trumpet, organ, lead guitar, and rhythm guitar; it settles into its bumptious groove early and keeps going for fifteen minutes, long enough to fill the left-over space on side 4 of *Get Up with It*.

Maiysha is more carefully made, and it became a fixture in the concert repertoire, one of the few fixed points that listeners could latch onto in the disorienting process of the live performances. Gaumont recalls, "It had no title until Miles met a woman named Maiysha. She was a real *conne.*"[97] The piece has two distinct and apparently unrelated parts: the first is a conventional samba, played softly and, in this studio performance, almost politely; the second is yet another rhythmic ramble, played loudly, with a whinnying guitar, probably Gaumont's, cantering above it. Even in the polite samba sequence, Fortune's flute, in its only turn, seems lost amid Davis's thick organ chords, which pose a challenge for any soloist; it is a challenge that Davis, when he picks up his trumpet, is spared, and perhaps one that he would have spared his reedmen if he had had to cope with it himself.

Both *Mtume* and *Maiysha* feature abrupt, momentary stops in the rhythm, a device first used, with extraordinary effect, on *Rated X*, also released on this LP. On the two new pieces, the stops seem otiose, and their frequency merely cheapens the dramatic effect, but within the limits of sonority and harmony in this rhythm band Davis apparently could find very few other options for relieving the music.

Onstage, the device was visually impressive. With congas beating, guitars wailing, and cymbals crashing, Davis would raise his finger and stop the commotion dead. Gene Williams, reviewing a concert in Washington, DC, in the fall, viewed Davis as a bwana leading his safari through "a dense electric rain forest": "Sensing a clearing, Davis extends his fingers in a signal and his group halts motionless as a soprano sax or electric guitar or even the leader's trumpet slips ahead alone, reporting what he sees. The leader listens, choosing a path. He arches his body, nodding his head to the desired pulse, beckoning the rhythm guitar, and his group falls in, resuming their journey. Echoing, reverberating electronically shaped notes and phrases form the strange beautiful foliage and strong life rhythms of Davis's musical world."[98] It was all in a night's work.

Davis took part of August off, his first complete break from recording and performing for over a year. Filling in time during the layoff, Sonny Fortune and Al Foster joined a quartet formed by bassist Buster Williams, with Onaje Allan Gumbs on piano, for a week-long engagement at Boomer's in New York. In the same period, Reggie Lucas assembled all the members of the working band except Davis for a recording session. "What cacophony!" Gaumont remarked. "We were obliged to face the fact that, without Miles, our getting together was totally useless."[99]

The busy schedule resumed in the fall with concerts at the Artpark in Lewiston, New York, and Washington, DC (September), club dates at the Bottom Line in New York (November) and the Troubador in Los

Angeles (December), and a tour of South America (November–December). Fortune had to adjust not only to the music he found himself playing but also to the audiences he faced. "The audience was mostly rock as opposed to jazz," he noted. "I've seen him [Davis] in two different settings. In the jazz situation he wasn't necessarily as visual as he was in the rock or fusion. For example, in the jazz situation, I remember Miles would play and walk off the stage after he had finished. But certainly when I was working with him in the band, he would never walk off the stage. The band was louder and Miles played fewer notes but whether all this was because of the rock setting or a matter of ifs, I can't say. Those things did happen but they may have more or less evolved to that."[100]

Gaumont was finding his adjustment difficult, but not because of the audiences. "I thought Henderson and Foster were fantastic," he said, "but when it came to playing the guitar, I told myself I could do better [than Lucas or Cosey]. I didn't even get the chance; there was too much vying for space among the guitarists. Still, it didn't stop Miles from keeping me on for a year. Miles had nothing to do with my leaving; I just couldn't transcend all the fuss. The guitarists would go and tell Miles that I couldn't play well, that I made them uncomfortable, when in fact I had done nothing. Well, they were wrong if they thought I was going to waste my talents by joining them in their pettiness."[101]

Gaumont quit several times, usually only for a few hours or a few days, but once more decisively. "It's for this reason that he kept me on for so long," he says. "I was the first person, me, the little French boy, to dare ask for a raise and then quit when it was refused. He was so surprised that he had his office send me a plane ticket in Paris to return."

In spite of the tension he felt onstage, Gaumont found his niche in the leader's affections. "In the group I was the *gamin*, the little foreigner," he says. "Miles called me 'the gypsy.'" Gaumont feels that the band eventually pulled together. "The last time we toured together, the band played really well, especially at the concerts in Brazil. It's too bad that tour wasn't recorded."[102]

Gaumont's last engagement was at the Troubador, at the end of the tour. Lee Underwood attended the opening night, with a crowd he describes as "a notorious bunch of cold-fish recording industry vinlypeddlers." Underwood was filled with anticipation because of what he had heard on the recently released *Get Up with It* LP, especially *Calypso Frelimo*, *He Loved Him Madly*, and *Rated X*. "Miles has reached a stage where he is concerned less with the *events* of sound (hummable melodies, standard phrases, standard structures, etc.) and more with the sound of sounds themselves," he reported in *Coda*. "He takes you into the dark and previously untouched places of your soul, opening a vast and relatively unexplored terrain of emotion." But not on this night. "He packed the Troubador his opening night, generated a tremendous amount of anticipatory excitement, but then went on to completely fizzle the gig ... Miles made no effort whatsoever to get across to them either musically or personally. Zero communication."[103]

Gaumont says, "Towards the end of the year, I was sick to death of all the pettiness that was going on and I left the u.s. depressed, at the beginning of 1975."[104] He blames his state of depression for his heroin addiction when he returned to Paris, and for leaving music for two years until 1978, when he formed a trio. He has been playing irregularly in France since then, trying diligently to make a fusion of the elements he learned from Davis and Hendrix.

For Davis, the year-end magazine polls again documented how he was losing his grip. *Down Beat* had honored him by dedicating its fortieth-anniversay issue in July to him, with Gregg Hall's interview and laudatory comments from sundry sources. But its readers' poll in December again ignored his current band and gave his former sidemen pride of place: Weather Report was named best group, and Davis's band showed a distant eighth, tied with Chuck Mangione's; Herbie Hancock was named Jazzman of the Year, with Davis sixth; and Weather Report's *Mysterious Traveler*, Keith Jarrett's *Solo Concerts*, and Hancock's *Headhunters* took the top three spots for LPs, with *Big Fun* a remote tenth. Only among the trumpeters did Davis make a good showing, placing second, again behind Freddie Hubbard. He could take some consolation, if he felt the need, from the fact that *Bitches Brew* had become a gold record during the year, with sales of 500,000 over four years, but even that was not unequivocal. *Headhunters*, a mélange of disco-funk, had done the same for Hancock within months of its release.

Davis found a more enthusiastic response early in the new year on a tour of Japan, his first in ten and a half years. Between 22 January and 8 February, he played fourteen concerts to capacity crowds in huge halls and won enthusiastic reviews. Keizo Takada praised his "magnificent and energetic band" and concluded: "Miles must be *the* genius of managing men and bringing out their hidden talent. He played his music with his band just as Duke Ellington did with his orchestra."[105] The two concerts at Osaka Festival Hall on 1 February were recorded and released as two double albums: *Agharta* appeared just six months later in Japan but waited another year for North American release; *Panagaea* came out in 1976 in Japan and has not yet been released elsewhere. The details are as follows:

Miles Davis Septet at Osaka Festival Hall
Miles Davis, tpt, org; Sonny Fortune, flt, ss, as; Pete Cosey, gtr, synthesizer, perc; Reggie Lucas, gtr; Michael Henderson, b; Al Foster, dms; James Mtume Foreman, perc. Osaka Festival Hall, Japan, 1 February 1975
Prelude; Maiysha; Theme from Jack Johnson; Interlude
(all on *Agharta*, CBS-Sony [Jap] SOPJ92–93, and Columbia PG 33967)
Priestley (1982) notes that *Theme from Jack Johnson* and *Interlude* are reversed on both label and liner of all issues. Fortune plays soprano on *Prelude*, alto on *Prelude* and *Jack Johnson*, and flute on *Maiysha, Jack Johnson,* and *Interlude.*

Zimbabwe 1 and 2; Gondwana 1 and 2
(all on *Panagaea*, CBS-Sony [Jap] SOPZ 96–97)
Fortune plays soprano on *Zimbabwe 2* and flute on *Gondwana 1*; he does not play on the other titles.

Although the music is from successive concerts on the same day, virtually nothing is repeated from one to the other. The quality also differs markedly, with *Agharta* vastly superior to *Pangaea*, and to most of Davis's music from this period.

Sonny Fortune takes a star turn on *Agharta*, especially in stating the samba theme on *Maiysha* and opening the *Theme from Jack Johnson* (side 3, not 4 as listed), where he plays flute and alto saxophone, respectively. On all his solos – six in all – the rhythm team seem much more responsive to him than they ever were to Liebman. Here, they support Fortune's improvisations in a manner much more similar to the rhythm section's traditional role in jazz. Then, inexplicably, Fortune virtually disappears during the second concert, taking only short turns at two points, and sounding careless.

The space created by Fortune's absence on *Pangaea* is filled by Pete Cosey, who finally gets a chance to extricate himself from the ensemble. He uses it advantageously, revealing a broader-based talent than he had otherwise shown. He closes *Gondwana 1* with a simple, thoughtful blues devoid of gimmickry, and his accompaniment of Davis's musing on *Gondwana 2* helps to make that sequence the high point of the concert; Cosey plays a delightful chiming figure behind Davis, and when Davis swings the tempo to 4/4, he reappears to play a jazz solo, his only one on record with Davis's band.

Agharta, in contrast, includes several high points in addition to Fortune's solos. Jazz buffs are likely to find *Prelude*, which covers one and a half sides, another wearying exercise in spinning out a two-chord theme, but *Maiysha*, immediately following it, gets the kind of treatment that might have done its namesake credit: it is tough and tender, and impossible to ignore. Best of all, for many reasons, is the *Theme from Jack Johnson*, which opens with Fortune's longest turn on his best horn, the alto, and after Lucas takes his turn swings into a shuffle beat built on Henderson's walking bass line and Cosey's non-psychedelic rhythm guitar. Henderson ends the long sequence playing the ostinato from *So What*. Davis makes a long, coherent statement on open trumpet that harks back to the days when he did it routinely. It is a treat, not for old times' sake but for the contrast it gives to the bristling, energetic context. Everything that precedes and follows it sounds fresher and brighter because of it.

On *Pangaea*, reviewer Howard Mandel observed, "Davis haunts its two sides like a spectre surveying the scorched earth."[106] On *Agharta*, he is the cooling element.

The wonder is not that Davis played hotly or coolly in Japan but that he played at all. He was suffering excruciating pain from his left hip, which had been operated on almost exactly ten years earlier. It now hurt him all the time, caused him to walk stiffly, and sometimes immobilized him when the femur slipped out of its socket. "I needed the operation," he told Cheryl McCall. "I was in Japan, and I was taking this codeine and morphine and didn't even know it [that he needed the operation]. They gave it to me to help my leg."[107]

Instead of slowing his pace, he had been working more frequently than he had in years, and covering more miles than he ever had. As soon as he returned from Japan, he continued the tour into the Midwest. As always, he acted in public as if nothing were wrong; the only clue to his deteriorating health showed in the lines around his eyes, and they were usually hidden, night and day, by dark glasses. The other clues were also hidden. Sy Johnson watched him painfully remove his right shoe and commented: "The bare foot is wheezed and old. I had the weird notion that Miles might be aging from the feet up." The cause of the pain was an open sore, "a dime-sized hole," on the middle toe, but Davis had been walking around all day apparently oblivious to the pain. "I realized," Johnson said, "that the medication for his hip and legs was probably so strong that he couldn't really feel his feet."[108] He was taking eight pills a day to kill the pain.

In public, all the pain was hidden behind his bravado. When he showed up for the first concert of the Midwestern tour at Northern Illinois University in DeKalb, he wore a maxi-length fur coat over his three-piece satin suit.[109] During the concert, he perched behind the organ and hardly touched his trumpet. Most of the audience had heard that he was playing more organ and less trumpet nowadays, but when he did the same the next night, at the Kiel Opera House in St. Louis, part of the audience suspected something was wrong, because he usually responded to his hometown crowd by burning some long trumpet choruses. He just could not find the strength. And as soon as he left the stage he collapsed, vomiting blood.

The next scheduled stop, at the Arie Crown Theater in Chicago on Easter Sunday, was played by Herbie Hancock and the Headhunters, with Bobbi Humphrey as the opening act. Hancock announced at the start that Davis was hospitalized in St. Louis with bleeding ulcers and invited the patrons to get refunds if they wished. According to one reviewer, "the audience didn't seem to care – or just had lost all faith in Davis and his perpetual excuses. To catcalls that Miles 'did it again,' the Sunday night concert got off to a bad start."

"I didn't even know I was sick from all this morphine and codeine until I got to St. Louis and I started throwing up blood," Davis said later, "and my *boys*, Dr. Weathers and a few friends of mine, they run the hospital, and they said, come on, and put me in the hospital ... You see, your liver gets fucked up, plus drinking, plus the pills – you throw up. And all that blood, it just sits in those little blood vessels down there."[110]

The bleeding ulcer was only the most obvious problem. The hip was a major one, but Davis chose to live with the pain rather than submit to surgery, which would keep him bed-ridden for weeks or even months. The nodes on his larynx impeded his breathing, especially when he slept, and he blamed them for making him winded when he played the trumpet and forcing him to cut short his solos. He entered a hospital in New York in April and had thirteen nodes removed.

His doctors were concerned about his use of analgesics and other drugs. After curing his heroin addiction in 1954 and leading bands in which he was sometimes the only musician not using drugs, the situation had reversed in the 1970s. "Drugs weren't important for the musicians in the band," Dominique Gaumont told his interviewer in

Jazz Hot, and then he added: "For Miles, drugs were perhaps important, you wouldn't be wrong in thinking that. In any case, I balance Miles out in all that. There is no doubt. He gave himself two shots in the hip. One wonders why."[111]

Davis's perception of drug use had also changed. He now viewed Charlie Parker's addiction in a different light. "He loved life, you know. He had a lot of fun," he told Cheryl McCall. "If people had left him alone, he would have been all right ... People saying you can't use this dope and to keep from getting busted you have to use all of it. You have to use all of it because if somebody catches you [with it], they'd put you in jail."[112] But Gaumont, who began using heroin in Paris after leaving Davis's band, disagreed: "For myself, I don't want my music to depend on drugs. Otherwise I wouldn't be making music, I would just be destroying myself. For years I was on horse [*cheval*, heroin] for three months at a time; then I would come off it to rehearse my trio for two months, give five concerts, then go back on heroin. I was risking my freedom, my health, my equilibrium. It was ridiculous! There is no Charlie Parker, it just isn't possible: you can't be a junkie and a musician."[113]

Davis's ulcers and other internal problems were aggravated by alcohol, and that seemed easier to solve. "What could be any worse than whiskey? It's got my liver all fucked up," he told McCall.[114]

He reassembled his band in June, after he had recovered from the throat surgery, for two nights (Tuesday the 14th and Thursday the 16th) at the Bottom Line, at 4th Street and Mercer in New York. Weekday prices at the Bottom Line, which booked heterogeneous bands ranging from Tony Williams's Lifetime to the Nitty Gritty Dirt Band, were normally $4, but for Davis's engagement they charged $5, the weekend price.

Sonny Fortune had formed his own quartet during Davis's layoff, and in his place Davis hired a young unknown named Sam Morrison. The hiring seemed to fit the pattern. Most members of Davis's band had been with him for years, and apart from Fortune and his predecessor, Liebman, they remained largely untried and almost unknown apart from their work with Davis. Michael Henderson had joined him at the end of 1970, James Mtume Foreman in 1971, Al Foster, Reggie Lucas, and Pete Cosey in the second half of 1972. Now Morrison joined them, and even the most avid fans in his audiences felt that Davis had surrounded himself with players incapable of adding the stamp of their own originality to his performances. And Davis himself seemed to be playing by rote.

His reviewers reflected a new response to his concerts. The reviews of the past three years, favorable or not, had usually been passionately stated; now the passion was replaced by resignation. When the band played a midnight concert on 1 July at Avery Fisher Hall as part of the 1975 Newport Jazz Festival, most reviewers noted Davis's return to George Wein's roster after refusing to play in 1972, but the performance itself received only blasé reports. "Wein's sound crew did wonders with Davis's thunderously loud and usually poorly balanced band," Robert Palmer reported in *Rolling Stone*; "for the first time in the memory of New York's Miles watchers, a concert by the current group came across with minimal distortion and feedback and with the contributions of individual sidemen clearly evident. For a band which has been together several years ... the musical transitions were astonishingly tentative. But Davis, the center of attention, played plenty of trumpet, occasionally recalling the sort of sensual lyricism he used to bring to ballad performances."[115] Whitney Balliett's review in the *New Yorker* was even more terse. "There was little that was new in his first number and set, which lasted close to an hour," Balliett wrote. "Davis went electric years ago, and he was surrounded onstage by amplifiers and electronic instruments. He played several solos, muted and open, electrified or not, and everything was as of old – the clams, the yearning tone, the highly melodic, free-time passages, the seeming disjointedness, and the incessant effort to get through to whatever it is musically that he has been trying to get through to for the past twenty years."[116] *Variety* reported: "Second half was better and better received than the first half because several auditors, expecting the old Davis, left during the long intermission ... Davis' trumpeting was fuller with the half more rewarding for the devotees."

On 8 August, Julian (Cannonball) Adderley died suddenly, five weeks before his 47th birthday. Wynton Kelly had died in 1971, also suddenly, and John Coltrane and Paul Chambers had both died in the 1960s, paring down the survivors among Davis's closest associates from his peak years. All of them were younger than he was. The ailing Davis received the news of Adderley's death grimly.

A performance at the Schaefer Festival in Central Park on 5 September drew a critical response as tepid as the Newport Festival performance from John S. Wilson in the *New York Times*. "Miles Davis's ability to leave his listeners languid was given pointed display," he reported. "His eight-piece group, which opened the program, performed for an hour. Mr. Davis was present for the first 50 minutes. He left during a solo by his bassist, who left during a solo by a conga player, who left during a solo by a second conga player." Wilson then described the performances that followed, by Raices, a Puerto Rican band, and John Blair, a jazz violinist, before returning to Davis's. "Before he worked his way down to this anticlimax," Wilson continued, "Mr. Davis took his group through the forest of electrified sounds that has been his vehicle for several years ... The steady flow [of percussion] was interrupted from time to time by brief breaks to allow Mr. Davis short passages in which dynamics, shading and even dramatic effect appeared. For the most part, the group produced a heavy-textured sound with a beat that seemed to be weighed down by the heaviness. It offered striking contrast to the seven musicians in Raices who, playing in a somewhat similar idiom, projected a light, bright, buoyant quality."[117]

These reviewers could not know – Davis himself did not know, although he must have suspected it sometimes, when he felt completely enervated by the pain in his hip – that they were among the last audiences that would see him for almost six years. His energy was all but drained, and his performances in the summer of 1975 showed that he could no longer hide it.

He kept trying, sometimes with unpleasant consequences. He was scheduled to appear two days after the Schaefer concert at Gusman Hall in Miami. By the time he sent the telegram announcing his cancellation, his musicians – and all the sound equipment, reportedly worth $25,000 – had arrived. The promoters, upset by the last-minute cancellation and the lack of any explanation for it, seized the equipment and sought a lien on it for their losses.[118]

One more concert was announced, for 12 October at the Auditorium Theater. It raised some anticipation, because it matched Davis with Michal Urbaniak, the Polish violinist whose strange fusions of jazz, rock, and European folk forms had been coming out on Columbia LPS since his arrival in New York in 1974; the advertisement announced, "The legendary jazz trumpet player is joined by the brilliant jazz violinist," and some of the fans who saw it hoped that Urbaniak's presence might signal a new or altered direction for Davis's music.

The advertisement was soon withdrawn. Davis now realized that he could no longer avoid the hip operation, or put it off much longer. And he suspected that, although he had recuperated fairly quickly before – covering the healing incision on his throat with a cravat when he played in Europe in 1956, hobbling around the stage in casts in western Canada in 1973 – he would not return as quickly this time.

The hip operation put an end to the most muddled and controversial period in Davis's career. For a long while, it seemed to have ended his career altogether. For almost six years he made no attempts to perform in public. He did make occasional forays into the recording studio – three or four sessions – but none of them resulted in record releases at the time. From his 49th year to his 55th, Davis was retired.

When he resumed playing again in 1981, after many people had given up hope that he ever would, he did not continue the musical directions he had left behind so abruptly in 1975. There would be echoes of that direction in his music, especially at first, but by and large those directions remain closed off, and so they stand strangely apart from what follows just as they do from what went before.

The music from 1972–5 is self-contained but hard to grasp, compact but hard to comprehend. It includes more than its fair share of contradictions. It began with an avowed attempt to find a black audience, but it baffled audiences of all colors. It drew sustenance from the easy blandishments of James Brown and Sly Stone, but its dense rhythms and often total lack of melody place it sound-years apart from them; it is probably the most forbidding and least accessible music that Davis ever made. It gained confidence from Stockhausen's example, but it found no cult among the European avant-garde composers; it was not so much ignored by Stockhausen's peers and students as it was unloved. It is often self-conscious and self-indulgent, but the self that fashioned it existed much of the time in a haze of pain and pain-killers.

Little wonder, then, that Davis's performances of this period, especially the recorded ones, so often evoked either confusion or sarcasm. Even the most positive comments – by Eugene Chadbourne, Ralph Gleason, Dave Liebman, and a few others – betray little real affection for the music. At best, they show respect for it, usually on the premise that Miles Davis can go ahead and do whatever he wants to do. But, of course, the authors of some of the negative comments – Ron Brown, Stan Getz, Clark Terry, and Betty Carter among them – would readily grant that premise. They knew as well as anyone that in approaching Miles Davis's music they would find no concessions to their tastes or anyone else's.

And Davis's critics hardly needed the scolding offered by trumpeter Oscar Brashear when he said: "They feel they can walk up to him and say, 'Miles, you ain't playin' shit now. Like, I dug you in 1965 when you had Wayne and them, but you ain't playin' shit now, Miles. You a drag, man. You don't sound nothin' like you sounded before.' They walk out on him ... They want you to be what *they* think is you."[119]

None of Davis's toughest critics took such a simple view. Most of them had followed his music closely, and they followed his new directions as closely as his mildest critics.

The crucial questions about the music of this period have nothing to do with whether Davis should be allowed to pursue a new direction in his music, or whether he should be permitted to sound different today from the way he sounded yesterday. Those questions are far too easy because they have only one obvious answer.

The real questions are so hard that they remain unanswered to this day. Was Davis's direction interesting? And was it productive? Even with a decade of hindsight, those questions have no clear answers.

Perhaps it is still too soon to try to answer them. Perhaps Davis was, as Dizzy Gillespie said, "hooked so far out in front" that ten years is too short for a perspective.

A couple of points are clear. Davis's music of 1972–5 has so far not proven interesting enough to entice listeners back to it. Whereas most of Davis's recordings since 1955 remain in print and have been continuously in print since they were issued, several of the recordings of 1972–5 are already hard to find. And the music was not productive enough to give rise to a school or to make a significant impact on any group of players. Dave Liebman and Sonny Fortune, the most conspicuous graduates of the bands from this period, have chosen to play music that bears little resemblance to what they played with Davis; their music draws much more inspiration from Davis's music of the late 1960s.

But the sound of Davis's rhythm band is not completely silent. It reverberates, incredible though it may seem, in the music Ornette Coleman plays when he surfaces sporadically with Prime Time, a double rhythm section (two guitars, two basses, two drums), both in the style and in the sound. Coleman's reviewers have seldom made the connection, either because Davis's music of the period is already a dim (or at least unattended) memory, or because the suggestion that Coleman has followed Davis's lead (or anyone else's) seems too fantastic. But whether Coleman was influenced by Davis or, more likely, came upon the style and the sound independently, as long as he keeps alive that thread of sound to Davis's recent past, there remains a chance that Davis's rhythm band may yet have their day.

They will not likely be resuscitated in the mainstream of jazz, where Davis's quintet of the 1960s now form the current, but they might yet be rediscovered by a select audience. Certainly Davis's music of this period, *at its very best*, has the qualities that cult revivals seem to require: it is highly idiosyncratic, and it is passionately stated.

15

Shhh
1975–81

His eyes give him away. That's why he wears those huge glasses. The pain, the hurt, the vulnerability, 48 years old, all there to see. But he puts those glasses on and it's the Black Prince, who knows no pain.   Sy Johnson

"I've been trying to retire," Miles Davis told Gregg Hall in 1974, but when Hall asked, "Do you really want to retire? You know the word is out on the street," Davis contradicted himself and said, "No, I really don't give a shit about retiring."[1]

The idea of retiring had been there for some time, forcing itself into his thoughts and occasionally into words when the aches and pains made a two-hour performance almost unbearable, but he never took it seriously for very long. It had become the kind of thing that he tossed into a conversation for its shock value, but as soon as it started provoking not surprise but expectancy, as with Hall, he retracted it. In the end, his retirement was not something he planned or wanted. It just happened.

He was young by the standards of most professions, just attaining the age at which attorneys become judges, professors become deans, and executives become vice-presidents. But he was long past the age when boxers hang up their gloves. More to the point, he was old for a jazzman – already older than Coleman Hawkins had been when he was the grey eminence of 52nd Street, and older than Lester Young had been when he displayed his spent talents in Europe, and much older than Freddie Webster, Charlie Parker, Fats Navarro, Bud Powell, Tadd Dameron, and so many of the other heroes of the bebop revolution had been when they died. On 26 May 1976, he would turn 50. When that birthday arrived, he had been out of the public view for almost eight months, and he would remain out of it for five more birthdays.

Most of the time, he just lay around his house with the shades drawn. When Cheryl McCall asked him, after it was all over, whether he had been depressed, he said: "*Bored* is the word. So bored you can't realize what boredom *is*. I didn't come out of the house for about four years ... Everything would come to my house. You know, anything you want you can get. All you have to do is ask for it. I didn't go to the store. I didn't go anywhere."[2] Whenever he woke up and saw sunlight streaming through the windows, he knew he was in the hospital, too sick and sore to get up and draw the shades.

The major operation, the one he most dreaded, took place in December 1975. The sickle cells caused thrombosis in several of his joints, including the shoulders and wrists, but the worst damage was in his left hip-joint. For almost two years he had been forced to curtail his gym workouts because the deteriorating joint allowed the thigh bone to slip out of its socket. The prosthesis that repaired the damage in the earlier operation had now deteriorated, and Dr Philip Wilson, the orthopedic surgeon, operated again to remove the bone chips and implant a rebuilt joint.

Davis began walking on it in January and seemed to be progressing normally. "He walks with a cane, but he's really fine," Teo Macero told a reporter. "He gets around pretty well. The fact that he stays home a great deal doesn't mean that he doesn't want to work. Miles wants to work."[3] But Davis was less certain. Afterward, he admitted, "That's what stopped me. That operation, man, I was so *disgusted* I just said fuck it for a while."[4] Macero was deceived by Davis's refusal to show his pain whenever it was possible for him to mask it. George Wein, who visited him in the hospital, noted that "Miles is not one to detail his suffering but you could see the agony on his face."[5] Looking back on it, Davis said, "I was all right," but he admitted: "It was just that I took so much medicine I didn't *feel* like playing the trumpet, didn't *feel* like listening to music. Didn't want to hear it, smell it, nothin' about it."[6]

By the time of his hip operation, he was still being treated for the stomach ulcer that had grounded him in St. Louis, and he had barely recuperated from the operation on his larynx. Still to come in the next three years were an operation to remove gallstones and further surgery on the hip socket.

None of these ailments was publicized, except in vague rumors that circulated throughout the jazz world, and Davis's absence became the subject of continuous speculation and gossip, mostly based on what was assumed to be the unsavory lifestyle of the Prince of Darkness.

One of the more persistent rumors pictured him withdrawing into a drug-induced catatonia behind the drawn shades of his brownstone. One of Davis gofers later admitted that his job entailed running to the liquor store for bottles of Mateus rosé, which Davis liked to sip after snorting cocaine. "It was weird," he told David Breskin. "Calls at 5:30 in the morning, he says, 'Get up here and keep me from killing Loretta.' That was one of his girlfriends. I'd get up there, and Loretta and him would be going at each other with these huge scissors that you could just put through somebody. I'd have to break the fight up and hide the scissors, and he'd punch her out and I'd cool him out and he'd cool the police out to keep from being arrested."[7] If such tales built his legend for a fringe of his fans, they also determined the critical perception of his recent music, as it became easier for his critics to dismiss it as the burblings of a man reeling out of control.

Another rumor, published in the French journal Le Point, claimed that Davis had been silenced by the Mafia for refusing to return the advances he received for cancelled concerts.[8] Another claimed he was underoing radiation treatments for throat cancer; this one gained credence after Davis returned to performing in 1981, because he reappeared wearing hats to cover a thin head of hair, and hair loss is one of the effects of radiation treatment. Like all the other rumors, this one has never been denied.

The rumor mills percolated wildly for five long years, and they were unchecked by any facts. Neil Reshen, Davis's manager, not only did not release any of the fact to the press, but he rebuffed all inquiries. Mark Zanger says: "I called Miles's manager Neil Reshen with some factual questions like, 'Who did the drummer play for before Miles?' Reshen wanted the questions in writing so he could ask Miles about them. So I mailed him the questions. Reshen doesn't return phone calls. A week later I talked to his associate, who asked me why I just didn't do some research. 'I am doing research,' I pointed out."[9] Sy Johnson had much the same success. "When I called Neil Reshen's publicity office for access to Miles," he says, "an arrogant and angry male voice said, 'How many times do I have to tell you – Miles Davis is not a jazz artist. Miles Davis makes his own music. Miles Davis will have nothing to do with a jazz issue of anything. I don't ever want you to bother me again.' Bang!!"[10]

After the first year of Davis's absence, many listeners remained cool to the claims that he was about to return. "Miles is a bad fucking man, and if he ever goes on the road again, I will not pay money to see him be an hour late and stand around, arrogant, condescending and spaced," a colleague told Ed Lowe of *Jazz* magazine. "Furthermore, I don't like all the electronic shit he's doing, and let's talk about something else."[11] Against that attitude, there were only a few scattered defenses. "He can turn people off and he has cancelled his concerts and this has hurt him in some areas, I'm sure," Macero told Gregg Hall, "but he probably didn't do it for the reasons people thought of at the time. I would say Miles is a well man but he has a tremendous amount of pain."[12]

Even Gil Evans, one of the few who knew exactly what Davis was going through, couched his explanation for his retirement in a crypto-mystical burn-out from creating a "new wave form." "He has to get that sound each time he plays and that's what people don't realize about someone who originates a tone – they have to recreate that tone every time the way they did it originally and it takes a lot of physical effort," he told Zan Stewart in 1981. "So when Miles plays he has to put out all that energy. That's why he took a five year vacation, because he did it for thirty years and he was exhausted. His total organism told him to quit."[13]

Lending credence to all the theories that his problems were not physical but mental or spiritual were the hints from Davis himself, starting well before his ailments put him in the hospital, that he was less than fully committed to his music. In 1972, Leonard Feather had asked him what he wanted to be doing in ten years, and Davis replied, "Nothing. If I don't have a deal lined up like I want it, ten years from now, I'd give up." Feather countered by saying, "It sounds to me as though you're not that interested any more, or not deeply concerned, about continuing in music," and, although Davis denied that immediately, he conceded, "If I started thinking about music – now – then I'll have to play the trumpet. But the minute I don't think about it, then I can be content doing nothing."[14]

He was not impervious to the critical lambasting he had taken for the past four or five years either. "I'm too vain in what I do to play anything really bad musically that I can help not doing," he told Nat Hentoff. "If I ever feel I am getting to the point where I'm playing it safe, I'll stop. That's all I can tell you about how I plan for the future. I'll keep on working until nobody likes me. When I am without an audience, I'll know it before anybody else, and I'll stop."[15] So the rumor persisted that he had stopped because of the catcalls drifting out of the audience wherever he had played since 1972, and the hostile reception to his recordings, especially *He Loved Him Madly*, the Ellington elegy into which, appropriately or not, he had poured so much feeling. The critical consensus on *He Loved Him Madly* formed immediately before he quit performing, and to some observers those two events seemed more than coincidental.

Davis had found himself not at the head of the current movement in jazz but all alone, doggedly pursuing a direction that no one else seemed inclined to follow. "In general there ain't much happening that I want to hear," he had told Feather in that interview a few years before. "All the groups are trying to play like somebody I know. I don't want to hear clichés: I don't want to get back into the past. What's important is what's happening now, the new music and the music of the future. I don't even want to think about what I was doing myself last year."[16] So Art Pepper, in his memoir, *Straight Life*, concluded: "Miles is panicked. He's stopped. He's got panicked trying to be different, trying to continually change and be modern and to do the avant-garde thing."[17] Lots of listeners found that convincing, and, perhaps, if it had been put to Davis by someone like Leonard Feather, even he might have gone along with it part way.

While Davis had spent more than a little energy repudiating his earlier music, during his retirement it became the only music that jazz fans heard. It came out of several sources, and probably the least important of them were the nostalgia buffs who, assuming Davis's career was spent, reached back into the stacks for the *Birth of the Cool* or *Walkin'* or *Kind of Blue*. Those phases of his career were securely fixed in jazz history, and replaying their consummations made a useful reminder of Davis's stature but added nothing new to it.

More significant was the thoroughgoing review of Davis's music of 1964–8, with the quintet of Wayne Shorter, Herbie Hancock, Ron Carter, and Tony Williams. That combination had been widely respected and highly successful in its day but had worked in a period when jazz was undervalued, with a dwindling general audience and a less than vigilant critical audience. In the rush to pick up on the early experiments in jazz-rock fusion that immediately followed, most listeners simply took the acoustic quintet for granted and shunted their LPs into a corner. With the rush ended and the fusion experiments, along with their patriarch, evidently played out, the time was ripe not just for a reminder but for a revaluation. Two long, detailed reviews, one by Harvey Pekar in *Coda* (1976) and the other by Scott Yanow in *Record Review* (1978), helped listeners to relocate the music of that quintet, and revivals of its style by strong new bands, especially one led – unexpectedly, in view of the music he had been marketing recently – by Herbie Hancock and later, as Davis was preparing to emerge into public view again, another led by a promising young trumpeter named Wynton Marsalis, Davis's achievement of the mid-1960s, which his band had not come close to exhausting when he abandoned it, came into its own.

Another source of Davis's earlier music came from Columbia Records, which pointedly ignored his 1972–5 backlog in the four LPs it compiled for release during his retirement. The first one, *Water Babies* (PC34396), in 1976, looked like a continuation from *On the Corner*, with its Corky McCoy cover illustration and its listings of electric keyboards, but the appearance was deceiving – so much so that John Norris, the co-editor of *Coda*, alerted his readers with a notice saying, "You should check out Miles Davis' *Water Babies*. It's with the classic 1960s quintet."[18] The music released two sessions from 1967–8 for the first time. Columbia's 1977 release (PC 34804) harkened back to May 1949, issuing nine transcriptions of the Miles Davis–Tadd Dameron quintet in Paris. Then two years passed in silence before Columbia issued *Circle in the Round* (KC2 36278) in 1979, a twofer compilation of music from 1955 to 1970, and it followed that two years later with a similar compilation called *Directions* (KC2 36472), containing tracks from 1960–70. The music was uneven, but it brought to light some buried gems, including *Two Bass Hit*, from Davis's first session for Columbia, Gil Evans's *Song of Our Country*, which had been left out of the *Sketches of Spain* LP, and several new pieces by the mid-1960s quintet.

A very different retrospective airing for Davis's music came about in New York in 1974–5, where the first significant attempts to form jazz repertory orchestras took place. The New York Jazz Repertory Company prepared an "in-depth, one-subject" concert of Davis's music as one program of a series that included similar concerts reprising the music of Louis Armstrong, Count Basie, Bix Beiderbecke, Jelly Roll Morton, and George Russell. The emphasis was placed on re-creating the sounds of the past, a less promising premise than that of New York's other repertory orchestra, the National Jazz Ensemble, directed by Chuck Israels, the composer and conductor who had once been Bill Evans's bassist. Israels was intent on capturing the spirit rather than the sound of jazz classics, and several of his programs incorporated Davis's music. On 21 November 1974, the Ensemble played *Israel*, Johnny Carisi's composition for Davis's nonet, in a score arranged for orchestra with Davis's original solo orchestrated for the brass section. The same concert featured Davis's *All Blues*, with Davis's solo and Bill Evans's original accompaniment arranged for the Ensemble and Evans as guest soloist; "Henry James would have relished such intricate footwork," Whitney Balliett noted in his review. The Ensemble's concert in January 1975 explored Davis's *Solar*, the melody that he played once in 1954 and promptly forgot, and in mid-April they ended their concert with (in Balliett's description) "big-band impressions of Ornette Coleman, John Coltrane and Miles Davis."[19]

The repertory orchestras both failed after one or two seasons, leaving jazz again with the most blatant gap in its long struggle toward cultural respectability. Their chances of success were doomed from the start by the fact that there were two of them, however different their premises, contending for audiences and foundation grants. Even if there had been only one – and even if that one had been Israels's imaginative and ambitious National Jazz Ensemble – it was probably doomed by the economic climate. North America was slipping into a long recession in 1974 as markets were being taken over by Japan, and for the time being, West Germany. Within a few years, West Germany would follow the rest of Europe into the same recession, and by then, in the United States, public funding was being diverted to bail out the textile, steel, and automotive industries. Even well-established symphonies, ballet companies, and universities faced sharp cutbacks in their grants, and there was nothing left over for an upstart from the world of jazz. But while they lasted, the two repertory orchestras made Miles Davis less inconspicuous.

It is hard to imagine anything more inimical to Davis's wont for burying the past than a repertory orchestra. His reaction would have been easy to predict, and Dizzy Gillespie suggested what it might have been. "The concerts they're having, where they go back through the music because so many people didn't hear it when it was first performed, are groovy," Gillespie said, but he added: "We need the followers to do that. The creators are supposed to step forward. That's why I can appreciate Miles. I don't care whether you like his music or not, he has stepped forward. It's up to your personal taste, but the music is there for you to taste whether you like it or not. He did have the courage to step up there."[20] From the mellower perspective of 1983, Davis could see some virtue in preserving the jazz tradition. "There's a place for it," he told Richard Williams in *The Times*. "That shouldn't be lost. Lester Young, Dexter Gordon – those styles shouldn't be lost. But I can't do that."[21]

Davis made a token effort to resume his activities in May 1976 by rehearsing and recording at the Columbia studios, probably with some of the men from his last working band. "He conducted and played the organ," Teo Macero reported. "The trumpet was there. He just didn't feel like playing the trumpet."[22]

The sessions ended abruptly when Davis's hip became severely infected. "He shoots happiness into his leg with a dirty needle," David Breskin said, "and pays no mind until one day he can't walk."[23] His doctors discussed the possibility of amputation and Davis shrugged. In the end, he faced further surgery and the leg was saved. So he marked his 50th birthday bedridden. Thoughts about resuming his career grew more remote.

Discussing the relapse with reporters, Macero tried to put it into a positive perspective. "Listen, a man gets sick, right," he said. "Sure a man gets sick. Sure he has to recharge his batteries. And with Miles, he knows – his body tells him when to play and when not to play. What's wrong with that?"[24] He sounded as if he were reassuring himself, or perhaps Davis.

Press releases for the 1976 Newport Jazz Festival, which had grown into an eleven-day slate held in various New York halls, announced that Davis would join the members of his mid-1960s quintet on 29 June for the first part of a concert called a "Herbie Hancock Retrospective." The centerpiece of the festival was intended to be four concerts devoted to phases of Duke Ellington's music, but the reunion of the Davis quintet became the main talking point when the program was released. In the end it did not happen, and Freddie Hubbard had to replace Davis, but the strength of the reunited sidemen produced what Robert Palmer, reporting for *Rolling Stone*, called "the magic moment of the festival." The quintet played the first part of the concert, followed by a reunion of Hancock's Mwandishi band of 1970–3 and a set by the current version of his jazz-funk group, Headhunters. "The surprise of the jam, which seemed to affect the musicians as much as the audience, was that the music they made together stood head and shoulders above their current efforts as individuals," Palmer wrote. "Neither saxophonist Shorter's Weather Report, pianist Hancock's post-Headhunters jazz-funk, bassist Carter's cti albums nor drummer Williams's Lifetime recordings compare with the barrage of music they laid down as a unit."[25] That point was not lost on Davis's former sidemen, and they decided to reunite the following summer for a tour.

As Davis's retirement entered its second year, attitudes toward him seemed to soften. Speaking to Sy Johnson in 1974, Davis had moaned about his isolation, mentioning that his old associates Thad Jones, Dizzy Gillespie, and Elvin Jones never went to hear him play, and that only Hancock of his younger associates ever visited him. "Chick [Corea] doesn't come to hear me ... Chick wouldn't be interested in my band," he said.[26] Now, two years later, Corea told Conrad Silvert in *Rolling Stone*: "This summer I'm going to take some time off, something I haven't done in four years. But I'll still do some composing. For years I've wanted to write solo orchestral compositions for certain musicians. One is Stanley [Clarke], another is Jean-Luc Ponty, and I'd love to write something for Miles Davis."[27]

Davis's most attentive companion during his extended convalescence was Cicely Tyson, the actress whose profile had graced the cover of his *Sorcerer* LP in 1967. Tyson's friendship with Davis persisted throughout his three-year marriage to Betty Mabry and probably a dozen other relationships. She seemed to be uncannily sensitive to his needs. "You know, she'll call and say, 'I'll be right over, I can feel something's wrong with you' – and I'll be sicker than a motherfucker," Davis told Gregg Hall. "She does it all the time. Remarkable! She's wonderful. She's a very talented woman!!"

By now, Davis's opinion of Tyson's talent was shared by almost everyone. In 1972–4 she became one of the most conspicuous actresses around with two brilliant successes, one on film and the other on television. In *The Autobiography of Miss Jane Pittman*, a television drama, she portrayed the title character from a young maid to a 110-year-old woman who takes a dignified stand for civil rights in the south, in a performance that won her an Emmy. Two years before, she portrayed a sharecropper's wife in *Sounder*, a Depression melodrama directed by Martin Ritt and co-starring Paul Warfield, for which she earned an Academy Award nomination. "Did you see her in *Sounder*?" Davis crowed to Gregg Hall. "That was a motherfucker!!" Of the climactic scene, where Tyson runs down the dirt lane to greet her long-lost, now-crippled husband, Davis said, "When she ran to Paul – UUHH!! brings tears to your eyes."[28]

Tyson's sympathetic contacts with Davis became increasingly important to him in the first year and a half of his convalescence, helping him to stave off the bouts of self-doubt and discouragement as his strength and stamina failed to return.

While Davis remained out of sight, Columbia seemed uncertain about how to respond. He was making no new records, but it still held a vast archive of his music in its vaults – some 80 unissued LPS, by Davis's reckoning – and 20 years of released material, amounting, in 1975, to 53 long-playing disks. Its choices seemed clear: either launch a systematic reissue program, resolving some of the anachronisms on the original issues, or delve into the archive for new LPS of unreleased material. Since most of Davis's releases on Columbia had remained in print from their initial release and were readily available, the most likely choice was the latter. Still, Macero seemed to favor a reissue program. "If there's anything at all that has held up the release of new records," he told Ed Lowe, "it's the fact that I wanted to put out a nine-album release in a series, one album a month for nine months, plus a final deluxe edition called *The Golden Years*, all taken from the recorded material CBS already has."[29] Preparations were apparently begun to clear the way for the reissues, because several of Davis's classic LPS on Columbia began to appear in record shops at discount prices around 1978, usually the first step in clearing out the backlog of stock to make way for the new issues. However, the only reissue that appeared was nothing but a repackaging; in 1980, Columbia put out a boxed set titled *Twelve Sides of Miles: Miles Davis Collection, Vol. 1* (c6x-36976), with the LPS *Miles Ahead*, *Porgy and Bess*, *Kind of Blue*, *Sketches of Spain*, and *Bitches Brew* inside.

Not much more was done about the archive, with only six disks of older material appearing in the six years of Davis's retirement, a potpourri of music excerpted from longer sessions in several phases of his career. Macero described the accumulation of music at CBS for Gregg Hall this way: "From the time the studio musicians start playing, we take down every note of music and all that music is intact in the vault at CBS. It's not cut. It's not edited. So there's an archive of Miles Davis that won't quit and it's all in perfect, mint condition. I take it and I make masters of everything [to be considered for a new release]. I may have fifteen reels of Miles and I cut those reels down; or I may have five and I may cut it down to two. I don't know. I keep listening to it over and over with the engineer and finally Miles comes in and listens to it and he smiles and he walks out. That's all there is to it."[30]

Much of the archive is probably useless for general release – the orchestral breakdowns for *Sketches of Spain* in 1959, when Macero started the practice of keeping the tape machines running continuously, the pure rehearsals intended only to introduce new players to the group, the four-hour experiments with "non-reaction" in 1973, and other sessions. But the archive includes also the unreleased half of the

Carnegie Hall concert with Gil Evans in 1961 and all of the UCLA concert with Evans in 1968, all the original music released with echoes, tape loops, and other artifices since 1969, and untold other sessions. Only a fraction of it has been touched.

Davis's most noticeable action in almost a year happened in February 1977, when he had a check for $500 delivered to the Jazz Museum in Manhattan as part of its fund drive to raise $5,000 for overdue mortgage payments.[31] The money helped save the museum for the time being, but it closed a few years later and its artifacts were removed to the Institute of Jazz Studies at Rutgers University in Newark, where they still await a new permanent home.

In the summer, many jazz fans heard a live reminder of Davis's music when Herbie Hancock reassembled the Newport reunion band of the summer before for a month-long tour. The band, called VSOP (for the designation on choice brandy), caused a sensation, drawing over 100,000 fans to its 25 concerts from New York to Los Angeles. Its high-energy, acoustic modal jazz not only recalled the spirit of Davis's music from ten years before but also revived it. In an interview with Conrad Silvert, Hancock explained that Davis wanted to attend the New York concert, but "he said he couldn't deal with all those people – because you know that when Miles comes around, especially since he's been off the scene ... everybody's going to jump on him." He added: "The night of the concert, me and Ron [Carter] went to see him at his house in between shows. He looked great, he looked *great*. He's been playing a little, I think, but not a lot."[32]

In his few pronouncements on VSOP, Davis seems less than enthusiastic. He told Sy Johnson, "I don't go to hear Freddie Hubbard only because I don't like him. I'd rather hear Thad [Jones] *miss* a note than hear Freddie make *twelve*."[33] (A few years later, Davis's objections to Hubbard seemed to be cleared away, when he told Cheryl McCall: "Well, I always try to have a good tone, 'cause I know if I don't it's gonna drag me, and it's gonna drag people I respect a lot, people like Dizzy and Freddie Hubbard and all the trumpet players."[34]) And in 1983, when Hancock was assembling the latest version of the summer band called VSOP II, with Wynton and Branford Marsalis as well as Ron Carter and Tony Williams, Davis told an English reporter: "Do you go back to Bernard Shaw for material? I only heard of VSOP three weeks ago. They wouldn't be able to get the same kind of intensity [as the original Davis band]. I wouldn't get the same thing now, either."[35]

Davis's lack of affection for Freddie Hubbard, who replaced him at the

Newport Festival in 1974 and 1976, placed ahead of him in *Down Beat*'s
readers' polls in 1973 and 1974, and joined Columbia's jazz roster in
1974, never developed into a general distaste for up-and-coming
trumpeters. In 1977, he recommended Woody Shaw to Columbia,
saying "he has a lot of heart."[36] Shaw was 32, and he played an
unamplified trumpet in a brisk, no-nonsense style; his tone, but not his
phrasing, is very similar to Hubbard's when Hubbard plays modal
music rather than disco-jazz or the other hybrids he attempted at
Columbia and elsewhere. Shaw began recording straight jazz for
Columbia, usually with his working quintet, and quickly gained a
following for both himself and his band, and Davis has remained
generous in his remarks about him. In 1982, when Leonard Feather
elicited Davis's responses to several younger trumpeters, he said that
Hubbard was all technique but no feeling, that Wynton Marsalis was
inspired mainly by Clifford Brown, and that Shaw could play differently
from all of them. "Now there's a great trumpet player," he said.[37]

In the summer of 1977, Robert Palmer reported in the *New York
Times* that Davis was actively preparing a band for his comeback, and
that Gil Evans was playing keyboards in it. The story caused a larger stir
than either Palmer or his source, which apparently was Columbia,
might have anticipated, and several reporters began checking it out.
While they did not get outright denials, the story quickly evaporated.
Dan Morgenstern sought out Evans, who could tell him only that the
Times story expressed "the merchandiser's point of view,"[38] although
he admitted he was pleased to be working with Davis again. Hubert Saal
sought out Davis, who would say only, "When I can stand on my leg I'll
play again." He could not be persuaded to comment one way or the other
on the report about his new band, but he pointed out: "I haven't been out
of the house more than seven times in the last two years."[39]

The fact that Davis and Evans were working together, or at least
thinking about music together, was not really newsworthy. While
Davis was suffering through his enforced inactivity, his shop talk with
Evans was uninterrupted by tours and rehearsals. "Gil Evans is my
favorite [musician]," Davis told Cheryl McCall. "Anything he does,
writes. He's also one of my best friends. He also guides me when I ask
him what I should do. He's a nice guy to ask a question 'cause he'll say, 'I
don't know.' (laughs) His favorite answer. He's all right. He's some
person, he's quite a man."[40] When there was nothing else to report on
Davis's music, even his friendly chats with Evans became news.

Columbia found other ways to keep Davis's name in the news. In

1977, it launched its Contemporary Masters Series, which included the Miles Davis–Tadd Dameron transcriptions from Paris and new releases by Charlie Parker, Lester Young, and Gerry Mulligan, by renting a Puerto Rican discotheque at 1674 Broadway for one night and converting it into its former glory, Birdland.[41] Davis, according to rumor, was to make an appearance in the audience, but he stayed away.

According to another rumor, Davis was expected to take a bow at a tribute for him organized by Lionel Hampton in February 1978. *Down Beat* reported that Hampton was putting together a program that included Gerry Mulligan, Woody Shaw, and the Jazz Workshop.[42] But the rumor, like all the others, fizzled out.

Rumors about Davis were so abundant that they became news in their own right. Ed Lowe reported to his readers in *Jazz* magazine: "The rumor that Miles is preparing himself for the Great Beyond is exaggerated, as is the occasional speculation that he has already taken up eternal residence there. Likewise, the story that he's been through enough corrective surgery on various parts of his innards to render him hashlike; and the tale of his having gone completely berserk, or at least more berserk than normal."[43] Another magazine, *Musician: Player and Listener*, found the Davis rumor mill easy fodder for its column of hip humor: "Keith Jarrett is having large bronze statues of himself cast for future installation in city parks across the nation. One of them will sub for him on his tour this spring," it reported, and "Miles Davis was in the studio again last week, but only to use the men's room, as he told the press upon leaving."[44]

Davis's contract with Columbia expired in 1976, and Teo Macero felt that the negotiations between the company and Davis on the new contract were deterring him from recording. "Once the contract is signed and things are worked out at CBS, we'll record again," he said. "When Miles is ready to record, we might record for ten months, every day. That's the way it is with Miles."[45] But the negotiations dragged on, probably not so much because of problems in coming to terms as Davis's reluctance to deal with music in any guise. The contract was settled sometime in 1977, but he apparently did not enter the recording studios at all that year; if so, it marked the only year he had failed to register a studio or an authorized live recording since 1945.

"I knew if I felt like playing I would play," he said later. "Even if it was just once. I didn't go places and sit in. Nobody had anything I wanted to sit in *with*." And then, probably in the first months of 1978, he felt like it. "I went down to the Vanguard once," he told Cheryl McCall, " and sat in the brass section, played everybody's trumpet, just once."[46] Thad Jones and Mel Lewis led their big band at the Village Vanguard on Mondays.

In February or March 1978, he phoned Macero and said, "I'm ready." The next day he resumed his recording career after almost two years of silence. He played the organ, and his recording band laid down the foreground backed by a set of pre-recorded brass arrangements by Bobby Scott, the singer who had had a smash hit with *Chain Gang* in 1955 and now worked as a freelance composer and producer. In the band Davis assembled, only drummer Al Foster had played for him before. Guitarist Larry Coryell was the best-known player; one of the young stars rising out of fusion music of the early 1970s, Coryell made his mark as a sideman in the bands of Chico Hamilton and Gary Burton, and then led his own band, Eleventh House, starting in 1973, when he turned 30. Keyboardist Masabumi Kikuchi also was experienced as a leader in Japan and as a sideman with Elvin Jones and Sonny Rollins, among others, in the United States; one of his compositions, *Lunar Eclipse*, was part of Gil Evans's new repertoire whenever he assembled a big band, as he had been doing more frequently since 1972. (Kikuchi often played with a young Japanese trumpeter named Terumasa Hino, who is said to have transcribed *every* Miles Davis solo ever recorded.) The third keyboardist, counting Davis, was George Paulis, and the bassist was T.M. Stevens.

The music remains unreleased, but *Down Beat* reported that it was "a cross between late '60s and late '70s disco."[47] If that made it sound unpromising for jazz listeners, their appetites might have been whetted by Larry Coryell's remarks about the session. "What I got from working with Miles was just one word: Stop! When in doubt, stop," he told Bill Milkowski. "Don't finish that phrase. So the spaces are starting to open up in my solos, and that came from just a few intense weeks of being around Miles."[48] Davis was apparently disappointed with the result, and when the session was completed he retired again for a year and a half.

His old triumphs were memorialized in the summer when he was named on one of the first twelve "Prez" plaques, commemorating the heyday of 52nd Street. The plaques were embedded on the sidewalk at the former sites of the Three Deuces, the Onyx, and the other jazz clubs, replaced long since by high-rises, one of them the CBS building, and the street signs along the block were marked "Swing Street." The other musicians so honored were Lester Young, Dizzy Gillespie, Charlie

Parker, Coleman Hawkins, Billie Holiday, Art Tatum, Roy Eldridge, Thelonious Monk, Sarah Vaughan, Kenny Clarke, and Stuff Smith, with a second set of presentations designated for Errol Garner, Slam Stewart, Red Norvo, Fats Waller, Oscar Pettiford, and Ben Webster. Davis's award was accepted at the official ceremony by Bruce Lundvall of CBS.

On 5 January 1979, Charles Mingus died of heart failure in Mexico, where he was seeking treatment for Lou Gehrig's disease (lateral sclerosis), which had confined him to a wheelchair for the previous year. Although completely immobilized, Mingus had stayed active, presiding over recording sessions in his name at the Atlantic studios, including the one in which songwriter-singer Joni Mitchell adapted some of his melodies and fitted them with her lyrics.

In 1980, Mitchell used Davis's music as the main motif for her segment of a movie called *Love*, with eight other segments devised by Lady Antonia Fraser, Edna O'Brien, and Liv Ullmann. Mitchell's screenplay, which lasts fifteen minutes and is directed by Mai Zetterling, has Mitchell portraying a black pimp. Both the plot and the character were evoked from the slice of Davis's music she started with. "My vision of the relationship between the soundtrack and the visuals is very precise," she explained. "The character I play, for instance, is a Miles Davis fan, and he carries the soundtrack around with him on a big portable cassette. I didn't think ... that they [the movie technicians] really understood the way I scc it, I wasn't sure Mai knew how articulate I wanted each gesture to be, to the beat, in some key scenes where there is no dialogue."[49] So far, *Love* has not been put into general release.

Davis's music was heard for six consecutive days and nights in the summer of 1979, when WKCR–FM in New York played every available tape and LP he ever recorded as a "Miles Davis fest," which also included interviews with Percy and Jimmy Heath, Bill Evans, Philly Joe Jones, Gil Evans, and Max Roach.

After years of inactivity by Davis, it was surprising that he made any showing at all on the year-end jazz polls conducted by *Down Beat* and other magazines. In the readers' poll for 1979, he placed tenth among trumpeters. As if to confirm the suspicions of some of his critics, the only musician associated with him in the 1972–5 period who made a showing was Sonny Fortune (ninth on alto saxophone), but the most significant indication of how jazz tastes had been reshaped as the decade neared its end came from the complete domination of Davis's sidemen and close associates from the period immediately preceding. Chick Corea came second for Jazzman of the Year, following Mingus; Weather

Report was the top jazz group; Wayne Shorter first soprano saxophonist; Corea, Josef Zawinul, and Herbie Hancock the top three electric pianists; the same three, with Zawinul first, the top three synthesizer players; Ron Carter the top bassist, with Dave Holland fifth; Tony Williams and Jack DeJohnette the top two drummers; and Airto Moreira the top percussionist. All of them had discovered their skills and shaped them under Davis's tutelage and then moved away in their own directions, like the drift from Pangaea, to establish their separate identities.

"All those guys, they came out of me," Davis told Hubert Saal. "Tell them [the fans] I'm still pregnant. I've been playing since I was thirteen. I don't turn the other cheek and I don't give up either."[50]

Another revival took place in 1980, when Lee Konitz was invited to re-create Davis's nonet orchestrations, now 30 years old, by Martin Williams of the Smithsonian Institution's jazz division. "I didn't know where the arrangements were, so I called Miles," Konitz told Whitney Balliett in a *New Yorker* interview. "I hadn't had any communication with him in years, and he wasn't interested. He didn't want to hear about it." When Konitz found it impossible to transcribe the arrangements from the recordings, he began tracking down the arrangers. Johnny Carisi supplied his chart for *Israel*, John Lewis filled in the details for Konitz's transcription of *Move*, and Gerry Mulligan rewrote his arrangements of *Godchild*, *Jeru* and *Rocker*. Konitz then phoned Davis to give him a progress report. "I said, 'Miles, remember my asking you for the arrangements of the *Cool* sessions? Well, we've transcribed them and rewritten them and put them together again.' He said, 'Man, you should have asked me. Those [motherfuckers] are all in my basement.'" Later, Konitz reported the conversation to Gil Evans, who said, "Miles wouldn't have told you he had everything in the basement if you hadn't first told him you'd gone to the trouble to transcribe the records."[51]

Davis apparently avoided the recording studio again in 1979, although he talked about making some recordings. Dominique Gaumont visited him from Paris and received what he took to be an invitation. "He told me that we should do some stuff, him, Al [Foster] and me," Gaumont reported. "But he's very paranoid [*très parano*], and when I talked to him about it again last year [1980] he told me that was a long, long time ago."[52] By then Davis was already hard at work recording music of a very different stripe.

What sent him into the studio in 1980 was a demonstration tape played for him over the telephone during one of his almost-daily calls to his sister, Dorothy, in Chicago. Davis's nephew, Vincent Wilburn Jr, a 22-year-old drummer, played him a tape he made with a quartet of his friends. Davis invited the young band to join him in Columbia's New York studios. Two of the fourteen pieces they recorded were released a year later, on *The Man with the Horn* (Columbia FC 36790), but most of the information about the sessions comes from a report filed by Howard Mandel in *Down Beat*, which appeared in September 1980.

Besides Wilburn, the Chicago quartet included Randy Hall, a 21-year-old guitarist and singer and a student at the Berklee School in Boston, who had grown up with Wilburn in Chicago; Robert Irving, a 26-year-old keyboard player who graduated from the University of North Carolina; and Felton Crews, a bassist. All were involved in playing reggae, funk, soul, rock, and some jazz, as pick-up players around Chicago. Wilburn, of course, knew Davis's earlier music well – he cited *Four and More* (1964) and *Bitches Brew* (1969) as his favorites for Mandel – and Hall, through Wilburn, knew it too. Neither Irving nor Crews had had much exposure to it. They soon learned. "Our concept in Chicago was different from what Miles told us to play," Wilburn said.

They arrived in New York in April and started rehearsing in the studio on 1 May with Davis, but the lessons spilled over outside the studio. "We all have a very close relationship," Wilburn said. "Miles talks to us, tells us not to mix with drugs, helps us get our business together, and cooks for us – a great dish called bouillabaisse."[53]

To fill out the group, Davis asked Dave Liebman to recommend a young reedman and was directed to Bill Evans, at 22 the same age as Wilburn and, coincidentally, from Hinsdale, Illinois, near Chicago; Evans's association with Davis was destined to be more enduring. The other players added for the recording came on the recommendation of Teo Macero and others. What was intended to yield a single 45-rpm release ended up as fourteen titles and sixty hours of studio time, spread over three different months. The details of the first sessions are as follows:

Miles Davis with Vincent Wilburn Jr: The Man with the Horn
Miles Davis, tpt; Bill Evans, ss; Robert Irving III, pno, el pno; Randy Hall, vcl, gtr, synthesizer, celeste; Felton Crew, b; Vincent Wilburn Jr, dms; Angela Bofill, backup vcl. New York, 1 May–June 1980
The Man with the Horn
(on Columbia FC 36790)
The Man with the Horn is written by Hall and Irving, as are some of the following titles, perhaps in collaboration with Glen Burris. On some of the

following titles, Sammy Figueroa, perc, is added, and Davis also plays el pno.
Spider's Web; Solar Energy; Space; Burn; I'm Blue; Mrs. Slurpey; Thanksgiving; 1980s; two unidentified titles
(all unissued)

Hall sings the lyric for *The Man with the Horn* in a rich baritone, with all
the colorations of soul music under good control; in his genre, he proves
himself to be a talented young singer. The background is dominated at
first by the synthesizer, and then by Davis's tightly muted trumpet with
wah-wah effects, which takes over between the second and third verses
for two choruses. The lyric is a paean to Davis that is extravagant and
sometimes awkward:

> Smooth, suave, debonair,
> describes a man so rare;
> like fine wine
> he gets mellower with age.

Each verse is marked by the refrain, "He's the man with the horn,"
echoed ("he's the man, he's the man, he's the man") by the backup
singers, Bofill and apparently Hall, dubbed in.

> His music sets the pace;
> the master never has to race,
> although he's much too fast
> to ever lose.

After Davis's trumpet choruses, Hall resumes:

> He's spent so many years
> crying melody for tears,
> but they don't understand
> what makes this man.
>
> The man keeps on blowing, yah,
> your mind keeps on growing;
> he's been up there for so many years
> blowing melody for tears.

If it seemed incongruous for Davis to resume his career by sponsoring a song extolling his stamina and by participating in his own eulogy, most listeners were willing to overlook that and notice, instead, that his trumpet playing, although constrained both in range and style in this framework, seemed to have lost little of its expressiveness.

Davis's recording sessions with the young Chicagoans were interrupted at the end of June, when Karlheinz Stockhausen joined him in the Columbia studios. "Stockhausen – I love him," Davis told Julie Coryell. "Gil [Evans] says, 'Stockhausen sounds like you.'"[54] Davis was accompanied also by Paul Buckmaster, the English composer and cellist who had introduced him to Stockhausen's works in 1972, and probably by Wayne Shorter and perhaps Josef Zawinul, among others. So far, the music they made together remains unissued.

After the interlude, Davis completed his work with his nephew's band. The details are as follows:

Miles Davis with Vincent Wilburn, Jr: The Man with the Horn
Miles Davis, tpt; Robert Irving III, el pno; Randy Hall, synthesizer; Barry Finnerty, gtr; Felton Crews, b; Vincent Wilburn Jr, dms; Sammy Figueroa, perc. New York, July 1980
Shout; two unidentified titles
(*Shout* on Columbia FC 36790; latter two unissued)
Shout is written by Hall, Irving, and Glen Burris.

Shout is an unpretentious little disco-rock dance tune with an infectious beat. Later, after the 45-rpm release scored a small success on the pop market, Davis said, "Randy Hall and my nephew and little Bobby [Irving], they all write great music for me. I need a bubble-gum song, I just call up Randy and say, 'Randy, send me a bubble-gum song. Like *Shout*.'"[55]

In the immediate aftermath, Wilburn and the others expected that their hours in the studio with Davis would give them an LP release by the fall, and they were ebullient about what it would show of them. "We're going to turn some heads around," Irving told Mandel. "People will be imitating songs, they'll be imitating Vince's drumming. Miles has been playing the stuff for other musicians and friends of his over the phone. Dave Liebman heard it, said it had a lot more changes to play over. Al Foster hear it; Miles played it for Cicely Tyson."

The unreleased material apparently follows the pattern of the two released tracks. "Well, there's something for everybody," Hall said, when Mandel asked for a description. "Vocals, electronics, to appeal to

young people. It's commercial enough that people who never heard
Miles before will get it. Older fans of his will dig, it, too. Some tunes are,
like, pop. It's into a wide spectrum. The music is mostly ballads, but
there's up-tempo funk, fusion, an open hi-hat sound with lots of drive
that Miles instructed Vince to play, hip melodies on the top, lots of
melodic changes ... The tracks average about five minutes each."
Wilburn added: "There's no one doing anything like it. It's beyond
sophisticated funk. Eddie Henderson? Hughie Masakela? Herb Alpert?
No, it's simply new Miles."

More significant than the music that resulted from these sixty hours
in the studio was the revival of Davis's ambitions. He proved to himself,
if he had ever doubted it, that his capability for playing the trumpet had
not disappeared after the years of neglect. "Miles has been talking about
coming out, and he's in good health, for all those who've been
wondering," Wilburn said. "He talks about touring Europe and Japan."[56]
As it happened, Davis's return to performing came soon enough that
Columbia did not have to delve into the funk tapes in order to come up
with an LP of new music. While the sessions with Wilburn and his
friends seemed important at the time, they were soon eclipsed.

Davis's worldly ambitions were also piqued by a grim reminder. On
15 September 1980, the pianist Bill Evans died suddenly, apparently
from complications after suffering a bleeding ulcer. He was 49, and,
although his period as a sideman with Davis has been much shorter than
Coltrane's or Adderley's, and his association with him less intense than
Mingus's, his death seemed to affect Davis more acutely. "It's too
painful for me to think of Bill Evans and his piano," Davis told Cheryl
McCall. "He's one of my favorite pianists. Or he was. But that's the way
it goes."[57] As soon as Davis emerged from his retirement, he began
playing *My Man's Gone Now* from *Porgy and Bess*, a striking incon-
gruity in a repertoire that was designed to bury the past, and, although
Davis never said so, he probably played it in homage to Evans.

Still months before the public would hear any of Davis's recent music,
Down Beat's letters column reflected some of the concern that focused
on Davis. "All over the world people have collected the music you
made, paid money to get hold of it," a Dutch fan chided him. "That's
more or less the same bread you received, which enabled you to live the
life you live nowadays. Dig? That is also why you owe it to the world to
come out wherever you are." In the same issue, an Australian fan asked
for clarification of some of the rumors. "I have been told: He's released
nothing in two years; his recording company is sitting on some new

material which it thinks is too far out; he's dead. What's going on? Can you put these tribal superstitions to rest? It's almost as bad as the pop scene."[58] A reader from New Jersey undertook to answer all the inquiries by declaring: "Let's all just *forget* about Miles Davis, huh? ... For all immediate purposes, Miles is gone – the past is over." He concluded: "The guy is obviously not doing anything worthwhile right now. Just as obviously, he doesn't care in the least for everyone's sobbing and lamentations for new material, an interview, or a live appearance. All Miles is doing now is showing up as every fifth or sixth word in every *Down Beat* article, no matter what the subject. The remedy for Davisitis? Get into what is happening *now* in jazz."[59] Davis would probably have agreed.

In his recording activities with the young Chicagoans, he seemed to be playing by rote, but those activities revived some deeper instincts. "Actually, see, you never retire from an instrument if you've been playing it since you were twelve because it's always in your head," he told Cheryl McCall. "I wasn't hearing any melodies or anything 'cause I wouldn't let myself hear anything, and all of a sudden those melodies started coming back to me."[60] He decided to try them out with a band in the recording studio.

For the first attempts, probably early in 1981, he brought back Al Foster, who had been playing with Sonny Rollins, and he re-called reedman Bill Evans, guitarist Barry Finnerty, and percussionist Sammy Figueroa, from the last sessions with the Chicago band. He needed a bassist, and Foster, Finnerty, and Evans all recommended Marcus Miller, one of the busiest young studio musicians in New York, on constant call for all kinds of funk and rock recordings. The details are as follows:

Miles Davis Sextet: The Man with the Horn
Miles Davis, tpt; Bill Evans, ss; Barry Finnerty, gtr; Marcus Miller, b; Al Foster, dms; Sammy Figueroa, congas. New York, probably January–March 1981
Back Seat Betty; *Aïda* [*Fast Track*]; *Ursula*
(all on Columbia FC 36790)
All titles are written and arranged by Davis.

Davis fulfilled some of the fears of his young sidemen by living up to his old reputation. He knew exactly what he wanted from them, and he let them know when he was not getting it. For *Aïda*, he told Miller to play an F and G vamp, but when Miller stuck resolutely to the chords, Davis stopped the band. "Is that all you gonna play?" he asked. "I heard you was *bad*. You ain't playin' shit." So Miller filled in his vamp ornately on the next take, and Davis stopped the band again. "What are you playin'?" he asked Miller. "Just play F and G and shut up."[61]

Some of the elements of Davis's post-retirement style are already intact in these recordings, although not as clearly defined as they would soon become. Where his working band of 1972–5 practiced a resolute collectivism, with the instrumental components fused together as if the surge of electricity had made a percussion-guitars-trumpet ingot, here they were restored as individual voices, charting their own space in the rock-jazz fusion. Davis plays trumpet solos instead of brass colorations, his two long turns playing muted over a walking bass line on *Ursula* comprising the longest, and most coherent, trumpet playing he had essayed for almost a decade. Al Foster, unencumbered in the new set up by the flotilla of players who formerly contributed to the dense bottom of the music, could play tough, elemental rhythms with only Figueroa's congas, sparse and tasteful, intervening.

Some of the music would persist when the retirement ended. *Back Seat Betty*, its title a left-handed compliment to Davis's ex-wife, became the concert opener in the first year of the comeback and, in a sense, for even longer than that, because the heavy-metal guitar and cascading percussion lick that starts it was retained when a new opener, called *Come Get It*, succeeded it. While *Ursula* is a long, meandering medium-uptempo ballad with a melody, perhaps entirely improvised, that is hard to locate, both *Aïda* and *Back Seat Betty* repeat simple four-bar declarations as their themes, the same kind of reduction of prepared material that Davis used in all his writing thereafter. His best compositions of the now-distant past, notably *Milestones*, *So What*, and *All Blues*, included similar proclamatory repetitions that gave way to longer melodies; in his new compositions only the proclamations remain.

Some of the other elements of these new recordings were destined to be shunted aside as his conception clarified. Bill Evans, soloing for the first time on record here, plays wailing, banshee cries on his too-sharp soprano saxophone, as if stepping into the old role of Davis's reedmen and supplying the foil for his more delicate trumpet. But Evans was clearly out of character. As his style developed in the next year when he became part of Davis's working band, he established a very different place for himself playing unassuming, cool solos on tenor saxophone, his preferred instrument, a foil instead for the fiery rock guitar that became the other component Davis used to spell himself off.

The most abiding composition, *Aïda*, underwent several changes after this initial recording. Retitled *Fast Track*, it became part of the new concert repertoire, but only after its simple theme was relocated in an easier context, usually played in future performances with a Spanish tinge. Few of the qualities that allowed it to endure in the repertoire are evident in this initial performance, which is heavily overlarded with rock effects. It seemed, if anything, the least distinctive of Davis's new themes.

Davis warmed to the task of making music on hearing the master tapes, and he realized that he had found some of the young sidemen he needed if he were going to make his return. He still wanted a more assertive guitarist, someone he could use as a soloist as well as the principal accompanist in the band; he asked Bill Evans if he knew anyone and was directed to Mike Stern. A young long-hair nicknamed 'Fat Time,' Stern looked like the epitome of the white rockers Davis sometimes complained about, but Evans's recommendation carried a lot of weight. "Now, if Bill plays that good, he's got it all," Davis reasoned, "and Mike plays that good, I'm goin' to play. Yeah, we played downstairs, and it was *nice*."[62] Davis soon returned to the studio with Stern in the band. The details are as follows:

Miles Davis Sextet: The Man with the Horn
Miles Davis, tpt, comp, arr; Bill Evans, ss; Mike Stern, gtr; Marcus Miller, b; Al Foster, dms; Sammy Figueroa, perc. New York, probably February– April 1981
Fat Time
(on Columbia FC 36790)

With Stern in the band, Davis located a new balance almost immediately. *Fat Time* is a longer theme – a tune, really – played over a lilting, funk bass line by Miller and chugging rhythm chords by Stern, a rhythm new to Davis's music and one that he would use frequently when he resumed performing. Evans's soprano solo, following Davis's muted solo, is relaxed and easy, a marked contrast to what he had played in the previous session, but he was allowed to ply his more natural style because he was now followed in the sequence by Stern, playing the high, reverberating notes over tougher rhythms that Evans had attempted earlier. Stern's rock-based electronics were not going to endear him to Davis's older fans, and after a year and a half of playing them for Davis even Stern began objecting to the stereotype he had settled into, but for the time being he was content. And Davis was delighted.

He started playing the new tapes for his visitors, and their reactions confirmed his feelings. Instead of the polite nods and vague murmurs they had given him for the tapes with Vincent Wilburn and his friends, they showed real enthusiasm. Gil Evans was impressed enough by Bill Evans that he lined him up to play in his band on 3 July 1981 at the Kool Jazz Festival (the Newport Festival, rechristened) and to tour Europe with his band immediately afterward. Herbie Hancock, a pillar of one of Davis's greatest bands, declared that these young players sounded like the best band Davis had assembled in years. George Wein, the Kool-Newport promoter who circled Davis warily throughout his retirement, had listened to some of the previous tapes with indifference. "Then one day he played something that gave me that old case of gooseflesh," he told George Goodman Jr. He added: "I didn't want to push him. I waited for him to say when."[63]

Davis was prepared to resume his career, and even Cicely Tyson, who had been encouraging him more actively than anyone, was surprised. "People say that it's thanks to me, but it's Miles who deserves credit for coming back," she told Leonard Feather in an interview published in *Jazz Hot* (translated into French and retranslated here). "We were together from 1966 to 1969. And at the end of each year after that I never forgot to phone him. I'd phone him New Year's eve, and I couldn't get over that he was still alive! I kept telling him that he still had a lot more things to do. Often he hung up on me, and I'd call him back again. He told me: 'I don't know any more if I've got anything to say.' He's a man who said from the start [*depuis les tripes*] if he had nothing to say, he wouldn't cheat." She could hardly argue with him on that, and his change of heart came without forewarning. "When he told me that he was rehearsing and that he was going to play again, I couldn't believe my ears."[64]

Wein was patient. He maintained an uncharacteristic silence with the press when he started talking seriously to Davis about ending the retirement, and in the end he scored the coup of his career. He and Davis had tangled dozens of times, usually noisily – "We have a love-hate relationship," Wein admits – but during the retirement he visited Davis in the hospital and at home several times. Once, according to Davis, Wein gave him $10,000: "I asked, 'What's this for?' and George told me, 'You might need it for cigarette money.'"[65] Now that Davis seemed ready to return, Wein was the only promoter he was talking to.

Still, it looked as if the comeback would have to wait another year. Wein's deadline for festival bookings passed and he faced the news conference to announce twenty-six concerts in seven days (28 June–5

July) in six different New York halls involving more than a hundred musicians, but Davis was not among them.

As soon as Wein sent out his press releases and placed his advertisements, Davis's discussions with him took a serious turn. He started complaining about the fee Wein had offered and dickering for a better deal. Wein knew then that Davis's retirement was over.

16

It Gets Better
1981 and After

Miles Davis is the only superstar that jazz has, not Mr. Basie, not Mr. Buddy Rich, not Mr. Kenton, none of these. Miles is the only superstar we've got. There are musicians who have made as much or more money but they weren't superstars. Jazz people need superstars just like rock people.   Chico Hamilton

Miles Davis's comeback concerts were the most publicized events in the history of jazz. *Down Beat* stopped its presses to squeeze this notice into its July issue: "BULLETIN: George Wein announced that the new Miles Davis Quintet will debut with two shows July 5." By the time that issue appeared on the newsstands in mid-June, newspapers all over the world had carried wire stories about the impending return. Tickets for the two concerts, scheduled for the Avery Fisher Hall in Lincoln Center at 7:00 and 10:30 on the final Sunday of the Kool Jazz Festival, were long gone. They sold out within two hours. Bill Cosby, the comedian, appeared on the NBC-TV *Tonight* show in August with a monologue explaining why he could not get tickets. "All these guys share the 'aura' of Miles Davis," he told ten million viewers, "so Miles Davis's show at the Avery Fisher Hall sold out without any advertising or anything, man, because they went in and bought all the tickets before they even went on sale – before they were even printed." Cosby was using comedic license; he had attended the concerts as Davis's backstage guest, but the comeback had turned into such a media event that he could use it as a springboard to put Davis's name in front of a mass audience.

The *New York Sunday Times* ran George Goodman Jr's interview on the front page of its entertainment section the week before the concerts, and Leonard Feather's *Los Angeles Times* column setting the background was syndicated and widely printed. Kiyoshi Koyama arrived from Tokyo to file reports for *Swing Journal*, and Michel Contat from Paris for *Le Monde*, which ran his review on its front page. Virtually every major newspaper in the world devoted some column inches to the event.

With all the publicity, the traditional squabble between Miles Davis and George Wein over Davis's fee seemed superfluous, but they had it anyway. Davis told Goodman that he would receive $90,000 for the two performances, and Wein, who had been berated by Davis in the past for discussing his fees in the press, replied, "I will not discuss the money issue except to say that $90,000 is not an accurate figure."[1]

Some of the anticipation may have dissipated when Davis decided to take his young band out in public *before* the Kool concerts, to try them out in what amounted to dress rehearsals. Davis took his new sextet into a small bar called Kix – described by one fan as "a really unpleasant club" – in Boston, probably arranged by Wein, where they played two sets a night from Friday to Monday, 26–29 June. One Boston fan who caught them there on the night of 29 June watched a first set of only 35 minutes and a second one of 75, and then wrote about them briefly in a personal letter: "He has a bunch of sidemen half his age and he *directs* them – the guitar player took too long a break and Miles went over and patted the guy's head. This 'direction' gave the whole thing a rather constipated tone." Davis, in his opinion, did not look or act like a healthy man. "I hope you get to see him for yourself," he added. "I had the feeling that his return wouldn't last long."

Another report, from Radio Paris in August, stated that Mino Cinelu, Davis's French-speaking percussionist, had massaged Davis's fingers for an hour and a half before the band could take the stand one night at Kix.

Columbia Records, apparently fearing that the comeback might be short-lived, stationed a remote recording crew in the Boston club and added the dress rehearsals to its archive. Some of the music was issued a year later on *We Want Miles*, a compilation of performances from Davis's first months back. (Columbia has never divulged the specific sources of the tracks on *We Want Miles*; sources listed here are based on inferences from incomplete private tapings, with the help of Jan Lohmann.) At Kix, the sidemen were obviously much less comfortable with Davis and with one another than they would become after a few months of working together; their concert in Tokyo in October, from which less than fifteen minutes was selected for the *We Want Miles* LP, is superior in every respect. But the Kix performances are much better than the band's frenetic playing at the pressure-packed Kool concerts in

July, which Columbia originally intended to issue as Davis's comeback LP. The details are as follows:

Miles Davis Sextet: We Want Miles
Miles Davis, tpt; Bill Evans, ts (on *Kix*), ss (on *Fast Track, My Man's Gone Now*); Mike Stern, gtr; Marcus Miller, b; Al Foster, dms; Mino Cinelu, perc.
Kix, Boston, 26–29 June 1981
Kix; Fast Track; My Man's Gone Now
(all on Columbia C2 38005)
Davis plays electric piano on the opening bars of *My Man's Gone Now*. Evans is not heard on the excerpt from *Fast Track*. Identification of these titles originating at this session is tentative.

Kix, which fills the fourth side of the LP, is built on a four-bar bass riff played by Marcus Miller, sometimes parroted by Cinelu's congas; Davis inserts a two-bar melody irregularly between the soundings of the bass riff, but it is the bass riff, not the trumpet melody, that recurs to form the theme. From this slender underpinning, the band take off in a varied and supple improvisation in 4/4 time, doubling the basic ballad tempo for long stretches and twice stopping the time, apparently leaving Miller to use his discretion in inserting his theme. The performance thus demands more than a little ingenuity from both Miller and the soloists – Davis, saxophonist Bill Evans, guitarist Mike Stern, Davis again, and Evans again. Although the band had played only a few hours in public when *Kix* was recorded, they had obviously been well drilled beforehand. The formal simplicity of *Kix* alleviated some of the potential problems they might have had in the transition from private to public rehearsals and may have been devised mainly for that purpose. In any event, the simplistic *Kix* was removed from the band's repertoire later in the summer.

The format gives the two young soloists, who were complete unknowns to most of the jazz audience, interesting exposure. Stern opens his solo with long, fast lines before moving into the choppy rock phrases and searing single notes that would become his usual register in this band; he functions more as the percussion leader than as soloist at the end of his turn, whipping Foster's drums along until they threaten to overpower him. Evans, soloing twice on tenor saxophone, plays longer here than he did in most performances later on. His first solo is redolent of John Coltrane. Joe Goldberg also noticed Evans's debt to Coltrane at a concert later in the summer and commented: "Most of Miles' saxophone players sound like that, perhaps because he tells them to ... It is understandable that, having heard that sound every night for years, Miles would miss it, and attempt to have it recreated. But if that was indeed his assigned task, the present saxophonist approached it with rather too much fidelity to the original. He evidently shares with me a fondness for the Coltrane solo on the original recording of *All Blues*, from which I heard several favorite phrases."[2] But Evans soon learned to control his tendency for aping Coltrane, and his playing, as it has become better known, is indebted to Coltrane no more (and no less) than many other tenor players his age.

For Davis, the *Kix* performance is ambiguous. His solos include moments of bright lyricism, unencumbered by any electronic tricks, making obvious references to his classic ballad style; it is impossible to tell whether he is revisiting his old style or rediscovering the old convictions that made that style, and his reviewers often vacillated between lauding it and damning it, depending on the assumption they made. But his solos also include some moments of flattened sonority, especially at faster tempos, and an attempted high note that emerges as a squeak.

Fast Track would soon become known, at least obliquely, under the title *Aïda*, in the studio version included on the LP *The Man with the Horn*, which Columbia rushed through production in order to catch the tide of publicity surrounding Davis's comeback. This version has the same spirit as the studio recording: it is an exercise in power rhythm, with a tough beat and echoing blasts of repeated notes from Davis and Stern. Much of its extra length is due to Mino Cinelu, whose conga playing is featured, sometimes in a dialogue with Foster. The harmonic range of the drums seems roughly equal to the trumpet and guitar, the way they are used on this piece. *Fast Track/Aïda* is a throwback to Davis's pre-retirement rhythm band style, but it lacks the libido that gave that style whatever fascination it had.

By far the most interesting music came on the title that pointed backward and updated Davis's old strengths. *My Man's Gone Now*, in a twenty-minute version, recapitulates many of the beauties of the six-minute version Davis recorded twenty-three years earlier with Gil Evans's orchestra. Here, as there, Davis plays the A sections of the melody full of respect for Gershwin and doubles the tempo at the bridge; here, Miller carries the tempo of the bridge throughout the A sections in a repeated bass vamp, where Paul Chambers and the brass choir had implied the faster tempo under the slow sections in Evans's score. Davis's intensity in his ballad reading is also remarkably preserved. But the retained elements are thoroughly transformed. In place of tubas and trombones, Davis relies on Miller's bass to supply resonance, and in place of the soaring brass he calls on Stern's guitar to supply color. Boosted electronically by devices unimagined at the time of the original recording, Miller and Stern become a space-age orchestra.

Other elements of the arrangement are entirely new. When Stern solos, he doubles the tempo of the bridge, thus quadrupling the tempo of the A melody. As this band settled into Davis's concept, Stern was asked more often than not to solo at double the tempo of the others, and in many contexts the rise in pitch whenever he moved into the foreground seemed gratuitous and ultimately wearying, apparently no less to Stern than to Davis's audiences. Here it is not gratuitous; Stern's redoubling of the tempo forms the climactic movement from the easy ballad and the accelerated bridge. Davis cannot resist joining Stern, coming in at an odd interval of the chorus and playing to the end, when he abruptly shifts the tempo back to the slow opening.

To this point, *My Man's Gone Now* makes a brilliant show of Davis's revitalized talents and his young sidemen's resources. The elements of Davis's rearrangement of the Evans-Davis orchestration are tightly controlled; as the band grew more familiar with it, it underwent certain mutations and the contrasting sections were only implied. In this performance, it stands as the best harbinger of Davis's return to form – to the point described above. Unfortunately, it does not end there. Instead, Davis resumes the arrangement from the top, but carelessly, only hinting at the A melody and allowing Stern another crack at high speed. Much of the feeling and all the freshness fade in this second run-through, and the fine performance that preceded it is somewhat sullied. Such excess seems a strange failing for a musician who spent much of his career extolling musical economy and practicing it as no one else ever had. But that was long ago. Davis started losing sight of the virtue of musical economy sometime in the late 1960s, and his first comeback performances served notice that, whatever old verities might be renewed in the music to come, economy would not be one of them.

Davis returned to New York from Boston on 1 July, the Wednesday before his Kool concerts, as guest of honor at a Columbia cocktail and caviar party held at Xenon, a discotheque. Davis stayed half an hour, meeting the press and posing for them, chatting briefly and accepting pats on the back, and smiling. No one complained that he left too soon.

He seemed to be enjoying a truce with the record company. "Columbia is so *vague* and *cheap*," he told Cheryl McCall, but he could not follow through with his old, familiar theme, and he added: "Now they're not cheap anymore, they think I'm a genius. They thought I was a genius before, but now they're *convinced*."[3]

Young Bill Evans played in Gil Evans's band for the Kool concert at Town Hall on 3 July. He was also booked to join Evans's band on their European tour as soon as Davis's Kool concerts were finished, but he had to change his plans. "At the last minute Miles decided that he was going to work," Gil Evans explained. "Miles went up to Boston and played those four nights and he was feeling so good that he decided to get booked around, so he wouldn't let Bill go. On the night of the Town Hall gig Bill told me he had to drop out. He felt terrible having to cancel at the last minute, but I told him, 'You'll get used to that. Your career will make you do that sometimes.' So luckily Steve Grossman was able to go at the last minute."[4]

Davis was nervous about his Kool concerts, and his nerves would continue to bother him before all his concerts for the next few years. "I get butterflies in my stomach before every concert," he told Leonard Feather. "I can't eat the day before, and I really suffer. But since I came back on the scene, my nervousness is disappearing, and the more I play, the stronger I get."[5]

The first Kool concert, scheduled for 7 p.m. Sunday, started and ended in confusion. After members of the audience had been assembled, waiting, for almost half an hour, the public address announcer informed them that they could leave the hall to get a drink. Many did, but some held their places, probably thinking, as Michel Contat did, that "having waited five years, one can easily wait a half-hour longer."[6] Almost as soon as the people were out of the hall, the announcer declared, flatly, "The event of the 80s," and Davis and his band walked onstage. The audience stood and began applauding, jostled by the rush of patrons back to their seats, but Davis, without a glance in their direction, raised the trumpet to his lips and started playing. The band played for seventy minutes without an intermission and walked off. The standing ovation turned to boos when Davis failed to return to take a bow.

Between concerts, Davis and the others cooled down at a reception in the green room, with Bill Cosby, Roberta Flack, Cicely Tyson, and other guests. Numerous musicians filed out of the hall as the audience made its slow retreat, among them Gato Barbieri, Carla Bley, Lee Konitz, Red Rodney, and the punk band called the Lounge Lizards – "this," Contat noted, "in a city where musicians never ordinarily go to hear a concert by a colleague."

The second concert went more smoothly, starting on time at 10:30, lasting more than ninety minutes, and ending with a standing ovation that Davis returned to acknowledge. There were no encores, but also no boos.

Whitney Balliett reviewed the first concert as part of his annual Newport/Kool report for the *New Yorker*. He saw it as a piece of musical theater and characteristically made the review into an indelible image. "Miles Davis ... turned up for two shows at Avery Fisher Hall tonight ... and, for the hour that the first show lasted, pretended he was in *Apocalypse Now*," he wrote. "Davis was dressed for the trip. He had on a fisherman's cap, a dark jacket, which he kept taking off, a singlet, gray pipestem pants, and clogs. It was night, and the darkness was broken by a searchlight that followed Davis as he stumped from side to side of the boat, ... raised his fist and brought it down to turn the ship of sound in a new direction ... The heavy-metal roar of guitar, bass, and drums was almost always present, and to make himself heard Davis had a small microphone fastened to his trumpet. His muted solos rose clearly above the din, and when he took out his mute and let loose an open-horn blast the crocodiles lining the banks jumped ... When the boat reached Kurtz's hideaway, Davis turned to the audience for the first time, and *waved*, as if to let us know that he is just one of us after all and that what we had been watching – it was a visual music – was only imaginary."[7]

Very little of the Kool concerts was issued on LP, notwithstanding Columbia's original intention of commemorating the event as Davis's comeback album. Sober evaluation of the concert tapes in the editing room after the excitement died down, and the availability of better performances when Davis remained active afterward, dictated a change of plans. Only an excerpt from *Back Seat Betty*, the concert opener, made the transition to record from the first concert. The details are as follows:

Miles Davis Sextet: We Want Miles
Miles Davis, tpt; Bill Evans, ts, ss; Mike Stern, gtr; Marcus Miller, b; Al Foster, dms; Mino Cinelu, perc. Avery Fisher Hall, New York, 5 July 1981
Back Seat Betty; My Man's Gone Now; Fast Track; Kix
(excerpt from *Back Seat Betty* on Columbia C2 38005; otherwise all unissued)
Evans is not heard on the issued excerpt from *Back Seat Betty*; he plays ts on *Back Seat Betty* and *Kix*, ss on the other titles.

Back Seat Betty gets a much more spirited reading than it had in the studio version, released on *The Man with the Horn*. Evans's solo, a gritty tenor ride, was sacrificed in the editing, and so were the other solos except for Davis's. The cascading intervals used both in the studio version and at the concert to open it and mark the transitions between soloists were shorn away too, but they are easily detached from the piece, and over the next years, after Davis stopped using *Back Seat Betty* as his concert opener, the cascading interval was retained as a kind of overture at all his concerts. Davis's solo begins with the simple muted melody, one part of it now further simplified into a playful schoolyard call ("He-ey, Be-e-etty"), and moves into an overlong sequence of exclamations on the open horn to rally the drummers. In the muted sections, Miller thumps out some fills that accent Davis's phrases perfectly.

The comeback concerts, for all their success as public relations events, placed Davis in a situation from which he had little chance of emerging unscathed. His presence on the stage guaranteed a standing ovation, but as soon as the curtain fell his performance was subjected to the closest scrutiny any jazzman had ever faced. Barely back on his feet after almost six years, supported by young and, except for Al Foster, inexperienced sidemen, he faced an audience as full of anticipation as any crowd at a world championship prize-fight, and critics almost as full of blood-lust. He could hardly expect to win the critical decision at the end, and in music, unlike boxing, there is nothing equivalent to a knockout for averting the decision.

The dominant impression of the critics after hearing no less than one hour and no more than three hours of music was that Davis had hardly changed at all since the last time he performed in public. "He neither regresses nor innovates," Contat wrote in *Le Monde*; "he recapitulates."[8] For Art Lange, that meant he had not changed enough. "Miles has emerged from a time-warp," he wrote in *Down Beat*; "his playing was stronger than anticipated – the same squirted, elliptical utterances which sounded so magical in the late '60s and early '70s ... Unfortunately, these are the '80s."[9] Cécile Tailleur, writing for *Le Point*, concluded: "His two concerts ... proved, above all, that [for Davis] the fusion between jazz and rock is irreversible."[10]

Most acknowledged that Davis was playing well technically. "Just one note and you knew Miles was back – that sound is as welcome and familiar as the first breezes of autumn," Lee Jeske wrote in *Down Beat*, in a review facing Lange's more caustic one. "Miles' tone was stunning, his chops were in excellent shape, and he quickly let us know it, removing the mute and wailing, with the trumpet bell not four inches off the stage floor."[11] "Davis's chops are in good shape," Balliett agreed, "but he played the same solo again and again. It went like this: an ascending shriek (Dizzy Gillespie, 1945) followed by a scurrying downward run; a second, lower shriek; silence; another run, broken off abruptly in the Bud Powell manner; silence; a three-note cluster, the last note flatted and held for a measure or two; an upward run; and a closing six-note cluster."[12]

The young sidemen bore the brunt of the critical beating. "Mr. Davis's latest group is reminiscent of his mid-70s units," Robert Palmer wrote in the New York Times. "Al Foster ... is the music's backbone. The other players are effective enough when Mr. Davis is soloing, but only the saxophonist Bill Evans seems to have a well-developed sense of pacing and at least a modicum of original ideas."[13] Contat largely shared that view, saying that the sidemen "are magnificent instrumentalists capable of playing everything, but not showing any inventiveness whatever."[14] Lange claimed that the sidemen "failed to sustain any extended solo or ensemble interest, culminating in guitarist Mike Stern's indulgent, exasperating forays."[15] Palmer added that "Mike Stern's guitar solos were rife with the most banal heavy rock clichés imaginable."[16] Stephen Brunt, in the Toronto Globe and Mail, said, "Most of their solos would have sounded more appropriate at a rock concert,"[17] but Lange claimed they were "neither good rock, nor good jazz." Jeske concluded: "The Man with the Horn is back – playing driving, aggressive trumpet – but the men with the guitar, bass and percussion were just not up to stylistic snuff."[18]

Lange viewed the late concert, as Balliett had the early one, as an exercise in showmanship: "This concert was more theater than music: the more appreciative members of the audience giving ovations at Miles' every move, Miles slapping fives with bandmates, his walking the stage, working it, worrying it to death, hunched over, notes aimed at the floor, braying like an elephant ... It's too easy to go out there and strut and vamp and jive this way."[19]

A few fans demurred. Down Beat printed a letter from a Minneapolis doctor stating that he had been "infuriated" by Palmer's review in the Times. "I traveled over 1500 miles to witness this concert," he said, "and I'm glad I was there."[20]

What infuriated him most was Palmer's contention that Davis should have been more aware of the music being played during his retirement.

"Apparently Mr. Davis did not listen to much contemporary electric music during his five-year absence from performing and recording," Palmer stated. "Bands like Ornette Coleman's Prime Time, Ronald Shannon Jackson's Decoding Society, and James (Blood) Ulmer's various groups have learned to make amplified ensemble music that is as harmonically challenging and melodically sophisticated as any contemporary jazz and as rhythmically bracing as the hardest funk. Compared to these groups, the Davis band's circumscribed harmonic language, heavy-handed rhythms, and hackneyed 60's guitar solos sounded positively old-fashioned."[21]

Palmer was right in assuming that Davis had not been keeping up with jazz in his retirement. The highest value he put on listening to records was a negative one. "It's useful, but mainly to see what you don't want to do, as always," he said. "It's nice to see someone else fall off the ladder! You can hear things that you wouldn't do yourself, without having to go through trying them out."[22] In various interviews granted in the wake of his comeback he responded to the inevitable question about whom he listened to by citing Stockhausen and Ravel, the pop-rock groups Journey and the Who, two young, teen idols named Michael Jackson and Prince, Weather Report, Willie Nelson, and singers who know how to exploit a melody, Frank Sinatra among them.

In his new band, he typecast Mike Stern in a Jimi Hendrix solo role and Marcus Miller in a funk support role. They worked capably, but both knew, and Davis would eventually find out, that their roles were far too narrow for the post-fusion climate they were playing in.

The critical perception of jazz-rock fusion had clarified considerably during Davis's absence. Musically, fusion music had crested almost a decade before, with the release of *Bitches Brew* and the further explorations that immediately followed it, many of them presided over by members of Davis's stock company. Commercially, it hit its peak a few years later in the mid-1970s, led by Hancock's Headhunters and Weather Report, but by then its jazz components had become so waterlogged that they were almost totally submerged. By 1981 the experiments were over and the audiences for rock and for jazz had gone their separate ways, with rock settling into punk banalities that were as vapid as, and not much different from 1950s rock 'n' roll. Tom Scott, the saxophonist who, as a young studio player and bandleader, had caught the fusion wave and ridden it to rock-style capital gains, now described its waning with no regrets. "As it turns out, I was in the vanguard of the fusion movement," he told A. James Liska in an interview in *Down Beat* that appeared on the newsstands just as Davis was unveiling his rock-based youth band. "It was an accident though. I was a serious Coltrane–Cannonball–Charlie Parker–Miles Davis student and all this fusion stuff was just a little departure that lasted ten years or so. There was nothing to it – nothing serious, that is."[23]

Several events at the Kool Jazz Festival, almost unnoticed in the hullabaloo of Davis's comeback, reflected the state of the art. Weather Report displayed their unrevised brand of jazz-tinged rock at Avery Fisher Hall the night before Davis, and almost half the audience, according to Stephen Brunt, left before the intermission. Two other erstwhile stars of jazz-rock revised their styles and kept their audiences. Chick Corea played acoustic piano at his concert – "having abandoned Electronic Heights, in Fusion City," as Balliett put it – with Roy Haynes, the bop drummer, in his quartet. Herbie Hancock assembled a quartet with Wynton Marsalis, Ron Carter, and Tony Williams and gave a concert that, for many observers, was the high point of the festival, without an electronic instrument or a wah-wah pedal in sight.

So Davis's comeback concerts presented a musical style that was out of step with the main currents of the day. That should not have been surprising: he had put himself out of step with those currents before retiring, when he formed his 1972 rhythm band and chose, whether he knew it or not at the time, to give up being the leader in jazz in favor of becoming its superstar. His return concert affirmed that he was going to stick with that choice, although the music he played on his return had little in common – certainly less than many reviewers assumed – with the music he was playing when he quit.

For the reviewers and many other members of the jazz audience, the realization that Davis would not reassume the mantle of leadership was disappointing, especially because no one had taken it up in his absence. But that was hardly Davis's fault.

"We deceive ourselves; we expect too much," Contat concluded, sounding a note that many other reviewers missed. "Five years of silence from one of the four or five great creators of jazz, when all the others are dead and the music is stagnating, creates a mythology: the myth of the Messiah. Miles Davis, and this should be enough to give us joy for the time being, is back."[24]

Davis's critics had more fodder soon after his concerts ended. Columbia released *The Man with the Horn* amid the swell of publicity, and it contained several performances that were far weaker than anything he had shown in his concert debut. W.A. Brower gave it three stars in *Down Beat*, and stated: "This record – parts of it – is pleasant.

That's all"; the rest of the review was a diatribe.[25] A more positive review in *Le Nouvel Observateur* welcomed Davis's return, but ended on this vague note: "Miles is always the man who walks on eggshells but the insidious sweetness – never cloying – of a piece like *The Man with the Horn* recalls how caramels also tease your teeth."[26]

Notwithstanding the reviews, the new LP sold briskly. It entered *Rolling Stone*'s list of the 100 best-selling albums in August at number 47 and moved up steadily. Radio Paris reported that it was selling "several hundred copies daily" there. Davis's only comment on the LP, when he played the tape to George Goodman Jr just before it was released in June, was, "To me, it's old. I can't stand it."[27]

Davis's comeback aroused at least as much curiosity about his well-being as about his music. The first report, from Goodman in the *Times*, was ebullient. "Mr. Davis is looking fit," he said, "and speaking with mischievous humor in the rasping whisper of a voice that is a Miles Davis trademark." That description hardly prepared his audiences for the changes that had transformed his appearance while he sat in his darkened brownstone.

He wore a cap or a wollen tam pulled down to his ears to cover a balding pate, where there had been, as far as anyone could remember, a thick Afro when last seen. He was down fifteen pounds from his "fighting weight" of 135, and the sparse new mustache and goatee only made his face look pinched. "When ... he re-emerged into the public arena, he seemed to a frightening degree physically reduced," Richard Williams wrote in *The Times* of London. "On stage ... he moved slowly and painfully; he appeared literally to have shrunk. The imperious carriage and the feline prowling which had contributed to his legendary presence were completely gone."[28] In fact, he now moved compulsively around the stage, as if he had been forbidden to give his weary bones any rest. His movements were impeded not only by his arthritic joints but also by the truss and rubber corset he wore to shore up the muscles of his abdomen.

Psychologically he seemed better off. He was full of confidence and claimed that he had never had any doubts about his ability to play the trumpet. "I never think about not being able to do anything," he said. "I just pick up my horn and play the hell out of it." His embouchure, he claimed, had never softened, and as soon as he started thinking about music again he was ready to play. He was now thinking about it all the time. "I can't stop once I start thinking about it," he told Goodman. "My mind is like this. I can't sleep for three days, four days at a time."

Gratuitously he offered Goodman his advice for staying young. "The way to stay young is to forget, to have a bad memory," he said. "You know, when a woman says to me, 'Do you remember when we were lovers five years ago?' I say, 'No.' Guys come up to me with their arms outstretched, I say, 'What's that for?' And they say, '1947, Chicago, remember? We got high together.' I say: 'Get out of my face.' ... Everything you do, you want to do, but then you don't want to be reminded of it."[29] If that attempt at hoary wisdom sounded out of character from a man who had just turned 55 and looked older, it is probably because it rightfully belonged to a man who was about to turn 70 and looked younger. Gil Evans had taken to expounding the same idea fairly often. "I read an interview in the *International Herald Tribune* with a man who was celebrating his 100th birthday and they asked the usual 'How do you account for such a long life?' and the man said, 'A poor memory.' That's all he said and I knew what he meant exactly," Evans told Zan Stewart in 1982.[30]

Apart from Davis's health, most of the curiosity was aroused by his young sidemen, whose professional careers began in an unusual glare of publicity. Following the Kool concerts, Davis took them on a round of American concert halls for three months, starting with a hastily arranged engagement at the Savoy in New York two weeks later, and moving on to other hastily arranged dates in various cities, including Washington, DC (28 July), and Detroit (16 August), until September, when his new manager, Mark Rothbaum, had enough lead time to put together a more carefully articulated tour that took in the Music Hall in Cincinnati (18 September), the University of Michigan at Ann Arbor (19), the Hollywood Bowl, Los Angeles (25), and Concord Pavilion, San Francisco (26). From California, they took off for a round of concerts in Japan.

As the American audience became exposed to the new band, it discovered that the young sidemen were not the ciphers that several of the New York critics had led them to expect. On the contrary, after the pressure of the comeback concerts they settled down and showed that they were among the brightest new talents in jazz.

The changing perception of the sidemen was boosted by Davis's respect for their talents, which he expressed at every opportunity. Asked by Cheryl McCall if he thought he was healthy enough to withstand all the traveling, he said, "Not really. It's just playing with Bill [Evans] and those guys. It turns me on. It makes the adrenalin start flowing. It's such a great bunch of guys, they play so well, it's a pity to let them down, you know."[31]

They had been stung by the caustic criticisms, and Davis constantly reassured them. Marcus Miller recalls Davis telling them, "Who you gonna believe, me or some guy who works for a newspaper?" And during one concert, Davis walked up to Miller and said, "Man, you swing better than them old motherfuckers."[32] Not all the critical barbs directed at them, Davis claimed, were strictly objective. "One guy did it 'cause I wouldn't do an interview with him," he said. "He kind of upset my guitar player. I said, man, look at me, I've been called a black motherfucker, and black this and that, some of this here and that there. Man, you just ignore it. The best thing is not to say anything at all."[33]

His feeling for the men in the band was undisguised, and his openness with them was part of a brand-new character that emerged after four years of sitting in the dark. "The Miles the band knows, no one else has ever known," Miller told Sam Freedman in a *Down Beat* interview. "This person is closer, I think, to the real person behind all the stories. Once on the phone, I was telling Miles I was feeling uptight about my playing, feeling a little insecure. Miles said, 'I felt the same way when I was your age.' And I said, 'You were playing with Bird and those guys.' He said, 'Man, Bird and them would leave me up on the bandstand, go downstairs to do their thing. The tempo would be goin' by and I played one chorus, two choruses. By the third chorus, I didn't care what I played. Wasn't my band.'" Miller adds, "It meant so much just to see everybody, even Miles go through those insecurities. And if Miles likes the way I play, I don't need to hear anything else."[34]

Davis dominated the new band musically, in much the way that he had dominated his earlier bands and in marked contrast to his melding into the collective sound of his last band. The music now was more carefully worked out, determining a context in which individual innovations were encouraged. "When you practice you take the *edge* off something," he said. "We don't practice, we *rehearse*, there's a difference. We rehearse and throw things around. After a couple of times they get the idea. And that's it."[35] Mino Cinelu told Gérald Arnaud: "Miles directs us very little. When Al [Foster] isn't playing what he wants, he just looks at him ... Lots of things pass between Miles and all of us. Since Mike [Stern] is responsible for the harmonies, it's good that he and Miles share a close communication." Although he said little to the young sidemen about their playing, Davis made sure that they would hear his opinions indirectly. "I simply know that Miles often tells Mike that I carry the whole band," Cinelu said, adding, "With Al, of course."[36]

"When Miles isn't playing, that doesn't mean he is absent," Miller noted in an interview for the French magazine *Jazz Hot*; "everything he touches carries his mark. He penetrates each of us and makes us play for him [*à sa guise*]. He transforms, inspires his band. His influence goes beyond his trumpet playing."[37]

The band members, Davis told Cheryl McCall, responded creatively to his indirect direction. "They pay attention," he said. "And they're all professionals, so professionally they know if they miss anything, it's gonna fall right back on them. Everybody in my band could have a band right now. I don't tell them what to do, I just *suggest* something and if they don't like it they'll suggest something else. Say, can we do this *and* this. Or they'll know what I mean and add something to it that makes it better."[38] In only a few months, the band pulled together musically and personally. "We're a group with a homogeneity truly astonishing," Cinelu said, "especially astonishing because our musical backgrounds are very different."[39]

As they made their first swing through several American cities that summer, the young sidemen gradually lost their anonymity.

Al Foster had been Davis's closest friend in his last working band, and he remained close to him during the retirement, one of a handful of friends that included Gil Evans, Herbie Hancock, and Dave Liebman who visited him regularly – "telling me," as Davis put it, "what's happening out on the street." Foster worked with numerous studio and pickup bands during Davis's layoff. His longest association was with the Milestone Jazz Stars, an all-star touring group assembled by Milestone Records, the heir to defunct Riverside, now a division of the Fantasy conglomerate. The Milestone Jazz Stars featured Sonny Rollins, McCoy Tyner, and Ron Carter, with Foster as the unbilled fourth man in the quartet. When tours took him away from New York, Foster talked to Davis almost daily on the telephone. "I stay in constant touch with Al no matter where he is," Davis told Cheryl McCall. There was no doubt in the minds of either of them that Foster would rejoin Davis if and when he formed a new band. "Al called me up from France," Davis recalled, "and said you should see the hotel I'm staying in. I said *I told you about that.* Why should you stay in a bad hotel, you don't live in a bad house? You lose half your money just trying to find a bed. He said, It's not like when we're travelling with you, chief, 'cause you had us the best food and rooms. I said, when you're with the best you get the best."[40]

The rehiring of Foster was surprising only because it went against

Bill Evans and Miles Davis onstage (Peter Jones)

Miles Davis (Brock May)

Davis's wont for hiring untried players. When Davis asked Dave Liebman to recommend a reedman for the new band, he explained that he could not use Liebman himself because he wanted new talents. "He doesn't like to go back to people he's played with before," Bill Evans said.[41] But the policy proved flexible when Foster was involved, and he was the veteran among the rookies in the new band.

Bill Evans became Davis's protégé, in the beginning, and the focal point for Davis's onstage wanderings. "Bill's my *right hand man*, boy. Without him I don't know what I'd do," Davis said.[42] At Davis's concerts, that description appeared to be true literally – Evans stood stage left, on Davis's right – but not figuratively. Only Liebman among Davis's reedmen got as little playing time, and Evans sometimes put in stretches of twenty minutes without raising his horn to his lips. He bided his time almost motionless behind his microphones in a three-quarter stance that let him keep his eyes on Foster and Stern at center stage without quite turning away from the audience. When Davis's wanderings on the proscenium took him close to Evans's position, sometimes catching him in a corner of the spotlight, Evans looked as if he had been caught stealing an apple, and when Davis raised his eyes from the floor and stared at Evans past the bell of his horn, Evans would flash a shy grin that suggested he would rather be anywhere else but there.

Evans's solos were often interrupted abruptly by Davis's trumpet re-entering at an odd juncture – the seventh bar, say, of Evans's second chorus – and taking over. Evans naturally got annoyed and frustrated, and toward the end of his two-and-a-half-year tenure he sometimes grumbled openly after concerts in which he had played less than his share. The interruptions, like everything else that passed between Davis and Evans onstage, seemed part of a relentless mind-game in which Davis preyed on Evans's diffidence, like a panther circling a treed potto.

Offstage, they showed deeper bonds – "a sick father/healthy son relationship," Breskin called it.[43] "There's my favorite pupil," Davis said, and among the lessons he claimed to have taught Evans were how to dress for concerts, apparently in the headbands and loose, decorative shirts that Evans favors, and how to tap his foot by bringing down the heel first.[44] Evans submitted graciously in the beginning. "It's my first time on the road, my first record, my first time being an important part of the band along with big names," he told Howard Mandel soon after the debut concerts. "This is, I would say, something major. And I like it – I like it a lot."[45]

Evans was 23 at the time of Davis's comeback and since leaving his Illinois home more than three years before had been an inveterate student. For a few terms he attended North Texas State University, home of a high-quality, high-pressure stage band program that had fed several players into the bands of Buddy Rich, Maynard Ferguson, Woody Herman, and others. He transferred to William Patterson College in New Jersey, where he could earn a degree in jazz performance while playing professionally in and around New York. Before Davis hired him, his best credential was an appearance with Art Blakey at the Village Vanguard. He met Dave Liebman and Steve Grossman at a summer clinic run by Jamey Aebersold, and through Liebman he met Davis in April 1980. Through Davis he met Gil Evans, who would have taken him on his first tour with a name band if Davis had not reclaimed him.

Evans's best horn was the tenor saxophone. He started playing the soprano saxophone, which he used more often in Davis's band, only after meeting Davis, and his first recorded efforts on it consisted of cautious, sustained notes quite unlike his more melodic, but still cautious, tenor solos. The gap between the two instruments narrowed noticeably in his first year of touring. By the summer of 1982 he also began carrying a flute onstage for some performances, using it seldom but, when he did, impressively.

Davis seemed to appreciate Evans's piano playing as much as his woodwinds. At every concert for the first two years, Davis edged him over to the electric piano at some point in the proceedings to take a turn, which Evans made as short as Davis would allow. "He used to play classical piano and give concerts of Rachmaninoff and stuff like that when he was sixteen," Davis says. "People don't know that. I wouldn't ask him to sit down if he couldn't play."[46]

Davis's conviction about Evans's ability on piano and Evans's reluctance to put it on exhibit developed into a piece of musical theater. In the early concerts, Davis directed Evans to the piano with an imperious motion of his head. On evenings when Evans held his place, smiling boyishly and pretending not to know what Davis wanted, Davis would stump over and escort him to the piano, one hand on the small of Evans's back. Early in 1983, the ritual expanded. Davis's onstage wanderings would lead him to Evans's microphone where he would challenge him to trade four-bar phrases; Evans, on soprano, would begin by parroting Davis's trumpet runs until one or the other of them, usually Davis, would unleash what the audience took to be an unparrotable tirade. Evans would then allow himself to be sheperded over to the piano as an act of submission. The ritual obviously pleased Davis immensely and unfailingly elicited whoops of delight from Davis's audiences. But Evans, cast as the fall guy, took less pleasure from it, and the ritual ended after a few months.

On nights when Evans had little opportunity to show his talents on reeds, he gave memorable performances playing Tom Jones to Davis's Squire Western. Some nights, he not only filled that role but also displayed a subtle touch on his horns, calmly developing handsome lines that floated over noisier rhythms than he would likely have chosen for himself. Davis's audiences recognized Evans's potential, but few of them saw it realized fully enough to share Davis's almost unbounded enthusiasm. "He's one of the greatest musicians I've ever come upon," Davis told Cheryl McCall, and he added: "He and Gil Evans. There must be something with those Evanses. Must be a *breed.*"[47] Davis's reluctance to let Evans prove his ability with fully elaborated solos or anything close to an equal share of the solo space baffled jazz fans and frustrated Evans.

Much more solo space was allotted to Mike Stern, who was recommended to Davis by Evans after they had played together in Boston in January 1981. "In order to recommend a guitar player to Miles, you've got to think about what Miles wants to hear," Evans told Howard Mandel. "He likes Jimi Hendrix and hot lines. A straight bebop guitarist wouldn't do it. Mike is a real good guy. He looks different, he thinks different, and he plays different; he has a real good technique, and he can handle the bebop bridges, where Miles swings. What else could you want?"[48]

Stern was born and raised in Washington, DC, and after high school went to Boston to study at the Berklee School of Music. There he took classes from Michael Goodrick, the guitarist who played briefly in the quartet of Gary Burton, another Berklee faculty member, in 1973 but whose considerable influence on young guitarists emanates from the classroom. "He was one of the first," according to John Scofield, another of his students, "to absorb Jim Hall's lyrical, legato approach and also have a real modern concept of harmony."[49] John Abercrombie and Pat Metheny also count Goodrick as an important influence, thus giving him a hand in the development of four of the most prominent young guitarists.

After Berklee, Stern made his home in Boston, traveling from there to play with the revived Blood, Sweat and Tears in the final attempt at restoring that band's commercial success and later with Billy Cobham's band. "That's where Miles first saw me," Stern told Howard Mandel. "But for me, playing with Miles is by far the best gig ever. I've always been a Miles fan but never expected to play with him. And he's real supportive. Like on the album [*Man with the Horn*], on my solo for *Fat Time*, that was the last thing recorded. I'd been brought in to replace Barry Finnerty. I thought the track we cut was an out-take. I didn't have my amps set right, and I was real depressed by the solo. But Miles really dug it. We get together now and listen to tapes we've made, and I'm never sure – but Miles is totally knocked out, and into it. He makes me do things I wonder about, but he's always right."[50]

Davis made Stern do things that Davis's audiences wondered about too, and none of the young sidemen absorbed such continual criticism. None of them was as conspicuous during Davis's performances. Stern stationed himself beside Foster's drum set in the center of the stage. The volume of his amplifier was set high. He played continuously, accompanying almost everything and soloing lengthily, usually with the tempo surging behind him. No matter if he sneaked in a bebop solo part way through the concert, the main impression was of frenetic, unmodulated, ear-busting verbosity.

He repeatedly claimed that much of what he played for Davis went against his better judgment. "I'll play bebop kind of lines – I've played hundreds of bop lines, but that's not what Miles wants – looking for the horn sounds on my guitar," Stern told Mandel. "Playing after horns, which I've been doing for several years now, that's what I tend to do. It's not Wes Montgomery or Jim Hall, though I try to do all of that, 'cause I'm into that. But I throw it all together and *think*, think about constructing solos, about putting Bill's and Miles' ideas together, and just hope it works. It's weird, but it's kind of big fun."[51]

The result often pleased Davis more than anyone else, Stern included. Stern found himself in a musical no-man's land in Davis's band, strafed by Davis if he moved too far from heavy-metal rock and shelled by the reviewers when he stuck with it. "Miles wants me to play loud," he told Bill Milkowski. "At Avery Fisher Hall ... he went over and turned my amp up at one point. And he's always saying thing to me like 'Play some Hendrix! Turn it up or turn it off!' Miles loves Hendrix. Jimi and Charlie Christian are his favorite cats as far as guitarists are concerned. So right now with this band he wants to hear volume. My own natural instinct is to play a little softer, which I've been able to do on tunes like *My Man's Gone Now*, where my playing is a little darker. But Miles wants me to fill a certain role with this band, so I'm playing loud and my solos are usually speeded to double-time where I have to play kind of rock-style, whatever that is." Stern had to separate his individual conception from Davis's conception: "While I'm going for Jim [Hall] and Wes [Montgomery], there's some Jimi in there too, I guess."[52]

Marcus Miller also found himself under heavy demands from Davis. When Davis was forming his band, he demanded, according to Miller, "Funk, funk, a funk bassist, I want funk!," and the other young players he was recording with automatically directed him to Miller. Miller had learned to play his instrument in the mid-1970s, when the line separating jazz and rock styles was almost imperceptible. "I found myself caught up at the same time in the history of jazz and funk," he explained to Klaus Blasquiz in *Jazz Hot*. "Everything was possible. You only had to play. In one period, the two musics became very close. Herbie Hancock, for example, after Miles, had reconciled two generations and two styles completely different."[53]

Miller's versatility made him one of the most active studio players in New York. After touring with Roberta Flack for more than a year, he settled into the studios, accompanying Luther Vandross, Grover Washington Jr, Aretha Franklin, and numerous others on record dates. He was working on a country and western recording when he received Davis's message in 1980 to show up in the Columbia studios.

Miller tried to break the ice at that first session by making a little small talk, with predictable results. "I walked into the studio," he recalled for Sam Freedman, "said, 'Hi, I'm Marcus Miller.' He said, 'I'm Miles.' Then he walked out. When he came back in, I said, 'I'm Wynton Kelly's cousin.' He didn't say anything."[54] Davis started Foster playing a straight 4/4 tempo and stood back to watch Miller and the others. "He gives this test to everyone," Miller said later. "You throw yourself into the water and he sees if you swallow more than a cupful. If you do, he knows it immediately."[55] Miller survived, and at the first break Davis walked over and said, "Did you ever play with your genius cousin?" Miller explained that he was too young; he was only 12 when Kelly died in 1971. "He was a genius," Davis said. "His touch, his touch."[56] At the end of the recording session, he asked Miller to join his band.

The last recruit was Mino Cinelu, a Parisian whose father had emigrated from Martinique. Cinelu arrived in New York as a guitarist and scrambled to find work. He recorded inauspiciously – "two or three times with European singers whose names I forget," he said – and accompanied a Haitian singer, and played a little jazz in pickup groups, including one with Roy Haynes. He started playing percussion in order to find more work. Then the immigration department rescinded his work visa. "To keep in shape," Cinelu told Gérald Arnaud, the editor of *Jazz Hot*, "I played with some African dance companies, without pay. But I regret nothing; I learned a lot and I succeeded in making myself a respectable conga player."

Davis heard him at Mikell's, a rhythm and blues club that had expanded its music policy to include ethnic bands, where Cinelu was playing in the last week of May 1981 with a group called Civily Jordan and Folk. "Lots of celebrities frequented the club and one night Miles came," Cinelu recalls,[57] but it was not a chance meeting, because Davis was actively organizing his band for the Kool concerts. Cinelu started rehearsing with Davis's band the next week.

Cinelu saw nothing unusual in his overnight elevation from impecunious freelancing to a steady job in the best-paid band in jazz. To him, it seemed preordained from the days of his Paris youth. "When I heard *On the Corner* I was touched by that conception of music," he said, "and I knew that if Miles had the chance to hear me, he would hire me."[58]

On the first round of American concert halls after the Kool concerts, the band grew more confident and settled into a freer style. Their reviews remained mixed, and there were ominous observations on the state of Davis's health, which was sometimes reported as robust and sometimes as flagging.

At the Savoy, the midtown rock auditorium named for the legendary uptown swing ballroom, their audience was mainly young and white, including the rock stars Rickie Lee Jones and the aging Rolling Stones, Mick Jagger and Charlie Watts. Davis played long and hard, reviving *All of You* from his old ballad repertoire as well as *My Man's Gone Now* as relief from the newer jazz-rock pieces. "Miles was full of energy and uncommonly extroverted onstage," Cheryl McCall reported, "and acknowledged the existence of the audience to the extent of French-kissing a blonde in the front row in the middle of one of his *moments musicaux*." But the onstage vitality was a façade. "When I went backstage," McCall said, "I was shocked to find Miles Davis in a state of collapse, sweating like a prizefighter between rounds and similarly attended by men with towels, drink, encouragement and aid."[59]

Joe Goldberg, author of a memorable profile on Davis sixteen years earlier in *Jazz Masters of the Fifties*, caught Davis's revival when it arrived in Washington, DC, driving 200 miles from his parents' home in West Virginia and finding a seat in the back of the balcony on a stifling night. Davis's performance, he reported in *International Musician*, "was a distillation of his most effective licks, his favorite things. It was by no means tired – on the contrary, it was played with tremendous energy – but it seemed immensely calculated."

So theatrical was Davis's presentation that Goldberg began to suspect that everything, including the photographer stationed on the balcony taking pictures of patrons for $4 each against a backdrop of a Rolls-Royce with MILES D on the licence plate, was stage-managed by Davis. "I have never heard him in more absolute technical command of his instrument, nor have I ever seen him more physically active onstage," Goldberg noted. "He used to stand in one place, hunched over, his intensity accentuated, like Charlie Parker's, by his lack of motion, but in Washington, he was all over the place. He was dancing ... He was playing the audience outrageously ... and they loved it." At the end, the audience chanted "We want *Miles*! We want *Miles*!," and eventually he returned to take a bow, carried on the shoulders of Evans and Stern.[60]

As the tour continued in the Midwest, all the reviews carried notices about Davis's energetic playing, his revival of *My Man's Gone Now*, his perpetual motion – "Davis now has a radio transmitter on his horn, enabling him to wander about the stage like an obsessed maniac," David Wild wrote in *Coda*, after the Ann Arbor concert.[61] Largely unnoticed, because the backstage areas were closely guarded, were the offstage collapses. Cheryl McCall, traveling in the entourage to prepare a feature on Davis for *People*, the high-circulation gossip magazine, saw them, and although *People* was no forum for a celebrity's health problems she later included them in the preamble to her remarkable interview with Davis for *Musician, Player and Listener*, perhaps the most thorough and certainly one of the most sensitive articles ever written about him. "Sometimes he was so stiff he was not able to bend sufficiently to put on his pants," McCall said; "the band had to help him. Concerts often exhausted him, but he had made a real commitment to working, his band, and even the audience. In Chicago and Detroit, Miles had to take oxygen from a portable tank in order to get through his concerts. He contracted pneumonia after a date in Ann Arbor, and although he's been a famous no-show in the past, got out of a hospital bed to make a gig in L.A."[62]

Whenever his entourage was penetrated by outsiders, Davis masked his health problems convincingly. Before the Chicago concert, McCall reported, he hosted a family reunion to introduce Cicely Tyson to his sister, Dorothy, and his brother, Vernon, both Chicago residents, and his daughter, Cheryl, who arrived from St. Louis. He also invited some childhood friends from St. Louis, and he presided over the occasion with high spirits in spite of the pneumonia.

The Los Angeles concert at the Hollywood Bowl near the end of September brought Davis one of the toughest critical rebukes of his career. Leonard Feather, reviewing the concert for the *Los Angeles Times*, maintained that Davis had surrendered to show business and seemed to have nothing left to contribute musically. Many of Feather's points echoed the critical comments that had followed the Kool concerts, but few reviewers rival Feather's authority. His critique, as a *Jazz Hot* editorial put it, "literally assassinated Miles."

Embittered by the review, Max Roach counter-attacked with a letter to *Jazz Magazine*, reprinted later in *Jazz Hot*. The letter was not so much a defence of Davis as an attack on Feather, declaring that "Feather has always had great difficulty understanding where the American music called jazz comes from, so it is almost impossible for him to know wht a creative artist is."[63] The hostilities caused a minor sensation for the jazz audience but amused Davis. "Max is like my brother and anything that anybody would say about me, Max is going to challenge them to fight or anything," he later told interviewers in Poland. "Max declares war on them." And then he added, "Poor Leonard."[64]

In 1982, Davis went out of his way to reconcile Feather, submitting to a four-hour interview with him and inviting him to prepare the liner notes for his 1983 LP, *Star People*. Few actions indicate so emphatically the character change that Davis had gone through during his retirement. "I wasn't bothered by your review of my concert at the Hollywood Bowl in 1981," Davis told him. "I was so sick that night that I could hardly walk."[65]

But Davis wanted to regain Feather's approbation badly enough that he not only consented to the interview but also took Tyson along and conducted himself decorously throughout. At the end, Feather observed that in their four hours together Davis had rarely used the obscenities with which he used to punctuate his sentences. Davis made no response to that, but Tyson averred he had finally learned that he did not need coarse language to make himself understood. That revelation caused at least one old acquaintance to wonder how Davis could possibly go on speaking with half his active vocabulary expunged, but the decorum did not outlast the occasion. At his next significant interview, Davis responded to a question from David Breskin for *Rolling Stone* with this diatribe about rock journalists: "Fuck that! Why do they ask all those rock stars that shit? ... Who they fuck and why they fuck and this song has a message. White people do that shit. What does it mean? I don't like that. It's all just music."[66] The rest of the interview was similarly couched in Davis's accustomed idiom.

By the time Breskin's interview was published, Feather had completed the conciliatory act of preparing the liner notes for *Star People*. The notes are restrained compared to the laudatory high style typical of the genre. Feather mainly discusses the reactions of Teo Macero and Davis as they listened with him to the master tapes. He concedes only that this music, in keeping with Davis's title for one of his new compositions, *It Gets Better*, represents an improvement over what Davis was playing after his comeback concerts: "It gets better. Miles could have been referring to his band, his playing, his health, or conceivably just his life at large. Whatever the thought behind it, the title applies on every level to the conception and execution of *Star People*."[67] Beyond that, Feather's reconciliation amounted to his willingness to be associated with Davis's new LP but not a retraction of the points he had made in his critique of the Hollywood Bowl concert.

Even Davis's staunchest defenders, Max Roach among them, conceded that he had imported some show business glitter into his performances. In part, it was a response to his longevity, which made him a celebrity – a superstar, in the argot of the baby boom – and allowed him to elicit adoring cheers effortlessly, with a sidelong glance at the audience or a grunt into the mike in his trumpet, the kind of *schtick* that Mick Jagger's idolatrous audiences always thrived on, and before him John Lennon's and Elvis Presley's and Frank Sinatra's and probably Caruso's.

The new repertoire offered few challenges. Formally, it was similar to *Agitation*, *Footprints*, *Nefertiti*, and the rest of the repertoire Davis had developed with Herbie Hancock and Wayne Shorter, consisting of open-ended melodies repeated irregularly and forming the touchstone for improvised variants of any length. Substantively, it was light-years removed from them, for it rejected their darker moods and exotic harmonies in favor of piquant, whimsical moods and hummable tunes.

The change in mood reflected a new accessibility, a kind of salutation to a populace that Davis seems to have become aware of only when he put himself into solitary confinement during his retirement. "Maybe he's widening the audience," Roach admitted, in a calmer tone than he had taken with Feather. "He knows that if you play things with a familiar ring to them, there's a market for them. The fact is that Miles is *never* going to play anything banal. He's going to play his way. But he's good at marketing, and if this is what the public will buy and accept, then he'll play that too."[68] If Roach harbored doubts about the musical virtues of Davis's new mood, another drummer, Bob Moses, harbored none at all. "Yeah, his new stuff is as good or better than what he did before, and is certainly better than anything else going on now," he told Howard Mandel. "I think his new band is wonderful – and what they're playing is people's music."[69]

Davis and his band left California for Japan, where they played seven concerts in less than two weeks, 2–14 October. Japan had been high on Davis's priorities whenever he had mentioned ending his retirement. His audiences there had always been large and appreciative – even his reviewers were appreciative – and the promoters were willing to pay in kind. Davis received $700,000 for this tour, more than triple his earnings for the 1975 Japanese tour, just before his retirement.

He explained his appeal to the Japanese in terms that seemed roughly equivalent to the lunch-bucket view of how the Japanese technocrats had brought the American automotive industry to its knees. "Japanese people are funny," he said. "They like anything that's good. You can't bring no bullshit over there. They know you're not coming back so they're gonna listen. So they can *copy*. You know how Japanese people are. They *copy*. And when they copy, they copy the *best*. And they *want* the best. They don't settle for anything but the best."[70]

At his concerts on this tour, as on the previous one, they saw a perilously unhealthy Davis hiding behind a bold front whenever he appeared in public. But his playing was stronger and surer than anything he had presented to his American audiences, judging from the Tokyo concert taped by CBS-Sony. Unfortunately only one title from the Tokyo concert was selected for the *We Want Miles* LP, and the others remain unissued, but that one title crystallized Davis's new style. Davis liked it so much that he had Columbia put two versions of the same performance on the LP, one a ten-minute track with the complete performance and the other a tightly edited four-minute version originally designed for 45-rpm release. The details are as follows:

Miles Davis Sextet: We Want Miles
Miles Davis, tpt; Bill Evans, ss; Mike Stern, gtr; Marcus Miller, b; Al Foster, dms; Mino Cinelu, perc. Tokyo, 4 October 1981
Jean Pierre
(on Columbia C2 38005)
This title is released in both an edited and unedited version on C2 38005. The

concert also includes *Back Seat Betty*, *My Man's Gone Now*, and *Fast Track*, all unissued.

The composition was unlike anything that Davis had played before, but listeners hearing it at this concert and all of Davis's concerts to come, including several million in the television audience for NBC's *Saturday Night Live* later in the month, reacted with the shock of recognition, of *déjà entendu*, although they could not quite place it. It sounded like a schoolyard catcall – "nyaaa-nyaa, nyaa-nyaa-nyaaa" – or a skipping song or something else dimly remembered from childhood, with its simple four-bar melody, endlessly repeatable, moving down a third of an octave on the first phrase and back up on the second.

When *We Want Miles* finally came out, it was identified as *Jean Pierre* and its composer was listed as Miles Davis. The title was unfamiliar and the composer seemed highly improbable, but Davis had had the wit to bring to the stage one of those melodies that belongs to every culture that uses the diatonic scale – a melody so simple and so deeply embedded in the collective unconscious that it was no one's invention and everyone's. It is the melody, for instance, of an old French lullaby, with words (though they vary slightly from region to region and from generation to generation) like these:

Do do, l'enfant do,
L'enfant dormira bien vite.
Do do, l'enfant do,
L'enfant dormira bientôt.

Davis's title provides a clue as to when the melody first impressed itself upon him. Jean-Pierre is the son of his second wife, Frances Taylor, by a previous marriage, and he lived with them as a youngster until their divorce.

Davis loved the melody, and he used it to close every concert for years, replacing *Kix* in the repertoire after the summer concerts. For the first year, its performance consisted of repeated assertions in rough harmony by Davis's trumpet and Evans's soprano saxophone, echoed in any order, even overlapping, by Miller's bass, Cinelu's congas, and Stern's guitar. Eventually, as the band added several other compositions stated in harmony by two or more of the instruments, a device for which *Jean Pierre* provided the prototype, Davis gave up on harmonizing *Jean Pierre* and began stating its theme on trumpet alone, sometimes playing no more than the first two notes and then standing back while the band made a free invention. Its form also became the favored form for much of Davis's new music: simple in structure, short in duration, and, he hoped, stunningly salient.

At the Tokyo performance, the four-bar theme recurs dozens of times, beginning with Cinelu patting it out on the congas, then Miller thumping it out on the bass, and then the harmonized trumpet-soprano statement. Davis does little more than repeat the theme over and over in his muted solo, except for interpolating the bridge from *Lullaby of Broadway*, which is also built on thirds ("Good night, ladies; good night, the milkman's on his way"). Stern leaves the theme further behind, with high screams that somehow resolve Miller's low repetition of the theme beneath him, and Evans comes along and parodies it by honking its final note.

It is a surprisingly resourceful performance, considering the slim underpinning that the theme provides; later performances retained the resourcefulness by relying less on the theme and exploring tangents that left the theme far behind.

Three days after returning from Japan, the band appeared on *Saturday Night Live* on NBC-TV playing *Jean Pierre*, live in a New York studio for a television audience of several millions. Davis's appearance on the show was widely publicized in spot announcements on the network the week before, and George Kennedy, the actor who hosted the show that night, used thirty seconds of the seven-minute spot introducing him: "...a man who has not appeared on network television in almost a decade ... Ladies and gentlemen, the *legendary* Miles Davis!" But the rendition of *Jean Pierre* was a shambles, taken at almost double the normal tempo, with missed cues and misshapen notes, especially by Davis. His appearance was frightening. He limped around the stage, the cameras losing him and finding him again awkwardly, his face taut, his eyes unseeing. Many viewers assumed he was in a drug-induced stupor; not one in a million could know that he had just returned from an international tour completely exhausted. He took two weeks off to recuperate before his next booking, on 4 November in Boston.

On 27 November, Davis married Cicely Tyson at Bill Cosby's home in Shelbourne, Massachusetts. Andrew Young, mayor-elect of Atlanta and ambassador to the United Nations during the Carter administration as well as a minister, performed the ceremony, with Max Roach and the political comedian Dick Gregory among the few guests. *People* magazine, probably via Cheryl McCall, noted the event and reported that

Miles Davis and Cicely Tyson (courtesy Canapress Photo Service)

John Scofield at Ontario Place Forum, 1983 (Bernard Lecerf)

Davis took the vows by rasping "Yeah," and that Tyson, when her turn came, mimicked his reply and his voice.[71] It was Tyson's second marriage and Davis's fourth.

Davis's brownstone on West 77th Street, originally bought for Frances Taylor and decorated by her, was being gutted and rebuilt to Tyson's specifications, in a massive overhaul that ended up taking two years. When Tyson and Davis were in New York, they lived either in a cottage at Montauk, on the tip of Long Island, or in an apartment on Fifth Avenue.

"I'm happy now," Davis told McCall. "I could have been happy years ago if I married Cicely. But years ago, no. Time takes care of that, time takes care of everything. If I had married Cicely she wouldn't have been a star now." In the same mood, he confessed that he had written some love songs, including one called *Love without Time*, scribbled on a paper bag. "Next album I'm singing," he said. "Sure. I'm going to siiiiinnng some soooulful ballads. *Love without Time*. (sings) 'Love without time, just don't give me no limit, don't need no limit.'"[72]

Not even the honeymoon interrupted his round of concerts. The day after the wedding, Davis emplaned with his band for Fort Lauderdale. By the time his tour reached Toronto on 13 December, Davis looked like a wraith. Mark Miller, reviewing the concert in the *Globe and Mail*, said: "Miles Davis' eyes – brooding, fixed, cold, once far-seeing but now simply distant – burned into the memory last night ... The band supplied the night with its exhilaration. Davis' contribution was more personal, more revealing, and, ultimately, more troubling."[73] A blond woman in the audience went around at intermission asking the scribes in the front-row seats what was wrong with him. "I saw him at the Colonial [a Toronto jazz club] in 1969," she said, "and he was *beautiful*. But when he came out tonight, I just felt like crying." She left at intermission because watching him, she said, was "too painful."

Notwithstanding the critical lambastings that followed some of Davis's concerts and the gathering portents of his deteriorating health, his return to performing restored his popularity. *Down Beat*'s readers voted him Jazz Musician of the Year by a wide margin and, in a dizzying show of sentiment over perspicacity, named *Man with the Horn* top album; *Directions*, his LP of older material, placed fourth. Among trumpeters, he placed third after Freddie Hubbard and Dizzy Gillespie, in front of Woody Shaw and Lester Bowie. *Down Beat*'s poll results were only one expression of the welcome. In Congo (Brazzaville) his portrait appeared on the 125-franc postage stamp.

Davis intended to carry on touring in 1982 with only a momentary rest in January. He had scheduled a series of concerts on the Pacific coast from Vancouver to San Diego for February. Then, only a week before they would have begun, the entire series was cancelled. Most fans speculated that he had had a change of heart about his comeback.

Instead, he was stopped cold by a new health problem that was more serious than any one of the myriad of problems that had caused him to stop for six years. He awoke one morning unable to move his right hand. The hand was bunched, the fingers immobile. Tyson was away in Africa, and Davis's doctor tried to cajole him into treating the affliction lightly. "I go to the doctor and he says I got the Honeymoon Paralysis," Davis told David Breskin in Rolling Stone. "Honeymoon Paralysis, that's when guys get so tired from fucking so much that they go to sleep on their hand and it wakes up numb."[74] But a battery of hospital tests confirmed that he had suffered a stroke, and he began physical therapy sessions at the hospital in an attempt to restore some mobility to the hand. When Tyson returned, his doctors told her that Davis would probably never regain adequate use of the hand and certainly never full use of it. They asked her to use her discretion about informing Davis of the seriousness of the injury, but she neither told him nor allowed herself to believe them. She watched and waited for the therapy sessions to give some signs of recovery.

For a month, nothing changed. Davis was despondent, lying around ready now to concede that he should never have attempted to return to performing. Apart from his mood and the useless right hand, both of which he tried to hide from his few visitors, he seemed little changed. The stroke, the doctors knew, was highly localized; it may have ended his career, but it need not prevent him from leading a reasonably normal life for the rest of his days.

Tyson knew that he could not lead anything like a normal life if he was not performing. She began inquiring about alternative treatment and learned about acupuncture, the Chinese medical tradition based on coaxing neural reflexes partly by stimulating nerve centers. Directed to a Dr Shin, she described Davis's state of health and received an optimistic prognosis.[75] It seemed to her to be worth trying. "I didn't want to go," Davis told Feather, "but she threw it at me all the time, and I finally gave in."

Within two months, his hand regained some mobility. "One night I woke up and I realized I could move it again," Davis said, as if describing a miracle, "and I could play the trumpet." Medically, the miracle was attributed to the brain's uncanny capacity for relocating functions to compensate for traumatic losses, part of the healing force of time, but Davis also needed to share the optimism of Tyson and his acupuncturist before it could happen. If his recovery was explicable in coldly clinical terms, it was still an explanation that ultimately came down to imponderables such as time and attitude, hardly removing it from the miraculous. Davis said, "After this, I'll never be afraid of anything that happens. Never again."[76]

Davis's general health lagged behind the recovery of his right hand. He began playing his trumpet almost immediately and soon began performing in public again, but his first concerts forced him to play sitting down part of the time until he developed enough stamina to resume his onstage roaming for the full ninety minutes.

The full recovery required a new regimen. He stopped smoking. He gave up beer and liquor in favor of Perrier water, of which he drinks two quarts a day; "that empties you, cleans you out, just what I need," he says.[77] He swims every day, explaining it this way: "Anything that helps the wind is good for a horn player. When I first started back playing, I got out of breath all the time. Swimming is good for that. If I don't do it, everything tightens up."[78] He eats Chinese herbs, prescribed by his acupuncturist, in a jelly for breakfast, and he has acupuncture sessions whenever he is in New York.

In a sense, the six months of hard touring before he suffered the stroke were only the prolegomena for the real comeback that followed it, when his theatricality became less forced, his playing brightened, and his conception clarified. "I'll stay active till I die, now," he says.[79]

In early April, he called the band back together and scheduled two rehearsals before taking them on the tour of Europe that he had been ready to cancel a month before. "It was an occasion for rediscovering ourselves," Mino Cinelu explained. "We hadn't played together for three months, and Miles wanted to see what had happened to us, to know if the feeling was still as strong."[80] Apparently he was satisfied, because he called off the second rehearsal.

Word about Davis's stroke had not circulated when he set off for Europe – it did not become common knowledge until Leonard Feather's interview appeared in the *Los Angeles Times* several months later – and most of the European reviewers assumed his enervation to be the result of his old pains rather than a new, and alarmingly recent, one.

The tour was jammed as usual, beginning at Konserthuset in Stockholm on 13 April and ending in Paris with two concerts at Théâtre musical on 2 and 3 May, with stops in between at Jazzhus Montmartre in Copenhagen, a jazz club rather than a concert hall, the Hammersmith Odeon in London, then Rome, Amsterdam, The Hague, and Châtelet, outside Paris. All tickets for both Paris concerts were sold in two hours on 18 April, the day they went on sale, at $80 for the best seats.

At the Hammersmith Odeon, Davis summoned up enough energy to walk onto the stage backwards, toying with the audiences that had often chided him for turning his back on them in the past. The concert was filmed by England's new independent television network and broadcast the following December, but it does not show Davis advantageously. Dave Gelly described him in his review of the concert for the *Observer* this way: "He is in constant pain, walks with difficulty and now has to play sitting down most of the time. The dashing young man-about-town has been replaced by a gaunt and dogged figure, expending every ounce of energy in two brief bursts per night."[81] That was early in the tour, and Davis seemed to be growing weaker as the tour continued. At Châtelet, the second-last stop, the reviewer Bayon, writing for *Libération*, thought he was viewing a walking corpse. Under the headline "Trompette de mort," he wrote: "The hero was fatigued, beat, bone-tired, his hips seized in rigor mortis, his limbs crumbling, the corpse visible, the face starved, staggering, coughing in fits that rattled his neck, the shadow of a shadow of a myth ... His vital signs reduced to a minimum, pinched, empty, and haunted, he had nothing to say ... It was as if he sat down before Paris to learn how to die."[82]

But the next day, in Paris, he seemed completely revived. "What happened between Sunday night and Monday?" asked Philippe Conrath, in a companion review to Bayon's. His only guess: "Obviously the little something that changed everything. Or a real joy about playing in Paris ... He entered like a boxer looking for a k.o. He put us on our knees, without giving us a second to catch our breath, piling chorus on chorus as at the best of times ... Sunday he made us pity him for his empty presence, but Monday there he was pirouetting at each ovation, smiling, full of affection for his guitarist whom he couldn't take his eyes off, bobbing in front of Al Foster to start up his drums, and gently admonishing the clowning Marcus Miller, the mad dog of the sextet."[83] In the weird counterpoint of the reviews of Davis's comeback, swinging from reports of well-being to imminent demise, the swing from one theme to the other had never been this sudden.

His young sidemen seemed aware only of Davis's revival and its effect on the band's music. "I wish we made a second album," Cinelu told a

French interviewer. "It would be so much better. Qualitatively, what we play now has nothing to do with our first recording [*We Want Miles*] ... The first record was important in the sense that it let people know that Miles could play, that he was always present."[84]

The new recordings had to wait, however, while Davis fulfilled some broken promises in North America and kept some new ones for George Wein. The 1982 Kool Jazz Festival expanded into a road show, headquartered in New York but moving into nineteen other cities with scaled-down programs. Davis played at Kool concerts in Washington, DC, at the end of May and in Atlanta in early June, left the lineup for independent festivals in Montreal (11 July, Festival International de Jazz), New York (17 July, Dr. Pepper Festival, at Pier 84), and in Vancouver (28 July, du Maurier Jazz Society), and then resumed his Kool connection in Seattle (31 July), Detroit (2 September), and Chicago (5 September). The Vancouver and Seattle concerts replaced cancellations there in the spring.

Between the New York and Vancouver appearances, he accompanied Cicely Tyson to Lima, Peru, where she was acting as a judge in the Miss Universe contest. They treated the trip as a holiday, sight-seeing in museums, with Davis swimming hours every day. The Miss Universe contest took place on Monday, two days before Davis was to appear onstage in Vancouver, some 5,000 miles from Lima, separated by three time zones, in the opposite hemisphere.

In Vancouver, Davis gave one of his strongest performances in years, playing long and full, and revealing a partly new repertoire, including a twenty-five-minute ballad improvisation that revived *Fran Dance* for several bars. "He strutted like a funky chicken, he smiled to the other musicians, he even acknowledged the crowd," one reviewer wrote.[85] More to the point, he played strongly.

The strong playing continued in Detroit. "Davis looked healthy, moved easily, and played with more confidence than he has in years," Stephen Brunt reported, and he noted some other changes: "Almost completely gone was the hard rock/funk sound of the *Man with the Horn*. In its place was a much more traditional form of jazz, including a straightforward blues ... There also seems to be a new Davis personality. He smiled at the crowd, spoke to them through the microphone in the bell of his trumpet in a raspy whisper, and reacted to shouts from the crowd."[86] Brunt was comparing Davis's music and deportment not to his appearances of ten or twenty years ago but to his comeback concerts only fourteen months before.

At the Chicago concert, Davis and his band made their entrance to the Grant Park stage by limousine and were stopped short by a burly policeman. Instead of trying to shout the policeman out of the way and inviting a confrontation, Davis and the others waited patiently. "Just in time the cop relented," Hank DeZutter reported, "and a puckish Miles not only played for but played with the audience. Infamous for his occasional sullen, brooding, damn-the-public behavior, Davis even mugged and posed for cameramen."[87] Peter Kostakis, covering the concert for *Down Beat*, wrote: "Davis played more trumpet than we had any right to expect, open horn mostly, with discrete spaces and that knockout *tone* basically unimpaired."[88]

Davis's new vitality finally silenced some of the nostalgia buffs who had populated his audiences for years, apparently harboring the impossible dream that he would transform himself, and perhaps them too, into what they had been twenty years ago. At Grant Park, an old fan noisily pleaded with Davis to play *So What*. "After four shouts of 'Play *So What*,'" DeZutter reported, "a man nearby shut him up, acidly suggesting, 'Go home and play the record.'"

Davis and his band also spent some time during the summer in the recording studios, and the recordings were released in June 1983 along with some subsequent sessions on *Star People*, the first studio recordings by the working band. The details are as follows:

Miles Davis Sextet: Star People
Miles Davis, tpt, synthesizer (on *Come Get It, Star on Cicely*); Bill Evans, ts (on *Star People*), ss (on *U 'n' I, Star on Cicely*); Mike Stern, gtr; Marcus Miller, b; Al Foster, dms; Mino Cinelu, perc. August–November 1982
Come Get It; Star People; U 'n' I; Star on Cicely
(all on Columbia FC 38657)
Gil Evans arranged the theme statement of *Star on Cicely*; Bill Evans is not heard on *Come Get It*, which may be an excerpt of a concert performance; Miles Davis is credited as composer of all titles, but *Star on Cicely* apparently originated as a phrase by Mike Stern; *Star People* includes a brief prelude and interlude by Davis on synthesizer and John Scofield on guitar, probably recorded December 1982–February 1983.

Come Get It is the new concert opener, replacing *Back Seat Betty* in the repertoire but retaining many of its features, including the cascading guitar-percussion introduction, a funk motif on the bass ("inspired by an old Otis Redding riff," Davis told Leonard Feather), and a simple scale on the trumpet as its theme. Some of the funk elements were weakening, notably in Mike Stern's contribution, where the rhythm softens behind him and allows him to play a more relaxed solo than he usually played, and leaving Davis to carry most of the heavy playing.

U 'n' I is a lilting ballad consisting of an eight-bar melody played over and over. The little tune shares some of the infectious simplicity of Jean Pierre and seems to beg for a silly little lyric to set if off. Listeners can easily supply their own, perhaps along these lines:

O, U 'n' I XL – we're gr8! –
4 U 'n' I alone R NTTs;
U lder what I MN8?
Only XTC.

Musically, U 'n' I has about as much substance as the doggerel it is likely to inspire, and in concert performances as well as in this studio version the musicians seem to be at a loss about what they can do with it. Often they do nothing at all, simply repeating the melody almost verbatim, as they do no less than thirteen times in six minutes on this recorded version, and the engaging little ditty begins to lose its charm after a few listenings. (Apart from their shared banality, Davis's U 'n' I is not related in any way to Betty Davis's You and I, a ballad released on her 1975 LP [Island ILPS 9329] that credits Gil Evans for its brass arrangement and Miles Davis for its "musical direction.")

Davis's long, winding blues solo at the beginning of the track called Star People gives the best evidence of his revitalized trumpet playing: it is unhurried and masterfully controlled, recalling the spirit – and a few of the phrases – of his older ballad style. Part of the length of Star People apparently comes from splicing two takes together, with an uninte-grated synthesizer interlude between them, but the spliced-in take preserves a country blues solo by Stern that contrasts effectively with Davis's urbane statements. The issued version is marred by an awk-ward, tinny percussion noise that sounds like an electronic distortion of the sock cymbal and was probably added after the session. If listeners allow it to distract them, the easy flow of the track is impeded, but Davis's solos are strong enough to override the arhythmic splashes in the background.

Gil Evans returns to Davis's music with the arrangement of the theme for Star on Cicely, an intricate blend of eighth-note and half-note harmonies played by the soprano saxophone and guitar, with the trumpet sometimes playing a third line. Evans's participation came about when Davis, listening to tapes of his band's performances, heard improvised phrases that he wanted developed into themes. The germ of *Star on Cicely* apparently originated in a solo by Stern, and Evans has turned it into a roller-coaster ride that comes to a sudden stop, but Davis gets composer credit for it. (An excerpt was released on 45 rpm for the teenage market as Columbia 38-03605, several weeks before the LP version.)

The news that Gil Evans was arranging some of Davis's new repertoire raised hopes that they would again collaborate on a larger project. "Gil still does a lot of things for me," Davis told Richard Williams. "He comes up with bass patterns, stuff like that. We just click together." But Davis had no elaborate plans. "We might do something, we might not," he said.[89] Evans, in an interview with Richard Cook for the *New Musical Express*, thought that their renewed collaboration was inevitable. "We'll be working together again," he said. "You could say we're in a musical and emotional condition where we can work together." The key to their working together again, in Evans's view, is Davis's health. "Miles is really feeling good," he points out. "He's had a lot of bad physical luck, but now – the way he plays a concert, he'll dance a little, play to the first rows. He's better." Evans also tossed out the tidbit that he had been talking to George Russell about all three of them working on a project. "He thought it was a good idea," Evans adds. "Maybe it'll happen."[90]

An innovation that might encourage Davis to work with Evans is his use of the Oberheim synthesizer, which joined the Rhodes electric piano at center stage at the end of 1982. "I haven't read the instruction book yet," he told Richard Williams, making light of his bemused noodling on it during performances. "It would take someone like Paul Buckmaster or Gil or Quincy [Jones] or J.J. [Johnson], one of those writers who'd really know what to do with it."[91]

Onstage, he tries for big-band effects on it, sounding chords with his left hand while playing the trumpet with his right, often with jarring results. He justifies it by saying, "Synthesizers are programmed to sound white – that's how prejudiced white people are – so if I don't play over it, it will sound mechanical."[92]

The synthesizer seems to have revived his ambitions to use orchestral effects in his music, and his further comments to Williams indicate that he understands not only its potential but also its limitations: "Now-adays instead of going on the road with a big band you just reach and grab a button and have the sound of brass or strings, but of course you can't replace the interplay – going in and out of those swells and lows. What you miss, too, is the unevenness of tone that gives it a thrill. You might have five different trumpet players, each with a different sound and attack, who make the sound you want." The simulated trumpet section of the synthesizer encodes five identical trumpet sounds, and to Davis that sound is anathema. "White people are so prejudiced that they make the trumpets on the Oberheim sound white," he says. "Imagine that. A prejudiced synthesizer. Ain't that something?"[93]

By the end of 1982, Davis had regained his position near the top of the jazz popularity polls, but he had to concede some of the top honors to Wynton Marsalis, one of the brightest young talents to emerge in a generation. Davis's *We Want Miles* won the Grammy Award, with Davis's band appearing on the televised proceedings to play *Speak*, part of their new repertoire, and it also won the gold medal in Tokyo's Jazz Disk Awards, but Marsalis's debut LP as a leader (*Wynton Marsalis*, Columbia FC 37574) won that honor in *Down Beat*'s readers' poll. Davis was named Jazz Musician of the Year in the *Jazz Forum* poll, but Marsalis took that honor in *Down Beat* and was also named top trumpeter, with Davis second. In a more bizarre sweepstakes, Davis was named in a press release by the United States space agency among a group of people thought to have the right qualities for space flight, including "strength of character, charm, glamor"; other nominees were Canadian prime minister Pierre Trudeau, science-fiction writer Arthur C. Clarke, comedians Richard Pryor and Dudley Moore, and Pope John Paul II;[94] Marsalis somehow failed to make that list.

Davis alone seemed unimpressed by Marsalis's talent. "All the trumpet players copy Clifford, Fats Navarro and Dizzy Gillespie," he said. "Just like the saxophonists imitate Coltrane, Wayne Shorter and Sonny Rollins. There aren't any original musicians any more. I know that the musicians in my band like Marsalis; me, I like to hear things with a different approach from what people call jazz."[95]

Ironically, Marsalis's music emanates directly from the modal and chordal styles that Davis explored in the 1960s. Technically and tonally his trumpet style makes a sharp departure from Davis's, but his genre was once primarily Davis's, and their conjunction is all the more obvious when Marsalis is heard with Davis's former rhythm team of Herbie Hancock, Ron Carter, and Tony Williams. He had been heard with them on two notable tours, the first in Japan in the summer of 1981, which brought the 20-year-old trumpeter international acclaim, and the second around the world in the summer of 1983, which added saxophonist Branford Marsalis, one year older than his brother Wynton, to make the quintet called VSOP II. Their repertoire naturally dips into Davis's short-lived book and has included Hancock's *The Sorcerer*, Carter's *R.J.*, and Williams's *Pee Wee*.

Son of a New Orleans jazz pianist, Marsalis left home in 1980 to join Art Blakey's Jazz Messengers, and since 1981 he has alternated between stints with Davis's former rhythm section and his own quintet. In all contexts he has consistently chosen to work in modal frameworks with acoustic bands, but the closer he comes to the exact context in which Davis has worked, as in his recordings of compositions first recorded by Davis, the easier it is to hear how distinctive his playing is. Marsalis provides the best object lesson jazz fans have ever had for showing that Davis failed to exhaust the styles he discovered before moving away from them in his restless search for innovations.

It is a lesson that Marsalis, with enormous self-assurance, not only proves with his music but also has articulated several times for those interviewers and fans who regard his music as a throwback to an "old" style. "Music has to be played before it gets old," he told A. James Liska. "The music that Ornette played, that Miles and Trane played in the '60s, some of the stuff that Mingus and Booker Little and Charlie Rouse and all those cats were starting to do – that music isn't old because no one else has ever played it."[96] Marsalis gave convincing demonstrations of the vitality of the style nightly, and his brother developed quickly into a forceful ally. "We're not playing this music because we're reacting against fusion," Branford told Peter Keepnews. "We're playing this music because it's harder to play than fusion. The way my mind works, I'm gonna play whatever is the most difficult music to play, intellectually and physically."[97] Davis's personal obsession with change and flux in musical style characterizes all his most productive periods, but the Marsalises prove that those obsessions are neither necessary nor sufficient for the creativity of other jazz musicians.

For Davis, change has always been the surest sign that he is healthy and deeply involved in his music. By the end of 1982, he was showing those signs again. The commissions for Gil Evans and the tinkering with synthesizers meant more in their potential than in their realization, with the former holding out the promise that Davis might broaden the slender compositional thread of his music and the latter that he might incorporate orchestral elements, synthesized or real, into it.

Another significant change took place on 31 December, when Davis's band appeared at the Felt Forum in Madison Square Garden with a new guitarist, John Scofield, in the band. The concert, with Davis's old friend Roberta Flack sharing the bill, started at 10 p.m. and had no more serious intent than greeting the new year, but Scofield's unexpected presence gave the occasion a special significance for jazz fans. Although Scofield belonged to the same age group as the other sidemen, his playing style was established before he joined Davis's band. He played jazz, and he was unlikely to submit to Hendrix imitations or hyperamplification.

A review of the Felt Forum concert by Lee Jeske in *Down Beat* emphasized the difference he made: "This was Scofield's debut with Miles, and Miles was quite generous in featuring him. Scofield, with his hollow-body guitar, played the kind of music that he has been playing for the past few years — scorching, clear, blues-drenched jazz, with a little smidgen of the avant garde and a small dollop of rock and roll. He is one of the finest guitarists around these days, and his playing brought a new hue to the band — he is a think-on-his-feet soloist who presents Davis with a challenge; if Miles scuffles, Scofield has the equipment to blow him away. The audience greeted every Scofield solo warmly, and his presence in the band bodes well for *musical* qualities of the organization."[98]

Davis first decided to replace Mike Stern with Scofield because, as Stern told a French interviewer, "last winter I started to coast a bit." He asked Bill Evans, who had recommended Stern in the first place, about a new guitarist, and he recommended Scofield. After the Felt Forum concert, Davis decided to carry both guitarists for six months, expanding the band to a septet. The band went through a period of adjustment in January, with Stern resuming his busy role as both accompanist and soloist and Scofield gradually working out his own role. "Little by little, Miles incorporated him into the group," Stern says. "At first I took all the solos, but now it's equal. We play as a duo, John and me, and we listen to one another very well."[99] In the expanded band, Stern still played in the rhythm section as well as soloing and Scofield worked mainly as a soloist, stationing himself stage left near Evans, whose role closely resembled Scofield's.

Asked why he added a second guitarist, Davis told Richard Williams, "I've always liked the sound of the guitar. And of the sitar. I like all the strings except the violin. It's too high-pitched for me. I can't hear that high."[100] (In the same interview, however, Davis observed that his inability to deal with high registers, a factor that forced him to depart from Dizzy Gillespie's model when he arrived in New York in 1945, was changing. "When I first started playing," he said, "it was low-middle to low register. I couldn't hear above that. Just lately, though, I've been able to hear up to octavissimo F, G, A sometimes.")

His only direct comments on Scofield's playing, one to Williams and another to Leonard Feather, have focused on Scofield's restrained note placement, one of the main devices of Davis's own playing when he developed what became known as the cool style. "John has a tendency to play behind the beat," he told Feather. "I had to bring him up; he really changed with Al's strong beat behind him."[101] And to Williams: "Denzil Best, the drummer, used to say to me, 'Don't play too far behind the beat because you'll work me too hard.' It's like stepping on your partner's feet." But Davis conceded that his own style altered in the new combination. "Having two guitar players makes me change," he says. "They don't have to breathe like a horn player does. They rub off on me."[102]

Scofield recorded with the band almost immediately, on a blues composition called *It Gets Better*, a theme statement composed by Davis and arranged by Gil Evans that probably originated as a phrase improvised by Bill Evans in a practice session. The details are as follows:

Miles Davis Septet: Star People
Miles Davis, tpt; Bill Evans, ss; John Scofield, Mike Stern, gtr; Marcus Miller, b; Al Foster, dms; Mino Cinelu, perc; Gil Evans, arr. Probably January 1983
It Gets Better
(on Columbia FC 38657)

In this studio version, the twelve-bar repetitions of the theme frame a long improvisation by Davis on muted trumpet, again revealing Davis's return to form in fashioning coherent lyrical statements at slow tempos. The theme itself is played ponderously in comparison to its freer, more emotional treatment in numerous concerts, where it had been played regularly since the summer of 1982. There it was usually stated by Evans on tenor saxophone and Stern on guitar, with Davis sometimes joining in, but the recorded version is a rearrangement, with Scofield as the lead voice and Stern the second voice, mixed low in the background. Its easy tempo is again marred by metronomic percussion noises not attributable to Cinelu and probably not directly attributable to Foster, although they may be post-edited electronic distortions of his drum kit. This straightforward blues makes a welcome change from the funk-cluttered backgrounds in which Davis couched his blues playing for several years, but Columbia holds several live versions that show off the band better than this one.

Long before *It Gets Better* was issued on the *Star People* LP in the late spring of 1983, word spread that Davis was playing a more or less straightforward twelve-bar blues at his concerts. It had made a striking impression at the Vancouver concert in the summer, immediately after his rejuvenating holiday in Peru, and audiences everywhere, steeled as they were now for a jazz-funk assault, greeted the sound of its traditional progressions enthusiastically. For the new Davis, that response was all he needed. The blues not only found a permanent place in his repertoire but dominated his concerts.

The blues segments grew stronger with Scofield added to the band for their first tour of 1983, a February swing through Dallas (two concerts on 1 February), Houston, Austin, and other Texas cities, Park West in Chicago, the National Arts Centre in Ottawa, and Roy Thompson Hall in Toronto (on 15 February). Above all, Davis seemed to bask in the response the blues elicited from his black audience, which he had tried to court with *On the Corner* a decade earlier. "Now, did you see last night, I was playing a blues and I go over and bend down and play to that fat woman in the second row?" Davis asked Breskin after one of the Texas concerts. "She says, 'That's right, Miles, come on over here, you can *stay* over here.' So then I play something real fast, and she says, 'Not like *that*, though. Go back over there if you're gonna play that shit.' Now, do you think a white person would tell me that? They don't even know what she's talking about. She's talking about the *bluuueeesss.*" After years of trying to unearth the essential blackness of his playing by immersing himself in electrified percussion barrages, Davis found it in his East St. Louis roots. "In my hometown, if you don't play the blues, shit, them motherfuckers go to ordering drinks, but if you play the blues, they'll stay right there. That fat bitch, she'd have me blowing all night."[103]

Scofield inched his way into the working band's métier on the February tour. At the same time, Davis tried a new bassist, Tom Barney, a small, boyish figure who broke into dance steps when the beat was up. Marcus Miller had always divided his loyalties among Davis's band, diverse recording sessions, and other bands, often with David Sanborn, the alto saxophonist whose distinctive sound attracted attention with Stevie Wonder, Gil Evans, the studio band of *Saturday Night Live*, and dozens of recordings. Shortly before he left Davis, Miller recounted his itinerary for Klaus Blasquiz in *Jazz Hot*: "I always kept close relations with Dave [Sanborn]. Even now I make the scene with Miles and him, and it's hard to bring the two together, but I really try. Today I'm with Dave in L.A., tomorrow in Detroit with Miles, then Phoenix, Chicago – pffff! Finally, on my holidays, I go back to New York to make some sessions!"[104] It was the kind of schedule that a few years earlier might have supplied enough work to support two or three musicians, and Miller was only one of a group of young, entrepreneurial successes – Sanborn, drummer Steve Gadd, and percussionist Ralph McDonald were others, and Ron Carter provided one of their first models – commandeering a lot of work both in jazz and on its pop fringes. As Davis packed his schedule with more playing dates spread across more miles th⌐n he ever had before, Miller had to choose between Davis and his diverse activities.

Most of the attention on the tour naturally focused on Scofield, not so much because of what he played, for he played sparingly, as what he represented. John Abercrombie, one of the leaders in the post-fusion generation that brought the guitar into jazz as a leading voice, told Lee Jeske: "The great thing about Scofield is he's got all this blues feeling in his playing that sets him apart from a lot of other jazz players; he's got this edge, this sort of bite which gives his playing – even when he's playing more abstract – a real foundation which I've always loved."[105] A reviewer at the Chicago Park West concert, Neil Tesser, commented: "I have no trouble calling Scofield the finest guitarist in modern jazz. His tone, his phrasing, and the sonorous intervals of his lines, all mark him an unabashed romantic; yet there is a razor's edge underneath, and a delightfully abstract logic, that shapes his music into something strong and supple ... He has been remarkable on records, and onstage [in Chicago] – perhaps because he has been with Miles less than three months – his solos were the only new music heard at Park West."[106]

Bill Evans and Mike Stern were beginning to establish their talents independently from Davis, recording with other bands and playing in pickup groups whenever time allowed, but Scofield came the closest to an established talent that Davis had admitted into his band in almost a decade.

The new band again recorded in the first months of 1983, and the track was, by recent standards, rushed into print to fill out the *Star People* LP. The details are as follows:

Miles Davis Septet: Star People
Miles Davis, tpt, synthesizer; Bill Evans, ss; John Scofield, Mike Stern, gtr;

Tom Barney, b; Al Foster, dms; Mino Cinelu, perc; Gil Evans, arr. Probably January–February 1983
Speak
(on Columbia FC 38657)

Though similar in tempo and key to *Star on Cicely* and featuring similar harmonies in Gil Evans's arrangement, *Speak* gets a much more spirited reading, with the arranged and the improvised elements almost equally uninhibited. It had been in the repertoire longer, and the players had thoroughly digested their parts. Davis plays simultaneous trumpet-synthesizer chords at the beginning and behind Stern and Scofield, the principal soloists, and seems distracted in his open trumpet solo at the end, played with a mellow tone that sounds like a flugelhorn, in order to get back to the synthesizer. He appears more than willing to let the guitarists take the honors. Stern solos first, in a series of sharp, short yelps into the highest register, and Scofield follows, after the second theme statement, building long lines that accelerate in intensity and eventually summon Davis's background riffs at the climax. Davis is left with the denouement.

More than any other track, *Speak* showed Davis's music in transition. It retained many of the elements that dominated his concerts, but it was also the harbinger of some innovations. The retained elements were carried over from the comeback concerts of 1981, and before that. The rhythmic pulse remained rocking (and sometimes rolling), with Al Foster showing none of the subtleties of touch or taste that once endeared Philly Joe Jones and Tony Williams to Davis. The new bassist, Barney, lacked Miller's assertiveness but remained essentially a funk bassist rather than a jazz player. Stern's presence guaranteed rock colorations in the ensemble and rock-derived improvizations, and the comparison between him and Scofield in the same context only emphasized his rock proclivities.

The new elements, still nascent in *Speak*, were the synthesized orchestral effects and the elaboration of arranged sequences beyond four or eight bars. *Speak* offered the first hint that Davis's music was taking a turn toward the kind of formal elaboration he seemed to eschew forever in the 1960s when he gave up on the thirty-two-bar song form and aborted several projects with Gil Evans. And in Bill Evans and John Scofield, he had two patient, thoughtful players with excellent technical abilities and jazz predilections.

Speak received a very different treatment when Davis selected it for a three-and-a-half-minute performance on the nationally televised Grammy Awards show on 23 February 1983. He kicked it off at a frantic tempo, and the playing, which squeezed in solos by Scofield, Evans (on soprano saxophone), and Stern in that order, was raw, with Davis often overpowering everyone including the sound engineers with his trumpet-synthesizer blasts. A. James Liska, in a *Down Beat* editorial, complained that the National Academy of Recording Arts and Sciences, the governing body of the Grammy Awards, "has become nothing more than an organization to serve the commercial side of the industry — an annual dog-and-pony show, replete with antics of the industry's lesser craftsmen and ignorant of the more artistic achievements of its membership." He reported, "Miles Davis kept his back to the audience for his excursion" on the telecast, and then he added: "His attitude at first seemed deplorable; upon reflection it was an admirable statement."[107]

Davis appeared anything but blasé in his brief showing, and the frenetic music he played seemed an honest reflection of nerves. He cared so much that, in the familiar, career-long pattern, he went out of his way to suggest that he cared not at all. Mike Stern told Jérome Reese that "Miles was overjoyed about winning his first Grammy since *Bitches Brew* although he hid it well."[108] Around the time that Davis was informed he had won, he told David Breskin, "I don't like to record at all, live or studio. I just do it to make money."[109]

In March and April, Davis revisited several of the European stages where he had last been seen, just one year earlier, playing from a chair as he recuperated from his stroke. He celebrated his regained health with concerts at Lille (29 March), Strasbourg (31), Turin (3 and 4 April), Bourg (10), Paris (12 and 13), Lyon (15), Vienna (18), Bordeaux (22), Angers (23), Brussels (25), and London (27 and 28). This was his first tour under the aegis of his new managers, Jerome and Robert Blank of Philadelphia, whose business card carried the unlikely designation "Delaware Valley Factors, Inc." Jerome Blank joined the entourage on this tour, and his nephew Robert accompanied him after this, and their presence made a difference. "You see, we didn't come into this knowing a whole lot about jazz, so we're not intimidated by Miles," Robert explained. "We want to find out why he's got this *reputation* — he's not like that, really — and see what can be done about it."[110] Starting with this tour, Davis has been calling his band back to the stage for encores and granting short newspaper interviews, often with Robert Blank clocking the interviewer in the background, in the cities where he plays.

Davis's return to health commanded more attention in Europe than his reconstituted band or his new repertoire. Richard Williams, who interviewed him at his London hotel for *The Times*, observed: "He still moved around the room with difficulty as he fetched himself bottles of mineral water, but the brightness of his eyes and the sheen of his skin suggested an altogether fitter man ... He talked freely and graciously, with dry humour and great animation, utterly dispelling the received image of surly arrogance."[111] Davis proudly flipped through a pad of his felt-pen sketches, mainly abstractions of female forms in whimsical attitudes and basic colors, the therapy of a restless man who spends hours on airplanes without drinking or smoking. He kidded Williams about requiring *The Times* to publish some of his drawings in return for the interview, but the public debut of Davis's sketches had to wait for the release of the *Star People* LP. Its cover carried three brightly colored, primitive stick musicians and some decorative borders, with this credit line: "All Drawings, Color Concepts and Basic Attitudes by Miles Davis." A year after that, on 26 May 1984, Davis would celebrate his 58th birthday and his return to performing after hip surgery with a slide-show of his sketches at a New York art gallery.[112]

Brian Case, reviewing one of Davis's Hammersmith Odeon concerts for *Melody Maker*, reported: "This time, lungs, plexus and chops were way up close on two hours, and he was not only committed to the swoop and flux but untypically warm towards the house." He also noted a change in his music: "This is very much the group that Miles wants, and they serve him magnificently. In keeping with the spirit of the time, it offers a broad recapitulation of one of the greatest careers in jazz."[113]

In May 1983, Davis made a quick tour of Japan, playing eight concerts to packed houses. Davis's band shared the billing with Gil Evans's orchestra, in which Evans's son Miles played in the trumpet section. Davis and Evans did not play together; throughout the tour, Davis's band played the opening set and Evans's took over after the intermission. Davis stuck with the concert format he had used in Europe. By the time they played at Yomiuri East, Kanagawa, on 29 May, he had eliminated the frail *U 'n' I* from the working repertoire, but the other titles – *Come Get It, Star People, Speak, It Gets Better, Star on Cicely*, and *Jean Pierre* – though all but the latter were new to Japanese audiences, already sounded tired from so many reworkings on so many stages.

CBS timed the release of the *Star People* LP to coincide with Davis's international travels, so that it received newspaper notices around the same time he was appearing in England, France, Japan, and the other countries. The concert promotions thus fed the record sales and vice-versa, in a marketing campaign perfected for touring rock stars such as the Rolling Stones, Bob Dylan and the Band, David Bowie, and The Jacksons. When Davis returned to North America, *Star People*'s release coincided with his summer schedule, which included Kool Festival concerts in Cleveland (12 June), New York (26) Minneapolis (13 July), and Pittsburgh (19 August), as well as independent festivals in Montreal (7 July) and Toronto (8).

The novelty of his comeback wore off long ago for Davis, but for his audiences it was only beginning to wear off by the summer of 1983, two years after it began. His full-time presence on concert stages brought a few adjustments by promoters. In Toronto he played not at one of the high-priced halls as he had in 1981 and earlier in 1983, but in a roofed amphitheater at Ontario Place, where for $4 patrons could jam the hillsides and peer down onto the stage. George Wein presented Davis's band paired with other bands, putting him with the McCoy Tyner quintet in Minneapolis and VSOP II in New York. If Davis had stayed after his performance to listen to the bands with which he shared those stages, he might have rediscovered more of his old musical virtues and perhaps even some new ones.

The novelty of his comeback had also obviously worn off for Davis's New York reviewers. They dealt with him perfunctorily at the Kool festivities, brushing past his performance to deal with some of the hundreds of other musicians who participated. Lee Jeske's notice of Davis's concert in *Down Beat* stated: "Opening for VSOP II was Miles Davis with his sextet. All I have to tell you about *that* is that Miles didn't play nearly enough, and his band played more than enough."[114] Whitney Balliett's annual Kool review for the *New Yorker* gave surprisingly short shrift to almost everyone; of Davis, he said: "His chops were in good shape, and he sounded like the old Davis of *Walkin'*. The rest of the time — he was disguised tonight as a sort of golfer, in white cap, baggy dark-blue windbreaker, and wide-legged 1930s pants — he played on an electric keyboard, let loose occasional trumpet shrieks, and allowed his group to scream its back-beated electronic head off."[115]

That nonchalance was beginning to crystallize into the American critical consensus on Davis's music of the 1980s. Neil Tesser, after watching Davis at Park West in February, concluded: "Miles has long personified 'cool'; now, like [a] glacial drift ... his music moves across the landscape, strewing stuff all over, some of it valuable, much of it worthless."[116] Even Greg Tate, in an eccentric revaluation of Davis's music since 1969 for *Down Beat* that otherwise inverted most jazz critics' perceptions, fell into line when he reached the music of the 1980s, stating: "I'll admit to being unable to take Miles' comeback seriously. Not that I'm alone in this mind you: I don't think Miles does either."[117] So far, the European and Japanese critics have been much more cautious about committing themselves on Davis's latest guise, and the American consensus remains local.

The force of that consensus may have obscured the critical perception of Davis's band after its return from Japan for its summer circuit. While Davis and his band played less freely and confidently in New York than in their subsequent concerts – apparently as a reflex of Davis's new vulnerability, which makes it impossible for him to contain his fretfulness in his so-what? disguise – they presented several changes for critical fodder.

John Scofield occupied center stage in place of Mike Stern, who left at the end of the Japanese tour. The difference that made to the ensemble sound could be measured in decibels, but it was more significant in the altered feeling. Scofield shares with Stern the command of high-pitched guitar colorations, but it is not the hallmark of his style as it is of Stern's.

The blues remained dominant, with *It Gets Better* joined in the repertoire by a new and similarly straightforward twelve-bar melody. That doubled Davis's opportunities for playing to the women in the front rows and stretched his powers of invention to the break-point, but it also played up one of Scofield's strengths, and Evans's too, when he was given enough space to develop his thoughts. No jazz audience agonized about hearing Davis play blues clichés instead of the funk clichés of his recent past.

The band's repertoire was almost entirely new. Sometime between the Kanagawa concert at the end of May and the first American concert in mid-June, Davis renovated his concert program. Even *Jean Pierre* was purged. The retained compositions – *Speak*, *It Gets Better*, and *Star on Cicely* – introduced intricately arranged passages, with Scofield and Evans playing tight harmonies, usually backed by Davis's trumpet-synthesizer riffs. Four new themes were built on similar arrangements.

The haste with which the new repertoire had been installed was also evident. Many sequences had rough edges, and the concerts had no more polish than dress rehearsals. In Toronto, the roughness was exacerbated toward the end when Evans, obviously annoyed about having so many of his solos cut short, began playing his long, difficult arranged parts half-heartedly, and at the very end the concert became a genuine rehearsal when Davis called the band back for an encore and kicked off a four-minute arrangement that the band were still learning.

What the concerts lacked in polish they partly gained in spirit, with the risks of a reorganized band searching for their new balance as they worked out new material. That new balance will not come easily. Without Stern to counterbalance the rocking rhythms, Foster and the new bassist, Darryl Jones, cast in the same funk role as his predecessors, often sounded ingenuous – an index of how suddenly the music had altered around them, but also a measure of how far they have to go to catch up with it.

Some of the rough edges in the summer repertoire were preserved when Davis selected excerpts of two of the new titles played at his Montreal concert for his new LP, *Decoy*. The details are as follows:

Miles Davis Sextet: Decoy
Miles Davis, tpt, synthesizer; Bill Evans, ss; John Scofield, gtr; Darryl Jones, b; Al Foster, dms; Mino Cinelu, perc. Festival international de Jazz, Montreal, 7 July 1983
What It Is; That's What Happened
(both on Columbia FC 38991)
Both are composed by Scofield and Davis and arranged by Davis.

Both titles feature tight uptempo unison passages by Scofield and Evans. *That's What Happened* adds Davis's simultaneous trumpet-synthesizer riffs in the background, but omits the solos. *What It Is* carries on into Evans's solo, his last on record as a member of the band although he would tour with them for four more months, and into Davis's, with an overdub of Davis's blues solo from the same concert superimposed.

The excerpts form the liveliest tracks on *Decoy*. The rest of the music was set down in studio sessions later that summer, as Davis resumed his once-familiar practice of rehearsing with the tapes running. The details are as follows:

Miles Davis Quartet: Decoy
Miles Davis, synthesizer; Darryl Jones, b; Al Foster, dms; Mino Cinelu, perc. New York, probably late August–September 1983
Freaky Deaky
(on Columbia FC 38991)

Miles Davis Septet: Decoy
Miles Davis, tpt; Branford Marsalis, ss; Robert Irving III, synthesizer; John
Scofield, gtr; Darryl Jones, b; Al Foster, dms; Mino Cinelu, perc. New York,
probably late August–September 1983
Decoy; Robot 415; Code M.D.; That's Right
(all on Columbia FC 38991)
Marsalis, Scofield, Jones, and Foster are not heard on the one-minute excerpt
titled *Robot 415;* Irving composed and arranged *Decoy* and *Code M.D.;* Davis
and Irving composed and arranged *Robot 415;* Davis and Scofield composed
That's Right, and Davis and Gil Evans arranged it.

Freaky Deaky pares down the ensemble to a quartet in order to give
some prominence to the new bassist, Darryl Jones, who had joined the
band in the spring on the recommendation of Vincent Wilburn, Davis's
nephew who now traveled with him as bodyguard and factotum. Davis
praised Jones's playing extravagantly at every opportunity, giving him
his highest accolade – "a motherfucker" – in fall interviews for French
and German radio and describing him this way for Leonard Feather in
the spring: "He has the same approach to music as Jimmy Blanton – in
fact, he's the greatest bass player since Blanton, and he's just 22."[118]
    Except for *That's Right,* the longest and best-elaborated track, the rest
of the music bears the imprint of Robert Irving, the keyboard player
from *The Man with the Horn* whom Davis was now readying for a place
in the working band. His funk charts are undistinguished but pleasant in
their brief airing, and the sparse solo spaces on them offer little interest
for the jazz listener. His synthesizer effects mix unobtrusively into the
background, as Davis's seldom did, and the ensemble seem tame.
    That tameness also pervades *That's Right,* notwithstanding the
collaboration of Davis, Scofield, and Gil Evans in its arrangement and
the presence of Branford Marsalis as a soloist. The track opens with a
blues solo by Davis and then swings into its arranged unison passage by
Scofield and Marsalis. The arranged passage recurs after solos by
Scofield and by Marsalis, and the track fades out during Davis's second
solo. Its form is orderly and its solos are generous, but the mood is
cautious. Davis and Scofield have played in this same blues context
nightly for over a year and have few surprises to offer, and Marsalis, with
a growing reputation as an earthy, swinging soloist, sounds uncertain.
He admitted to no uncertainty when Peter Keepnews questioned him
about the session. "It was pretty much the stuff I used to play in high

school," he said. "It was, you know, vamp music. But it was good. I definitely had fun."[119]

Davis was satisfied with Marsalis's work in the studio but could not add him to the band because he was committed to his brother's quintet. Bill Evans rejoined Davis for the remaining tour of the year, an October swing through Europe, but the tension between them was palpable. In Rome, Davis told an interviewer, "I'm trying to make my saxophone player understand the problem of phrases ... He throws them away, he wastes them, like a boxer making useless jabs and wasting his energy."[120] In Paris, after having his solos cut short, Evans said, "Hey, Miles, you don't even like saxophone players anymore, do you?" "I didn't even answer that nonsense," Davis told Leonard Feather.[121]

Davis was received royally in Warsaw, where the tour opened on 23 October. he was waved through customs by officers wearing "We Want Miles" buttons, whisked away in a Russian-made Chaika limousine, and escorted to a two-bedroom suite at the Victoria Hotel, where the swimming pool had been scrubbed and freshly filled for his use.[122] After his performance at the Warsaw Jazz Jamboree, the 5,000 fans stood and chanted "Sto lat" (May you live a hundred years), and Davis reciprocated by calling his band back for three encores.[123]

His reception in Berlin on 29 October was no less noisy but much less friendly. Before leaving the United States, Davis had given a long, relaxed interview to Ute Büsing for German radio. He dispatched the promotional business early, saying, "I hope you fuckin' Germans come out an' see us," and then offered numerous opinions for the German public to ponder. Many of them involved Beethoven. "I don't like to listen to Beethoven," he said. "He's just too old for me. You got Stockhausen. Not Beethoven. He's too fuckin' old." Prodded by Büsing, he returned to the theme: "I just don't like Beethoven. That's my personal feeling about his music." And later, in response to a question about his use of electronics, he said, "You can't fuck around, like old Beethoven." By the time he landed in Berlin, his opinions had aroused a storm of controversy in the press and he faced a horde of reporters wherever he went. His two concerts for Jazz Fest Berlin at Philharmonic Hall, on the same day as Master Srinvas Group from India and the Sun Ra All Stars with Philly Joe Jones, Archie Shepp, and Don Cherry, were received enthusiastically by sellout crowds.

The European triumphs were capped on Davis's return to New York by a gala retrospective at Radio City Music Hall, "Miles Ahead: A Tribute to an American Music Legend," on 6 November. Co-produced by the Black Music Association, the tribute received press coverage that rivaled Davis's 1981 comeback concerts. "We think this will be a once-in-a-lifetime experience," said George Butler, Columbia's vice-president for jazz. "The program is an attempt to entertain, and to inform people about Miles's impact. We'll take the styles of music he has been involved with from the late 1940s to the present." The roster of performers stretched the outer limits even of Davis's many genres, with a contingent of rhythm and blues singers including Angela Bofill, Shalamar, and the Whispers, reflecting Davis's current listening tastes rather than his music. "It is also designed to entertain Miles," Clayton Riley, the director, said.[124]

Parts of the four-hour show became a genuine retrospective. With Bill Cosby as host, revolving stages, a videotaped encomium from Dizzy Gillespie, and numerous speeches, there was still time for brief performances by Davis's early associates Walter Bishop Jr, Roy Haynes, J.J. Johnson, and Jackie McLean, his alumni George Benson, Ron Carter, George Coleman, Herbie Hancock, Jimmy Heath, Philly Joe Jones, Buster Williams, and Tony Williams, and an all-star orchestra conducted by Quincy Jones playing Slide Hampton's rearrangements of some of Gil Evans's arrangements for *Porgy and Bess* and *Sketches of Spain*. At midnight, Davis received an honorary degree in music from the president of Fisk University while Cosby and Cicely Tyson enrobed him in purple. The evening ended with a half-hour set by Davis and his current band.

When it was over, Cosby cajoled Davis to make a speech. Finally he took the microphone and whispered, "Thank you." He grew more talkative backstage as the NBC-TV cameras recorded him chugging a litre of Perrier water. Asked if the tributes overwhelmed him, he took the bottle away from his lips, furrowed his brow, and said, "No, I wonder why they waited so long."[125]

The gala ended a long, sustained period of touring and performing for Davis and preceded a long layoff. He entered the hospital two weeks later for a left-hip prosthesis. The operation was expected to take two hours but ended up taking ten. The recuperation was expected to take six weeks, with Davis back onstage in January 1984, but took six months because he caught pneumonia in December. *Decoy*, announced for release in January, came out instead at the end of May, to coincide with Davis's return to performing, which started with a concert at the Beverly Theatre in Los Angeles on 2 June. The summer schedule had the familiar look of recent years, with Kool festival appearances in June and

August and European festivals in July. The band looked and sounded only slightly different. Bill Evans, as expected, left to try his hand at freelancing, and Mino Cinelu joined Weather Report. Their places were filled by Bob Berg and Steve Thornton, as unknown as Evans and Cinelu had been when they joined and indeed as most of Davis's sidemen had been for more than a decade. The repertoire continued to change too and, with it, Davis's notion of what improvising musicians should sound like. He is still not willing, or perhaps not able, to coast.

As long as he retains that restlessness there is some chance that he may yet rise above his superstardom and, against the odds of most of his current critics, influence another generation of jazzmen. The odds are, of course, long and grow longer daily in a young person's art form. In the life cycle of most jazz players, Davis is already well into what ought to be his dotage. One is reminded of André Hodeir's question, "Why do they age so badly?" and of his ominous answer: "The history of both jazz and jazzmen is that of creative purity gradually corrupted by success. In his youth, the great musician has to struggle to impose his art; if he succeeds in doing so, he must then struggle daily *against* his own success. How many men have won *this* struggle?"

When he wrote this in 1962, Hodeir could name only one who had: "Charlie Parker undoubtedly did, because he never reached the peak of success and because he died at the age of thirty-five." And he was willing to hazard a guess about two others: "Monk and Miles Davis may win it, either because of their tough, incorruptible characters, or because they took Pascal's advice and fled success rather than try to stand up to it."[126]

For Thelonious Monk, Hodeir's guess proved prophetic. He never wavered in imposing his art. In 1955, when he began recording for Riverside, Orrin Keepnews persuaded him to record two LPs of Ellington melodies and standard ballads in an attempt to make his music more accessible, but Monk simply translated them into his own singular idiom. It never occurred to him to tailor his music for commercial success; he used all his energy pursuing his own muse and had none left for the bitch goddess. By 1964, when his portrait appeared on the cover of *Time*, he had succeeded in bringing the audience to him. After that, he felt less need for performing, recording, or composing. He disbanded his quartet with tenor saxophonist Charlie Rouse in 1970 and emerged into public only on special occasions. After an international tour with Dizzy Gillespie, Sonny Stitt, Kai Winding, Al McKibbon, and Art Blakey in 1972, billed as the Giants of Jazz, he appeared with the New York Jazz Repertory Company in 1974, at the Newport Jazz Festival in 1975, and

Bill Evans at Ontario Place Forum, 1983 (Bernard Lecerf)

Miles Davis at Ontario Place Forum, 1983 (Peter Jones)

at Carnegie Hall in 1976. He shrugged off countless inducements. His seclusion was rumored to be caused by a mysterious biochemical disorder, which may or may not translate into schizophrenia, but sporadic reports confirmed that he was fit to perform more often than not, if he had wanted to. When he died at 64 in February 1982, his art was uncorrupted, its stunning integrity one of the great achievements in jazz.

For Miles Davis, Hodeir's guess seems equally secure. He has already succeeded in imposing his art four or perhaps five times, toughly and incorruptibly, all the while fleeing success for bitches more to his taste. Only now, as Davis enters his fifth decade as a jazz artist, Hodeir's terms of reference are harder to apply. His music keeps changing, but the character guiding it seems neither incorruptible nor particularly tough. He feels no need for imposing his art again, and when Ute Büsing asked him what he saw in the future of jazz, he replied, "Bullshit." Success finally caught up to him, and he seems genuinely relieved that the race is over. "Struggling musicians," he told Büsing, "are bad musicians."

So he pokes fun at the tough, incorruptible character he used to be. He interpolates eight bars of *Surrey with the Fringe on Top* and then casts a sideward look – a Jack Benny take – at the audience, or he snatches his trumpet away from his lips and sticks out his tongue just as a front-row photographer clicks his shutter, or he hoists his pant legs and invites the audience to cheer his bright red boots. "Yeah, I'm an entertainer," he admitted to Cheryl McCall. "I've got a certain amount of ham in me. I don't know. I'm doin' what I'm doin' but I know I'm a big ham. It doesn't take away from the music, because I enjoy what I'm doin' at that particular time."[127]

"I've earned an enormous amount of money since my comeback," he told Leonard Feather,[128] and he revels in the glitter that goes with show-biz. The $60,000 yellow Ferrari no longer represents thoroughbred recklessness but celebrity status. He had it flown to Los Angeles from New York when he went there to perform on the Grammy Awards show and towed to the curb in front of his hotel, L'Ermitage in Beverly Hills; it could not be driven because of mechanical problems, according to David Breskin, "but it's a stage prop that makes him feel good."[129] Of Breskin's *Rolling Stone* profile, Davis said, "I read a little bit and threw it away, because it was evident from the first paragraph that he didn't like me." But even his disdain for the press is wavering, and he added, "One of these days, maybe if I've just made love real good and I'm in the right mood, I'll read the whole thing and it won't drag me."[130]

On the road, he stays at the best hotels while his sidemen stay elsewhere. ("They're in a different hotel," Breskin says, "even on the same stage."[131]) Off the road, the renovated Manhattan brownstone is now joined not only by the Long Island retreat but also by a seaside villa in Malibu, California. "New York is great," Davis told George Goodman in 1981. "I've got so much noise. Subways. Horns. I can't stand nothing quiet. I go nuts."[132] But the villa is quiet, and Davis told Leonard Feather: "I love California more and more. It's a place where you should be able to add fifty years to your life, even with the smog."

"It's a good sign of your social status when you know you can have whatever you want in the world," he added. "I love clothes and I love cars. And I love to have a good band. My manager makes life easy on tours. I only have to show up and play. I like the California lifestyle, and if I miss New York I can always go back. Really, it's a good life."[133]

AFTERWORD

Miles Davis (Peter Jones)

So What?

If I didn't play trumpet, I don't know what I would have done. I couldn't stay in an office. I'd do some kind of research. That W-H-Y is always my first word, you know. I'd do research, 'cause I like to see why things are how they are, the shape and flesh and everything. I'm one of them motherfuckers. Miles Davis (1983)

I have not called Miles Davis a genius. He does not call himself a genius, although he comes close once, in a bantering mood, on page 313.

   Charlie Parker was a genius, and the young Louis Armstrong was too. Their music burst out of them as flashes of insight. It seemed to depend more on intuition than on introspection, and once they were rightly heard all the music around them had to change.

   Miles Davis did not do that. But he did something no less difficult, and as inexplicable. He sustained a long creative life in the second half of the twentieth century, when creative lives are seldom long and long lives are seldom creative. He grew and changed and renewed himself, and with him the music grew and changed and renewed itself. He leaves behind not a flash of insight but a luminous trail.

   Davis's achievement is a rare one, and not only in jazz. Hemingway discovered a unique, powerful voice for fiction, and then he spent the last two-thirds of his time parodying his own voice. Brando transformed dialogue and stage directions into illusion, and then he made the dialogue inaudible and the actions stupefying. Joseph Heller filled *Catch-22* with hilarious indignation and grotesque joy, and then he followed it, after thirteen years of near-silence, with stylish voids. Orson Welles passed from masterworks in several media to so-so ads for *vin ordinaire*. The spirit slumps or the will weakens.

   Not always. Davis's achievement is rare in jazz, but it is not unique.

Duke Ellington's creativity lasted at least as long and shone at least as brightly. Some, perhaps many, would say more brightly. It hardly matters, because, in the end, it is immeasurable.

So Davis's place among jazz musicians is secure. He ranks at the top with Armstrong and Ellington and Parker and very few others – probably Jelly Roll Morton and Thelonious Monk, perhaps Coleman Hawkins and John Coltrane and, if one is permitted to look beyond the point where music intersects with myth, Buddy Bolden.

All of them made highly personal responses to the way we are in our time and sublimated them into art so they could be felt and shared. They help form the sensibility of our time as surely as do our painters, poets, composers, novelists, directors. If they have not had the same audience and their art form remains undervalued in the cultural reckoning, that may yet change.

Davis's music tapped resources of metaphor among those who took the time to be moved by it. His performances, Charles Fox said, were like "a man reading aloud from his diary."[1] In an image by Barry Ulanov that stuck doggedly to his playing for years, through several changes, Davis was "a man walking on eggshells."[2] To that, Ira Gitler responded, "Miles may be a man walking on eggshells, but he is also a diamond cutting into opaque glass."[3] Whitney Balliett heard in Davis's music "young-Werther ruminations ... – a view of things that is brooding, melancholy, perhaps self-pitying, and extremely close to the sentimental."[4] Martin Williams pointed out that Davis was far removed from that picaresque romantic by stating, "Davis the musician walks firmly and sure of foot; if he ever encounters any eggshells, his intensity will probably grind them to powder."[5]

We are told that one of the wellsprings of Davis's music is his essential shyness. That seems a peculiar, even exotic, piece of psychologizing in the face of the facts. Davis's strengths have always been the converse of those of a shy man. As Gil Evans puts it: "Miles Davis is a leader in jazz because he has a definite confidence in what he likes and he is not *afraid* of what he likes. A lot of musicians are constantly looking around to hear what the next person is doing and they worry about whether they themselves are in style. Miles has confidence in his taste, and he goes his own way."[6] Teo Macero agrees: "He has never been bound by convention. You wouldn't expect Miles to go back and do something the way he did it years ago any more than you would expect Picasso to go back to what he was doing in his blue and rose periods."[7]

Another point against the easy explanation of shyness is that Davis has felt the adulation of his fellows and his fans, often presupposed as in Macero's unhesitating comparison with Picasso but usually much more directly, performing before millions of people all over the world. Surely such an experience reinforced countless times over the years would be an effective antidote for anything but the most pathological shyness, and surely anyone who suffered from acute shyness could not in the first place bear to hone his art — which requires, after all, *performing* — so that it invited such exposure.

But if not shyness, what then? I would suggest, at some risk, that arrogance fits better. The risk arises from the baffling fact that whenever arrogance has been associated with Davis, the association has almost always been made by someone who deplores him — by promoters for whom he has refused to work cheaply, or audiences miffed at his refusal to bow, or antagonists on whom he has figuratively or literally spat. It sometimes seems that the protestations of shyness show up more frequently after he has committed some impudent public act, as if designed by well-meaning acquaintances to shield him from the charge of arrogance.

It is worth wondering why the attribution of arrogance has, where Davis is concerned, been appropriated by people lodging a complaint against him, so that any attempt to associate the term with him in a neutral or well-meaning way requires vindication. No one ever hesitated in applying the term to Shaw, or Pavlova, or Stravinsky, or any number of our cultural bellwethers.

Perhaps the reluctance to recognize Davis's arrogance positively, as a wellspring of his art, merely reflects the fact that the art for which he is the bellwether, jazz, is less secure among our arts than most others, having ascended so recently into the concert hall from the black folk roots of field songs, spirituals, and funeral marches. Or perhaps it is because Davis lives in a world where, for some, an arrogant black man is "uppity," a social taboo that was supposed to die with the Emancipation Proclamation.

Davis has suffered for being a black man in other ways too. Apart from the social and occupational indignities visited on blacks during their tedious rise from the plantations, he has suffered by spending his creative energies on a music that is making its own tedious rise from brothels and dance halls. True, Davis has earned more material rewards than all but a very few jazzmen. Even so, his affluence probably came harder than that of people in other cultural pursuits, the leading divas, conductors, actors, directors, novelists. True too, Davis has received some measure of artistic recognition, but, again, it has hardly been comparable to his counterparts in other art forms – if indeed it is possible to identify counterparts to Davis in other art forms, for one would be hard pressed to name an individual in those other arts who maintained such an utterly commanding position for even half the length of time that Davis dominated his.

Perhaps the rewards he has gathered are the harbingers of a more tolerant cultural climate, with a better future for jazz in it. Just ten or fifteen years ago, any mention of Davis or any other jazz musician in the same breath as Maria Callas, Leonard Bernstein, Marlon Brando, Elia Kazan, or Saul Bellow might have been dismissed as ludicrous among the guardians of our culture. It is less likely to be so dismissed nowadays, I think, at least in many circles.

If so, it is partly Davis's doing. At his best, when he was willing to make the fewest concessions, he not only created the music, he dignified it. When Bud Powell told him, "I wish I was blacker than you,"[8] it was presumably not the hue of his skin that he envied so much as his undenigrable character.

In a tradition where the musicians had been treated like vaudevillians and buskers for generations, Davis found a liberating stance. It worked only because he, unlike anyone who came before him except Duke Ellington, had the conviction to do it his way and the strength to make it stick – the arrogance, if you will. Ralph J. Gleason put it this way: "The fact that he is now, like Picasso and a very few other artists, a great commercial success in his own lifetime is a tribute to his courage and his sanity and his basic good sense. It is also, whether or not he wills it, a rare symbol to all artists everywhere of the complete triumph of uncompromising art."[9]

If the comparison with Picasso works it is not only because both men achieved commercial success on their own terms but also because both men, as Macero said, spent their careers in a constant search for expression. "Like Picasso, he has made change into style," Gleason added, "and wherever you go you bump into little fragments of his music."

In the shape of their careers and the restlessness of their vision, Davis and Picasso seem to invite comparison. Jazz writers, if no one else, find it compelling. David Breskin recently added this one: "Restless, relentless, [Davis] synergizes new vocabularies, masters the language, then moves on with another generation in tow. He's the Picasso of the invisible art."[10] And Greg Tate, on Davis's 1980s incarnation, says,

"Like Picasso when he ran out of ideas, Miles has taken to enjoying poking a little fun at himself."[11]

The comparison will soon be a cliché. In jazz journalism it may already be a cliché. Is it enlightening? Does it mean anything at all?

Davis, for one, does not think so. Some wag, charged by a corporate sponsor with preparing program notes for a 1982 concert, tried it out on him. Lots of people, he told Davis, were comparing him with Picasso. Did he have any thoughts on that? Davis stared at him a long time, his eyes impassive and his lips fixed, until the adman's smile wavered and came unglued. Then he whispered, "I'm in a class by myself."[12]

As is Picasso, of course.

References

CHAPTER NINE:
PFRANCING: 1960–2 (pages 3–50)

1 Adderley 1964, pp. 261–3
2 Simpkins 1975, p. 90
3 Sussman 1980, p. 28
4 Sy Johnson 1976, p. 22
5 Gordon 1980, p. 99
6 Hentoff ca 1960
7 Hall 1974b, p. 14
8 Hentoff ca 1960
9 Hall 1974b, p. 14
10 Martin Williams 1970b, p. 160
11 Harrison 1976, pp. 140–1
12 Cook 1983, p. 15
13 Hentoff ca 1960
14 Harrison 1976, p. 141
15 Martin Williams 1970b, p. 160
16 Martin 1960, p. 3
17 Stewart 1982, p. 65
18 Cook 1983, p. 15
19 Stewart 1982, p. 65
20 Liska 1982, p. 20
21 Thomas 1975, pp. 108–9
22 Simpkins 1975, p. 109, p. 111
23 *Melody Maker* 14 July 1965, p. 6
24 Goldberg 1965, p. 231
25 Spellman 1970, p. 128
26 Feather and Gitler 1976, p. 34
27 Silvert 1980, p. 18
28 Feather and Gitler 1976, p. 34
29 Goldberg 1965, p. 230
30 Stewart 1981, p. 22
31 Spellman 1970, p. 14
32 Spellman 1970, p. 6
33 Berendt 1976, p. 97
34 Johnson 1976, p. 24
35 Cole 1974, p. 152
36 Liska 1982a, p. 20
37 Martin 1960, p. 3
38 Goldberg 1965, p. 63
39 Martin 1960, p. 3
40 Simpkins 1975, p. 116
41 Goldberg 1965, p. 86
42 DeMicheal 1969b, p. 18
43 Feather 1974b, p. 225
44 Goldberg 1981, p. 59
45 Gordon 1980, p. 102
46 DeMicheal 1966, p. 18
47 Cotterrell 1967, p. 4
48 Goldberg 1965, p. 80

49 Goldberg 1965, p. 208
50 Hailey 1964, p. 167
51 Gleason 1961
52 Primack 1979, p. 37
53 Gleason 1975, p. 133
54 Quoted by Carr 1982, p. 128
55 Wilson ca 1961
56 Balliett 1962, p. 143
57 Simon ca 1961
58 Ronald Atkins, in Harrison et al
    1975, p. 99
59 Norsworthy 1974
60 Goldberg 1965, p. 63
61 Taylor 1977, p. 11
62 Nyhan 1976, p. 82
63 Scott 1980, p. 92
64 Martin Williams 1970a, p. 107
65 Interview Toronto August 1976
66 Feather 1967, p. 16
67 Max Harrison 1976, p. 140
68 Martin Williams 1970b, p. 160
69 Feather 1967, p. 16
70 Hall 1974a, pp. 17–18
71 Hall 1974b, p. 13

CHAPTER TEN:
SO NEAR, SO FAR: 1963–4
(pages 51–75)

1 Sussman 1980, p. 28
2 Martin 1960, p. 3
3 Underwood 1979, p. 54
4 Taylor 1977, p. 13
5 Coryell and Friedman 1978, p. 88
6 DeMicheal 1969b, p. 20
7 Bouchard 1980, p. 22
8 Taylor 1977, pp. 11–12
9 McRae 1975, p. 10
10 Feather 1974b, p. 237
11 Goode ca 1970

12 Gleason ca 1963
13 Gleason 1975, p. 249
14 Evans 1981
15 Hawes and Asher 1974, p. 130
16 Gillespie and Fraser 1979, p. 454,
    p. 457
17 Gilmore 1978, p. 20
18 Sussman 1980, p. 61
19 Hennessy 1977, p. 46
20 Spellman 1970, p. 15
21 Tinder 1980, p. 6
22 Cole 1974, p. 95
23 Palmer ca 1975
24 Palmer ca 1975
25 Ullmann 1980, p. 135
26 Coryell and Friedman 1978,
    p. 259
27 Ullmann 1980, p. 135
28 Liska 1982a, p. 20

CHAPTER ELEVEN:
CIRCLE: 1964–8 (pages 76–134)

1 DeMicheal 1969b, p. 20
2 Jones 1968, p. 82
3 Jones 1968, p. 85
4 Pekar 1976, p. 8
5 Lyons 1983, p. 145, p. 150
6 Hawes and Asher 1974, p. 138
7 Gordon 1980, p. 102
8 Carter 1982, p. 44
9 Mialy 1983
10 Hall 1974a, p. 20
11 Ramsey ca 1975
12 Williams 1970b, p. 162
13 Silvert 1977, p. 16
14 Coryell and Friedman 1968,
    pp. 3–4
15 Balliett 1983a, p. 169
16 Jeske 1983e, p. 24

17 Goodman 1981, p. 12
18 Taylor 1977, p. 13
19 Pekar 1976, p. 9
20 Yanow 1978, p. 58
21 Collier 1978, p. 433
22 McCall 1982, p. 43
23 Jeske 1983e, p. 24
24 Morgenstern 1966, p. 32
25 Gordon 1980, p. 98
26 Zwerin 1966, p. 39
27 Siders 1973b, p. 45
28 DeMichael 1969b, p. 20
29 McCall 1982, p. 43
30 Gordon 1980, p. 101
31 Feather 1967, pp. 16–17
32 Feather 1967, p. 17
33 Quoted by Hentoff 1975, p. 199
34 Clark 1977, p. 13
35 Wilmer 1970, p. 73
36 *Down Beat* 6 April 1976, p. 13
37 DeMicheal 11 Dec 1969, p. 32
38 Wilmer 1969, p. 17
39 Russ Wilson 1967, p. 30
40 Siders 1973b, p. 19
41 Hawes and Asher 1974, p. 147;
   Siders 1973b, p. 19
42 Blumenthal ca 1981
43 Hentoff 1978
44 Feather 1969, p. 28
45 Hall 1974a, pp. 17, 18
46 Feather 1967, pp. 16–17
47 Stewart 1982, p. 64
48 Feather 1967, p. 16
49 Blumenthal 1979, pp. 65–6
50 Blumenthal 1979, p. 65
51 Clark 1977, p. 14
52 Lyttleton 1978, p. 68
53 Gitler 1967, p. 26
54 Wilmer 1982, p. 68
55 Quoted by Thomas 1975, p. 226

56 Balliett 1981b, p. 40
57 Gillespie 1976, pp. 9–10
58 DeMicheal 1969b, p. 21
59 Walton 1972, p. 129
60 Taylor 1977, p. 18
61 DeMicheal 1969b, p. 21
62 Taylor 1977, pp. 16, 18
63 Wilmer 1967, p. 19
64 McRae 1975, p. 10
65 Taylor 1977, p. 17, p. 18
66 Coryell and Friedman 1978, p. 98
67 Birnbaum 1979, p. 44
68 Silvert 1977, p. 17
69 Martin Williams 1970a, p. 272
70 Martin Williams 1970a, p. 272
71 Coryell and Friedman 1978,
   p. 103
72 Martin Williams 1970a, p. 273
73 Martin Williams 1970a,
   pp. 272–3
74 Williams 1970a, p. 276
75 Taylor 1977, p. 13
76 Jeske 1983c, p. 31
77 Taylor 1977, p. 15
78 Mitchell 1968, p. 37
79 Mitchell 1968, p. 37
80 Kart 1968, p. 24
81 Pekar 1976, p. 11
82 Morgenstern 1977b, p. 14
83 Stewart 1982, p. 65
84 Stewart 1982, p. 64
85 Nisenson 1982, p. 204
86 Quoted by Carr 1982, p. 166
87 Nisenson 1982, p. 204
88 Feather 1974b, p. 255
89 DeMicheal 1969b, p. 20
90 Feather 1974b, p. 240
91 Feather and Gitler 1976, p. 133
92 Feather 1974b, p. 240
93 Johnson 1976, p. 27

CHAPTER TWELVE:
MILES RUNS THE VOODOO DOWN:
1968–9 (pages 135–75)

1 Taylor 1977, p. 14
2 Avakian ca 1967
3 Hentoff 1978
4 Avakian ca 1967
5 Carter 1982, p. 44
6 Saal 1977, p. 41
7 Saunders 1975, p. 30
8 Coryell and Friedman 1978, p. 162
9 Jagajivan 1973, p. 15
10 Sy Johnson 1976, p. 24
11 Sy Johnson 1976, p. 25
12 Silvert 1976, p. 24
13 Coryell and Friedman 1978, p. 148
14 DeMicheal 1969b, p. 21
15 Coryell and Friedman 1978, p. 27; Feather and Gitler 1976, p. 332
16 Grime 1979, p. 84
17 Smith 1973, p. 4
18 Grime 1979, p. 84
19 Feather 1976, p. 54
20 Feather 1976, p. 53
21 Feather 1975, p. 41
22 Townley 1975, p. 17
23 Townley 1975, p. 17
24 Albertson 1971, p. 87
25 Underwood 1979, p. 60
26 Down Beat 20 February 1969, p. 10
27 Underwood 1979, p. 60
28 Stern 1978, p. 52
29 Feather 1974a, p. 35
30 Coryell and Friedman 1978, pp. 128–9
31 DeMicheal 1969b, p. 18
32 Coryell and Friedman 1978, p. 129
33 Heckman 1974, p. 75
34 Pekar 1976, p. 12
35 Birnbaum 1979, p. 44
36 Jeske 1982, p. 17
37 Townley 1975, p. 17
38 Birnbaum 1979, p. 44
39 Miles Davis ca 1971
40 Jeske 1982, p. 17
41 Hall 1974b, p. 15
42 Feather 1979, p. 17
43 Siders 1969
44 Jeske 1981, p. 18
45 Jeske 1981, p. 18
46 Hall 1974b, p. 14
47 Clive Davis 1974, p. 43
48 Albertson 1971, p. 69
49 Clive Davis 1974, p. 299
50 Clive Davis 1974, p. 300
51 Taylor 1977, p. 223
52 Albertson 1971, pp. 68–9
53 Hall 1974a, p. 18
54 Albertson 1971, p. 69
55 Clive Davis 1974, p. 299
56 Albertson 1971, p. 69
57 Clive Davis 1974, p. 299
58 Cole 1974, pp. 104–5
59 Morgenstern 1976, p. 211
60 Albertson 1971, p. 69
61 Rollins 1982, p. 44
62 Coryell and Friedman 1978, p. 84
63 Meadow 1973, p. 16
64 Jeske 1982, p. 17
65 Feather and Gitler 1976, p. 32
66 McRae 1975, p. 11
67 Birnbaum 1979, p. 44
68 Feather and Gitler 1976, p. 32
69 Feather 1974b, p. 239
70 Feather 1976b, p. 148

71 Feather and Gitler 1976, p. 35
72 Clive Davis 1974, pp. 300–1
73 Clive Davis 1974, p. 302

CHAPTER THIRTEEN:
FUNKY TONK: 1969–71
(pages 179–232)

1 DeMicheal 1969a, p. 12
2 Quoted by Carr 1982, p. 194
3 McCall 1982, p. 48
4 Nyhan 1976, p. 87
5 Nyhan 1976, p. 88
6 McCall 1982, p. 48
7 DeMicheal 1969b, p. 21
8 Hall 1974a, p. 18
9 McCall 1982, p. 48
10 DeMicheal 1969b, p. 18
11 DeMicheal 1969b, p. 18
12 Coryell and Friedman 1978, p. 41
13 Feather 1976b, p. 49
14 Breskin 1983, p. 49
15 McCall 1982, p. 47
16 New York Post 3 March 1970
17 McCall 1982, p. 47
18 Johnson 1976, p. 27
19 Pepper and Pepper 1979,
   pp. 111–12
20 Berendt 1976, p. 101
21 Grime 1979, p. 84
22 Gordon 1980, p. 102
23 Albertson 1969, p. 31
24 DeMicheal 1969b, p. 19
25 Miller 1982, pp. 200–1
26 Blumenthal 1979, p. 66
27 DeMicheal 1969b, p. 18
28 Feather 1960, pp. 477–8
29 DeMicheal 1969b, p. 18
30 Underwood 1978, p. 16
31 Morgenstern 1973b, p. 20
32 Clive Davis 1974, p. 302

33 Clive Davis 1974, p. 302
34 Coryell and Friedman 1978, p. 68
35 Priestley 1974, p. 15
36 DeMicheal 1969b, p. 18
37 Clive Davis 1974, pp. 101–2
38 McCall 1983, p. 42
39 Down Beat April 1982, p. 10
40 Hall 1974b, p. 15
41 New York Post 4 March 1970
42 Isaacs 1979
43 Quoted by Walton 1972, p. 121
44 Coon 1977, p. 66
45 Albertson 1971, p. 68
46 Albertson 1971, p. 68
47 DeMicheal 1969b, p. 18
48 Jazz Journal June 1972, p. 16
49 Priestley 1974, p. 15
50 Hall 1974a, p. 19
51 Jarrett 1973
52 O'Reilly 1975, p. 17
53 Coryell and Friedman 1978,
   pp. 172–3
54 Feather 1974b, p. 247
55 DeMicheal 1969b, p. 18
56 Feather 1975, p. 41
57 Feather and Gitler 1976, p. 33
58 Jones and Chilton 1971, p. 247
59 Hentoff 1958, p. 165
60 Hailey 1962 (reprinted 1964),
   pp. 168–9
61 Feather 1974b, p. 258
62 Noë 1974, p. 57
63 McRae 1975, p. 11
64 Yanow 1978, p. 61
65 Clive Davis 1974, p. 302
66 Underwood 1981, p. 15
67 Stewart 1982, p. 66
68 Gaumont 1981, p. 36
69 Feather 1976b, p. 45
70 Balliett 1976, p. 209

71 Coryell and Friedman 1978, p. x
72 Coryell and Friedman 1978, front matter
73 Berendt 1976, p. 100
74 Nisenson 1982, pp. 209, 217
75 Underwood 1978, p. 15
76 Feather 1974b, p. 245
77 Hailey 1962 (reprinted 1964), p. 169
78 Quoted by Yanow 1978, p. 61
79 Hall 1974a, p. 18
80 Stewart 1982, p. 66
81 Silvert 1976, p. 24
82 Smith 1973, p. 2
83 Berendt 1976, p. 42
84 Grime 1979, p. 84
85 Ullmann 1980, p. 210
86 Hall 1974a, p. 20
87 Sy Johnson 1976, p. 25
88 "The Inner Sleeve" Columbia Records ca 1971
89 Albertson 1971, p. 87
90 "The Inner Sleeve" Columbia Records ca 1971
91 McRae 1972, p. 24
92 Hall 1974b, pp. 13, 15
93 Jeske 1982, p. 17
94 Feather 1974b, p. 246
95 Ames ca 1970
96 Feather 1974b, p. 247
97 Siders 1973c, p. 11
98 Ames ca 1970
99 Grime 1979, p. 84
100 Hill 1977, p. 5
101 Traill 1979, p. 26
102 Feather 1974b, pp. 248–9
103 Nisenson 1982, p. 217
104 Clive Davis, p. 134
105 Clive Davis, p. 303
106 Feather 1974b, p. 247

107 McRae 1975, p. 11
108 Albertson 1971, p. 67
109 Hall 1974a, p. 19

CHAPTER FOURTEEN:
SIVAD SELIM: 1972–5 (pages 233–82)

1 Feather 1974b, p. 242
2 Prince 1979, p. 14
3 Feather 1980, p. 186
4 Freedman 1982a, pp. 24–5
5 Feather 1974b, pp. 244–5
6 Hentoff 1976, p. 228
7 Perla 1974, p. 26
8 Stewart 1982, p. 66
9 Watts 1973, p. 124
10 Zanger 1976, pp. 14–5
11 Morgenstern 1973a, p. 31
12 Brown 1973b, p. 38
13 Feather 1974b, p. 243
14 Watts 1973, p. 124
15 Cole 1974, p. 165
16 Sy Johnson 1976, p. 23
17 Watts 1973, p. 126
18 Primack 1979, p. 26
19 Gaumont 1981, p. 36
20 Choice 1974, p. 4
21 Perla 1974, p. 26
22 Johnson 1976, pp. 24–5
23 Johnson 1976, pp. 22, 25
24 Watts 1973, pp. 124, 126–7
25 Baggenaes 1974, p. 5
26 Feather 1974b, p. 241
27 Balliett 1976, p. 31
28 New York Times 19 July 1972
29 Carr 1982, pp. 211–13
30 Sy Johnson 1976, p. 24
31 Smith 1972, p. 14
32 Gleason 1974, p. 13
33 Perla 1974, p. 26

34 Yanow 1978, p. 61
35 *Down Beat* 18 January 1973, p. 44
36 Quoted by Yanow 1978, p. 61
37 Watts 1973, p. 126
38 Hall 1974a, p. 18
39 Saunders 1975, p. 30
40 Hall 1974a, p. 19
41 Watts 1973, p. 126
42 Feather and Gitler 1976, p. 33
43 Orysik 1973, p. 32
44 Ron Johnson 1973, p. 37
45 Noë 1974, p. 57
46 Breskin 1983, p. 46
47 Hall 1974a, p. 20
48 The following four paragraphs are based on Chadbourne's report (Chadbourne 1973b).
49 Chadbourne 1973a, p. 4
50 Hall 1974a, p. 17
51 Watts 1973, p. 127
52 Sy Johnson 1976, p. 26
53 Zanger 1976, p. 15
54 Grime 1979, p. 84
55 Fox 1972, p. 106
56 Perla 1974, p. 26
57 Brown 1973a, p. 18
58 Noë 1974, pp. 55–6
59 Hall 1974a, p. 19
60 McCall 1982, p. 40
61 Bloom 1981, p. 19
62 Choice 1974, p. 6
63 Diliberto 1983, p. 23
64 Murphy 1975
65 Noë 1974, p. 55
66 Choice 1974, p. 4
67 Saunders 1975, p. 30
68 Choice 1974, p. 4
69 Quoted by Carr 1982, p. 218
70 Zanger 1976, p. 16
71 Saal 1977, p. 44

72 Choice 1974, pp. 3–4
73 Perla 1974, p. 26
74 Coryell and Friedman 1978, p. 40
75 Noë 1974, p. 56
76 Choice 1974, p. 4
77 *Coda* December 1974, p. 27
78 Offstein 1974, p. 27
79 Goddard 1974
80 Gleason 1974, p. 13
81 Sy Johnson 1976, p. 27
82 Noë 1974, p. 56
83 Noë 1974, pp. 56–7
84 Gaumont 1981, p. 37
85 Hall 1974a, p. 18
86 Gaumont 1981, p. 35
87 Hall 1974b, p. 14
88 Hall 1974a, p. 19
89 Gaumont 1981, p. 38
90 Johnson 1976, p. 22
91 Coryell and Friedman 1978, p. 37
92 *Down Beat* 25 April 1974, p. 16
93 Reese 1981
94 Tepperman 1976, p. 27
95 *Jazz Journal* December 1975, p. 6
96 Gleason 1975, p. 147
97 Gaumont 1981, p. 38
98 Quoted by Hentoff 1976, p. 145
99 Gaumont 1981, p. 37
100 Fortune 1982, p. 44
101 Gaumont 1981, p. 36
102 Gaumont 1981, p. 37
103 Underwood 1975a, p. 28
104 Gaumont 1981, p. 38
105 Takada 1975, p. 32
106 Mandel 1982, p. 44
107 McCall 1982, p. 40
108 Sy Johnson 1976, p. 26
109 Saunders 1975, p. 30
110 McCall 1982, p. 40
111 Gaumont 1981, p. 37

112 McCall 1982, p. 43
113 Gaumont 1981, pp. 37–8
114 McCall 1982, p. 43
115 Palmer 1975
116 Balliett 1976, p. 24
117 Wilson 1975
118 *Variety* 17 September 1975
119 Underwood 1975b, p. 42

CHAPTER FIFTEEN:
SHHH: 1975–81 (pages 283–307)

1 Hall 1974a, p. 20
2 McCall 1982, p. 41
3 Lowe 1976, p. 20
4 McCall 1982, p. 40
5 Goodman 1981, p. 1
6 McCall 1982, p. 41
7 Breskin 1983, pp. 49–50
8 Tailleur 1981
9 Zanger 1976, p. 15
10 Sy Johnson 1976, p. 21
11 Lowe 1976, p. 20
12 Hall 1974b, p. 15
13 Stewart 1982, p. 64
14 Feather 1974b, pp. 255–6
15 Hentoff 1976, p. 136
16 Feather 1974b, p. 256
17 Pepper and Pepper 1979,
   pp. 112–13
18 "Odds & ..." *Coda* June 1977
19 Balliett 1976, pp. 134, 135, 230
20 Gillespie and Fraser 1979, p. 487
21 Richard Williams 1983
22 Lowe 1976, p. 21
23 Breskin 1983, p. 50
24 Lowe 1976, p. 21
25 Palmer 1976, p. 10
26 Sy Johnson 1976, p. 27
27 Silvert 1976, p. 24

28 Hall 1974a, p. 17
29 Lowe 1976, p. 21
30 Hall 1974b, p. 15
31 Morgenstern 1977a, p. 20
32 Silvert 1977, p. 58
33 Sy Johnson 1976, p. 27
34 McCall 1982, pp. 43–5
35 Richard Williams 1983
36 Ullmann 1980, p. 105
37 Feather 1983b, pp. 18–19
   (retranslated)
38 Morgenstern 1977b, p. 14
39 Saal 1977, p. 42
40 McCall 1982, p. 42
41 Feather 1980, p. 33
42 *Down Beat* 26 January 1978, p. 9
43 Lowe 1976, p. 20
44 *Musician, Player and Listener* 17
   (April 1979), p. 7
45 Lowe 1976, pp. 20–1
46 McCall 1982, p. 45
47 *Down Beat* 20 April 1978, p. 9
48 Milkowski 1984, p. 68
49 McGrath 1980, p. E1
50 Saal 1977, p. 42
51 Balliett 1983b, p. 182
52 Gaumont 1981, p. 37
53 Mandel 1980, p. 17
54 Coryell and Friedman 1978, p. 40
55 McCall 1982, p. 43
56 Mandel 1980, p. 17
57 McCall 1982, p. 42
58 *Down Beat* September 1980, p. 8
59 *Down Beat* December 1980, p. 9
60 McCall 1982, p. 41
61 Freedman 1983, p. 19
62 McCall 1982, p. 41
63 Goodman 1981, p. 1
64 Feather 1983b, p. 19
   (retranslated)
65 Goodman 1981, p. 1

CHAPTER SIXTEEN:
IT GETS BETTER: 1981 AND AFTER
(pages 308–60)

1 Goodman 1981, p. 1
2 Goldberg 1981, p. 56
3 McCall 1982, p. 45
4 Stewart 1982, p. 66
5 Feather 1983b (retranslated),
  p. 18
6 Contat 1981, p. 1
7 Balliett 1981a, p. 58
8 Contat 1981, p. 24
9 Jeske and Lange 1981, p. 23
10 Tailleur 1981
11 Jeske and Lange 1981, p. 68
12 Balliett 1981a, p. 58
13 Palmer 1981, p. 17
14 Contat 1981, p. 24
15 Jeske and Lange 1981, p. 23
16 Palmer 1981, p. 17
17 Brunt 1981
18 Jeske and Lange 1981, p. 68
19 Jeske and Lange 1981, p. 23
20 Down Beat December 1981,
  p. 84
21 Palmer 1981, p. 17
22 Richard Williams 1983
23 Liska 1981, p. 31
24 Contat 1981, p. 24
25 Brower 1981, p. 33
26 Zylberstein 1981
27 Goodman 1981, p. 1
28 Richard Williams 1983
29 Goodman 1981, p. 1
30 Stewart 1982, p. 65
31 McCall 1982, p. 43
32 Freedman 1983, p. 19
33 McCall 1982, p. 43
34 Freedman 1983, p. 19
35 McCall 1982, p. 42

36 Arnaud 1983, pp. 22, 23
37 Blasquiz 1983, p. 21
38 McCall 1982, p. 45
39 Arnaud 1983, p. 21
40 McCall 1982, p. 42
41 Mandel 1981, p. 52
42 McCall 1982, p. 48
43 Breskin 1983, p. 50
44 McCall 1982, pp. 48, 40
45 Mandel 1981, p. 52
46 McCall 1982, p. 42
47 McCall 1982, p. 42
48 Mandel 1981, p. 52
49 Freedman 1982b, p. 18
50 Mandel 1981, pp. 52–3
51 Mandel 1981, p. 53
52 Milkowski 1982, p. 17
53 Blasquiz 1983, p. 23
54 Freedman 1983, p. 17
55 Blasquiz 1983, p. 58
56 Freedman 1983, p. 17
57 Arnaud 1983, p. 22
58 Arnaud 1983, p. 21
59 McCall 1982, p. 38
60 Goldberg 1981, pp. 55, 56, 59
61 Wild 1981, p. 30
62 McCall 1982, p. 40
63 Quoted (in French) with Feather
  1983b (retranslated)
64 Brodowski and Szprot 1983
65 Feather 1983b (retranslated),
  p. 19
66 Breskin 1983, pp. 46–9
67 Feather 1983a
68 Roach 1982, p. 44
69 Mandel 1983, p. 29
70 McCall 1982, p. 43
71 People Weekly 14 December
  1981, p. 176
72 McCall 1982, pp. 45, 41
73 Miller 1981

74 Breskin 1983, p. 52
75 Richard Williams 1983
76 Feather 1983b (retranslated),
    p. 18
77 Feather 1983b (retranslated),
    p. 17
78 Richard Williams 1983
79 McCall 1982, p. 47
80 Arnaud 1983, p. 21
81 Gelly 1982
82 Bayon 1982, p. 28
83 Conrath 1982, p. 28
84 Arnaud 1983, p. 23
85 Andrews 1982
86 Brunt 1982, p. 17
87 DeZutter 1982, p. 39
88 Kostakis 1982, p. 58
89 Richard Williams 1983
90 Cook 1983, p. 15
91 Richard Williams 1983
92 Breskin 1983, p. 52
93 Richard Williams 1983
94 *Sunday Star* (Toronto) 7
    November 1982, p. D2
95 Feather 1983b (retranslated),
    p. 18
96 Liska 1982b, p. 16
97 Keepnews 1984, p. 18
98 Jeske 1983b, p. 46
99 Reese 1983, p. 19
100 Richard Williams 1983
101 Feather 1983a
102 Richard Williams 1983
103 Breskin 1983, p. 49
104 Blasquiz 1983, p. 58
105 Jeske 1983a, p. 43
106 Tesser 1983, p. 40
107 Liska 1983, p. 62
108 Reese 1983, p. 19
109 Breskin 1983, p. 52

110 Interview Philadelphia
     December 1983
111 Richard Williams 1983
112 *Rolling Stone* 5 July 1984,
     p. 11
113 Case 1983, p. 16
114 Jeske 1983d, p. 23
115 Balliett 1983a, p. 75
116 Tesser 1983, p. 40
117 Tate 1983b, p. 24
118 Feather 1984, p. 91
119 Keepnews 1984, p. 18
120 Pellicciotti 1983, p. 34
121 Feather 1984, p. 91
122 Brodowski and Szprot 1983
123 *Down Beat* February 1984,
     p. 13
124 Pareles 1983, p. E3
125 "Entertainment Tonight" NBC-
     TV 7 November 1983
126 Hodeir 1965, p. 19
127 McCall 1982, p. 43
128 Feather 1983b (retranslated),
     p. 18
129 Breskin 1983, p. 52
130 Feather 1984, p. 91
131 Breskin 1983, p. 52
132 Goodman 1981, p. 13
133 Feather 1983b (retranslated),
     pp. 18, 19

AFTERWORD: SO WHAT?
(pages 363–7)

1 Fox 1972, p. 106
2 Attributed to Ulanov by
   Goodman 1981, p. 13
3 Quoted by Goodman 1981,
   p. 13
4 Balliett 1962, p. 142

5 Martin Williams 1970b, p. 159
6 Hentoff 1976, p. 135
7 Albertson 1971, p. 69
8 Mingus 1971, p. 65
9 Gleason 1975, p. 132
10 Breskin 1983, p. 49
11 Tate 1983b, p. 54
12 Program note, Vancouver 28 July 1982

Bibliography

Adderley, Julian 'Cannonball' (1964) "Paying dues: the education of a combo leader" *The Jazz Review* reprinted in Martin Williams ed *Jazz Panorama* New York: Collier Books

Albertson, Chris (1969) "Caught in the Act: Garden State Jazz Festival" *Down Beat* 11 December

— (1971) "The unmasking of Miles Davis" *Saturday Review* 27 November

Ames, Morgan (ca 1970) Liner note *Miles Davis at Fillmore* (Columbia G 30038)

Andrews, Markc (1982) "Miles magic" *Vancouver Sun* 29 July

Arnaud, Gérald (1983) "Mino Cinelu: 'Les sentiments dépassent les ethnies'" *Jazz Hot* 399 (April)

Avakian, George (ca 1967) Liner note *Charles Lloyd: Love-In* (Atlantic SD 1481)

Baggenaes, Roland (1974) "Interview with Mary Lou Williams" *Coda* July

Balliett, Whitney (1962) *Dinosaurs in the Morning* Philadelphia: J.B. Lippincott

— (1976) *New York Notes: A Journal of Jazz, 1972–75* Boston: Houghton Mifflin

— (1981a) "Down the river" *The New Yorker* 27 July

— (1981b) *Night Creature: A Journal of Jazz, 1975–80* New York: Oxford University Press

— (1982) "Good tidings" *The New Yorker* 14 June

— (1983a) "Jazz: Wein world" *The New Yorker* 25 July

— (1983b) *Jelly Roll, Jabbo, and Fats* New York: Oxford University Press

Bayon (1982) "Trompette de mort" *Libération* 5 May

Berendt, Joachim (1976) *The Jazz Book* St Albans, Herts: Paladin

Birnbaum, Larry (1979) "Weather Report answers its critics" *Down Beat* 8 February

Blasquiz, Klaus (1983) "Marcus Miller: 'servir, pénétrer et respecter un climat'" *Jazz Hot* 399 (April)

Bloom, Steve (1981) "Freddie Hubbard: money talks, bebop walks" *Down Beat* November

Blumenthal, Bob (1979) "The eight year Weather Report" *Rolling Stone* 11 January

— (ca 1981) Liner note *Miles Davis: Directions* (Columbia KC2 36472)

Bouchard, Fred (1980) "Alan Dawson: teaching the traps, gigging with the greatest" *Down Beat* November

Breskin, David (1983) "Searching for Miles: theme and variations on the life of a trumpeter" *Rolling Stone* 405, 29 September

Brodowski, Pawel, and Janusz Szprot (1983) "Miles speaks: 'I don't wanna be like I used to be'" *Jazz Forum* 85

Brower, W.A. (1981) Review of Miles Davis *The Man with the Horn* (Columbia FC 36790) *Down Beat* November

Brown, Ron (1973a) Review of Miles Davis *On the Corner* (Columbia KC 31906) *Jazz Journal* May

— (1973b) "Miles at the Rainbow" *Jazz Journal* September

Brunt, Stephen (1981) "Davis dumps cool style and some don't like it" *The Globe and Mail* (Toronto) 7 July

— (1982) "The year of the trumpeters" *The Globe and Mail* (Toronto) 7 September

Carr, Ian (1982) *Miles Davis: A Biography* New York: Morrow & Co

Carter, Ron (1982) "Memories of Miles" *Musician, Listener and Player* 41, March

Case, Brian (1983) "Miles Davis: Hammersmith Odeon, London" *Melody Maker* 7 May

Chadbourne, Eugene (1973a) "Astral travelling: a dialogue with Lonnie Liston Smith" *Coda* December

— (1973b) "Heard and seen [Miles Davis in Calgary]" *Coda* June

— (1975) "Review of Miles Davis *Big Fun* (Columbia PG 32866) *Coda* May

Chambers, Jack (1972) Review of Miles Davis *Live-Evil* (Columbia G-30954) *Coda* August

— (1973) Review of Miles Davis *On the Corner* (Columbia KC 31906) *Coda* October

— (1974a) Review of Miles Davis *In Concert* (Columbia KG 32092) *Coda* March

— (1974b) "Someday, Miles, someday" *The Globe and Mail* (Toronto) 19 October

Choice, Harriet (1974) "Miles Davis, solo: brews concocted and broods
    begotten" *Chicago Tribune* (Arts and Fun section) 20 January
Clark, Douglas (1977) "Miles into jazz-rock territory" *Jazz Journal* June
Coker, Jerry (1975) *The Jazz Idiom* Englewood Cliffs, New Jersey: Prentice-
    Hall
Cole, Bill (1974) *Miles Davis: A Musical Biography* New York: William
    Morrow and Co. Ltd
Collier, James Lincoln (1978) *The Making of Jazz: A Comprehensive History*
    Boston: Houghton Mifflin
Conrath, Phillippe (1982) "Les variations de Miles" *Libération* 5 May
Contat, Michel (1981) "Le retour de Miles Davis" *Le Monde* 10 July
Cook, Richard (1983) "Gil Evans: still smiling after all these years" *New
    Musical Express* 26 March
Coon, Caroline (1977) *1988: The New Wave Punk Rock Explosion* London:
    Omnibus Press
Coryell, Julie, and Laura Friedman (1978) *Jazz-Rock Fusion: The People, the
    Music* New York: Delta Books
Cotterrell, Roger (1967) "Interlude: Miles Davis with Hank Mobley" *Jazz
    Monthly* October
Davis, Clive, with James Willwerth (1974) *Clive: Inside the Record Business*
    New York: Ballantine
Davis, Miles (ca 1971) Liner note *Zawinul* (Atlantic SD 1579)
DeMicheal, Don (1966) "A long look at Stan Getz, part 1" *Down Beat* 19 May
— (1969a) "And in this corner the Sidewalk Kid" *Down Beat* 11 December
— (1969b) "Miles Davis" *Rolling Stone* 27 December
DeZutter, Hank (1982) "Improvising" *Reader* (Chicago) 10 September
Diliberto, John (1983) "The Karlheinz Stockhausen interview: the electronics
    of eternity" *Down Beat* April
Dobbin, Len (1974) "Around the world: Montreal" *Coda* December
Evans, Gil (1981) Liner note *Where Flamingos Fly* (Artists House AH 14) June
Feather, Leonard (1960) *Encyclopedia of Jazz* (revised) New York: Bonanza
    Books
— (1966) *Encyclopedia of Jazz in the Sixties* New York: Bonanza Books
— (1967) "The modulated world of Gil Evans" *Down Beat* 23 February
— (1969) "Blindfold test: Bobby Bryant" *Down Beat* 20 February 1969
— (1974a) "Blindfold test: Larry Coryell" *Down Beat* 18 July
— (1974b) *From Satchmo to Miles* London: Quartet Books
— (1975) "Blindfold test: Ron Carter" *Down Beat* 18 December
— (1976a) "Blindfold test: Miles Davis" *Down Beat* reprinted in
    Encyclopedia of Jazz in the Seventies by Feather and Gitler
— (1976b) *The Pleasures of Jazz* New York: Horizon Press

— (1979) "Joni Mitchell makes Mingus sing" *Down Beat* 6 September
— (1980) *The Passion for Jazz* New York: Horizon Press
— (1983a) Liner note: Miles Davis *Star People* (Columbia FC 38657)
— (1983b) "Miles Davis: Mis à nu ... par son contestataire même!" *Jazz Hot* 399, April
— (1984) "Miles – sketches of pain" *Los Angeles Times* 29 April
Feather, Leonard, and Ira Gitler (1976) *Encyclopedia of Jazz in the Seventies* New York: Horizon Press
Fortune, Sonny (1982) "Memories of Miles" *Musician, Player and Listener* 41, March
Fox, Charles (1972) *The Jazz Scene* London: Hamlyn
Freedman, Sam (1982a) "Archie Shepp, embracing the jazz ritual" *Down Beat* April
— (1982b) "John Scofield: music for the connoisseur" *Down Beat* September
— (1983) "The Thumbslinger: bassist for hire [Marcus Miller]" *Down Beat* April
Gaumont, Dominique (1981) "Comment j'ai rencontré Miles" *Jazz Hot* 388, September
Gelly, Dave (1982) "Unique gifts [Miles Davis in London]" *The Observer* 25 April
Gillespie, Dizzy (1976) "Foreword" in Dan Morgenstern *Jazz People* New York: Harry N. Abrams Inc
Gillespie, Dizzy, and Al Fraser (1979) *To Be or Not To Bop* New York: Double-day 1979
Gilmore, Mikal (1978) Review of Herbie Hancock *VSOP* (Columbia C2-34976) *Down Beat* 26 January
Gitler, Ira (1967) "Newport echoes" *Down Beat* 7 September
Gleason, Ralph J. (1961) Liner note *Miles Davis: Friday and Saturday Night at the Blackhawk* (Columbia 1669–70)
— (ca 1963) Liner note *Miles Davis in Europe* (Columbia CL 2183)
— (1974) "Miles Davis still accepts the challenge" *Rolling Stone* 23 May
— (1975) *Celebrating the Duke ... and Other Heroes* Boston: Little, Brown and Co.
Goddard, Peter (1974) "Trumpeter Davis in his classic form" *Toronto Star* 27 January
— (1981) "Miles Davis' good taste just about all he has left" *Toronto Star* 14 December
Goldberg, Joe (1965) *Jazz Masters of the Fifties* New York: Macmillan
— (1981) "Miles Davis: the king in yellow" *International Musician* November

Goode, Mort (ca 1970) Liner note *Miles Davis at Fillmore* (Columbia G 30038)

Goodman, George, Jr (1981) "Miles Davis: 'I just pick up my horn and play'" *New York Times* Sunday 28 June

Gordon, Max (1980) *Live at the Village Vanguard* New York: St Martin's Press

Grime, Kitty (1979) *Jazz at Ronnie Scott's* London: Robert Hale Ltd

Hailey, Alex (1962) "Playboy interview: Miles Davis" *Playboy* September (reprinted in *The Best From Playboy – Number One* Playboy Press, 1964)

Hall, Gregg (1974a) "Miles: today's most influential contemporary musician" *Down Beat* 18 July

— (1974b) "Teo [Macero]: the man behind the scene" *Down Beat* 18 July

Harper, Michael S. (1970) *Dear John, Dear Coltrane* Pitt Poetry series, University of Pittsburgh Press

Harrison, Max, Alun Morgan, Ronald Atkins, Michael James, and Jack Cooke (1975) *Modern Jazz: The Essential Records* London: Aquarius Books

Harrison, Max (1976) *A Jazz Retrospect* Boston: Crescendo Publishing Co.

Harrison, Tom (1982) "Miles Davis playful" *The Province* (Vancouver) 29 July

Hawes, Hampton, and Don Asher (1974) *Raise Up off Me* New York: McCann and Geohegan

Heckman, Don (1974) "Jazz-Rock" *Stereo Review* November

Hennessy, Mike (1977) Review of Elvin Jones *Live at the Village Vanguard* (ENJA 2036) *Jazz Journal* October

Hentoff, Nat (1958) "An afternoon with Miles Davis" *The Jazz Review* December, reprinted in Martin Williams ed *Jazz Panorama* New York: Collier Books, 1964

— (ca 1960) Liner note *Miles Davis, Sketches of Spain* (Columbia CL 1480)

— (1975) "The eye of the beholder" in *Esquire's World of Jazz* revised and updated, New York: Thomas Y. Crowell

— (1976) *Jazz Is* New York: Random House

— (1978) Liner note *Herbie Hancock: Speak Like a Child* (Blue Note BST 84279)

Hill, Hal (1977) "Art Pepper speaks with Hal Hill" *Buffalo Jazz Report* August

Hodeir, André (1965) *Toward Jazz* trans Noel Burch, London: The Jazz Book Club

Humphreys, Norman (1970) "Concert" *Jazz Journal* January

Isaacs, James (1979) Liner note *Miles Davis: Circle in the Round* (Columbia 36278)

Jagajivan (1973) "Musing with Mwandishi" *Down Beat* 24 May

Jarrett, Keith (1973) Liner note *Solo-Concerts* (ECM 1035-37 ST)

Jepsen, Jorgen Grunnet (1969) *A Discography of Miles Davis* Copenhagen: Karl Emil Knudsen

Jeske, Lee (1981) "Chick Corea" *Down Beat* June
— (1982) "Johnny McLaughlin, acoustic guitarist" *Down Beat* April
— (1983a) "Blindfold test: John Abercrombie" *Down Beat* April
— (1983b) "Caught: Miles Davis at the Felt Forum" *Down Beat* April
— (1983c) "Howard Johnson: center of gravity" *Down Beat* January
— (1983d) "Kinda Kool" *Down Beat* October
— (1983e) "Ron Carter: covering all basses" *Down Beat* July
— (1984) "Stateside scene – east coast: Miles" *Jazz Journal International* February
Jeske, Lee, and Art Lange (1981) "Two bites from the Apple" *Down Beat* October
Johnson, Ron (1973) "Around the world [Miles Davis in Minneapolis]" *Coda* March
Johnson, Sy (1976) "Miles" *Jazz Magazine* fall
Jones, Leroi (1968) *Black Music* New York: Morrow & Co.
Jones, Max, and John Chilton (1971) *Louis* Boston: Little, Brown
Kart, Lawrence (1968) Review of *Miles in the Sky* (Columbia CS 9628) *Down Beat* 3 October
Keepnews, Peter (1984) "Family fortune: the mysterious making of a new jazz traditionalist [Branford Marsalis]" *Musician* 69, July
Kostakis, Peter (1982) "Caught: Chicago Kool Jazz Festival" *Down Beat* December
Liska, A. James (1981) "Tom Scott" *Down Beat* July
— (1982a) "Wayne Shorter: coming home" *Down Beat* July
— (1982b) "Wynton and Branford Marsalis: a common understanding" *Down Beat* December
— (1983) "Grammys on hold" *Down Beat* May
Lowe, Ed (1976) [no title] in *Jazz* fall
Lyons, Len (1983) *The Great Jazz Pianists Speaking of Their Lives and Music* New York: Quill
Lyttleton, Humphrey (1978) *The Best of Jazz: Basin Street to Harlem* Harmondsworth: Penguin
McCall, Cheryl (1982) "Miles Davis" *Musician, Player and Listener* 41, March
McGrath, Paul (1980) "Joni enters movies, backwards" *The Globe and Mail* (Toronto) 29 November
McRae, Barry (1972) "Avant courier no. 7: Funky Tonk" *Jazz Journal* July
— (1975) "Avant-courier: Miles Davis since Philharmonic Hall, Berlin-1964" *Jazz Journal* June
Malson, Lucien (1982) "Miles Davis à Paris" *Le Monde* 26 April
Mandel, Howard (1980) "Miles Davis' new direction is a family affair" *Down Beat* September

— (1981) "Profile: Bill Evans, Mike Stern, and Mino Cinelu" *Down Beat* November
— (1982) "Waxing on: getting down to brass attacks" *Down Beat* August
— (1983) "Bob Moses: surreal swing" *Down Beat* May
— (1984) "Tribute to Miles Davis: Radio City Music Hall" *Down Beat* February
Martin, John (1960) "Miles out" *Jazz News* 1 October
Massett, Larry, and E.W. Sutherland (1975) *Guide to Drugs and Medicines* New York: Luce Inc.
Meadow, Elliot (1973) "Meet Benny Maupin" *Down Beat* 18 January
Meeker, David (1977) *Jazz in the Movies* New Rochelle, New York: Arlington House
Mialy, Louis-Victor (1983) "Ron Carter: un géant des profondeurs" *Jazz Hot* 400, May
Michener, James A. (1971) *Kent State: What Happened and Why* New York: Random House
Milkowski, Bill (1982) "Jimi Hendrix: the jazz connection" *Down Beat* October
— (1984) "Larry Coryell: back to the roots" *Down Beat* May
Miller, Mark (1981) "A change of tune Miles Davis-style" *The Globe and Mail* (Toronto) 14 December
— (1982) *Jazz in Canada: Fourteen Lives* Toronto: University of Toronto Press
Mingus, Charles (1971) *Beneath the Underdog* ed Nel King, New York: Alfred A. Knopf
Mitchell, Sammy (1968) "Caught in the act [Miles Davis-Gil Evans at Berkeley]" *Down Beat* 13 June
Morgenstern, Dan (1966) "Caught in the act: Miles Davis at Village Vanguard" *Down Beat* 13 January
— (1973a) "Blindfold test: Stan Getz" *Down Beat* 10 May
— (1973b) "Different Strokes [Airto Moreira]" *Down Beat* 15 March
— (1976) *Jazz People* New York: Harry N. Abrams Inc.
— (1977a) "Doggin' Around" *Jazz Journal International* June
— (1977b) "Doggin' Around" *Jazz Journal International* August
Murphy, Frederick D. (1975) "Miles Davis" *Encore* 21 July
Nisenson, Eric (1982) *'Round About Midnight: A Portrait of Miles Davis* New York: Dial Press
Noë (1974) "I mean, I mean, I mean, I mean ... [Dave Liebman]" *College Monthly* October
Norsworthy, Fred (1974) Liner note *Kenny Dorham/Rocky Boyd: Ease It* (Muse 5053)

Nyhan, William L. (1976) *The Heredity Factor* New York: Grosset & Dunlap

Offstein, Alan (1974) "Around the world [Miles Davis in Toronto]" *Coda* March

O'Reilly, Ted (1975) "Keith Jarrett and the muse" *Sound* April

Orysik, John (1973) "The scene: Montreal [Miles Davis concert]" *Coda* June

Palmer, Robert (1975) "Newport plays it famous, plays it safe" *Rolling Stone* 14 August

— (ca 1975) Liner note *Sam Rivers: Involution* (Blue Note BN-LA453-H2)

— (1976) "Newport jazz standing in the shadow of the past" *Rolling Stone* 12 August

— (1981) "Jazz scene: Miles Davis comeback" *The New York Times* 7 July

Pareles, Jon (1983) "New York jazz concert a milestone in music" *The Globe and Mail* (Toronto) 5 November

Pekar, Harvey (1976) "Miles Davis: 1964–69 recordings" *Coda* May

Pellicciotti, Giacomo (1983) "Mode et mood de Miles" *Jazz Magazine* 323, November

Pepper, Art, and Laurie Pepper (1979) *Straight Life: The Story of Art Pepper* New York: Schirmer Books

Perla, Gene (1974) "Dave Liebman" *Coda* January

Priestley, Brian (1974) "Alone ... he's cool: Billy Cobham" *Down Beat* 14 March

— (1982) "Discography," Appendix C in Ian Carr *Miles Davis: A Biography* New York: Morrow & Co.

Primack, Brett (1979) "Profile: Eddie Moore" *Down Beat* 22 February

Prince, Linda (1979) "Betty Carter: bebopper breathes fire" *Down Beat* 3 May

Ramsey, Doug (ca 1975) Liner note *Ron Carter: Spanish Blue* (CTI 6051 SI)

Reese, Jérome (1981) "Miles électrique" *Jazz Hot* 388, September

— (1983) "Miles + Gil Evans = Star People" *Jazz Hot* 399, April

Roach, Max (1982) "Memories of Miles" *Musician, Listener and Player* 41, March

Rollins, Sonny (1982) "Memories of Miles" *Musician, Listener and Player* 41, March

Roura, Phil, and Tom Poster (1981) "Fans trek to see Davis but they boo when he stops" *New York Daily News* 7 July

Ruppli, Michel (1979) "Discographie: Miles Davis" *Jazz Hot* February and March

Saal, Hubert (1977) "Jazz comes back!" *Newsweek* 8 August

Saunders, Jimmy (1975) Interview with Miles Davis *Playboy* April

Scott, J.T. (1980) *Arthritis and Rheumatism: The Facts* New York: Oxford University Press

Siders, Harvey (1969) "Caught in the act [Miles Davis at Monterey]" *Down Beat* 27 November
— (1973a) "Drum shticks" *Down Beat* 15 March
— (1973b) "Group Therapy" *Down Beat* 10 May
— (1973c) "The Manne-Hole chronicles" *Down Beat's Music '73: 18th Annual Yearbook*
Silvert, Conrad (1976) "Chick Corea's changes: a return is not forever" *Rolling Stone* 15 July
— (1977) "Herbie Hancock: revamping the present, creating the future" *Down Beat* 8 September
— (1980) "Old and new dreams" *Down Beat* June
Simon, George T. (ca 1961) Liner note *Miles Davis at Carnegie Hall* (Columbia CL 1812)
Simpkins, C.O. (1975) *Coltrane: A Biography* New York: Herndon House
Smith, Bill (1972) "Ann Arbor Blues and Jazz Festival" *Coda* December
— (1973) "Song for the newborn [David Holland]" *Coda* March
Spellman, A.B. (1970) *Black Music: Four Lives* (originally *Four Lives in the Bebop Business* 1966) New York: Schocken Books
Stern, Chip (1978) "Jack DeJohnette: South Side to Woodstock" *Down Beat* 2 November
Stewart, Zan (1981) "Buell Niedlinger" *Down Beat* June
— (1982) "Gil Evans" *Musician, Player and Listener* 39, January
Sussman, Andrew (1980) "George Coleman: survival of the grittiest" *Down Beat* March
Tailleur, Cécile (1981) "Miles Davis: magie intacte" *Le Point* July
Takada, Keizo 1975) "Around the world [Miles Davis in Japan]" *Coda* May
Tate, Greg (1983a) "The electric Miles, part 1" *Down Beat* July
— (1983b) "The electric Miles, part 2" *Down Beat* August
Taylor, Arthur (1977) *Notes and Tones: Musician-to-Musician Interviews* New York: Perigee 1977
Tepperman, Barry (1976) Review of Miles Davis *Get Up with It* (Columbia KG 33236) *Coda* February
Tesser, Neil (1983) "Blowing on empty: Miles Davis at the altar of showbiz" *Reader* (Chicago) 18 February
Thomas, J.C. (1975) *Chasin' the Trane* New York: Doubleday
Tinder, Clifford (1980) "An interview with David Baker" *Coda* 176, December
Townley, Ray (1975) "The mysterious travellings of an Austrian mogul [Josef Zawinul]" *Down Beat* 30 January
Traill, Sinclair (1979) "The Shelly Manne story" *Jazz Journal International* August

Ullmann, Michael (1980) *Jazz Lives* Washington: New Republic Books

Underwood, Lee (1975a) "Around the world: Los Angeles [Miles Davis at the Troubador]" *Coda* April

— (1975b) "Profile: Oscar Brashear" *Down Beat* 18 December

— (1978) "Airto and his incredible gong show" *Down Beat* 20 April

— (1979) "Tony Williams: aspiring to a lifetime of leadership" *Down Beat* 21 June

— (1981) "Devadip Carlos Santana: instrument of light" *Down Beat* January

Walton, Ortiz M. (1972) *Music: Black, White and Blue* New York: Morrow & Co.

Watts, Michael (1973) "Miles Davis" in Ray Coleman ed *Today's Sound* A Melody Maker Book, London: Hamlyn 1973

Wild, David (1981) "Around the world [Miles Davis in Ann Arbor]" *Coda* 181, December

Williams, Ed (1978) "Ron Carter: the compleat artist, part 1" *Down Beat* 26 January

Williams, Martin (1970a) *Jazz Masters in Transition: 1957–69* New York: DaCapo

— (1970b) *The Jazz Tradition* New York: New American Library

Williams, Richard (1983) "On top of all the beat" *The Times* (London) 28 April

Wilmer, Valerie (1967) "London Lowdown" *Down Beat* 28 December

— (1969) "What Charles Tolliver can use" *Down Beat* 20 February

— (1970) *Jazz People* New York: Bobbs Merrill Co.

— (1982) "A shaman for the '80s [Ronald Shannon Jackson]" *Down Beat* August

Wilson, John S. (ca 1961) Liner note *Miles Davis at Carnegie Hall* (Columbia CL 1812)

— (1966) *Jazz: The Transition Years 1940–60* New York: Appleton-Century-Crofts

— (1975) "Miles Davis leaves them limp, waiting for more" *New York Times* 7 September

Wilson, Pat (1972) "Conversing with Cannonball" *Down Beat* 22 June

Wilson, Russ (1967) "Caught in the Act [Miles Davis at Berkeley]" *Down Beat* 1 June

Yanow, Scott (1978) "Miles Davis: the later years" *Record Review* April

Zanger, Mark (1976) "Miles Davis blowing hot and cool at 50" *The Real Paper* 11 August

Zwerin, Michael (1966) "Miles Davis: a most curious friendship" *Down Beat* 10 March

Zylberstein, Jean-Claude (1981) "Les rendez-vous" *Le Nouvel Observateur* 8 August

Index

Authors and composers are cited in parentheses following the titles of books and musical works.